Beer in The Netherlands 2

CAFÉS · BEER · PUBS · BREWERIES

TIM SKELTON

Skelton ink

Second edition published by Skelton Ink
Eindhoven, the Netherlands

© Skelton Ink 2020

First edition published in 2014 by
The Homewood Press Limited.
The original concept for *Beer in The Netherlands*
came from Tim Webb, Managing Editor of
Cogan & Mater Limited.

Publisher and author: Tim Skelton
Text editor: Des de Moor
Book design/typography: Dale Tomlinson
Maps: John Macklin

ISBN 978-90-9032724-2

A catalogue record for this book is available from the
British Library and the Dutch Koninklijke Bibliotheek.

Printed and bound in the United Kingdom by
Cambrian Printers Ltd.

FSC
www.fsc.org
MIX
Paper from
responsible sources
FSC® C005094

Every effort has been made to ensure the contents of this book
are correct at the time of printing. Nevertheless the Publisher
cannot be held responsible for any errors or omissions,
or for changes in the details given in this publication, or for
the consequences of any reliance on the information provided
by the same. This does not affect your statutory rights.

Symbols used in the book

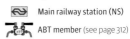

Main railway station (NS)

ABT member (see page 312)

Picture credits

Front cover photograph: Tim Skelton

Back cover Tim Skelton portrait: Amanda Cliff

All other photographs by the author except:
Page 233: Amanda Cliff

The author has not accepted advertising or
received any other form of payment or deal from
any of the beer outlets featured in this guide.
All entries were chosen entirely on merit.

skeltonink.eu

Contents

Foreword

The development of brewing in the Netherlands in the past century has mirrored almost perfectly the history of beer in Europe.

A century ago, travelling the country would have revealed a nation of two halves. North of the great rivers a reserved, Protestant culture reflected the Germanic trend towards cleanly conditioned, increasingly blond lager brewing, while in the more Catholic south, brewers still adhered to older ways, piecing together traditional, sharp light ales, their edges sugared away.

After the 20th century's first catastrophic war it was legislation that saw off the older styles. After its second, new business methods and the mighty power of advertising, skills learned from America, shaped the dominance of blond lagers brewed on an industrial scale. Nowhere was the drive to a one-size-fits-all brewing monoculture stronger, or more successful.

Whether the three café owners who in 1968 banded together to import a few Belgian ales to break up the monotony of Dutch lagers, thought that they were starting a counter revolution is questionable. Either way, the Netherlands now has one.

Gone are the days when the newer breweries that made the most expressive new beers lacked the technical skills to prevent them going bad within a week or two, along with the desire of those brewers who had mastered sound technique to keep their imaginations in check.

The emergence of several hundred new breweries, hitting local markets and beyond with confident brews often of types never seen before in this essentially conservative beer scene, has been awesome. Of a sudden the humble *pintje* has come to look inadequate, however deftly the waiter decapitates its foam. Writers about the Belgian beer scene must adjust to finding better Dutch craft ales in cafés in Antwerp, Brussels and even Bruges.

Beer in the Netherlands has likely never been as accomplished as it is at present. Not all is great – some remains poisonous. Not all the new brewers will survive – but provided the best of the new breed are allowed access to markets, there is no reason why the Netherlands' journey to becoming Europe's most diverse beer culture will not continue.

Nobody knows this extraordinary and ever-evolving scene better than Tim Skelton – and you will not find a better guide to it than the one that you are holding.

TIM WEBB
Author, *The World Atlas of Beer*

Welkom

What a difference a few years and a global craft beer revolution can make.

When CAMRA's *Good Beer Guide to Belgium & Holland* was published in 2002, the Netherlands had a mere 40 breweries and 150 places in which to drink decent beer. When the first edition of this guide appeared in 2014, there were 200 brewing companies and 400 good beer pubs. Five years on, the total of physical breweries has grown to 350, with almost as many brewers who make their beers elsewhere. The number of specialist beer cafés has passed 500, despite us raising our definition of what actually constitutes a 'specialist café'. To say that trying to keep abreast of everything has been an exhausting rollercoaster ride would be an understatement.

Quality is also on the up. Back in 2002, drinking a competently-made beer that wasn't a mainstream lager more often than not meant ordering something Belgian. That no longer need be the case. Now with the words 'Dutch beer' and 'scene' are happily reunited in the same phrase and the country's beer culture decisively renewed, the Netherlands can once again take its rightful place among the big league of brewing nations.

That's not to say that a delicious experience is guaranteed. There are still some shockers out there, and while the consistency and infection problems that once plagued beers from Dutch micros have become rarer, they have not disappeared completely. But the ratio of good eggs to rotten is becoming ever-more encouraging, as mediocre brewers either up their game or find themselves replaced by young pups who take pride in their craft.

Despite this, industrial-scale pilsener remains the *bier* of choice for a majority of drinkers, with half a dozen names enjoying the lion's share of an easily pleased market. Such conservatism means that some smaller producers still have trouble breaking into the mainstream café sector, with most relying on sales through specialised shops and appearances at festivals to get themselves known. But we are happy to report that even that is finally changing. While the dominance of pils isn't exactly under threat, it's certainly been drawn into question, with a growing sense that the craft beer scene has come of age.

And this is where we come in. We want the world at large, including the owners of Dutch cafés, to realise that new Dutch beer is worth checking out and deserves respect.

On these pages we have listed all existing breweries and their most regular beers, as well as recommending the best places to drink and to buy beer to take away. There is also a calendar listing beer festivals where you may find some lesser-known brewers, and some history and practical advice to make it all simple.

In short, this book will tell you why to come; how to get here; what to drink once you arrive; and where to find it. Everything you need for a voyage of discovery through the world of Dutch beer. *Goede reis* and may your glass always be half-full.

Proost!

TIM SKELTON
Eindhoven
January 2020

Redemption and Rebirth
The Dutch beer revival since 1975

ANY beer-loving time traveller who chose to visit the Netherlands around 1970 would be horrified. A land that a few centuries earlier boasted hundreds of ale breweries had fallen head first into a bottomless ocean of a skinny froth-topped blond called pilsener. Even the Trappist monks at the brewing abbey of Koningshoeven had succumbed.

The popularity of pilsener, brewed for looks and inoffensiveness rather than flavour in quantities the size of Olympic swimming pools, was one of several factors that led to the closure of most smaller brewing concerns. In 1970, only 22 breweries remained and most of them were operated by conglomerates. Moreover, few cafés showed any interest in unusual beers. In those days, *Beer in the Netherlands* would have been a pamphlet.

The tide began turning in the late 1960s when landlord Piet de Jongh of the Beyerd in Breda (page 220), spotting how much more interesting beer was south of the border in Belgium, joined with two colleagues to import ales from Belgium to improve their offer. Then a few other brave publicans began encouraging customers to try something more daring, including the original Gollem in Amsterdam (page 249) in 1974. To Piet de Jongh, who died in 2019, we doff our caps.

Yet despite the enthusiasm of their owners, these places remained oases in a national beer Sahara, their crusade seeming futile as brewery acquisitions and closures continued. By 1980, the total number of operating breweries was below 20, producing fewer than 100 beer brands, with all the top-selling names tasting virtually identical.

Then something pivotal happened. A small band of Dutch members of a UK beer consumer group called the Campaign for Real Ale (CAMRA), inspired by early successes in reviving the UK's pub and brewery scene, put out a rallying cry in the organisation's magazine *What's Brewing*, calling on Dutch readers to establish a regional branch.

This request was dismissed by the parent organisation, which, in the manner of all revolutionary groups set on changing the world, decreed that the Netherlands was not a North Sea too far. Undeterred, the pioneers created their own association, launching PINT in 1980 (with £50 start-up capital donated by CAMRA) as a means of persuading Dutch brewers to make, Dutch cafés to sell and Dutch drinkers to buy decent beer.

A few years later, a second group joined the fight from the other side. The handful of publicans specialising in beer realised they were getting nowhere alone. So at a PINT meeting in 1983, the landlords of the Locus Publicus in Rotterdam (page 287), Jan Primus in Utrecht (page 295) and Breda's Beyerd banded together. By the time they launched the Alliantie van Biertapperijen (Alliance of Beer Tappers, ABT) in 1986, they had been joined by a dozen others. Three of the founders – the Beyerd, the Vlaamsche Reus in Wageningen (page 198) and Amsterdam's In De Wildeman (page 253) – are still members today.

To begin with, the Dutch beer revival was heavily dependent on imports. Belgium, Germany and the UK, three nations surrounding the Netherlands, had resisted the tide of homogenous industrial lager more than most and retained some variety and tradition in their beer culture. Reviving Dutch brewing would take a little longer.

Among the first of the new wave small ale breweries, De Hemel in Nijmegen (page 73) opened in 1983, followed in 1985 by both 't IJ in Amsterdam (page 77) and Friese in Friesland (page 67). Their numbers continued to grow, albeit slowly, and by the turn of the millennium, the brewery total stood at around 40.

With the brewing revival came a renaissance of beer styles. Dark Dutch autumnal *bokbier* was embraced as a 'new-old' institution, said to be inspired by dark German bocks from Einbeck, but actually closer to Norwegian *bokøl*, a black lager brewed to see off the previous year's grain. By the 1980s, most breweries had given up on it, but the majority of Dutch brewers today see it as their national duty to brew one in the appropriate season.

Brewers went on to resurrect other defunct styles, most notably stout, a popular Dutch drink in the days before the pilsener tsunami breached the dykes. The revival also leaned heavily on Belgian styles, with new breweries making imitations of spiced wheat beer and abbey-style dubbels and tripels, usually not as well as their southern neighbours.

This was partly due to the very low number of breweries in the country prior to the revival, which meant professional brewing skills and knowledge were scarce. Most of the newcomers were homebrewers, hobbyists who had taught themselves at a time when the available information and support on how to make beer was a fraction of what it is today. Thus it was no surprise if each batch turned out differently from the last, or if bottles exploded on opening with the vigour of an unwanted wild yeast infection. Many brewers struggled to deal with these problems, and rather too many simply shrugged them off.

Nevertheless, things were heading in the right direction, even if you needed a stop-motion camera to spot the changes. While a devoted core of enthusiasts sought out new microbrews and the few remaining specialities from old-established producers in a growing number of good bars, most drinkers who preferred something with more flavour than standard pils were content with Belgian imports. Few noticed the winds of change blowing through the wider beer world or demanded that Dutch brewers wake up and smell the coffee notes in the roasted malt.

For things to become really interesting, the industry needed a hefty kick up the backside.

And it got one, in 2004.

Although lauded as the Dutch brewing sector's white knight, De Molen's first head brewer Menno Olivier did not appear out of nowhere. He had 12 years' experience of making beer before his now globally famous brewery opened for business in 2004. Beginning as a homebrewer, he worked his way through the ranks at microbreweries Texel and De Prael before taking over brewing duties at De Pelgrim in Rotterdam's Delfshaven.

But when Menno and his upstart friends installed a brewery at the Arkduif windmill, in the prim and proper South Holland town of Bodegraven, things caught fire. Unlike most of their peers, they took little notice of what had gone before in Belgium or the Netherlands. They looked further afield for inspiration, to the new craft brewers making waves in the USA and elsewhere.

De Molen embraced the hop, and the instinct that bold flavours should be relished, not feared. Menno also understood, as many US colleagues had already begun to do, that quality and consistency were vital in expanding interest in flavourful beers beyond a small coterie of enthusiasts. And his company recognised that brewing great beer didn't mean much unless drinkers were persuaded to buy it through strong presentation and branding. Soon, De Molen's contemporary pale ales and strong porters and stouts, usually bearing two-word names conjoined with a prominent '&' on smart but simple and informative labels, were feted as the equals of anything on the planet.

Even so, one brewery does not a revolution make. Nevertheless, the impact of all this on the Dutch brewing scene cannot be overstated. Numerous established Dutch microbreweries were inspired to up their game and begin looking beyond Belgian styles, with IPAs and stouts becoming the new mainstays. A new generation of homebrewers saw there was a market beyond their living rooms for the expressive, bold beers they loved to make. Dozens took the plunge and turned professional. The game was most definitely on.

Unprecedented growth
Dutch beer since 2014

WHEN the first edition of this guide emerged in 2014, the number of Dutch beer-making companies, both with and without their own brewing equipment, slid past the 200 mark to much fanfare. Everything seemed set for steady if unremarkable progress. But someone turned up the heat.

For the next few years, new brewing outfits appeared at a rate of 100 every year, two per week in a country of 17 million people. Ridiculous. Their combined numbers broke through the 600 barrier in 2018, and while the growth rate has slowed (fortunately, for those of us trying to keep tabs), that figure could soon reach 700.

Part of this breathtaking rise has been down to availability of new sources of financing such as crowdfunding, but it is also simply because beer is currently on-trend.

The availability of money has also allowed many of those featuring in this guide's first edition as 'Brewers without breweries' to become 'Brewers *with* breweries'. Using someone else's facilities is reasonable so long as a business is honest about it, and has enabled many talented brewers to enter the field. But a brewhouse of one's own can make a big difference in terms of flexibility and consistency, particularly as output grows.

As more Dutch brewers create more craft beers, their availability has also widened, with more and more café owners willing to stock them alongside familiar and, if we are honest, cheaper Belgian and German brands. That, too, we celebrate.

But let's not get carried away. Just four firms produce around 90% of all the beer brewed in Netherlands, and industrial pilsener still accounts for around 85% of all the beer

drunk. Half of that is produced by Heineken. The three other big players are multinationals AB InBev and Asahi, the latter in its capacity as the owner of Grolsch, plus independent but fast-becoming-global Bavaria, or Royal Swinkels Family Brewers as it prefers to be known these days.

An ongoing problem is the government's imposition of disproportionate duties on beer compared to other alcoholic beverages, aligning with the European Union's apparent policy of subsidising wine-making far more than brewing through the Common Agricultural Policy, to the tune of many billions of euros. Of course this has nothing to do with the politicians' and bureaucrats' personal fondness for wine over beer. The duty burden, along with the lack of economy of scale, means smaller brewers cannot compete on price, either with the large breweries or with their Belgian and German counterparts, while maintaining sufficient quality. They, and many café owners, live in fear that tax may drive them out of business.

Meanwhile, as we enter the third decade of the new millennium, two new trends have appeared, one welcome, the other less so. Firstly, as in several comparable countries, low- and non-alcoholic beers have firmly established a beachhead on the Dutch market, and resourceful brewers have discovered ways of making something that was once thoroughly unpalatable rather good.

Secondly, and also in line with developments elsewhere, the major players have woken up to the potential profits in craft beer and decided they want in. Over the past few years, Duvel-Moortgat, a smallish multinational with interests in the US and the

Czech Republic as well as at home in Belgium, has added 't IJ in Amsterdam to its portfolio. Lindeboom has a piece of De Prael, while Heineken has minor stakes in Jopen, Oudaen, Oedipus and others. Bavaria has its fingers in several pies, including a small slice of Maallust and Maximus, and 100% of early trailblazer De Molen, although the circumstances behind the latter takeover were extenuating. Whilst all this is enabling the new subsidiaries to expand production and enter new markets without notable 'dumbing down', it's already restricting the field for new entrants and raises questions about the future direction of the breweries concerned.

So where is Dutch beer heading next, seven decades on from Freddy Heineken's discovery of the power of advertising?

Events could unfold in several different ways. The boom is unlikely to last forever, and there are signs that the end is already in sight. The market could also soon become saturated, leading to stagnation. Beer may even stop being cool, leading to the collapse of the whole craft market.

But we can at least enjoy the ride while it lasts. For now at least, Dutch craft brewers find themselves lying in a bed of roses, albeit one from which someone forgot to remove at least some of the thorns.

The Netherlands
A brief history of a nation of traders

BEFORE cheap airfares made criss-crossing the globe routine, the world had the Dutch. Always a home to many of the great merchant traders of Europe, the Netherlands began to increase its influence as the domination of the Spanish and Portuguese waned, and its power diminished with the emergence of the growing British and French empires. Yet to this day, this small nation punches well above its weight.

Much of the story of the Netherlands is linked inextricably to water – no surprise when half the country lies below sea level.

We know there were tribes here in the Bronze Age, though much of the land remained too boggy to be cultivated.

By the time the region lay on the northern fringes of the Roman Empire, it was occupied largely by three Germanic peoples: the Frisians, the Low Saxons and the Franks. But it was another Germanic tribe, the Batavians, who established the regional identity.

The Romans respected the Batavians as fine soldiers and employed them to defend the borders of their Empire. But in the year 69, after the Romans executed a Batavian leader on false charges of treason and paraded another in chains in Rome, the tribe mounted a rebellion. Despite early successes, the revolt ultimately failed, but the tribe's name would later be used in a foundation myth established by 16th-century writers linking the moment with the uprising against Spanish rule. The original capital of the Dutch East Indies was named Batavia, as were several ships.

Despite the early glimmer of nationalism, throughout the Dark Ages the lights in the western half of the Netherlands went out. It remained barely inhabited until the 11th

century, when local farmers began an ambitious project of draining the swamps, starting a millennium-long obsession with reclaiming land from the sea.

The name Holland first appeared in 1083, referring to a region now comprised of the province of South Holland and the southern part of North Holland. The area's power grew and the Counts of Holland added neighbouring Zeeland and West Frisia to their portfolio.

Guilds were established, with trade flourishing as new markets were developed. New towns sprang up and merchants grew in wealth and power, buying privileges as Holland expanded. Some cities became semi-independent and joined the powerful trading bloc called the Hanseatic League, a medieval forerunner of the European Union.

Eventually, Duke Philip the Good of Burgundy gained control of the region through a skillful mix of natty trade deals, lucky

inheritance and brute force, the 'Good' clearly short for 'good old-fashioned violence'. Nevertheless, many Dutch noblemen welcomed him, taking advantage of a chance to integrate with Flanders. As a result, the Burgundian Netherlands was constituted in 1433.

Consolidation paid off. The unified state broke the trade restraints of the Hanseatic League in key sea battles and the regional economy rocketed. Amsterdam became the leading port of Northern Europe.

Holy Roman Emperor Charles V (1500–58), at the time the most powerful man who had ever lived, introduced religious tolerance of sorts, and declared the Netherlands independent of German and French rule. But he was suceeded by the considerably less sympathetic and vehemently Catholic Philip II of Spain, also a familiar figure as an adversary of England under Elizabeth I.

During the 16th century, Reformation fever swept the northern Netherlands, mainly in the form of Calvinism. Many Calvinists excoriated the abuses of the Catholic church,

associating it with foreign, Spanish influences, and claimed their own moral superiority and piety in opposition to it. Philip responded with persecution and the deployment of the Inquisition.

In 1566, an outbreak of iconoclastic riots known as the *Beeldenstorm* (Iconoclastic Fury), where Calvinists stormed churches and vandalised graven images, was met with brutal repression by Spanish troops under the command of the 'Iron' Duke of Alva. This culminated in a revolt led by Dutch nobles, the most prominent of whom was Willem van Oranje, known in English as William the Silent, *stadhouder* (governor) of the provinces of Holland, Utrecht and Zeeland. The revolt escalated into a much larger conflict that would become known as the Eighty Years' War. Under Willem's leadership, the northern provinces formed the Republic of the Seven United Netherlands, or the United Provinces, which declared independence in 1581. The south became the Spanish Netherlands, covering an area encompassing much of modern Belgium, Luxembourg and the Dutch provinces of North Brabant and Limburg.

As its name implies, this was a war that dragged on. It was not until 1648 that independence was finally recognised, and the new country became known as Holland, and entered a period of spectacular national growth. Or so reads the simple version of history.

The reality was more complex. The heartland of Holland was peaceful and entered an age of prosperity long before 1648. In 1585, the Spanish had captured Antwerp after a long siege, closing the river Schelde (Scheldt) to navigation and driving trade northwards to Amsterdam, which prospered even more vigorously than before.

But around the periphery of the nascent Netherlands, skirmishes and sieges ebbed and flowed, and the commitment of its citizens to the emerging nation state was by no means uniform. Many towns in the east and south with Catholic majorities were content to live under the Hispanic regime and did not want to be 'liberated', especially not by people with whom they fundamentally disagreed on theological grounds.

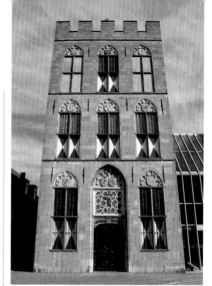

Despite that friction, when peace finally dawned, it heralded an era of unprecedented prosperity. Trade, industry, the arts and sciences all flourished, and for a time Holland was the most economically powerful nation in Europe, supported by a massive fleet of ships used primarily for trading, but also for bullying rivals when the occasion arose. It had to import barley for its own brewing needs but records survive of massive importation and onward export of beers from all its barley-growing neighbours.

One name rose above all others at this time: the Verenigde Oostindische Compagnie (VOC, Dutch East India Company). Founded in 1602, it was in effect the world's first multi-national and for much of the 17th century the world's largest business. Financed by share issues that created the first modern stock exchange, it got rich from the spice trade, dealing mostly in India and Indonesia. A lucrative trade monopoly with the tightly self-sufficient empire of Japan did not hurt either.

The Netherlands dominated northern European trade through its strategic location on the continent's northern coast and at the mouth of two large rivers, the Rijn (Rhine) and the Maas (Meuse). Elsewhere, the more adventurous Dutch were founding colonies, not only in the East Indies, in what became Indonesia, but in North America at Nieuw Amsterdam (New York), in South Africa and the West Indies.

At home, a climate of humanism and tolerance, begun a century earlier with Erasmus, attracted religious refugees. Jewish merchants from Portugal and French Huguenot shop-keepers arrived, adding to the melting pot and propelling the economy. Scientists and free thinkers came from across Europe. The arts flourished, nurturing world-class talents like Rembrandt van Rijn and Johannes Vermeer.

Meanwhile, big-thinking civil engineers were fighting and winning another battle, expanding the land mass by the use of hydraulics. Windmills pumped water from lakes and marshes, turning them into polders. Canal networks spread across cities like cobwebs and merchants built grand waterside houses to show off their wealth.

All this prosperity made the neighbours, most notably England, deeply envious, resulting in three Anglo-Dutch wars. The second, in 1667, famously ended when the Dutch fleet raided Kent by sailing up the river Medway, a victory that marked the peak of Dutch power, even though it barely gets a mention in British history books.

Events took a turn for the worse only five years later, in the *Rampjaar* (disaster year) of 1672. First, England declared war, then France, and then the city states of Münster and Cologne. An Anglo-French sea invasion failed, but only just. To thwart a French land attack, the Dutch had to breach dykes and flood their own land. Defeating Cologne and Münster required the equally dodgy manoeuvre of buying support from other German states with chunks of territory. Peace was restored, but the dazzling performance of the Dutch economy was not.

Then in 1688, perhaps ironically, *stadhouder* Willem III van Oranje was invited to take the throne of England by Protestant nobles opposed to its Catholic king, James II. Hence England got its William III, of Orange, and the Dutch gained a crucial ally in wars against the French.

But the 'Golden Age' was over. Northern European trading shifted focus from Amsterdam to London and Dutch power waned throughout the 18th century. In 1795, Holland became the Batavian Republic, initially a satellite of Napoleon's French empire and later a full imperial province.

When Napoleon's laurel crown began to slip, the Dutch seized their moment. The United Kingdom of the Netherlands was declared in 1813, with the House of Orange as its monarchy. Initially, the territory included most of modern Benelux, but in 1830, an eruption of local tensions in Brussels, stoked by the British, led to the creation of a breakaway state called Belgium. The borders of the Netherlands were finally agreed in 1839 and the country became a parliamentary democracy with a constitutional monarch in 1848.

The Netherlands remained neutral during the First World War (1914–18), the German Schlieffen Plan requiring the invasion of Belgium only as a way of reaching Paris. The deal enabled the country to avoid trench warfare, but its enforced isolation from the trade routes affected the economy badly and imposed massive deprivation.

The Dutch responded to the Great Depression of the 1930s with an ambitious programme of public building works, pre-empting US President Franklin Roosevelt's New Deal as a creative approach to tackling high unemployment. Most prominent among these projects was the Afsluitdijk, the sea dyke that closed off the Zuiderzee inlet and created the freshwater IJsselmeer lake in 1933.

With Nazism and fascism on the rise across Europe, most Dutch people assumed German Führer Adolf Hitler would respect their neutrality. He did not, instead launching an invasion on May 10 1940 that plunged the Netherlands into the Second World War. When the Dutch showed signs of holding out, the Luftwaffe flattened Rotterdam, killing 900 and leaving 78,000 homeless. A threat to repeat the exercise on Utrecht persuaded the government to capitulate.

The occupation was harsh, prompting many to join the Resistance, though worse befell the country's 140,000 Jews. Some 40,000 went into hiding, like the family of Anne Frank in Amsterdam, or fled. Of the 100,000 who stayed, only 1,000 survived.

In 1944, following D-Day, much of the Netherlands was liberated, though parts remained occupied into 1945. Angered by Dutch defiance, the Nazis cut off food supplies, resulting in mass starvation during the *Hongerwinter* (hunger winter) of 1944–45. Many died, with others kept alive mainly by being bombed with bread by the Allies.

After the war, the Netherlands once more focussed on rebuilding itself, a plan that pushed steadily forth even in the face of massive flooding in 1953, when a huge storm caused dykes to collapse in Zeeland, inundating the land. Around 1,800 people drowned, prompting the government to commission the building of the Delta Works flood barrier, yet another wonder of the modern world, which eventually became operational in 1986.

The modern Netherlands is again prosperous thanks to its trading prowess and its capacity to cooperate with neighbours. Even as the war was ending in 1944, it formed a customs union with the neighbouring, and historically related, territories of Belgium and Luxembourg, extended into the Benelux Economic Union in 1958. This created an early blueprint for what would become the European Union, of which the Netherlands is a founder member.

The country's liberal values have led to it being famed as a land where prostitution and soft drugs are accepted. Yet the Netherlands is as prone to economic downturns as anywhere else. Joblessness brings out the worst intolerance in some, putting discontent about immigration on the political agenda. As in many other European lands, the far right has made advances by exploiting people's fears and prejudices.

So yes, there are blips, but I have lived here long enough to know that, while not everything is perfect, there are far worse places to be.

As you would expect from a country that has for centuries sat at the centre of world trading, there are almost infinite ways to get here.

Getting there

By SEA

The traditional way of reaching the Netherlands from the UK is by ferry. It's inevitably also the slowest option but can be remarkably civilised if you treat the crossing itself as part of the experience.

Drivers starting their journeys in the south of England will likely find it faster and more convenient to travel from Dover to Calais or Dunkerque and take to the motorways rather than using a direct ferry. This isn't recommended for foot passengers and cyclists as integration with public transport at the ports is very poor, with Eurostar trains and direct ferries providing more practical options.

Individual ferry company websites are listed below, but aferry.com and ferrysavers.co.uk are handy one-stop shops for comparing fares. For short visits, five-day excursion fares booked at least a week in advance can be significantly cheaper than last-minute bookings.

Note that cabin reservations are compulsory on all overnight services.

Direct

Harwich–Hoek van Holland is operated by Stena Line (stenaline.co.uk) using two very comfortable vessels, the largest of their kind in the world. There are two crossings daily in each direction, with the day service taking around 6½ hours, the night service taking an extra hour but allowing three more hours on board. This can be an excellent option for foot passengers and cylists as both ferry terminals are integrated with rail stations. Harwich International has trains to/from London Liverpool Street and is directly accessible from many other parts of Britain. Hoek van Holland Haven station has connections to Schiedam, the interchange for Amsterdam, and Rotterdam Centraal, and a long-overunning project to integrate it into the Rotterdam Metro finally opened in late 2019. Good value Dutchflyer through tickets cover the journey between Liverpool Street (and other stations in eastern England) and any Dutch station: look for Sail & Rail on the Stena website.

Hull–Rotterdam Europoort, operated by P&O Ferries (poferries.com), takes 12 hours. Nightly crossings leave at 20.30 from both ports, arriving the following morning. Transfer buses for foot passengers connect with both Hull and Rotterdam Centraal stations, and there's also a direct bus from Europoort to Amsterdam, though it may be quicker and more comfortable to catch the Rotterdam bus and change to a train.

Newcastle–IJmuiden, operated by DFDS Seaways (dfdsseaways.com), takes 16 hours. Nightly crossings leave Newcastle at 17.00 and IJmuiden at 17.30, arriving the following morning around 09.30. There are transfer buses for foot passengers from Newcastle station to the ferry port, and from IJmuiden to Amsterdam Centraal.

Rosyth–Eemshaven. As we went to press, a company called TEC-Farragon was in talks to create a direct freight and passenger link between Scotland and the northern Netherlands. The plan was to start services by the end of 2019, with the journey time expected to be 20 hours.

Via France or Belgium

Dover–Calais, operated by P&O and DFDS, is still the most frequent, popular and fastest route from Britain to mainland Europe, with up to 40 sailings a day in high season, taking around 90 minutes. Calais is a 2½-hour drive from the nearest Dutch city, via the unpredictable Antwerp Ring. Only P&O accepts foot passengers, who will likely face a long walk to or from the nearest stations at both ports and no convenient rail connections from Calais Ville to the Netherlands.

Dover–Dunkerque has sailings at least every two hours and a two-hour crossing time. This is a slick DFDS operation which is often the cheapest for drivers and deposits you 20km closer to the border, but doesn't carry foot passengers.

Hull–Zeebrugge, operated by P&O, has a similar pattern to the Rotterdam route, departing a bit earlier, but with no other obvious advantage for travel to the Netherlands.

By CAR via The Channel Tunnel

Le Shuttle, operated by Eurotunnel (eurotunnel.com), is the fastest road-to-road connection from southern England. Transporter trains run through the Channel Tunnel up to four times an hour, linking to the French coastal autoroute. From here a series of motorways takes you east and north to the Netherlands via Belgium. Fares are charged per vehicle, with the cheapest prices available airline-style to those who book the least popular slots in advance. Fast, efficient and as entertaining as watching paint dry.

By TRAIN

From the UK

Eurostar (eurostar.com) is Britain's token high speed train service from London St Pancras International and Ebbsfleet International to Rotterdam Centraal (3¼ hours) and Amsterdam Centraal (four hours) via the Channel Tunnel and Brussels. Advance booking is obligatory and, as with airlines, fares vary dramatically depending on how early you book and the level of demand on your chosen service. Also reminiscent of air travel is the minimum 30-minute check-in for security and immigration procedures at the UK stations. Disagreements over the implementation of these controls at the Dutch end have resulted in the bizarre circumstance that, while three trains daily travel directly from St Pancras to Amsterdam, in the opposite direction passengers have to disembark at Brussels, go through checks there and board a second train, adding 45 minutes to the journey. We are told this will be sorted out in 2020, but it is already years overdue. For other major Dutch cities, the best option is usually to head for Rotterdam and Amsterdam and change where necessary: use the journey planner at ns.nl.

From Belgium and France

High-speed Thalys services (thalys.com) connect Amsterdam and Brussels in two hours via Schiphol, Rotterdam and Antwerp, with some trains continuing to or from Paris Gare du Nord (about 3½ hours). Seat reservations are required, with cheaper prices for advance tickets.

Hourly Intercity Direct services take 45 minutes longer between Amsterdam and Brussels via Breda and Brussels Airport, but are cheaper and operate on a turn-up-and-go basis so you don't have to book a specific train. Slower but regular trains run on the Maastricht—Liège and Roosendaal—Antwerp routes. More details on all these options are at nsinternational.nl.

From Germany

Intercity Express (ICE) runs direct trains to Amsterdam and Utrecht from a large number of German cities with remarkable efficiency, as you would expect from Deutsche Bahn (DB, bahn.de). Seat reservations are required, with cheaper prices if you book ahead on specific trains.

Five local rail services connect border towns with Germany: Hengelo—Bad Bentheim; Enschede—Münster; Enschede—Dortmund; Venlo—Hamm (via Düsseldorf); and Heerlen—Aachen. These are turn-up-and-go services and no reservations are required. A sixth route from Groningen—Leer is now an express bus service.

By BUS

If you have more time than money, you can travel from most major European centres to Amsterdam and some other Dutch cities by bus, though it is a buttock-numbing experience, with the trip from London to Amsterdam taking 12 hours or longer. The most comprehensive European long-distance bus network is operated by Eurolines (eurolines.eu); among its competitors are German-owned Flixbus (flixbus.com) and BlaBlaBus (ouibus.com), linked to French rail operator SNCF.

By AIR

The continued success of low-cost airlines means that, from the UK and most other parts of Europe besides Belgium and Germany, the fastest and cheapest way to get here is to fly, whatever the environmental impact. For those arriving from beyond Europe, who have no other option, the good news is that Amsterdam's Schiphol airport – the only one constructed on the site of a major sea battle – is one of Europe's largest international hubs.

The range of options for travelling by air from the UK has gone, er, skywards but study the price carefully as few companies are entirely transparent about how much you pay. Up-front fares are designed to look tempting but may not include airport charges, credit card fees and tax, which can push the price considerably higher. You may also incur charges if you bring more than hand luggage or cannot check in online.

Some budget airlines herd their customers like cattle, although all allocate seats beforehand these days, so it is less of a scrum at the gate than it once was. Most then spend the whole flight trying to sell you stuff. It is all part of the price paid for saving.

Full-price airlines give you more legroom and aren't always that much more expensive, though in-flight catering on short-haul routes has been cut back, typically to a free drink and a snack, often nothing more than a slice of dry sponge cake.

Cheap ticket websites may provide a good way of comparing fares but seldom offer better value than buying directly from airlines. Try several before settling on the best deal.

Airports

Amsterdam Schiphol (schiphol.nl), known in the Netherlands simply as Schiphol, is by far the largest Dutch airport, accounting for 92% of all air arrivals, with over 70 million passengers passing through each year. More than 10 million of those are transiting to/from the UK, with direct flights to around 20 British airports at the last count, many operating several times daily. Flying time is roughly an hour from England, 90 minutes from Scotland or Northern Ireland. Be warned budget services from the UK often arrive at the remote H gates, located a bracing walk away in a neighbouring parish.

Up to eight trains every hour connect the airport directly with Amsterdam Centraal station. Standard rail fares apply and trains even run hourly throughout the night. Additional direct trains serve most major Dutch cities, plus Antwerp and Brussels, some of them using high-speed lines.

The second-largest Dutch airport is **Eindhoven** (eindhovenairport.nl), with around six million passengers annually. Its direct connections to the British Isles are the Ryanair flights from London Stansted, Edinburgh, Manchester and Dublin. Bus 400 provides a regular and fast service from the airport to Eindhoven railway station, stopping only twice along the way; it's supplemented by bus 401 which is marginally slower.

British Airways flights from London City serve **Rotterdam-The Hague** airport (rotterdamthehagueairport.nl) but as these are marketed at business travellers they rarely offer the cheapest fares. The airport is linked o central Rotterdam by bus 33.

Up north, **Groningen** airport (groningenairport.nl) has direct Flybe flights from London Southend, Newquay and Guernsey. Bus 9 gets you from there to the city.

In the south, **Maastricht-Aachen** airport (maa.nl) sometimes has UK-bound traffic, but it is currently only used for holiday charter flights to the Mediterranean.

Airlines

Air France-KLM (klm.com) may have acquired a semi-Gallic moniker but is still considered by the Dutch to be Royal Dutch Airlines, the national flag carrier. It operates its many short-haul routes, including to regional UK airports, as KLM Cityhopper.

British Airways (ba.com) leaves the regional services to the competition and only flies to Schiphol from London's Gatwick, Heathrow and City airports, the latter as BA CityFlyer.

EasyJet (easyjet.com) was the low-cost pioneer that shrunk North Sea prices and still offers some of the most convenient and cheapest services from UK regional airports.

Jet2.com (jet2.com) flies to Amsterdam Schiphol from Leeds—Bradford airport. **FlyBe** (flybe.com), or 'Fly mayBe' as it is known by regular customers, flies to Schiphol from half a dozen UK airports. **Ryanair** (ryanair.com) provides its famously no-frills services between London Stansted, Edinburgh or Manchester and Eindhoven. It also flies from Dublin to both Eindhoven and Schiphol.

Being

Novice travellers need not fear. English is spoken almost everywhere, prices are generally as displayed and those locals who are not friendly are usually incredibly efficient, unless they have sunken eyes and a crack pipe sticking out of their pocket.

there

SLEEPING

The Netherlands has all the various sleeping options you would expect in a First World country, from campsites, hostels and B&Bs, via small family-run guesthouses, to chain franchise or international standard five-star hotels.

The ease of finding a room depends on when and where you go, though Amsterdam is always a special case where accommodation is often in short supply. Many hotels there appear to be permanently full so book as far ahead as possible, as last-minute deals tend to favour daylight robbery over basement clearance rates. Alternatively stay somewhere outside the city and make use of the efficient rail network to travel in.

Elsewhere, except during special events, finding somewhere to stay is generally not a problem. And while cute country inns may fill at weekends, business hotels that are full on weekdays may offer substantial discounts.

If you arrive somewhere without a reservation, the best place to head is the local tourist office (VVV), though most ask a small booking fee to cover costs.

Hotels

Dutch hotel star ratings fall more or less in line with other international systems. Three stars and up should mean a comfortable room with bathroom en suite. Like anywhere, ratings only measure facilities, while real quality will vary depending on intangibles like design, how recently a place was renovated and how charming the staff are feeling.

Like-for-like, room rates tend to be higher than in neighbouring Germany and Belgium. Prices in Amsterdam skyrocket in high summer. On the other hand, a room in a backwater town out of season can be a steal. Most cheaper hotels include breakfast in the room rate; the top international chains charge extra for the pleasure.

Small hotels are not required to have lifts and older Dutch staircases can be notorously steep, tight and narrow. Do your research beforehand if this is a consideration. Be aware too that some older city centre places are not always properly soundproofed against nearby bars that stay open with loud music into the early hours.

Pensions and B&Bs

There are B&B options throughout the country, priced cheaper than hotels, though quality can vary from superb to not. This is one area where the arrival of **airbnb.com** has upended the market, opening up countless new options but also upsetting many people along the way. Its success in Amsterdam has resulted in more visitors than ever crowding into the capital, lengthening queues at every tourist sight. Longer-established **bedandbreakfast.nl** is an alternative booking site worth considering.

Youth Hostels

If you don't mind sharing with strangers, hostels offer cheap, basic accommodation. Most hostel beds are in shared dorms, though some have a few twin-bed rooms with en-suite bathrooms, though the twins might be bunks and you might pay extra for bedding. Most hostels include breakfast and can provide other meals with advance booking.

The official Dutch youth hostel chain Stayokay (**stayokay.com**) runs 22 places up and down the country. There are a fair number of independent places in Amsterdam but few in other cities.

MOVING ABOUT

Public transport

For train information, use **ns.nl**. For the broader public transport network, try **9292.nl**. As a last resort, call the premium-rate phoneline 0900 9292 and prepare to be fleeced.

Trains

The train is generally the most efficient way to travel round the Netherlands. The network is extensive, services on most routes run at least twice and sometimes up to six times an hour, most trains run to time and the delays that do occur tend to be minor. Fares are generally much lower than in the UK.

There are broadly two types of service. Intercity trains stop only at major stations, while Sprinters defy their name by stopping everywhere. Intercity and many local trains are provided by the national operator NS (Nederlandse Spoorwegen, Dutch Railways,

ns.nl). Some local services are franchised to private operators like Arriva: NS tickets are usually valid on these.

Seat reservations are not possible on domestic services, so if you need to be seated, travel outside peak hours or get good at pleading with busy commuters.

Smoking is not permitted on trains or outside designated zones at stations.

Metro

Only Amsterdam and Rotterdam have suburban metro networks, though one of Rotterdam's lines goes to Den Haag. The tram and bus systems can be more convenient, though the opening of Amsterdam's long-awaited Noord–Zuidlijn (North–South line, officially line 52) in 2018 has provided new options for getting to outlying districts, particularly in the north.

Buses and trams

City and regional buses, and in some places trams, are excellent and frequent. Many bus and tram routes start or end at a railway stations, making connections both logical and simple. Buses are clean and increasingly benefit from dedicated lanes. Routes are clearly marked on maps in bus stations and at many stops. On board, a recorded voice and electronic displays inform passengers of approaching stops.

The longer bus routes essentially substitute for trains in areas the railways never reached. We have no hesitation in recommending them to inexperienced travellers.

Metro, tram and bus tickets

The **OV-chipkaart** (ov-chipkaart.nl) is a national electronic payment card that covers the whole domestic public transport network of buses, trams and metro: OV stands for *openbaar vervoer* (public transport). It works similarly to London's Oyster card and other city-based travel smartcards: load it with a balance then hold it against detectors whenever you enter and leave buses, trams or metro stations and it will be debited for the actual distance travelled. For trams and buses, you have to check off one vehicle and onto the next each time.

'Anonymous' cards valid for five years are available from metro, train and bus stations and some magazine kiosks and supermarkets. The card itself costs €7.50 and will also need to be loaded with credit before use, either over the counter or using a machine. You can also buy disposable pre-loaded paper tickets for short journeys at stations and from bus and tram drivers, and in Amsterdam from conductors in the booth at the rear of trams, but for anything other than an occasional journey these work out much more expensive. Note that cash is no longer accepted on many buses and trams for security reasons.

If staying longer, a personalised card is a good investment as you can manage it online and set up automatic subscriptions. Residents of Benelux and Germany can order one for the same price as an anonymous card via the website. If you live elsewhere, ask for an application pack at an Arriva or Connexxion bus station or an RET (Rotterdam transport) ticket office, pay €10.50 and have the card sent to a Dutch address such as a hotel. In both cases, you'll need a digital photo.

If you're just staying in Amsterdam, Rotterdam or another big city, an alternative option is a one, two or three-day card valid on the local network. The Amsterdam day card includes the train from Schiphol: see gvb.nl.

Rail tickets

The OV-chipkaart system also works on domestic trains, using pillars within the station, or, as is increasingly the case, electronic gates. As rail fares are usually more expensive, you will need a minimum balance of €20.00 to use an anonymous card or €10.00 to use a personalised card. You only need to check out and in when changing trains if switching to a different rail operator.

If you're making a long rail journey or several short journeys on the same day, the best option may be a *dagkaart* (day ticket) which covers you for unlimited second class travel on NS for only €53. See panel for how to get these even more cheaply.

The ultimate plan is to replace all traditional train tickets with direct electronic payments. For now, you can still buy a ticket online or from machines found on all stations, loading it onto an OV-chipkaart if you prefer. At busier stations, there are even human beings sitting behind counters who can sell you tickets, though at a modest extra cost. You cannot buy a ticket once on board a train and there are hefty fines for travelling without one.

You can break your rail journey as much as you wish before midnight. First-class travel costs 50% more than second. The only advantage of return (*retour*) tickets is a minor increase in convenience if travelling out and back on the same day, as they cost the same as two single fares (*enkele reis*) and are only valid until 04.00 the following morning.

Non-folding bicycles (€6.90) and any animal not carried in a bag (€3.20) need their own day ticket. Guide dogs travel free. Non-folding bicycles are banned from trains on Mo-Fr 06.30–09.00 & 16.00–18.30.

Taxis

Convenient they may be, cheap they are not. You cannot hail a taxi in the street but will need to book by phone or pick one up at a designated rank. Licensed cabs have blue number plates. Most drivers are helpful and courteous and do not expect a tip as the fare is already damaging enough. The history of Uber in the Netherlands has been a controversial one: it only operates in the Randstad area and in Eindhoven and is obliged to use licensed drivers with no price advantage.

IDER'S TIP

Dutch chain stores – Albert Heijn, Blokker, Hema and Kruidvat – regularly offer heavily discounted train ts that can save a fortune on long journeys, for example selling *dagkaarten* for under €20 rather than the dard €53. Some tickets have restrictions preventing travel at peak times on weekdays, so read the small print. ome of these offers are physical tickets that must be checked in and out in the normal way at stations on day of travel. Others are codes that you enter online, either to create a bar code for downloading to your e, or to generate a PDF ticket that you print off and carry with you.

he consumer website **treinreiziger.nl** keeps tabs on the best-available current offers. It is in Dutch only, but ring the search term *goedkope treinkaartjes* (cheap train tickets) will help you find what you need.

Private transport

Cycling

The Dutch are enthusiastic cyclists and make considerable provision for cycles in towns, across the countryside and both at stations and on trains. That said, pedal power demands concentration in busy cities and we do not recommended it to the inexperienced, especially after a few beers.

You can rent a bicycle from most railway stations for a reasonable daily rate but be warned that standard models often use a disconcerting braking system that relies on back-pedalling gently. This can throw the uninitiated, sometimes off the bike altogether. Machines with handlebar brakes usually cost extra.

Driving

A dense network of well-maintained motorways and other roads traverses the country, though traffic can be heavy, especially in the Randstad. Tolls are mostly reserved for tunnels and river ferries.

The Dutch authorities are about as keen on drunk driving as the rest of us. The legal alcohol limit is 0.5g/l, which is lower than in the UK. The Netherlands also has a campaign to encourage drivers not to drink at all and be 'Bob', the designated driver. Punishments for exceeding the limit include imprisonment.

Fuel prices fluctuate around the higher end of the European norm, though diesel is significantly cheaper than in the UK. Fuel is available 24/7 on motorways, elsewhere from 06.00 to 22.00 without difficulty, though rural areas can be awkward on Sunday.

Parking Street parking is difficult in many towns, especially Amsterdam, where the risks of taking your car often outweigh the benefits.

Many urban centres are pedestrianised or 'shared space' where pedestrians and cyclists have priority, town centres are metered and other areas reserved exclusively for resident permit-holders (*vergunninghouders*). In Blue Zones you need to display a blue timer disc on the dashboard, which you can buy from ANWB motoring shops, some newsagents, and police stations. Illegally parked cars may get clamped or towed.

All big towns have multistorey car parks, often the most convenient option but rarely cheap. Parking may be free in suburban areas, smaller towns and villages, at Park & Ride centres and almost anywhere besides city centres and tourist spots on Sundays.

Tips and rules On motorways, as from March 2020 the speed limit is 100 km/h from 06.00–19.00; at other times it is 130 km/h unless otherwise stated; on rural highways it is 80 km/h unless clearly marked as 100; in built-up areas it is 50, dropping to 30 in some shopping or residential areas and around schools.

In towns or on minor roads, English-speaking drivers can be alarmed by traffic merging from the right that acts like it owns the road. In fact it probably does, unless a yellow diamond sign indicates you are on a road with priority. Local drivers who have the right of way often pull out without looking.

The Dutch veer towards aggressive driving in other ways too, for example pulling out into implausibly small gaps between cars travelling at speed in the outside lane of a busy motorway. Many take the view that using their indicator when doing so might cause it to wear out.

Other national driving games include beeping the driver in front if they fail to react within a millisecond of a traffic signal turning green, and ploughing through amber signals.

Be wary of cyclists, especially at night when they may have had a few. Most seek self-preservation by observing the rules of the road but many do not, preferring to ignore red lights and to swerve in front of you on the assumption that you will give way. They know that in any legal tussle the law will favour them, no matter whose fault the accident may have been. They will also claim priority from the right, as above, to the occasional horror of all concerned.

Although map makers and transport planners have applied the Europe-wide E-numbering system to Dutch motorways, sign makers in the Netherlands have not. Motorways (*snelwegen*) are designated *autoweg* or A roads, while other main roads are called *nationaal* or N roads.

Seatbelts are compulsory, front and back. Using a handheld mobile phone while driving is illegal as well as moronic. Front fog lights must only be used in fog when visibility drops below 200m, and rear fog lights only when it falls below 50m. Winter tyres are not compulsory as in Germany but are advisable in colder winters, which are often harsher than in the UK. By law, all cars must carry a first aid kit and a warning triangle for breakdowns. The French requirement to carry two breathalyser kits does not apply, yet.

For breakdowns on the road, contact the ANWB on **T** 088 269 2888 or via **anwb.nl**.

Oh, and drive on the right.

Island hopping

The Frisian island chain dribbles like a string of massive bulwarks protecting the northern coast of the Netherlands and German Lower Saxony from being ravaged by the North Sea.

The Western Frisian or Wadden Islands have a windswept, solitary beauty.

Listed below is the ferry information for islands with a beery draw. The Vlieland boats are operated by the same company as for Terschelling, and those for Schiermonnikoog by the Ameland crew.

Texel

Car ferries between Den Helder, at the northern tip of North Holland, and Texel are operated by TESO (**teso.nl**). Tickets can be bought at the port or online. Boats leave the mainland on the hour and Texel on the half hour, from 06.00 to 21.30 each day, starting later on Sundays and running more frequently in high summer. The crossing takes 20 minutes and it is neither necessary nor possible to book a specific sailing. There is no check-in on the return leg: just turn up and board. Den Helder port is a 20-minute walk from the station, or take bus 33.

Terschelling

Ferries between the Friesland port of Harlingen and West-Terschelling are operated year-round by Rederij Doeksen (**rederij-doeksen.nl**), sailing between five and 10 times daily, with more departures in summer. The car ferry takes two hours, while the 45-minute *sneldienst* (fast service) takes foot passengers only: bicycles must use the car ferry. Buy tickets online, or at the port, which is next to Harlingen Haven train station. For short stays, it is cheaper to leave your car in Harlingen's long-stay car park.

Ameland

Ferries between the Friesland coastal village of Holwerd and the quay at Nes on Ameland are operated by Wagenborg (**wpd.nl**), typically six times daily with fewer on Sunday and more in summer. Crossings take 45 minutes each way and tickets can be bought online or at the port. As for Terschelling, for short stays it is cheaper to leave cars on the mainland. Bus 66 or 166 from Leeuwarden station takes 36 minutes to reach Holwerd.

EATING

In years gone by, before the likes of Delia Smith, Jamie Oliver and Hugh Fearnley-Whittingstall up-ended our meagre culinary traditions, when French, Belgian and Italian friends poked gentle jibes at British cooking, one easy defence was, "Have you tried Dutch?"

Traditional Dutch cooking tends towards simple, filling and frankly unexciting. The emphasis at the national horeca (hotel-restaurant-catering) cookery course was always on competence and cleanliness rather than imagination and pizzazz. Thus there were few shockers in cafés and restaurants, but not much to make a song and dance about either. Flair is a word that has only belatedly entered the average Dutch chef's lexicon.

But over the three decades since we began observing the Dutch culinary scene, restaurants and bistros have made huge strides. And in the past several years pub grub has also moved away from the familiar and comforting. You are as likely to find pulled pork or gourmet burgers on a bar menu these days as tomato soup from a tin.

Meals and mealtimes

A typical breakfast (ontbijt) in a mid-range hotel means sliced bread or rolls with thin-sliced cheese and ham, yoghurt, jams, fruit and a hard-boiled egg, the last of these being the only warm item. Fancier hotels will offer greater variety, leaning on overseas traditions to present a cooked breakfast. The distinctly Dutch addition is chocolate hagelslag (hailstones), which generations of Netherlanders have sprinkled on their daily bread since early childhood. Also popular among those with a sweet tooth is ontbijtkoek, a spiced breakfast cake.

Lunch is typically sandwiches, rolls or soup, with cheese and ham featuring once more. Most cafés will start serving at 12.00, and some continue until 17.00, making a seamless transition to an early supper.

Dinner is generally heartier and may be advertised as fixed-price three-course menu (3-gangenmenu). Most places start serving it at 17.00 or 17.30. Kitchen closing times vary but most have stopped by 22.30. To err on the safe side, arrive by 21.00 and note that the Dutch eat out early on Sundays, when restaurants may be packed at 17.30 and empty by 20.00.

Portions can be huge and, as elsewhere, the more expensive the dish, the smaller the plate. Café food is often more generous than restaurant fare.

Etiquette dictates that, once your food is served, your server will say eet smakelijk, literally 'eat tastily' and the equivalent of the French bon appetit. Smile warmly and thank them politely. Halfway through eating, or when they clear your plate, they will ask if you are enjoying or have enjoyed your food. The correct response is lekker, an untranslatable word that transmits positive regard and means 'tasty' in this context, regardless of whether it was.

Beer snacks

The national bar snack is bitterballen, made from meat mechanically recovered from the bones of a cow, ground to a mush, rolled into balls, deep-fried in breadcrumbs and served searingly hot. Dipping them into bland yellow mustard (mosterd) cools them a little.

Other popular drinking snacks (borrelhapjes) include cubes of semi-hard cheese (kaas) and/or salami, served with the same dull mustard. Ossenworst is raw or lightly cured beef sausage, like a tubular variant of steak tartare. Nuts (noten) in various formats are normally dispensed free, peanuts in shell being popular in wooden-floored bars where the shells should be thrown on the floor and trodden in to provide wood-preserving oils, allegedly. Hard-boiled eggs in the shell may appear in traditional brown cafés.

Other snacks

The national staple is frietjes (also patat friet or frites), the local incarnation of chips/frites/fries. Street stalls serve these up in cardboard cones, smothered in a great gob of some high-calorie mayonnaise-like ooze, to be eaten with a wooden fork. Besides the default topping, there's often a battery of pump-topped containers dispensing other

varieties, sometimes in combination. Most pub main courses also come with *frietjes*.

Another streetside favourite is a *Hollandse nieuwe* or *matjes haring*, a beheaded, scrubbed and largely filleted raw herring offered with chopped raw onion and some variety of pickled gourd. Eat cut into squares or else grab it by the attached tail, tip your head back, lower the fish into your waiting mouth and devour like a performing dolphin bobbing for rewards. We do not recommend eating the tail.

Other fish snacks found at altogether grander stalls include pickled herring, marinaded cooked herring, breadcrumbed or *kibbeling* (battered fish bits) and variations on smoked, cured and sauced sea and freshwater fish.

At the other end of the dietary health scale are the hole-in-the-wall, coin-operated vending machines that dispense alleged food items through a bank of small glass doors, often found in stations or alongside shops selling *frietjes*. We urge you to leave these to the experts: drunks, students, drunk students and those who have lost all sense of taste and smell following an unfortunate injury. Higher-end contents include dry burger patties, descending via all manner of deep-fried objects such as *kroketten* (big *bitterballen*) to *frikandellen* (skinless tributes to the science of meat rendering).

Soup

Soup (*soep*) is considered an essential starter to any meal. The most sought-after are tomato (*tomaten*), onion (*uien*), oxtail (*ossenstaart*), and mustard (*mosterd*). Vegetarians should be aware that vegetable soup (*groentensoep*) often contains a type of meatball (*soepballen*), though some are now soya-based.

Head-and-shoulders above all of the above is *erwtensoep*, a pea soup also informally called *snert*. Served in winter and hearty enough to be the main meal, it is made from dried split peas boiled at length with leek, celeriac, carrot, parsley, smoked sausage (*rookworst*) and a bit of bacon (*spek*) for flavour, then served with *katenspek*, a smoked bacon eaten cold like ham, on slices of dense, chewy rye bread (*roggebrood*). Vegetarian versions are occasionally seen.

Pub grub

After simple filled rolls (*belegde broodjes*), perhaps the most common lunchtime pub standard is *uitsmijter*, often translated prosaically on an English menu as 'three fried eggs on bread'. Depending on the café, this can be overcooked eggs on processed white bread with tasteless cheese and watery ham, or a nostalgia-forming gastronomic epiphany complete with tasty bread, quality bacon and flavoursome melted cheese.

Then there is pub grub with colonial influence. In Indonesia, *satay* or *saté* means bamboo sticks threaded with delicate morsels of grilled meat, often served with chillied peanut sauce. In café-speak this becomes a giant metal skewer spearing industrial chunks of pork or chicken, served with chips and swamped in a puddle of thick, sweet peanut goo.

Pancakes (*pannenkoeken*) are popular, served with a range of savoury as well as sweet fillings. Do not expect delicate lacy *crêpes* – these are thick and hearty discs designed to keep draughts out and intended to be doused in syrup (*stroop*) before eating, whatever the other toppings.

Although originating from the Alsace, *flammkuchen* have become a staple of many a Dutch pub menu and festival food stall. They are similar to very thin-crust pizza, with cream replacing tomato sauce.

Filet americain is a more finely ground form of steak tartare imported from Belgium, consisting of spiced raw minced beef. Do not order it medium rare.

Uitsmijter

Indigenous restaurant food

Most but not all traditional Dutch dishes are designed to allow the locals to survive the winter gales that whip in off the North Sea.

Stamppot and *hutspot* are one-pot meals in which (usually) smoked sausage (*rookworst*), potatoes (*aardappelen*) and one or more vegetables, most commonly curly kale (*boerenkool*) or cabbage (*kool*), are boiled up together, sometimes with onion (*ui*). The sausage is then temporarily removed while the rest is mashed with hot milk, butter and nutmeg. These domestic favourites, once a rare find on professional menus, are starting to appear more often in restaurants and pubs showing a renewed confidence in local classics.

The Dutch share the German love of eating pigs in various forms, either as pork (*varkensvlees*), ham or bacon (*spek*), accompanied at home by apple purée (*appelmoes*).

Everything but the oink, as the French say, is considered edible, and if something appears meaty but its origins are unspecified, it is probably pig.

Appelmoes is also considered an acceptable accompaniment to chicken (*kip*), which is enormously popular in grilled or roasted form.

For a nation that in large part arose out of, and continues to share half its border with, the sea, the Netherlands is not especially noted for fishy delicacies beyond the ubiquitous herring. Mussels (*mosselen*) are common in the late summer, when the new season for farmed shellfish begins, but at other times most of the crop is sold to the Belgians. The largest stocks come from the Zeeland delta around the town of Yerseke (pronounced 'ear sucker'). The majority are steamed in the shell, using stock made with celery and onion only (*natuur*), or with the addition of white wine (*witte wijn*), cream (*room*), garlic (*knoflook*) or curry (*kerrie*).

Other fish dishes feature salmon (*zalm*), Dover sole (*slibtong*), lemon sole (*tongfilet*) or cod (*kabeljauw*), with occasional appearances for a more-expensive but highly prized local favourite, smoked eel (*gerookte paling*).

On the vegetable side, much is grown, particularly in the massive acreage of greenhouses that light the way for pilots descending into Schiphol from the North Sea, but is mainly of boy band quality: good looking but insipid. One exception is white asparagus (*asperges*), seen mostly in May, particularly in Limburg where the majority is produced. It is cultivated in the dark, inside mounds of earth beneath lightproof plastic sheeting, keeping the shoots colourless, the green variety being considered unsubtle and inferior.

Ethnic restaurants

Just as the British have adopted curry from their colonial past, so the Dutch have *rijsttafel* (rice table). Served in restaurants designated Indonesian, often run by third or fourth generation descendants of Javanese immigrants, the dishes served have authentic origins but the dining concept is Dutch.

The core of a *rijsttafel* is based on West Sumatran *nasi padang*, in which you are served a dish of everything available but only pay for what you eat. This being the Netherlands, the tweak is that you pay for the lot, with diners ordering one apiece, ordering fewer and sharing is often frowned upon. Most include 15–20 dishes of variable spiciness, cooled with pickled vegetable (*atjar*) or spiked with chilli sauce (*sambal*). Much food is wasted and doggie bags jettisoned after breakfast.

Some Indonesian places offer the more manageable mixed rice (*nasi rames*), a one-plate variant involving rice with spoonful-sized portions of several other dishes.

Besides straight Indonesian cuisine, every Dutch town has a *Chinees-Indonesisch* restaurant serving an amalgam of Chinese and Indonesian cuisine that falls short of either. The red-orange sauces that cover most dishes vary so little from one place to another that we suspect all are prepared in a giant central kitchen and then piped nationwide.

Vegetarian and vegan

Though the variety of vegetarian (*vegetarisch*) and vegan food is perhaps not as wide as in the UK or the US, it has certainly increased in recent years, and those who avoid meat will find eating out much easier than in France, for example. Many more traditional Dutch restaurants and even pubs now offer at least one *vegetarische schotel* (vegetarian dish), a welcome change from the times when veggie options were mainly limited to a few specialist outlets besides ethnic places such as Indian (*Indiaans*) restaurants and pizza and pasta joints.

Desserts and sweet things

Dame Blanche is vanilla ice cream with hot chocolate sauce and whipped cream. A good insight into Dutch restaurant psyche can be gained by asking for flavours other than vanilla.

Dutch fruit pies are legendary, particularly apple (*appeltaart* or *appelgebak*). The whipped cream (*slagroom*) offered alongside is usually from an aerosol, an accoutrement also often wielded by streetside ice cream sellers to add yet further fat content to their wares. Traditional stone-baked tarts (*vlaai*) include the excellent fruit-filled Limburg variety (*Limburgse vlaai*) topped with a sweet lattice pastry, baked sweetened rice tart (*rijstevlaai*) and creamy variations on custard, egg and advocaat, which are personal favourites.

Cheese

The Netherlands is famous for cheese (*kaas*). For the most part we cannot fathom why. Though the days when there was little beyond flavourless Edam or Gouda have thankfully gone, the country remains some way behind France, Italy, Belgium, Spain and, let's not be modest here, Britain in terms of quality and interest.

Most Dutch cheesemaking relies on variations of a hard cheese of the Gouda type: firm, yellow and no more than moderately tasty, labelled and sold according to how long it has matured. Young cheese (*jonge kaas*) gets to sit around for a month: it has the mildest flavour and the softest, most flexible texture. *Jong belegen* is matured for two months; mature (*belegen*) for four months; *extra belegen* for seven or eight; old (*oude*) for up to a year; and vintage (*overjarige*) for 18 months and longer. The oldest versions are the most interesting, though inevitably the most expensive, with a darker, harder consistency, a more intense flavour and a crumbling graininess built on the formation of salt crystals. Other variants involve the addition of spices such as cumin seeds (*komijn*) or clove (*kruidnagel*), usually to *jonge kaas*.

Boerenkaas (farm cheese) is in broadly the same style and subject to the same ageing variations, but is handmade from unpasteurised milk and tends to have more flavour. There are also craft producers creating or re-creating soft, blue-veined or goat cheese, but their products are hard to come by and generally only sold in specialist delicatessens.

DRINKING (OTHER THAN BEER)

With Dutch beer nose-diving in originality in the latter half of the 20th century, it was inevitable that wine would rise in popularity. Most restaurants stock a plausible variety, though those sold by the glass in bars are often worthy of caution. There is a local wine industry, but this is a tiny niche, only slowly beginning to justify its prices.

In contrast, the Dutch spirits industry is massive, in more ways that one.

All gin is descended from *jenever*, named for the juniper berries used to flavour it. The origins of distilled alcohol flavoured with juniper are obscure, with references found as early as the 13th century, though its official launch date is 16th century.

There are two basic types, distinguished by process, not age. *Oude* (old) jenevers are closer to the original style and must contain at least 15% of spirit distilled from barley malt using a similar process to malt whisky. *Jonge* (young) jenever contains less malt and is otherwise a blend of spirits distilled more cheaply using mixed grains and neutral alcohol from other sources like sugar beet.

Oude jenevers containing only grain-derived distillate are termed *graanjeenver*. *Moutwijn* is made entirely from barley malt, rather like a malt whisky but without the ageing process. *Korenwijn* (literally corn wine) is typically 50 to 70% malt-derived and usually aged in oak.

It is a question of taste. If you want flavour, choose something *oude* and drink it at room temperature, ideally in a specialist tasting room (*proeflokaal*), though not as a spirit chaser, for reasons expressed in the Dutch name for that: a *kopstoot*, or head butt.

In a traditional *proeflokaal*, shot glasses are poured to the brim. Before picking them up, lean forward to take a first sip (*nippen* or *slurpen*) without using your hands.

Distillers also produce a bewildering variety of fruit and herb liqueurs, which vary from the crystal clear, sickly sweet and 'chemical' to some perfectly lovely and sophisticated alcoholic fruit juices, the best of which are steeped with whole fruit like a good sloe gin.

In the Netherlands, the generic name for bottled mineral water is Spa, regardless of the brand, ordered as red (*rood*) for sparkling, blue (*blauw*) for still and green (*groen*) for in-between. Cola is 'cola', or 'cola light' if you prefer sugar-free and aspartame-rich. Ask for 'coca' and you may get you more than you bargained for, and arrested.

At home and at work, the Dutch like to wash down food with milk (*melk*) or butter-milk (*karnemelk*), which seems odd to everyone else. This habit is rarer in cafés.

Despite the popularity of alcohol and the reputation for dope, the Netherlands' national drug of choice is caffeine. Dutch coffee (*koffie*) is universally excellent and great care goes into its preparation, often involving an Italian-style espresso machine. No business meeting or social gathering can commence without a regulation cup (or two), served with evaporated milk (*koffiemelk*). If you prefer fresh, warm milk, ask for a *koffie verkeerd*. Decaffeinated (*cafeïnevrij*) is available in most places. Don't even consider asking for instant, which rarely appears except in sachets beside the kettle in some hotel rooms.

As regards tea (*thee*), shall we just say that English or Indian entrepreneurs have thus far missed a major trick by allowing tasteless grit packaged in bags to flagship the world's most popular beverage in mainland Europe. Tea in the Netherlands is, in our opinion and perhaps literally, the dregs of the beverage world.

Brewing &

Deftige Aap, Helmond, North Brabant

beer styles

HOW BEER IS MADE

There may be tens of thousands of different beers in the world, but virtually all follow the same fundamental life cycle: growing, selecting & preparing the ingredients; mashing, boiling & filtering; fermentation & conditioning; packaging; selling; drinking; and then returning the nutrients to the soil to start over.

The ingredients

Grain

Play around all you like, but no beer is beer without grain (*graan*), the ultimate source of its alcohol as well as providing flavour, aroma, colour and texture. In principle, you can use any grain, though malted barley remains the one best suited to the task.

Barley (*gerst*) contains plentiful starch, enzymes to convert that starch into sugar, and proteins to keep the yeast healthy. It becomes malt (*mout*) by being partially germinated then heated to arrest the process.

The grains are first soaked in water for several days, then aerated to induce germination. They are considered fully modified when the young roots reach the same length as the original kernel. By now the grains have softened and become a little sweet, while retaining ample quantities of starch and enzymes.

The next step is to heat the grain. This drives off the moisture, stops the biological processes, wilts away the unwanted rootlets and creates a dry ingredient, easily transported and stored. Varying the time and the manner in which the grain is heated introduces colour and flavour variations which the brewer can later exploit in creating different styles.

Heating also progressively destroys the precious enzymes, so most beers are made mainly, if not entirely, with the palest types of 'base' malt – pale ale malt and even paler pilsener malt – with small proportions of darker, 'speciality' malts as required. These include more heavily toasted malts like Munich and Vienna, which add nutty flavours and an amber colour, and roasted, chocolate and black malts which add intense coffee and chocolate notes and dark brown colours. Variations such as crystal malt and caramalt are produced by keeping the grains moist during part of the heating process, forming caramelised sugars that do not ferment but add caramel and toffee flavours to a finished beer.

Almost all beers contain barley malt, but other grains in both malted and unmalted form may be added as 'adjuncts' to introduce new textures and flavours. The most popular is wheat (*tarwe*), which, besides affecting flavour, also gives a creamy, stable head. Rye (*rogge*), oats (*haver*), spelt and others are also used.

More controversial are rice (*rijst*) and maize (*mais*, corn). While interesting results can be coaxed from these, their reputation is tarnished by their inclusion in many industrial beers where they add alcohol without troubling the drinker with additional flavour.

Bigger brewers have their own mills, enabling them to grind the grain to exactly the desired consistency. Smaller brewers often don't have this luxury so buy their grain ready-ground.

Stronger beers made with 100% malted grain have a tendency to be heavy and overpowering. For lightness and balance, brewers may replace a proportion of the malt with cornflour, starch, syrup or sugar (*suiker*). This practice is frowned upon in certain brewing traditions, for example in Germany, but is almost a defining feature of strong Belgian-style monastic ales.

Water

In terms of liquid, almost everything in a beer that is not alcohol is water. Any unpolluted source will do, but the mineral content affects flavour and, historically, determined to some extent what kinds of beer worked where. In the UK, Burton upon Trent's water contains sulphates, perfect for creating hoppy pale ales. Munich's water is low in sulphates, but rich in calcium carbonate, making hoppy beers unpalatable but softening a malty Dunkelweizen. In the Czech Republic, the waters of Plzeň and České Budějovice have a very low mineral content, ideal for delicate Pilsener and Budweiser lagers. Today, most brewers work with the local mains supply, filtering it if desirable or affordable then tweaking it with the appropriate minerals for the beer they intend to brew.

Yeast

Without yeast (*gist*) there is no beer. Introduce these micro-organisms to anything sweet and they start to convert simple sugars into alcohol, producing carbon dioxide gas as a by-product. As the sugar reduces and the alcohol level rises, they become dormant and sink, partially clarifying the beer as they plummet.

There are many thousands of yeast strains, each suited to working best under certain conditions, adding its own thumbprint flavours. Brewers' yeasts are divided into two species: warm- or top-fermenting ale yeasts that work best at room temperature, and cold- or bottom-fermenting lager yeasts that prefer a chill. A third option, mastered by the lambic makers of Belgium, is spontaneous or wild fermentation, in which open tanks and oak casks attract various species of natural yeasts and other bacteria from the immediate environment.

Besides alcohol and carbon dioxide, yeasts also produce small quantities of flavour and aroma compounds that vary according to the strain and the way fermentation was carried out. The long, cold fermentation and conditioning of a lager eliminates most of these to leave what brewers describe as a 'clean' flavour, but the fruity notes of esters are part of the signature of most ale styles and spicy, clove-like phenols add interest to Bavarian wheat beers and some Belgian-style ales. The complex array of fermentation-related flavours exhibited by 'wild' beers like lambics is almost the entire point of the style.

Hops

Put grain, yeast and water together in the right way and you can make beer, though the result will likely be relatively bland and unpalatable with poor keeping qualities. While various herbs and spices have been tried over the centuries to help remedy this, today's overwhelming people's champion is the hop. The bitter acids and essential oils in its fruiting bodies, known as cones, combine antibacterial and other properties to create a perfect natural preservative. Moreover, they add a pleasant bitterness which helps balance the bland sweetness of the grain, and a myriad of other flavours and aromas, ranging from earthy, floral and fruity, to you name it.

There are hundreds of hop varieties, each with indiviual characteristics, and their numbers increase every year as growers experiment with cross-pollination to introduce new flavour profiles. Traditional German and Czech hops such as Saaz and Hallertau are floral and grassy, providing a crisp, clean taste. British hops like Fuggles or East Kent Goldings are earthier and spicier. American hops such as Cascade typically have a pronounced grapefruit-citric character, sometimes with a 'catty' blackcurrant note, with new varieties like Citra and Mosaic adding powerful tropical fruit and pine, while New Zealand varieties like Motueka and Nelson Sauvin give softer tropical fruit and grape-like notes.

Hop cones are dried before use, and are available either as 'whole hops' or ground and compressed into pellets. Some brewers believe the former provide more delicate flavours and aromas, but the latter take up less space, have a longer shelf life and are

a perfectly good substitute. Industrially-produced extracts are also used, but like any ingredient, the more you process it, the more its subtleties are lost.

Other ingredients

Besides the big four ingredients, brewers may add a variety of other substances. Fruits and spices have been revived in recent years but experimental brewers love throwing in weirder stuff, ranging from vegetables to whey, or in the case of one Swedish brewer, beaver musk.

The brewing bit

The first stage of brewing is a process called 'mashing' (*maischen*), in which the appropriate blend of ground grains is mixed with hot water and left to soak for 60–90 minutes in a mash tun (*maischkuip*) to activate the enzymes. At a constant temperature of around 60–70°C, it is mostly simple sugars that are extracted. Anything hotter speeds the process, but releases unfermentable dextrins, which can make the finished beer taste sweet. Some beers are mashed in stages at a series of different temperatures to achive the optimum result, sometimes by extracting part of the mash, boiling it and returning it to the mash tun.

The result is a high-sugar, hazy brown liquid called 'wort', which is run off from the mash tun through a simple filter. Further, though thinner, wort may then be obtained by rinsing (*afspoelen*) the remaining grains with hot water. The spent grain (*bostel*) is often used as cattle feed, and increasingly for making bread.

The next stage involves boiling (*koken*) the wort with hops for an hour or so, essential to release their bittering and preservative properties and to stablise the mixture. Depending on the brewery's kit, this may be done in a separate vessel known as a 'copper' or 'kettle' (*brouwketel*), or the wort may be filtered into a vessel called a lauter tun (*klaringskuip*) then returned to a combined mash tun/kettle for boiling. The result is hopped wort (*gehopt wort*) which is then cooled and clarified, sometimes by centrifuge, to remove residual solids.

The traditional method of boiling with hops is excellent for bittering and shelf-life purposes, but it can also drive off many of the volatile aroma compounds for which hops are so prized today. One way of mitigating this is to add additional hops just before or at the end of the boil, known as 'late hopping'. Many of today's hoppier beers acquire their pronounced character by being dosed with hops even further down the line: in the centrifuge, the fermentation and conditioning tanks, or even in the keg. This is known as 'dry hopping' or 'cold-side hopping'. Some brewers now avoid adding hops at all during the boil when producing beers with intense hop aroma and flavour but little bitterness.

Fermentation and conditioning

Cooled, hopped wort is a drinkable, extremely sweet, non-alcoholic beverage. It is not beer. To complete the metamorphosis it must be transferred to a fermentation vessel (*gistingsvat*) with added yeast.

Primary fermentation

Traditionally, fermenting vessels were simple open tanks, but today, most are sealed and pressurised stainless steel tanks to reduce the risk of infection. The first, or primary, fermentation (*eerste gisting*) typically takes three to seven days, during which the yeast converts most of the sugar to alcohol and CO_2. The final strength of the beer is determined by how much fermentable sugar is dissolved in the wort, in turn determined by the proportion of grains to water in the mash tun, and how efficiently the process of converting starch to sugar to alcohol has been carried out.

Fermentation temperatures can be tightly controlled. Ale yeast, also known as top-fermenting yeast because in an open fermenting vessel it tends to clump on the surface of the liquid, is most content at 15–21°C, or even a little higher for some strains. Warmer fermentation is faster and cheaper, but tends to leave behind more esters, phenols and other flavour components which may or may not be palatable. Lager yeasts, also known as bottom-fermenting yeasts as they tend to sink lower in their tanks, evolved to work in the cold surroundings of the caves where Bavarian brewers stashed their beers in summer when it was too warm to control fermentation. They work slowly and efficiently at around 7–13°C to produce cleaner-tasting beers with fewer volatile by-products.

Some stronger ales may go through several fermentation steps using various yeast strains that work best at different alcohol levels.

Conditioning

Once primary fermentation is complete, the liquid in the tanks is technically beer but may not yet be ready to drink. Most beer benefits from at least a day or so of rest to break down flavour components that leave 'green', buttery and other undesirable flavours in the liquid. And depending on the style, it will improve further if given enough time and the right microorganisms, allowing some character to develop before it is packed up and sold. Such 'conditioning' (*rijping*) can happen in stainless steel tanks, oak tuns or in the container in which the beer finally leaves the brewery gates.

In a classic lager, nowadays a rare beast though undergoing something of a revival, low temperature tank-conditioning at 3–4°C for anything up to 12 weeks sweeps up all the compounds that cause odd and sub-standard tastes. This is the 'lagering' process that gives the style its name, *lagern* being German for 'to store', though the big brewers have found ways to accelerate it greatly, hiding any unpalatable flavours by serving the beer at temperatures low enough to render them undetectable.

Those brews that condition far longer, usually at cellar temperature and sometimes in oak casks or tuns, may be subject to the attention of slower-acting yeast species capable of breaking down more complex sugars, as well as lactic acid-producing bacteria like *Lactobacillus* and *Pediococcus*.

Some brewers induce further conditioning by adding fruit, which among other things contains sugar that reinvigorate the yeast, though most modern fruit beers are created by simpler shortcuts, more along the lager-and-lime principle.

Packaging

However much or little a beer is conditioned at the brewery, it will at some point be packaged into a sealed keg (*fust*), bottle (*fles*), can (*blikje*), or on some occasions a cask or barrel (*vat*).

The simplest way of capturing a beer in peak condition is to pasteurise and recarbonate it, then drink it as soon as possible. Even the tiniest amount of yeast will allow the beer to continue to condition and develop in the container.

Some brewers bottle-condition beer by adding a dose of yeast, sugar or unfermented wort just before packaging, prompting a continued fermentation which in ideal circumstances will extend the shelf life and add character and complexity. If this is miscalculated, the beer may either end up flat and dull or too highly carbonated. Insufficient hygiene risks wild yeast and bacterial infections which can result in a 'gusher', often smelling or tasting foul in addition to, well, gushing. But if such problems are avoided, bottle conditioning works particularly well for beers designed to age, such as strong stouts, barley wines, monastic ales or oude geuze.

Fermentation control has become so precise in recent years that it is now possible to continue some fermentation or conditioning in cellar tanks, kegs, casks, bottles and cans without the need for additional yeast or sugar. Many craft brewers now package their beer unfiltered and unpasteurised direct from the fermentation vessels once it has reached the optimal point of carbonation and alcohol content, perhaps with the addition of modest amounts of carbon dioxide to tweak the sparkle.

Selling the beer

It does not matter how fantastic your drink is; if it does not look the part, few will be tempted.

Some amateurish labels put you off before you start. On the other hand, look too slick and professional and you may also be shunned. Our advice to buyers is to be wary of any beer where there is a lack of clarity on the label about its brewery of origin.

Something simple and clear works best, with a common image across the product range, precise information about where a beer was brewed and by whom, and maybe some non-promotional, useful facts and figures.

Choosing the right format is important. The same beer tastes different when presented in different forms, for reasons that are part real, part imagination. Light, heat and oxygen damage beer, so sealed, darkened, heat-proof containers preserve quality best.

Cans, once shunned by beer enthusiasts and seen as the preserve of park bench tramps, are now on-trend and openly embraced, for their convenience and low weight compared to glass bottles, their superior light-excluding preservative attributes and for their hipster promise of containing something wonderful.

Finally there is the appearance of the beer itself. Continuing fermentation in a bottle or can throws a yeast sediment that, if it mingles with the beer on pouring, can add its own flavour, for better or worse. Many beer consumers once viewed hazy and cloudy beers with suspicion and some still do, though opacity has become almost emblematic of fashionable recent craft styles.

For larger brewers, who inevitably follow the shiny beads route, packaging becomes more important than product, though none will admit this openly. It is, after all, the look of the logo, bottle or advert that first catches a punter's eye.

If there were a dictionary definition of how to market beer to a global audience, it would simply read: see Heineken. Did you really think those little smiley upturned 'e's in the name got there by accident?

BEER STYLES

If a world is ever created in which all beers are defined by their style, Michael Jackson and the other great beer writers will have lived in vain. Beer styles simply provide a few basic signposts to help drinkers navigate the breadth and depth of possibilities in beer making.

There are few surviving styles of beer native to the Netherlands. Most have been collected magpie-like from elsewhere. In the past, Dutch brewers wishing to create something other than pilsener imitated Belgian abbey beers or witbier. Nowadays, many follow global trends and produce types of beer more associated with North America, Germany and the imagined past of UK brewing, though a few defunct historic Dutch styles are re-emerging in a small way.

Here are some names with which to conjure, defined as for their current Dutch use:

Altbier: a lagered ale speciality of Düsseldorf in Germany, typically amber and 4.5-5.5% ABV.

Amber ale: similar to pale ale (qv), but typically less bitter, redder and 5-5.5%. Most are imitations of well-known Belgians.

Amber lager: lager modelled on an American steam beer, a shade darker, hoppier and more characterful than pilsener, typically 6%.

Barley Wine: generic British description of strong beers, 8% and up. Similar to a Belgian strong or massive ale or a Dutch quadrupel, so the terms have become interchangeable. The bulk are amber or brown and sticky-sweet to balance the alcohol.

Berliner Weisse: variant of the classic German wheat beer, typically low alcohol (3–4%), with a (sometimes face-inverting) tartness created by the use of *Lactobacillus* bacteria.

Blond ale: light-coloured ale made with pilsener malt (6–6.5%). A relatively recent Belgian style adopted wholeheartedly in the Netherlands. Some can be great but too many are bland and sweet, low in bitterness and indistinguishable from one another. We call these LBJs: Little Blond Jobs.

Bok or **Bock**: brown beers, traditionally bottom-fermented and 6.5–7%, for release as an autumn or winter seasonal. They now appear in September and are often top-fermented. Also termed Bo(c)kbier or Herfstbo(c)k (autumn bock: the word *bok* itself also means 'billy goat'). The tradition may originate from the habit of using up old grain from the previous year in a harvest-time superbrew.

Dubbel: brown ale (6.5–7%) of a type first popularly designated by the brewery of the Westmalle Trappist abbey in Belgium, and much imitated. At their best, dubbels are rich and rewarding, but too often there is excessive caramel sweetness. The name originates from the practice of marking casks with multiple crosses to indicate ascending strengths, rather than an actual doubling of alcohol content: see also Tripel.

Dubbelbok or **Dubbelbock**: a stronger version (8%+) of bok (qv).

Geuze or **Gueuze**: see Lambic

Gose: wheat ale (4–5%), originally from Goslar in Germany, traditionally flavoured with salt and coriander, with a tartness gained from *Lactobacillus* bacteria but normally less sour than Berliner Weisse.

Herfstbok or **Herfstbock**: see Bok

India Pale Ale or **IPA**: usually assertively hoppy American styles of medium-strength pale ale (5.5–7%), originally derived from a historic English pale ale popular in the outposts of empire. Sub-genres include Red, Rye, Black (with roasted malts), New England (NEIPA, a 'hazy, juicy' beer with lots of hops but low bitterness), West Coast (in the style of early American examples from the 1990s, with a distinctly bitter finish), Double (DIPA, around 8%) and Triple (TIPA, around 10%). Most Dutch examples are constructed with American or Australasian hops to the fore, though English IPAs using traditional English varieties in similar quantities are occasionally found.

Kölsch: a top-fermented, lagered blond ale (4.5–5.5%), of a type that originated from the German city of Cologne (Köln, Keulen in Dutch). Legally, the term should only be applied to examples brewed in and around that city as it has Protected Geographical Indication status, so 'Kölsch-style' or variants thereof are sometimes used instead.

Kuit or **Kuyt** or **Koyt**: a recently revived traditional Dutch style of pale mixed-grain ale (5–8% ABV), classically hopped only with noble varieties (Saaz, Hallertau, Tettnanger or Spalt). It should contain a minimum of 45% oats and 20% wheat or malted wheat.

Kriek: see Lambic

Lambic or **Lambiek**: a collective term for beers fermented without the addition of cultured yeasts, traditional to the city of Brussels in Belgium and the neighbouring Pajottenland. The process is often called 'spontaneous fermentation' but 'wild fermentation' is technically more accurate. The wort is left overnight in a shallow vessel called a 'coolship' (*koelschip*) and then placed in oak barrels or vats, where it undergoes a complex fermentation and conditioning involving numerous wild yeasts and bacteria resident in both the brewery and the wood. Young (*jonge*) lambic is fermented for four to 12 months, old (*oude*) lambic for up to three years, starting musty and going on to develop citrus flavour and aromas of old bookshops and horse barns. Lambics are

Oud Bruin (Flemish): a 1980s designation of the oak-aged brown ales (4.5–7%) found in parts of Belgian Flanders, featuring lactic sourness gained from a year or two of maturation in oak tuns. Originally influenced by early 19th-century English porter brewing practices and similar in principle to Gulpener's lower-ABV Mestreechs Aajt.

Pale ale: derived from the much undersung classic, crisp and polished British ale style of the 19th century that once enjoyed global fame. Typically 4.5–5.5% with firm but balanced hopping in contrast to a hop-forward modern IPA.

Pils or **Pilsener**: bottom-fermented blond lager, typically 5% ABV, descended more or less from a style perfected in the 1840s in Plzeň (Pilsen in German), now in the Czech Republic. The use of the name was effectively deregulated by a Court in Munich in 1899; the Germans and other nations sometimes spell it 'Pilsner' but the Dutch usually add an extra 'e'. The local variant is crisp and malty with low hopping, lots of pizzazz but not much taste. It accounts for 90% of the beer market and should be ordered as 'pils', not 'lager'. The latter marks out an ignorant foreigner.

Porter: see Stout.

Quadrupel: a 1990s term invented to define a single product from the Koningshoeven brewery that was stronger than dubbel and tripel, then picked up by beer enthsiasts seeking to be equally vague. Interchangeable, for now, with strong or massive ale. And barley wine in common usage.

Rauchbier or **Rookbier**: originally a smoked lager from the days before maltsters could control their kilns, preserved by brewers in the German town of Bamberg in Upper Franconia. Nowadays the smoking is deliberate, using beechwood to give the beer (5–7%) the aroma of bonfire and a fruity, smoky taste.

Rosé: vile pink-washed witbiers created by marketing people to sell to those who don't like beer. Most are patronising alcopops. If Hell has a reception area for newly deceased beer lovers, this is what the Devil would serve as a welcome drink.

sometimes served on draught but are more common in other forms. Blended lambics of various ages refermented in the bottle become Oude G(u)euze, compared by some to champagne and by others to cider. Oude Kriek is made by steeping young lambic with sour cherries in wood, while raspberries are used to make Framboos or Frambozen. Other fruits are possible, but some big-name commercial variants are actually blends of lambic and more conventionally fermented beer with artificial flavours and sweeteners. These are not allowed to describe themselves as *oude*. EU-protected lambics must originate from the traditional area, but a few Dutch brewers are experimenting with the principle.

Lentebok or **Lentebock**: seasonal spring gold-blond beers (6.5–7%), sometimes called Meibock but mostly rebranded since their release moved to April, which also broadened the linguistic gap with German Maibock lager. Can be sweet, but quite alluring when done right.

LBJ: see Blond ale.

Meibok or **Meibock**: see Lentebok.

Oud Bruin (Dutch): low-alcohol (2–3.5%), dark, malty and typically overpoweringly sweet concoctions. Derived from low-alcohol Donker lagers that were popular a century ago and possibly related to German *Malzbieren*, Belgian *tafelbieren* and British 'Invalid' stouts.

Saison: originally a low-alcohol pale ale brewed to quench the summer thirst of Belgian farm workers, now a middle strength (5.5–6.5%), refreshingly dry, near-blond ale using a distinctive farmhouse yeast. US-brewed versions sometimes involve wild yeasts and bacteria and this practice appears to be spreading.

Schwarzbier: in Germany, a black lager typically from the East. Most Dutch versions are dryish ales (4.5–5.5%) with crisp, fruity overtones.

Scotch ale: heavy sweetish brown ale, around 8%, that the Belgians preserved long after the Scots had stopped drinking the beer from which it is derived.

Stout and **Porter**: a family of dark brown and near-black beers that derive their colouring and flavour from the inclusion of dark and roasted malts, descended from a style perfected in London in the early 18th century that was the catalyst for the emergence of the modern brewing industry. Originally, a stout was simply a stronger type of porter. Today, the differences between them are hotly debated, but in common Dutch usage there is no clear and consistent distinction, so in this guide we bow to the brewers' judgement. Stouts and porters range from dry to sweet, in every degree of strength and bitterness, and gain complexity with liquorice, coconut, vanilla, blackcurrant, cocoa or burnt coffee notes. Lighter stouts begin around 4.5%, with their heavier-hitting imperial cousins ranging from 8% upwards. Milk stout implies the use of lactose, an unfermentable sugar derived from milk that contributes sweetness and texture to the finished beer; Baltic references the strong but smooth versions once widely brewed along the Baltic coast, often using lager rather than ale yeast; Irish or Oyster should mean salty and dry, with the latter occasionally indicating the inclusion of real bivalves; and Oatmeal just that, the addition of the porridgey grain contributing a creamy texture. Stout was brewed widely in the Netherlands in the 19th century, but went all-but-extinct in the 20th, only to undergo an impressive revival in the 21st. Most are reasonable; some outstanding.

Tripel: a strong ale (8–9.5%), usually golden-blond and sometimes lightly spiced, its name indicating the next step up from a Dubbel (see above) in terms of strength. The designation was first popularised by the Westmalle Trappist abbey in Belgium and the Belgian versions have been widely copied in the Netherlands.

Vienna: deep amber lager with a slight malty sweetness, typically around 5%, featuring Vienna or Wiener malt.

Weizen or **Weissbier**: Bavarian-style wheat beers (5–6%) top-fermented from a blend of wheat malt and barley malt, the banana and clove flavours emerging from fermentation with a particularly untidy yeast strain rather than added spices. Usually unfiltered and hazy with suspended yeast, a variant more properly known in German as Hefeweizen (yeast wheat) to distinguish it from a filtered version labelled Kristallweizen. Amber versions are known as Dunkelweizen or Dunkelweiss, the latter literally 'dark white'. Weizenbock is a stronger interpretation at around 7–7.5%.

White beer: see Weizen and Witbier.

Witbier: 'white beer', a surviving Belgian style of wheat beer (4.5–5.5%), nowadays with added spices, typically coriander and dried citrus peel. Until recently, almost all Dutch wheat beers were in this style, but the trend has swung towards Germany. They can be refreshingly citric or intrusively sweet.

Winterbier: seasonal ales, often dark, heavy and sometimes sweet. The nearer to Christmas the name, the higher the chance of heavy yuletide spicing with a combination of nutmeg, clove, cinnamon or ginger. Strength tends to be 8% and up, to keep out the chill.

Other useful beer terms

Abbey beer or **Abdijbier**: see Trappist.

ABV: Alcohol By Volume, the routine measurement of a beer's strength, often rendered an inexact science by the effects of continuing fermentation.

Alcoholvrij: any drink with less than 0.5% alcohol. The first such beers in the Netherlands were introduced by Bavaria in 1978. Once not very appealing, they have improved in leaps and bounds and some are now not only palatable but even enjoyable.

EBU or **IBU**: European or International Bitterness Units, both of which are interchangeable and indicate the proportion of bittering acids in the beer. Though increasingly quoted on labels, EBU is only a rough guide for drinkers as the perceived bitterness varies according to other factors such as sweetness, mouthfeel and alcohol content. Wheat beers and industrial pils may be as low as 15-20 EBU, while an IPA could go beyond 60 but is unlikely to taste three times as bitter due to the additional alcohol balancing it out. A hoppy presence becomes more obvious at 30 and up.

Green hopping: see Wet hopping.

High-density brewing: the technique of brewing to a higher ABV then diluting the beer with water before packaging, thus saving space and energy during production, invariably at the expense of quality. Some brewers can the undiluted version as extra-strength 'winobeer' targeted at those whose primary concern is affordable oblivion.

hl: short for hectolitre, or 100 litres, the standard international bulk measurement for beer, used in the industry to measure things like equipment capacity and annual output, and by governments for calculating their slice of the pie. In old money, 1hl is 0.61 UK brewers' barrels, 0.85 US brewers' barrels and 176 imperial pints.

Imperial: very strong, as in 8% and up. Originally applied to the strong stouts exported from the UK to Imperial Russia, but generalised in modern craft beer parlance to a variety of other styles.

Radler: pilsener and lemonade, known to the British as shandy. The makers often claim real lemons are added, which is very sweet of them.

Session beer: any beer designed to be quaffed in volume with minimal ill effects, often a lower-strength (3-4.5%) version of a particular style, most commonly IPA.

Trappist: beers that can be called an 'Authentic Trappist Product' must be produced under the supervision of the Trappist Order and within the walls of an abbey, with the proceeds from sale spent on charitable works or the upkeep of the Order. At the time of writing, 12 breweries meet these criteria: six in Belgium, two in the Netherlands and one each in Austria, Italy, the UK and the USA. Some Dutch café owners still offer grenadine syrup with the dark beers, a prospect that makes us shiver. Numerous Belgian secular brewers, and a few Dutch ones, also make beers in a broadly monastic style, some under license from a genuine abbey, others just with monks and Gothic windows on the label: these are known as *abdijbieren* (abbey beers).

Wet hopping: Also known as green hopping, this is the increasingly popular seasonal practice of making beers with freshly harvested, undried hops. As hops deteriorate quickly after they are picked, the few breweries with their own hop gardens or close to one of the small number of commercial hop growers operating in the Netherlands have the advantage here.

Wisseltap: a 'changing tap', in other words a line reserved for frequently changing guest beers.

The Dutch brewing industry

BACK in 2002, the Netherlands' 40 beer producers made about 200 regular beers. When the first edition of this guide emerged in 2014, that figure had swelled to 200 brewers making well over 1,000 beers. Today's equivalent figures are treble that and rising, without including one-off brews.

Once upon a time, growth proceeded at a sedate pace and newcomers were easily monitored, but for a period between 2015 and 2018 more than 100 new producers entered the market annually, a rate both dizzying and absurd. And unsustainable. The market simply cannot support that rate of expansion indefinitely.

As of late 2019, the madness has calmed a little. Nevertheless, more will doubtless have launched in the period between this guide going to press and hitting the *straatjes*.

Around 370 have their own brewing equipment, though may not necessarily produce everything in house: several smaller operations still use other people's facilities for larger runs. There is a huge gulf in size between the largest and smallest Dutch breweries. At the top end, Heineken's Zoeterwoude site is the largest beer production plant in Europe. At the other extreme are brewers working in little more than a home kitchen. Those who think of breweries the size of all-steel brewpubs and upwards may have to downgrade their concepts of scale.

The Netherlands also possesses an unusual number of individuals or companies – call them gypsy, nomad or cuckoo brewers if you like – who are legally classed as breweries and market their own beer brands but don't produce commercially on their own kit, instead having various arrangements with other breweries. Some still achieve greatness, despite this apparent disadvantage; others do not. For more on this thorny and divisive issue, see Brewers without breweries (below).

Beer ratings

There was a time when we tried to sample every commercially available Dutch beer. Sheer numbers mean this is no longer sensible. Space restrictions have also necessitated the omission of many seasonal brews. Although most breweries make at least a meibock and an autumn bock, we have only included those that are unavoidably ubiquitous or otherwise worth seeking out.

Star ratings (see below) for listed beers should be considered approximate, as beers from smaller brewers often fluctuate from one batch to the next. Beers with no rating are simply those we have not yet tried. Don't ignore them as they might be wonderful.

We do our best to keep tabs on every beer, producer and brewery, but new brands appear and existing ones evolve at a dizzying rate, with older brands disappearing just as suddenly. Let us know if you find something outstanding that isn't listed here.

Dutch beers that are not

We have excluded two high-volume but otherwise inconsequential 'Dutch' beer brands that are made abroad, their breweries of origin being long gone. These are **Leeuw Pilsener**, which is made by Haacht in Belgium; and **Oranjeboom Pilsener**, which originated from the long-levelled Drie Hoefijzers brewery in Breda but is now manufactured in Germany for a Breda-based importer misleadingly called United Dutch Breweries.

The **Schelde** brewery is trickier. Originally based in Zeeland, it has since moved just over the Belgian border to Meer. It remains Dutch-owned and has a distribution warehouse in Flevoland but, as it is now listed in CAMRA's *Good Beer Guide Belgium*, we consider it to have emigrated.

The various beers brewed under the **Mongozo** brand also claim Dutch nationality via a Boxmeer office but as the Huyghe brewery in Belgium lists them as its own, we exclude them here.

★ Pointless or inadequate: buy something else.
★+ Could do better, but something's not right: try only if you want to tick it off.
★★ Competent: buy once at least.
★★+ Worth looking out for: buy when you can.
★★★ Among the best in class: take some home.
★★★+ Among the Netherlands' finest beers: keep a stock.
★★★★ Among the world's finest beers: keep a secret stock.

Breweries and brewpubs

In most cases, except where stated otherwise, the brand name on any beer range, if any, will be the name of the brewery as it appears in the heading. In a few cases, the brand appears on labels with an extra final letter for grammatical reasons, usually an 'e' or 's'. For more details on those brewpubs and taprooms that have regular opening times, see where to drink (below).

SIZE IS IMPORTANT

The size of a brew run can say a lot about the ambitions of an operation. Serious kit starts at 30 hectolitres (hl) and above, although many established craft brewers can and do work profitably in the 10 to 15hl range. On the other hand, an aspirant brewer may start from 5hl, while it could also be argued that someone making 2.5hl batches and below is still a hobbyist at heart.

013

Piushaven 1, 5017 AN Tilburg
T 013 207 00 98
adsbrouwerij013.nl

Brewery and taproom named after Tilburg's local dialling code, founded in 2018. Housed in a historic boat-shaped Amsterdam School building dating from 1935, it brews 20hl around twice per week. The owners are also a part of Stadsbrouwerij Eindhoven, but this business is separate.

BEERS INCLUDE: lightweight dry session IPA **'n Steekje Los** (3.5%: ★★); acceptable witbier **Witte Koning** (5%: ★★); malty but dull **Piuspils**

(5.1%: ★★); dry-hopped **Rooie Stien** (6%: ★★) IPA; lightweight dry and malty **Kruikje Blond** (6.5%: ★★); likeable dubbel **Op den Ophef** (7%: ★★+); blond tripel **Tilburgse Heer** (8%: ★★); malty bitter 'Belgian strong ale' **Lumunus** (8.5%: ★★); dark and rich quadrupel **Schering & Inslag** (9%: ★★+); and rounded imperial stout **Mooi de Klos** (10%: ★★+).

16.30

Plein 25, 3991 DL Houten
T 030 208 094
deroskam.com

The home of this microbrewery in Utrecht province, founded in 2018, is shared with the Roskam bar and restaurant (see cafés), which was built in 1630, thus the name. The kit, in an events hall towards the rear of the building, is used only occasionally, so the beers are often unavailable even on the premises.
BEERS INCLUDE: a **Märzen** (6%) and a **Saison** (8.4%).

1923

Burgemeester Brandtstraat 23, 2841 XB Moordrecht
T 06 1411 8945
brouwerij1923.nl

Four brewers from South Holland making small quantities of Belgian-style beers since 2014, using recipes that usually feature malted spelt.
BEERS INCLUDE: banana-edged blond **Het Gouden Uur** (5.5%: ★★); sweetish dubbel **De 5e Tocht** (9%: ★★); and equally sweet tripel **Traveys** (9%: ★★).

3 Horne

Brouwerij De 3 Horne
Marktstraat 40-A, 5171 GP Kaatsheuvel
T 0416 275666
de3horne.nl

This veteran North Brabant microbrewery, established in 1991, currently uses a 7.5hl installation, renting out excess capacity to numerous nomadic outfits and also selling brewing equipment in the Gruithuys shop (*Sa 10.00–17.00*). Its bottled beers are often seen in the shops but its draught products are rarer. Visits for groups of 10 or more by appointment.

BEERS INCLUDE: perfumed **Blondy** (5.3%: ★★); sweetish **Dobbelaer** (6%: ★★) dubbel; cherry-flavoured **Kerselaer** (6.5%: ★★), with a cocoa edge; sharply citrussy wheat ale **Horns Wit** (7%: ★★+); easy-drinking **Trippelaer** (8.5%: ★★) tripel; and golden, honeyed **Wiegeleir** (8.7%: ★★). Also brews **Bosrijkse Brouw** (5.5%) for the nearby Efteling theme park.

3 Vrouwen

Giek 2, 1276 JD Huizen
T 06 4681 9606
brouwerij3vrouwen.nl

North Holland brewery in operation since 2017. We think the name 3Women refers to the brewer's daughters.

BEERS INCLUDE: blond sour **Suurtje** (4.9%); lightweight blond **Boerbier** (5.5%); bitter IPA **Ouwe Vrijster** (6.5%); and blond tripel **Twee keer Drie** (7.5%); *SEASONAL:* herbal amber winter ale **Dubbel D** (8%: ★★).

58e Genot

Achtmaalseweg 137A, 4881 AZ Zundert
58egenot.nl

The 58th Delight was founded in 2017, with the idea of making 58 different beers, the last of which would in its view be "perfect". The first 10hl batch only appeared in late 2019, so there is still a way to go.

7 Deugden

Brouwerij De 7 Deugden
Akersluis 8d, 1066 EZ Amsterdam
T 020 667 3221
de7deugden.nlw

Founded in 2009, the Seven Virtues brewery in west Amsterdam outgrew itself in 2018, moving to a larger site with a 40hl kit beside a windmill and a cooperage museum (**molenvansloten.nl**). As at fellow Amsterdam brewery De Prael (below), it employs people with learning difficulties and other disabilities, helping them integrate into society. Brewer Garmt Haakma is fond of adding unusual spices, usually with successful results. In theory you can drink in at the shop (*Mo–Th 09.00–17.30; Fr 09.00–19.00; Sa 14.00–19.00*), but to call it a taproom would be stretching things. Tours and tastings by arrangement.

BEERS INCLUDE: assertive juniper-spiced rauchbier **Arm+Zalig** (5%: ★★★); light wheat ale **Ruw+Bolster** (5%: ★★+) with lime; cardamom-laden dunkelweizen **Wijs+Neuzig** (5%: ★★+); pils **Scherp+Zinnig** (5%: ★★), dosed with chilli; lemongrass-spiced saison **Ruim+Hartig** (5.5%: ★★+); citrussy IPA **Vol+Mondig** (5.7%: ★★+) with ginger and lemongrass; hoppy **Koor+Blond** (7.3%: ★★+); rounded **Dubbel+Dik** (6.5%: ★★+), spiced with star anise and clove; accomplished **Stout+Moedig** (7%: ★★★); and clove-spiced tripel **Scheeps+Recht** (7.5%: ★★).

SEASONAL: **Spring+Bock** (6.5%: ★★+), with lemon balm; thyme-infused **Spring+Tijm** (6.5%: ★★★); summer saison **Zij+Zon** (5%: ★★+); autumn honeyed **Bezig+Bij** (6%: ★★+); raisiny autumn **Bock+Sprong** (7%: ★★+); and winter **Vuur+Gloed** (8.5%: ★★+) with star anise.

74

Adriaen van Ostadelaan 74, 3583 AL Utrecht
T 06 2705 4431
facebook.com/brouwerij74

Brewing "retro beers with a retro look" since 2017, and named after the founding friends' birth year.
BEERS INCLUDE: sweetish, almost amber **Blond Jochie** (6%: ★★); hazy golden **Tripel Tempeest** (8%: ★★).
SEASONAL: dark, vinous, cocoa-edged winter quadrupel **Cuvée de 74** (11%: ★★★).

A

Woudenbergseweg 19 D4, 3707 HW Zeist
T 0343 212000
abrewery.nl

Founded in 2017, A Brewery makes no beers under its own name but instead contract brews for others using a solar-powered 10hl kit. It's part of umbrella group Dutch Brewery & Beer Trading (**dbbt.nl**), which also owns Thorhem and Brasser (see Brewers without breweries), both of which brew here.

AAA

Zwaanhoefstraat 102G, 4702 LC Roosendaal
T 06 2440 8534
aaa-brouwerij.com

North Brabant micro founded in 2017, and seemingly content for now only to produce seasonals, with no core range planned.

Admiraals

Admiraals Bierbrouwerij Aldtsjerk
Rhaladijk 7, 9064 DD Aldtsjerk
T 06 2255 4538
admiraalsbierbrouwerij.nl

Friesland-based outfit founded in 2014 with a 10hl brewing capacity, operating mainly as a contract brewery for hire though marketing its own **Aldtsjerker** beers since 2018.

Currently used by a dozen or so regional beer producers, most prominently Grutte Pier. Group tours and tastings by appointment.
BEERS INCLUDE: dry citrussy **Witbier** (5.5%: ★★+); fruity autumnal bock **Stoarmmok** (7%: ★★); and darkly warming **Quadrupel** (8%: ★★+).

Alfa

Thull 15–19, 6365 AC Schinnen
T 046 443 2888
alfabier.nl

Founded in 1870 in rural South Limburg, Alfa is now one of the largest independents. Its focus remains on unadventurous large-volume lagers, with its superior unfiltered pils hard to find on tap. Tours by arrangement. A taproom in Heerlen with its own brewhouse, **Beerkompanie** (Pancratiusplein 46; beerkompanie.nl), is on the site of the former Romein brewery. Small-scale seasonals are brewed there "a few times a year" under the mouthful dialect name **Heëlesche Sjtadsbroewerie**.
BEERS INCLUDE: malty sweet **Donker Bruin** (3%: ★+); unambitious **Edel Pils** (5%: ★+); far superior unfiltered pilsener **Ongefilterd Puur** (5%: ★★+); bittersweet **Krachtig Dort** (7.5%: ★★+); and **Super Strong** (9%: ★), which is strong but not super.
SEASONAL: sweetish **Lentebok** (6.5%: ★★) and autumnal **Herfstbok** (6.5%: ★★).

Ambrass

Gats 13, 6131 EM Sittard
T 046 400 9300
ambrass.nl

Small outfit brewing since 2014 on copper vessels in a historic building. Tours and tastings for groups of at least 10; smaller groups can visit on Saturdays once a month (pre-book via website). A taproom in a brick-vaulted cellar is technically open Fr&Sa but reservations are preferred.
BEERS INCLUDE: malty sweet Vienna lager **Asor** (5.5%: ★★); middling honeyed amber

Rosamunde (6.5%: ★★), almost rescued by added ginger; lightly bitter **Brats IPA** (6.5%: ★★); and sweetish multi-grain tripel **Ambrosius** (8%: ★★).
SEASONAL: **Winter Warmer** (7.8%: ★+) brown ale spiced without love.

Amelander

Smitteweg 6, 9162 EC Ballum
T 0519 554365
amelanderbier.nl

Nanobrewery set up in 2010 on Ameland by a husband and wife team, currently brewing 2hl of beer weekly in a barn. Call ahead if you want to visit the taproom, as the brewer is also one of the island's bus drivers and often out.
BEERS INCLUDE: rounded blond **'t Leste Lot** (6%: ★★); bittersweet brown wheat **Skutehôn** (6.3%: ★★+); its lighter sister, bitter witbier **Butenbiëntke** (6.5%: ★★); hoppy amber **Barnstiën** (6.5%: ★★+); fruity stout **Bikkelha'd** (6.5%: ★★+); and sharply refreshing **Bij 't Roaie Hek** (6.5%: ★★+), an amber ale flavoured with cranberries.
ALSO: **Ballumer Sap** is a 'surprise' beer that appears occasionally, in different forms.

Animal Army

Riviervismarkt 1, 2513 AM Den Haag
T 070 365 1955
animalarmybrewery.nl

City centre pub originally opened in 1996 as the Fiddler & Firkin, part of a UK-based brewpub chain, closed in 2007 and reopened simply as the Fiddler in 2012. The 10hl brewery has been rebranded but remains the only Dutch producer of UK-style cask-conditioned ales, with seasonals brewed for keg.
BEERS INCLUDE: lightly bitter pale ale **Albino Fox** (4.5%: ★★); not very bitter bitter **Lion's Den** (4.5%: ★★); easy-drinking red ale **Redhead** (5.6%: ★★+); **Black Mamba** (6%: ★★+), a decent burnt-edged stout; a token Belgian-style blond **Fuzzy Bear** (6%: ★★+); and quaffable English-style **Sea Lion's IPA** (6.2%: ★★+).

Antonius

Staddijk 1, 6603 LM Alverna
T 06 1003 7110
brouwerij-antonius.nl

Brewing small batches on the site of a farm and the Eijkenhorst tearoom (same address) outside Nijmegen since 2015. Visits on request.
BEERS INCLUDE: dark, nutty **Dubbel** (6.2%: ★★+); dry, golden **Eikenhorster Boerenblond** (6.9%: ★★), made for the abovementioned tearoom; and a **Tripel** (8%), **Imperial Stout** (10%) and **Barley Wine** (10.6%).
SEASONAL: **Speculator** (6.9%: ★★+), a cinnamon and liquorice-spiced dark Christmas ale.

Argentum

Achterwetering 22a, 2871 RK Schoonhoven
T 06 1055 6140
brouwerijargentum.nl

A South Holland company brewing in 10hl batches at a site near Gouda since 2015 and renting out excess capacity to others. It changed ownership in 2018 but we believe the brewer has remained.

BEERS INCLUDE: **Hooibouw** (3.3%), a historic blond style originally intended for farmers to sup at harvest time; dry, bitter **Golden Ale** (4.8%: ★★+); citrus-hoppy **IPA** (5.6%: ★★+); an **Imperial Dunkel Weizen** (7%); and hazy amber **Tripel** (7.7%: ★★).

Artemis

Reveweg 12, 8251 PW Dronten
T 06 4578 2749
brouwerijartemis.nl

Flevoland microbrewer since 2017, originally producing 4hl per month with larger runs made elsewhere. A subsidy in 2019 funded an expansion to a 10hl installation, with a taproom likely to follow around publication time.
BEERS INCLUDE: witbier **Wit** (5.5%); bittersweet **Blond** (5.6%: ★★+); a **Saison** (6.2%); hoppy, chilli-spiced, multi-grain amber **Farmhouse Ale** (6.5%: ★★+); and cherry-laden **Kersen Porter** (6.8%).

Asperius

Bilderdijkstraat 188, 1053 LE Amsterdam
T 020 412 9631
asperius.com

Microbrewery in the Zest Food & More restaurant (see cafés), founded in 2018, now selling some bottled beers in shops.
BEERS INCLUDE: hazy blond **Helles** (5.5%: ★★); lightly bitter **IPA** (5.8%: ★★); fruity bitter single-hopped IPA **Mish Mash** (7%: ★★); and rounded **Russian Imperial Stout** (7.8%: ★★+).

Avereest

Langewijk 362, 7701 AR Dedemsvaart
brouwerijavereest.nl

Overijssel brewer founded in 2017 with a 10hl brewing kit inherited from Ootmarsummer when the latter relocated. Pre-booked tours and tasting Sa 16.00 and on request at other times for groups of eight or more; shop Sa 14.00-17.00.
BEERS INCLUDE: **Bluswater** (4.6%) pilsener; English-style pale ale **Shakespeare** (4.6%); multi-grain weizen **Eigen Wiez** (5%); **Lanter Fanter** (6.2%) dunkelweizen; **Blonde Bertha** (7.2%); and **Dikke Bolle** (8%) tripel.

Axes Castellum

Assendorperdijk 2, 8012 EH Zwolle
axes-castellum.nl

Founded in 2017 by a brewers guild in the historic 16th-century cellars of a former Dominican cloister, although there is no current monastic link. Beers are mainly sold in the local area. Tours and tastings for groups of 10 or more.
BEERS INCLUDE: **Zondagskind** (5.2%) weizen; **Praedicare** (6.5%) blond; lightly bitter **Saison de Martín** (7%: ★★+); Belgian-style **Tripel Dominicus** (9%); and spicy heavyweight quadrupel **Paradisus** (10%: ★★+).

Barelds & Sabel

Veenakker 80, 9411 LX Beilen
barelds-sabel.nl

Named after the two homebrewing friends
who started it, this new Drenthe nanobrewery
founded in late 2019 was set to launch its first
beers as we went to press.

Barwin

Doortocht 8, 2411 DS Bodegraven
T 06 4271 0559

Founded by two South Holland friends in
2019, the name deriving from their names:
Barry and Erwin. Currently using a 2hl kit
housed next door to De Molen to make its
I Am Barwin range.
BEERS INCLUDE: hoppy, peachy **Tripel** (9%:
★★); and bubblegum-tinged imperial stout
Deep Dark Wood (11.1%: ★★).

Bavaria –
see Swinkels

Bax

Frieschestraatweg 201/2A, 9743 AC Groningen
T 050 211 2040
baxbier.com

Brewing since 2014, Bax currently has a 20hl
brewery with a taproom in a canalside industrial area in north Groningen. Quality wavered
in 2018 but has rebounded following the
arrival of a new brewer.
BEERS INCLUDE: dry witbier **Kon Minder
Wit** (4.4%: ★★+); hoppy blond flagship
Kon Minder Blond (5.1%: ★★+); accomplished
smoked porter **Koud Vuur** (6.5%: ★★+),
sometimes found **barrel-aged** (★★★);
standard **Kon Minder Dubbel** (6.6%: ★★);
and standout fruity **Ketter** (8.5%: ★★★),
an imperial smoked porter. *SEASONAL:* hoppy
spring blond **Rokkenjager** (6.6%: ★★+).

Bax brewery

ALSO: experimental one-offs in the **050 Series**
can go any way in style and quality.
For **Solt**, a company run by fishermen and
specialising in shrimp and beer (no, really):
bitter IPA **Soltcamp** (5.3%: ★★); nutty-edged
blond **Thomas van Seeratt** (5.8%: ★★); and
Grondzee (8.5%: ★+), a too-sweet herbal tripel.

Bekeerde Suster

Kloveniersburgwal 6, 1012 CT Amsterdam
T 020 423 0112
debekeerdesuster.nl

The Repentant Sister opened in 2004 on the
site of the city's first new wave brewpub,
Maximilian. It's owned and run by the Beiaard
Group, which sells the beers on tap in its cafés.
Friday is usually brewday.
BEERS INCLUDE: malty blond **1450 Kloosterpils**
(4.8%: ★★); witbier **Witte Antonia** (5.4%: ★★);
fruity **Blonde Barbier** (6.2%: ★★); and
sweetish tripel **Manke Monnik** (7.2%: ★★).

Berghoeve

Achteres 15, 7683 SX Den Ham
T 06 1827 8345
berghoevebrouwerij.nl

A husband and wife team, both food nutrition-ists, started this excellent farmhouse-based outfit in rural Overijssel in 2010, adding their own 7.5hl brewhouse in 2013. They are slowly working towards self-sufficiency using solar panels for power. Visits by appointment.
BEERS INCLUDE: thirst-quenching session saison **Hènig An** (2.5%: ★★+); hugely quaffable hoppy IPA **Khoppig** (4.5%: ★★★); sourish Brett-infected porter **De Oale Piepe** (5%: ★★★); easy-drinking hoppy 'red saison' **Rooie Neuze** (5%: ★★★); bitter Scotch ale **Warm Applaus** (6%: ★★+); gently smoky rye ale **Ontrustoker** (6%: ★★+); disconcertingly amber **Hammer Blont** (6%: ★★); well-rounded double IPA **Tevreden Oordeel** (7%: ★★★); dry dubbel **Goede Buur** (7%: ★★); lightly perfumed tripel **Verre Vriend** (8%: ★★+); lovely imperial black IPA **Tsjuster** (10%: ★★★); dark prune-tinged barley wine **Uut Eerder Tijd** (10%: ★★★+); deeply warming dark American-style barley wine **Klabats!** (10%: ★★★); and delicious five-malted imperial stout **Zwarte Snorre** (11%: ★★★★). Several beers also crop up in barrel-aged versions, usually well worth trying.
SEASONAL: rich, raisiny autumnal bock **Windbuul** (7%: ★★+), made with seven malts.

Berging

Jaagweg 6, 1441 PA Purmerend
T 06 4100 9363
bergingbrouwerij.nl

North Holland brewery established in 2013, initially producing 2hl batches with different recipes each time. It moved to a larger location with a 10hl kit in a former milk factory in 2016. The core range has settled into six numbered '**B**' beers.
BEERS INCLUDE: improving hoppy **B5 IPA** (5.5%: ★★+); spiced **B1 Weizen** (5.6%: ★★); average **B4 Saison** (5.7%: ★★); Belgian-style **B2 Blond** (6.5%: ★★); decent **B3 Tripel** (8.4%:

★★); and full-bodied, sweetish **B6 Quadrupel** (9.5%: ★★+).
ALSO: a self-explanatory **Oak** series and other barrel-aged and experimental brews.

Bevlieging

Oranjelaan 20 A, 2741 ER Waddinxveen
T 06 5363 0381
maleier.com

Founded in 2017 in a small-scale residential complex for people with disabilities or other special care needs, helping residents enter the labour market. Beers, sold under the **Maleier** brand, are rarely seen outside the local area. Visits on request.
BEERS INCLUDE: a **Pils** (5%); blond ale **Gold**; **Stout**; strong dark **Dubbel Bruin**; and a **Tripel**.

Beyerd

Boschstraat 26, 4811 GH Breda
T 076 521 4265
beyerd.nl

Long-established café that began brewing for itself in 2004, starting with a resurrection of the Drie Hoefijzers (Three Horseshoes) brand, defunct since AB InBev closed the town's Oranjeboom brewery. Group tours by arrangement.
BEERS INCLUDE: above-average **Dirk Urtyp Pilsener** (5%: ★★+); moderately successful revived icon **Drie Hoefijzers Klassiek** (5%: ★★+) pilsener; standout burnt-edged **Schwarzbier** (5%: ★★+); sweetish **Hefe Weisse** (5.5%: ★★); occasionally brewed English **IPA** (5.8%: ★★); dry, bitter **Blond** (6.8%: ★★); and seldom-seen **Tripel** (8%: ★★).

Biberius

Derde Baan 12, 6561 KH Groesbeek
T 06 2501 6085
brouwerij-biberius.nl

Gelderland homebrewers selling beer made on a 1.2hl kit since mid-2019.

BEERS INCLUDE: lightweight **'t Genomen Blondje** (5%); oak-aged **Lady Luck** (6%); IPA **Aurum** (7.5%); and **Muli Tripel** (8%)

Bierfabriek (Alfa)

Koetsierbaan 2, 1315 SE Almere
Nes 67, 1012 KD Amsterdam
Burgwal 45–49, 2611 GG Delft
bierfabriek.com

Not one but three breweries, the Beer Factories are all Alfa-owned brewpubs. The first opened on Rokin in Amsterdam in 2011 and relocated one block east in 2016. The second appeared in Delft in 2014 and the third in Almere a couple of years later. The beers at all three are brewed to the same recipes and only sold in house.
BEERS INCLUDE: airhead blond **Bianco** (5.2%: ★★); amber **Rosso** (5.6%: ★★); and porter **Nero** (5.8%: ★★), arguably the best of the bunch.

Bierfabriek

Biertafel

Kruisdijk 7, 7251 RL Vorden
T 06 2509 3314
debiertafel.nl

Since opening in 2015, Gelderland-based Beer Table has focused on just one core beer, sweetish straw-blond **Hackfort Bier** (6%: ★★), brewed roughly weekly on a 5hl kit. Visits, tastings and workshops for at least eight people on request.

Bjuster

Raadhuisstraat 9, 9001 AG Grou
T 0566 652345
facebook.com/BrouwerijBjuster

Bjuster ('unusual' in Frisian) started out in 2018 brewing tap beers to order for local cafés with a 3hl kit, but now produces its own bottled range, starting with **Grouster Blond** (6%). Tours and tastings on request.

Blauwe Knoop

Tongelaar 12, 5451 WP Mill
T 06 2939 0569
deblaauweknoop.com

North Brabant outfit brewing mostly Belgian-style ales since 2014, with its own nanobrewery since 2016, supplying mainly local outlets and festivals. Tastings on request.
BEERS INCLUDE: thinnish witbier **Witte Willems** (4.8%: ★+); **Stoute Millenaar** (5.2%: ★★) with blackcurrant fruit pastille hints; lightweight brown **Dubbele Dorus** (5.6%: ★★); sweetish **Bennie Blond** (7.9%: ★★); hazy **De Moss Tripel** (8.1%: ★★); and too-thin **Damen Quadrupel** (9%: ★+), which punches below its weight.

Boegbeeld

Uilenburg 1, 5211 EV 's-Hertogenbosch
T 06 5315 9196
brouwerijboegbeeld.nl

Figurehead, a nanobrewery founded in 2015, is in a historic building in one of the oldest areas of the city. We believe larger runs are brewed elsewhere. Workshops and tours by arrangement.
BEERS INCLUDE: standout hoppy blond **Wanne Klets** (5.9%: ★★+); brown ale **Houdoe & Bedankt** (6%: ★★); **Kutbier** (6.3%: ★+), a hazy blond with prunes that includes a Dutch obscenity in its name but is otherwise unremarkable; witbier **Siberië** (6.3%: ★★); cocoa-tinged stout **Sjekeláde Bol** (6.5%: ★★); and blond tripel **Bossche Beul** (7%: ★★), spiced with non-noticeable Szechuan pepper.

Boei

Rommelpot 11, 1797 RN Den Hoorn
T 0222 314180
landgoeddebontebelevenis.nl

Texel micro founded in 2002 at the Bonte Belevenis farm museum, where the entry fee includes a tour of the brewery and on-site distillery. With only a 5hl kit used twice a month, this is a small-scale operation but still extends to a cold room for lagers. Bottled beers only, mostly sold in house and at a few local shops.
BEERS INCLUDE: aromatic, flowery, honeyed pilsener **Noorderzon 6** (6%: ★★); wheat ale **Dichte Mist** (6%: ★★); **Windkracht 6** (6%: ★★+), a soft-spoken blond with bog myrtle; bitter tripel **Windkracht 8** (8%: ★★); warming barley wine **Windkracht 10** (10%: ★★+); and super-strength **Windkracht 12** (12%: ★★+), brewed once a year with whisky malt.

Bogt

Calandkade 157, 2521 AA Den Haag
T 06 4501 0451
brouwerijbogt.nl

Occasional brewer of 1hl batches since 2014, re-emerging on a new site in 2015 after an enforced break for licensing reasons.
BEERS INCLUDE: **Blonde Dolly** (5.5%: ★★), a kuit with saison yeast; and occasional one-offs.

Bohemean

Parkweg 3, 8011 CK Zwolle
T 06 5340 8448
bohemean.nl

Bohemian and German-inspired producer founded in 2016, originally brewing elsewhere but with its own 2hl kit since 2019.
BEERS INCLUDE: **Edelweis Weizen** (5%); Kölsch clone **Zwölsch** (5%); and its stronger sister **Zwölsch 2B** (8%).

Bolle Brouwketel

Helleneiend 24, 5531 BV Bladel
T 06 2238 3280
debollebrouwketel.nl

North Brabant microbrewery established in 2019.
BEERS INCLUDE: dubbel **Zwarte Kaat** (7.8%), named after a local witch; and her blond sister **Tripel Kaat** (8%).

Bolschout

Hopperzuigerstraat 55, 1333 HM Almere
T 06 2299 2553
bolschout.nl

Another drop of rain in the Flevoland desert, creating Belgian-style ales since 2014. Originally working at 50l scale, it moved to a larger location with a 6hl installation in 2017.
BEERS INCLUDE: hazy organic pilsener **Urtyp** (5.5%: ★★); undemanding pale ale **Belga** (6%: ★★); fruity IPA **Hopvol** (6%: ★★); and multi-grained **Blond** (7%: ★★+).
SEASONAL: superior witbier **Blom** (5.5%: ★★+), made with elderflower for spring and summer; and spiced winter bock **Ster** (6%: ★★+).

Bonifatius 754

Diepswal 5, 9101 LA Dokkum
T 06 1368 7839
bonifatius754.nl

This Frisian brewery and distillery claims to be the modern successor of a brewhouse started by

(6.8%: ★★); sweetish dark **Dubbel** (7.2%: ★★); and **Kindelbier** (8.4%: ★★), an export stout with liquorice notes.

Borne

Beerninksweg 67, 7621 XS Borne
T 06 2036 3635
bierbrouwerijborne.nl

Overijssel microbrewery with improving beers, founded in 2017.
BEERS INCLUDE: orange-spiced **Spanjaard Blond** (5.8%: ★★); nutty dark **Spanjaard Donker** (6.5%: ★★+); dry amber **Deeps Duudter** (7.6%: ★★+); and **Boris Bier** (8.1%: ★★+), dark and stout-like barley wine with added coffee.

Borrelnoot

Beellanen 13, 3445 TD Woerden
T 06 2166 3956
brouwerijborrelnoot.nl

Homebrewers who went pro in 2013, with their own 2.5hl kit since 2017 but still brewing larger runs elsewhere, possibly at Naeckte Brouwers.
BEERS INCLUDE: summery blond **Zilte Zonderling** (4.2%: ★★) with liquorice and seaweed; red ale **Rebelse Rooie** (5.7%); and standard **Brutaal Blondje** (6.8%: ★★).

Bossche

Bossche Brouwers aan de Vaart
Tramkade 29, 5211 VB 's-Hertogenbosch
T 06 5141 4836
bosschebrouwers.nl

Founded by music-loving friends in 2017 with a tiny 50l kit housed in their music café on an industrial site north of the station. No tours, but tastings on a boat (maximum 12 passengers). Quality is reasonable but ratings are challenging as all beers are one-off brews. We have tried **Winternacht** (5.5%: ★★+), an aniseedy seasonal.

monks following the assassination of Anglo-German preacher St Boniface in the year 754, though the line of continuous brewing was broken between 1876 and 2016. The kit, on the first floor of a historic building with a taproom below, is used mainly for test brews and one-offs, with bulk runs often done at Dockum (below). They also distill spirits.
BEERS INCLUDE: **Klooster Fruit** (3.8%: ★★), a sweetish, pink concoction using mulberries from a nearby churchyard tree; blond **Maerte Saison** (4.9%: ★★), spiced with star anise; fruity witbier **Wad Wit** (5.2%: ★★); and vinous dark quadrupel **Acht Guldens** (10%: ★★+).

Borghman

't Zand 25, 7126 BG Bredevoort
T 0543 450089
borghman.nl

Gelderland brewery and taproom founded in 2015 in a 1950s former school on the site of a 16th-century castle, although nothing of that remains. Tours with tastings for groups of four or more.
BEERS INCLUDE: citrussy witbier **Rondje** (4.2%: ★★); less-than-regal **Royaal Blond** (5.2%: ★★); lightly fruity **Blond** (6.6%: ★★); fruity but dull **APA (Achterhoeks Pale Ale)**

Bourgogne Kruis

Wilhelminakanaal-Zuid 104, 4903 RA
Oosterhout
T 06 3964 8631
bourgognekruis.com

North Brabant brewery established in 2009
by descendants of a family who owned a
brewery on the same site 50 years previously.
Beers brewed in 7.5hl batches always include
wheat. Open on some Saturdays (*13.00–17.00*),
but check before travelling. Tours by
arrangement.
BEERS INCLUDE: citrussy witbier **Goud van
Tarwe** (5%: ★★); dark dubbel **Bronze van
Tarwe** (6.5%: ★★+); and **Zilver van Tarwe**
(8%: ★★), a decently balanced tripel.

Brand (Heineken)

Brouwerijstraat 2, 6321 AG Wijlre
T 043 450 8282
brand.nl

The roots of what is now the Netherlands'
oldest brewery reach back to 1340. The Brand
family took over in 1871 and its members have
retained a role since Heineken took over in
1989. A copper brewhouse from 1937 remains
for the admiration of visitors and as a backdrop
to photoshoots, though hasn't been used
since 1981. The beers from the production
brewery are more adventurous than those
of the parent and benefit from new recipes
harvested through an annual homebrewing
competition.
BEERS INCLUDE: yucky sweet **Oud-Bruin**
(3.5%: ★+); lightly fruity **Session IPA** (3.5%:
★★); citrussy **Gose** (4.8%: ★★); industrial
blond **Pilsener** (5%: ★★); its unfiltered cousin
Ongefilterd Pilsener (5.2%: ★★); far better,
full-bodied, best-in-show pilsener **UP**
(5.5%: ★★★); citrussy but sweetish **Weizen**
(5.3%: ★★); restrained but balanced **Porter**
(6%: ★★+); malty amber lager **Imperator**
(6.5%: ★★); entry-level simplistic **IPA** (7%: ★★);
and almost-tripel **Blond** (8.5%: ★★), which
started out complex but has been simplified
for the masses.

SEASONAL: average **Lentebock** (6.5%: ★★);
bittersweet **Dubbelbock** (7.5%: ★★+);
and treacly winter **Sylvester** (7.5%: ★★).
ALSO: alcohol-free versions of the **IPA**
and **Weizen**.

Brave Hendrikus

Molenstraat 15, 6961 DS Eerbeek
T 06 1016 6930

Nanobrewery making elusive Belgian-style
ales using local ingredients since 2014.
BEERS INCLUDE: IPA **Hopje** (5.2%);
dubbel **Bruintje** (8.2%); a **Tripel** (8.1%);
and a **Blonde** (9%).

Breda

Takkebijsters 37A, 4817 BL Breda
T 06 2953 1203
bierbrouwerijbreda.nl

Substantial 20hl brewery-for-hire working
since 2017 for a range of clients including
locally based Bliksem and Witte Anker,
brewing own-label beers very occasionally.

Breuster

Breusterstraat 27, 6245 EH Eijsden
T 043 737 0202
breusterbrouwers.ursulinenconvent.com

Limburg brewery in the cellars of the Ursuline
Convent international museum for family history
(**ursulinenconvent.com**) since 2017, brewing
more-or-less weekly on a simple 2hl kit, with
beers sometimes sold in the adjacent café.
Tours and tastings for groups of 10+.
BEERS INCLUDE: citrussy blond **Pieth** (7%: ★★)
and quadrupel **Mère de Boebe** (9%: ★★+).

Brewboyz –
see Utrecht

Brielsch/Kont Van Het Paard

Brielsch Brouwers Gilde/
Brouwerij 't Kont Van Het Paard
Kaatsbaan 1-3, 3231 XL Brielle
T 0181 416161
brielschbrouwersgilde.nl, kontvanhetpaard.nl

South Holland collective making beer at the
back of the Kont van het Paard pub since 2016.
The pub also makes its own **Dorstige Ros**
brand on the same kit, and as it's unclear
whether they operate as one or two companies,
we lump them together here. No tours, but
the café is worth the effort and the best place
to find the brews.
Brielsch BEERS INCLUDE: dry bitter-finishing
Belgian-style blond **Angelus** (5.7%: ★★+)
and autumnal, dark and cocoa-laden
De Gecroonde Bock (7.8%: ★★).
Dorstige Ros BEERS INCLUDE: dry, fruity
hoppy **American Pale Ale** (5.7%: ★★+);
amber **Hefeweizen** (5.8%); and hazy blond
Zware Saison (8%: ★★)

Broeders

Heulenslag 13, 2971 VE Bleskensgraaf
broedersbier.nl

Two South Holland-based brothers nano-
brewing for the local market since 2018,
but scaling up leads us to believe that larger
runs are now made elsewhere.
BEERS INCLUDE: IPA **Gulle Broeder** (6.5%)
and tripel **Stevige Broeder** (9%).

Broer & Zus

Schans 10, 1947 JR Beverwijk
cafebroerenzus.com

North Holland brewpub at first brewing at
Naeckte Brouwers when launched in 2016.
The taproom opened in 2017 and a dedicated
10hl kit has been in operation since 2019.
BEERS INCLUDE: lightweight oatmeal stout
Ochtenddauw (4.8%: ★★+); dark amber red
IPA **Klaproos** (5.5%: ★★+); standout American
IPA **Duinpan** (6.2%: ★★★); easy-drinking blond

Levenslicht (6.4%: ★★); rich, dark porter
Bitterzoet (8.2%: ★★+); raisiny quadrupel
Nachtschade (10%: ★★+); and evening-closing
barley wine **Kopergloed** (11%: ★★+).

Bronckhorster

Rhabergseweg 9, 7224 NA Rha (Bronckhorst)
T 0575 452149
bronckhorster.beer

Middle-of-nowhere Gelderland brewery
founded in 2010 by expat Yorkshireman Steve
Gammage. Initially named Rodenburg, it takes
its current name from the local municipality,
as does the New York City borough of Bronx.
Beers are brewed in 10hl batches at least twice
weekly and the results are often outstanding,
winning numerous international awards.
The taproom beside the kettles is usually
open Sa&Su (*13.00–17.00*) but call ahead to be
sure as it's occasionally closed for brewing.
BEERS INCLUDE: easy-drinking limbering-up
beer **Slimme Rhakker** (2.5%: ★★+); improving
pilsener **Hooge Heeren** (5%: ★★+); superior
weizen **Eigenweiss** (5.5%: ★★+); suaver-than-
most **James Blond** (6%: ★★+); fruity, hoppy
English IPA **Royal Rha** (6%: ★★★); fresh and
lovely New England IPA **OurRidgeinAle**
(6%: ★★★+); cleverly restrained smoked
Altbier **ALTernative** (6.5%: ★★★); warming
amber **Saison Nouvelle** (7%: ★★); dry dark
Dubbelganger (7.5%: ★★); subtly bitter
Angus Tripel (8.5%: ★★+); intensely hoppy,
moreish double IPA **Hoptimist** (9.5%: ★★★);
treacly, rich and imperious **Nightporter**
(8%: ★★★★); and heavy-hitting black
quadrupel **BBC Four** (11%: ★★+).

SEASONAL: refreshingly dry blond **Hop into Spring** (6%: ★★★); golden, ginger-spiced quaffer **Hop into Summer** (4.5%: ★★+); fruity red ale **Hop into Autumn** (7%: ★★+); hoppy bitter autumn **IJsselbock** (7%: ★★★); rich dark dubbelbock **Brok-in-de-Keel** (8.5%: ★★+); and superbly rounded dark dry **Hop into Winter** (10.5%: ★★★).
ALSO: a number of ever-changing **Barrel-Aged** beers that are rarely less than great.

Brood

Kerkstraat 3, 4761 CA Zevenbergen
T 0168 327140
cafedebakkerij.nl/brouwerij-brood

Bread was founded in 2016 as an offshoot of De Bakkerij down the road (see cafés) and now brews more-or-less weekly. Tours on request.
BEERS INCLUDE: **Blond Sneetje** (6%); dry, fruity dark IPA **Broodnodig** (6.5%: ★★); and its fruitier and more successful sister **Broodnodig Grapefruit** (6.5%: ★★+).

Brouwdok

Nieuwe Willemskade 8, 8862 RZ Harlingen Haven
T 06 4416 9174
hetbrouwdok.nl

Brewing since 2014 behind the owner's home, Brew Dock moved to a harbourside site with a 20hl kit in 2016, adding a taproom in 2019. Most beers are named after nautical and sailing terms – these guys know the ropes. Tours on request for groups, or without reservation for individuals Sa 14.00.
BEERS INCLUDE: light, dry quaffing blond **Slim Slimmer** (4.2%: ★★+); bitter American pale ale **Ús Ale** (5.2%: ★★+); dry-hopped witbier **Toplicht** (5.8%: ★★+); red ale **Captain's Daughter** (6%: ★★+); easy-drinking **Wad Weizen** (5.5%: ★★+); fruity, almost milkshake-smooth IPA **Hophûn** (6.5%: ★★+); golden tripel **Vlaams Paard** (8%: ★★, 'Flemish horse' is a rigging term not an animal); **Dokwerker** (8.5%: ★★+), a cocoa-laden Baltic porter; and heavyweight imperial stout **De Dude** (10%: ★★★).

Brouwerij

Piet Heinkade 4, 1019 BR Amsterdam
T 020 811 0381
deliriumcafeamsterdam.nl

The Brewery is a 1hl installation behind the Delirium Café Amsterdam, in place since 2016 and mainly used for workshops, although beers are occasionally made sale at the bar.

Brouwerslokaal

Blekestraat 16 4503 BG Groede
T 06 1153 2712
brouwerslokaal.nl, dutchbargain.com, marckensteijn.com

Originally founded as Marckensteijn in 2012 at the nearby Drie Koningen café, the brewery was rebranded to accommodate a second range of beers, Dutch Bargain, and a third brewer. A larger crowdfunded facility with tap-room and restaurant in a former village school and gym around the corner (address as above) should be open by the time you read this.
As **Dutch Bargain:** ginger-spiced sweetish blond **Seawise** (4.3%: ★★); heavy-handed sweetish **Imperial Zeeuws Blond** (7.4%: ★+); hoppy, perfumed **Imperial Pale Ale** (10%: ★★),

a barley wine in all but name; and deceptively drinkable, chocolatey **Imperial Russian Stout** (11.5%: ★★+) with cocoa nibs.

AS *Marckenstein:* standard blond **Nr 1** (6.5%: ★★); fruity-edged dubbel **Nr 2** (6.5%: ★★); competent but undemanding tripel **Nr 3** (7.2%: ★★); solid amber **Nr 4** (6%: ★★); and average saison **Nr 5** (5%: ★★).

ALSO: **Het Lab** is Marckenstijn's experimental range, while Dutch Bargain's is labelled **Signatures**.

Brouwersnös

Eibergseweg 1, 7141 CD Groenlo
T 0544 221009
brouwersnos.nl

The owner of this large new-build brewery in the Gelderland Achterhoek formerly made beers as Eastgreen (Yellow Moon) before upscaling in 2018. The taproom is in the stately house across the park. Brewery tours and boat trips by appointment.

BEERS INCLUDE: sweetish amber **Ne Toffen** (3.8%: ★★); dry fruity pale ale **Frolijke Frans** (4.8%: ★★+); multi-grained blond **Willemken** (5.8%: ★★); sweetish dubbel **Tweeduuster** (7.3%: ★★); coffee and cocoa-tinged imperial stout **Dikke Toon** (8.2%: ★★+); sweetish tripel **Mooien Muiter** (9%: ★★); and full-bodied amber quadrupel **Zwaar Gesschut** (10.5%: ★★+).

ALSO: **Kopstoot** (6.6%: ★★+), an odd gin and beer blend created for and with the Michelin-starred Librije restaurant in Zwolle.

Brouwersnös

Brouwkamer

Baarnschedijk 6B2, 3741LR Baarn
T 06 2428 4466
brouwkamer.nl

Microbrewery based in Utrecht province since 2018, launching its first commercial beer, **Baarns Blondje**, a year later.

Brouwschuur

Brouwschuur
(Weerter Stadsbrouwerij)

Parallelweg 143, 6001 HM Weert
debrouwschuur.nl, weerterstadsbrouwerij.nl

Founded in 2014, and since 2016 with a permanent base at the Weerter Stadsbrouwerij, which operates as a separate business. The brewer makes a solid and ever-expanding range under the Brouwschuur name on the 10hl kit, which is also rented out to a dozen or more others, most notably Natte Gijt. The taproom (see cafés) is worth a visit.

BEERS INCLUDE: dry-hopped **Toch Unne Pils** (5%: ★★); hoppy IPA **Nog Eine Dan** (6.2%: ★★+); drinkable blond **Gust z'n Zus** (6%: ★★); bitter rye pale ale **Gouwe Rog** (7%: ★★+); and smoky porter **Doef Van D'n Daeke** (7.3%: ★★+), among many others.

SEASONAL: **Kaoj Veut** (8.8%: ★★+), a bitter-finishing winter stout with chilli hints.

Brouwtoren

Binderkampweg 29 U31, 6545 CA Nijmegen
brouwtoren.nl

Founded in 2014 and initially brewing elsewhere, Brew Tower acquired its own 5hl kit in 2017. *BEERS INCLUDE:* lightly spiced red IPA **Graodus** (5.5%: ★★); fruity 'Mexican' pale ale **Güero** (5.8%: ★★); Belgian-style pale ale **Berta** (7%: ★★); and sweetish tripel **Saga** (7.6%: ★★).

Bruusk

Kijkuit 52, 4001 XD Tiel
T 06 4226 5344
facebook.com/bierlapbruusk

Gelderland brewery founded in 2017 with the main intention of renting out its small 1.5hl kit for workshops, but with occasional one-off brews on sale locally.

Bruut

Cruquiusweg 83D, 1019 AT Amsterdam
T 020 331 2727
bruutbier.nl

In business as a nomadic brewer since 2014, Bruut added a brewpub four years later. The brewhouse is mainly used for experiments

and one-offs sold at the bar, with most of the core range still made elsewhere in longer runs. *BEERS INCLUDE:* dry-hopped citrussy 'English Bitter' **Vogt** (4.5%: ★★+); refreshing witbier **Eigenweiss** (5.5%: ★★+); dry, bitter **Saison** (5.5%: ★★+); bitter, hoppy blond **Stennis** (5.5%: ★★+); hazy pale ale **Wazig** (5.5%: ★★+); strong blond **Soelaas** (7.5%: ★★); and standout **Gajes** (8%: ★★★), a bitter dry-hopped golden tripel.

Budels

Nieuwstraat 9, 6021 HP Budel
T 0495 491369
budels.nl

Established in 1870 and now run by the fourth generation of the Arts family, this North Brabant independent with a conscience and a generally reliable output strives to be carbon neutral, brewing its mostly organic beers using renewable energy. After decades of little change, the brewery is finally adding adventurous new styles to its repertoire, although they could be bolder. Visits and tastings by arrangement for groups of 30 or more Mo-Sa.
BEERS INCLUDE: sticky sweet **Oud Bruin** (3.5%: ★+); new kid, lightly sour **White Gose** (4.5%: ★★+); honeyed blond **Honing** (4.5%: ★+); standard **Pilsener** (5%: ★★); malty organic **Bio Pilsener** (5%: ★★); **Ongefilterd** (5%: ★★+), the bio pils in unfiltered form; balanced wheat **Witte Parel** (5%: ★★); hazy, golden blond **Weizen** (5%: ★★); malty amber **Batavier** (5%: ★+); herbal and bitter **Golden Ale** (6%: ★★+), dry hopped with Sorachi Ace; above-average dry **Goudblond** (6%: ★★+); faintly sweet-and-sour dubbel **Capucijn** (6.5%: ★★+); an **IPA** (7%: ★★) that errs on the safe side; coriander-spiced amber **Kolos** (7.5%: ★★); and warming barley wine **Zware Dobber** (8.5%: ★★+).
ALSO: several no and low alcohol beers and radlers that are yet to hit the mark. We really want to like (dry-)**Hopped 0.0%** (★), but it tastes like hop-infused watery cornflakes.

Bulkse Hoek

Valeriaan 24, 5331 DA Kerkdriel
T 06 4378 0836
bulksehoek.nl

Gelderland homebrewer who turned pro in 2016. Beers are sold locally under the **Drielse Bieren** brand but rarely seen elsewhere. *BEERS INCLUDE:* blond **Hopbel** (5.8%); **Karakter** (7.6%); and **Expreszo** (7.9%) double stout.

Bunnik's

Nieuwe Gouwe Westzijde 4A, 2802 AN Gouda
T 0182 512324
bunnikbier.nl

South Holland homebrewer who turned pro in 2018. A dozen beers are planned over three 'lines': allegedly 'accessible' **BasisBieren**, 'moment-specific' **BierBeleving** and experimental **BontBier**, but they have been slow to roll out so far. *BEERS INCLUDE:* Belgian-style pale ale **Burengerucht** (6.7%); and spiced blond **Baby** (7.3%).

Burg

Putterweg 45, 3851 GB Ermelo
T 0341 564934
burgbieren.nl

Beers from this small-scale Gelderland brewery, founded in 1995, are largely sold bottled in a shop on one side of the brewhouse or draught in a taproom on the other, and occasionally seen elsewhere. Tours Sa 14.00; also We 15.00 (*mid-May to mid-Sep*) and Th 15.00 (*Jul&Aug*). *BEERS INCLUDE:* slowly improving **Veluws Blond** (5.5%: ★★); malty, caramel dubbel **Veluws Bruun** (7%: ★★); sweetish golden **Tripel-B** (8%: ★★); and dark barley wine **Gulle** (9.5%: ★★), which has oomph but little else.

Butcher's Tears

Karperweg 45, 1075 LB Amsterdam
T 06 5390 9777
butchers-tears.com

A Swedish head brewer oversees the production of high quality, sometimes-exceptional beers at this brewery and taproom, opened in 2013 in a former factory in Amsterdam South. *ONLY TWO BEERS MAKE THE CORE RANGE:* bitter amber session ale **The Last Possession** (5%: ★★+); and deliciously quaffable hoppy blond **Green Cap** (6%: ★★★). **Lipreader** (usually ★★+—★★★) appears in autumn, but tends to shapeshift in style and strength from one year to the next. There are also many other one-offs and specials.

Cambrinus

Houtmarkt 56B, 7201 KM Zutphen
T 0575 546688
hanze-stadsbrouwerij.nl

City-centre brewpub founded in 2006 as Hanze but renamed in 2013, making draught beers of solid if unexceptional quality for sale exclusively in house. Group tours by arrangement. *BEERS INCLUDE:* witbier **Witte Wolf** (5.3%: ★★); safe blond **Liesje** (6.8%: ★★); dubbel **Broedertje** (8%: ★★), with caramel notes; sweetish tripel **Droge Nap** (9.5%: ★★); and mighty **Magistraat** (12.5%: ★★+), a tangled witches' brew of alcohol, walnut and aniseed.

Ceijser

Schoolstraat 13, 7634 PT Tilligte
T 06 1456 2288
deceijser.nl

Overijssel nanobrewery making 30l batches since 2018, with plans to upgrade to 1hl. It may also use other locations to upscale. *BEERS INCLUDE:* standard blond **Weizen** (5%: ★★) and deceptively easy-drinking hoppy **Citra IPA** (8%: ★★+). Others are in the works, alongside one-off experimental brews.

Chamaven

De Stoven 31, 7206 AZ Zutphen
T 06 2824 5061
chamaven.nl

Undergoing enlargement in 2019, this
brewery was founded in 2017 by a group of
friends who named it after the Germanic
tribe inhabiting the area in Roman times.
BEERS INCLUDE: session IPA **Grijp** (5%);
blond **Walburg** (6.1%); and dark quadrupel
Rijkhard (9.8%).

Comenius

Vestingwerken 1-B1, 1411 WC Naarden-Vesting
T 035 737 0168
comeniusbrouwerij.nl

North Holland microbrewery since 2018,
brewing on a micro-scale in a vaulted room
inside the old city wall. First beer was
Kölsch-style **Courtine**, with half a dozen
others expected to follow.

Commies

Essenseweg 37, 4709 BK Nispen
decommies.nl

North Brabant outfit founded in 2017 close
to the Belgian border, currently brewing in
4.5hl batches twice per month.
BEERS INCLUDE: German pale ale **(H)alt** (5.4%);
Cascade-hopped wheat ale **Amerikaans Wit**
(5.5%); noble-hopped **Saison** (7%); and
Gouden Commies (8%) tripel.

Cornelis

Meerkoetenweg 9, 8218 NA Lelystad
T 06 2825 0198
stadsbrouwerijcornelis.nl

Flevoland brewery founded in 2018 by a
homebrewer with 25 years' experience,
producing beers under the **Schuurbier** label.
Visits by arrangement.

BEERS INCLUDE: dry session IPA **Hop Groen**
(3.5%: ★★+); nutty red ale **Rood** (5%: ★★);
subtle rauchbier **Botterbier** (6%: ★★+);
and sweetish **Donker Blond** (8%: ★★).
ALSO: **Sea Bottom** experimental one-offs.

Corviri

Hoge Hereweg 33, 9756 TG Glimmen
corviri.nl

Brewing in 1.5hl batches in the basement of a
rural pancake restaurant south of Groningen
since 2015.
BEERS INCLUDE: straw-blond dryish **Weizen**
(5.5%: ★★); amber **IPA** (7.2%: ★★+); sweetish
blond **Tripel** (8%: ★★); and dark-brown spicy
sweetish **Quadrupel** (8.5%: ★★).

Crooked Spider

Jagerslaan-Noord 10, 2242 SZ Wassenaar
T 06 1463 5872
crookedspider.nl

Brewery near Den Haag, started in 2014 with
a 1hl kit but since expanded to 2.5hl. The
name recalls an unfortunate arachnid who
fell into a brewing vessel. Tours, tastings and
a taproom are planned.
BEERS INCLUDE: lightly peachy session ale
Blond d'Eté (4.5%: ★★); dry, amber **California
Gold** (5.5%: ★★); hoppier **American Amber**
(6.5%: ★★+); gently bitter **English IPA** (6.5%:
★★+); and warming, lovely **Russian Imperial
Stout** (9.6%: ★★★), also appearing around
Christmas in variously barrel-aged form as
R.I.B.A.C.S. (usually ★★★).

Croy

Croylaan 9, 5735 PB Aarle-Rixtel
T 0492 381348
croybier.nl

Lovely middle-of-nowhere North Brabant
tavern brewery with its own hop garden,
opened in 2011 but claiming a heritage back
to 1671. Brewing once took place in the pub;

it's since expanded into an adjacent building but we believe the core bottled range is still made at Van Steenberge in Belgium. Beer cheese and jars of *stoofvlees* beef stew with beer are made in house. Pre-booked tours every last Sa of each month.

BEERS INCLUDE: unfiltered pilsener **Croy 1671** (4.5%: ★★); session blond **Echt bier** (4.5%: ★★); lightweight, drinkable **Stout** (5.5%: ★★+); nondescript **Blond** (6.5%: ★★); average **Dubbel** (7.5%: ★★); lightly fruity **Tripel** (9%: ★★), sold in 75cl bottles as **Grand Cru**.

Dampegheest

Achterweg 22, 1906 AG Limmen
T 06 5194 0176
dampegheest.nl

Founded in 2008 in a North Holland village with a 3hl kit homemade from salvaged dairy tanks but since upgraded to 8hl. A pop-up taproom appears down the road (Schoolweg 1), every third Su of the month (*15.00-20.00*). Tours by arrangement for groups of 10 or more.
BEERS INCLUDE: coriander-spiced thirst-quencher **Manus** (4.7%: ★★); standard blond **Antje** (6%: ★★); crisp **Alkmaars Blondje** (7.5%: ★★); sweetish amber **Skoftig** (7.6%: ★★); bittersweet blond **Merakels** (8%: ★★+), made with 30% whey; and raisin-tinged barley wine **Zware Hufter** (10%: ★★+).
SEASONAL: fruity meibock **Ut 1e Kieft-ai** (7%: ★★) and spiced wheat **Winterwit** (9%: ★★+).

Davo

Sluisstraat 6, 7411 EG Deventer
T 0570 866431
davobieren.nl

This enthusiastic crew had been cuckoo brewing for four years when they acquired their own 5hl brewery and taproom in 2016, producing an evolving range of good quality, widely-distributed beers. Saturday afternoon tasting sessions can be pre-booked via the website.
BEERS INCLUDE: quaffing blond **Café Racer** (5.8%: ★★+); hoppy blond **Surf Ale** (6.4%: ★★+);

spicy hoppy **Indie IPA** (7.5%: ★★+); **Darkness** (7.5%: ★★), a not-entirely-successful dubbel/stout hybrid; rich, dark **Weizenbock** (8.8%: ★★★), with banana and bitter chocolate hints; fruity tripel **Road Trip** (8.5%: ★★+); and chewy imperial stout **The Don** (10%: ★★★).

Deftige Aap

Markt 14, 5701 RK Helmond
T 06 2152 7704

North Brabant's Posh Ape was founded in 2017 in the village of Gerwen, evolving into a brewpub at the currrent site late in 2019. Beers include a competent, dark **Dubbel** (7.5%: ★★+) and a golden **Tripel** (8%: ★★).

Delftse

Hippolytusbuurt 43, 2611 HM Delft
delftsebrouwers.nl

Noted De Molen brewer John Brus launched
this side project in 2019, using a 6.5hl brewery
in the Delfts Brouwhuis pub. The brewhouse
is used for one-offs and experimental brews
sold in house, but for capacity reasons the
core range is made at De Molen.
BEERS INCLUDE: clean crisp **Oerpils** (5%: ★★+);
safe, crowd-pleasing **Weizen** (5.2%: ★★);
superior saison **Bronstig Bijtje** (5.6%: ★★+);
banana-tinged **Blond** (6.2%: ★★); tropical
fruity bitter IPA **Klunzig Kuiken** (6.2%: ★★★);
a sweeter less bitter **IPA** (6.5%: ★★); fruity
blond **Tripel** (8.5%: ★★); and orange-peel
infused **Sinaaspril Tripel** (8.5%: ★★).

Demoersleutel –
See Moersleutel

Dijk

Balsem 16, 9285 KD Buitenpost
T 06 5414 8796
dijk-bier.nl

Friesland-based 2hl mobile brewery that can
also be hired for workshops and brewing
demonstrations, launched in 2017.
BEERS INCLUDE: triple-grained **Wonderlijk
Wit** (5.9%: ★★); restrained amber IPA **Hemels
Hop** (6.1%: ★★+); lightly bitter **Trotse Tripel**
(8.2%: ★★+); and standout cocoa-laden
imperial **Stevige Stout** (9.5%: ★★★).

Dikke

Veldpoortstraat 15, 3961 BK Wijk bij Duurstede
T 06 3854 2178

Utrecht microbrewery making unfiltered
kuit beers to traditional recipes since 2015,
rehoused in a larger crowdfunded location
in 2019. A taproom may follow.
BEERS INCLUDE: oat-heavy **Dikke OPA**
(5.5%: ★★); **Dikke MAAi** (6.5%: ★★), which
contains cherry juice but avoids sweetness;
sharp blond **Wijkse Dikke** (6.5%: ★★+); and
fruity amber **Dikke Donder** (7.5%: ★★).

Dockum

De Hogedijken 20, 9101 WV Dokkum
T 0519 740004
brouwerijdokkum.nl, kaldkletske.nl

Started as a cuckoo known as **Kâld Kletske**
in 2014, this Friesland producer survived the
death of its founder in 2017 and went on to
gain its own copper brewhouse and taproom
with restaurant the following year. The
brewery is named Dockum but the original
brand has been retained for the beers.
BEERS INCLUDE: citrussy saison **Jiertid**
(5.1%: ★★); weizen **Weet** (5.5%: ★★); rounded
stout **Krêftich** (5.6%: ★★+); golden blond
Ljocht (6%: ★★); standard blond **Blûn** (6.5%:
★★); **Galjes** (6.5%: ★★+), a herbal and spicy
amber gruit beer with bog myrtle; bitter-
finishing IPA **Hoppig** (6.5%: ★★); and tripel
Trijedûbel (8%: ★★).

Doetinchem

Grutstraat 31, 7001 BW Doetinchem
T 0314 820993
grandcafehendrixen.nl

Gelderland micro producing **Walters** beers
for sale exclusively in the adjacent HendriXen
taproom since 2014.
BEERS INCLUDE: fruit-edged **Blond** (5%: ★★);
dryer **Amber** (5%: ★★); and golden **Tripel**
(8.1%: ★★).

Dokjard

Noorderhaven 63, 9712 VJ Groningen
T 050 364 2420
dokjard.nl

Begun as a cuckoo at Bax in 2018 before expanding into its own brewpub a year later, Dockyard currently produces only one beer: bitter IPA **Kluusbaas** (6.8%: ★★+), spiced with kaffir lime and chilli.

Dommelsch (AB InBev)

Brouwerijplein 84, 5551 AE Dommelen
T 040 208 7911
dommelsch.nl

This historic North Brabant brewery, founded in 1744, was taken over in 1950 by the Snieders family and sold in 1968 to Belgian giant Interbrew, a predecessor of what's now the world's largest drinks company, AB InBev. It makes only three beers, but produces 1,000,000hl per year, so someone clearly likes them. *BEERS INCLUDE:* woeful liquid breakfast cereal **Oud Bruin** (2%: ★+); and bog-standard dull **Pilsener** (5%: ★+). Alcohol-free **0%** (★★) is fair in comparison to its peers.

Dordrecht

Buddingh'plein 20, 3311 BV Dordrecht
T 078 750 7227
stadsbrouwerijdordrecht.nl

A 1hl brewery installed in 2008 in an early 17th-century building which was once the malt store of De Sleutel (the Key) brewery, founded in 1433 and the oldest surviving brewery in the Netherlands when it was closed

by Heineken in 1968. The current operation employs youngsters from disadvantaged backgrounds to help brew **Schapenkopje** beers at least weekly. Tours every last Sa of the month (except Dec) 15.00 & 16.30, at other times on request for groups of 10–15. *BEERS INCLUDE:* floral-tinged **Blond** (5%: ★★); orange peel-laden **Amber** (6%: ★★); relatively dry but toffee-tinted **Dubbel** (6.5%: ★★); and coriander-spiced **Triepel 1433** (8.5%: ★★+).

Draok

D'n Draok Bossche Brouwerij
Musselstraat 55, 5215 HE 's-Hertogenbosch
T 073 642 6865
draok.nl

Brewing in 40l batches since 2015, with larger runs now made at the Brouwstudio in Berlicum, shared with Uthoka (below). *REGULAR BEERS INCLUDE:* **Bossche Bol** (5.5%: ★★), a lightly bitter stout with a vanilla edge; superior **Bosch Blond** (6.5%: ★★+); dry dubbel **Houdoe & Bedankt** (7.3%: ★★+); and clove-tinted **Tripel Twelve** (7.7%: ★★). *ALSO:* numerous limited-edition one-offs.

SOCIALLY CONSCIOUS BREWERIES

Several Dutch breweries offer a social service beyond providing good beer, by helping to rehabilitate those who have otherwise failed to find work. Some, like Dordrecht, employ the educationally or socially disadvantaged. Others, most notably De Prael, have a workforce mainly comprised of people who have suffered major mental disorder and struggled to rejoin mainstream society. Their principle is that many jobs in a brewery are quite complex yet easy to learn from experience, which gives people both the confidence and the skills to work constructively. We applaud all their efforts.

Drie Heerlijkheden

Waaijenbergstraat 17, 4881 NB Zundert
T 06 3065 1388

North Brabant-based Three Glories, founded in 2016 with a 1hl kit, brews mainly Belgian-style ales with tongue-twisting names. *BEERS INCLUDE:* blond **Bettieakkemaaij** (6.5%); dubbel **Durdouwer** (7%); imperial stout **Dikkenambras** (8%); tripel **Houdoewentoot** (8.5%); and quadrupel **Kunniekwoadblijve** (10%).

Drie Ringen

Kleine Spui 18, 3811 BE Amersfoort
T 033 465 6575
dedrieringen.nl

Longstanding microbrewery operating since 1989 in a riverside building beside a medieval gate, making reasonable beers which are unexpectedly hard to source outside the taproom and a few other Amersfoort bars. Group tours by appointment. *BEERS INCLUDE:* lightly bitter **Amersfoorts Blond** (5%: ★★); malty, Kölsch-leaning **CorDeux** (5%: ★★+); spiced wheat **Wit** (5%: ★★); bitter blond **Stadsbier** (5%: ★★); healthily non-sweet **Dubbel** (6.5%: ★★); golden **Tripel** (6.8%: ★★); and hoppy blond **Vuurvogel** (7.5%: ★★+).

Drift

Brugwachter 5, 3034 KD Rotterdam
driftbrouwers.nl

Founded in 2016, making small batches in house but commissioning larger runs from Anders in Belgium. *BEERS INCLUDE:* hoppy blond **Neustadt Weizen** (5.1%: ★★+); fruity **Beetje Stout** (6.2%: ★★+); and strongly bitter **Hijs IPA** (6.5%: ★★).

Drul & Stollenberg

Wylerbaan 14A, 6561 KR Groesbeek
brouwerijdendrul.nl

Two breweries merged to create this new business in 2019, which at first continued to brew 5hl batches using the kit of one of its predecessors, D'n Drul (Dorpsstraat 7, Groesbeek), while constructing a new site with a 20hl brewhouse and bottling line in the middle of the Operation Market Garden landing zone. This should be online by publication date, but as far as we know the Drul taproom will stay open as a bar (see cafés). Which of the founding breweries' beers will survive the transition is as yet unclear. **D'n Drul** *BEERS INCLUDED:* lovely bitter black IPA **Eloy** (6.5%: ★★★); peach-tinted **Hofs Blondje** (7%: ★★); and **Sgoer** (8.5%: ★★+), a deceptively easy-drinking imperial black IPA dry-hopped with Cascade. **Stollenberg** *BEERS INCLUDED:* lazy blond **Heerlijkheid** (5.4%: ★★); decent but simple **Tram IPA** (6.2%: ★★); and ginger-spiced tripel **Het Uitzicht** (7.8%: ★★).

Ducaat

Brouwerij in Speciaalbier Gebroeders Ducaat
Jupiterweg 17, 3893 GC Zeewolde
T 06 2183 3367 · gebroedersducaat.nl

Founded in Flevoland in 2014 by two brothers who produce mainly Belgian-style brews on a 6hl kit. *BEERS INCLUDE:* dry, hazy **Saison** (6%: ★★); Cascade-hopped **Polderblond** (6.2%: ★★); copper-brown bitter **IPA** (7.8%: ★★+); sweetish, almondy **Tripel** (9%: ★★); five-grained malty imperial **Lekker Stout** (10%: ★★+); and dark, sweetish, strongly alcoholic quadrupel **Ducator** (11.8%: ★★).

Duits & Lauret

Noodweg 2, 4121 KK Everdingen
T 06 1425 1923
duitslauret.com

Daniëlle Duits and Marco Lauret began cuckoo brewing in 2009, and following success in

international competitions conceived an ambitious project to restore an 1840s fort in Utrecht province as a permanent home. Brewing began there in 2017, and the site now has a campsite as well as a taproom in which to display all the prizes. Tastings and tours bookable for groups of eight or more. *BEERS INCLUDE:* easy-drinking Kölsch-style **Wiess** (5%: ★★+); fruity **Amber** (5.5%: ★★+); gently bitter **Blond** (6.5%: ★★+); coffee-tinged **Stout** (6.5%: ★★+); amber French-style farmhouse ale **Bière de Garde Brune** (7.5%: ★★+); and near-tripel **Extra Blond** (8.5%: ★★+). *SEASONAL:* rounded meibock **Kiem** (6.5%: ★★+); complex, wood-aged, peat-smoked **Houtgerijpte Rook Dubbelbock** (7.5%: ★★★); warming chocolatey **Winterstout** (8.5%: ★★★), which develops tones reminiscent of Belgian Trappist Rochefort with cellaring; and **TeVreden** (★★★), a year-end special sold for charity.

Duiyk

Hortensiastraat 9, 8013 AA Zwolle
denduiyk.nl

Overijssel outfit brewing small batches in house since 2015, although we believe larger runs are made elsewhere, possibly at Huttenkloas. *BEERS INCLUDE:* blond pilsener **IJsselwaen** (4.9%); Belgian-style **Blondgenoot** (5.8%); floral IPA **Intergalactic Guardians of Love** (6.5%: ★★+); bitter-finishing saison **Seizoensmeester** (7%: ★★); and hoppy coriander-spiced tripel **Spice Cowboy** (7.4%).

Dukes

Dr. H. B. Wiardi Beckmanplein 60,
4207 NC Gorinchem
T 0183 750297
stadsbrouwerijdukes.nu

Brewery and taproom opened by two friends in 2016 in a modern eastern suburb, currently on the lookout for a larger location. *BEERS INCLUDE:* clean-tasting IPA **Orange** (5%: ★★+); Belgian-style **Amber** (5%: ★★);

malty pilsener **Hamel** (5.5%: ★★); citrussy **Weizen** (5.5%: ★★); the rather better **Dunkelweizen** (5.5%: ★★★+); well-balanced **Saison** (6%: ★★+); an unfiltered **Stout** (6%: ★★) which tastes fine despite its muddy appearance; decently dry **Blond** (6.7%: ★★+); too-sweet **Dubbel** (6.7%: ★★); and fruity blond **Tripppel** (8.7%: ★★).

Durs

Klarendalseweg 534, 6822 GZ Arnhem
T 026 202 2200
durs.nl

Gelderland brewery originally known as Kleefse Waard, which produced its first beers under its new name at the end of 2019. The aim is to brew 50hl per week in 10hl batches. *BEERS INCLUDE:* pilsner **Karel** (5%); amber **Geutpisser** (5.9%); blond **Dakhaas** (6.5%); and IPA **Leip Hert** (6.5%).

Eanske

Weverstraat 35, 7545 TJ Enschede
T 06 1267 9028
brouwerijeanske.nl

Oscar Moerman worked for numerous Dutch micros before branching out in his own right in 2013, at first as a cuckoo at Ootmarsummer. Since 2019, he's been brewing three times weekly on his own 10hl kit. *BEERS INCLUDE:* quaffable IPA **Heilige Jacobus** (4.5%: ★★+); easy-drinking American pale ale **1325** (5.8%: ★★+); light, fruity schwarzbier **Donkere Dagen** (6%: ★★+); hoppy '70-minute red ale' **Ei van Columbus** (7%: ★★+); standout bitter porter **De Stadspoorten** (7.2%: ★★★); and strong brown ale **Hoog & Droog** (8.5%: ★★). *SEASONAL:* dry summer saison **Zomertijd** (5.5%: ★★+). *ALSO:* moderately successful past experiments with lambic-style wild fermentation may be repeated in future.

Eembier

Eembier

Havenstraat 5b, 8081 GN Elburg
T 033 461 6391
eembier.nl

A tireless nomad since 2006, Amersfoort-based Ruud van Moorst originally used the slightly different name De Eem. He finally opened his own 20hl brewery and taproom in a picturesque Gelderland town in 2018. Pre-booked tours Mo–Fr 15.00; Sa 12.00, 13.30, 15.00, 16.30. *BEERS INCLUDE:* session IPA **Dorstig** (3.5%: ★★+); dry blond **Jolig** (6.2%: ★★+); gently bitter hoppy pale ale **Tierig** (6.5%: ★★+); currant-tinged dubbel **Potig** (7.5%: ★★+); fruity red IPA **Grillig** (7.5%: ★★+); sweetish dark ale **Stadig** (7%: ★★); amber rye ale **Prachtig** (9%: ★★+); darkly dangerous imperial stout **Krachtig** (9%: ★★+); and standout imperial black IPA **Machtig** (9.5%: ★★★). *SEASONAL:* superior autumnal bock **Bronstig** (6.5%: ★★+). *ALSO:* beers made with the five-woman Tasty Lady team (tastylady.nl), including original spiced blond **Tasty Lady** (6.2%: ★★+) and cocoa-tinged **Darkside Porter** (7%: ★★+).

Een Kwestie Van

Oude Baan 9, 4681 RM Chaam
eenkwestievanbier.nl

A Question Of was founded in 2018 with the original intention of distilling whisky but ended up brewing instead. *BEERS INCLUDE:* IPA **Hip-Hop** (5.2%) and autumnal dark **Boks** (6.5%).

Egmond

Weg over de Bisschop 1b, 1934 CS Egmond aan den Hoef · **T** 06 5537 0787
sanctiadalberti.nl

Egmond is one of the few Dutch breweries with a genuine monastic connection, marketing beers under licence from the Benedictine Egmond Abbey since 2010. Its '90% organic' **Sancti Adalberti Egmondse** range was at first brewed in Belgium, but a 25hl crowdfunded brewery finally opened on an industrial estate in 2017. A taproom and pre-booked tours are available in summer. *BEERS INCLUDE:* sweetish **Weizen** (5%: ★★), which inexplicably replaced a far better witbier; run-of-the-mill **Blond** (5.7%: ★★); cocoa-tinged bitter **Dubbel** (6.5%: ★★); and aromatic amber **Tripel** (7.5%: ★★), flavoured with coriander and lime blossom. *SEASONAL:* dark amber winter **Pastorale** (8.1%: ★★+).

Egmond

Eigenwijs

Coba Ritsemastraat 49, 2642 CE Pijnacker
facebook.com/brouwerijeigenwijs

A South Holland brewery since 2017, Stubborn was founded by former homebrewers. BEERS INCLUDE: American pale ale **Fris en Fruitig** (6.7%); tripel **Eigenwijs Blond** (8%); strong blond **AJLB** (8.3%); and **Eigenwijs Zwart** (9.6%) quadrupel.

Eiland Brouwers Texel

Bosrandweg 202, 1796 NK De Koog
eilandbrouwerstexel.nl

This tiny brewery in the Hotel Tatenhove was the third of five on the island of Texel, making just 120 bottles per batch since 2015. It fell dormant in the summer of 2019 when the hotel business took priority, and we don't know yet if or when it's likely to resume production.

Eindhoven

Vestdijk 280, 5611 CZ Eindhoven
T 040 842 8000
stadsbrouwerijeindhoven.com

Eindhoven got its second working brewery in 2015 following a merger of former nomads Eijkenrode and Brasserie Bours. Both predecessors' ranges have been absorbed, with new brands added as **100 Watt**. A 10hl kit in a former carpet factory produces dozens of generally excellent beers. There's a taproom with tours and tastings on offer, and the adjacent Bottle Distillery (bottledistillery.nl) makes its neighbour's beer into a spirit besides producing London-style dry gin. BEERS INCLUDE: **15 Watt** (5%: ★★), the taproom's house pilsener; hoppy session IPA **Fine Fleur** (4.2%: ★★★); coffee-forward porter **110 Volt** (5.8%: ★★+); **Dancing Queen** (5.9%: ★★★), a sharp, hoppy buckwheat IPA; fresh New England IPA **Orchestra of Angels** (6.3%: ★★★); dry farmhouse ale **Pas de Saison** (6.5%: ★★+); hop-forward American pale ale **Allure** (7%: ★★★); deeply flavoursome black

IPA **Zwarte Bliksem** (7.3%: ★★★); strongly bitter IPA **Euforie** (7.5%: ★★★); cocoa-edged stout **240 Volt** (7.7%: ★★+); Scotch ale **Quilty Pleasures** (8.4%: ★★+); **Non de Jus** (8.8%: ★★+), a fruity triple with camomile and grains of paradise; rich imperial stout **400 Watt** (10%: ★★★), even better in its barrel-aged expressions (★★★+); and full-bodied evening closer barley wine **200W** (12%: ★★★). SEASONAL: US-hopped meibock **Naar De Knoppen!** (5.6%: ★★+); summer blond **Route de Soleil** (6.4%: ★★+); winter spiced pumpkin ale **Cinderella's Ride** (6.4%: ★★+); and wintry heavy hitter, **Nuit Noire** (10%: ★★★), a glass of dark, coffee-tinged luxury. ALSO: a historic range including spiced wheat ale **Witte Dame** (5.1%: ★★); sweetish dubbel **Oude Haas** (7%: ★★); golden tripel **EvoluWonder** (9%: ★★); and tripel **Heeren van Eynthoven** (9%: ★★).

EleganT

Rozemarijntuin 47, 2353 PC Leiderdorp
T 06 2271 5517
elegantbier.nl

This nanobrewer in a Leiden suburb has ploughed its own furrow since 2003, selling bottled beers locally and occasionally elsewhere.
BEERS INCLUDE: lightweight IPA **Hooimeid** (5%: ★★); Belgian-style saison **Geisha** (5%: ★★); English-style porter **Nimf** (5%: ★★); reasonable weizen **Callgirl** (6.5%: ★★); slightly sharp amber **Deerne** (6.5%: ★★), with added cherries; and tripel **Groupie** (8.5%: ★★).
SEASONAL: burnt-edged dubbelbock **Bruintje** (7%: ★★+).

Eleven

Eendrachtlaan 100, unit 15, 3526 LB Utrecht
T 06 8116 1884
brouwerijeleven.com

Begun as a nomad in 2017, Eleven acquired its own 5hl kit in 2018 and now rents out excess capacity to others. Tastings and workshops by appointment.
BEERS INCLUDE: ginger-spiced saison **UTCA** (5.5%: ★★); bittersweet New England IPA **Papa Beer** (5.5%: ★★+); mellow IPA **Matse** (7%: ★★+); and rounded imperial stout **Met Jan naar de Maan** (9%: ★★+).

Emelisse –
see Slot Oostende

Eric's

Eric's Beer Craft (EBC)
Oliemolenhof 90, 3812 PB Amersfoort
T 06 4339 2545
ericsbeercraft.nl

A 2.5hl brewery in Het Lokaal, a market for local food and drink producers, opened in 2016 by experienced homebrewer Eric Bergacker.

BEERS INCLUDE: ginger-spiced Belgian-style blond **Zonnestraal** (5%: ★★); 'Belgian-style' **Stoute Quibus** (6.5%: ★★+); and dry tripel **Hooi en Klomp** (8.5%).

Erve Kots

Brouwhoes Achterhoek
Eimersweg 4, 7137 HG Lievelde
T 0544 371691
ervekots.nl, brouwhoesachterhoek.nl

Lager brewery with a 10hl kit opened in 1998 in the Erve Kots open air museum, since tranformed into an audiovisual self-guided tour, the Bier Experience (see Beer tourism). Beers under the name **Stadsch** are sold at the museum shop and café, accessible without paying an admission charge.
BEERS INCLUDE: decent straw-blond **Pilsner** (4.6%: ★★); lightly bitter **Weizen** (5%: ★★); malty blond **Glorie** (6%: ★★); and sweetish amber **Schemer** (6%: ★★).

Excosa

Rijneveld 153, 2771 XV Boskoop
T 06 5755 9909
excosa.nl

South Holland microbrewery founded in 2017 in a green recreation area, the Proeftuin van Holland (proeftuinvanholland.nl). Tours, tastings and workshops by arrangement.
BEERS INCLUDE: pilsener **Heat** (4.9%); weizen **Eigenweiz** (5.2%); IPA **Fennek** (5.9%); dubbel **Dubter** (7.2%); blond **Viper** (7.5%); and tripel **Brisant** (8%).

Fire Power

Henri Osewoudtstraat 6, 4906 ES Oosterhout
firepowerbrewery.nl

North Brabant micro launched in 2019 with **Ballista Blond** (7%) and **Katapéltis Tripel** (7.3%).

Fontein

Ondergenhousweg 15, 6171 GW Stein
T 046 426 2858
brouwerijdefontein.nl

Semi-rural south Limburg farm brewery founded in 2006. Besides a reliable house range, the 10hl kit produces commissioned beers for local bars and restaurants and accommodates several cuckoo brewers. *BEERS INCLUDE:* marshmallow-tinged **Steinder Wit** (4.9%: ★★); safe **Limburgs Blond** (5.9%: ★★); dunkelweizen **Maaskanter** (6%: ★★); chocolatey **Limburgs Dubbel** (6.4%: ★★); straw-coloured, citrus-fruity **Sakamai** (8.4%: ★★), made from Japanese sake rice; and lightly fruity **Limburgs Tripel** (9%: ★★+). *SEASONAL:* summer **Euleteul Zomer** (5.1%: ★★+) and **Euleteul Winter** (8.5%: ★★+), both with pleasant floral notes from added elderflower.

Fortuna –
see Vlieland

Freonskip

Noordersingel 5, 9251 BL Burgum
T 06 4623 2022
itlulkewiif.frl

Friesland outfit launched in 2015, since 2017 using a kit from the defunct Sneeker Stadsbrouwerij Meerpael. Beers are labelled **It Lulke Wiif** (The Angry Woman), though only one has appeared to date: sweetish, coriander-spiced **Heechblond** (7%: ★★).

Friekens

Meteorenweg 272, 1035 RN Amsterdam
friekens.nl

Based since 2016 in an odd edge-of-town Amsterdam North location where now-defunct Vriendschap once had its Brouw Lab tester facility. An English head brewer produces beers mainly sold in the Proost taproom and Stroop pancake house in the same building.

BEERS INCLUDE: session ale **B.S. The Bright Side** (4.4%); sweetish brown **P.A. Philosopher's Ale** (4.4%), made with English yeast; floral blond **Tuin Garden Ale** (4.8%); malty **N.A.P. Normaal Amsterdams Pils** (5%: ★★); bitter-finishing, US-hopped **A.P.A. Amerikaanse Pale Ale** (5.5%: ★★+); and multi-US-hopped **I.P.A.** (6.6%).

Friese

Snekerstraat 43, 8701 XC Bolsward
T 0515 577449
usheit.com

Part of the microbrewing vanguard, Friesland's first contemporary brewery was founded in 1985 in the hamlet of Uitwellingerga, moving to its current site, a former food and drink technology college, in 1995. It now has its own maltings, whisky distillery, shop and taproom besides a 20hl brewhouse for creating its **Us Heit** (Our Father) beers. Individual tours (*Fr 16.00; Sa 11.00, 14.00, 16.00*) must be booked online; group tours for 20 or more at other times by arrangement.

BEERS INCLUDE: malty **Twels Pilsener** (5%: ★★); improved malty amber **Twels Speciaal** (5%: ★★+); unsubtle brown **Buorren Bier** (6%: ★★); rounded wheat **Dubbel Tarwe Bier** (8%: ★★+); oddly spiced **Houtgelagerd** (8%: ★★), a herbal mouthwash aged 12 months in house whisky barrels with star anise; and **Elfstedenbier** (8%: ★★+), a warming bitter-sweet brown ale for when it's Frisian outside. *ALSO:* alcohol-free **Nuchtere Heit**.

Frontaal

Liniestraat 31; 4816 BG Breda
T 06 1560 5900
brouwerijfrontaal.nl

A star of Dutch craft brewing since 2015, Roel Buckens successfully crowdfunded a small brewery in a shipping container in 2016 before moving to a bigger location with a 30hl kit near Breda station in 2019. His adventurous and often excellent beers are widely available but best enjoyed in the taproom.
BEERS INCLUDE: exceptionally quaffable session ale **Tankard** (3.9%: ★★★); balanced Belgian-style wheat ale **Author** (5%: ★★+); **Juice Punch** (5.8%: ★★★), a fresh New England IPA that gets a tweak with each new batch; **Freehand** (7.2%: ★★+), a saison with orange blossom, honey and pepper; bitter hoppy American IPA **Bulldog** (7.5%: ★★★); cocoa-forward, earthy, imperial coffee oatmeal stout **Billiard** (9.5%: ★★★); and American barley wine **Rhodesian** (11.3%: ★★★), which retains subtlety despite being heavy on the date and prune flavours. *ALSO:* among a bewildering variety of one-off brews, the experimental **Compass** series includes beers named after compass points which riff on (usually) IPA or stout themes, often with great success.

Gansje

Magdalenastraat 9, 4461 AL Goes
T 0113 269416
hetgansje.nl

Little Goose is the creation of a homebrewing husband and wife team with more than 25 years' experience. They went commercial in 2018 but still produce on a tiny scale of no more than 27l per batch, nonetheless achieving consistently good results. Beers are only available in the taproom to drink in or take away.
BEERS INCLUDE: accomplished, fruity English-style **Bitter** (4.4%: ★★★); wheat ale **Tarwe** (4.9%: ★★+); lightly bitter **Blond** (5%: ★★+); fruity-hoppy but not very New England **NEIPA** (5.5%: ★★+); light, nutty English-style **Porter** (6.6%: ★★+); dry **Dubbel** (7%: ★★+); fruity **Amber** (7%: ★★); hazy elderflower-flavoured **Vlier Tripel** (7.6%: ★★+); lightly honeyed **Honing Tripel** (7.6%: ★★+); bean-forward, bitter **Koffie Stout** (7.8%: ★★+); and solid dry **Tripel** (8%: ★★+).

Gaperd

Staarten 4B, 5281 GR Boxtel
T 088 116 1285
gaperd.nl

An extraordinary enterprise which since 2015 has been touring the country with a large, bullet-style aluminium caravan containing a 6hl kit, used for brewing at festivals and other events. Beers for a more international audience occasionally appear under the **Ducktail Brewing** banner.
BEERS INCLUDE: sweetish amber pale ale **De Goedsack** (6%: ★★) and **De Klerelijer** (6.6%: ★★+), a rich, coffee-heavy stout.
AS Ducktail: **Miss Otis** (5.5%: ★★+), an easy 'Cole-inspired' (their words) honey Porter.

Gele Kanarie

Goudsesingel 284, 3011 KH Rotterdam
T 010 333 5444
degelekanarie.com

City centre brewpub launched in 2018 with "support" from Heineken, though we're unsure of the global giant's level of involvement. The cellar brewery currently produces only one beer, unfiltered **Hoppie Blond** (4.5%: ★★+), which hits the middle ground between a Belgian blond and an IPA.

Gerlachus

Burgemeester A. Campostraat 17, 6336 BN Hulsberg
T 045 710 0520
gerlachus.com

South Limburg whisky distillery that added a microbrewery in 2017, rumoured as likely to expand but spirits appear to remain the core business. Tours of both distillery and brewery by arrangement. *BEERS INCLUDE:* dull weizen **Limburgs Veldbier** (5%: ★★); spiced dubbel **Limburgs Genieten** (6.5%: ★★); Dortmunder lager **Beumer Walder** (7%); and needlessly heavy **Limburgse Tripel** (10%: ★★).

Ghoplin

Wildeman 5, 3905 TK Veenendaal
T 06 4126 4458
ghoplin.nl

Founded in 2016 with a 7.6hl kit, this micro names its beers after colours, though not always as a meaningful clue to the flavour. *BEERS INCLUDE:* fruity **Red** (5%) with raspberries and strawberries; weizen **White** (5.8%); IPA **Silver** (6.5%); blond **Gold** (6.5%); tripel **Orange** (6.7%); double IPA **Blue** (8.2%); and imperial stout **Black** (11%). **Green** is reserved for one-off experiments.

Gieterij

Klokkengietersstraat 1, 5735 EH Aarle-Rixtel
T 06 1418 4248
brouwerijdegieterij.nl

The Foundry near Eindhoven, opened in 2016, is so-named for its location in a former bell foundry which it shares with Laarbeek (below), though it has its own 2.5hl kit. *BEERS INCLUDE:* English-hopped amber **Alese Ale** (6%: ★★); an occasional **Black IPA** (7%: ★★+) that appears at festivals; dark **Dubbel** (7%: ★★); moreish **Koffiestout** (7%: ★★+), laced with Ethiopian beans; a **Tripel** (8%: ★★) with rye malt for spiciness; and bold, rich **Imperial Stout** (9%: ★★+).

Goede & De Stoute

Emmalaan 2, 1862 ET Bergen
T 06 8187 5743
degoedeendestoute.nl

North Holland brewers since 2017, The Good & The Bold's focus is sparkling beers using Champagne yeast. First effort **Vuurzee** (8.5%) was made with pinot noir grapes, but other varieties may follow.

Gooi en Eemland

Schapendrift 35, 1261 HM Blaricum
degooischemoordenaar.nl

Utrecht province brewer established in 2019 and at the time of writing about to inherit a 5hl installation from D'n Drul (above). Beers will appear under the **Gooische Moordenaar** (Gooi Murderer) label, the nickname of a historic steam tram still operating on the nearby Medemblik to Hoorn heritage line (**stoomtram.nl**), acquired after it was involved in a deadly accident in 1927.

Gooimeer

Binnendelta 4L, 1261 WZ Blaricum
T 035 204 2005
gooimeerbrouwerij.nl

Formerly the homeless Gooische Biergilde, founded in 2012, this company rebranded in 2017 following a move to a purpose-built brewery on a North Holland industrial estate. It's named after the nearby lake that separates the brewery from Almere, just to the north. *BEERS INCLUDE:* sweetish witbier **Anna's Witte** (4.8%: ★★); bitter-finishing Irish red **Avondrood** (5.2%: ★★); **Indian Black Ale** (5.5%: ★★+), which is actually copper-brown; average **Hilferts Blond** (6.2%: ★★); and decent dubbel **Gooische Bertus** (7.5%: ★★+). *SEASONAL:* spiced brown **Winter Koning** (9.2%: ★★+).

Gooisch

Marktplein 3, 1211 DZ Hilversum
T 035 631 6747
gooischebierbrouwerij.nl

Not to be be confused with either of the above, Gooisch began in 2011 by using other people's facilities, but now brews several times weekly on its own 20hl installation in the central Mout food hall (see cafés). Its beers are organic wherever possible and often feature buckwheat. Tours and tastings are bookable through the website and can also be arranged at other times for groups of at least 10. *BEERS INCLUDE:* unfiltered old-school pilsener **Goud** (5%: ★★+), designed to be

drunk fresh; sweet and sour **Wit** (5.5%: ★★); light-golden bitter **IPA** (5.9%: ★★+); bittersweet **Blond** (6%: ★★); standout dry schwarzbier **Zwart** (6%: ★★+); amber 'red ale' **Rood** (6%: ★★); and dryish **Bubbel** (9%: ★★+), made with champagne yeast. *ALSO:* rye-based **Larens Saison** (6.8%: ★★) and **Larens Tripel** (9%), made with and for a local agricultural foundation.

Goudsche Leeuw

Volmolenhof 7, 2807 ES Gouda
T 0182 338211
stadsbrouwerijdegoudscheleeuw.nl

Conceived in 1999 but unrealised until 2012, the Gouda Lion has boasted its own 2hl kit since 2018, although we believe larger runs are still brewed elsewhere. Its products are seen mostly in the Gouda area. *BEERS INCLUDE:* sweetish witbier **Goudsch Wit** (5%: ★★); fruity **Goudsch Kuyt** (6%), allegedly brewed to an ancient recipe; blond **Erasmus Bier** (7.5%: ★★); and sweetish **Goudsch Tripel** (8%: ★★).

Grolsch (Asahi)

Brouwerslaan 1, 7548 XA Enschede
T 053 483 3333
grolsch.nl

The Netherlands' third-largest brewer traces its orgins to De Klok (The Clock) brewery in Groenlo, founded in 1615: its name means 'from Grol', from an obsolete version of the city name. In 1922, De Klok merged with a brewery in Enschede which subsequently became the main production site. That brewery was severely damaged by fire following a disastrous explosion in a nearby fireworks warehouse in 2000, prompting the company's move to its current edge-of-town site. Grolsch was independent until 2008 when it was sold to SABMiller, before being handed to Japanese giant Asahi in a game of corporate pass-the-parcel to placate the competition watchdogs when AB InBev gobbled up the rest of its rival multinational in 2016.

BEERS INCLUDE: drinkable but thin **Session IPA** (3.5%: ★★); stuff-strutting **Premium Pilsner** (5%: ★★); simpler pilsener **Kornuit** (5%: ★+); standard **Weizen** (5.3%: ★★); banana-edged **Weizen-IPA** (6%: ★★), more the former than the latter; a reasonable blond **Saison** (6.5%: ★★); sweetish less-than **Klassieke Blond** (6.7%: ★★); standout **Kruidige Tripel** (8.3%: ★★+), spiced with lemongrass and cardamom; and **Kanon** (11.6%: ★+), a shortcut to oblivion and little else.
SEASONAL: malty **Lentebok** (6.5%: ★★); clean-tasting blond **Zomerbok** (6.4%: ★★+); caramel-tinged **Herfstbok** (6.5%: ★★); and spiced **Winterbok** (7.5%: ★★+), which is unsubtle, but so is Christmas.
ALSO: Grolsch brews the **Brouwers** range for Albert Heijn supermarkets and makes at least half a dozen alcohol-free beers and radlers, of which only the **0.0%** (★★) pilsener and **Weizen 0.0%** (★★) pass muster.

Gulpener

Rijksweg 16, 6271 AE Gulpen
T 043 450 7575
gulpener.nl

This South Limburg family brewer is one of the country's oldest, founded in 1825, and remains defiantly independent, despite Grolsch, and consequently Asahi, taking a chunk. Gulpener claims to be Europe's only sizable brewer fermenting in all three ways, making lagers, ales and mixed fermenation beers, the last represented by star turn Mestreechs Aajt. Its core beers are doggedly mainstream but it has dipped a toe into the craft scene with a series of collaborations. Test brews and one-off experiments happen in a 2.5hl microbrewery located in the BrouwLokaal taproom. Pre-booked tours and brewing courses.
BEERS INCLUDE: malty, sugary **Oud Bruin** (3%: ★+); lovely, quaffable sweet-sour wood-aged **Mestreechs Aajt** (3.5%: ★★★), now on tap in Gulpen and Maastricht; average **Pilsener** (5%: ★★); crisper, better-balanced pilsener **Chateau Neubourg** (5%: ★★+); organic, unpasteurised **Ur-Pilsener** (5%: ★★+); competent **Ur-Weizen**

(5.3%: ★★); malty India Pale Lager **Ur-Hop** (6%: ★★+); shallow **Gerardus Blond** (6%: ★★); its better, drier-edged sister **Gerardus Dubbel** (7%: ★★); and beefier eldest sibling **Gerardus Tripel** (8.5: ★★).
SEASONAL: sweetish spring **Lentebock** (6.5%: ★★); classy summer witbier **Korenwolf** (5%: ★★+); thinnish sweet **Herfstbock** (6.5%: ★+); and sweetish dark **WinterVrund** (8.5%: ★★).
ALSO: **Aan Lager Wal** (3.5%: ★★+) session lager made with De Prael; **Op Stoom** (6%: ★★+) California steam beer with VandeStreek; and Uiltje collab, double IPA **Spicy Roger** (8%: ★★+) subtly dosed with chilli.

Gulzige Gans

Van Heutszsingel 90, 7741 EW Coevorden
T 0524 518772
degulzigegans.nl

A husband and wife team making 1.8hl batches at their home-based Greedy Goose brewery in Drenthe, established in 2008. Quality is surprisingly high for such a tiny operation and their beers are found in numerous local shops and bars. Visits by appointment.
BEERS INCLUDE: dry witbier **Fladder** (5.5%: ★★+); gentle blond **Snaterwater** (6.5%: ★★); fruity, bitter wheat ale **Spring in 't Veld** (7%: ★★+), with linden blossom; restrained bitter IPA **Vreemde Eend in de Bite** (7%: ★★+); amber **Kasteelheer** (8.5%: ★★+), which balances a fruity edge with a bitter finish; beefy tripel **Waggel** (9%: ★★); warming barley wine **Kachel** (10%: ★★+); and **Rook in de Kachel** (10%: ★★★), which adds smoke to the former.

Haagsche Broeder

Oude Molstraat 35, 2513 BA Den Haag
haagschebroeder.nl

Monastic microbrewery started in 2013 at the city centre abbey of the Brothers of St John, making 1hl batches for sale in 75cl bottles at the monastery shop (*We-Sa 13.00-16.30*).
BEERS INCLUDE: entry-level amber **Postulant** (4.5%: ★★); blond **Novice** (7%: ★★); standout **Prior** (8.5%: ★★★), a Baltic porter or strong

dubbel depending on who you believe, also found in barrel-aged versions (★★★); and **Johannes** (9%), a quadrupel brewed annually on December 27, the feast of St John the Evangelist.

Halve Tamme

Koperslagerij 11, 4762 AR Zevenbergen
halve-tamme.nl

Half Tame are nano-scale North Brabant brewers making traditional Belgian styles alongside contemporary craft ales since 2015.
BEERS INCLUDE: India pale lager **Blonde Donny** (5%); dubbel **Doppelgänger** (7%); multi-grained **Tripelzone** (7.6%); many-hopped double IPA **Hopgesodemieterd** (8%); caffeine-rich black IPA **Zwarte Koffie** (8.1%), with espresso beans; and barley wine **Gerstederrie** (11.2%).
ALSO: the **Project Series**, the experimental range where the brewer lets his hair down.

Hart4bier

Newtonstraat 16, 4702 RT Roosendaal
hart4bier.weebly.com

Nanobrewery producing 50l batches in a garage for the local market since 2014, although flagship Jumelange is brewed in larger runs at nearby Pimpelmeesch.
BEERS INCLUDE: porter **Dark Angel** (6.1%); American pale ale **Jumelange** (6.2%); and stout **Dark Dream** (7.5%).

Heer en Meester

Barnseweg 92, 3771 RP Barneveld
T 06 3058 7238
brouwerijheerenmeester.nl

Lord and Master began in June 2016 as a Gelderland village brewery with a 2hl kit. Brewing stopped in late 2018 pending a change of ownership and a move to South Limburg which was due to be completed by publication time.

Heeren van Beerta

Schipvaart 32, 9883 PP Oldehove
T 06 3972 6737
deheerenvanbeerta.nl

Microbrewery established in Groningen province in 2018, selling mainly via its own webshop.
BEERS INCLUDE: American IPA **Ho(o)pvol** (6%) and coriander-spiced tripel **Gronings Goud** (8%).

Heerlijkheid

Kerkbuurt 56, 3354 XK Papendrecht
brouwerijdeheerlijkheid.nl

The Glory microbrewery and farm shop opened in 2011, across the river from Dordrecht in a 16th-century building that once housed the lords of Papendrecht. It brews 3hl batches, more or less weekly, for sale in bottles at the shop, at one off licence in town and rarely elsewhere.
BEERS INCLUDE: fruity amber **Steegtbier** (4.2%: ★★); hop-forward blond **Dijkbier** (4.8%: ★★+); and multigrained blond **Boezembier** (4.9%: ★★+), sweetened with apple and pear juice.

Heineken

Burgemeester Smeetsweg 1, 2382 PH Zoeterwoude
Rietveldweg 37, 5222 AP 's-Hertogenbosch
T 071 545 6111 (Zoeterwoude), 073 620 9911 (Den Bosch)
heineken.com

The world's second-largest brewing company began in 1864 when Gerard Adriaan Heineken bought a brewery in Amsterdam, converting it five years later into one of the early adopters of lager brewing in the Netherlands. It was the marketing genius of Gerard's grandson Alfred 'Freddy' Heineken (1923–2002) that transformed a relatively small family business into the producer of one of the world's most recognisable brands. Like arch-rival AB InBev,

it focuses on high-profile industrial pilseners, though they're no longer produced at the historic Amsterdam site, which hasn't brewed since 1988. The main Zoeterwoude facility is Europe's biggest brewery, a colossal beer factory covering 30 hectares and producing 10 million hl of pilsener per year, 60% of which is exported. A further 6 million hl per year of the same staple is produced alongside other lines like 'Mexican' brands Sol and Desperados at a second plant in 's-Hertogenbosch. Between them, these two sites account for half the beer output of the nation. No tours.
REGULAR: watery mess **Lingen's Blond** (2%: ★+); unbalanced sweet **Heineken Oud Bruin** (2.5%: ★+); thin, bland **Amstel Blond** (4%: ★); sickly pink mouthwash **Wiekse Rosé** (4%: ★); inexplicably popular simpleton **Amstel** (5%: ★+); unerringly competent but dull **Heineken** (5%: ★★); maltier **Amstel 1870** (5%: ★★); half-decent witbier **Wiekse Witte** (5%: ★★); and disturbingly sweet **Amstel Gold** (7%: ★+).
ALSO: a variety of seasonals, alcohol-free lagers and shandy-like radlers.

Helderse Jongens

Westoever 1, 1785 PB Den Helder
T 06 2183 6172
heldersejongens.nl

Beginning on a tiny scale in 2013, the Boys from Den Helder expanded in 2017 to a brewpub in a Napoleonic fort. Tours Sa&Su 13.00, 15.00.
BEERS INCLUDE: inoffensive weizen **Dorus** (5%: ★★); raspberry rye red ale **Lange Jaap** (5%); lightly bitter **Lekker Stout** (8%: ★★+);

blond **Kouwe Snuffel** (5.5%), made with local rainwater; and spiced **Helderse Tripel** (7.9%: ★★).
SEASONAL: deeply dark dubbelbock **Napoleon** (7%: ★★+).
ALSO: a numbered **Labrat** series of experimental brews.

Hemel

Franseplaats 1, 6511 VS Nijmegen
T 024 360 6167
brouwerijdehemel.nl

Heaven, opened in 1983, is now the country's oldest brewpub, and has expanded to supply numerous outlets in Nijmegen and beyond. Its brewhouse and a museum are below the café in the cellars of the Commanderie van Sint Jan, a 12th century cloister where spirits, vinegar and mustard are also produced. Public tours Sa&Su 13.00–17.00 with no booking required, or at other times for pre-arranged groups. A 1.2hl kit in the same building is used for workshops and demonstrations under the name **Vaghevuur** (Purgatory, vaghevuur.nl).
BEERS INCLUDE: grassy blond **Luna** (5%: ★★); rounded witbier **Serafijn** (5%: ★★); malty amber **Godelief** (5%: ★★); fruity blond **Mariken** (6.5%: ★★); lightly smoked amber **Moenen** (6.5%: ★★+); nettly hoppy IPA **Hopverdomme** (7%: ★★+); bitter tripel **Helse Engel** (8%: ★★+); and dangerously drinkable **Nieuw Ligt** (10%: ★★★), a barley wine that becomes sublime in its cellared version, **Grand Cru** (12%: ★★★+).
SEASONAL: smoky autumnal **Eikenbock** (6.5%: ★★+), matured in oak.
ALSO: tripel **Rooie Tiep Top** (8%: ★★+) for the Blaauwe Hand in Nijmegen.

Hemursbier

Willem de Zwijgerlaan 2, 3958 GT Amerongen
hemursbier.nl

Three Utrecht brewers producing beer under the name **Hemurs** in tiny amounts since 2015, sold locally and at festivals.

BEERS INCLUDE: **Borre** (6.5%: ★★) dubbel; summery blond **Greetje** (6.9%); fruity tripel **Amerongen Bree** (7.2%: ★★); and ginger-spiced amber **Gruppel** (8.1%).

Herder

Rijksweg 57B, 5941 AA Velden
T 06 4768 0109
herderbier.nl

Limburg nanobrewer near Venlo making beer in 75l batches since 2018, most of which is sold through the website. Tours on request.
BEERS INCLUDE: Citra-hopped session blond **Albino Schaap** (4.5%) and **Kwietwaeg** (8.6%) barley wine.

Heren 3

Zambezilaan 268, 1448 RB Purmerend
deheren3.nl

North Holland friends who turned pro in 2013, at first content to brew 20l and 40l batches of **Mooi Blond** (6%) for local bottle shops, though now planning to upscale using someone else's kit, at which point they may lose their 'brewery' status.

Hert

Hert Bier Brouwerij
Keizerswoert 26, 3881 LE Putten
T 0341 353335

Founded in 2015 as a nomadic brewer named Puttense, Stag acquired its own kit in 2017. There's no relationship with cuckoo brewer Het Hert from Nijmegen (below). Pre-book tours online (*We&Sa 15.00*).
BEERS INCLUDE: pilsener-ish **Mooi Leven** (5%); **Nieuw Leven** (5.3%: ★★) weizen; sweetish honeyed blond **Dorps Leven** (6.5%: ★★); Belgian-style **Dubbel Leven** (6.5%); thinnish dry amber **Lang Zal Ze Leven** (7.2%: ★★); and spiced tripel **Zwaar Leven** (7.7%: ★★).

Hertog Jan (AB InBev)

Kruisweg 44, 5944 EN Arcen
hertogjan.nl

The chequered history of this north Limburg ale brewery begins during the First World War in 1915 when it was founded as the Stoombierbrouwerij de Vriendenkring (Circle of Friends Steam Brewery), its name reflecting the fact that it was equipped with a steam engine. The crippling costs of reconstruction following extensive damage in the next war resulted in half a century of corporate pass-the-parcel. It was known as the Arcense Stoombrouwerij by the 1980s when it began brewing a range of beers for a distributor under the name Hertog Jan, a reference to the 13th century Duke John I of Brabant, the legendary 'King of Beer', also known as Gambrinus. These Belgian-style abbey ales were among the first modern Dutch brews to challenge the hegemony of pils and played an important role in the early days of the Dutch beer revival. The business was acquired by Interbrew (now AB InBev) in 1995 on condition it remain an ale brewery, and renamed after its best-known brands three years later. We assume its Pilsener is either top-fermented or made elsewhere. Despite corporate ownership, it's now a pleasing anachronism with a lovely taproom.
BEERS INCLUDE: lightweight metallic blond **Enkel** (4.5%: ★+); uninspiring **Pilsener** (5%: ★★); reasonable **Weizener** (5.7%: ★★); half-decent **Dubbel** (7.3%: ★★); amber not much **Karakter** (7.5%: ★★); bittersweet **Tripel** (8.5%: ★★); and unbalanced barley wine **Grand Prestige** (10%: ★+), which tastes like it has fallen downstairs, but rebounds to ★★+ or better in its various **Vatgerijpt** barrel-aged versions.
SEASONAL: **Lente Bock** (7.2%: ★★) and **Bockbier** (6.5%: ★★) tick the boxes without shining.
ALSO: **Bastaard** (2.7%: ★+) has an eye-catching name for a sugary radler.

Hettinga

Zwolse Stadsbrouwerij Hettinga Bier
Esdoornstraat 3, 8021 WB Zwolle
T 038 466 2902
hettingabier.nl

Founded in 2008, the brewery moved in 2013 to a new 5hl installation in a business complex north of the city centre, making reliable beers that are mainly sold locally. Group visits, brewing workshops and tastings by appointment. *BEERS INCLUDE:* top-fermented **Zwolse Pils** (5%: ★★); spiced wheat **Ijssel Wit** (5.5%: ★★); competent amber **Agnietenbier** (5.5%: ★★); moreish dark **Sassenporter Robuust** (6.8%: ★★+); non-sweet **Hanze Dubbel** (7%: ★★); and sweetish **Hanze Tripel** (9%: ★★). *SEASONAL:* bitter, autumnal **Zwolse Bok** (6.5%: ★★+).

Heusden

Burchtplein 6, 5256 EA Heusden
T 0416 660039
kareltje.info

Established in 2002 as a brewpub occupying an attractive building in a picturesque North Brabant town, brewing in 1.75hl batches that are becoming harder to find, and also making liqueurs. Its **Kareltje** beers, only sold in house, are named after the owner's dogs. *BEERS INCLUDE:* quaffable **Blond** (5%: ★★); clean-tasting **Wit** (5%: ★★); and honeyed brown **Kanjer** (6%: ★★).

Hoek

Houtweg 5, 7451 DV Holten
T 06 3390 3327
hoekbier.nl

Overijssel picobrewer in operation since 2018. *BEERS INCLUDE:* copper-brown **Dunkelweizen** (5%) and **Hoolter Blond** (5.5%).

Hoevebrugsch

Walenburgerweg 62B, 3033 AE Rotterdam
hoevebrugsch.nl

Nanobrewery making occasional batches above the Walenburg pub in Rotterdam since 2017. *BEERS INCLUDE:* Belgian-style spiced wheat ale **Wit** (5.4%); **6-ON** (6.2%: ★+), a sharpish amber saison that misses the mark; and sweetish **Blond!** (6.8%: ★★).

Holevoort

Hollevoort 1, 5761 PC Bakel
T 06 3040 0073

North Brabant outfit billing itself as a local brewer using local ingredients, opened in 2017. *BEERS INCLUDE:* lightly sour rose-infused **Rosa** (5.4%: ★★); bittersweet **Blond** (6%: ★★); and too-malty **Tripel** (8.2%: ★+), also cellared in whisky barrels as **Barrel Aged** (10.8%).

Homeland

Kattenburgerstraat 5 – building 6,
1018 JA Amsterdam
T 020 723 2555
homelandbrew.nl

Brewery with an impressive 10hl installation, opened in 2016 in the Homeland Pension hotel, a former naval building beside the National Maritime Museum. It began by brewing draught beers for the house bar but its products are now widely available in cans. *BEERS INCLUDE:* floral summery session IPA **Luwte** (3.5%: ★★+); straw-blond dry **Speltbier** (4.3%: ★★); Citra-hopped **Pieremegoggel** (5.9%: ★★+) saison; bitter if unchallenging IPA **Katzwijm** (6.5%: ★★); nettly, bitter New England IPA **Zeebonk** (7.1%: ★★+); lightly bitter tripel **Kielzog** (7.3%: ★★); and chewy bitter imperial stout **Zwartbaart** (10.5%: ★★★).

Hoop

Lagedijk 71, 1544 BC Zaandijk
brouwerijhoop.nl, hoopbier.nl

Ambitious 20hl brewery with taproom and restaurant north of Amsterdam, making beers of overall high quality since 2016. Former head brewer Patrick Breugem also uses it to make his own beers under the Breugem name (see Brewers without breweries), while experimental beers and specials emerge from a second smaller brewery in the Lab-44 restaurant (see cafés).

BEERS INCLUDE: fruity session weizen **Anker** (3.4%: ★★+); dry-hopped pilsener **1862** (4.5%: ★★+); blond pale ale **Bleke Nelis** (4.9%: ★★); dry, beautifully rounded **Water Wolf** (5.5%: ★★★), one of the best Dutch saisons; subtly honeyed blond **Queen Bee(r)** (5.5%: ★★+); balanced, light East Coast IPA **Kaper** (6.4%: ★★+); and fruit-and-nutty **Oudt Heyn en Syn Wyf** (9%: ★★★), a rare example of Dutch old ale.

SEASONAL: self-explanatory **Spring Spring Bock** (6.6%: ★★+), so good they named it twice; dangerously quaffable **Summer Session IPA** (5%: ★★+); **Awesome Autumn Rum Bock** (6.9%: ★★+), with a clue in the name about its secret ingredient; and **Winter Warming Chocolate Porter** (6%: ★★+) with cocoa nibs.

ALSO: a numbered **Limited Edition** series and an endless string of collaboration brews.

Hoorns Nat

Van Goghhof 83, 1628 XE Hoorn
T 06 1435 5574
hoornsnat.nl

North Holland microbrewery launched in 2018 with an accomplished hoppy black IPA **HN.03** (7.1%: ★★+)

Hopper

Brouwerij D'n Hopper
Vaartstraat 55, 5171 JH Kaatsheuvel
T 043 450 3967
denhopper.com

North Brabant-based brother and sister team with a 2hl installation, brewing commercially since 1996. Once a regular at festivals, they may have fallen dormant or even stopped, hence no beers listed below.

Hopperveld

Steenbergseweg 31, 4671 BC Dinteloord.
facebook.com/hopperveld

A North Brabant outfit new in 2019, likely using its own kit only for small runs and recipe development and brewing on a commercial scale elsewhere. First beer was **'n Bietje Hoppig** (8.2%), a US-hopped IPA containing sugar beet, for better or for worse. It was followed by Belgian-style tripel **Kom uit de Cask** (9.5%).

Huttenkloas/Sallands

Ootmarsumseweg 95, 7665 RW Albergen
T 074 259 0805 (Huttenkloas), 074 259 1311 (Sallands)
huttenkloas.nl, sallandslandbier.nl

These two Overijssel companies ostensibly operate separately but with a common management and brewery, so we combine them here. Huttenkloas began as a nomad brewer in 2002, working at Sallands when that was established in the town of Raalte in 2009. The waters became muddied when both moved to larger premises in a former meat-processing plant in 2017. New kit installed in 2018 doubled capacity and excess is now rented out to a legion of homeless brewers. Walk-up tours We&Sa 14.30, also Th in school holidays, with a taproom open 14.00–17.00 on tour days.

Huttenkloas BEERS INCLUDE: malty, sweet **Pilsener** (5%: ★+); solid **Weizen** (5.2%: ★★); delicately perfumed **American Pale Ale** (5.9%: ★★+); dry-hopped **IPA** (6.5%: ★★); dependable **Blond** (7.5%: ★★); down-the-middle **Dubbel** (7.5: ★★); refreshingly light **Tripel** (8%: ★★+); and coffee-tinged **Russian Imperial Stout** (9.5%: ★★+).

Sallands BEERS INCLUDE: competent **Witte Franciscus** (5%: ★★) weizen; vastly improved crisp, dry **Blonde Johannes** (6%: ★★+); malty dunkelweizen **Donkere Henricus** (6%: ★★); citrussy **India Pale Ale** (6.5%: ★★+); fruity-edged **Lebuïnus Dubbel** (7%: ★★); fruitier **Lebuïnus Tripel** (8.5%: ★★); and a **Russian Imperial Stout** (9.5%: ★★+) that may use the same recipe as the Huttenkloas version.

Huygenmeester

Eikenlaan 11, 1702 TA Heerhugowaard
T 06 2035 6341
huygenmeester.nl

A long-standing North Holland homebrewing group, brewing commercially more or less monthly since 2017. Past beers have included everything from elderflower-infused blonds through saisons to stouts, but appear to change with each batch, rendering ratings pointless.

IJ (Duvel Moortgat)

Funenkade 7, 1018 AL Amsterdam
T 020 622 8325
brouwerijhetij.nl

Brouwerij 't IJ is a pioneer of the Dutch beer revival, founded in 1985 in an old bath house with a popular taproom out front. It takes its name from the nearby body of water, best approximated by English speakers as 'uht ay', to rhyme with 'bay', and certainly not 'tidge' as we've heard from time to time. In 2013, a second 40hl brewery opened nearby at Zeeburgerpad 55, tripling capacity. Belgian-based minor multinational Duvel Moortgat bought an undisclosed but 'significant' portion of the business in 2015, making further expansion likely, although we are assured this will not affect artistic independence. Some but not all beers are organic, and quality and consistency have improved significantly in recent years following decades of unpredictability. Tours Fr–Su 15.30, 16.00.

BEERS INCLUDE: bitter, dry **Session IPA** (4%: ★★+); dry, lightweight blond **Flink** (4.7%: ★★+); anaemic but OK 'tropical Lager' **Biri** (4.7%: ★★); date and raisin-tinted dubbel **Natte** (6.5%: ★★); lightly spiced witbier **IJwit** (7%: ★★); copper-brown **IPA** (7%: ★★+); dry blond tripel **Zatte** (8%: ★★+); chocolate-edged barley wine **Struis** (9%: ★★+); and rich, dark amber **Columbus** (9%: ★★+).

SEASONAL: standard blond meibock **PaasIJ** (7%: ★★); autumnal **IJbok** (6.5%: ★★); and unsubtle winter barley wine **IJndejaars** (9%: ★★+).

OTHERS: all manner of often-excellent one-offs.

Jeronimo

Tweede Oude Heselaan 476, 6542 VK Nijmegen
T 06 3013 5094
brouwerij-jeronimo.nl

Launched in Gelderland in 2017 with a 2hl kit, upgrading to 10hl in 2019 and planning to rent excess capacity to others.
BEERS INCLUDE: restrained hoppy saison **Yellow Angel** (5.5%: ★★); subtly citrussy **Blue Pistol** (6%: ★★), which calls itself an American wheat ale but curiously contains no wheat according to the label; and lightly bitter but unassertive IPA **Red Devil** (6.2%: ★★+).

Jonge Beer

Fabrieksweg 14, 7902 NM Hoogeveen
T 06 2908 8711
jongebeer.nl

Drenthe-based Young Bear has brewed with a 1.5hl installation in a former wooden toy factory since 2014. Group visits by arrangement.
BEERS INCLUDE: golden quaffer **Sesjun HobBlont** (3.5%: ★★); hefeweizen **Weyte** (5.3%: ★★); bitter amber **Humber** (5.5%: ★★), aiming at but not quite hitting a German-style altbier; citrussy dry-hopped **HobBlonder** (6.2%: ★★+); standout dark smoky rauchbier **Wadder** (6%: ★★+); and **Jopper** (9%: ★★+) barley wine.

Jongens van de Wit

Hofvijver 4, 5223 MC 's-Hertogenbosch
T 073 302 0014
jongensvandewit.com

Brewpub with a 10hl installation opened south of the station in 2016. Group tours can be arranged, but are limited by how busy the bar is.
BEERS INCLUDE: bottom-fermented dark **Donkerfris Dunkel Lager** (3.5%: ★★); undemanding but good **Bossche Schermering** (3.8%: ★★+) porter; fruity **PIPA** (Paleiskwartier IPA) (4.7%: ★★) easy-drinking **Maagdelijk Blond** (5.1%: ★★); amber wheat ale **Gerrit de**

Struikrover (6.5%: ★★+); standard **Tripel H4** (7.2%: ★★), named with an abbreviation of the street address; bitter imperial stout **Bossche Duisternis** (10%: ★★+); and sweetish barley wine **Boze Griet** (10.5%: ★★+).

Jopen

Emrikweg 19, 2031 BT Haarlem
T 023 210 0133
jopen.nl

Jopen has long been a familiar name in Dutch brewing, launching as a contractor in 1994. In 2010, it finally returned brewing to Haarlem with the opening of the Jopenkerk (see cafés), a lavish brewpub complete with a 20hl brewhouse in a decommissioned church. In 2014, it brought all production back to the city and boosted its output further by adding a second facility with a bottling line and taproom on an industrial estate at the address above. Its widely sold beers are getting bolder and receiving broader recognition internationally. A distribution deal with Heineken has also made the name a common sight in bars at home and abroad. Tours for individuals (*Sa 13.30 & 16.00; Su at 14.00*) can be booked online.
BEERS INCLUDE: refreshing blond **Gerstebier** (4.5%: ★★); citrussy witbier **Adriaan Wit** (5%: ★★+); intense rye IPA **Jacobus RPA** (5.3%: ★★★); fruity, bitter dunkelweizen **Malle Babbe** (5.5%: ★★+); easy-drinking **Extra Stout**

(5.5%: ★★+); world-class floral-hoppy IPA **Mooie Nel** (6.5%: ★★★★), which garners accolades wherever it goes and is exported under the name **North Sea IPA**; dry, hoppy blond **Hoppen** (6.8%: ★★+); strong brown original **Koyt** (8%: ★★+), launched in 1998 as the first modern revival of the style; characterful **Trinitas Tripel** (9%: ★★★); and hoppy barley wine **Ongelovige Thomas** (10%: ★★★). *SEASONAL:* hoppy spring **Lentebier** (7%: ★★★); multigrained autumnal **4-granen Bokbier** (6.5%: ★★+); above-average bock **Johannieter** (6.5%: ★★+); and annual winter barley wine **Meesterstuk** (10%: ★★+).

ALSO: summery session IPA **Life's a Beach** (3.3%: ★★+), not part of the core range but almost always available; **Mashing Pumpkins** (9%: ★★★), a spiced pumpkin ale brewed with SNAB (see Brewers without breweries); **Grateful Deaf** (usually ★★★), an annual IPA collaboration with deaf American brewer Ken Fisher; and **Jopen Limited**, a series of one-off brews (often ★★★ or better).

AND: **Non IPA** (0.3%: ★★+), one of the better additions to the low alcohol ranks.

Jouster

Groenendalstraat 5, 8502 ET Joure
T 06 5350 3390
jousterbrouwerij.nl

Founded in a Friesland village in 2018, brewing under the **Van Baerdt** label for sale online and in local outlets.
BEERS INCLUDE: **Weizen** (5.4%); **Amber** (5.6%); **Blond** (6.4%); **IPA** (6.5%); and **Tripel** (8.2%).

Jovius

De Liesbosch 14F, 3439 LC Nieuwegein
T 030 410 0424
brouwerij-jovius.nl

Named after the brewer's cat Julius when launched in 2016, the brewery was absurdly forced to rebrand in 2018 after complaints from AB InBev, maker of Hoegaarden Julius. Its beers are mainly in traditional European styles, made on a 2hl installation which is rented out to others when not in use. Visits, workshops and tours by arrangement.
BEERS INCLUDE: sweet, malty **Blond** (7%: ★★); banana-edged **Imperial Dunkelweizen** (7.2%: ★★+); fruity amber **Vienna** (8.5%: ★★); sweetish **Tripel** (9%: ★★); and too-sweet brown alcohol bomb **Quadrupel** (10.5%: ★+).

Juliana

Julianastraat 2, 2361 TA Warmond
julianabrouwerij.nl

South Holland brewery founded in 2017 by four homebrewing friends, making their own 50l batches of some beers, like the **Quadrupel** (10.3%), but relying on Noord-Hollandse for longer runs of recipes that include an **IPA**, **Weizen** and **Blonde**.

Kaapse

Veerlaan 19D, 3072 AN Rotterdam
T 06 1841 7773
kaapsebrouwers.nl

Brewpub and shop in a dockside warehouse opened in 2014 with the help of De Molen (below), using the kit that first saw service in the latter's windmill. Beers have a frustrating tendency to vary in quality but at their best can touch on world class. Group tastings by arrangement.
BEERS INCLUDE: pilsener **Nelis** (4.6%: ★★); hoppy American pale ale **Maria** (4.7%: ★★★); lychee-laced session IPA **Karel** (4.9%: ★★+); outstanding black rye IPA **Bea** (6%: ★★★+); lightly bitter saison **Harrie** (6.1%: ★★+); fruity

red IPA **Carrie** (6.5%: ★★★); zingy West Coast IPA **Zweipac** (6.5%: ★★+); 'New England' saison **Jane** (7.5%: ★★+); too-sweet oatmeal stout **Gozer** (9.8%: ★★); and prune-tinged copper-amber barley wine **Leen** (10.7%: ★★★), brewed annually.
SEASONAL: autumn bock **Matador** (6.5%: ★★+) and Christmas-spiced ale **Klaas** (9.8%: ★★+).
ALSO: **Karloff** is a series of experimental one-offs.

Kaarschot

Slikstraatje 5, 4891 RH Rijsbergen
T 06 3041 2383
facebook.com/kaarschot

The products of this North Brabant nano-brewery, active since 2013, are rarely seen outside its immediate area though sometimes reach Breda.
BEERS INCLUDE: witbier **Wit** (5.5%); American-style **Amber** (7.5%); and a **Triple** (9%) with anglicised spelling.

Kantelaer

Nieuweweg 79, 5853 EP Siebengewald
T 06 3831 7758
facebook.com/kantelaer

Limburg brewer making occasional 1hl batches for the local market since 2015. The only beer we are aware of is Belgian-style blond **D'n Afgod** (6%).

Kaper

Louis Couperushof 10, 4207 SH Gorinchem
T 06 2450 8592
brouwerijdekaper.nl

South Holland brewers producing monthly 2hl batches since 2017, mainly for local sale.
BEERS INCLUDE: fruity hoppy IPA **Kaailoper** (5.3%: ★★+) and less successful sweetish amber **Gods Genade** (5.8%: ★★).

Katwijks

Heerenweg 6 A11, 2222 AM Katwijk
katwijksbier.nl

Founded in 2014, this South Holland micro mainly produces traditional European styles for local sale on a 4hl kit.
BEERS INCLUDE: hefeweizen **Zeebries** (5.6%); double-hopped 'English-style' IPA **Hoppy Daze** (5.8%); Franconian-style rauchbier **Eròòkt** (6%); North Sea-hopping **Export Stout** (6.5%); and abbey-style **Tripel** (8.2%).

Kasparus

Karwijhof 15, 8308 AJ Nagele
T 06 1519 5454
facebook.com/BierbrouwerijKasparus

This Flevoland village nanobrewery, founded in 1994, went into recess in 2017 so owner Kasper Katuin could help his nephew start up Katuin (see Brewers without breweries), but was due to resume production at a new location in late 2019. Kasper used to brew a bewildering range of beers of variable quality, but it's not yet clear which if any of his old recipies will be revived.

Kees!

Voltaweg 16, 4338 PS Middelburg
T 0118 436228
brouwerijkees.nl

Former Emelisse brewer (see Slot Oostende below) and craft beer superstar Kees Bubberman opened his own crowdfunded 25hl brewery on an industrial site in southeast Middelburg in 2015, quickly gaining a deserved international reputation for excellence. Kees brews two or three times a week, with consistently impressive results, widely distributed in kegs and cans. The name is pronounced closer to 'case' than 'keys'. No tours, but a city centre taproom is planned.
BEERS INCLUDE: lightweight quaffer **Session IPA** (3.5%: ★★+); refreshingly hoppy **Pale Ale Citra** (4.6%: ★★★); super-dry, nettly bitter IPA **Mosaic Hop Explosion** (5.5%: ★★★+);

clean-tasting **It's Blond** (6%: ★★+), with a name that can't be questioned; moreish **East India Porter** (6.5%: ★★★); strongly bitter-hoppy New England IPA **Hazy Sunrise** (7.1%: ★★★); beautifully perky espresso stout **Top of the Morning** (8.6%: ★★★+); deceptively understated rye- based **Double IPA** (8.7%: ★★★); superbly rich **Export Porter 1750** (10.5%: ★★★+); **Caramel Fudge Stout** (11.5%: ★★★+), which is elegantly restrained despite the name; and deliciously complex **Barley Wine** (11.5%: ★★★+).
SEASONAL: amber **Spring Blossom** (6%: ★★+); fruity summer stout **Strawberry Fields** (6%: ★★★); summer IPA **Pink Grapefruit** (5.5%: ★★★); autumnal bock **Indian Summer** (6%: ★★+); and Scotch ale **Wee Heavy** (9.5%: ★★+), an intense winter warmer.
ALSO: a self-explanatory **Barrel Project** series, usually ★★★+ or better.

Kemphaan

Kemphaanpad 4, 1358 AC Almere
T 06 3390 1730
stadsbrouwerijdekemphaan.nl

It seems wrong that pan-flat Flevoland's brewers sometimes have to cling onto a cliff, yet that's been the predicament of the Ruff brewery (as in bird, not medieval fashion accessory), run by a local beer guild. The original location where it opened in 2002 had to close after just two years, and the restaurant where it re-emerged in 2006 also closed soon afterwards. When this location reopened under new management in 2012, the brewery was forced to move to its current site in an adjacent farm shop, where 2hl batches are brewed twice weekly. Tours, tastings and workshops by arrangement, with a taproom that only opens for pre-arranged groups.
BEERS INCLUDE: session ale **Waterkasteel** (2.5%); witbier **Madeleine** (5%: ★★) with lemon verbena; refreshing lightweight **Blond** (5.5%: ★★); stronger blond **Weerwater** (7%: ★★); lightweight IPA **Oostvaarders** (7%: ★★); and overly sweet **Tripel** (8.5%: ★★).

Kievit

Rucphenseweg 38, 4882 KC Zundert
zunderttrappist.nl

The Maria Toevlucht abbey, close to the Belgian border south of Breda, became the Netherlands' second Trappist brewery when it was awarded the Authentic Trappist Product mark in 2013 for its beers sold under the **Zundert** label. No visitor facilities at present, but a country café around the corner, In Den Anker (**indenanker.nl**), operates as an unofficial taproom.
BEERS INCLUDE: solid sweetish copper-amber **8** (8%: ★★★) and **10** (10%: ★★★+), its darker sister, more intense and complex with hints of bonfire.

Kinhem

Hofgeesterweg 6, 1991 AD Velserbroek
kinhem.atspace.cc

Started as a cuckoo in 2009, Kinhem now develops recipes at a site in IJmuiden and brews at scale at the present address on a 5hl brewhouse shared with Santpoorts (below), although as the two remain different companies we list them separately here. The only regular beer is sweetish honeyed blond **Hooglander** (8.5%: ★★), with others appearing as the experimental **Flex** series.

Kip

Kipstraat 2, 4589 KR Ossenisse
T 0114 682096
brouwerijdekip.nl

The Chicken started in 2014 as a nomadic brewer but increased capacity hugely in 2017 when it inherited a 10hl kit from 't Hofbrouwerijke in Belgium. All beers have suitably poultry-themed names.
BEERS INCLUDE: session wheat ale **Krielkip** (3.9%); standard amber **Scharrelkip** (5.7%: ★★); dryish blond **Kiplekker** (6.5%: ★★); and tripel **Haantje de Voorste** (8%).

Kleiburg

Hullenbergweg 6, 1101 BL Amsterdam
brouwerijkleiburg.nl

A loosely ecclesiastical outfit founded by a group of lay monks in 2015, initially nomadic but with their own brewery and the Proefzaak taproom in a prefabricated hut in Amsterdam Bijlmer since 2017. The landowners have long-term plans to build a hotel on the site, and the brewery may or may not be part of that, but any redevelopment is still several years away. The core beers are mostly hybrids of different styles. Tours and tastings by arrangement for groups of eight of more.
BEERS INCLUDE: hoppy witbier **Siciliaans Wit** (5.5%: ★★+); quaffable, bitter **Porter Saison** (6.5%: ★★+); dry amber **Dubbel Blond** (7.5%: ★★); robust, hoppy and balanced **Tripel IPA** (9.5%: ★★★); and aniseedy dark heavyweight **Quadrupel Poorter** (10.7%: ★★+).

Klein Duimpje

Hyacintenlaan 2a, 2182 DE Hillegom
T 0252 531186
kleinduimpje.nl

Tom Thumb is a longstanding presence on the Dutch beer scene, brewing commercially at various locations since 1996. It got its own premises with weekend taproom in the heart of the South Holland bulbfields in 2012, and currently brews 15-20hl at a time. Pre-booked tours and tastings for individuals and groups. *BEERS INCLUDE:* decently roasted schwarzbier **Blackbird** (4.6%: ★★+); dryish blond **Gerstebier** (4.9%: ★★); fruity **Porter** (6%: ★★+); black rye IPA **BRIPA** (6.5%: ★★); wheaty **Bollenstreek Ale** (7%: ★★); golden IPA **ZevenMijlsLaarzen** (7%: ★★+); run-of-the mill **Dubbel** (7.5%: ★★); better tripel **Blauwe Tram** (8%: ★★+); bog myrtle-infused **Gagel Tripel** (8.5%: ★★); Christmas cake Scotch ale **Hillegomse Hangkous** (8.5%: ★★); longstanding but too-sweet winter ale **Erik de Noorman** (9%: ★★); and chewy, face-filling **Imperial Russian Stout** (10.5%: ★★+). There are more than 40 regularly-brewed beers so this list is highly selective. *ALSO:* Bierhistorie Delft commissions historical beers including unhopped **Gruytbier** (5.5%: ★★); **VOC Stout** (5.5%: ★★); amber **Luyks Bier** (7%: ★★); and herbal **Kuyte Bier** (8.5%: ★★). **St Bonniefatius** brands are made for Café De Gooth in Haarlem.

Klinker

Muntstraat 45, 6211 EH Maastricht
T 06 2784 9301
brouwerijklinker.nl

Nanobrewery opened in 2015 at the Knijnspiep pub (see cafés), run by the brewer's parents, making European-style beers sold locally. *BEERS INCLUDE:* hop-shy English-style IPA **Klinker Pale Ale** (6%: ★★); sweetish **Dubbel** (7.5%: ★★); dry golden **Tripel** (8.5%: ★★); and soulless blond **Batteraof** (9%: ★★).

Klinkert

Brouwerstraat 16, 8356 DV Blokzijl
T 06 2295 9138

Not to be confused with the above, this Overijssel outfit, founded in 2018, brews 1hl batches weekly in a delicatessen shop (*Th 08.00-13.30, Fr 9.00-13.30, Sa 10.00-17.00*). The 1614 building in the centre of a well-preserved medieval town once housed De Zwaan brewery. Tours by appointment. *BEERS INCLUDE:* gently bittersweet blond **De Vuurtoren van Blokzijl** (6.5%: ★★) and **Het Kanon van Blokzijl** (8.5%: ★★), a decent fruity tripel. A **dubbel** sometimes appears.

Kluys

Sint Jansstraat 1, 5371 LN Ravenstein

Former North Brabant homebrewers who went pro in 2017. They claim to have their own kit, although larger runs may be made elsewhere. *BEERS INCLUDE:* metallic **Blonde Godfried** (6.5%: ★★); fruity tripel **Godfried Met Den Baard** (8%: ★★); and barley wine **Het Wapen Van Godfried** (10%).

Kompaa

Kollenburg

Korenbrugstraat 5–7, 5211 EG
's-Hertogenbosch
T 073 613 6915
cafebarleduc.nl/location

Microbrewery founded in 1999 beside the
Café Le Duc taproom, brewing 5hl batches
more-or-less weekly. Quality issues that
plagued **'t Kolleke** beers in their first decade
have happily become a distant memory.
Tours and tastings for groups of 10 or more.
BEERS INCLUDE: improving dry, spiced
wheat **Jonge Jan** (5.5%: ★★); amber **Kleine
Jan** (5.5%: ★★); bitter blond **Ome Jan** (6.5%:
★★); a decent amber **IPA** (7%: ★★+) multi-
grained dubbel **Oude Jan** (7%: ★★); honeyed
blond **Jheronimus** (7%: ★★), named in honour
of local hero artist Hieronymus Bosch; and
golden **Tripel** (8.5%: ★★).
SEASONAL: agreeable dark **Winterbier**
(9.2%: ★★+) with a dry burnt edge.

Kompaan

Saturnusstraat 55, 2516 AE Den Haag
T 06 5260 1344
kompaanbier.nl

Three friends who began running a small
installation in 2012, expanding to a 35hl
brewery and taproom in 2015. Beers were
always good but now deserve a place in the
award-winning category.
BEERS INCLUDE: hoppy pilsener **Kameraad**
(5%: ★★+); superior blond **Bondgenoot**
(5.2%: ★★+); citrussy American-style wheat
ale **Badgast** (5.7%: ★★+); strongly bitter
triple-hopped double IPA **Handlanger** (8.2%:
★★★); and standout port-laced imperial stout
Bloedbroeder (9.1%: ★★★★).
SEASONAL: hoppy pale ale **Spring Break**
(5.5%: ★★+); summery **Mango Unchained**
(3.7%: ★★+), a Brett-infused fruity session IPA;
and bitter-finishing autumnal **Bocks** (6.8%:
★★+). *ALSO:* a 'Foreign Legion' of occasionally
brewed boundary-pushing beers, among
which the most frequently recurring are
Jerry Sauertopf (3.7%: ★★★), a super-sharp

Berliner weisse; strongly hopped IPA **Joey
Greenhorn** (6%: ★★); and **Tommy Double-
Barrel** (11.5%: ★★★+), a smoky, intense and
quite lovely twice barrel-aged strong ale.

Koningshoeven

Eindhovenseweg 3, 5056 RP Berkel-Enschot
T 013 535 8147
latrappetrappist.com

What was for many years the Netherlands'
first and only Trappist brewery was founded
in 1884 at Schaapskooi Abbey on the outskirts
of Tilburg. By 1970, it was producing only one
beer, billed as Abdij Pilsener, though it was
conceivably a dry blond ale. Inspired by the
growing success in the Netherlands of the
classic monastic ales from the Trappist abbey
of Westmalle in Belgium, a brown dubbel and
golden tripel began to appear under a variety of
names including Tilburgs, Abdij Koningshoeven,
Trappist Koningshoeven and eventually
La Trappe. An extra-strong dark ale was added
to the range in 1991 under the name Quadrupel,
a term later appropriated by beer geeks and
retroactively applied as a style category.
Ownership flip-flopped between God and
Mammon, as secular companies gradually
acquired the brewhouse, the production methods,
the brands and the distribution, until in 1998
the operation became part of national giant
Bavaria (Swinkels) and was consequently stripped
of its Authentic Trappist Product status. This was
soon restored following intense negotiations,
and now the monks are technically back in
overall charge of the production from a
brewhouse that remains within the walls of the
abbey. That said, the facility also appears to be
used for making non-Trappist ales for Swinkels.

In recent years, the range has expanded and notably improved, regardless of who is responsible. Pre-booked tours are in Dutch (*Mo-Fr 14.00; Sa&Su 13.30, 15.30*) or English (*Tu&Th 12.00; Sa 11.30*).
BEERS INCLUDE: malty organic not-a-Kölsch **Puur** (4.7%: ★★); citrussy wheat **Witte Trappist** (5.5%: ★★); safe **Blond** (6.5%: ★★); disappointing by Trappist standards **Dubbel** (7%: ★★); dry amber **Isid'or** (7.5%: ★★+); golden **Tripel** (8%: ★★+) with bitter orange hints; and warming amber barley wine **Quadrupel** (10%: ★★+), developing massive complexity in its **Oak Aged** version (10%: ★★★+) which can further improve to world class (★★★★) with cellaring. SEASONAL: decent if slightly thin **Bockbier** (7%: ★★).

Kont van het Paard –
see Brielsch/Kont van het Paard

Kobold
Hatertseweg 5, 6581 KD Malden
brouwerijdekobold.nl

Originally known as Brouwbarrel and using its 50l installation solely for brewing to order for parties and workshops, this Gelderland brewer switched to making beer commercially in late 2019, although at the time of writing we yet to witness the fruits of these efforts.

Koperen Kat
Schieweg 15M, 2627 AN Delft
T 06 4212 3398
koperenkat.nl

The Copper Cat, based on an industrial estate south of Delft, has expanded substantially since it was founded in 2011 to a 10hl kit producing 700hl per year, with a corresponding increase in quality. No tours, but the on-site taproom is open Th-Su.
BEERS INCLUDE: malty low-strength pale ale **Poeslief** (1.9%: ★★); hazy blond saison **Parel van Delft** (4.5%: ★★); bittersweet,

easy-going **Blonde Anouk** (5%: ★★+); malty bitter pilsener **O15** (5%: ★★+); evolving **Schorem** (5.5%: ★★+), which began life as a brown ale but is now an IPA; dryish honeyed wheat ale **Lindebier** (6%: ★★+); malty amber **Princebier** (7%: ★★); fruity tripel **Balthasar** (8%: ★★); multi-layered **D'oostPorter** (8.5%: ★★+); and heavyweight quadrupel **De Kater** (10%: ★★+).
SEASONAL: the wonderfully designated **Brrr...** (6.3%: ★★+), a dark, sweetish winter ale.

Koperen Ster
Het Wolbert 23B, 7545 WK Enschede
T 06 1069 8709
dekoperenster.nl

The Copper Star's brewery and whisky distillery, launched in 2015, has the capacity to produce 25hl in a day but only makes occasional beers under its own name, as it's otherwise rented out to cuckoos like Black Baron and Crazy Black Cat. The brewer's wife distils a range of malts aged in Pedro Ximénez sherry vats from a base beer brewed on site. A smaller 1hl installation is used for workshops and demonstrations.
BEERS INCLUDE: fruity bitter **OPA (Oliver's Pale Ale)** (6.5%: ★★+) and dry blond **Symbiose Pinot Brut** (10.5%: ★★★+), an outstanding triple-fermented beer made with pinot grapes and champagne yeast, hand-finished champagne-style using the *méthode traditionelle*.

Kraan

Overtocht 6, 2411 BV Bodegraven
T 0172 615558
brouwerijkraan.nl

Bodegraven gained a second beer producer besides mighty De Molen (below) in 2013, thanks to the owner of the Speciaal Bierwinkel shop. Initially working elsewhere, he now brews fortnightly in 2hl batches under the label **Kraanwater**, which means tap water but clearly isn't.
BEERS INCLUDE: lightweight stout **4.2** (4.2%: ★★); blond **5.2** (5.2%: ★★); English pale ale **6.3** (6.3%: ★★); spicy blond **8.2** (8.2%: ★★); improving imperial stout **9.9** (9.9%: ★★+); and unsubtle quadrupel **10.2** (10.2%: ★★).

Kromme Haring

Europalaan 2C, 3526 KS Utrecht
dekrommeharing.nl

Founded by American expat brewer Stephen Grieg and Dutch friend Gijs van Wijchen in 2014, the Crooked Herring began life as a nomad brewer but opened its own brewpub in 2016. The beers were daring from the word go. Tastings for groups of eight or more.
BEERS INCLUDE: hoppy session wheat ale **Whitebait** (4.5%: ★★★); sour session IPA **Dolphin's Cry** (4.5%: ★★+); strongly bitter American amber **Rockfish** (5.5%: ★★★); beautifully dry, bitter blond IPA **Twisted Kipper** (6.3%: ★★★); rounded black IPA **Inktvis** (6.5%: ★★★), with a burnt currant background; dry saison **Les Perles du Homard** (8%: ★★+); and **Original Smokey** (8.5%: ★★★+), a gloriously rounded smoked porter.
Other specials making occasional appearances include: dry Anglo-American pale ale **The Otter** (5%: ★★★), made with Maris Otter malt, Fuller's yeast and US hops; strongly bitter New England IPA **Barbarian Fishing** (8%: ★★+), brewed in small runs to keep it fresh; and **Lactic Fantastic** (ABV varies; usually ★★★), a sour beer made with *Lactobacillus* bacteria, *Brettanomyces* yeast and a changing guest fruit for each batch.

Kuipertje

Appeldijk 18, 4161 BH Heukelum
T 0345 611839
hetkuipertje.nl

This hard-to-find one-man concern on the outskirts of a tiny Gelderland village was founded by Frits Kuiper in 1987 and is now run by his son Henk. Using organic hops, it remains wilfully uncommercial, an approach we love. The taproom, open Saturdays, is the only reliable place to find the beers, though they are occasionally seen at festivals and in shops. *BEERS INCLUDE:* pale ale **Vriendenbier** (5.5%: ★★+); bittersweet hefeweizen **Eige Weisse** (5.5%: ★★); rounded golden **Blondie** (6.5%: ★★); subtly banana-dabbed dunkel-weizen **Donker Tarwe** (6.5%: ★★); and bitter-sweet barley wine **Nachtvorst** (10%: ★★).

Kwartierbier

Hunzestraat 18, 3812 HT Amersfoort
kwartierbier.nl

Founded in 2017, this small outfit makes one-off beers every few months in a 2hl installation, usually spiced with ingredients ranging from juniper berries to lemongrass. The last one we saw was a sweetish, honeyed **Honing Saison** (7%: ★★).

Kwartje

Zamenhofstraat 90, 2518 LB Den Haag
T 06 5240 7290
brouwerijkwartje.com

Three young ex-schoolfriends began brewing on other people's kit under this name in 2015, adding their own 5hl brewhouse the following year.
BEERS INCLUDE: fruity and lightly bitter American pale ale **Any Key** (4.5%: ★★+); slightly smoky, easy-drinking wheat IPA **Refresh** (5%: ★★+); bitter-finishing peated porter **Firewire** (5.5%: ★★+); fruity-edged smoked rye IPA **RSI** (6.5%: ★★+); and **Brute Force** (10.7%: ★★+), a warming malty imperial stout.

*Kromm[e]
Inktvis [*

ALSO: the **Upgrade** series of imperial stouts. variously spiced with mixed results, and the **Zero-Day** series of wide-ranging experiments.

Laarbeeks

Klokkengietersstraat 1, 5735 EH Aarle-Rixtel
brouwerijlaarbeek.nl

A group of six North Brabant homebrewers developed several Belgian-style abbey-style beers at Sint Servattumus before launching their own brewery in 2016. Tours for groups of 10+ by arrangement.
BEERS INCLUDE: elderflower-spiced wheat ale **Linde Wit** (5%); honeyed **Blond** (7%: ★★); lychee-tinged amber **Urtyp** (7%: ★★+); malty dark amber **Brunette** (7%: ★★); sweetish stout **Vanille Zwart** (8%: ★★); and coriander-spiced tripel **Goud** (9%: ★★).

Lab54

Waalbandijk 16 (Unit 54), 6541 AJ Nijmegen
T 06 5065 1952
lab54.nl

Founded in 2016, Lab54 is one of three breweries currently operating in the former Honig Fabriek starch factory, alongside Nevel and Oersoep. As the name hints, it occupies the old laboratory.
BEERS INCLUDE: English-style porter **London Calling** (5%: ★★+); bittersweet American pale ale **Brave New World** (6%: ★★+); refreshingly fruity IPA **Ticket to the Tropics** (6.4%: ★★+); and oddly dill and chilli-spiced Japanese-inspired pale ale **Samurai** (7.5%: ★★).

Leckere

Schaverijstraat 15, 3534 AS Utrecht
T 030 231 2343
deleckere.nl

The beer shelves of every healthfood shop in the country are apparently carved up between Budels and this longstanding organic brewery, founded in an Utrecht suburb in 1997. It moved

in 2019 to a much larger site, with a taproom nearby, where output is expected to increase to 50,000hl a year. Quality has varied over the years but newer arrivals show far more pizzazz.
BEERS INCLUDE: malty **Pilsener** (5%: ★+); standard witbier **Witte Vrouwen** (5%: ★★); dark amber **Willibrord** (5%: ★★); dry blond **Gulden Craen** (5.2%: ★★); blond saison **Sonnen Borgh** (6.2%: ★★+), lifted by star anise; rounded dubbel **Crom Hout** (6.5%: ★★+); sweetish golden tripel **Paulus** (7.5%: ★★); too-sweet tripel **Razende Swaen** (8%: ★★); and malty brown barley wine **Blauwe Bijl** (10%: ★★).
SEASONAL: lightly fruity meibock **Spring Haver** (6.5%: ★★); quaffable summer ale **Lichte Gaard** (3.4%: ★★+) with sour raspberry hints; and dubbelbock **Rode Toren** (8.5%: ★★).
ALSO: dry bitter schwarzbier **Black Saxon** (4.9%: ★★+), officially a one-off, but likely to return; **Low Alc. IPA** (0.5%: ★★), good in its class but could be hoppier; too sweet and malty **Low Alc. Weizen** (0.5%: ★+).

Leiden

Aalmarkt 1–3F, 2311 EC Leiden
T 071 532 7646
stadsbrouwhuis.nl

Frustratingly, since it opened in 2016, this city-centre brewpub appears to have produced mainly one-off specials, making it difficult to review, though the beers we have tried were in the ★★-★★+ range. **Witte Catharina** (6%: ★★+), a lightly bitter witbier with lemon meringue tartness, has made at least a few repeat appearances.

Leidsch

Flevoweg 6 B, 2318 BZ Leiden
leidschbier.nl

Jan-Willem Fukkink has twice expanded his original 90l facility since it opened in 2004 and now has an 8hl installation and pilot kit, though we believe demand is such that commercial runs of the Aaipiejee and Blond are still outsourced to Proef in Belgium. The beers are good, sometimes great. Visits by appointment.

BEERS INCLUDE: frisky, dry blond **La Dixième** (4%: ★★+), made with champagne yeast; above-average kuit **Moons** (5%: ★★+), brewed to an ancient recipe; dry, bitter **Blond** (6.5%: ★★+); accomplished chocolatey and chewy standout **Morsporter** (6.1%: ★★★+); and lovely, rounded hoppy **Aaipiejee** (6.4%: ★★★), just as an IPA should be.

SEASONAL: summery golden saison **SingelBier** (6.5%: ★★+); slightly nutty autumn **Klompenbock** (6.5%: ★★+); and spiced dark winter ale **Boisot** (8.8%: ★★+).

★★+); **Razor** (7%: ★★+), a lightly fruity dry farmhouse ale; and amber tripel **Eldorado** (8%: ★★).

Lepelaer

Grote Sloot 481, 1757 LR Oudesluis
T 0299 683722
lepelaer.nl

This rural North Holland brewer was founded back in 2002 but took over a decade to get its own kit. The 1.2hl installation is now used for small batches, with larger runs still accomplished at Proef in Belgium.

Beemster BEERS INCLUDE: faintly bitter **Blond** (6%: ★★); malty, sweet golden **Tripel** (8.5%: ★★); and balanced dubbelbock **Bock Bock** (8%: ★★). And yes, that is its name.

Leroy Brown

Nieuwe Havenweg 13, 6827 BA Arnhem
T 06 2474 7525
leroybrownbrewery.com

Brewing since 2018 on an industrial estate in Arnhem's southeast suburbs, this outfit maintains a more conveniently placed taproom opposite the main station (see cafés). Beer names borrow fragments of lyrics from the not-'Bad Bad'-at-all Jim Croce song, an inspiration to the brewers. Workshops and tastings by arrangement.

BEERS INCLUDE: hazy blond American-style wheat ale **Treetop Lover** (4.7%: ★★); currant-tinged oatmeal stout **Junkyard Dog** (6.2%:

Lindeboom

Engelmanstraat 52–54, 6086 BD Neer
T 0475 592900
lindeboom.nl

The Linden Tree is one of the larger old-established Dutch independents, founded in 1870 on the outskirts of a small Limburg village. If its managers were a little more adventurous, it could make a killing with a range of bolder craft lager styles, but it remains sadly risk-averse despite dramatically widening its range in recent years. Book tours and tastings in advance online (Fr 14.00).

BEERS INCLUDE: anaemic, oddly sweet **Pilsener** (5%: ★+); copper-amber Düsseldorf-ish altbier **Venloosch Alt** (5%: ★★+), the best of the range; run-of-the-mill spiced **Venloosch Wit** (5.2%: ★★); and middling **Saison** (5.8%: ★★). Alongside these are the **Gouverneur** abbey brands: blond, grassy **Speciale 140** (5.5%: ★★); up-market hooker (no flaws, little class) **Blonde** (6.5%: ★★); sweetish **Dubbel** (6.5%: ★★) with a bitter finish; an oak-aged **Stout op Hout** (7.5%: ★★) that wants to be cool as craft, but is too restrained; and too-sweet **Tripel** (8.2%: ★★).

SEASONAL: undistinguished **Herfstbock** (6.5%: ★★); and better **Gouverneur Dubbelbock** (7.5%: ★★+), with some character.

ALSO: driver's pilsener **Lindeboom 0.5** (0.5%: ★+), which hasn't realised such things can now be tasty; and several low and non-alcoholic **Radlers**, best left to those with a sweet tooth.

Lion's Head

Van Woustraat 34 H, 1073 LM Amsterdam
T 06 4845 0378
lionsheadbrewing.com

Opened in 2018 by a German and a South African, this gastro brewpub often reflects its owners' origins in its range of styles. More than 20 different beers emerged from the 2.5hl kit in the first couple of years but most were one-offs. They're keen to expand but have limited space.
BEERS INCLUDE: flagship Kölsch-style **Frau Schultz** (4.5%: ★★+); blond **Blueberry Hefeweizen** (5%: ★★+), made with UK malt; dark, dry **Schwarzbier** (5%: ★★+); and dry, fruity **Lion's IPA** (5%: ★★+).

LOC

Burgemeester Brokxlaan 8–82 (Gebouw 84), 5041 SJ Tilburg
T 06 4208 2884
locbrewery.nl

Four friends with children attending the same school began brewing with often excellent results on a 5hl kit in 2015. Their current site is

an old railway building behind Tilburg station, explaining the name LOC, short for locomotive, as well as some of the brands. A taproom opened in 2018, and tours are offered by arrangement.
BEERS INCLUDE: refreshingly tangy session IPA **Dinky Citra** (4.7%: ★★+); fruity-hoppy American pale ale **Hogger** (5.7: ★★+); dry, fruity IPA **Lord Nelson** (6.2%: ★★★); bitter IPA **Sleeper** (6.6%: ★★+); admirably rounded imperial IPA **Train Hopper** (8.4%: ★★★); and rich, chewy imperial stout **84** (10.5%: ★★★). Also: a seemingly endless train of one-offs, including experimental brews in the **Platform** series.

LOK

Reggelaan 94, 8033 AX Zwolle
T 06 1523 2740
lokdrank.nl

Not to be confused with the above, this brewery was founded in 2018 by a homebrewer of 20 years' experience who makes liqueurs as well as beers, both usually only available locally.
BEERS INCLUDE: bittersweet **Tripel** (8.8%) and copper-amber quadrupel **Holy Shi** (10.5%).
SEASONAL: meibock **Spring** (7%); session IPA **Summer** (4.5%); imperial IPA **Autumn** (7%); and **Winter** (8.5%), an imperial stout.

Loon

Graaf van Lynden van Sandenburgweg 6, 3945 PB Cothen
T 0343 725090
deloonbrouwerij.nl

Founded in Utrecht province in 2015, this brewery-for-hire has a 20hl brewhouse and enough fermentation and conditioning tanks to give it an annual capacity of 10,000hl. It hosts around a dozen homeless brewers and doesn't yet produce its own brands. *Loon* in Dutch means 'wage' and is pronounced closer to English 'loan', so there's no suggestion of mental incapacity, though the brewery's street address is surely the daftest in this guide.

Maallust

Hoofdweg 140, 9341 BL Veenhuizen
T 0592 388971
maallust.nl

Microbrewery founded in 2011 in the former grain mill of a Drenthe colony to which the 19th-century Dutch poor were deported. Solid and reliable ales are brewed several times a week in an impressive 15hl installation and served in a regularly-open taproom (see cafés), with tours by arrangement. Swinkels (Bavaria) took a undisclosed stake in 2017 in a deal that covered distribution and possibly more.
BEERS INCLUDE: refreshingly rounded weizen **De Kolonist** (5%: ★★); impressively bitter, malty Vienna lager **De Vagebond** (5%: ★★★); dull spelt beer **De Pauper** (5.5%: ★★); bittersweet blond **De Weldoener** (6.7%: ★★); chestnut-brown dubbel **Mooie Madam** (7%: ★★); and grassy tripel **Zware Jongen** (9%: ★★+), which evokes images of summer meadows.
SEASONAL: standard meibock **De Deerne** (7%: ★★); autumnal bock **Veldwachter** (6.7%: ★★+); and winter barley wine **1818** (10%: ★★★), with aniseed and banana riding waves of warming alcohol.

Maar

Maar 2, 6454 AM Jabeek
T 06 5278 7992
dorpsbrouwerijdemaar.nl

Beers from this farmhouse brewery established in 2003 in a tiny Limburg village near the German border are mainly sold locally in porcelain-stoppered bottles salvaged from the former Leeuw brewery in Valkenburg. A gorgeously quaint taproom is sadly now open only irregularly, with tours by arrangement.
BEERS INCLUDE: pleasantly rounded **Jabeeks Blond** (5%: ★★+); lightly bitter amber **Genhoots Genot** (6.5%: ★★); stronger and better date-laced amber **Bengelder Bengel** (7.5%: ★★+); fruity **Witte Juffer** (7.5%: ★★), witbier-inspired but made with unmalted rye rather than wheat; and above-average bittersweet **Jabeeks Tripel** (8.5%: ★★+).

Maastrichter Maltezer

Oeverwal 12, 6221 EN Maastricht
T 043 855 3258
stadsbrouwerijdemaastrichtermaltezer.nl

Following a year of working elsewhere, this project revived brewing activity, albeit on a small scale, at the site of Maastricht's historic Ridder (Knight) brewery in 2018. The building, which dates from 1825, produced beer between 1857 and 2002, when it was shut by Heineken. There's a  taproom, and individuals can book tours and tastings at set times through the website, also offered at other times for groups of eight or more. The only regular product is **Maltezer** (6.5%: ★★+), a dry, amber Dortmunder-style beer from a tweaked historic recipe. The brewery trains landlords in serving this at its best and offers a download-able self-guided walk, the Via Malta, linking ten accredited historic pubs in the city.

Mannenpap

Plataanstraat 9, 6522 JG Nijmegen
T 06 2707 6916
mannenpap.com

Two friends cuckoo brewing since 2017 who successfully crowdfunded this 5hl installation in 2019 and plan to open a taproom shortly. *BEERS INCLUDE:* **Cocktail** (5.8%: ★★+), an hoppy New England IPA; fruity, bitter-finishing IPA **Fruitcake** (7%: ★★+); and standout malty imperial stout **Black Oxx** (10.2%: ★★★).

Markebier

Kazerneplein 6, 7211 BM Eefde
T 0575 540166
markebier.nl

Gelderland brewery founded in 2017 with a tiny 30l installation in the gatehouse of a former barracks. The first beers to appear were **Aevede Tripel** (8.5%) and **Risselt Saizon** (6.5%), with a **Stout** and a **Bock** expected to follow.

Markies

Statenlaan 299, 5223 LG 's-Hertogenbosch
brouwerijdemarkies.nl

Established in North Brabant in 2011, the Marquis brews up to 100l per session in 25l batches. Their brand **Ons Vergist** means both 'Our Mistaken' and 'Us Fermented'. *BEERS INCLUDE:* improving **Is Stout!** (5%: ★★); weizen **Gebroken Wit** (5.5%); citrussy IPA **IetsiePietsieAnders** (6%:★★+); dry wheat ale **Signature** (7%: ★★); strongly hoppy wheat beer **Hop d'r op en d'r Over** (8%: ★★+); a golden **Tripel** (8.5%: ★★); American amber **Rood** (8.5%: ★★+); and amber tripel-ish **Grand Cru** (9%: ★★).

Martinus

Kostersgang 32–34, 9711 CX Groningen
T 050 311 6310
brouwerijmartinus.nl

City-centre brewery with 10hl kit founded in 2015, sold widely across the region as well as in its own taproom and restaurant. Walkup tours possible (*Fr&Sa 15.30, 16.30; Su 15.30*), but may be cancelled at short notice if fewer than four people join.

BEERS INCLUDE: lightly bitter dark **Bruin** (5%: ★★+); fruity hoppy American-style **Pale** (5%: ★★+); wheat ale **1717** (5.3%: ★★); rounded golden IPA **Peerd** (5.8%: ★★+); golden pale ale **Nuchter** (6%: ★★); malty dry **Blond** (6.5%: ★★); dry, restrained **Saison** (6.7%: ★★+); triple-grained fruity **Tripel** (8.6%: ★★); full-bodied imperial stout **Calmix** (9%: ★★+); dark, rich and improving standout **Imperial Smoked Porter** (9%: ★★★); and a raisin and fig-tinged **Quadrupel** (9.5%: ★★+).

Maximus

Pratumplaats 2A, 3454 NA Utrecht (De Meern)
T 030 737 0800
brouwerijmaximus.nl

Experienced brewer Marcel Snater, previously of Snaterende Arend, started afresh in 2011 with this project, moving a year later into a purpose-built site in a western Utrecht suburb, complete with 15hl brewhouse and

(5%: ★★+); Belgian-style witbier **Limburgse Witte** (5.5%: ★★); **Lekker Bekske** (7.2%: ★★+), a malty stout/porter hybrid; and dubiously named triple-hopped tripel **Sex Sells** (9%: ★★).

Met Maten

Uilenwaard 46, 5236 WB Empel
brouwerijmetmaten.nl

North Brabant-based With Friends was set up in 2017, co-funded by 150 investing 'friends'. **Maatwerk** (8.5%: ★), its first effort, was a sour and seriously off-kilter blond tripel. We trust things will only improve from there.

Middelburg

Korte Geere 17, 4331 LE Middelburg
T 06 8107 9149
stadsbrouwerijmiddelburg.nl

Known as Dienges when it began commissioning beer from others in 2014, this Zeeland operation got more interesting when it added its own city-centre brewpub in 2016. It produces around 250hl per year from a 5hl brewhouse, most of which is sold under the **Hosternokker** label.
BEERS INCLUDE: fruity dry saison **Bier van Ier** (4.5%: ★★); superior malty dry lagered **Ké Dost** (5.5%: ★★+); citrus-finishing bitter IPA **Ék Zinin** (5.5%: ★★+); banana-edged weizen **Whats Ab** (5.8%: ★★+); odd-tasting fruit beer **Rooie Rakker** (6%: ★+); sweetish blond **Lekker Dieng** (6.5%: ★★); dry spiced blond **Middleburgs Stadsbier** (6.5%: ★★+); sweetish blond **Madam Babette** (7%: ★★); lightly bitter dubbel **Môk Ôk Èh** (7.5%: ★★+); dry imperial wheat ale **Cuvée** (8%: ★★+); **Lekker Stout** (8.4%: ★★), which is thinnish and not especially *lekker* in its basic form but gains body and depth in its **Whisky-Infused** version (★★+); sweetish tripel **Afslag 39** (9.1%: ★★); and **Middelburgs 800 Winters** (9.5%: ★★+), a stout given a tart edge by added blackcurrants.

expansive taproom. His beers, reliably decent with frequent splashes of brilliance, are widely available nationally, even more so since 2018 when Swinkels (Bavaria) bought a stake that included distribution rights.
BEERS INCLUDE: easy-drinking session rye pale ale **Little Fred** (3.5%: ★★+); dryish amber dunkelweizen **Dakhaas** (5.5%: ★★+); superbly hoppy American-style amber lager **Brutus** (6%: ★★★+); immensely likeable IPA **Highhops** (6%: ★★★); floral, hoppy pale ale **Pandora** (6%: ★★★); bitter **Stout 6** (6%: ★★+); and **Stout 8** (8%: ★★★), its enticingly imperial big sister.
SEASONAL: dry, unassuming **Bock** (7%: ★★) and spiced winter ale **Arcticus** (8%: ★★+).

Menkes

Groenseykerstraat 8e, 6161 SG Geleen
T 06 5268 1749
demenkes.nl

The South Limburg duo behind this 5hl operation, making beers since 2015, treat it as a side project to their day jobs, with no grand ambition other than to sell good beers locally.
BEERS INCLUDE: fruity IPA **Hey Enne!?** (4.7%: ★★+); lightly bitter pale ale **Einde Slag**

Mieghelm

Venkant 19, 5271 SP Sint-Michielsgestel
T 06 8135 7668
brouwerijmieghelm.nl

This veteran North Brabant micro, established in 1994, fell silent in 2015 following the death of its founding brewer, but the 10hl copper brewhouse has recently been returned to action by his grandson.
YEAR-ROUND: fruity amber **Abraham** (5%: ★★); simple wheat **Gestels Withelm** (5%: ★★); and sweetish **Mieghelms Tripel** (7%: ★★).

Moersleutel

Diamantweg 9, 1812 RC Alkmaar
T 06 2002 0351
brouwerijdemoersleutel.nl

The Wrench (as in spanner) made an instant impression when it was launched by four brothers in 2015 with a range of hop-forward IPAs and supercharged imperial stouts. In 2018, it moved down the road from its original location in Heiloo to an expanded 25hl brewery on the current site, with the Scrapyard taproom following a year later (see cafés). The brand appears on labels as **DEMOERSLEUTEL**, without a space after the definite article, which may be confusing to non Dutch speakers. The bold-flavoured, sometimes unsubtle beers are aimed squarely at a contemporary audience for whom more is more, though some of the heavyweight double IPAs have morphed into lighter, fresher and more fashionable 'hazy, juicy' form recently.
BEERS INCLUDE: fruity, hoppy New England IPA **Punch Line** (5.5%: ★★★); its fresh citrussy near-twin **Juiced Up** (6%: ★★★); rich, oaty brown ale **Rusty** (8%: ★★+); burnt sugar-tinged imperial stout **Smeerolie** (10%: ★★★), also appearing chilli-spiced as **Smeerolie Mexicake** (10%: ★★★); peated imperial stout **Octane Overload** (11%: ★★★); and inky, bitter-finishing imperial stout **Motorolie** (12%: ★★★).
ALSO: **Hoptimized**, a numbered series of hoppy IPAs in various strengths and forms

(usually ★★★); **Je Moer** (10%: usually ★★★), a varously barrel-aged imperial porter; and **Willy Tonka** (10%: usually ★★★), a numbered series of imperial stouts with tonka beans.

De Molen (Swinkels)

Overtocht 43, 2411 BT Bodegraven
T 0172 610848
brouwerijdemolen.nl

Founded in 2004, the Mill quickly became a standard bearer for the next phase of the Dutch beer revolution under the guiding hand of head brewer Menno Olivier (see Redemption and Rebirth). Its name references its original site in a landmark waterside windmill, de Arkduif (ark dove), which still houses the shop and restaurant (see cafés), but demand forced a huge expansion into new facilities on a small industrial estate 100m away, currently equipped with a 50hl brewhouse and still growing. De Molen's international status was boosted by hosting the annual Borefts festival (see Festivals and events), which since 2009 has brought some of most talked-about breweries from across the world to this small Protestant town of sober tastes. In many people's eyes, its once unassailable reputation began to tarnish when Swinkels (Bavaria) first took a minority stake in 2016 then bought out the business

entirely in 2019 as a means, according to the founders, of making it sustainable, but we prefer to let the beers do the talking. Beers are sold nationwide and by high-end craft brew importers around the world. Tours by arrangement.

BEERS INCLUDE: fruity hoppy session IPA **Hugs & Kisses** (3.5%: ★★+); American/British pale ale hybrid **Licht & Lustig** (4.5%: ★★★); hoppy blond thirst-quencher **Op & Top** (4.5%: ★★★+); delicately balanced middleweight IPA **Hop & Liefde** (4.8%: ★★★+); full-mouthed porter **Hamer & Sikkel** (5.2%: ★★★); lightly restrained saison **Heksen & Trollen** (6.1%: ★★+); former best-in-show IPA **Vuur & Vlam** (6.2%: ★★★+), which remains a classic though arguably surpassed by some more recent challengers; supremely sour Flemish-style oak-aged brown **Lief & Leed** (6.2%: ★★★+); quaffable bergamot-infused IPA **Dag & Dauw** (7.1%: ★★★); bittersweet English-style ale **Molenbier** (7.5%: ★★+); darkly rich smoked stout **Bloed, Zweet & Tranen** (8.2%: ★★★); smoked, chilli-stoked stout **Rook & Vuur** (8.2%: ★★★); bittersweet tripel **Heen & Weer** (9.2%: ★★★); intense yet dangerously quaffable double IPA **Storm & Bliksem** (9.6%: ★★★+); rich, smoky, chocolatey stout **Hemel & Aarde** (10%: ★★★+); classic imperial stout **Hel & Verdoemenis** (10%: ★★★+) with smoky coffee; chocolate-laced **Mooi & Meedogenloos** (10.2%: ★★★+), a stout/quadrupel hybrid; beautifully understated, treacly cocoa-rich stout **Moord & Doodslag** (10.4%: ★★★★), aka **Rasputin**; deeply

moreish vanilla and coffee-tinged imperial porter **Tsarina Esra** (11%: ★★★★), a star that shines even more brightly in its barrel-aged incarnations; and barley wine **Bommen & Granaten** (11.9%: ★★★), which has dipped in strength but remains laden with sweetness and alcohol, still deserving its 'bombs & grenades' designation.

ALSO: a relentless stream of collaborations and one-offs which are nearly always at least interesting.

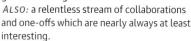

Molengraaf

Vaanakker 26, 5731 JM Mierlo
T 06 2728 4847
facebook.com/demolengraaf

North Brabant homebrewers who turned pro in 2018, now producing beer for the local market in tiny 120-bottle batches. First effort was strong blond **De Klap Van De Molen** (8%).

Möllinkwoner

Noordmolen 3, 7495 VK Ambt Delden
T 06 1529 4885
mollinkwoner.nl

One-woman Overijssel microbrewery and cheesemaker founded in 2016 by the sister of one of the Hemursbier brewers (above).
BEERS INCLUDE: raspberry-infused **Frambozenbier** (5.5%); light-blond **Berghöpke** (6.5%); and tripel **Noaste Noaber** (9%).

Mommeriete

De Oostermaat 66, 7783 BX Gramsbergen
T 0524 562511
mommeriete.nl

Founded in 2004 by husband and wife brewers Gert and Carina Kelder, Mommeriete moved its altogether quieter brilliance to its current canalside spot in an Overijssel village in 2008. The products of their copper brewhouse stick resolutely to traditional European styles with no new world hops added. They're best appreciated at the idyllic taproom in a former lock keeper's house but are also seen in better beer shops and at some festivals. Tours by arrangement.
BEERS INCLUDE: malt-edged **Klokhenne's Weizen** (5%: ★★); rustic, entertaining **Blond** (6%: ★★★), which uses Chouffe yeast to give a Belgian hint; fruity-hoppy **IPA** (7%: ★★★); lightly fruity **Scheerse Tripel** (9%: ★★★), made with Westmalle yeast; voluptuous barley wine **Vrouwe van Gramsbergh** (10.2%: ★★★+), with alcoholic raisiny notes; and its male stablemate **Heer van Gramsbergen** (11%: ★★★+), once a barley wine but now a fine imperial stout.
SEASONAL: delightfully bitter and complex German-style **Meibock** (6.7%: ★★★+) and rich, smoky and fruity autumnal **Rookbock** (7%: ★★★), Bamberg in a glass.

Mop van Dalfsen

Pastoriestraat 45, 7721 CV Dalfsen
T 06 5283 9075
demopvandalfsen.nl

Tiny Overijssel outfit brewing commercially since 2017 but founded five years earlier as a "joke". The 50l kit is mainly used for workshops and demonstrations, with surplus production and other small-run batches sold on the local market.
BEERS INCLUDE: spiced **Amber** (6.5%: ★★+) with ginger and cinnamon; and heavyweight **Quadrupel** (11%).

Muifel

Vikingenweg 5, 5349 BT Oss
T 06 4056 0581
muifelbrouwerij.nl

One of the Netherlands' more adventurous brewers, Martin Ostendorf started the Muffle in 2006, at first specialising in subtly rounded big-hitters brewed at various locations. He found a permanent home in North Brabant in 2018, with a 17.5hl kit in operation since 2019. For the moment, some large runs are still brewed elsewhere, but this may change as capacity grows. An on-site taproom opens only for groups by appointment.
BEERS INCLUDE: low-alcohol **Crazy IPA** (0.7%: ★★+), one of the best in its class; lightly spiced wheat ale **Weizen** (5%: ★★+); dry, fruity cranberry ale **Messentrekker** (6%: ★★+); malty blond **Graaf Dicbier** (6%: ★★), with orange peel; rounded bitter amber **Berghs Bier** (6.5%: ★★+); pleasingly fruity **USA IPA** (7%: ★★★); sweetish malty blond **D'n Ossekop** (7.5%: ★★); intensely dry and bitter hop-forward double IPA **Dr. Hop** (8.5%: ★★★+); richly satisfying coffee-edged imperial stout **Black Bastard** (9.5%: ★★★); bittersweet tripel **Broeder Everardus** (9.5%: ★★+); equally bittersweet barley wine **Zuster Agatha** (10%: ★★+), which gains complexity in its **Houtgerijpt** (wood-aged, 10.5%: ★★★) version; and amber heavyweight **Beerskey** (11%: ★★+), complete with the peat smack of whisky malt.
SEASONAL: US-hopped India pale lager **Lentebier** (5.5%: ★★+) and autumnal **D'n Ossebock** (7%: ★★+), with prune-like sweet and sour flavours.

Nacht

Heuvelstraat 7, 5101 TB Dongen
T 06 1100 4518
nachtbrouwerij.nl

Founded in 2016, the Night takes its name from the brewer's preference for working undistractedly in the hours of darkness, when he produces small-runs for the local North Brabant market. Larger batches are brewed elsewhere.
BEERS INCLUDE: banana-forward dunkelweizen **Weizzz...zzz...** (5.2%: ★★); US-style **InsomIPA** (6%: ★★); lightly bitter blond **Ochtendgloren** (7.7%: ★★); off-kilter fruity honeyed tripel **Nachttrip** (9%: ★+); and warming, dark quadrupel **Nachtzuster** (9.5%: ★★+).

Naeckte Brouwers

Amsterdamseweg 22, 1182 HD Amstelveen
T 020 789 5689
naecktebrouwers.nl

Formed in 2012, the Naked Brewers opened their first 10hl brewery on a business park in Amstelveen (Weverij 5) in late 2013. Their confidence boosted by growing popularity, they added a second brewhouse with taproom in a former church in 2018. Excess capacity is rented out to numerous others.
BEERS INCLUDE: blond session ale **Amazone** (3.8%: ★★+) with bladderwrack seaweed; dry gold-blond kuit **Elser** (5.5%: ★★+); improved dry-edged saison **Zonnegloed** (6.5%: ★★+); variously single-hopped **SHIPA** (6.8%: usually

★★★); hoppy blond **Hop-X** (6.8%: ★★+); sweetish blond **Feeks** (7.5%: ★★); superior Belgian-style dubbel **Naeckte Non** (8%: ★★★); rich imperial stout **Leprechaun** (8%: ★★+); full-bodied tripel **Nimf** (9%: ★★+); and **Elegast** (10%: ★★+), a bittersweet barley wine.

Natte Cel

Prins Willem Alexanderlaan 8, 1611 EV Bovenkarspel
T 0228 512451

Microbrewers established in 2008 in a North Holland village. Flagship brand Skeetje is usually brewed in quantity elsewhere, we believe at Proef in Belgium, while others are made in house and sold in 75cl bottles.
BEERS INCLUDE: multigrained fruity blond **Skeetje** (6%: ★★+); spiced white **Cipiertje** (6%: ★★); tartly fruity blond **Veelpleger** (6%: ★★); too-sweet **India Pale Ale** (7%: ★+); soft, sweet **Blonde Ann** (7%: ★★); peaty citrus **Whisky Honey Beer** (7.5%: ★★+), matured on whisky-soaked wood chips; dry herbal tripel **Vrije Voeten** (8%: ★★); fruity-edged porter **Gladjanus** (8.5%: ★★); and distinctive tripel **Zware Jongen** (8.5%: ★★+).

Nederlands Openluchtmuseum

Schelmseweg 89, 6816 SJ Arnhem
T 026 357 6123
openluchtmuseum.nl

Founded in 2007 in the impressive National Open Air Museum and based in an incongruously modern glass building, this brewery produces beer under the name **Goeye Goet**. Visitors with museum tickets can wander in to observe brewers at work (*daily 10.00–17.00*), or visit the displays in the adjoining building, a preserved 18th-century brewhouse. Groups of 10 or more can pre-book a tasting hosted by the brewer. For more about the Budel taproom next door, which sells the beer on draught, and the extraordinary wider surroundings, see cafés. Bottled beers are sold at the museum shop and in several Arnhem outlets.

BEERS INCLUDE: refreshingly balanced **Pilsener** (5%: ★★+); simple spiced **Witbier** (5%: ★★); copper-brown sweet-and-sour **Dubbel** (7%: ★★); sweetish **Tripel** (9%: ★★); and full-bodied brown quadrupel **Zware Barrie** (10%: ★★+).

Nemeton

Grotestraat 222, 5141 HE Waalwijk
T 0416 534727
facebook.com/Nemetonbrewing

The owners of the Vinotake shop and Proeflokaal bar founded this adjacent brewery in 2017, though haven't yet brewed commercially due to licensing issues. For now, beers like **Ritual Series No.1 Opening Ceremony** (10%: ★★★), a dark, full-bodied barley wine, are produced elsewhere, but we expect this to change in the near future.

Nevel

Waalbandijk 8d, 6541 AJ Nijmegen
T 06 4675 2003
nevel.org

Originally known as Katjelam when created in 2014, Mist is led by two young brewers who inherited Oersoep's old kit and, like their mentors, continue to make bold, experimental and almost always excellent beers, mostly medium-alcohol wood-aged and wild ales. They rebranded on moving to their current location in 2016, after acquiring 150 wine barrels as Brett-infected playthings, and added a taproom in 2019.
BEERS INCLUDE: hazy golden 'kvass' **Aard** (5.2%: ★★★), a Slavic/Baltic-style wild ale made from rye bread; variously hopped golden farmhouse ale **Erve** (5.2%: usually ★★★); dark, fruity 'not a bock' autumn wild ale **Tumult** (5.3%: ★★★); **Teerling** (5.5%: ★★★+), a dry, sharp and delicious dark wild ale aged in whisky barrels; **Tenger** (5.5%: ★★★), a lightly sour barrel-fermented wild ale with southern wormwood; and Brett-tinged partly wood-aged pale ale **Loof** (5.7%: ★★★).

Nicolaas

Gorps Baantje 1, 5051 PX Goirle
T 06 4634 2278
brouwerijnicolaas.nl

A group of friends began this North Brabant brewery at a 1.2hl scale in 2017, then grew into a new 3.5hl installation in 2019. Beers are primarily available in the Roovertsche Leij (roovertscheleij.nl), a thatched café and restaurant next door.
BEERS INCLUDE: multi-grained, juniper-spiced blond session near-witbier **Droeftoeter** (4.8%: ★★) and unassuming blond **Blije Bakkes** (6%: ★★).

Nieuwe Ketelhuis

Zinkweg 35, 3262 BC Oud-Beijerland
T 06 8126 4882
hetnieuweketelhuis.nl

South Holland nanobrewery founded by three friends in 2017, producing only around 1.5hl per month.
BEERS INCLUDE: a self-explanatory **Blond** (5.9%); wheat ale **Weissen** (5.9%); and citrussy, balanced **Citra IPA³** (7.5%: ★★+), a hoppy IPA/tripel hybrid.

Nijver

Heuvel 1, 5664 HJ Geldrop
T 040 286 7000
kaffeepeijnenburg.nl

North Brabant microbrewer founded in 2016
with a 1.3hl kit in the Hotel Nijver. Beers are
sold in 75cl bottles, mainly in the on-site
Kaffee Peijnenburg (see cafés).
BEERS INCLUDE: dry, light, bitter-finishing
Geldrops Blond (5%: ★★+); dark dubbel
Donkerbruin Vermoeden (7%: ★★); and
bittersweet, honeyed **Tripel Carlo** (7.5%: ★★).

Noarder Dragten

De Bolder 76, 9206 AR Drachten
T 06 5137 5460
bierbrouwerijnoarderdragten.nl

Friesland microbrewers making a slowly
expanding and improving range of beers in
6hl batches since 2016, renting out excess
capacity to others. They plan to open a
taproom but the preferred location, above the
Apen & Bieren bottle shop (Oosterstraat 23),
may require the brewery to downsize.
Group tastings by arrangement.
BEERS INCLUDE: witbier **RAL 9010** (4.8%: ★★),
named after the colour code for white; dry,
bitter IPA **Drachtster Pale Ale** (DPA, 5.6%: ★★+);
nutty, rounded **Porter** (6.5%: ★★+); sweetish,
honeyed **Tripel** (7%: ★★); fruity and drinkable
black IPA **Mat Zwart** (7.1%: ★★+); and banana-
tinged, sweetish **Sinneblond** (7.2%: ★★).

Noord-Hollandse

Lagendijk 7, 1911 MT Uitgeest
T 06 4565 8051
dnhbb.nl

Started in 2012, the brewery doubled its space
with a move across town in 2017, allowing 29
(at the last count) fermentation and conditioning tanks to be installed alongside a 20hl
brewhouse. Own-branded beers appear only
occasionally as practically all this capacity is
rented out to a lengthening list of brewers

without breweries, attracted by a reputation
for solid quality and a policy of engaging clients
in the brewing process. Tours by arrangement.
BEERS INCLUDE: witbier **Centaur** (5.5%: ★★)
and balanced blond **Compromis** (5.5%: ★★+).

Noordt

Zaagmolenkade 46, 3035 KA Rotterdam
T 010 223 0566
brouwerijnoordt.nl

This ambitious brewery, founded in 2015,
creates widely distributed beers of improving
quality in a kaleidoscope of styles at a 20hl
installation with shop and taproom in the
north of the city, and also rents space to others.
Pre-booked tours with tastings Fr 17.00.
BEERS INCLUDE: lightweight session **New
England IPA** (3%: ★★+); citrussy single-hopped
US wheat ale **Noordtsingle** (4.5%: ★★+);
banana-tinged **Weizen** (5%: ★★); crisply
bitter **Blondt** (6%: ★★+); fruity, dry pale ale
Seven Hops (7%: ★★+); a standard **Dubbel**
(7%: ★★); and fruity blond **Tripel** (7.5%: ★★).
ALSO: Kölsch-style **Herrie** (4%: ★★+), made
with and for celebrity chef Herman den Blijker;
and **Dark Chocolate Porter** (8%: ★★+), with
and for celebrity baker Hidde de Brabander,
alongside half a dozen seasonals and all
manner of one-offs.

Norem

De Kleine Elst 48, 5246 JJ Rosmalen
brouwerijnorem.nl

North Brabant microbrewery since 2019,
its first commercial beer was Belgian-style
Kort Blontje (6.7%).

Oedipus

Gedempt Hamerkanaal 85, 1021 KP Amsterdam
T 020 244 1673
oedipus.com

A group of friends connected through
Amsterdam's Beer Temple began making

beers commercially at various locations under the Oedipus name in 2011. They opened a 6hl brewery and taproom in 2015, but soon outgrew it and had to upgrade to a 25hl installation. Such is their beers' popularity that this has in turn become too small, especially after Heineken took an undisclosed stake in 2019, a move that will doubtless further increase distrbution and demand.
BEERS INCLUDE: dry and balanced blond **Slomo** (3.5%: ★★+), possibly the Netherlands' only grisette, a light saison style; citrussy sharp Berliner weisse **Vogelen** (4%: ★★★); slightly less sharp **Swingers** (4%: ★★★), a lemon gose with sea salt; light dry-hopped wheat ale **Offline** (4.5%: ★★+); clean-tasting **Oedipus Pilsner** (5%: ★★+); admirably restrained mango sour **Polyamorie** (5%: ★★★); dry pale ale **Mama** (5%: ★★★); golden-blond saison **MannenLiefde** (6%: ★★+), spiced with lemongrass and Szechuan pepper; full-bodied stout **Panty** (6%: ★★★); fruity bitter IPA **Gaia** (7%: ★★★); **Thai Thai** (8%: ★★+) tripel spiced with galangal, lemongrass, chilli and coriander; and chewy, dark and lovely imperial stout **Kinder Yoga** (11%: ★★★).
SEASONAL: dry-hopped spring lager **Avatar** (4.5%: ★★+); summer grapefruity session IPA **Pais Tropicale** (4.5%: ★★★); and winter double IPA **Hosanna** (9%: ★★+).
ALSO: **Rubberen Robbie** (6.7%: ★★+), a subtly rounded smoked porter brewed with Prael. **Studio Oedipus** is a numbered experimental series.

Oersoep

Waalbandijk 14D, 6541 AJ Nijmegen
T 06 2506 4611
oersoepbrouwerij.nl

Founded in 2012, Primordial Soup moved in 2014 to its current location in the former Honig Fabriek starch factory, installing a 10hl kit and opening the Stoom taproom later that year (see cafés). It's particularly noted for producing wild and mixed fermentation, wood-aged and sour beers and other non-standard styles, with usually excellent results. Several barrel-aged brews develop their character in huge 75hl vats on site, but, for capacity reasons and to reduce the risk of cross-contamination, the more conventional products are made in bulk at Proef in Belgium. The landowner plans to redevelop the site so the brewery may have to move, but this appears still to be years away. Tours with tastings for groups of 10 or more.
BEERS INCLUDE: strongly hoppy session IPA **Hopfather** (4.9%: ★★★); dry, wheat-based saison **Freewheel** (5%: ★★+); and fruity, hoppy saison **Sergeant Pepper** (7%: ★★★). Other beers change regularly but recent stars have been: **Popsicle** (4.5%: ★★★+), a complex raspberry sour; dry-hopped sour **Berlin, Berlin** (4.7%: ★★★); and **Lawnmower** (6.6%: ★★★), a dry and bitter IPA with Brett yeast.
SEASONAL: refreshing spring session ale **Offspring** (5.5%: ★★+); summer sour **Juicebox Hero** (3.9%: ★★★); and cocoa-heavy dubbelbock **Sexy Motherbocker** (8.4%: ★★+).
ALSO: **Load** (usually ★★★), a series of extra-hoppy IPAs.

Oijen

Oijense Bovendijk 61, 5394 LA Oijen
T 0412 492217
speciaalbierbrouwerij.nl

Small farmhouse brewery and distillery founded in 2002 near the Maas in North Brabant, mostly supplying its own taproom and restaurant. Beers are brewed in 2hl batches, with spent grain used to feed the pigs kept in pens by the car park. Tours on request.

BEERS INCLUDE: malty blond **Pilske** (5%: ★★); balanced **Witbier** (5%: ★★); reasonable **Blond** (6%: ★★); standard dryish dubbel **Donker** (6%: ★★); fruity-hoppy **IPA** (6%: ★★+); caramel-tinged **Amber** (6%: ★★); and unsubtle blond barley wine **Kaboem** (10%: ★★).
SEASONAL: chestnutty **Bokbier** (7.2%: ★★+) and sweetish alcoholic blond **Help Henk de Winter Door** (9%: ★★), Henk being one of the abovementioned pigs.

unfiltered pilsener **Goud** (5.3%: ★★); solid amber **Dunkel Weizen** (5.5%: ★★+); refreshing **Weizen** (5.8%: ★★); standout, peaty smoky **Rauch** (6.2%: ★★★); a bitter-finishing **Blond** (6.5%: ★★); strong wheat ale **Doppel Weizen** (8%: ★★+); and sweetish **Tripel** (8.9%: ★★).

Onder de Linden

Haagsteeg 16, 6708 PM Wageningen
T 0317 843559
onderdelindenwageningen.nl

This café-based microbrewery was founded in 1989 but closed in 2012 following the death of the original brewer. It restarted under new ownership a couple of years later, reviving the old recipes mainly for sale in the café and a few other places locally, and also making liqueurs under the name Moonshine.
BEERS INCLUDE: standard dry **Wagenings Blond** (7.4%: ★★); bitter blond **Wagenings Tripel** (7.5%: ★★+); and delicately restrained **IPA** (8.1%: ★★+).

Ootmarsummer

Commanderieplein 6, 7631 EA Ootmarsum
T 0541 760808
othmarbier.nl

Founded by two friends in 2012 after one inherited a 10hl brewery, fermentation and lagering tanks and a bottling line from his father, who we infer was a pretty serious home brewer. They started out making their **Othmar** beers, compliant with the Bavarian purity law, in an edge-of-town industrial site, but moved in 2016 to a more central location in a restored building beside an open air museum (openluchtmuseumootmarsum.nl) with a 20hl copper brewhouse and taproom. Tours and tastings for groups of 10 or more.
BEERS INCLUDE: nettly but thin **Session IPA** (2.9%: ★★); malty blond **Pilsner** (5%: ★★);

Opener

Veepad 33, 5105 AG Dongen
T 0162 223200
opener.nl

North Brabant brewery with its own kit since 2015. Shop open Sa 09.00–13.00; visits, workshops and tours by appointment.
BEERS INCLUDE: blond hefeweizen **White Now** (5%: ★★); bitterish multi-hopped English IPA **Hopsession** (5.5%: ★★); dry saison **Saisoff** (6.7%); inoffensive **Simply Blonde** (7%: ★★); spicy tripel **TripleX** (9.5%: ★★); and bitter-sweet barley wine **Jackhammer** (10%: ★★+).

Oproer

Westkanaaldijk 5-10, 3542 DA Utrecht
T 06 1891 4623
oproerbrouwerij.nl

'Riot' was the result of the 2016 merger of Rooie Dop and RUIG, at first making 4.5hl batches in the CAB buildng for the onsite taproom (see cafés) and beyond. Growing demand for its uniformly high-quality beers spurred an expansion to a 25hl kit at a separate location.
BEERS INCLUDE: highly hopped quaffable pale ale **24/7 Session Ale** (3.9%: ★★★); superb hop-forward **Uncut IPA** (6.2%: ★★★+); dry hoppy **Blonde Enigma** (6.2%: ★★+); black IPA **Black Flag** (6.5%: ★★★) with liquorice hints; nettly-fresh fruity blond double IPA **Refuse/ Resist** (8.5%: ★★★); bittersweet **Imperial Oatmeal Stout** (9.5%: ★★★), a heady mix of roasted malt, chocolate, oats and prune,

even better in its **barrel-aged** form (★★★+); and no-holds-barred barley wine **Dark Storm** (10%: ★★★).
ALSO: dozens of collaboration brews and one-off experiments.

Oudaen

Oudegracht 99, 3511 AE Utrecht
T 030 200 4276
oudaen.nl

Brewery installed in 1990 in the basement of a historic canalside manor house in the city centre, mainly selling its beer in the bar above (see cafés). Heineken acquired a stake in 2017, although we're unclear about the level of control. Group visits by appointment.
BEERS INCLUDE: a **Pilsener** (5%: ★★+) with more character than many; soft unfiltered **Witbier** (5%: ★★); and inoffensive little brown job **Dubbel** (7%: ★★).

Oude Rijn

Rijndijk 269, 2394 CE Hazerswoude-Rijndijk
T 06 5171 6271
deouderijn.nl

Homebrewer with a commercial licence since 2009, making occasional 50l runs of **Bruno** beers from organic ingredients in a garden shed. The restricted output and negligible distribution ensure extreme rarity.
BEERS INCLUDE: wheat ale **5.2** (5.2%); blond **6.3** (6.3%: ★★); warming dubbel **8.2** (8.2%: ★★); IPA/tripel hybrid **9.5** (9.5%); and dark-brown barley wine **10.2** (10.2%: ★★+).

Oudeland

Trompetstraat 74, 3335 DH Zwijndrecht
T 085 060 9787
brouwerijoudeland.nl

South Holland microbrewery founded in 2017 by two friends using a 2.5hl installation.
BEERS INCLUDE: weizenbock **De Witte** (4.6%); coffee stout **Stoute Ellen** (5%); **Swindregts Dubbel Blond** (7%); and dubbel **Dark Ale** (7%).

Parkzicht

Museumplein 3, 9641 AD Veendam
T 0598 666888
bogdike.com

This brewery in the hotel of the same name began in 2018 with distinctive 5hl glass brewing vessels inherited from the defunct Graaf van Heumen brewery. Brewing usually takes place weekly on Sundays, and beers appear under the **Bogdike** brand, named after a local cultural society and pronounced as in English. The head brewer also makes his own beers here under the name Melessen (see Brewers without breweries). Tours and tastings by arrangement.
BEERS INCLUDE: sweetish gold-blond **Weizen** (4.8%: ★★); dry, citric, unchallenging **Veendammer Wit** (4.8%: ★★); sweetish unfiltered pilsener **Ongefilterde Puur** (4.8%: ★★); tropical-fruity amber **Hazewinkel's IPA** (4.9%: ★★+); dryish **Tammo's Blond** (6%: ★★+) with hazelnut hints; and coriander-spiced **Adriaan's Tripel** (8%: ★★).

Pauw

Achterbroekweg 1, 7731 PN Ommen
T 0546 671363
pauwbier.nl

Two brothers founded the Peacock brewery in 1996, moving in 2011 to a 5hl installation in a thatched barn on the remote farm where they were born, 20 minutes' walk from the nearest road. They brew with homegrown barley "in the old way", using scales, thermometers, a watch and "common sense", and sell the results through regional outlets. Visits can be arranged but bring a map and boots.
BEERS INCLUDE: citrussy **Wit** (5%: ★★); lightly honeyed **Blonde Trots** (6.5%: ★★); fruity, dry **Bokbier** (6.5%: ★★); rounded dubbel **Pauw's Trots** (6.5%: ★★+); and sweetish, aniseedy barley wine **Zwaar Bier** (8%: ★★+). Seasonal **Zometrots**, **Herfsttrots** and **Wintertrots** are simply repackaged versions of the Wit, Bok and Zwaar respectively.

Pelgrim

Aelbrechtskolk 12, 3024 RE Rotterdam (Delfshaven)
T 010 477 1189
pelgrimbier.nl

This long-established brewpub (see cafés) on the historic quayside at Delfshaven, opened in 1996, now brews roughly 10hl a week of reliably good quality beer. Most is for the house taps although bottled beers are seen elsewhere. Some is also used to make mustard, pâté, chocolates, cheese and syrups. Group tours for eight or more people.
BEERS INCLUDE: unfiltered dry pale ale **Stoombier** (5%: ★★+); lightly bitter English-style **India Pale Ale** (5%: ★★+); drinkable **Weizen** (5.2%: ★★+); dry **Saison** (6%: ★★); lightly bitter tripel **Mayflower** (7.8%: ★★); liquorice-laced imperial stout **Vagabond** (8%: ★★+); and sledgehammer barrel-aged stout **Armada** (11%: ★★★).
SEASONAL: spring meibock **Lammetjes** (6.5%: ★★); its beefier blond sister **Dubbellam** (7.6%: ★★+); sharply refreshing

summer wheat **Zonnelief** (5.8%: ★★+) with raspberry; sweetish autumn **Bock** (6%: ★★); and more complex **Dubbelbock** (8%: ★★+).

Pimpelier

Grootschoterweg 24, 6023 AS Budel-Schoot
T 06 3067 0163
pimpelier.nl

The founder of this 2018 North Brabant brewery, a homebrewer with 30 years' experience, had the advantage of a day job working in AB InBev's quality team, enabling him to acquire a 14hl copper vessel once used at the Stella Artois brewery in Leuven, although it has a leak and can't be filled above 10hl. His 40hl fermentation tanks are from the old Oranjeboom site in Breda. Shop open Fr 13.00–19.00, Sa 13.00–17.00; tours at other times on request.
BEERS INCLUDE: citrussy witbier **De Witte van Schoet** (5%: ★★); bitter-finishing peachy blond **Bittersweet Symphonie** (6%: ★★+); fruity dubbel **Secretum** (6.4%: ★★); lightly bitter blond **Het 8ste Sacrament** (6.5%: ★★); golden, lightly fruity **Helleveeg** (7%: ★★); bittersweet amber **Hoppy** (7%: ★★+); dry dark saison **Kietelaar** (7%: ★★); Cascade dry-hopped IPA-ish **Boemel** (7.6%: ★★+); and coriander-spiced brown ale **Moppie** (8%: ★★).
ALSO: a wide variety of fruit beers, mostly as one-offs.

Pimpelmeesch

Ginderdoorstraat 4a, 4861 CC Chaam
T 0161 491615
pimpelmeesch.nl

Created in 2010 in rural North Brabant,
Blue Tit now brews in 6hl batches in a
lovingly restored thatched farmstead,
and also hires itself to other brewers.
The adjacent café is technically a separate
business but sufficiently joined at the hip
to be considered a taproom (see cafés).
Tours for groups of 10+ by appointment.
BEERS INCLUDE: sweet-edged **Chaams
Hefeweizen** (5.5%: ★★); multigrained
oversweet blond **Baken van Breda** (6%: ★+);
better blond **Zilverpel** (6.5%: ★★); balanced
Chaamse Dubbel (7%: ★★); waning star hoppy
pale ale **Goudpel** (7%: ★★+); improved dry
Chaamse Tripel (8.5%: ★★+); **Tripel Oak**
(8.5%: ★★+), as the last but aged in oak;
and standout **Socius Oak** (8.5%: ★★★) which
travels the more-familiar wood-matured
imperial stout route.
SEASONAL: fruity session IPA **Pracht van
Chaam** (4.2%: ★★+) intended for spring and
summer; autumnal **Chaams Bockbier** (6.8%:
★★), which gains subtle vanilla in its **oak-aged**
form (★★+); and copper-amber barley wine
Chaams Winterbier (8.5%: ★★+).
ALSO: blond **Toontje Schoen** (6%: ★★),
made for the adjoining café. Some core beers
are also repackaged with dubiously sexist
labels: Hefeweizen appears as **Heisse
Weissen**; Dubbel as **Vurige Non**; Tripel as
Blonde Snol; and Winterbier as **Kerst Snol**.

Pinas

Pinaskade 70, 2725 ER Zoetermeer
brouwerijdepinas.nl

Named after a class of sailing ship, nano-scale
Pinas was founded in 2017 by a long-term
homebrewer, currently making around 100l
each week for local sale.
BEERS INCLUDE: blond **Stien** (6.5%); dubbel
Stijn (8%); and dark heavyweight seasonal
Winterbier (10%).

PochPoater

Elsener Bierbrouwerij PochPoater
Diependaalseweg 14, 7475 SW Markelo
T 0548 521479
elsenerbierbrouwerij.nl

The address given for this Overijssel village
brewery, founded in 2014, is for administration:
brewing in 50l batches takes place around the
corner at the Herberg de Kemper (Kemperweg
4, Markelo; **herbergdekemper.nl**), also a
virtual taproom as the beers are sold there
as well as in numerous other local outlets.
Visits and tastings by arrangement.
BEERS INCLUDE: session saison **Boajngengr**
(2.5%: ★★); fruity wheat-based IPA
Skiethoppe (5%: ★★+); lemon and chilli-spiced
blond **Flantuutn** (6.5%: ★★+); stout-leaning
black IPA **Zwatn Kedoes** (7%: ★★+); citrussy
double IPA **Hopzoep** (8%: ★★+); banana-tinged
but balanced dark saison **Doesterik** (8%: ★★+);
imperial stout **Ondog** (9.5%: ★★+); warming
amber barley wine **Prookereur** (10%: ★★+);
and dozens more.

Poesiat & Kater

Polderweg 648, 1093 KP Amsterdam
T 020 333 1050
poesiatenkater.nl

This brewpub opened in 2015 in the ammonia
plant of a former gasworks is named after two
1890s employees of Amsterdam's Gekroonde
Valk brewery. Heineken continued to produce
beers from its **Van Vollenhoven** range for a
while after closing it in 1949. These were much
missed when they were discontinued and have
since been revived here, albeit in tweaked
versions. Beers under the current brewery's
own brand are more modern in style, though
named after former Gekroonde Valk workers.
Poesiat & Kater BEERS INCLUDE: crisp dry
session IPA **Little Smuling** (3.1%: ★★+);
drinkable **Kercken Porter** (4.7%: ★★);
hazy pale ale **Muuke** (5.7%: ★★); hoppy IPA
Smuling (6.5%: ★★+); and sweetish multi-
grain tripel **Kaintz** (8.5%: ★★).
Van Vollenhoven BEERS INCLUDE: citrussy

witbier **Princesse Bier** (5.5%: ★★); light pale ale **Falcon Ale** (6.2%: ★★+); gentle blond IPA-ish **East India Pale Ale** (6.5%: ★★+); autumnal, chestnutty **Bokbier** (6.5%: ★★+); and balanced, warming flagship **Extra Stout** (7.1%: ★★★).

Prael

Oudezijds Voorburgwal 30, 1012 GD Amsterdam
Nieuwe Hemweg 2, 1013 BG Amsterdam (Houthavens)
Boterdiep 75, 9712 LL Groningen
Esperantoplein 20, 2518 LE Den Haag
T (main) 020 408 4470
deprael.nl

De Prael isn't just a brewery but a work rehabiliation scheme for people who are living with significant mental illness, and its head brewer and guiding light, Fer Kok, is a fully qualified mental health professional. It began in 2002 in an industrial area in the Amsterdam suburbs and was originally to be called De Parel (the Pearl) after a 17th century brewery, but the spelling was changed to avoid a clash with the Budels beer Parel. In 2008, it moved to the Red Light District in the city centre where it soon added a shop (*daily 12.00–19.00*) and taproom (see cafés). Its beers have grown steadily in quality and confidence and its empire has since expanded, with brewpubs in Amsterdam Houthavens, Den Haag and Groningen, and a fifth location in Utrecht (Oude Vleutenseweg 33) in development, although not every site was yet brewing at the time of writing. Lindeboom, a long-time supporter, took an undisclosed minor stake in 2017. Group tours and 'brew yourself' days by arrangement.

BEERS INCLUDE: glorious **Milk Stout** (4.9%: ★★★), with macaroon and burnt caramel hints; dry **Code Blond** (5.1%: ★★+), made occasionally with rainwater when available; lightly spiced **Weizen** (5.4%: ★★); gently bitter **Bitterblond** (5.7%: ★★); dry and bitter **IPA** (6.5%: ★★+); sensibly smoked amber **Rookbier** (5.7%: ★★★); hazy, hoppy IPA **New England Style** (5.7%: ★★+); solid dry **Pale Ale** (6.1%: ★★+); German-style amber **Dortmunder** (6.4%: ★★+); strong blond **Tripel** (7.5%: ★★); sweetish **Scotch Ale** (7.9%: ★★+); fruity, strongly bitter double IPA **DIPA** (9%: ★★+); bittersweet amber **Barley Wine** (9.6%: ★★); and malt-forward **Quadrupel** (11.5%: ★★+), for cold evenings. Also: three regular collaboration brews are English-style bitter **Klassieker** (4.5%: ★★+) with Bijdehand; **Rubberen Robbie** (6.7%: ★★+) smoked porter with Oedipus; and **Kinky Koos** (5.4%: ★★+) saison with Two Chefs.

Praght

Staalwijk 8C, 8251 JX Dronten
T 0321 329321
brouwerijpraght.nl

Founded in 2007 to offer work experience to people with disabilities and the long-term unemployed, this Flevoland brewery produces well-made and improving beers that are unfiltered, unpasteurised, compliant with the Bavarian purity law and widely found across the region. It was forced to relocate from its original semi-rural spot on a farm to an industrial estate in 2018. Tours and tastings for groups of 10 or more.

BEERS INCLUDE: straightforward bitter blond **Polderpionier** (6%: ★★); multi-grained US-hopped 'Polder IPA' **P.I.PA.** (6.5%: ★★+); dry beech-smoked **Rookbier** (7%: ★★+); solid, dry-edged **Tripel** (8%: ★★); bitter, full-bodied **Stout Export** (8%: ★★+); and perilously drinkable, warming barley wine **Zware Blonde** (10%: ★★+).
ALSO: various one-offs, mostly found at festivals.

Princen

Princen Brouwerijen
Haarlemmerstraatweg 73G, 1165 MK Halfweg
T 085 666 1111
princenbier.nl

Housed near Haarlem, this North Holland brewery rose in 2013 from the ashes of Olm Bier, a company that went out of business after Heineken sued it for filling branded kegs with its own products. That should tell you much of what you need to know. Its single core product **Princen** (5%: ★+) is a dull pilsener brewed in industrial quantities for café drinkers with low expectations. **Van Buuren** pilsener, ostensibly made for another 'brewing' client, is probably the same recipe in a different jacket, or very close to it.

Pronck

Langegracht 70D, 2312 NV Leiden
T 06 2244 3814
brouwerijpronck.nl

Pronken means to show off or flaunt, and these confident South Holland brewers have every right to. Production of good quality beers in a variety of styles has grown since founding in 2014 to around 50hl a month in 8hl batches. Individual tours and tastings every third Sa of each month (14.30, 17.00; or by arrangement at other times for groups of 12 or more.
BEERS INCLUDE: refreshingly bitter **Citra Rye IPA** (5%: ★+), with Earl Grey tea; herbal, flowery multi-grained **Witbier** (5.5%: ★★+)

with lavender; aromatic, variously hopped **White IPA** (5.5%: ★★★); fruity golden **El Dorado IPA** (6.3%: ★★★) with apricot hints; bittersweet English-style **Nut Brown Ale** (7%: ★★+) with chestnuts and date palm juice; bittersweet **Tripel** (9%: ★★+); and nutty, rich **Imperial Porter** (11%: ★★★), spiced with cardamom, vanilla and juniper.

Puik

Oude Apeldoornseweg 70A,
7333 GD Apeldoorn
puikbieren.nl

Former homebrewer selling beers through local outlets since 2015, usually in bottles featuring 1950s-style pin-ups on the labels, for better or worse. A new city centre brewpub (possibly Beekstraat 12) is at the planning stage as we write.
BEERS INCLUDE: multi-grain citrussy witbier **Stout Witsje** (5.7%: ★★+); sweetish **Blonde Donder** (6%: ★★); fruity-bitter US-hopped IPA **Dartele Deerne** (7.1%: ★★+); bittersweet tripel **Zwaar Blond** (8.2%: ★★); **Krachtpatser** (9.5%: ★★+) imperial porter; and unsubtle quadrupel **Vurige Bliksem** (10.2%: ★★).
ALSO: **Kiekeboe**, an ever-changing experimental brew, and various seasonals.

Puzzelaer (Terheijden)

Munnikenhof 20, 4844 PK Terheijden
T 06 3025 6465
bieruitbrabant.nl

North Brabant's Puzzler brewery began at 3 Horne in 2015, moving to its own 3hl single-vessel kit two years later. It shares a site with the Munnickenheid B&B and campsite (munnickenheide.nl), but has no taproom. Group tours can be booked via the website. NB The name changed to Terheijden in 2020.
BEERS INCLUDE: **Experimental Saison** (5%: ★★), which appears to have an unchanging recipe despite the name; inoffensive **Brabants Blondje** (6.5%: ★★); and sweetish blond **Traais Tripeltje** (8.2%: ★★).

Radboud

Gedempt Achterom 4, 1671 AG Medemblik
T 0227 823393
stadsbrouwerijradboud.nl

This North Holland brewery was founded in
2016 in an attractive town beside the
IJsselmeer, in a building that was once home
to another brewery but more recently served
time as a garage. It normally produces 40hl
per week with two double brewdays on a
10hl kit, and facilitates other brewers
including Die. Tours, tastings and cooking
workshops by arrangement.
BEERS INCLUDE: flagship hoppy pale ale
Lord Murray (4.5%: ★★+); dryish blond **Floris
V** (4.8%: ★★+); dry, bitter Weizen (4.9%: ★★);
De Eerste (6.6%: ★★+), a dry witbier with
bog myrtle; sweetish copper-amber **Dubbele
Blik** (7.2%: ★★); and lightly perfumed tripel
Kwaaie Pier (9.5%: ★★+).

Ramses

Thijssenweg 20a, 4927 PC Wagenberg
T 06 2951 7085
ramsesbier.nl

Ramses Snoeij worked at craft breweries in
the US before starting to brew under his own
first name in 2009, initially working elsewhere
but with his own 15hl brewhouse in a village
near Breda since 2013. His mainly single-hopped
beers rapidly entered the Dutch Premier

League and have stayed there ever since, even
when he's playing with exotic ingredients such
as dried Amazonian lemon ants. No taproom
or tours on site, but BRACK, a shared taproom
with Bliksem, opened in Breda in 2019 (see cafés).
BEERS INCLUDE: fruity weizen **Zwaluws Nat**
(4.8%: ★★+); top-fermented hoppy lager
Ibis (5%: ★★+); dryish UK-hopped kuit saison
Kuiter (5.5%: ★★+); mocha-starting, fruity-
bitter ending **Mamba Porter** (6%: ★★★+);
Naar de Haaien (6%: ★★★), a zingy golden
'seaman's ale' made with oak and sea water;
triple-hopped blond **Hop** (6.5%: ★★+), with
Irish moss; **Koele Kikker** (6.6%: ★★+), a
Munich-style dark lager containing bison grass;
all-round excellent IPA **Den Dorstige Tijger**
(6.6%: ★★★★); superior dry-edged dubbel
Willem Bever (6.9%: ★★★); its occasionally
seen fruity variant **Eduard Bever** (6.9%: ★★★+)
with 300kg of cherries in each batch; subtly
double-hopped double IPA **We Are Hop**
(7%: ★★★); dry-hopped bitter 'golden ale'
Rotskruiper (7.5%: ★★+); honeyed, balanced
Antenne Tripel (8.8%: ★★★), also sometimes
seen as citrussy **Ant-Tenne Tripel** (8.8%: ★★★)
with the aforementioned ants; superbly bitter
but rounded imperial IPA **Trilobiet** (9%: ★★★);
and occasional imperial rye stout **Roggestout
VOC** (10%: ★★★★), brewed to a 17th-century
recipe then lagered in whisky casks.
ALSO: dozens of specials.

RBM

Ringbobbel Bier Mate Rooise Bierbrouwers
Kremselen 2, 5492 SM Sint-Oedenrode
T 06 8394 0691
rbm-brouwerij.nl

This rural North Brabant brewery with a name that's mercifully usually abbreviated was founded in 2018 by six friends in a barn at the Gasthuishoeve, partly a folk museum, partly a working farm. Its neighbours include a clog factory, a hay store, the local tourist office, a shop, bakery, café and greenhouse terrace (see cafés). Tours and workshops by arrangement.
BEERS INCLUDE: light, nutty-dry **Kremsels Blond** (6%: ★★); chestnut-tinged standout **Dubbel** (7%: ★★+); and spiced **Rooysche Tripel** (8%: ★★).
SEASONAL: amber spring **Vûrjaor Bier** (7%: ★★+).
ALSO: beers labelled as **Heren Van Rode's Vrijheid** are experimental one-offs.

Redbad

Neptunusweg 5, 8938 AA Leeuwarden
T 06 1252 6222
facebook.com/redbadbeer

Named after an ancient king of Leeuwaarden, this Friesland operation was founded by friends in 2015 to make German-style beers, some on their own tiny 50l kit, the rest elsewhere.
BEERS INCLUDE: a restrained **Weizen** (5.3%: ★★+); dry amber dunkelweizen **Zwarte Ridder** (5.8%: ★★+), and fruity, banana-edged **Weizenbock** (7%: ★★+).

Reeuwijk

Edisonstraat 39a, 2811 EM Reeuwijk
T 06 2785 6001
brouwerijreeuwijk.com

Launched in 2018, this South Holland brewery claims to work in traditional ways "without machines", and early results indicate a preference for IPA variants.

BEERS INCLUDE: dry, bitter **NEIPA** (6.5%: ★★+); unexciting **IPA-TJE** (6.5%: ★★); stoutish cocoa-edged **Dark IPA** (7%: ★★+); and sweetish dark **DIPA** (8.5%: ★★).

Reijngoud

Vijverhofstraat 10, 3032 SN Rotterdam
T 010 503 6327
brewpubreijngoud.nl

Brewpub established in 2019 by the owner of the Reijngoud and Boudewijn bars (see cafés). Early beers showed promise but were brewed at Brouwerij Utrecht – the in-house kit went into operation at the end of 2019.
BEERS INCLUDE: summer pale ale **Hoppa** (4.3%: ★★+); weizen **Je Bennie Weiss** (5.6%; ★★); and lightly hoppy grapefruit IPA **Natte T** (6%: ★★+).

Reuzen

Heizenschedijk 1, 5066 PL Moergestel
T 06 2650 4546
reuzenbieren.nl

Giants is a collective of former homebrewers who went commercial in 2010. Beers were initially brewed elsewhere, but a brewhouse and taproom opened in the North Brabant countryside in 2018, inside the Reuselhoeve events venue (see cafés).
ReuZ BEERS INCLUDE: light hoppy quaffer **Session Pale Ale** (3.5%: ★★+); delicate, subtly fruity **Imperial Lager** (6.8%: ★★); lightweight **Dubbel** (7%: ★★); dry, hoppy **Blond** (7.5%: ★★+); malty blond **Tripel** (8%: ★★); fruity-hoppy **IPA** (8.5%: ★★+); a **Stout** (9.5%: ★★+) with strong cocoa and burnt coffee; rich amber **Barley Wine** (10%: ★★+) with hints of crème brûlée; intense, hoppy and delicious **Black IPA** (10%: ★★★); full-bodied **Koffie Porter** (10.5%: ★★+); and sweetish amber **Quadrupel** (11.5%: ★+), with too much banana ester for its own good.
SEASONAL: above-average **Lentebock** (5.5%: ★★+) and autumnal **Dubbelbock** (7.8%: ★★).

Rigters

Alsteedseweg 38, 7481 RW Haaksbergen
rigtersbier.nl

A 10hl brewhouse in a former cheese factory
south of Enschede, launched in 2014 and also
renting out excess capacity to others. Its
beers are stocked at the Hooge Esch pancake
restaurant (hoogeeschbuurse.nl) next door.
Tours with tastings by appontment.
BEERS INCLUDE: citrussy witbier **Lust** (4.5%:
★★+); dry-hopped gold-blond **Better
Together** (5.3%: ★★); intense six-hopped IPA
I Like Big Hops and I Cannot Lie (6.6%: ★★+);
cocoa-edged black IPA **Ptch Blck** (7.6%:
★★+); and full-bodied **D-IPA** (8%: ★★+).
SEASONAL: spring blond **Please Don't
Feed the Lamb** (6.7%) and autumnal dark
Please Don't Feed the Goat (7.5%).
ALSO: standard Belgian styles in the **Buurse**
range, including a dull **Blond** (6.1%: ★★) and
restrained **Tripel** (7.2%: ★★).

Rijkshotel

Dorpstraat 203 A, 5504 HG Veldhoven
T 06 1851 3283
brouwerijhetrijkshotel.nl

This nanobrewery founded by two friends in
2019 is in former police cells, thus its ironic
name the State Hotel. Early efforts such as
Goelag 2.0 (10.8%: ★★+) show promise and
a preference for strong stouts and porters.

Rijpelaer

Zeelandhof 11, 5709 EL Helmond
T 06 1183 7990
derijpelaer.nl

North Brabant brewery founded in 2016,
currently working on a small scale in the
owner's garage.
BEERS INCLUDE: lightly smoked wheat ale
Straakven (5.4%: ★★); herbal blond **Allodium**
(6%: ★★+) spiced with coriander and Irish
moss; dubbel **Broedersbos** (7.3%: ★★);
golden tripel **Maria Oord** (8%: ★★); dry,

bitter IPA **Het Vliegveld B86** (8.9%: ★★+),
named after a nearby British wartime airfield;
and rounded porter **Buurtschap** (9.7%: ★★+),
with subtle star anise

Rock City

Mijnbouwweg 15, 3812 RT Amersfoort
T 033 202 2230
rockcitybrewing.com

Established in 2014, Rock City shed its skin and
moved into a bespoke brewpub on a business
park in 2018. Besides the adventurous core
range, it is licensed to brew more traditional
styles under the historic **Phoenix** label.
Tours and tastings by arrangement.
Rock City *BEERS INCLUDE:* aromatic session
blond **Peach Squeezer** (4%: ★★+); hoppy
golden **Amersfoort Pale Ale** (5.8%: ★★+);
flagship sweetish tripel **Koene Ridder** (8%:
★★); **Maker's Monk** (8%: ★★+), a raisiny,
bourbon-infused 'abbey ale'; and all manner
of one-offs.
SEASONAL: hoppy spring blond, the beautifully named **Brews Springsteen** (4.5%: ★★+).
Phoenix *BEERS INCLUDE:* cocoa-heavy
Porter (4.9%: ★★+); lightly perfumed **Weizen**
(5%: ★★); above-average dry **Blond** (6%: ★★+);
and tripel-ish **Sterk Blond** (7.5%: ★★).

Rockin' Ludina

Turfsingel 12–14, 9712 KP Groningen
T 050 721 0901
rockinludina.nl

Two employees of the Toeter (see cafés) began brewing in 2015 with a 50l test kit on the 'tjalk' sailing boat *Ludina*, built in 1910, which serves as the café terrace. The brewery is now land-based a few doors down the road, with a 3hl installation bought from Leidsch when that brewery upgraded.
BEERS INCLUDE: dry milk stout **Noah's Ark** (4.5%: ★★+); bitter IPA **Barbarossa** (5.5%: ★★+); lightly bitter blond **Belgian Mermaid** (6.6%: ★★+); and fruity saison **De Tromp** (6%: ★★).
ALSO: **Ludina Specials** are one-off, usually barrel-aged beers.

Rolduc

Stichting Brouwgilde Abdij Rolduc
Heyendallaan 82, 6464 EP Kerkrade
T 06 3040 8140
rolduc.com

This Limburg microbrewery founded in 2013 is based in Rolduc abbey, now a hotel. It operates as a separate business, though its beers are often sold in the hotel's Kanunnik brasserie (*Mo-Th 11.30–20.30; Fr-Su 10.30–21.00*). Tours for groups of 10 or more.
BEERS INCLUDE: Belgian-style blond **Rolduc Abdijbier** (6.3%: ★★); fruity hoppy IPA **Kloeëster** (6.5%: ★★); dark **Rolduc Dubbel** (7%: ★★); and golden **Blonde Non** (8%).

Roodbaard

Leerlooijerij 8, 4651 SM Steenbergen
gebroedersroodbaard.nl

This North Brabant nanobrewery, founded in 2016 by two red-bearded brothers-in-law, numbers its beers from 2 upwards: No.1 is held back for whenever they succeed in brewing their 'best beer ever.' It hasn't yet been allocated, though the output so far is decent enough.

BEERS INCLUDE: middling dubbel **No.2** (7%: ★★); coriander-spiced tripel **No.3** (8.6%: ★★+); sweetish if unsubtle barley wine **No.4** (11.1%: ★★+); blond wheat ale **No.5** (6.6%: ★★); bitter-finishing American IPA **No.6** (6.7%: ★★+); multi-grained citrussy tripel **No.7** (8.3%: ★★+); easy-going, cleverly balanced smoked coffee porter **No.8** (7.7%: ★★★); and bitter double IPA **No.9** (8.9%: ★★+). Beers numbered **10** and above are one-off barrel-aged brews.

Roos

Sint Sebastiaanstraat 4, 5081 ZG Hilvarenbeek
T 013 505 5045
bierbrouwerijderoos.nl

A former 19th century brewery building in this North Brabant village was restored by volunteers and opened as a museum in 2002, with a new brewhouse initially working under the name Museumbrouwerij De Roos. Though the brewery dropped its 'Museum' prefix in 2016, its beers, which have improved over the years, are still on sale in the on-site café.
BEERS INCLUDE: golden, lightly bitter **Roos Ale** (5.5%: ★★+); bitter but unassertive IPA **Waggelèèr** (6%: ★★); bittersweet, herbal red ale **Rooie Fik** (6.5%: ★★+); balanced amber **Konjel** (7%: ★★); improving **Bikse Tripel** (8%: ★★+).
SEASONAL: unsurprising **Meibok** (6.5%: ★★); spiced summer white ale **Witte Roos** (5.5%: ★★); autumnal **Herfstbock** (6.5%: ★★); and chestnutty **Winterbier** (8%: ★★+).

Rubelijn

De Roerdomp 69, 7609 WB Almelo
facebook.com/rubelijn

This one-man operation began ambitiously in 2015 by brewing at Rigters, but downsized in 2018 and now makes occasional 70l batches at home for local outlets.

Sallands –
see Huttenkloas

Santpoorts

Hofgeesterweg 6, 1991 AD Velserbroek
santpoortsbier.nl

Founded in 2013, this North Holland producer
has been based since 2018 at the Landzicht
farm B&B and events venue
(boerderijlandzicht.com) since 2018, using a
5hl kit which it shares with Kinhem (above),
although the two are separate businesses.
Tours and workshops by arrangement.
BEERS INCLUDE: lightweight **Session IPA**
(4.9%: ★★); blond **Speltweizen** (5.5%: ★★);
reasonably balanced amber **Rood Mout** (6.5%:
★★+); dubbel-like run-of-the-mill **Black IPA**
(7%: ★★); sweetish strong blond **Goud Gele
Rakker** (7.5%: ★★); standard gold-blond
Tripel (8.5%: ★★); and a rich, dark **Quadrupel**
(9.5%: ★★+) that ducks cloying sweetness.

Schans

De Schans 17–21, 1421 BA Uithoorn
T 0297 522106
schansbier.nl

This sleepy small brewery has quietly gone
about its business since 1998 in a sleepy
North Holland commuter town, gaining a
reputation for quality without marketing
splash. Beers can be hard to track down,
though there's now a taproom, bottle shop,
distillery and one-room B&B on the premises.
BEERS INCLUDE: fruity, nutty copper-amber
DMA (Dark Mild Ale) (3.5%: ★★+), with more
depth than its alcohol content suggests;
darkly bitter **Schwarz** (5%: ★★+) with
strong vanilla overtones; dryish, lightly

bitter **Guus Blond** (5.8%: ★★), named after
the late founding brewer; well-rounded dry
Saison (6%: ★★+); rich, dark, bitter, full-
bodied **Stout** (6.5%: ★★+); chocolatey,
porterish **Dubbel** (6.5%: ★★+); decent dry
Tripel (8.2%: ★★+); and richly rewarding
strong stout **Imperial** (8.8%: ★★★).
SEASONAL: spring blond **Lentedruppel** (5.5%:
★★+) and coffee stout-like **Winter** (8%: ★★★).

Schoemrakker

Torenstraat 47, 8881 BH West-Terschelling
schoemrakkerbierterschelling.nl

Terschelling's first proper brewery, named
with a local dialect word for 'sandpiper', has
made Belgian-style beers with dune water in
a 5hl installation since 2014. It is gradually
taking over the island, though rarely seen
on the mainland. The adjacent pub Storm
(see cafés) acts as the taproom.
BEERS INCLUDE: quaffing blond **Halmblond**
(5%: ★★); dry golden-blond **Brandaan** (6%:
★★+), good within its style; and cocoa-tinged
dubbel **Tjuster** (7.4%: ★★). *ALSO:* various
one-offs in a numbered **Craft Series**.

School

Koekoekslaan 14A, 1171 PJ Badhoevedorp
T 020 334 8056
brouwerijdeschool.com

Founded by two childhood friends in 2016 as
De Twee Knaapjes, this North Holland microbrewery changed a year later to its current
name, which means the same in Dutch as it
does in English. The beers are widely available
in nearby Amsterdam and beyond.
BEERS INCLUDE: above-average blond **Juffie**
(5.5%: ★★+); solid dry saison **Krijtje** (5.8%: ★★+);
light, citrussy IPA **Π (Pi)** (6%: ★★+); and unassuming golden tripel **Strafwerk** (8.2%: ★★).
SEASONAL: citrus-flavoured summer session
pale ale **Heilig Boontje** (3.5%: ★★+); and
'tiramisu stout' **Ouderavond** (8.5%: ★★+),
a liquid dessert.
ALSO: **'t Kofschip**, a changing series of
barrel-aged experiments (★★+ to ★★★).

Sint Crispijn

Gedempte Haven 1, 5141 JW Waalwijk
T 06 4529 7770
brouwerijsintcrispijn.nl

Founded in 2013, this North Brabant brewery originally worked at 3 Horne but acquired its own 5hl installation and taproom in a former grain warehouse in 2018. Brewing takes place once or twice a week and quality has improved. Individual tours Sa 14.30, 16.00, at other times for groups by arrangement.
BEERS INCLUDE: hoppy American pale ale **A.P.A.** (6%: ★★+); bitter red ale **Furieus** (6%: ★★+), with hints of blood orange; hoppy red IPA **Ruby Ruby Ruby** (6.2%: ★★+); bitter-finishing cocoa-edged stout **Swart** (6.5%: ★★+); improved Belgian-style **Blonde** (6.8%: ★★+); balanced smoked porter **1722** (7.8%: ★★+); dry and deceptive tripel **Zonnewende** (8.4%: ★★); and malty dark ale **Noir** (8.8%: ★★+).

Sint Joris

Grote Markt 19, 4811 XL Breda
T 076 889 8180
brouwerijstjoris.nl

Microbrewery established in 2016 in the cellars of the Boterhal (see cafés) since 2016. Group tours by arrangement, with the cellar taproom occasionally open to the public.
BEERS INCLUDE: dry witbier **Witte Geit** (5%: ★★); standard **Weerloos Blondje** (6%: ★★); its dark sister **Dubbele Tong** (7%: ★★); and blond tripel **Koppige Draak** (8.5%: ★★).

Sint Servattumus

Ericastraat 11b, 5482 WR Schijndel
T 06 1932 8967
sintservattumus.nl

Veteran North Brabant micro in an edge-of-town industrial building, brewing with variable results since 1996, with a sometimes regrettable tendency to throw fruit of all sorts into the mix. A radical revamp of the range announced in 2019 could herald better times ahead.

Group tours by appointment.
BEERS INCLUDE: pleasingly hoppy blond **Hopbelleke** (5.6%: ★★+); amber raspberry beer **Frambozen** (5.6%: ★★); and amber **Knalbier** (7.5%: ★★). A new **Speltbier** series includes citrussy **Weizen** (5.6%: ★★); blond **Enkel** (5.6%: ★★); wheatless spiced white ale **Wit** (6%: ★★); sweetish but drinkable **Stout** (6%: ★★+); sweetish **Dubbel** (7.5%: ★★); not too sweet honeyed amber **Honing** (8.5%: ★★+); and a standard **Tripel** (8%: ★★).
ALSO: bespoke house beers for several restaurants and cafés.

Slot Oostende

Singelstraat 5, 4461 HZ Goes
T 06 1456 2981
slotoostende.nl, emelisse.nl

This Zeeland brewpub with a 20hl installation has been housed since 2016 in an impressively restored ruined castle. Alongside the house range, **Emelisse** beers are brewed here under licence following the closure of that brewery in 2016, alongside head brewer Jens van Stee's Bad Hair brands (see Brewers without breweries). Individual tours Sa 15.00, 17.00 and at other times for groups.
Slot Oostende BEERS INCLUDE: malty wheat ale **Wit Voetje** (4.5%: ★★); decent bitter-finishing **Blonde Jacoba** (5%: ★★+); rounded gold-blond IPA **Straffe Non** (6.5%: ★★+); bittersweet ruby-brown **Dubbele Slot** (7%: ★★+); chocolatey bitter porter **Poortwachter** (7%: ★★); and malty tripel **Gouden Gans** (8%: ★★).

Emelisse *BEERS INCLUDE:* quaffable, bitter **Session IPA** (3.3%: ★★+); dry **Blond IPA** (5.8%: ★★+); lightly smoky **Smoked Rye IPA** (6.2%: ★★+); **DIPA** (7.9%: ★★+), still eminently drinkable but something of a faded star; intensely bitter **Black IPA** (8%: ★★★); moreish coffee-laden **Espresso Stout** (9.5%: ★★★); unsubtle golden **TIPA** (10%: ★★+); full-bodied **Imperial Russian Stout** (11%: ★★★); and toe-warmer **Barley Wine** (12%: ★★+).

ALSO: the **Emelisse White Label** series of barrel-aged imperial stouts and barley wines (usually ★★★).

Solaes

Oostdijk 36, 3245 AS Sommelsdijk
T 06 4912 0474
solaes.nl

This South Holland micro was established in 2016 with its own 4.5hl kit though we believe some longer runs are brewed elsewhere. No tours, but it has a lovely taproom (see cafés). *BEERS INCLUDE:* sweetish blond **Zes Gemeten** (6%: ★★); dry, perfumed amber IPA **Brut** (7%: ★★+); dry, nettle-hoppy amber wheat ale **Acht Gemeten** (8%: ★★); rounded, oak-aged dark barley wine **Stellebos** (10%: ★★★); and multi-grain imperial stout **MD10** (10%: ★★+).

Spierbier

Baljuwsstraat 3, 3641 BE Mijdrecht
T 06 1173 6464
spierbier.com

Utrecht brewer making mainly Belgian-style beers in 50l batches since 2014, sold relatively widely through local outlets. We believe an expansion is planned. No tours. *BEERS INCLUDE:* witbier **SpierWit** (5.5%: ★★); dry blond **InSpieratie** (6%: ★★); fruity tripel **Spierkracht** (8.3%: ★★+); and barrel-aged Baltic porter **ShakeSpier** (9.5%: ★★★).

Spinoza

Tulpenstraat 47, 2231 GV Rijnsburg
T 06 2423 3270
brouwerijspinoza.nl

South Holland nanobrewer making no more than 100l per month since 2016, so its beers are rare even in local outlets. *BEERS INCLUDE:* session **Vicus IPA**; dubbel **Geminus** (6%); **IPA** (6.9%); and **Blonde** (8.2%).

Stanislaus Brewskovitch

Stadsgravenstraat 59, 7511 ER Enschede
T 053 203 2470
stanislausbrewskovitch.nl

Founded in 2016, this former roaming outfit opened its own city-centre brewpub and shop with a 5hl installation in 2018. Its reliable and widely available products veer towards modern craft in style. *BEERS INCLUDE:* Australian-hopped session IPA **Koala Beer** (3.5%: ★★+); rounded red IPA **Tukr.** (5%: ★★+); banana-laced fruity **Barry Weizen** (5.2%: ★★+); 'coffee milk oatmeal stout' **Cappu Dei' Capi** (5.3%: ★★+), in which the coffee just wins in a gentleman's fight; subtly chilli-spiced and honeyed blond **Sambal Bij** (5.6%: ★★★), New Zealand-hopped stout **All Black** (7.5%: ★★); and **Triple Rock Church** (8%: ★★+), a multi-grained tripel. *ALSO:* numerous seasonal brews and collaborations.

Steffelaar

Industrieweg 93–95, 3044 AS Rotterdam
T 06 1044 7193
steffelaarbier.nl

A brewery-for-hire which has been making beer for others in 4hl batches since 2015, occasionally brewing under its own name between commissions.
BEERS INCLUDE: pils-like blond **Goud** (4.8%: ★★) and thinnish **Stout** (5%: ★★).

Sterck

Bosstraat 7, 4611 NA Bergen Op Zoom
T 0164 319000
brouwerijsterck.nl

Known as Merck when it was founded in 2018, this North Brabant brewery, currently based behind a town-centre delicatessen and selling through local outlets, took its current name a year later. Beers are numbered, using odd numbers for light and even ones for dark recipes, beginning with blond ale **5** (6.2%) and Belgian-style dark ale **10** (9.4%).

Stijl

Fellinilaan 151, 1325 TW Almere
T 06 1002 7270
brouwerijstijl.nl

This Flevoland outfit brewed at Berging when launched in 2015 but has since added its own kit.
BEERS INCLUDE: grapefruit-hoppy **Ally Pale Ale** (5.5%: ★★+); spicy **Dennentoppen Blond** (6.5%: ★★+) with added pine tops; clean-finishing dark **Basterd Dubbel** (7%: ★★); and **Russian Imperial Stout** (10%: ★★+) with sea salt and vanilla, rounded by bitterness.
ALSO: one-off experiments appear as **Bierlab**.

Strijder

Sonseweg 39, 5681 BH Best
brouwerijstrijder.nl

North Brabant microbrewery founded in 2017, currently making 2hl batches on the site of the Bevrijdende Vleugels (Wings of Liberation) military museum (bevrijdendevleugels.nl). Tastings and workshops for groups of 10 or more.
BEERS INCLUDE: solid witbier **Amerikaans Wit** (6%: ★★) and sweetish rye-based **Roggetripel** (8%: ★★).

Swambacchus

Korte Brouwersstraat 3, 6658 AC Beneden-Leeuwen
swambacchus.nl

Gelderland brewery opened in 2012, producing beers rarely seen outside the immediate area in 1hl batches on a more-or-less weekly basis.
BEERS INCLUDE: bittersweet **Lauwes Blond** (6%: ★★); a middling **Dubbel** (7.5%: ★★); hazy amber dunkelweizen **Bôjum** (8%: ★★); and Belgian-style **Drie Dijken Tripel** (8%: ★★).

Sweeler

Vereenigde Sweeler Bierbrouwers
Kloosterdwarsweg 2, 7851 AL Zweeloo
facebook.com/SweelerBier

This Drenthe brewer began in 2014 by using other people's kit before acquiring its own small setup in a former doctor's surgery near Emmen in 2016.
BEERS INCLUDE: clean blond flagship **Oes Pils** (5%: ★★); blond wheat ale **Wisper Witte** (5%); and brown ale **Machtige Möpper** (6.2%).

Swinkels (Bavaria)

De Stater 1, 5737 RV Lieshout
T 0499 428111
swinkelsfamilybrewers.com

Founded as Bavaria in 1719 and run by the Swinkels family since 1764, this historic North Brabant company has grown into the Netherlands' biggest independent brewing

group. It became a lager brewery in 1924, introduced one of the world's first alcohol-free beers in 1978 and in 1989 sold the first Western beer to the Soviet Union. It's now a global player of some clout, with an interest in several other breweries: it owns the brewhouse at Koningshoeven abbey (above), which we believe it uses to make its own ale-style brands; took full possession of De Molen (above) in 2019; and has a majority stake in Belgium's Palm group, which in turn owns Rodenbach among others. Its portolio also includes two maltings which between them control much of the Dutch market. Despite a cosmetic name change to Royal Swinkels Family Brewers in 2018 to play up its heritage, the branding of its core products as **Bavaria** has been left untouched. Group tours by arrangement.

BEERS INCLUDE: liquidised cereal **Oud Bruin** (3%: ★), less sweet than some; anaemic **Premium Pilsener** (5%: ★★), lacking much of anything, and also sold in **Gluten-Free** form and as **3.3** (3.3%: ★+), which tastes watered down; and unpasteurised pilsener **Swinckels' Volmaakt** (5.3%: ★★).
SEASONAL: sweetish **Bok** (6.5%: ★★), fermented as a lager.
ALSO: several low-alcohol and alcohol-free 'beers', some fruit-flavoured and all lacking in finesse; a subtlety-free **8.6** range for uncritical alcohol consumers on a budget; and own-label beer with tweaked recipes, notably **Kordaat** (5%: ★★), a light, unchallenging pilsener for the Lidl chain.

Techum

It Uleboerd 79, 8941 AS Leeuwarden
T 06 1293 4712

Friesland-based homebrewers who turned professional in 2018, making occasional beers using a 50l kit. To date they have only brewed seasonals: blond **Summer Ale** (5.2%) and autumnal **Hjerst Bock** (5.5%).

Tesselaar

Tesselaar Familiebrouwerij Diks
Spinbaan 11, 1791 MC Den Burg
T 06 3023 0277
biervantexel.nl

Maurice Diks, a co-founder of nearby Texelse (below), created this new, entirely family-run enterprise in 2017 by hand-building his own impressive 30hl kit. Beers are sold in the taproom and elsewhere on the island, with no ambition to export to the mainland. Walkup tours for a maximum of 20 people Tu-Su 14.00.
BEERS INCLUDE: dry, straw-blond wheat ale **Witte Tessel-aar** (4.9: ★★+); superior, crisp unfiltered pilsener **Eilandbier** (5%: ★★+); and dry blond **Eilandkriebel** (6.4%: ★★+).

Texelse

Schilderweg 214b, 1792 CK Oudeschild
T 0222 320325
texels.nl

Brewing in a rural corner of Texel since 1994, this is now among the Netherlands' largest micros, with nationwide distribution as well as a claimed 100% coverage of the island itself, including the bar on the ferry. Walkup tours throughout the year, with taproom and shop open on every tour day: check website for times.

BEERS INCLUDE: flagship dunkelweizen **Skuumkoppe** (5%: ★★+); fruity Irish red **Vuurbaak** (5%: ★★+); witbier **Wit** (5%: ★★); malty amber **Eyerlander** (5.5%: ★★); understated sweetish **Dubbel** (6.4%: ★★); golden-blond **Goudkoppe** (6%: ★★); and improved **Tripel** (8.5%: ★★+).
SEASONAL: sweetish but appealingly off-beat meibock **Springtij** (7.5%: ★★); straw-blond summer wheat ale **Seumerfeugel** (3.9%: ★★); full-bodied **Bock** (7.5%: ★★+); alleged dubbelbock **StormBock** (10%: ★★+), actually more a barley wine; and amber **Noorderwiend** (7.5%: ★★), too thin and sweet for cockle-warming on cold evenings.

Theodorus

Burg van Hulstlaan 44, 5384 LS Heesch
T 06 2043 4707
obunto.nl

Nanobrewery founded in 2018, producing Belgian-style beers labelled **Obunto**. Tastings by appointment.
SELF-EXPLANATORY BEERS INCLUDE: **Weizen** (5.9%); **Brabants Blond** (6.2%); a stronger variant **Sterke Blonde** (7.6%); **Tripel** (8.1%); and **Quadrupel** (9.6%).

Thissen's

Brouwerspad 14; 5397 GG Lith
T 06 5322 8614
thissensbrouwerij.nl

This semi-rural North Brabant brewery, founded in 2015, uses a10hl kit to produce **Henry's** beers named after owner-brewer Henry Thissen, renting out excess capacity. Tours for groups of 8–15 by arrangement.
BEERS INCLUDE: lightly bitter **Blond** (6%: ★★); sweetish herbal **Dubbel** (7%: ★★); and equally sweetish blond **Tripel** (8%: ★★).

Thoms

Halvemaanpassage 1, 3011 AH Rotterdam
T 010 333 5322
thoms.nu

City-centre brewpub opened in 2018 with a 5hl kit, its beer exclusively sold in house.
BEERS INCLUDE: more session than New England-style **N.E.I.P.A.** (3%: ★★+); pleasingly dry Kölsch-style blond **Keilen** (4%: ★★+); a not-bad **Pilsener** (5%: ★★); dry blond **Weizen** (5%: ★★+); and a sweetish **Hoppy Pale Ale** (6%: ★★) that seems to be holding back.

Thuis

Harnaschdreef 7, 2635 BT Den Hoorn
T 015 785 0049
raadhuisschipluiden.nl, biervanthuis.nl

This South Holland microbrewery, founded in 2016, uses a 3hl brewhouse at the Raadhuis café in Schipluiden (see cafés). A new-build brewery a little closer to Delft should be open by publication time, with a taproom to follow.
BEERS INCLUDE: straw-blond quaffing saison **Het Zonnetje** (5.4%: ★★); fruity, Amarillo-hopped **Schipluidens Pale Ale** (6.6%: ★★+); herbal, chilli-spiced amber **Otto's Liefje** (7%: ★★+); golden **Raadhuis Tripel** (8%: ★★); and another eight beers not considered part of the core range.

Tilburg

Noordhoekring 75, 5038 GC Tilburg
T 06 5337 7444
stadsbrouwerijtilburg.nl

Established in 2017, this brewery in a former coach house has only a 2hl kit but is still able to rent out capacity to others. Tours and tastings by arrangement.
BEERS INCLUDE: Kölsch-stlye blond **Tölsch** (4.7%); light, golden **Broken Arm Cream Ale** (6.5%); blond ale **Charactère** (6.6%); English-style **Beeldhouwers' IPA** (6.9%); and **Champenoise** (7%), with added grapes.

Toebes

Kloosterlaan 24, 5435 XD Sint Agatha
T 06 1814 3417
toebesbier.nl

North Brabant outfit founded near Nijmegen in 2015 with a home-built 2hl kit located in a monastery, although the ecclesiastical connections end there.
BEERS INCLUDE: citrussy wheat ale **Witte Nie** (5.5%: ★★); lightly fruity amber **D'n Urste** (6.3%: ★★); gold-blond **Tripelke** (7.7%: ★★); and malty **Kwadruppel** (9.5%: ★★).
ALSO: the **Wa Denk'te** experimental series.

Toekomst

Wilhelminastraat 9, 4793 EL Fijnaart
T 06 3974 2197
brouwerijdetoekomst.nl

The Future began in 2018 by brewing 1hl batches in a North Brabant home kitchen, with larger runs commissioned elsewhere, though was due to expand modestly to a garden shed in 2019.
BEERS INCLUDE: triple-hopped **IPA** (5.6%); and a Belgian-style **Dubbel** (7.2%), **Blonde** (7.5%) and **Tripel** (7.8%).

Tommie Sjef

Middenweg 109, 1782 BC Den Helder
T 06 4386 5835
tswildales.com

Talented young beer magician Tommie Sjef rapidly took the Dutch and wider beer world by storm when he launched his first wild farmhouse ales in 2015. He cellar-ages base beers brewed at various locations in wooden barrels for six to 12 months, sometimes with added fruit, usually with exceptional results. A taproom should open in 2020, a date for the diary.
BEERS INCLUDE: sharp, dry crimson **Braam-Vlier** (5%: ★★★), with blackberry; sharp but balanced **Cassis-Braam** (5%: ★★★+), with blackcurrant and blackberry; Riesling-based sour **Cuvée** (5%: ★★★+), like a vintage champagne but better; moderately sour, well-balanced **Mandarin** (5%: ★★★), with Mandarina Bavaria hops; almost-sour, prune-laden dark ale **Opal** (5%: ★★★+); subtly sour **Rosé** (5%: ★★★★); superbly balanced, citrussy oak-aged blond **Sici** (5%: ★★★★); and sharp and sour **Druif** (6%: ★★★+), with added red wine grapes.

Torens

Piushaven 22, 5017 AN Tilburg
torenstilburg.nl

North Brabant brewer making beer at Sint
Servattumus from 2014, switching to its own
micro-installation behind Burgemeester
Jansen (see cafés) in 2017.
BEERS INCLUDE: dark dubbel **Tweeling** (7%:
★★); drinkable fruity tripel **Wapen** (8.2%:
★★+); and coffee-slanting dark quadrupel
De Bonte Kraai (10%: ★★+).

Troost

De Pijp: Cornelis Troostplein 23,
1072 JJ Amsterdam
Westergasfabriek: Pazzanistraat 25–27,
1014 DB Amsterdam
T 020 737 1028
brouwerijtroost.nl

This small chain began in 2014 as a brewpub
with a 10hl kit in Amsterdam's De Pijp district.
A second brewpub at Westergasfabriek
opened a year later with the potential to brew
7,000hl per year, and most production has now
shifted there, with the original site reserved
for small runs and experiments. A third outlet
in Amsterdam West (Bilderdijkstraat 205) has
no brewery.

BEERS INCLUDE: hoppy **Black IPA** (3.8: ★★+);
improved **Weizen** (4.7%: ★★); lightweight
Pilsner (4.8%: ★★); citrussy witbier **Extra Wit**
(5%: ★★); dry-finishing **Smoked Porter** (5.1%:
★★+); hazy blond **New England I.P.A** (5.5%:
★★+); lightly bitter **Saison** (5.5%: ★★);
copper-amber **IPA** (6.5%: ★★+); sweetish,
honeyed **Honingblond** (7%: ★★); and a
reasonable **Tripel** (7.5%: ★★).
ALSO: weizen **Bammetjes Bier** (4.5%: ★★),
made with waste bread, and pale ale **Pieper
Bier** (4.7%: ★★), made with waste potatoes,
both for Instock, a restaurant chain
specialising in upcycling surplus food.

Tsjerkebier

Doarpsstrjitte 2, 9021 CL Easterwierrum
T 06 3949 8645
tsjerkebier.nl

Frisian brewery founded in 2018 in a former
church, albeit a modern low-rise brick affair,
as far as possible using green energy
generated locally.
BEERS INCLUDE: lightly fruity blond **Lichte
Preek** (5.8%: ★★); bitter dubbel **Alderling**
(6%: ★★); and coriander-spiced tripel **Swiere
Dûmny** (6.9%: ★★).

Twee Leeuwen

Keizersdijk 5C, 4941 GC Raamsdonkveer
T 06 5731 1866
detweeleeuwen.com

This North Brabant company gained its own
copper brewhouse and taproom in 2018, also
available for hire, though it had already been
producing beer for four years in Belgium.
Tours on request.
BEERS INCLUDE: fresh, fruity New England
IPA **Hazy Sunshine** (3.5%: ★★+); sweetish
Blond (5.8%: ★★); and cocoa-laden **Imperial
Porter** (9.5%: ★★+).

its beers across the country. There's a taproom, Bar Alt (see cafés), but no tours. *BEERS INCLUDE:* fruity dry-hopped weizen **Tropical Ralphie** (5%: ★★+); refreshing spiced wheat ale **White Mamba** (5%: ★★+), made with kaffir lime leaves; delightfully hoppy pale ale **Funky Falcon** (5.2%: ★★★); strongly hoppy IPA **Green Bullet** (5.7%: ★★+); and rounded imperial porter **Howling Wolf** (8%: ★★+).

ALSO: a wide range of occasional specials, including some that appear more regularly, such as refreshing Helles lager **Holy Gunther** (5.6%: ★★+); golden-red IPA **Red Rocket** (5.6%: ★★★); floral double IPA **Crying Merman** (8.6%: ★★★); and bitter-finishing imperial stout **Dirty Katharina** (10.5%: ★★+).

Twentse

Haaksbergerstraat 51, 7554 PA Hengelo
T 06 2127 4890
twentsebierbrouwerij.nl

Opened in 2008 with a 5hl kit in an industrial building near the town centre, this moved to a larger out-of-town site with a taproom and restaurant in 2018, but at the time of writing hasn't yet begun brewing again, instead making its beer elsewhere. We give them the benefit of the doubt for now, as the expectation is that the site will one day at least be used for workshops and experimental one-offs. *BEERS INCLUDE:* bland **Premium Pils** (5%: ★+); significantly better **Oerpils** (5%: ★★); standard witbier **Wit** (5%: ★★); sweetish **Amber** (6%: ★★); full-bodied Belgian-style blond **De Gusteau** (6.5%: ★★+); and crisply sweetish **Honing Tripel** (8%: ★★+).

Two Chefs

Moezelhavenweg 6, 1043 AM Amsterdam
twochefsbrewing.nl

Genuinely founded by two chefs, this enterprise began nomadically in 2012 but installed its own 35hl brewery in a warehouse near Sloterdijk station in 2016 and now sells

TX

Slotskolk 22c, 1794 BG Oosterend
T 0222 760150
brouwerijtx.nl

On opening in 2018, this Texel brewery sold beer from its 10hl kit only in keg. Its products have been more widely distributed since it began bottling in 2019. *BEERS INCLUDE:* easy-going spiced wheat ale **Wit** (4%: ★★); banana-forward dunkelweizen **Donkerblond** (5.5%: ★★+); and standout floral-hoppy **Hop Blond** (6.8%: ★★+).

Uddelaer

Staverdenseweg 283a, 3852 NV Ermelo
T 06 5377 8994
uddelaer.nl

This Gelderland brewpub, opened in 2017, is the brainchild of local celebrity Jacques Brinkman, who twice won Olympic gold with the Dutch men's hockey team. His 20hl operation couldn't have a grander setting, in the partly moated coach house and stables of country manor Kasteel Staverden. The beers are yet to match the surroundings but are developing nicely.

BEERS INCLUDE: lightly bitter quaffing session **IPA 4.0** (4%: ★★+); slightly sweetish **Pilsener** (5%: ★★); citrussy **Witbier** (5%: ★★+); fruity golden **Blond** (6.5%: ★★); sweetish multi-grained **Tripel** (8.4%: ★★); and deceptively delicate bitter-finishing **IPA** (8.5%: ★★).

Uiltje

Bingerweg 25, 2031 AZ Haarlem
T 023 844 6395
uiltjecraftbeer.com

Now one of the country's foremost craft breweries, Little Owl began in 2012 by developing recipes at home which were then upscaled at Jopen. Brewer Robbert Uyleman quickly outgrew this model and now has his own 40hl brewery and taproom on an industrial estate. With a deserved international reputation, his creations are bold, uncompromising, and seldom less than superb.

BEERS INCLUDE: outstandingly tart Berliner weisse **Crybaby** (2.4%: ★★★+); easily likeable white IPA **Miss Hooter** (4.4%: ★★★); gloriously dry, bitter IPA **Bird of Prey** (5.8%: ★★★★); rounded American pale ale **Trackdown**

(5.2%: ★★+); strongly bitter-hoppy pale ale **Dikke Lul 3** (5.6%: ★★★); watermelon wheat ale **Wingman** (6%: ★★); deeply bitter and complex **Me Myself & IPA** (7%: ★★★+); grassy Northwest imperial IPA **El Patron** (8.2%: ★★★+), designed to be drunk fresh; richly chewy and bitter black IPA **Little black Dress** (8.8%: ★★★); restrained double IPA **Dr Raptor** (9.2%: ★★+); and occasionally brewed **Flaming Ass Owl** (10%: ★★★), a richly smoked imperial porter with chilli. *SEASONAL:* summery quaffing session IPA **FF Lekker Met Je Bek in Het Zonnetje** (3.5%: ★★+) and German-style doppelbock **Commisaris Rex** (8%: ★★+).

ALSO: a numbered **Grandma's Recipe** series largely consisting of super-strong and richly textured imperial stouts (often ★★★★), and all manner of outrageously daring one-offs and specials.

Uthoka

Nederhof 3A, 5258 CB Berlicum
T 06 2414 7747
biersommelier.biz, batchesbrewery.nl

This North Brabant outfit derives its name
from that of its founder, German-born beer
sommelier Uwe Thorsten Kalms, and has
shared a 5hl installation with Draok (above)
since 2017.
BEERS INCLUDE: sweetish, honeyed blond
Bee 52 (4.8%: ★★+); German-style
hefeweizen **Petrus** (5.5%: ★★+); gold-blond
IJzeren Man (5.8%: ★★); fruity-edged
Heideblond (5.6%: ★★); and decent blond
tripel **Belgian Buddy** (9%: ★★+).
ALSO: **Batches**, a series of one-off collaborations with Draok's brewer.

Utrecht (Brewboyz)

Anton Koolhaasstraat 1, 3544 HV Utrecht
T 06 2883 9527
brewboyz.com

Born in 2017 under the name of **BrewBoyz**, the
brewery was rebranded to reflect its location
in 2019, although core beers retain the original
label. Five other brewers use the 5hl kit.
BEERS INCLUDE: balanced American pale ale
APA (5%: ★★+), fruity **IPA** (6.5%: ★★+);
standard dry **Blond** (6.5%: ★★); coriander-
spiced **Tripel** (8%: ★★); restrained **Stout**
(8%: ★★); and more assertive **Russian
Imperial Stout** (8.5%: ★★+).

Vaan

Deventerseweg 9b, 2994 LE Barendrecht
T 06 8115 3611
vaanbrouwers.nl

South Holland brewers since 2018, with their
own micro-installation since 2019. Visits on
request.
BEERS INCLUDE: citrussy blond **Citroen** (5%);
and Belgian-style **Zwaar Blond** (7%), **Dubbel**
(7%), **Tripel** (9%) and **Quadrupel** (10%).

Vagabond

Ridderplein 33, 5421 CX Gemert
vagabond.nl

Another group of homebrewers who let their
hobby get out of hand, turning pro in 2019.
Tours and tastings by appointment.
BEERS INCLUDE: **Dapper Blond** (4.5%);
witbier **Witte Woestaard** (4.5%); and spiced
Trotse Tripel (7%).

Vaghevuur –
see Hemel

Van Kinsbergen

Prins Hendrikplein 15, 2518 JC Den Haag
T 070 310 7892

The small kit at this gastropub is used for
draught specials, while the flagship house
beer, a lightly bitter but quaffable **Pale Ale**
(4.5%: ★★+), is brewed elsewhere.

Van Moll

Keizersgracht 16a, 5611 GD Eindhoven
vanmollcraftbeer.nl

This central brewpub became Eindhoven's
first commercial brewery for 60 years when it
opened in former offices in 2013. The application
of consistently high standards has earned it a
place at the top table of Dutch craft brewing.
Draught specials and one-offs for festivals
are made on site in 1.5hl batches, but rising
demand for the nationally distributed bottled
range is now satisfied by outsourcing.
BEERS INCLUDE: refreshingly grapefruity
session IPA **Wanderlust** (2%: ★★+); super-
hoppy hefeweizen **Langharig Tuig** (5.5%:
★★★); gently bitter blond **Toewijding** (6.5%:
★★+); outstanding assertive IPA **Doerak**
(6.5%: ★★★★); crisp, dry, easy-drinking
Triple Trouble (8.5%: ★★+); and chewy
imperial stout **Ons Blackie** (9.5%: ★★+).
ALSO: variously single-hopped quaffer

Eenvoud (4%: ★★+); citrussy witbier/saison hybrid **Luikse Vechter**(5.5%: ★★+); **Kiss From a Rose** (5.5%: ★★★+), a lightly fruity wheat ale with rose water, lime and lychee; moreish, burnt-edged dark IPA **Black Metal Manita** (7.5%: ★★★); and **Zoltan** (11%: ★★★), a cocoa-heavy imperial stout, usually encountered in superb barrel-aged form (usually ★★★★).

Vandenbroek

Midwolde D22, 9355 TL Midwolde
brouwerijvandenbroek.com

Groningen-based Toon van den Broek became a homebrewer in 1969 but was only persuaded to turn pro in 2015. He now makes his generally excellent sour and wild ales using a self-built wood-fired 6hl copper vessel, with an open coolship tank for wild fermentation.
BEERS INCLUDE: magnificent geuze-style **Watergeus** (6%: ★★★★), 100% wild-fermented and oak-aged; its super-sharp kriek-style sister **Fruity Watergeus** (6%: ★★★+), with cherries; gently fruity **Vlaamsbruin** (Flemish Brown, 7%: ★★★), even better as **Vlaamsbruin Kersen** (7.8%: ★★★+) with added oomph and sharpness from cherries; and comparitively staid Brett-infused oat ale **Cluyn** (7%: ★★+).

Vandeoirsprong

Koestraat 20, 5688 AH Oirschot
T 0499 572002
vandeoirsprong.nl

The Kroon (Crown) brewery in North Brabant was one of the Netherlands' oldest family businesses when it was closed by Bavaria (Swinkels) in 1996, with a history of brewing on the site dating back to at least 1659. New owners revived beer production in 2015 with a modern 20hl kit and a taproom: the current name reads as 'from the source' but also puns on the spelling of the place name. The old brewhouse, now a museum (see Beer tourism), is included in tours and tastings for groups of 10 or more.
BEERS INCLUDE: lightly fruity **Session IPA** (3%: ★★); dry, malty unfiltered pilsener **Zwickel** (5%: ★★+); fruity **Amber** (5.5%: ★★+); decently dry **Weizen** (5.6%: ★★+); standard golden **Blonde** (6%: ★★); amber, dry **Dunkelweizen** (6%: ★★+); perfumed, hoppy and bitter-finishing **OPA – Oirschots Pale Ale** (6.1%: ★★+); improving balanced **Dubbele** (6.7%: ★★+); bittersweet golden **Tripel** (8.4%: ★★); and heavily dark and spicy **Quadrupel** (9.8%: ★★+).

vandeStreek

Ontariodreef 43, 3565 BC Utrecht
T 030 737 1255
vandestreekbier.nl

Two talented brothers began brewing commercially in 2013 at De Leckere but now boast their own substantial 35hl installation, with a long-awaited taproom that finally opened in late 2019. Individual tours Sa 14.00.
BEERS INCLUDE: low alcohol hoppy **Playground IPA** (<0.5%: ★★+), accomplished within its class; refreshing driver's beer **Fruit Machine** (0.5%: ★★) with raspberry and blueberry; easily likeable IPA **Hop Art** (5% ★★★); bitter amber **Broeders** (6%: ★★+); dry rye pale ale **Koper** (7%: ★★+); coffee-tinged stout **Dark Roast** (8%: ★★+); and **Turf 'n' Surf** (8.5%: ★★), a tripel with peat and sea salt.
SEASONAL: superior meibock **Zonnesteek** (6%: ★★+); summer wheat ale **Dewitt** (5.5%: ★★+); porter-ish autumn **Blackbock** (6%: ★★+); and **Bock jij of Bock ik?** (0.5%: ★★+).

Vechtdal

Molendijk 11, 7721 AB Dalfsen
T 06 1917 4403
vechtdalbrouwerij.nl

This Overijssel outfit has been brewing mostly Belgian-style ales since 2015, at first at Admiraals but since 2016 with its own 6.5hl kit. Tours by appointment.
BEERS INCLUDE: lightweight but drinkable dubbel/stout hybrid **Dame van Dalfsen** (5%: ★★+); rounded **Vechter Blond** (6%: ★★); restrained American pale ale **Bleke Alie** (6%); strong blond **Goed Goan** (7%: ★★); and sweetish tripel **Jan van Dalfsen** (9%: ★★+).

Veem

Torenallee 86, 5617 BE Eindhoven
T 06 1381 2616
brouwerijhetveem.nl

Eindhoven's third working brewery was founded in a food market in a former Philips factory in 2015 but licensing problems delayed regular production on its 10hl kit for a further two years. The beers, sold on draught in the taproom and in bottles in the adjacent shop, are slowly finding their feet.
BEERS INCLUDE: improved session IPA **Pentode Passion** IPA (4.5%: ★★+); dry floral **Transistor Weizen** (5.4%: ★★); fruity **Innovator Blond** (6%: ★★); bitter IPA **Hop Creator** (6.5%: ★★+); sweetish **Techno Tripel** (8%: ★+); and inoffensive quadrupel **Forbidden City** (10%: ★★).

Veens

Vivaldisingel 151, 2151 GP Nieuw-Vennep
T 06 2126 7341
veensbier.nl

North Holland former homebrewer who went pro in 2019 at nano scale making 30l and 50l batches, and also offering workshops and tastings. Beers so far appear to be variations on a Belgian-style **Quadrupel**, with recipes changing between batches.

Veldhovense

Binnenweg 9, 5502 AM Veldhoven
T 06 1809 2609
veldhovensebierbrouwerij.nl

Ellen Verhoeven Jannes began this project in 2017, and currently brews 2hl weekly for local sale, using organic ingredients where possible.
BEERS INCLUDE: citrussy wheat ale **Witte Boordencrimineel** (5.5%); hoppy amber **Verbitterde Weduwe** (6%); IPA-ish **Het Licht Vergrijp** (6%); **Stoute Schoen** (7%) stout; and spiced tripel **Boefke** (8%).

Verdwenen Bock

Kabeljauwallee 8, 6865 BN Doorwerth
T 06 2122 0905
deverdwenenbock.nl

The Vanishing Goat began near Nijmegen in 2018 with a numbered series of light **Dry Hopped Session** beers in various styles with spicing.

Vergulde Pul

Markt 26B, 5541 EA Reusel

Tiny North Brabant brewery founded in 2016, mainly distributed locally.
BEERS INCLUDE: lightly bitter Belgian-style IPA **D'n Koenschoof** (5.5%: ★★); standard blond **D'n Scheeper** (6.5%: ★★); malty tripel **D'n Smokkelear** (7.5%: ★★); chocolatey rich dubbel **Unne Streuper** (7.5%: ★★+); and raisin and vanilla-tinged quadrupel **D'n Gloeiige** (10%: ★★+).

Vermeerssen

Absdaalseweg 2, 4561 GG Hulst
T 0114 310660
vermeersen.com

This brewery in southern Zeeland was founded as Halve Maan in 1991 but renamed after its

owner in 2016 following pressure from the well-known pub and brewery in Bruges. This change also seems to have spurred a near-dormant operation back into action.
BEERS INCLUDE: too-sweet cherryade **Kriek** (3.5%: ★+); tedious pilsener **Java Premium** (5%: ★+); spiced witbier **Zeeuwse Witte** (5%: ★★); dull **Zeeuws Blond** (6.5%: ★★); sweetish **Dubbel XX** (6.5%: ★★); vanilla-honeyed amber **Lazarus** (6.5%: ★★); sweet brown **Grof Geschut** (8%: ★★); citrussy **Tripel XXX** (8%: ★★); and wheat tripel **Illabefactus Autopous** (8%: ★★).

Vet & Lazy

Maasboulevard 100, 3063 NS Rotterdam
T 06 5161 0250
lazy.vet

Fat & Lazy launched in 2015 in BlueCity, a former resort swimming pool complex that now houses numerous businesses striving to establish a zero-waste circular economy. It currently brews several times a month in 8hl batches and offers tours for groups of 10 or more.
BEERS INCLUDE: coffee-laced porter **Bean Me Up Scotty** (6.3%: ★★+); harshly bitter and not at all fluffy IPA **Fluffy** (6.4%: ★★+); citrussy wheat ale **Dubbel Wit Zomerfit** (7%: ★★), spiced with Szechuan pepper; gold-blond tripel **Je Moeder** (8.5%: ★★); and **Le Phallus** (8.5%: ★★★), a full-bodied multi-grain English porter with mercifully indistinct oyster mushrooms.

Veteraan

Jacob Le Mairestraat 253, 7825 XE Emmen
deveteraan.com

Drenthe-based nanobrewery whose products have rarely been seen outside the local area since it started in 2015. Beers follow well-trodden Belgian paths and include a **Wit** (4.4%), **Blond** (6%), **Dubbel** (7%), and **Tripel** (9%).

Vijfheerenlanden

Energieweg 17P, 4143 HK Leerdam
T 0345 618857
glassbier.nl

Founded in 2012 in a small town which gave its name to a big cheese, this 2.6hl 'beer studio' moved from South Holland to Utrecht in 2019 without lifting a finger when the provincial boundaries were redrawn. Ill health interrupted production in 2018 but we believe it is now back in business and slowly rebuilding its range.
BEERS INCLUDE: caramel dubbel **Zwarthut** (7.2%: ★★); sweetish **Glassbier Tripel** (7.5%: ★★); more rounded **Cope Tripel** (7.8%: ★★); and **Glashut** (8.3%) tripel with whisky malt.

VIS

Louis Pasteurstraat 4F-H, 1821 BL Alkmaar
brouwerijdevis.nl

The Fish began in 2016 by working at Noord-Hollandse but has been brewing its own beer since 2017, also renting out its kit to others and offering 'brewer for a day' sessions. Tours and tastings by arrangement.
BEERS INCLUDE: Vienna lager **Goudvis** (5%); kuit beer **Hom & Kuit** (5.5%); porter **Duivelsvis** (7%); and dubbel **Bruinvis** (8%).

Vlaardingse

Oosthavenkade 90, 3134 KA Vlaardingen
vulcaanbier.nl

Founded in 2012 and based since 2016 in an old warehouse by a historic herring fishing harbour, this South Holland brewer took its **Vulcaan** brand from the name of another local harbour rather than a science fiction franchise. Shop every first Sa of each month 14.00–16.00, with informal brewery tours if it's not too busy.
BEERS INCLUDE: citrussy **Wit** (4.7%: ★★+); lightly bitter flagship amber **Vulcaan** (5.4%: ★★+); and dubbel **Mammoet** (7%: ★★), plus various one-offs.

Vleeghel

N.C.B.-laan 52A, 5462 GE Veghel
wittern.nl

North Brabant brewer making 2hl batches in and for the Wittern restaurant (see cafés) since 2014.
BEERS INCLUDE: drinkable hazy gold-blond **Jonge Vleeghel** (5%: ★★+); malty amber **Oude Vleeghel** (5%: ★★); thinnish stout **Duistere Vleeghel** (5%: ★★); and less-than-successful double IPA **Brabants Zen** (8.1%: ★+).

Vlieland (Fortuna Vlieland)

Fortweg 10, 8899 CC Oost-Vlieland
fortunavlieland.nl

Began in 2016 as Selkiebrouwerij, cuckoo brewing their amber ale **Rampzalig** (6.8%) at Naeckte Brouwers, this island-based company was constructing its own site next to a theatre as this book went to press. The brewery also re-branded itself as Fortuna Vlieland in late 2019.

Vlijt

Vlijtseweg 130, 7317 AK Apeldoorn
T 06 1443 9518
veluweschavuyt.nl

This Apeldoorn producer began with a 3hl kit at city centre brewpub het Achterom (see cafés) in 2010. Growing demand encouraged expan-

sion in 2013 to a 10hl brewhouse and taproom in a renovated former baby cream factory, offering a broadening range of beers widely sold locally and beyond under the **Veluwse Schavuyt** brand. The original site has been retained as a taproom and the kit is still in place, though we're not convinced it's still in use.
BEERS INCLUDE: citrussy but standard **Witbier** (5%: ★★); hazy, fruity **Blond** (5.6%: ★★) with peach hints; improving, increasingly dry flagship **Amber** (6.5%: ★★+); also improved fruity **IPA** (6.5%: ★★+); and coriander-spiced wheat **Tripel** (7.5%: ★★).

Volendam

Morseweg 12, 1131 PK Volendam
T 06 5356 0875
bierbrouwerijvolendam.nl

Founded in 2000 on an industrial estate in an otherwise picturesque tourist town north of Amsterdam on the shores of the Markermeer, this brewery achieves consistent quality on a small scale. Its beers are found over much of North Holland but are less common elsewhere. Group tours by appointment.
BEERS INCLUDE: balanced **Weizen** (5.5%: ★★); fruity bitter **VPA** (Volendams Pale Ale) (5.5%: ★★+); dry golden **Zeebonck** (6.5%: ★★+); sweetish dubbel **Bap** (7%: ★★); and full-bodied tripel **Ootje** (8.5%: ★★+), with some barley wine character.
SEASONAL: well-balanced autumnal **Vølenbock** (6.5%: ★★+),

Volle Maat

Asschatterweg 233, 3831 JP Leusden
devollemaat.nl

Brewing on others' kit from 2013 and installing its own kit a year later, this producer in Utrecht province can usually be visited Fr 13.00–16.00 or Sa 10.00–16.00, but call ahead to be sure.
BEERS INCLUDE: US-hopped fruity **Saison Mosaic** (5.5%: ★★+); dry blond **Vliervluiter** (5.5%: ★★+) with elderflower; weizen **Weizhijt** (5.5%: ★★); blond **Hoppekee** (5.5%: ★★); bitter-finishing **Hoogblond** (6.5%: ★★+);

coffee-laced porter **Corretto** (7.5%); rounded brown **Dubbelaar** (7.5%: ★★+); golden **Tripel** (8.5%: ★★+); rich, bitter standout black IPA **Tomahawk** (8.5%: ★★★); and **Maate Hari** (9.5%: ★★+), a dark, full-bodied barley wine.

Vorstin

Vorstinnenhof 19, 4751 BE Oud Gastel
facebook.com/BrouwerijdeVorstin

North Brabant-based nanobrewery Princess was founded in 2018, and makes its **Gastelse** beers in 40l batches for local bottle shops and bars.
BEERS INCLUDE: **Hopnar** (5.1%) IPA and Belgian-style blond **Goud** (7.5%).

Vrijstad

Nijverheidsweg 6, 4104 AN Culemborg
T 06 1130 6385
brouwerijvrijstad.nl

Founded by two friends in 2012 and currently brewing in 7hl batches, mainly sold in Gelderland and Utrecht provinces.
BEERS INCLUDE: märzen-style lager **Keller** (5.6%: ★★+); **Pumpkin Ale** (5.6%); **I.P.A.** (5.6%); and **Scottish Ale** (7.5%).

Vrolijcke Joncker

Bolmeer 1, 9354 VL Zevenhuizen
T 06 5114 2122
vrolijckejoncker.nl

Nanobrewer making a wide range of **Joncker** beers on a 60l kit since 2016 in rural southwest Groningen, rarely seen outside the local area. *BEERS INCLUDE:* weizen **Wijze** (6.5%); IPA **Dolle** (7%); **Stoute** (8%); **Blonde** (8.5%); golden tripel **Malle** (8.5%: ★★); imperial stout **Zwarte** (9%); strong dubbel **Rode** (9%: ★★) warming dark-brown quadrupel **Zware** (9.5%: ★★+); and strong blond **Duivelse** (10%: ★★). *ALSO:* beers under the **Westerkwartbier** label for the local market, likely minimally tweaked versions of the above.

Waallicht

Roggeweg 28X, 6534 AJ Nijmegen
waallicht.nl

Homebrewers who turned pro in 2018, mainly selling through local outlets. *BEERS INCLUDE:* sweetish but not bitter enough IPA **Estus** (7.3%: ★★); fruity golden IPA **Cervonaut** (7.4%: ★★); imperial stout **Supermassive** (10.8%: ★★+), massive if not quite super; and sweet copper-amber barley wine **Nachtbraker** (11.3%: ★★+).

Wageningen

1e Kloostersteeg 5, 6701 DL Wageningen
T 06 3630 0440
brouwerijwageningen.nl

This Gelderland brewery, founded by friends in 2013 and initially brewing elsewhere, opened its own crowdfunded 10hl town centre brewpub, the Rad van Wageningen (see cafés), in 2017, using local ingredients wherever possible. *BEERS INCLUDE:* softly restrained IPA **Hop Lovin' Criminal** (5.4%: ★★+); dry weizen **Hermelijn** (5.6%: ★★); medium-bodied saison **Successor** (5.9%: ★★); hoppy amber lager **Otto II van Gelre** (7.3%: ★★); rich, strong

dunkelweizen **Mordicus** (7.5%: ★★+); dry, full-bodied saison **Drost van Wageningen** (8.4%: ★★+); and deceptively drinkable imperial oatmeal stout **Tsaar van Wageningen** (10.5%: ★★+).

Walhalla

Spijkerkade 10, 1021 JS Amsterdam
T 06 1139 1675
walhallacraftbeer.nl

Walhalla opened its own crowdfunded brewery and taproom in Amsterdam-Noord in 2018 after two nomadic years. Its widely available beers, mostly named after ancient gods, have a growing reputation for excellence. *BEERS INCLUDE:* dry, hoppy blond **Juno** (4.5%: ★★+); dry-hopped golden IPA **Loki** (5.5%: ★★★); lightly hoppy American amber **Ares** (6%: ★★+); boldly dry gold-blond farmhouse ale **Osiris** (7%: ★★★); strongly bitter blond imperial IPA **Shakti** (8.2%: ★★★); and subtly rounded copper-amber barley wine **Wuldor** (9.8%: ★★+). *SEASONAL:* dry, autumnal dubbelbock **Heimdall** (8.5%: ★★+) and **Nanouq** (9%: ★★★), a hoppy, warming dark brown winter ale. Also: regular specials and collaborations.

Walnoot

Bosscherweg 10, 6336 XK Hulsberg
T 06 3051 6997
facebook.com/BrouwerijDeWalnootAalbeek

South Limburg nanobrewery founded in 2018, using locally sourced ingredients where possible, in beers which are elusive outside the immediate area.
BEERS INCLUDE: sweetish dark **IPA+Sjroap** (6.9%: ★★), hindered not helped by the addition of apple syrup; gold-blond **Maretak Honey Ale** (7%); and tripel **Vliegenzwam** (7%).

Waterland

Galgeriet 4, 1141 GK Monnickendam
T 0299 407647
bierderijwaterland.nl

Originally brewing since 2015 at other locations, Waterland opened its own brewpub by a yachting marina in 2018, billing it as a *bierderij*, a pun on *boerderij*, 'farm'. It brews using organic ingredients on a 10hl installation and also smokes its own sausage and fish.
BEERS INCLUDE: galangal-spiced session blond **Hemelse Heks** (3%: ★★+); citrussy wheat ale **Marker Maagd** (5%: ★★); dry schwarzbier **Suiverswart** (5%: ★★+); clean-tasting superior pilsener **Waterlander** (5%: ★★+); pleasantly herbal amber **Kattekwaad** (6%: ★★+), made with willow bark; hoppy **Broeker Blonde** (6%: ★★+), better than many of its ilk; bittersweet red IPA **Hoppy Hannah** (6.3%: ★★+); lightly bitter New England IPA **Blije Bart** (6.5%: ★★+); cocoa-edged **Purmer Porter** (7%: ★★+); golden tripel **Monnicker Moker** (8%: ★★); strong, dark **Dubbelduts** (8.5%: ★★), more barley wine than dubbel; honey-edged blond **Gouden Bocht** (9%: ★★); and take-no-prisoners quadrupel **Duiveldauw** (12%: ★★+).

Weerter –
see Brouwschuur

Waterland

Wentersch

Groenloseweg 75, 7101 AD Winterswijk
T 0543 769080
wentersch.nl

Brewing good quality beers for regional
distribution in an edge-of-town former
petrol station in the Gelderse Achterhoek
since 2016, this 20hl brewery was as we write
looking for a new home. Its taproom is now
only open for group visits (Fr&Sa), with
pre-booked individual tours Sa 14.30.
BEERS INCLUDE: nettly hoppy **Achterhoek
Pale Ale** (5%: ★★+); citrussy weizen
Wentersweiss (5.5%: ★★+); spiced white
Wentersch Wit (5.5%: ★★); easy-drinking
coffee porter **Gerrit** (5.7%: ★★+); sweetish
blond **Druuf** (6%: ★★), with grape juice;
bitter-finishing, medium-hoppy **IPA** (6.5%:
★★+); golden **Blondelle** (7%: ★★+), spiced
with curaçao orange and coriander; spicy
golden **An de Tripel** (9%: ★★); delicious
occasional brew **Black IPA** (9%: ★★★), almost
a hoppy stout; cocoa-laden imperial stout
R.I.S. (9%: ★★+); and **Pomp 4** (10%: ★★+), a
dark-brown quadrupel with burnt sugar hints.

Werf

Paktuinen 6, 1601 GD Enkhuizen
T 0228 222160
brouwerijdewerf.nl

The Wharf was founded as De Compagnie in
2012, with the intention of brewing in the
like-named pub around the corner (see cafés),
but it morphed into a new-build waterside
warehouse-like brewpub with a 20hl kit in 2018.
Beers initially promised more than they deliver-
ed but are developing in the right direction.
Some other brewers rent capacity here.
BEERS INCLUDE: lightly fruity session IPA
Vonkel (4.2%: ★★+); fruity weizen **Wahja!**
(5.2%: ★★); **Wahja! Meloen** (5.2%: ★★),
the same with added melon; dry amber
Meermoid (5.7%: ★★); sweetish blond **Porno**
(6%: ★★); clean-tasting tripel **Tunus** (9%: ★★+);
malty sweetish quadrupel **Hemelsbruin**
(9%: ★★+); strongly bitter triple IPA **Skitter**
(9%: ★★★); and rounded, burnt-edged
imperial stout **Diepdonker** (9.5%: ★★+).
ALSO: numbered experiments appearing
under the name **Batches**, and a self-
explanatory **Barrel** series.

Wertha

Bassin 6, 6001 GZ Weert
T 06 5241 5859
werthabrewpub.nl

At the time of writing, this was a brewpub in name only, its beers being made down the road at Weerter, but it should begin brewing on its own 5hl kit in 2020. Beers so far have included a cocoa-tinged **Bock** (7%: ★★+) and a coriander and cardamom-spiced **Tripelll** (7.3%: ★★).

Westeinder

Ype Poortingawei 35, 8915 KE Leeuwarden
T 06 4104 9898
westeinder.com

Homebrewers who turned pro in 2017, currently only producing seasonal beers. *BEERS INCLUDE:* spring blond **Lentekracht** (6.8%); summer pilsener **Zomergenot** (6.8%); autumn bock **Herfsttooi** (6.8%); and stout-like **Winterpracht** (6.8%: ★★).

Westerwolde

Burgermeester Buiskoolweg 35,
9541 XM Vlagtwedde
brouwerij-westerwolde.nl

A father and son team brewing in 5hl batches since 2017 in rural southeast Groningen province. Shop Sa 11.00–15.00; tours and tastings by appointment.
BEERS INCLUDE: session blond **Summer of '69** (3.5%: ★★+); hoppy pilsener **Frisse** (5.5%); wheaty pilsener **Rijke** (5.5%); strong blond **Sterke** (7.8%); gold-blond **Tripel** (8.5%); rounded but heavy hitting **Imperial Stout** (11%: ★★+); and warming barley wine **Westerwolder Gerstewijn** (12%: ★★).

Westfriese

Komodovaraan 33, 1704 VH Heerhugowaard
T 072 888 5208
westfriesbier.nl

This North Holland microbrewery began in Enkhuizen in 2015 but relocated the following year.
BEERS INCLUDE: amber **Ientje Toe** (5%); American IPA **Skeef** (7.5%); and tripel **Groôs** (8.5%).

Wijchense Schone

Kastanjepad 18 6602 BK Wijchen
T 06 1811 4093
wijchenseschone.nl

This Gelderland producer began at Sint Servattumus in 2014, gaining its own 5hl kit in 2016, also rented out to other brewers.
BEERS INCLUDE: spiced blond **Dukzat** (7%: ★★); lightly bitter 'India Brown Ale' **Hittepetit** (7%: ★★); better **Blonde Dern** (7.1%: ★★+); and bittersweet tripel **Wannekwats** (9%: ★★).

Wildervanker

J. Kammingastraat 89, 9648 KK Wildervank
T 06 4073 4058
wildervankerbrouwerij.nl

Launched in 2014 by a Groningen homebrewer with 30 years' experience.
BEERS INCLUDE: ginger-flavoured **Gember Bier** (5.5%: ★★+); blond tripel **Klokje Breuer** (9%: ★★); cocoa-tinged **Imperial Stout** (9%: ★★+); and amber quadrupel **Scheepsjoager** (9%: ★★).

Wilskracht

Molensingel 6, 5371 AW Ravenstein
T 06 5570 8153
stadsbrouwerijravenstein.nl

This 5hl North Brabant brewery and taproom in an old village windmill was started in 2016 by two men called Wil, thus the name Wils' Power.
BEERS INCLUDE: honeyed elderflower blond **Vlierbier** (5%: ★★+); honey-tinged **Wiener Weizen** (5.5%: ★★); standard **Blonde Kolonel**

(6.5%: ★★); sweetish dubbel **Bolwerck 8** (8%: ★★); spiced tripel **Bastion** (8.5%: ★★); and beefy quadrupel **Bolwerck 10** (10%: ★★+).

Wispe

Herengracht 16, 1382 AE Weesp
T 06 2451 4518
wispe.nl

This North Holland organic brewer was content to make beer at De Leckere for its first decade, but finally opened its own crowdfunded brewery and taproom in the former St Laurentius church in late 2019.
BEERS INCLUDE: average **Wit** (5%: ★★); maltier **Blond** (6%: ★★); cocoa-heavy **Porter** (6.3%: ★★+); nettly bitter **IPA** (6.4%: ★★); and sweetish **Tripel** (7.6%: ★★).

Witte Klavervier

Oudezijl 1, 9693 PA Bad Nieuweschans
T 06 2200 1711
witteklavervier.nl

The original White Four-Leaf Clover is a house in Zwolle with a brewing history dating back to 1651. This brewery began there in 2011, but moved in 2018 to its current location in a former rail station in Groningen province, complete with a micro-maltings.
BEERS INCLUDE: self-explanatory fruity blond **Koyt-Kuit-Kuyt** (5.8%: ★★+) and **Hopjumper** (6%: ★★+), a bitter-finishing kuit.

Wittenburg

Markt 7, 6901 AE Zevenaar
T 0316 253520
stadsbrouwerijwittenburg.nl

First installed in 2008 in a handsome old building near the town centre, Wittenburg became a fully fledged brewpub in a prime spot on the main square in 2014. Its **De Jonkheer** beers are sold in the pub and adjacent shop, and elsewhere. Tours and tastings by arrangement.
BEERS INCLUDE: straw-blond **Stadsbier** (5.25%: ★★); dry bitter **Blond** (6.2%: ★★); above-average **Wit** (6.2%: ★★+); standout bitter amber American pale ale **Stoommachine** (6.5%: ★★+); sweetish **Dubbel** (7%: ★★); unsubtle, sweetish **Tripel** (7.8%: ★★); vanilla-edged stout-ish **Straffe André** (7.8%: ★★+); and an oddly unbalanced **Stout** (8.4%: ★★).

Woest

Elementenstraat 3, 1014 AR Amsterdam
woestbier.nl

Founded in 2017 and currently brewing in batches of up to 2.5hl for local sale, with no ambition to scale up.
BEERS INCLUDE: **Wit** (5%); **Pale Ale** (7.5%); and a **Tripel** (8.5%).

Zaltbommelse

Nieuwstraat 6, 5301 EW Zaltbommel
T 06 1649 9070
zaltbommelse-stadsbrouwerij.nl

Brewing **De Kroniek** beers, named after a former local paper, in 1hl batches beside the Orion café since 2014, with plans to scale up to 5hl when funds allow.
BEERS INCLUDE: sweetish **Blond** (6%: ★★); standard **Dubbel** (6.5%: ★★); lightly bitter blond **Zuster Thaddea** (6.5%: ★★); strongly bitter **IPA** (8.2%: ★★); and golden **Tripel** (8.5%: ★★).

Zotte Kalf

Trekweg naar Onderdendam 46, 9951 SE Winsum
hetzottekalf.nl

Founded in 2017 with a 1hl kit on a farm in Groningen province, Mad Calf brews beers named after cow breeds, usually on Saturdays, not that those facts are linked.
BEERS INCLUDE: hoppy blond **Barrosa** (6.5%: ★★+); fruity porter **Galloway** (7.4%: ★★); golden tripel **Salorn** (9%: ★★); and warming quadrupel **Brangus** (10%: ★★+).

Zundert –

see Kievit

Zuyd

Tapijnkazerne 20, 6211 ME Maastricht
T 06 3987 6145

South began in 2015 with a 5hl installation in the cellar of a former army barracks that's now the Tapijn (see cafés). It's rumoured the building's owner Maastricht University has other plans for it, so the brewery may have to relocate during the life of this guide.
BEERS INCLUDE: lightly hoppy India pale lager **Mosa 5** (5%: ★★); sweetish red ale **Via 6** (6%: ★★); and standout fruity-bitter pale ale **Novum 7** (7%: ★★+).

ALSO: malty blond **Project-K** (6%: ★★), made with and for Tapijn; and six-hopped IPA **'t Gouverneurke** (6%: ★★+) for the Gouverneur beer pub.

Zwaluw

Noordeinde 19, 8428 HL Fochteloo
zwaluwbierbrouwers.nl

A Friesland homebrewer of 30 years' experience created Swallow in 2017 to brew small runs in European styles for local sale.
BEERS INCLUDE: Czech-style amber lager **CZ Amber** (5.5%); Düsseldorf-style altbier **Fochteloër Alt** (6.5%); and Belgian-style **Tripel** (8.5%).

Brewers without breweries

One feature of the Dutch brewing scene is the high proportion of businesses registered with the Chamber of Commerce (KvK) as brewing companies who do not possess a physical brewery, but instead make their beers using other people's facilities. These are sometimes known in English as contractors, and more recently as cuckoo brewers if they work mainly in one location, or as gypsy brewers if they regularly change locations, though this last term is increasingly being replaced by 'nomad' to avoid any potential ethnic insult. Dutch speakers prefer *brouwerijhuurders* (brewery hirers), though all these terms are imprecise and cover a wide variety of arrangements.

At the more ethical end of the spectrum are skilled brewers who either brew themselves at someone else's site or collaborate actively in the design of their beers before another brewer makes them. The usual reason for this is that they simply cannot afford the financial risks of leasing premises and investing in equipment. Some of the most talented and daring beer makers in the Netherlands are among this group and many excellent brewers have used such arrangements as a stepping stone to acquiring their own brewhouse.

More typical are those who sketch out ideas which a professional brewer turns into reality, with whatever degree of input the customer is willing or able to provide.

At the other extreme are those who simply order existing beers from others, perhaps with a minor tweak or two, then label them as their own. A complete absence of information on the package about a beer's origins should alert you to such dubious practices. Not so very long ago, it was possible for anyone to order a pallet of an industrial beer of any colour, strength and sweetness from the Bavaria (Swinkels) brewery for relabelling, provided the name was unique.

In the descriptions below, we have tried to indicate where a producer stands on this spectrum, with more detail afforded to genuinely original products. As the scene is progressing rapidly and information is sometimes hard to obtain, we may occasionally have got this wrong, so apologise in advance to both readers and brewers.

The use of the term 'brewery' (*brouwerij*) implies the existence of a building with stand-alone equipment for making beer. If a company does not have this, it should not suggest to customers that it does. We disapprove of anyone practising this deceit.

1573

El Grecohof 1, 1816 MV Alkmaar
T 06 1259 9829
brouwerij1573.nl

Above-average beers made at Noord-Hollandse since 2016, named for the year Spanish occupation of the Alkmaar region ended.
BEERS INCLUDE: rounded, fruity dunkelweizen **Sonoy** (5%: ★★+); New England IPA **Metius** (5%: ★★+); easy-drinking hoppy blond **Trijn** (5.3%: ★★+); fruity golden amber **Drebbel** (5.5%: ★★+); tripel **Pinksterdrie** (7.4%); and beefy imperial stout **Caesius** (10%: ★★+).

4 Islands

Zomerhofstraat 71 unit 232, 3032 CK Rotterdam
T 06 8714 5257
4islands.com

Brazilians in the Netherlands making beer in Germany and the US since 2017. No, really.
BEERS INCLUDE: five-hopped guava IPA **Geronimo!** (4.8%: ★★+) and sharp cashew gose **Road Trippin'** (5%: ★★+).

7de Hemel

Klassenweg 13, 5975 PR Sevenum
T 077 467 3326
brouwerijde7dehemel.nl

Seventh Heaven, based in northern Limburg since 2006, originally brewed in nearby Horst but now gets its generally very good beers made at Proef in Belgium.
BEERS INCLUDE: blond New England IPA **Bengeltje** (5%: ★★+); dry saison **Bengel** (5.5%: ★★+); superior blond **Zonnestraal** (6.5%: ★★+); bitter red IPA **Diva** (7%: ★★+); standout hoppy IPA **Hopla** (7.5%: ★★★); and rounded black IPA **Visioen** (8%: ★★+).

84

Heerenveenseweg 2, 8471 BE Wolvega
T 06 2387 3207
brouwerij84.nl

Friesland homebrewers who turned pro in 2019, making their first commercial beer, elderflower-infused **Vlierbloesem IPA** (6.5%), at Brouwdok, mainly for sale in their own Pub '84 (address as above).

Alderbastend

Molenstraat 25, 7391 AA Twello
alderbastend.nl

Gelderland homebrewers who went commercial in 2019 using the facilities at De Werf.
BEERS INCLUDE: blond **Jolige Joppie** (6%); amber **Bennie Bang** (6.9%); and tripel **Flinke Freek** (8%).

Amazing Bliss

Weidehof 114, 1403 PN Bussum
facebook.com/amazingblissbrewing

North Holland-based brewers making great beers occasionally at Huttenkloas, such as **The Blissert** (11%: ★★★), a super-rich chewy imperial stout.

Amsterdam Brewboys

Seranggracht 15, 1019 PM Amsterdam
T 06 5478 0822
amsterdambrewboys.nl

Friends brewing mainly hop-forward beers at various locations including Lindeboom and Noord-Hollandse since 2014. A co-owner runs Bar Langendijk beside the IJ brewery in Amsterdam (Zeeburgerstraat 1), in effect their taproom.
BEERS INCLUDE: dry-hopped wheat ale **Kama Citra** (4.4%: ★★+); quaffable session ale **SIPA** (4.6%: ★★+); crisp, bitter-finishing **Amsterdam Pale Ale** (5.2%: ★★★); intensely hoppy IPA **Bombay Bastard** (6.2%: ★★★); and **Hophead Heaven** (7.5%: ★★+), a fine double IPA.

Amsterdam Brewing Company (ABC)

Vrolikstraat 160-H, 1092 TP Amsterdam
T 06 2695 9241
amsterdambrewing.com

Brewing at Huttenkloas since 2014, with a *de facto* taproom at Café Saloon in Amsterdam (Lijnbaansgracht 271).
BEERS INCLUDE: spiced **Flower Power** (5%: ★★+) with ginger, coriander and mountain tea; fruity IPA **Lost Identity** (6%: ★★+); and bitter double IPA **Guilty Pleasure** (9.2%: ★★+).

Apenzaken

Voorhelmstraat 9 RD, 2012 ZM Haarlem
brouwerijapenzaken.nl

Homebrewer turned pro in 2017, originally as Brouwer Zonder Baard (Beardless Brewer) but rebranded in 2018. First beer, brewed at Noord-Hollandse, was IPA **Kalia** (6.5%).

ARN

Strijplaan 168, 2285 HW Rijswijk
T 06 1099 2307
bierbrouwerijdearn.nl

Brewing at Huttenkloas since 2013, and with a licence to use the historic name Zuid-Hollandsche Brouwerij (ZHB) since 2018. A real brewery is planned once the right location in Rijswijk is found.

BEERS INCLUDE: weizen **Eigenweize Arn** (5.5% ★★); standard **Blonde Arn** (6.2%: ★★); dry, subtle **Stoute Arn** (6.6%: ★★+); sweetish **Dubbele Arn** (7.5%: ★★); restrained IPA **Iris' Pale Arn** (7.5%: ★★); and sweetish blond **Triple Arn** (8%: ★★).

SEASONAL: summer thirst quencher **Zomerse Arn** (3.5%: ★★+); dubbelbock **Bokkige Arn** (8%: ★★+); and darkly appealing **Winterse Arn** (9%: ★★+). *AS ZHB:* sweetish **1894 Weizen** (5.5%: ★★); golden **1881 Blond** (6.2%: ★★); and candy-sweet **1921 Dubbelbok** (8%: ★★).

Arnulfus

Energietdijk 9, 4706 HX Roosendaal
T 06 1092 0206
arnulfusbieren.nl

North Brabant company making beer since 2006, currently at 3 Horne.

BEERS INCLUDE: fruity blond **1809** (5.5%: ★★); coriander-spiced **Dubbel** (6%: ★★+); sweetish honeyed **Tripel** (7.5%: ★★+); and fruity, bitter-finishing **Zeer Stout** (8.8%: ★★+).

Arrr!

Ambachtweg 47, 2841 MB Moordrecht
T 06 1094 4345
arrr.beer

A pirate-obsessed South Holland outfit brewing at an unknown location since 2018.

BEERS INCLUDE: session IPA **Cali** (4.6%); weizen **Bruhaha** (5.2%); and pale ale **Waiho** (5.6%).

Assen

IJselstraat 19, 9406 TN Assen
T 0592 750585
wapenbier.nl

This Drenthe company first used the name Wapen Drents in 2016, but renamed itself in 2018. It produces **'t Wapen** beers at Veteraan.

BEERS INCLUDE: lightweight **Drents Edel Pils** (5%: ★★); timid IPA **Dutch Pale Ale** (6.5%: ★★+); unsubtle stout-ish **Dubbel** (7%: ★★); and dull blond **Tripel** (8%: ★★).

SEASONAL: autumnal **Herfstbok** (7%: ★★+), decent within its class.

Baardaap

Prinsenlaan 35, 4336 HJ Middelburg
baardaapbrewing.com

Founded in 2017 as De Krab, Bearded Ape now brews at Middelburg.

BEERS INCLUDE: chilli witbier **Zeeuwse Zonneschijn** (6%: ★★); pale ale **Uitmuntend** (6.5%: ★+), which adds mint tea to detrimental effect; hop-forward passion fruit IPA **Hoppy Howler** (7%: ★★+); and dry marshmallow milk stout **Chubby Chimp** (7.4%: ★★+).

Backstage

Laan van de Lemenhees 78, 7823 JK Emmen
facebook.com/Backstagebrewers

Longtime Drenthe homebrewers who went pro in 2018 with **Backstage Blond** (6.5%), brewed at Rockin' Ludina.

Bad Hair

Kapellerie 7, 4421 KZ Kapelle
T 06 3613 9141
badhairbrewing.nl

Zeeland-based father and son Bram and Jens van Stee have been brewing commercially since 2013 and currently work at Slot Oostende, where Jens is also head brewer.

BEERS INCLUDE: dry bitter **Hizug Blondje** (6%: ★★+); well-balanced triple-hopped IPA **Ut Bittere Eind** (6.5%: ★★+); and spiced, herbal **Stevug Tripel** (8%: ★★).

Barbier

Geuzenstraat 18, 4521 CC Biervliet
T 06 1173 2855
biermetstijl.com

Barber, active in Zeeland since 2016,
currently brews at Vermeersen.
BEERS INCLUDE: dull but dry **Irish Stout** (4.5%:
★★) and citrussy **Tarwe Tripel** (7.6%: ★★+).

Baros

Julianalaan 78, 5161 BC Sprang-Capelle
barosbier.nl

North Brabant company producing citrussy
blond witbier **First Summer** (5%: ★★) at
3 Horne since 2018.

Batjes

Walramplein 11 A, 6301 DC Valkenburg

The Ragamuffins, based in south Limburg,
have worked at various locations since 2018.
First beers were hoppy American pale ale
Batteraaf (5%: ★★+) and bitter dry-hopped
tripel **Verrèkkeling** (8%: ★★+).

Bavels (BABB)

Nieuwe Daalakker 6, 4854 PV Bavel
bavelsebierbrouwerij.nl

North Brabant company which debuted with
Bavels Blond (5.5%) in 2018.

Bazen

Pieter Zeemanweg 30T, 3316 GZ Dordrecht
T 06 2827 0889
bazenbrouwerij.nl

We believe this South Holland company,
founded in 2016, brews at Steffelaar.
BEERS INCLUDE: lightly bitter session IPA
Huisbaas (4.5%: ★★); crisp, blond dry-
hopped **Wit** (5%: ★★+); and golden dry rye
pale ale **Arye** (5.8%: ★★+).

BE+ER

PO Box 47, 2140 AA Vijfhuizen
T 06 1511 0131
be-er.nl

Launched in 2014 and now among the better
nomads, brewing hands-on at Noord-Hollandse.
BEERS INCLUDE: likeably quaffable **Session
IPA** (3.9%: ★★★); smoky schwarz/rauchbier
mashup **Rokerige Zwarte** (5.6%: ★★+);
Laurier Porter (5.9%: ★★+), spiced with bay;
herbal-spiced **Tripel Saison** (8.7% ★★); and
rounded, dangerously quaffable imperial
stout **RISPoetin** (10%: ★★★).

Bebaarde Brouwer

Jonker Fransstraat 113C, 3031 AR Rotterdam
debebaardebrouwer.nl

Begun in 2014, the Bearded Brewer is a side
project of Kaapse brewer Étienne Vermeulen,
making his own beer using his employers'
facilities.
BEERS INCLUDE: India Pale Lager
Pornstache (4.5%: ★★); hoppy wheat ale
Melksnoer (4.5%: ★★+); strongly bitter IPA
Mosaic Moustache (6.5%: ★★+);
StoppelBaard (6.5%: ★★+) stout with a burnt
sugar edge; and full-bodied rye IPA **Midnight
Moustache** (7%: ★★+).

Beekdal

Kerkstraat 33, 6871 BH Renkum
T 06 4150 9235
bkdl.nl

This Gelderland company, founded in 2018,
brews at a variety of Dutch locations under
the brand **BKDL**, which stands for Beter Koud
Dan Lauw (better cold than lukewarm).
BEERS INCLUDE: American amber **Oranje
Nassau's Rood** (5.2%)

Belgica

Marktstraat 42A, 4921 BG Made
belgica.nl

This one-man North Brabant producer, launched in 2015, commissions its only beer, multi-grained 'white saison' **Wittekop** (6.5%: ★★+), from Ter Dool in Belgium.

Bennebroecks

Bijweglaan 50, 2121 BJ Bennebroek
T 06 5147 9756
bennebroecks.nl

North Holland outfit since 2018, developing recipes at home in 15l batches and scaling up at Noord-Hollandse.
BEERS INCLUDE: Belgian-style **Het Blonde Hert** (5.5%) and barley wine **Het Edele Hert** (7.5%).

Berne

Abdijstraat 49, 5473 AD Heeswijk-Dinther
berneabdijbier.nl

This North Brabant-based outfit with monastic links has brewed at Val-Dieu in Belgium since 2015. It claims it will have its own kit in 2020, but we have heard that story before.
BEERS INCLUDE: standard **Norbertijn Blond** (6%: ★★); superior **Prior Dubbel** (8%: ★★+); and sweetish golden **Tripel** (9%: ★★).

Beste Maten

Parnassialaan 86, 2211 NW Noordwijkerhout
bestematenbrouwerij.nl

Three Best Mates from South Holland have made beers named after themselves since 2018, beginning with witbier **Fabian** (5%) and red ale **Maarten** (5.1%), with **Vincent** to follow.

Bezwooren Kerf

Hoofdweg 54, 1433 JW Kudelstaart
facebook.com/debezwoorenkerf.nl

North Holland company selling Belgian-style ales labelled as **Buck** since 2017, likely brewed at School.

BEERS INCLUDE: hefeweizen **44** (4%) and lightweight hoppy tripel **17** (7.1%: ★★).

Bierboerderij

Monseigneur Zwijsenstraat 10, 5076 NW Haaren
bierboerderij.nl

North Brabant-based since 2016, Beer Farm makes beers labelled **Bieren van de Nar**, most recently at Noord-Hollandse.
BEERS INCLUDE: standard **Blond** (6.1%: ★★); sweetish amber **Vienna** (6.5%: ★★); and golden **Tripel** (7.6%).

Bierbroeders

Ossenweide 12, 1689 MR Zwaag
T 06 2879 4233
facebook.com/De.Bierbroeders

North Holland's Beer Brothers have made numbered beers at Noord-Hollandse since 2014.
BEERS INCLUDE: five-hopped 'West Fries Pale Ale' **#1** (7%: ★★+); fruity Scotch ale **#2** (9%: ★★+); malty blond **#3** (6.5%: ★★); and dubbelbock **#4** (8.5%: ★★).

Bierkout

J.H.van Kinsbergenstraat 24, 1901 WT Castricum
bierkout.nl

Founded in 2018 by students from Amsterdam High School, who now make their only product, **Ontzettend Blond** (5.5%), at Noord-Hollandse.

Bierkwartier

Castellum 13, 2211 ZN Noordwijkerhout
brouwerijhetbierkwartier.nl

South Holland Beer Quarter, brewing at Steffelaar since 2017.
BEERS INCLUDE: subtle thyme-infused blond **Dauwtrapper** (5%: ★★+); citrus-hoppy white IPA **Nachtbraker** (5.7%: ★★+); and golden tripel **Herrieschopper** (9%: ★★+).

Bierverbond

Het Aambeeld 9B, 1969 NC Heemskerk
T 06 5511 7639
bierverbond.nl

Two North Holland friends making lager-style beers at Huttenkloas since 2018.
BEERS INCLUDE: amber California common beer **Hey Dude** (5%); amber lager **Oh Vienna** (5%); and India Pale Lager **Bombay** (5.5%).

Big Belly

Achterom 17, 4811 LS Breda
T 06 1123 1652
bigbellybrewing.nl

moerige
st

Ambitious young brewers making adventurous beers at various locations since 2016, though sometimes forgetting that less can be more.
BEERS INCLUDE: citrussy American-style wheat ale with lemongrass **Mo Phi** (4.5%: ★★+); fruity IPA **Smooth Louis** (6.9%: ★★+); even fruitier double New England IPA **Ahanu** (8%: ★★+); sweetish apple-infused tripel **Adam** (8.5%: ★★); complex, vanilla and cinnamon-spiced amber **Papa Midnight** (9%: ★★+); and peated imperial porter **Athelstan** (10%: ★★+).

Bijdehand

Poldermolen 29, 2661 LB Bergschenhoek
T 06 1737 5153

Side project since 2012 of current Bekeerde Suster head brewer Wesley Aarse.
Provenier *BEERS INCLUDE:* spring **Dubbellam** (7.8%: ★★+); and liquorice-tinted autumn **Dubbelbock** (7.8%: ★★+).

Billy The Mountain

Balloërweg 5, 9409 TN Loon
T 06 2475 0568
brouwerijbillythemountain.nl

Drenthe brewers named after a Frank Zappa song, scaling up their own test brews at Noord-Hollandse since 2018. Their promising

first beer was strongly bitter IPA **Holy Moses!** (7%: ★★+).

Bird

Diemerbospad 3, 1118 PZ Diemen
T 06 2689 9409
birdbrewery.com, houseofbird.nl

This Amsterdam-based business, founded in 2015, produces its confident, award-winning range at Jopen. It plans to open a House of Bird taproom with a pilot brewery at the above address in the city suburbs in 2020, but will still brew at commercial scale elsewhere.
BEERS INCLUDE: session IPA **Fuut Fieuw** (4.6: ★★+); dry, fruity saison **Datisandere Koekoek** (5.4%: ★★+); American amber **Rumoerige Roodborst** (5.8%: ★★+), with tropical fruit hints; malty IPA **Vink Heerlijk** (6.2%: ★★); raisin and coffee-tinged American-style brown ale **Nognietnaar Huismus** (6.4%: ★★+); and sweetish Scotch ale **Datsmaaktnaar Meerkoet** (6.8%: ★★+).
SEASONAL: easy-going meibock **Nog Eendje** (6%: ★★+) and sweetish dubbelbock **Lekker in de Kauw** (7%: ★★).

Black Baron

Rijssensestraat 179, 7441 AC Nijverdal
T 06 3640 4825
black-baron.nl

Overijssel brewer making beer with and at Koperen Ster in Enschede since 2017.
BEERS INCLUDE: rounded **Mandarina IPA** (5.5%: ★★+); golden **Citra Weizen** (5.6%: ★★+); an **American Pale Ale** (6.5%: ★★+); and a **Russian Imperial Stout** (8.7%).

Blauwe IJsbeer

Vuurkruidstraat 3, 2965 CJ Nieuwpoort
T 06 5349 2330
brouwerijdeblauweijsbeer.nl

The Blue Polar Bear began in South Holland in 2012 and is currently brewing at De Hemel.

BEERS INCLUDE: refreshing weizen **Weijsbeer** (5%: ★★); fruity gold-blond **Gouwe Ouwe IJsbeer** (6%: ★★); amber tripel **Mooie Weer IJsbeer** (8%: ★★); and tasty Scotch ale **Schotse IJsbeer** (8%: ★★+).

Bliksem

Vondelstraat 35, 4819 HD Breda
T 06 1868 9680
brouwerijbliksem.nl

Founded in 2015, Lightning currently makes its heavy metal-inspired beers, each with a recommended song pairing, at Breda brewery. Its BRACK taproom (see cafés), jointly run with Ramses, should gain a pilot brewery over the life of this guide.
BEERS INCLUDE: malty session IPA **Rye the Lightning** (4%: ★★); rounded pale ale **Pale Rider** (6.9%: ★★); dry blond **Saison in the Abyss** (7%: ★★); full-bodied black IPA **Kermis in de Ale** (7.3%: ★★+); sweetish honeyed tripel **Hemel Vuur** (9%: ★★); and fruity dark quadrupel **Black Sabbath** (10%: ★★+).
ALSO: **Grom**, an ever-changing, usually barrel-aged, imperial stout.

Blue Sheep

Dr. Schaepmanstraat 19, 7557 JA Hengelo
T 06 3809 2629
bluesheepbrewery.nl

Founded in 2017 by two brothers-in-law, working at Huttenkloas.
BEERS INCLUDE: **Blue Monday Saison** (6.2%) and **Goldy Locks Tripel** (8%);

Bluswater

Schijfmospad 11, 1314 MG Almere
T 06 4008 6477
brouwerijbluswater.nl

Firewater was founded in 2018 by three home-brewing firemen who also work at 7 Deugden.
BEERS INCLUDE: white ale **Witje** (5%); **Blondje** (5%); and quadrupel **Ladderzat** (10%).

Bombazijn

Molenstraat 24, 7571 CN Oldenzaal
T 06 5128 5351
debombazijn.nl

This Overijssel company has been planning its own brewery since 2014 but the site was still open ground when we last looked in 2019. Its beers, including a **Blond**, **Dubbel** and **Pale Ale**, are clearly made elsewhere.

Bommelaar

Prins van Oranjestraat 3, 5301 RA Zaltbommel
T 06 2000 6001
bommelaar.nl

Founded in 2013, likely brewing at Noord-Hollandse.
BEER: Düsseldorf-style **Alt** (5%); sweetish wheat ale **Mispelbier** (5%: ★★), made to a 1748 recipe; and mediocre **Stout** (6.5%: ★★).

Borst

Spanbroekerweg 29, 1715 GH Spanbroek
T 06 8338 0031
borstbier.nl

The name of this North Holland producer means 'breast' though also happens to be the last name of the owner, who launched it in 2019 with lightweight **Betrouwbaar Blond** (5.5%), brewed elsewhere as a first step towards opening a brewpub.

Boschdal

Groenstraat 16A, 4841 BD Breda-Prinsenbeek

Founded in 2017 and named after a local castle, brewing at 3 Horne.
BEERS INCLUDE: **Wit** (5%) and **Blond** (7%).

Boslust

Pastoriehoef 2, 5131 EH Alphen
brouwerij-boslust.nl

Two North Brabant friends working at 3 Horne since 2017.
BEERS INCLUDE: **Blond** (6.6%); Belgian-style pale ale **Blom** (7.2%); and tripel **Bazuin** (8.2%).

Boys

Korte Papaverweg 15, 1032 KA Amsterdam
boysbier.com

Begun in 2016 by design studio La Bolleur, brewing its pilsener **Boys Bier** (5%) at Troost.

Braaf

Sint Eloystraat 12, 6024 BS Budel-Dorplein
braafbrewery.nl

One-man company founded in 2017, seemingly content to experiment at home with bold ingredients. The only beer released on a commercial scale to date has been grapefruity IPA **Brave Gijt** (5.9%: ★★★), a collaboration with Nate Gijt made at Weerter.

Brabants Gevoel

Rubensstraat 13, 5102 DT Dongen
T 06 5511 1284
tbrabantsgevoel.nl

The Brabant Feeling, founded in 2017, pilots organic beers in house before upscaling at Weerter.
BEERS INCLUDE: witbier **Witte Tonnie** (6.3%) and sweetish tripel **d'n Dieje** (8%: ★★).

Bracque

Brinkhuisburg 63, 7511 MK Enschede
bracque.nl

Brewing company founded in 2015, currently working at Huttenkloas. Its name is a reference to BRAK, a student group at Twente university.
BEERS INCLUDE: pale lager **Single Blonde** (6%) and white IPA **Zon Zuiper** (6%).

Brakkerij

Jupiterstraat 5, 3582 PT Utrecht
facebook.com/debrakkerij

Founded by a group of bread bakers in 2016, working at Oproer.
BEERS INCLUDE: dark rye ale **Black Velvet** (5.5%: ★★); banana-dominated weizen IPA **Whale Rider** (6%: ★★+); and smoky, whisky-malted Vienna lager **Whisky Wiener** (6.9%: ★★+).

Brasser

Oude Postweg 118, 3711 AL Austerlitz
T 0343 491010
brouwerbrasser.nl

One-man business from Utrecht province, working at the A Brewery since 2017.
BEERS INCLUDE: sweetish, fruity **Amber 1804** (6.3%: ★★); sweet, banana-tinged **Austerlitzer Pale Ale** (6.4%: ★★); and standout vanilla-tinted **Oude Post Blond** (6.4%: ★★+).

Braxzz

Keizersgracht 391A, 1016 EJ Amsterdam
braxzzamsterdam.com

We applaud the intentions of this Anglo-Dutch team who started making no and low alcohol craft beers in 2018, though the results so far have been middling at best. The brewing location is also annoyingly vague.
BEERS INCLUDE: pointless **Session IPA** (0%: ★+); chocolate-tinged but thin **Porter** (0%: ★★); lightly bitter **Rebel IPA** (0.2%: ★★); and its fruitier sister **Orange IPA** (0.2%: ★★).

Breugem

Lagedijk 192, 1544 BM Zaandijk
T 088 130 8890
brouwerijbreugem.nl

Patrick Breugem rescued his **Saense** brands after his own brewery went to the wall in 2013 by cuckoo brewing them elsewhere.

They are currently produced at Hoop where he previously also worked as head brewer.
BEERS INCLUDE: dry-hopped quaffer **Session** (3%: ★★); citrussy **Wit** (4.3%: ★★); mildly bitter-hoppy **IPA** (6.2%: ★★); dry blond **Zoentje** (6.3%: ★★); occasionally brewed cocoa-forward **Dark IPA** (7.4%: ★★+); **Heet & Stout** (8%: ★★★), subtly spiced with sambal; full-bodied, bitter-finishing **Tripel** (8.1%: ★★+); strongly bitter golden **Double IPA** (8.3%: ★★★); sweetish **Quadrupel** (9.5%: ★★+); and aromatic Palo wood-infused **Kracht Hout** (9.5%: ★★★).
SEASONAL: superior spring blond **Lente Kus** (7%: ★★+).

Bridge

Wethouder Teselinglaan 6, 3972 GB Driebergen-Rijsenburg
bridgebrewhouse.com

Company in Utrecht province making beers at an unknown location since 2018.
BEERS INCLUDE: American pale ale **Mistico** (5.4%); hefeweizen **Skinny** (5.6%); New England IPA **Longfellow** (5.9%); US-hopped **Golden Gate IPA** (6.8%); and imperial stout **Tower** (8.5%).

Briljant

De Genestetstraat 19, 2032 ZJ Haarlem
briljantbrouwhuis.nl

Rob Alphenaar, landlord of the Lokaal in Haarlem (see cafés), has brewed occasionally since 2015 at various locations including Oproer and Noord-Hollandse.
BEERS INCLUDE: hoppy golden pale ale **Hannes de Vijfhoek** (5.5%: ★★) and smoky, fruity imperial **Stoeien met Stout** (9.8%: ★★+).

Broederliefde

Perzikkruid 10, 4823 CH Breda
brouwerijbroederliefde.nl

Established by two North Brabant brothers-in-law in 2019, Brotherly Love makes its beers at an unknown location.
BEERS INCLUDE: **Blonde Monster** (6.4%); **Triple Trouble** (7.7%); and quadrupel **Bomb's Quad** (8.7%).

Bronzen Ezel

Spoellaan 7, 1964 TA Heemskerk
debronzenezel.nl

Founded in 2019 by the brewer of now-defunct 5Hoog, North Holland-based Bronze Donkey brews no more than a few times a year at various Dutch locations. The name derives from a statue in the town centre.

Broodnodig

Janzenstraat 78, 1781 RD Den Helder
T 06 4053 1726
broodnodigbier.nl

North Holland company founded in 2017, brewing bread-based beers at Helderse Jongens.
BEERS INCLUDE: **American Pale Ale** (4%) and **American Brown Ale** (4.5%).

Brothers In Law

Eerste Anjelierdwarsstraat 12A, 1015 NR Amsterdam
T 06 2996 7123
brothersinlawbrewing.nl

Founded in 2017, indeed by three brothers-in-law, one of whom works as a brewer at Loon where the beers are currently made.
BEERS INCLUDE: stress-free **0.5 Hoppy Lager** (0.5%); bitter **India Pale Lager** (4.9%: ★★+); rounded **Australian Pale Ale** (5.8%: ★★+); US-hopped **American Brown Ale** (5.8%: ★★+); a competent **Blond** (5.9%: ★★); sweetish **East Coast Porter** (6%: ★★); and golden **Tripel** (8.5: ★★)

Brouwbeesten

G.J.M. Sarlemijnstraat 34, 1064 DK Amsterdam
brouwbeesten.nl

The Brewing Beasts are homebrewers who began working commercially at various locations in 2018.
BEERS INCLUDE: chilli IPA **Anacondor** (6.5%) and lovely black IPA **Nacht Vlinder** (6.8%: ★★★).

Brouwhuys

PO Box 1160, 3840 BD Harderwijk
T 06 1000 2425
hetbrouwhuys.nl

Despite its name, the Brewhouse, founded in Gelderland in 2017, does not have a brewhouse and is less than clear about where its beers are actually made.
BEERS INCLUDE: blond **Hoge Brugge** (4.7%); amber **Lage Brugge** (6.1%); and tripel **Lutteke** (8.5%).

Brouwvakkers

Scheltemastate 50, 8926 LT Leeuwarden
T 06 1879 1899
debrouwvakkers.nl

The Brew Workers, founded in 2018, claim to brew in Leeuwarden though we think the Brouwdok in Harlingen may be closer to the truth.
BEERS INCLUDE: blond gose **Gosse** (4.2%) and imperial stout **Dokter O.** (12%).

BrouwVrouw

Dijk 6, 1601 GJ Enkhuizen
T 0228 315767
facebook.com/debrouwvrouw

The Brewing Woman is the owner of the Ankertje pub in Enkhuizen (see cafés), who has brewed at Noord-Hollandse since 2016.
BEERS INCLUDE: witbier **Witte Kaatje** (5.5%: ★★); dryish amber **Alex Ankertje** (6%: ★★+); nutty black IPA **Black Enkertje** (6%: ★★+); unassuming blond **Lecker Blontje** (6%: ★★), rounded **Dubbel Leckertje** (6.5%: ★★+); and bittersweet tripel **Tankertje** (8%: ★★).

Bûsdoek

De Kastanje 34, 9251 NT Burgum
brouwerijbusdoek.nl

Named in Frisian as Handkerchief, this business was founded by five friends in 2018, though it's unclear where they are currently brewing.
BEERS INCLUDE: hoppy, zesty witbier **Wiis Prater** (6.2%: ★★+) and sweetish brown IPA **Nachtdraver** (7.1%: ★★).

Callantsoger

De Gorsen 30, 1759 XN Callantsoog
facebook.com/callantsogerbier

North Holland business which turned pro in 2018 after the owners won a brewing competition, launching their first beer in 2019: Belgian-style pale ale **Duinmannetje** (4%).

Casle

Markt 1, 5995 BB Kessel
T 06 5316 3616
facebook.com/caslebier

The name of this Limburg brewer, founded in 2017, is a corruption of and pronounced Castle. Another one with an obscure brewing location.
Kessel *BEERS INCLUDE:* **Blondj** (4.8%); witbier **Witte** (6.7%); and **Triepel** (7.5%).

CC

Sonsbeeksingel 105, 6822 BJ Arnhem
T 06 1641 4608
brouwerij.cc

Created in 2015 to make house beers for the Caspar in Arnhem at various locations with guidance from Dennis Kort of Oldskool (below).

BEERS INCLUDE: amber **American Wheat Ale** (6.1%) and dangerously drinkable, full-bodied old ale **Walden** (8.5%: ★★★).

Ceaux

PO Box 3041, 3502 GA Utrecht
T 06 4302 5021
ceaux.nl

Pronounced as in the name of owner Ko Hendriks, with accomplished beers made at a variety of locations since 2013.
BEERS INCLUDE: dry, hoppy American-style wheat ale **Bastard** (5%: ★★★); full-bodied oatmeal stout **Breakfast** (7%: ★★+); and beefy brown triple IPA **Cane** (10%: ★★★) with smoked peppers and sugar cane, like a rauchbier on steroids.

Christoffel

Raadhuisstraat 28, 4835 JB Breda
christoffelbieren.com

Fallen angel (Sint) Christoffel was a pioneering Dutch microbrewery that challenged conservative tastes when it launched in 1986 with a double-hopped pilsener. It closed in 2013, but the brand survived and is currently produced at Proef in Belgium.
BEERS INCLUDE: crisp **Blond** (5.4%: ★★); dry-hopped weizen IPA **W-IPA** (6.5%: ★★+); and spiced blond **Tripel** (8.5%: ★★).

Cinema

Korte Papaverweg 2H, 1032 KB Amsterdam
T 06 4507 0995
cinemabrewers.com

Another of the better nomads, producing often-excellent beers with movie-inspired names at various locations since 2014, most commonly De Molen.
BEERS INCLUDE: dry-hopped American-style lager **Lebowski** (4.5%: ★★+); passion fruit pale ale **Dancing Dirty** (5.3%: ★★+); fruit and vanilla-infused pale ale **$5 Shake** (5.5%: ★★★); lemongrass IPA **Apocalypse** (6.5%:

★★+); bitter red ale **Brimstone** (6.5%: ★★+) with blood oranges; and tripel **King Kong** (8%: ★★), which merely reinforces our distrust of coconut in beer.

Crans

Edelhertweg 75, 1338 KB Almere
T 06 1459 7190
facebook.com/cranscraftbeer

Flevoland brewer working at various locations since 2016, most recently at Martinus.
BEERS INCLUDE: blond/saison hybrid **Fem** (5.1% ★★); fruity bitter IPA **Ciprianus** (7%: ★★+); and rich, if a little thin-bodied, Baltic porter **Sicco** (7.6% ★★+).

Crazy Black Cat

Het Wolbert 23b, 7545 WK Enschede
irishbeer.nl

Overijssel brewers since 2017, making their Irish-inspired **Dublin** range at Koperen Ster.
BEERS INCLUDE: dry **Red** (5.1%: ★★+); marshmallowy **Dark Red** (5.8%: ★★+); and lightly bitter **Dry Stout** (6.8%: ★★+).

Cuijks

Cuijkse Brouwbrigade
facebook.com/cuijksebrouwbrigade

Gelderland brewers based in Cuijk, making their **Kuuks** beer range at Wilskracht since 2017.
BEERS INCLUDE: hazy bitter **New England IPA** (5.8%: ★★) and dry blond **Brut Saison** (6%).

Daan's Moonshine

Arenberglaan 350, 4822 ZS Breda
facebook.com/Daansmoonshine

North Brabant brewer since 2017, working at Opener.
BEERS INCLUDE: pilsener **Allemansvrind** (6%) and blond tripel **Drie Keer Nee is Ja** (9%).

Die

Maasstraat 281, 1823 XL Alkmaar
brouwerijdedie.nl

North Holland company founded in 2015,
currently brewing pseudo-historical beers at
Radboud.
BEERS INCLUDE: intrusively ginger-spiced
blond **8 October** (5.5%: ★★), almost an
alcopop; herbal blond **'t Cieraedt van Alkmaar**
(5.8% ★★); honey-tinged, sweetish **Dirk Duyvel
Blond** (6.3%: ★★); and sweetish Belgian-style
amber **'t Swaart van Cabeliau** (8%: ★★).

Diggelfjoer

Bosschawei 5, 9212 RG Boornbergum
brouwerijdiggelfjoer.nl

Fries brewer since 2016, upscaling home-
developed recipes at Admiraals.
BEERS INCLUDE: faintly hoppy blond **Naflik**
(5%: ★★); blond tripel **Suver Nuver** (9%: ★★);
and dark quadrupel **Grutsk** (10%: ★★+).

Doesburgh

De Bogaert 37, 6983 HE Doesburg
T 06 2110 6605
dorstigedriftkop.nl

Gelderland company founded in 2017 and
making **Dorstige Driftkop** beers at an
unknown location for the local market.

Door Mannen

Burgemeester van Roosmalenstraat 20,
1911 EZ Uitgeest
bierdoormannen.nl

North Holland-based Beer By Men has
produced its only beer, tripel **Staal** (7.5%),
at Noord-Hollandse since 2018.

Dorstige Mees

Mezenlaan 21, 2566 ZB Den Haag
dedorstigemees.nl

The Thirsty Tit, founded by homebrewers in
2018, works at Naeckte Brouwers.
BEERS INCLUDE: IPA **North Seapâh** (6.2%);
saison **Rokjesdag** (6.7%); and imperial **Houtje
Stoutje** (10%).

Drentsche Schans

Den Hool 4, 7845 TG Holsloot
T 0591 564160
drentscheschans.nl

This business founded in 2002 in a Drenthe farming hamlet sends local grain to Van Steenberge
in Belgium for use in its beers. Its café-taproom
is only open for darts nights (*Th from 19.30*).
BEERS INCLUDE: mediocre **Pilsener** (5%: ★+);
standard spiced white **Olde Witte** (5.2%: ★★);
Boeren Blond (7%: ★★); and dubbel-strength
amber **Turfsteker** (7%: ★★).

Duin

Buitenduinstraat 8, 1361 BE Almere
T 06 2879 2775
duinbrouwerij.nl

Flevoland company since 2019, making beers
such as elderflower-spiced **American Pale Ale
Vlierbloesem** (6%) and orange peel-infused
Tripel Sinaasappelschillen (7.5%) at an
unknown location, but with long-term plans
for their own brewpub.

Duindaw

Meester Ludwigstraat 20, 1901 PT Castricum
T 06 1046 1057
duindauw.nl

North Holland's Dune Dew has been making
beers at Noord-Hollandse since 2017.
BEERS INCLUDE: dry-hopped IPA **Hoppige
Hilde** (5%); standard **Blozend Blond** (6%: ★★)
with a secret ingredient that could be ginger or
galangal; and peachy tripel **Dorps Gek** (8.8%: ★★).

Ebontree

Wega 83, 3328 PG Dordrecht
T 06 4411 5675
ebontree.nl

South Holland brewer making **Ebon** beers at Weerter since 2017.
BEERS INCLUDE: session IPA **Rye 2.0** (5.5%); fruity **IPA** (6.6%: ★★+); nettly, aromatic **3C IPA** (7.2%: ★★+); and **Dark Ale** (9%: ★★+), with caramel flavours.
SEASONAL: zesty **Summer Wheat** (4.6%: ★★+) and autumnal **Smoked Bock** (7.5%: ★★+).

Eeuwig Zonde

Slievenstraat 46, 5711 PL Someren
T 06 2003 1349
brouwerijeeuwigzonde.nl

North Brabant-based Eternal Sin, launched in 2016, currently brews at Loon and Weerter.
BEERS INCLUDE: lightly refreshing **Session IPA** (3.5%: ★★+); blond **Eeuwig Zon** (4.9%); herbal **Blond** (6.3%: ★★); raisiny **Dubbel** (7.4%: ★★); and sweetish spiced **Tripel** (8.2%: ★★).

Eeuwige Jeugd

Linnaeusstraat 37A, 1093 EG Amsterdam
T 06 1420 3868
deeeuwigejeugd.nl

Founded in 2016, Eternal Youth initially brewed locally at Troost, but most of its beers now come from Anders in Belgium. A *de facto* taproom opened in late 2019 (page 304).
BEERS INCLUDE: bitter-finishing white IPA **Gladjanus** (5.2%: ★★+); fruity blond **Lellebel** (5.7%: ★★+); dry IPA **Belhamel** (6.5%: ★★+); and sweetish weizen-tripel **Bullebak** (7.7%: ★★).

Eggens

Van Goghstraat 22, 9718 MP Groningen
T 06 4007 7207
eggenscraftbeer.com

Founded in 2017 and currently working locally at Bax.

BEERS INCLUDE: standard **Weizen** (5.8%: ★★); bitter blond **IPA** (6.7%: ★★+); sweetish **Zwaar Blond** (7.9%: ★★); and malty blond **Tripel** (8.1%: ★★).

Eiber

Den Helderstraat 64, 2547 SN Den Haag
T 06 4399 2522
eiberbier.nl

South Holland producer since 2016, likely working at Noord-Hollandse.
BEERS INCLUDE: balanced American-style wheat ale **Achter De Duinen** (4.5%: ★★+); dull, malty **Hof Blond** (6.4%: ★★); copper IPA **Zeer Hoppig Bier** (6.8%: ★★), not that hoppy despite the name; and chestnut-brown, coffee-laden **De Baron** (6.8%: ★★).

Eigen Schuld

Tolsteegbarrière 2, 3511 ZD Utrecht
T 030 234 3538
facebook.com/Brouwerijeigenschuld

Own Fault has brewed for the owner's cafés (including Lijn 4: see cafés) at Kompaan since 2017.
BEERS INCLUDE: pale ale **Blonde Saar** (5.5%) and IPA **Dikke Bult** (6%).

Elfen

Elfenbank 5, 9404 ME Assen
T 06 2524 3614
de-elfen.nl

Drenthe homebrewers working commercially at Noarder Dragten since 2018.
BEERS INCLUDE: **Elfendubbel** (7%); **Elfenblond** (7.2%); and **Elfentripel** (8.2%).

Engelbertus

Oderlaan 34, 5691 MB Son en Breugel
engelbertus.be

Begun in North Brabant in 2017 and currently making its promising beers at Weerter.

BEERS INCLUDE: fruity rich IPA **Het Doet Leven** (7.5%: ★★+); strongly bitter dry-hopped double IPA **Hop Doet Beven** (8%: ★★+); and superbly rounded, cocoa-edged Baltic porter **Zachte Hemelmeester** (8%: ★★★).

Enkhuizer

Parklaan 14, 1601 EK Enkhuizen
T 06 4672 4834
enkhuizerbierbrouwerij.nl

Founded as Pierewaaier in 2016, this brewer specialises in wheat beers named **Witte Hulck** after a medieval brewhouse, with recipes developed on a 35l kit and upscaled at Huttenkloos.
BEERS INCLUDE: faintly perfumed **Weizen** (5.5%: ★★); and cocoa-tinged **Weizenbock** (7.4%: ★★+).

EPE

Epe Bier Collectief, Laar Enk 4, 8162 CH Epe
T 06 2335 3387
epebier.nl

Homebrewers working commercially at various locations since 2012.
BEERS INCLUDE: lemongrass and ginger-spiced blond **Zzzoef** (4%: ★★); burnt-edged schwarzbier **Afschot** (5.5%: ★★+); dunkel-weizen **Duuster Wit** (6.2%: ★★+); bitter, wet-hopped IPA **Praotnat** (6.2%: ★★★); and copper-amber quadrupel **Rein** (10%: ★★).

Floembier

Hoofdweg 36, 9905 PD Holwierde
floembier.nl

This Groningen outfit brewed its first beer, IPA **Grote Verbond** (6.5%), at Parkzicht in 2019.

Folkingebrew

Folkingestraat 18, 9711 JW Groningen
folkingebrew.nl

Brewing spinoff from the Just in Beer bottle shop (see cafés), producing one-off beers at various locations since 2018.

Fontaine

Vogelschordreef 8, 4551 MH Sas van Gent
T 06 1828 4547
brouwerijlafontaine.com

The Fountain has been based in Zeeuws-Vlaanderen since 2012, but commissions its beer from De Graal in Belgium.
BEERS INCLUDE: blond **Belle & Elegante** (6.5%: ★★) and amber **Belle & Forte** (7%: ★★+).

Frankendael

Entrada 100, 1114 AA Amsterdam
frankendaelbrewing.com

Brewing at various locations since 2015.
BEERS INCLUDE: lightweight saison **Tramp Stamp** (3.5%: ★★+); citrussy witbier **White Bastard** (5.5%: ★★); fruity pale ale **Billy Balster** (6%: ★★+); sweetish, not-very-English 'English-style' **Mello Pale Ale** (7.5%: ★★); herbal weizenbock **Uberweizen** (8.5%: ★★+); and Sichuan pepper-spiced tripel **TITS** (Three Idiots Tripel Spiced, 9.5%: ★★).

Gallivant

Hondsdraf 3, 7491 LH Delden
T 06 5788 4749
gallivant.nl

Overijssel company formed in 2018, working at Huttenklaos.
BEERS INCLUDE: citrussy **Wit** (5.2%: ★★+); New Zealand-hopped IPA **Maori Madness** (7.5%); sweetish **De Blonde Amber** (8%: ★★), which can't decide what it wants to be; and dry, bitter tripel **Wingman** (9%: ★★+).

Gebroeders Hop

Dieze 18, 5032 XH Tilburg
T 06 2901 4347
gebroedershop.nl

Active in North Brabant since 2016, the Hop Brothers brew at 3 Horne.
BEERS INCLUDE: witbier **Witte Wè** (4.5%); weizen **El Blanquito** (6%); fruity IPA **Grapefruit**

145

Coby (7.6%: ★★+); double IPA **Standje Gemak** (7.6%); and chilli tripel **Scoville** (7.7%);

Gebrouwen Door Vrouwen

Nieuwe Hemweg 4F, 1013 BG Amsterdam
T 06 3807 6029
gebrouwendoorvrouwen.nl

Two friends founded Brewed by Women in 2015, working at Noord-Hollandse with a taproom, De Bar, in Amsterdam (see cafés). *BEERS INCLUDE:* seaweed-dosed witbier **Zonnig Zeewit** (3.8%: ★★+); ginger-laced pale ale **Gember Goud** (4.6%: ★★+); juniper-spiced **Gin Weizen** (6%: ★★+); sweetish **Strawberry Blond** (6.3%: ★★); hoppy **Bloesem Blond** (6.7%: ★★+), with elderflower; and easy-drinking **Tricky Tripel** (7.8%: ★★+).

Geusz!

Violiervaart 32, 2724 VT Zoetermeer
geusz.nl

Founded in South Holland in 2015, with a **Blond** (5.5%), **Dubbel** (8.5%), and **Tripel** (8.5%) made at Boelens in Belgium.

Gierbier

Peelkant 61, 5845 EG Sint Anthonis
T 06 2903 3582
gierbier.nl

North Brabant operation which launched its first beer, a **Blond** (5.8%), in late 2019.

Goat

Sonmansstraat 62 B 02, 3039 DL Rotterdam
thegoatrotterdam.nl

Brewing at various Dutch locations since 2018. *BEERS INCLUDE:* nutty **Pale Ale** (5.5%: ★★+) and superior US-hopped **Bad Kid IPA** (6%: ★★★).

Goede Kant van het Spoor

Korenland 28, 5663 HE Geldrop
T 06 3419 4249
goedekantvanhetspoor.nl

Right Side of the Tracks, launched in North Brabant in 2016, brews occasionally at Weerter. *BEERS INCLUDE:* cocoa-laden, bitter-finishing barley wine **Chocolate Monster** (8.4%: ★★+).

Goede Verwachting

Hortensialaan 75, 9713 KL Groningen
T 06 4129 1291
facebook.com/bdgv.nl

Founded in 2017 by homebrewers who were half a notch less optimistic than Dickens, Good Expectations makes its beer at Noarder Dragten. *BEERS INCLUDE:* dry, bitter **OPA** (Oosterpakker Pale Ale) (7%: ★★).

Goorsch Gruyt

facebook.com/GoorschGruytBier

This Overijssel outfit began in 2012 by recreating historical beers. Activity ceased in 2016 following the untimely death of a co-founder, but there were signs of a resurgence in 2019.

Gouden Leeuw

Jan Smuldersstraat 24, 5512 AZ Vessem
T 0497 591252
brouwerijvessem.nl

The Golden Lion housed a brewery from the 17th century until 1954, ultimately run by the grandmother of the current owner of the pub on the site, who since 2011 has commissioned house **Beerze** beers from Malheur in Belgium. *BEERS INCLUDE:* lightweight blond **Bier** (5.5%: ★★); more complex blond **Brave** (7.5%: ★★); and triple-hopped blond barley wine **Bold** (10.5%: ★★+).

Graafsch Genot

Reigershorst 1, 5361 TJ Grave
graafschgenot.nl

Active in North Brabant since 2014, upscaling home-developed recipes at Wijchense Schone. *BEERS INCLUDE:* witbier **Witte Reiger** (5%: ★★); banana-tinged dubbel **Sint Elisabeth** (6.5%: ★★); **Pothuus** (8%) tripel; and whisky-malted quadrupel **Strafpaard** (9%).

Graansilobier

Griffeweg 4, 9724 GG Groningen
T 050 200 3600
graansilobier.nl

Brewing at Martinus since 2018 using only local ingredients. *BEERS INCLUDE:* standard **Blond** (6%: ★★); lightly hopped **IPA** (5.7%: ★★+); and a golden **Tripel** (8%: ★★).

Grits

Burgemeester de Bruïnelaan 83, 3331 AC Zwijndrecht
T 06 2313 5175
brouwerijgrits.nl

Two South Holland friends who turned pro in 2019. *BEERS INCLUDE:* weizen **Yeoman** (5.6%); blond **Gold Miner** (6.1%); rye pale ale **Farmhand** (6.9%); and dark barley wine **Blacksmith** (10.3%).

Groninger

Noorderhaven 25, 9712 VG Groningen
groningerbier.nl

Founded in 2015, working at Huttenkloas. *BEERS INCLUDE:* malty but balanced **Spelt Pale Ale** (5%: ★★+); citrussy **Oerspelt Weizen** (6%: ★★); more liquorice than **Sweet Stout** (6%: ★★); bitter-finishing **American Pale Ale** (8%: ★★); and heavyweight **Zwaar Blond** (9%).

Groningse

PO Box 5091, 9700 GB Groningen
T 050 318 3563
grunn-speciaalbier.nl

Not to be confused with the above, this Groningen-based business has long cast a dark shadow, commissioning what we believe are off-the-peg brews from Belgium and Germany with a variety of local-sounding brand names like **Grunn**, **Hunebed**, **Zeebier** and **Kruisheren**.

Groos

Marius Richtersstraat 78, 3059 TH Rotterdam
T 06 5425 1244
facebook.com/BrouwerijGroos

Two South Holland-based homebrewers who went pro in 2019, using Noord-Hollandse to make their first commercial beer, **Tripel Twee** (8%).

Grutte Pier

Slauerhoffweg 9a, 8912 BH Leeuwarden
T 06 8151 7844
gruttepierbrouwerij.nl

Brewing locally at Admiraals since 2014. *BEERS INCLUDE:* lightweight but competent **Blond** (4.5%: ★★); faintly fruity **Dubbel** (7%: ★★); bittersweet **Tripel** (7.5%: ★★+), also made with rainwater as **Frieze Boezem**; sharpish Brett-infused wood-aged tripel **Bretttûne** (8%: ★★★); raisiny dark **Quadrupel** (9.5%: ★★+); and chewy, malty **Kracht in de Nacht** (10%: ★★+).

Gudzekop

It Hôf 44, 8511 AG Goingarijp
gudzekop.nl

Based in Friesland, working at Bax. *BEERS INCLUDE:* raspberry wheat ale **Opgedirkt** (5.6%); American pale ale

Overzees (6%); and juniper and coriander-spiced blond **Opsteker** (6.4%: ★★).

Gula

Randweg 60, 7944 BM Meppel
T 06 3197 3882
facebook.com/gulabeers

Drenthe homebrewers who turned pro in 2018 after winning a competition, now working at Noord-Hollandse.
BEERS INCLUDE: dry **Zonneblond** (5.8%: ★★) and multi-hopped, mercifully not **Sweet IPA** (6.5%: ★★+).

Haas

Faunalaan 186, 3972 PS Driebergen-Rijsenburg
haasbieren.nl

Founded in 2016 in Utrecht province, Hare brews at Wijchense Schone and the A Brewery, and earns a gold star from us for the transparency of its labelling.
BEERS INCLUDE: rounded, copper-amber English-style bitter **Hop of the Old Block** (5.2%: ★★+); lightly smoky, well-balanced peated ale **Peatje Precies** (6.3%: ★★+); beatifully rounded inky-black IPA **Once You Go Black** (6.3%: ★★★); and sweetish tripel **Haasje Over** (8.4%: ★★).

Hagemeester

Rijksstraatweg 174, 6573 DG Beek-Ubbergen
T 024 684 2294
hagemeester.nl

Gelderland brewer since 2015, making beers locally at Drul & Stollenberg.
BEERS INCLUDE: a **Weizen** (5.5%); **Saison** (6.5%); and **Tripel** (8%).

Halsche

Groenestraat 15, 6681 DW Bemmel
halschestoombierbrouwerij.nl

Gelderland company founded in 2013, following what it claims are old recipes for beers commissioned from Den Triest in Belgium, such as gold-blond **Goud** (6.5%) and amber **Isabella** (7.5%).

Halve Ton

Akkerstraat 47, 5025 ME Tilburg
T 06 2312 3944

The name Half Ton refers to the combined weight of its five portly co-owners, who have been brewing normal beer styles in abnormal strengths at Tilburg brewery since 2019.
BEERS INCLUDE: pilsener **Mannenpils** (7%) and witbier on steroids **Frisse Jongen** (7.8%).

Hanneker

Hannekerveldweg 17, 7581 BC Losser
brouwerijhanneker.nl

Overijssel brewers active since 2017, making German-style beers at Ootmarsummer.
BEERS INCLUDE: **Weizen Licht Gebrand** (5%) and dark **Weizen Dubbel Bock** (7.5%).

Hapj

Scheepersdijk 2A, 5062 EC Oisterwijk
hapj.nl

Launched in 2018 with hefeweizen **Weissneus** (6%), North Brabant-based Snack works at Vandeoirsprong.

HappyFace

Kempenlaan 21, 1966 PA Heemskerk
happyfacebeers.com

The two brothers who founded this cheerfully-named brewery in 2016 are the Netherlands' and possibly the world's tallest brewers, unmissable at every beer festival they attend. They brew at Koperen Kat.
BEERS INCLUDE: bitter but rounded session IPA **SIPA** (3.5%: ★★★); dry, lightly hoppy **Stout**

(6%: ★★★); fruity, hoppy weizen/IPA **Scapegoat** (6.5%: ★★+); standard **Weizen** (6.5%: ★★); quaffable, lightly bitter **IPA** (7%: ★★+); and coriander and orange-spiced **Tripel** (8%: ★★+).
SEASONAL: superior cocoa-tinged autumnal **Bock 666** (8%: ★★+) and darkly spiced heavyweight **Winter Frost** (10%: ★★+).

Heaps of Hops

Diamantstraat 17B H, 1074 GA Amsterdam
heapsofhops.com

Founded in 2016 with a range of hop-forward but session-strength beers brewed at Troost. The owner's name is Bjørn, hence the odd spelling of the names.
BEERS INCLUDE: citrussy, floral session IPA **Bøcketlist** (3.5%: ★★+); UK-hopped saison **Vønkelwater** (3.5%: ★★); copper-amber 'Bohemian' pale ale **Bjørning Man** (3.8%: ★★+); and citrussy golden ale **Gøld** (3.8%: ★★+).

Heer van Oranje

PO Box 155, 4650 AD Steenbergen
heervanoranje.nl, witkruis.nl

Brewing at Argentum since 2016 but actively looking for a suitable location to install its own brewhouse.
BEERS INCLUDE: hazy blond **Weizen** (4.8%: ★★+); bitter **Pale Ale** (5%: ★★+); fruity amber **IPA** (6%: ★★); nutty, dry **Saison** (6.5%: ★★); and spiced blond **Tripel** (8.5%: ★★).
ALSO: beers for the local market branded **Het Wit Kruis**.

Heeren van Borculo

Geesterse Binnenweg 4a, 7271 VX Borculo
heerenvanborculo.nl

Based in the Gelderland Achterhoek since 2017, the Gentlemen of Borculo make their beers locally at Erve Kots.
BEERS INCLUDE: sweetish blond **Sufferd** (5.2%) and **Cycloon Weizen** (5.5%).

Heerlijk & Eerlijk

Daalderstraat 4, 4285 AV Woudrichem
woerkumer.nl, altenabier.nl

Not-for-profit Delicious & Honest, founded in 2007, makes beers under two separate brands at Van Steenberge in Belgium.
Woerkumer *BEERS INCLUDE:* witbier **Witte** (5%); **Blondje** (8%); and a **Tripel** (8%).
ALSO: **Altena** beers made with local North Brabant hops, such as **India Pale Al(T)e(NA)** (8%).

Heesakkers

Orthen 159, 5231 XR 's-Hertogenbosch

This North Brabant brewer created its debut beer, a white **IPA** (6.2%), at Danny in Belgium in 2018.

Heidebrouwerij

Venturistraat 12 A, 6718 XW Ede
T 0318 785428
heidebrouwerij.nl

Known as Veluwse Heidebrouwerij when it started in 2011 in the kitchens of a decommis-sioned barracks, the Heath 'Brewery' has simplified its name and switched to selling rather than making beer, with brewing now happening at an undisclosed location.
BEERS INCLUDE: half-decent pilsener **EEF** (5.2%: ★★+); fruity **Vlinder Blond** (6.2%: ★★) with intrusive orange peel; bittersweet honeyed **Bijen Blond** (6.2%: ★★+); herbal **Valk IPA** (7.5%: ★★+); flowery **Everzwijn Tripel** (8.5%: ★★); and quadrupel **Edelhert Donker** (9%: ★★+).

Heimans

Europalaan 300, 7543 DN Enschede
T 06 4818 2007
heimansbier.nl

Overijssel brewers who made their first beer, IPA **Juicy** (7%), at Rigters in 2018.

Hemelwater

Puttelaar 40, 5411 AB Zeeland
T 06 1219 9185
facebook.com/Hemelwater

North Brabant-based Rainwater has made beers at nearby Wilskracht since 2016.
BEERS INCLUDE: lemongrass-hoppy pale ale **Cirrus** (6% ★★); tea-infused citrussy blond **Wuyún** (6%: ★★); and bittersweet American amber **Cumulus** (7% ★★).

Hert

Prinsenlaan 6, 6542 TB Nijmegen
brouwerijhethert.nl

Not to be confused with Hert Bier (above), Het Hert ('The Stag') has brewed at Troost since 2015.
BEERS INCLUDE: coffee-tinged schwarzbier **Damhert** (6%: ★★+); Citra-hopped **Pampahert** (6%: ★★+); and citrussy blond **Edelhert** (6.5%: ★★).

Heuvel

Langbroekerdijk A 26, 3947 BH Langbroek
brouwerijheuvel.nl

Founded in 2014, Utrecht-based Hillock currently brews at Loon.
BEERS INCLUDE: multi-grained blond **Helena** (4%: ★★+); bitter blond **Zon** (6.5%: ★★+); and lightly smoky quadrupel **Focoldus** (8%: ★★+).

Heyloo

E. J. Potgieterweg 6, 1851 CH Heiloo
T 072 533 4196
heyloobier.nl

This North Holland team, active since 2011, upscales beers developed in house at Radboud, Klein Duimpje and De Schans.
BEERS INCLUDE: spiced **Heilooër Blond** (7%: ★★) and dark **Ter Coulster Dubbel** (7%: ★★).

HillDevils

Plantagebaan 103, 4725 RB Wouwse-Plantage
T 06 2219 7086

This North Brabant producer, active since 2014, is one of the country's better cuckoos, working commercially at nearby Pimpelmeesch.
BEERS INCLUDE: dry, hoppy summer ale **Thirsty Mosquito** (5%: ★★+); bitter dry-hopped **HillDevil IPA** (6.5%: ★★★); darkly lovely black IPA **Not Totally Black** (6.7%: ★★★), also infused with oak chips as **American Black Horse** (6.5%: ★★+); strongly bitter double IPA **Exploded** (9%: ★★★), also sold in a French-oaked version **Exploded Barrel** (9.4%: ★★+); and gloriously cocoa-forward imperial stout **Big Black Boltini** (10%: ★★★), matured in various woody ways as the **Basement Barrel Aged** series (★★★+).

Hobbel

Heemsteedseweg 10, 3992 LS Houten
brouwerijdehobbel.nl

Three homebrewing friends who made their first commercial beer, hoppy American Pale Ale **Blijvertje** (5.6%), in 2019 at nearby Utrecht brewery.

Hommeles

Fresiatuin 20, 3994 PJ Houten
T 06 1325 5615
brouwerijhommeles.nl

Only one of the three Utrecht-based friends who founded this business in 2011 remains: the others sold their shares in 2019 to Huttenkloas, where the beers are now brewed.
BEERS INCLUDE: dryish saison **Dorstvlegel** (6%: ★★+); improving IPA **Hopdonder** (6%: ★★+); triple-US-hopped **Kuitenbijter** (6.3%: ★★+); honeyed amber **Goede Raat** (7.5%: ★★+); and fruity tripel **Gluiperd** (8%: ★★+), with added apple, pear and elderberry.
ALSO: experimental one-offs in the numbered **Untaped** series.

Hooglander

Kerkstraat 14, 5735 BZ Aarle-Rixtel
hooglanderbier.nl

Started in North Brabant in 2015, Highlander brews with aplomb at Weerter and Sint Servattumus.
BEERS INCLUDE: hoppy American-style wheat ale **Wit** (5.9%: ★★★); sharp-edged **Milk Porter** (6.5%: ★★+); rounded, strongly bitter English-style **IPA** (6.8%: ★★★); above-average **Saison** (7%: ★★+); and coffee and chocolate-laden **Russian Imperial Stout** (9%: ★★★).

Hoornse Hop

Vredehofstraat 5, 1624 XG Hoorn
T 06 5191 4286
hoornsehop.com

This North Holland company, founded in 2013, has its range of mostly seasonal beers brewed at Hofbrouwerijke in Belgium.

Hootch

Oude Groenestraat 6–98, 6678 MB Oosterhout
T 06 2276 4940
brouwerijhootch.nl

Founded in Gelderland by two college friends in 2018, currently working at the A Brewery.
BEERS INCLUDE: reduced alcohol American-style wheat ale **Power To the Flower** (2.5%); US-hopped saison **Mr. Baboon** (6%); and bourbon-infused dark ale **Darkness My Old Friend** (8%).

Hop Bird

Akeleilaan 53, 2343 VV Oegstgeest
T 06 1104 0535
hopbird.nl

This South Holland outfit, launched in 2017 as Hop Op Hop, develops recipes with a home 50l kit, upscaling them at Leidsch.
BEERS INCLUDE: **Bakkerbier** (5%), made with unsold bread; and an **IPA** (6%).

Hopleverancier Prins

Kerstraat 310, 1017 HC Amsterdam
hopleverancier-prins.nl

Founded by two friends in 2016, working at Huttenkloas.
BEERS INCLUDE: pilsener **Kroonprins** (5%); weizen **Op Het Witte Paard** (5%); unadventurously restrained IPA **Maharadja** (6.5%: ★★).

Hosenhym

Gelderspad 3, 6851 DZ Huissen
T 06 1208 1247
hosenhym.nl

This Gelderland company, founded in 2016, brews German-style wheat beers at Wittenburg.
BEERS INCLUDE: blond **De Witte Wieve Weisse** (6.2%) and dunkelweizen **De Düstere Wilde Weisse** (6.2%).

House of Pint

Wittevrouwenkade 4, 3512 CR Utrecht
T 06 5158 0761
houseofpint.com

This outfit founded by three friends in 2016 lost its facilities with the closure of InBier and is currently looking for a new home.
BEERS INCLUDE: bitter IPA **Chop Chop** (6%: ★★+) and delicious black IPA **Arrr!** (8%: ★★★).

Húflo

Húflo Originals
Zuidende 154, 5701 MG Helmond
T 06 4430 6903
huflo.nl

North Brabant-based since 2017 and currently making beer at Weerter.
BEERS INCLUDE: **Ambachtelijk Pilsener** (5%) and cherry-laden **Amarene Stout** (10.5%).

HuZo

facebook.com/HuZoBier

Roermond-based family team brewing at Weerter since 2018.
BEERS INCLUDE: IPA **Grab 'em By the Ale** (7.3%) and imperial **Stoute Poetin** (10.2%).

In de Nacht

Klaasstraat 23B, 5911 JN Venlo
brouwerijindenacht.nl

Limburg-based In The Night has been brewing beers at Weerter since 2016.
BEERS INCLUDE: gold-blond **Ties** (6%: ★★); champagne-yeasted dry blond **Cuvée la Nuit** (7.7%: ★★+); subtly restrained quadrupel **Donker Sur Lie** (9.2%: ★★+); and sledgehammer barley wine **Belhamel** (11%: ★★). Both Donker Sur Lie and Belhamel also appear in a string of **Barrel-Aged** versions, often ★★★ or better.

Inspiratie

De Zaan 14, 3448 BS Woerden
bier-en-inspiratie.nl

Founded in Utrecht province in 2016, currently working locally at Jovius.
BEERS INCLUDE: herbal blond **Daphne** (4%).

Iron Door

Bilt 8, 6107 BM Stevensweert
irondoorbrewing.com

These Limburg brewers, inspired by San Diego brewing culture, began brewing at the ill-fated InBier in 2017 and will need to find a new location, although there are plans to open a brewery in Roermond.
BEERS INCLUDE: session IPA **Roadrunner** (4.1%); red **Copperhead IPA** (6.66%); and double IPA **Diablo Drop Off** (8.5%).

IV:UUR

Garvesingel 76, 7672 AM Vriezenveen
facebook.com/4uurbieruur

Overijssel company founded in 2018, making beer locally at Rigters.
BEERS INCLUDE: aromatic session IPA **Fred Dorst** (3.5%: ★★+); mildly bitter double IPA **Zwärrechie** (7.6%: ★★).

Jantjes

Saxofoonstraat 80, 5402 CG Uden
T 0413 269361
jantjesbieren-uden.nl

One-man North Brabant operation working quietly since 1993, mostly at Sint Servattumus.
BEERS INCLUDE: standard **Amber** (5.5%: ★★); spiced **Witbier** (6%: ★★+); malty **Blond** (6%: ★★); standard **Dubbel** (6.5%: ★★); overly sweet **Tripel** (7.2%: ★+); and sweetish **Barley Wine** (9%: ★★).

Jauk's

Graaf Lodewijklaan 53, 3818 DP Amersfoort

This outfit has produced beer only occasionally since it was founded in 2013, most recently **Amersfoorts Blond** (7.5%), likely brewed at Van Steenberge in Belgium.

JD

Elisabethsdal 28, 6004 JN Weert

This elusive enterprise was founded in 2010, then disappeared for years before re-emerging in 2019 with lightly smoked **De Porter van Limburg** (6.9%: ★★+), made at Weerter.

Johnny Thursday

Emmastraat 158, 7513 BG Enschede
facebook.com/JohnnyThursdayBeer

Overijssel brewer active since 2016, making beers at Rigters with names inspired by the works of Johnny Cash.

BEERS INCLUDE: hoppy dry pale ale **A Boy Named Citra** (4.3%: ★★★) and easy-drinking **Hey! Porter** (5.7%: ★★+), derived from a recipe that won the Brand amateur brewing competition.
ALSO: **Beiaard Zwarte Ros** beers for the Beiaard café in Enschede.

Jotner

Kastanjelaan 18, 9741 CP Groningen
T 06 4161 4548
Jotner.nl

Founded in 2016, upscaling production at Ootmarsummer following recipe development on a 30l kit.
BEERS INCLUDE: unfiltered **Pils** (5.1%) and various **barrel-aged** stouts and quadrupels.

Kaetelkøp

Sint Gillisstraat 12, 6181 GC Elsloo
kaetelkop.nl

Based in Limburg and working commercially at Weerter since 2019.
BEERS INCLUDE: hoppy pale ale **Frische** (6%: ★★+) and black IPA **Nox Duuster** (8%: ★★+).

Kat

Deken van der Hagenstraat 7, 5707 TV Helmond
brouwerijdekat.nl

At first content to use their own nano-scale kit when they began brewing commercially in

2013, the Cat brewers have since responded to growing demand by switching production to Weerter, though they plan to revive brewing in Helmond.
BEERS INCLUDE: malty golden **Bots** (4.8%: ★★+); amber pale ale **Peel Ale** (6%: ★★); raisiny copper-amber dubbel **Nicodemus** (7.5%: ★★); and peachy golden tripel **Hemelrijk** (8.5%: ★★).

Katuin

Soesterweg 165, 3812 AE Amersfoort
T 06 1519 5454

Founded in 2017, this family collaboration of Kasparus brewer Kasper Katuin and his nephew Edo brews occasional **Katuiner** beers at the A Brewery.
BEERS INCLUDE: **Saison** (6.5%); **Dubbel** (7.2%); and imperial **Amersfoort Stout** (8.5%: ★★+).

Kek!

Rondehoep Oost 16,
1191 KB Ouderkerk aan de Amstel
kek-bier.nl

Founded in 2015, this North Holland company has most recently been spotted working at Steffelaar.
BEERS INCLUDE: witbier **Wit** (5.2%); honeyed **Donkerblonde Honing** (5.4%); and a **Tripel** (8%).

Keuvel

Smaragd 5, 1625 RE Hoorn
T 06 4022 3026
keuvelbier.nl

North Holland-based company founded in 2015 and working at Noord-Hollandse.
BEERS INCLUDE: sour wheat ale **Westfriese Lambiek** (5%: ★★★), which is well worth drinking if not technically a lambic; less-exciting blond **Zonnegroet** (6%: ★★); and spiced **Tripel** (8%: ★★).

Kleine Beer

PO Box 188, 8530 AD Lemmer
kleinebeerbrouwerij.nl

Friesland-based Little Bear began brewing on a nano-scale in a shed in 2013, but long ago outgrew this and switched to working on a larger scale at various Dutch locations. *BEERS INCLUDE:* hoppy pale ale **Goldilocks** 2019 (5.2%: ★★+); standard blond **Beer Uit Lemmer** (6%: ★★); restrained, dry dubbel **LE-4** (7%: ★★+); banana-edged tripel **De Toer** (7%: ★★+); and bitter double IPA **Double Trouble** (8%: ★★).

Klep

Keizerstraat 13, 5911 JW Venlo
T 077 463 3287
cafedeklep.nl

The owner of the like-named café (see cafés) has been brewing his house beers at Fontein since 2012. *BEERS INCLUDE:* **Alt** (4.8%) and **Pilsner** (5%).

Koe en Kalf

't Goor 6, 8336 KL Baars
T 0521 345411
koeenkalf.nl

Rural Overijssel brewers working at Vechtdal since 2018. *BEERS INCLUDE:* Belgian-style dubbel **Ome Henk** (6.5%); blond **Wildebras** (7%); tripel **'t Olde Wief** (8.5%); and IPA **De Izeren Brogge** (8.5%).

Kolkbier

Prins Clausstraat 38, 3433 EP Nieuwegein
kolkbier.nl

Small enterprise in Utrecht province making occasional beers at Loon since 2015. *BEERS INCLUDE:* ginger-spiced **Blond** (6.5%: ★★) and a **Tripel** (9.2%).

Koningshert

Smaragd 82, 9207 GH Drachten
T 06 1244 9314
koningshert.nl

Friesland company founded in 2015 as Drachtsterbrouwer, working at Admiraals. *BEERS INCLUDE:* solid **Drachtster Weizen** (5.7%: ★★) and nutty **Chico Amber Ale** (6%: ★★).

Kopstoot

2e Virulystraat 4 A 04, 3022 ZM Rotterdam
facebook.com/brouwerijdekopstoot

Founded in 2018, Headbutt has since 2019 been making its beer at Reijngoud, where the owners work as head brewers. *BEERS INCLUDE:* wheat pale ale **Tarwelijer** (4.8%: ★★+) and black IPA **Brak Obama** (6%).

Kraft

Kapitein Hatterasstraat 1-10, 5015 BB Tilburg
T 06 3488 7200
kraftbier.nl

This North Brabant oddity, founded in 2015, has taken the opposite route to most brewers, disposing of its own kit in 2019 and now working at Loon. *BEERS INCLUDE:* perky American pale ale **Hoppakee** (5.2%: ★★+); refreshing white IPA **Schoôn Mèdje** (6.2%: ★★★); sweetish blond **Groote Kweek** (7.9%: ★★); and dry tripel **Het Witte Kasteel** (8%: ★★).

Kroon op Leeuwarden

De Oerset 16, 8934 DA Leeuwarden
T 06 1521 7525
dekroonopleeuwarden.frl

Friesland company founded in 2014, brewing its hefty beers locally at Admiraals and elsewhere. *BEERS INCLUDE:* cocoa-heavy **Stoutzen** (8.6%: ★★+); sweet blond **Cambier** (9%: ★★); unsubtle barley wine **Swiete Swiere** (11%: ★★); and rich imperial stout **Kammeraat** (11.3%: ★★+).

Kwadrant

Hoornbladstraat 20, 6841 KD Arnhem
brouwerijkwadrant.com

Gelderland company which debuted in 2019
with pale ale **De Pionier** (6.2%).

Lange Lijs

Hazerswoudestraat 59, 2729 CK Zoetermeer
langelijs.nl

Founded in South Holland in 2017, Tall Liz
brewed its early beers at Ghoplin.
BEERS INCLUDE: weizen **Solar Flare** (6%);
black IPA **Lunar Landing** (7%); and quadrupel
Eclipse (9.5%).

Lastige Broertjes

PO Box 32, 4900 AA Oosterhout
delastigebroertjes.nl

The North Brabant-based Awkward Brothers
have been brewing beers at 3 Horne since 2016.
BEERS INCLUDE: improving nettly IPA
Janksmoel (6.5%: ★★+); sweetish blond
't Wosterhouts Snollebolleke (8.5%: ★★); and
warming imperial stout **Joa Zééti** (10.5%: ★★+).

Laveloos

Boutenslaan 6, 4707 NC Roosendaal
brouwerij-laveloos.nl

Plastered (as in drunk, not interior decoration)
has been active in North Brabant since 2015,
though its beer is made at Boelens in Belgium.
BEERS INCLUDE: IPA **Sikker** (7%); tripel **In
d'n Olie** (8%); and imperial stout **Kachel** (9%).

Leeghwater

Luttik Oudorp 40C, 1811 MX Alkmaar
T 06 4302 8211
brouwerijleeghwater.nl

North Holland brewer established in 2017 and
currently working at Jopen.

BEERS INCLUDE: lightweight red ale **Rijper
Liefde** (3.5%: ★★); hoppy blond **Beemster
Boezem** (4.7%: ★★); and standout fruity white
IPA **Ruys** (4.7%: ★★+).

Licht

PO Box 17, 3500 AA Utrecht
T 030 879 7399
brouwerijhetlicht.nl

Founded in 2014, the Light brews mostly
seasonal beers at De Leckere, with only pale
ale **Nieuwe Maan** (6%) and amber saison
Volle Maan (6.2%) available year-round.

Lossers Gruitrecht

Hogeweg 77, 7582 CB Losser
defilantroopbier.nl

This Overijssel brewer, active since 2017, makes
beer at Rigters under the name **De Filantroop**.
BEERS INCLUDE: sweetish but balanced **Blond**
(6.2%: ★★+) and honeyed **Tripel** (7.2%: ★★).

Louis Loyal

Sprokenpad 1, 3813 DP Amersfoort
T 06 5339 6053
louisloyal.nl

Brewer based in Utrecht province since 2015
and working at Noord-Hollandse.
BEERS INCLUDE: dry-hopped blond **Celeste**
(5.3%: ★★+); not smoky **Smoky Wan** (5.5%: ★★)
brown ale; fruity copper-amber **American
Pale Ale** (5.6%: ★★+); standard **Blond** (6.2%:
★★); and sweetish blond **Tripel** (7.9%: ★★).

Lowlander

Nieuwe Hemweg 14F, 1013 BG Amsterdam
T 020 752 9726
lowlander-beer.com

The young brewer who created this company
in 2015 uses his background working in the
botanicals department of a gin distillery to
create unusually spiced ales brewed at Jopen.

BEERS INCLUDE: light and sharp session ale **Ginger & Kaffir Lime** (2.5%: ★★+), which also contains Darjeeling tea; similar but better **Yuzu & Grapefruit** (2.5%: ★★★) with Earl Grey tea; subtly fruity, spiced wheat-based **White Ale** (5%: ★★+); lightly smoky dark **Poorter** (6%: ★★+); and delightfully refreshing **IPA** (6.3%: ★★★), with coriander and white tea.

Luie

Zandzuigerstraat 12-73; 5222 AH 's-Hertogenbosch
luiebrouwers.nl

The Lazy Brewers are two North Brabant-based friends who brewed their first commercial beer, blond **Stoute Maud** (6.3%), in 2019.

Luie Nond

Oliemolenstraat 38, 4791 JV Klundert
T 06 5329 3570
jakobusbuijs.nl

North Brabant-based friends making **Jakobus Buijs** beers for the local market since 2018. BEERS INCLUDE: a light **Blond** (5.5%) and dark dubbel **Bruin** (7%).

Lux

Herzenbroekenweg 66, 5642 NP Eindhoven
T 06 4444 4339
luxbrewery.nl

Martijn van Damme has been working as a one-man business since 2014, developing his often-excellent recipes on a 60l kit before upscaling at various locations. BEERS INCLUDE: spiky blond **Cactus Ale** (6%: ★★+), also featuring lime; dry blond **Weizen** (6%: ★★+); biscuity golden **Quinoa Pale Ale** (6%: ★★+); sharp and raspberry-rich but beautifully balanced **Frambozen Stout** (7.5%: ★★★+); sweetish dark **Quadrupel** (10%: ★★); and richly alcoholic barley wine **Rye of the Storm** (10%: ★★+). ALSO: a string of occasionally recurring specials, the best of which include sharp 'sort

of Berliner' **Paradise Weisse** (4.5%: ★★★) with grapefruit and lemon grass; lovely dry, hoppy **Brut IPA** (6.5%: ★★★); and super full-bodied **Luxe BA Barley Wine** (9.5%: ★★★+).

LVR

LVR 'Breweries'
Marsmanhove 112, 2726 CS Zoetermeer
lvrbreweries.nl

These South Holland friends with the initials L, V and R have been making beer since 2017, currently at the equally abbreviated A Brewery. Quite why they need more than one imaginary brewery in their name is beyond us. BEERS INCLUDE: witbier **White Walter** (4.5%); stout **Black Brian** (6.1%); and **Z.IPA** (6.5%).

Maatbier

Koningsweg 31, 4191 HA Geldermalsen
maatbier.nl

Three Gelderland brothers working together since 2017 and currently brewing at Rigters. BEERS INCLUDE: self-explanatory **The Red Ale District** (4.5%) and **Betuwse Blonde** (5.5%).

Maatje

Van der Ploegstraat 1, 1964 SK Heemskerk
brouwerijhetmaatje.nl

Four North Holland friends brewing commercially since 2017, currently at Noord-Hollandse. BEERS INCLUDE: dry-hopped IPA **Primaat** (6.5%) and tripel **'t Maatje Aan de Maat** (9%).

Maestrichter

PO Box 3081, 6202 NB Maastricht
demaestrichterbrouwerij.com

Limburg company founded in 2014, brewing up the road at Fontein. BEERS INCLUDE: witbier **Pottemenneke** (5%); sweetish blond **Lansmenneke** (6.1%: ★★); and brown ale **Vääske** (7.1%).

Lux, Qua

Mag

Le Sage ten Broekstraat 18, 5041 CM Tilburg
facebook.com/Brouwerijtmag

North Brabant brewer active since 2018, currently working at Breda brewery. Heineken appears to be involved, at least as far as distribution is concerned.
BEERS INCLUDE: spiced wheat **Wit** (4.9%); **IPA** (5.5%); and a **Tripel** (9.2%).

Magnus

Witte Paal 318, 1742 LD Schagen

Founded in North Holland in 2015, though we believe its **Skager** brands – pilsener **Stierenbier** and blond **Molenbier** – are made at Scheldebrouwerij in Belgium.

Mahabier

Handwerkerszijde 158, 9201 CR Drachten
mahabier.eu

Friesland-based company founded in 2018 and currently commissioning beer from Noord-Hollandse. *BEERS INCLUDE:* golden pale ale **Caribbean** (4.5%: ★★), with lime, and a **Blond** (5%).

Manskerel

Assumburgstraat 12, 4834 KP Breda
manskerel.nl

North Brabant outfit founded in 2018, brewing locally at Breda brewery.
BEERS INCLUDE: **Weizen** (4.5%) and tripel/IPA hybrid **Hopler** (8.5%).

Marco

Karseboomstraat 4, 1601 KP Enkhuizen
T 06 5316 4908
facebook.com/brouwerijmarco

North Holland brewer producing occasional beers since 2016, last spotted making a bock locally at De Werf.

Melessen

Beneden Oosterdiep 88, 9641 JG Veendam
T 0598 383100
m-bier.nl

Jakob Melessen, head brewer at Parkzicht, has also made his own experimental **M-Bier** range there since 2016.
BEERS INCLUDE: easy-drinking champagne-yeasted blond **M-Champagne** (2.4%: ★★); **Süsses Schwarz** (3.5%: ★★+), a black lager with liquorice; lightweight 'Dutch East India' Pale Ale **VOC** (4.5%: ★★+); and smoky whisky-malted blond **M-Label Black** (6.5%: ★★+).

Meuleneind

Moleneindsestraat 21, 4741 RG Hoeven
T 06 1091 8668
brouwerij-tmeuleneind.nl

Founded in 2017, this North Brabant company makes its **Halderbergs** beers at 3 Horne.
BEERS INCLUDE: rounded **Weizen** (6%: ★★); sweetish **Blond** (6%: ★★); superior roasted-edged **Dubbel** (7%: ★★+); malty **Tripel** (8.5%: ★★); and imperial stout **Bombast** (9%: ★★+).

Mijn Streek

Bongerd 18, 6411 JM Heerlen
T 045 577 2288

Irony is clearly lost on the My Region restaurant, which commissions its **Dubbel** and **Tripel Bijdehand Honingbier** from across the border at Grain d'Orge in Belgium. It was known as Kameraad when it launched in 2015.

Mirakel

Puccinistraat 9, 3816 VE Amersfoort
brouwerij-mirakel.nl

Ten ex-schoolfriends have made beers commercially at Hoop since 2016.
BEERS INCLUDE: blond **Lieve Vrouw** (6.4%) and sweetish spiced tripel **De Vondst** (8.4%: ★★).

Mokums Mout

Den Texstraat 11H, 1017 XW Amsterdam
mokumsmout.nl

Another group of friends, making beer at various North Holland locations since 2016. Mokum is a nickname for Amsterdam, while *mout* is 'malt'.
BEERS INCLUDE: bitter American red ale **Kolenkit** (6.5%: ★★); tarragon-spiced saison **Duivelseiland** (6.7%: ★★); and **Van Der Pek** (9.6%: ★★), a quadrupel with cinnamon and orange.

Molenduyn

Terrasweg 43, 2071 BB Santpoort-Noord
T 06 5160 5176
brouwerijmolenduyn.nl

North Holland outfit brewing at 7 Deugden but aiming to use its 2hl kit 'in the near future' when licensing issues are resolved.
BEERS INCLUDE: **Dubbel** (6.9%); sweetish **Blond** (7.2%: ★★); and dark **Klooster** (7.3%: ★★+).

Monnick

Dissel 46, 1141 ZM Monnickendam
T 06 5151 3715
brouwerijdemonnick.nl

North Holland-based one-man enterprise brewing at an unknown location since 2014.
BEERS INCLUDE: blond **De Witte Lelij** (5.5%: ★★); malty amber **Sneetjes Bier** (5.6%: ★★), made from old bread; and unsubtle fruity amber **De Roode Vos** (7.5%: ★★).

Moondance

Rosendaal 73, 1851 RK Heiloo
moondancebrewing.nl

Founded in North Holland in 2017 by a US expat who makes her one beer, the imperial stout **Total Eclipse** (8.3%), at an unknown location.

Morebeer

Funenpark 199, 1018 AK Amsterdam
morebeer.nl, meerbier.nl

Amsterdam beer café chain owner Peter van de Arend began this pet project in 2015, working at half a dozen regional breweries. *BEERS INCLUDE:* hoppy pale ale **Dutch Eagle** (5.5%: ★★+); dry saison **Eastern Farm Eagle** (5.5%: ★★+); fruity rauchbier **Smoke House Eagle** (7.5%: ★★+); multi-hopped dark tripel **Eye of the Eagle** (7.9% ★★+); and fabulous **Big Fat 5 Double IPA** (8%: ★★★★), brewed at Uiltje.

Natte Gijt

Mauritsstraat 35, 6006 EJ Weert
T 06 4495 4207
brouwerijdenattegijt.nl

Limburg-based Wet Goat, founded by two brothers in 2011, currently creates its generally impressive hop-forward range locally at Weerter, a business in which the brewers had intended to invest but they missed the crowdfunding boat.
BEERS INCLUDE: intensely bitter and delightful flagship IPA **Hop met de Gijt** (6.5%: ★★★+); subtly smoked IPA **Vredesgijt** (6.8%: ★★★); moreish double IPA **Gijt UT?** (8%: ★★★); burnt coffee-tinged imperial **Stoute Gijt** (8.8%: ★★+); and variously barrel-aged imperial stout **Hellegijt** (11.5%: ★★★+).
ALSO: a numbered series of experimental one-offs.

Neo

Korfoedreef 27, 3562 SB Utrecht
T 06 2676 4488
projekt-neo.nl

The friends who founded this outfit, known as Neobosski when it launched in 2016 and rebranded some years later, are saving up for thieir own brewery while making beer at Loon and elsewhere.

BEERS INCLUDE: Mexican chilli-laced amber **Swearing Senorita** (6.5%: ★★+); porter **Porta Belgica** (7.4%); dry dark tripel **Kandy Express** (7.5%: ★★+); tangy weizen **Wicked Lemon** (7%: ★★+); grappa-laced tripel **Grappapolis** (8.2%); and black IPA **Sooty Otter** (8.5%: ★★+).

Neptunus

Camphuysendreef 10, 2353 CJ Leiderdorp
T 06 5271 7669
neptunusbier.nl

South Holland company founded in 2015, brewing mainly at Leidsch.
BEERS INCLUDE: cocoa-tinged oatmeal stout **Peko** (5.9%: ★★+); standout moreish bitter coffee porter **Erebus** (8.7%: ★★★); and citrussy tripel/kuit hybrid **Ceres** (8.9%: ★★+).

Nooitgedacht

Oudendijk 74a, 4285 WL Woudrichem
T 06 4842 3806
brouwerijnooitgedacht.nl

Never Thought was founded by North Brabant-based friends in 2017, working at an unknown location.
BEERS INCLUDE: amber **Nooit Genoeg** (6.5%) and spiced honeyed tripel **Nooit Op** (7.5%: ★★).

Nowhere

Carolina van Nassaustraat 11, 2595 TK Den Haag
T 06 5154 8428
nowherebrewing.com

This company founded in 2016 is firmly Dutch-based, brewing at Steffelaar, but curiously sells most of its beer in Luxembourg, rather frust-ratingly as creations such as New England IPA **Necessary Evil** (6%: ★★★) are well worth trying.

Nuenhem

Egelantierstraat 13, 5672 XJ Nuenen
brouwerijnuenhem.nl

Founded in a North Brabant village in 2016, working at Weerter.

BEERS INCLUDE: dependable witbier **Lust** (5%: ★★); dry, fruity saison **Trots** (5.5%: ★★); quaffable black IPA **Lef** (6.9%: ★★+); and rich, curranty **Stout** (9.5%: ★★+).

Oerbron

Drontermeer 33, 3825 XK Amersfoort
T 06 1309 0751
facebook.com/brouwerijoerbron

Utrecht-based since 2019, Original Source last seen working at Stijl to make beers such as American IPA **Butch Cassidy** (5.5%) and Belgian-style blond **Ugly Kid Joe** (6.4%).

Oldskool

Cavallilaan 189, 5654 BD Eindhoven
T 06 2752 8036
oldskoolbrewery.nl

Beer sommelier and brewer Dennis Kort has been developing recipes, mostly in purity law-compliant German and English styles, on a 60l home kit then upscaling them at various locations since 2013.
BEERS INCLUDE: classic English-style Extra Special Bitter **<3 Hops** (6%: ★★★); Munich-style festbier **Festen** (6%: ★★+); rounded fresh-hopped IPA **Hopplukker** (6.5%: ★★★); fruity amber **Altskool** (7%: ★★+); bitter Mandarina-hopped tripel **Triple Sec** (8%: ★★★); variously single-hopped **Hopfen Weisse** (8%-ish: usually ★★★); dark, chewy UK-hopped **My Imperial Brown Ale** (8.5%: ★★★); and deliriously bitter **The Great Emperial IPA** (9%: ★★★). *SEASONAL:* banana-tinged dubbelbock **Shut the Bock Up!** (5.2%: ★★+).

Ooijevaer

Pater Celiestraat 1, 6591 ZG Gennep
dooijevaer.nl

Stork was founded by Limburg-based friends in 2015 who now brew at De Hemel.
BEERS INCLUDE: nutty Alt **Driekus** (4.8%: ★★) and balanced imperial stout **Loc 94** (9.9%: ★★+).

Oudewater

Westerwal 2, 3421 BX Oudewater
bierwaarjevoorblijft.nl

Brewing company based in Utrecht province since 2019, its first commercial beer was blond ale **'t Swaert** (6.5%).

Ouwetoeter

Ring 52, 3227 AS Oudenhoorn
T 06 1286 3183
ouwetoeter.nl

North Holland homebrewers producing commercially since 2018, currently at Noord-Hollandse.
BEERS INCLUDE: **Eigen Weizen** (6%) and **Sterke Blond** (8.2%).

Paap

PO Box 1117, 3350 CC Papendrecht
T 06 4117 6244
paapbeer.com

Whinchat are South Holland twins brewing professionally since 2018, currently at Breda brewery.
BEERS INCLUDE: weizen **Oerpaap** (5.8%: ★★); too sweet and malty Blond (5.9%: ★+); lightly bitter IPA **IPAAP** (6.5%: ★★); and **Krachtig Dubbel** (7.5%).

Pannes

Groenstraat 16, 6151 CS Munstergeleen
T 06 3618 2785

These Limburg brewers have been working to historical recipes at an undisclosed location since 2017, with results like **Fonto** (5%: ★★+), a citrussy weizen using ancient wheat types emmer and einkorn.

Paoter Gustaaf

Graaf Hendrik III Laan 137-c, 4819 CE Breda
T 06 2446 5432
paotergustaaf.nl

This North Brabant outfit founded in 2017 claims its own brewery, but we believe blond ale **Eej Kul** (6.6%) has been made commercially elsewhere.

Peelander

Verseputseweg 38, 4321 TD Kerkwerve
T 06 4433 0216
peelander.nl

Peelander was a founded in 1998 as a village brewery, but in 2009 the name was sold to the Spennekot Groep, which now commissions dull clone beers from Van Steenberge in Belgium.
BEERS INCLUDE: boring **Tripel** (8%: ★★) and blond **Zeeuws Goud** (8%: ★★).

Peelreus

Fitissingel 6, 5754 CA Deurne
depeelreus.nl

North Brabant-based Peel Giant, founded in 2016, orders its witbier **De Witte** (5.5%) and blond ale **Zwaar Blond** (8.5%) from Boelens in Belgium.

Penose

Jan Witheijnstraat 16, 1018 WM Amsterdam
T 06 5314 9387
penosebrouwerij.nl

Founded in 2015 and mainly working at Huttenkloas.
BEERS INCLUDE: standard fruity **Blonde Mien** (6.5%: ★★) and rounded, superior rye IPA **Haring Arie** (7%: ★★★).

Pieke

Pieke Broodbier
Hoogzwanenstraat 141, 6211 BZ Maastricht
piekebroodbier.nl

One-woman company launched in 2018 to make beer using surplus bread from local shops. We think English-style golden ale **Pieke Broodbier** (6.3%) is made at Fontein.

Pinterman

Korhoenstraat 77, 5022 BG Tilburg
pinterman.nl

This North Brabant company began in 2016 by sourcing beer from Boelens in Belgium but may now be brewing at Dutch locations.
BEERS INCLUDE: witbier **Route de Soleil** (4.8%); blond **Gouden Collega** (5.7%: ★★+); stoutish dubbel **Pelsjager** (6.5%: ★★); and dry tripel **Heilige Verlosser** (7%: ★★+).

Plan100

Walstein 65, 3848 AP Harderwijk
biervanplan100.nl

Gelderland brewer active since 2018, making beer at Noord-Hollandse.
BEERS INCLUDE: cardamom-spiced ginger beer-like tripel **Drie Keer Niks** (8.3%: ★★).

Platte Harnas

Brabanterlaan 4, 3772 PK Barneveld
T 06 2488 1718
brouwerijhetplatteharnas.nl

Based in Gelderland since 2018, Flat Harness develops recipes in 20l batches and upscales them at Noord-Hollandse.
BEERS INCLUDE: IPA **Tommy Gun** (6%); standard blond **Groot Geschapen** (7%: ★★); dubbel **Dwars** (7%); and tripel **Lamme Jan** (9%).

Pontus

Johan Huizingalaan 262-2, 1065 JM Amsterdam
T 06 2951 6898
facebook.com/PontusBrewing

Brewer Nando Servais and a friend who is no longer involved founded this as Pampus in 2013. It was rebranded in 2016 after pressure from Huyghe in Belgium, which bizarrely claimed that the original name sounded too much like its Campus brand. Nando makes beer at Naeckte Brouwers, which became a co-owner in 2019.
BEERS INCLUDE: white session IPA **Jolly Dolphin** (4.5%: ★★+); juniper-spiced pale ale **Siren's Song** (5.5%: ★★+); hoppy black IPA **Nautilus** (6%: ★★+); bitter-finishing IPA **Oceanic Flight** (6.3%: ★★+); fruity saison **Lighthouse** (6.5%: ★★+); hop-forward double IPA **Gigantic Sailor** (8%: ★★★); smoked porter **All Mouth** (9.5%: ★★+); and imperial stout **Kraken** (10.5%: ★★+)
ALSO: **Monster Brews** imperial stouts, triple IPAs and barley wines, usually ★★★.

Poort

Zuiderpoort 46, 2152 RG Nieuw-Vennep
brouwerijpoort.nl

North Holland brewer Gate upscales home-developed recipes at Noord-Hollandse.
BEERS INCLUDE: crisp blond **Bietenbrug** (6%: ★★), with sugar beet; sweetish dubbel **Schaduw** (6.5%: ★★); straw-blond tripel weizen **Maaidorser** (8.5%: ★★); and dull **Tripel** (9%: ★★).

PUNT.

Van Lenneplaan 301, 9721 PK Groningen
facebook.com/Puntgroningen

The former brewer of now-defunct Vechter has been making beer at Breda brewery since 2018.
BEERS INCLUDE: dry, citrussy **Blond** (6%: ★★+) and assertively dry hoppy **IPA** (6.6%: ★★★).

Puuro

1e Maasveldstraat 39, 5921 JL Venlo
T 06 2170 6998

This Limburg company began by commissioning from Boelens in Belgium in 2015 but has since transferred brewing to Fontein.
BEERS INCLUDE: US-hopped IPA
Hopfalderie (6.5%: ★★+); dry-hopped pale ale
Josefien II (7%: ★★+); and fruity IPA
Sluukske (7%: ★★).

Rakker

Van Pallantstraat 42, 6081 BJ Haelen
Rakkerbier.nl

Limburg producer brewing commercially on other people's equipment since 2016.
BEERS INCLUDE: pineapple and mango IPA
Lu'au Rakker (6%: ★★+); fruity, bitter IPA
One in a Melon (7%: ★★+); and orange peel and coriander-spiced tripel **Royale Rakker** (7.5%: ★★+).

Rare Jongens

't Zand 52, 3454 PB De Meern
T 030 233 4105
rarejongens.com

Brewer making beer at Spierbier for the like-named restaurant in Utrecht province since 2017.
Beers include witbier **Witte Woeste** (6%) and **Tripel Trappel** (7%).

Raven Bone Hill

Vincent van Goghlaan 163, 3141 KT Maassluis
T 06 5733 2123
ravenbonehill.nl

The name of this South Holland outfit founded in 2010 derives from anglicisations of the owners' names: Raaf (Raven), Bot (Bone) and Vreugdenhil. Recipes are developed in house then brewed at Ramses.

BEERS INCLUDE: citrussy wheat ale
Crowdsurfer (5.5%: ★★+); coffee-laden black IPA **Jolly Roger** (6.66%: ★★+); whisky-malted imperial stout **Black Peat** (8%: ★★★); and hoppy honeyed blond **Styx** (8.5%: ★★+), sold locally as **Maassluis Stadsbier**.

Remunj

Beemdenlaan 19, 6041 NL Roermond
stadsbroewerieremunj.wordpress.com

Limburg producer brewing its only beer, tripel **Lurrie** (8.1%), at Weerter since 2019.

Ridder Bliek

Veerstraat 19 H, 1075 SL Amsterdam
T 06 4613 6223
facebook.com/RidderBliekBeer

Founded in 2017 and currently brewing at Noord-Hollandse.
BEERS INCLUDE: blond **Kannenkijker** (5.5%) and IPA **Pimpelaar** (6.5%).

Riethoff

Schielandweg 8, 2741 MA Waddinxveen
ikwil.gouwebier.nl

South Holland homebrewer who since 2015 has upscaled his **Gouwe** beers developed on a 40l kit at other people's breweries.
BEERS INCLUDE: pale ale **Glinster** (4%); witbier **Rietpluim** (5%); lightweight, banana-tinged red ale **Gouwe Bier** (5%: ★★); and dark dubbel **Veenbonk** (7%).

Rodanum

Weststraat 33, 4527 BR Aardenburg
biertainment.com

This company in Zeeuws-Vlaanderen, founded in 2015, makes its beer at Eutropius in Belgium.
BEERS INCLUDE: fruity **Saison Jane** (5.5%: ★★+) and clean-tasting **Tripel Jules** (8%: ★★+).

Raven Bon

Romondt

Sparrenhof 40, 6951 MB Dieren
brouwerijromondt.nl

One-man operation founded in Gelderland in 2018, currently working at Huttenkloas.
BEERS INCLUDE: witbier **Elderwit** (4.8%); blond **Goudheerlijk** (5.5%); and tripel **Blaauw Garrit** (7.5%).

Rotjoch

Spant 11, 1628 GJ Hoorn
T 06 3127 1682
facebook.com/brouwerijrotjoch

Junkie was founded by three North Holland friends in 2018, who brew their white IPA **Gele Maagd** (6.5%) "locally".

Rott.

Kortebrantstraat 7D, 3031 PM Rotterdam
T 06 3077 3559
rottbrouwers.nl

City brewer making confident beers at various Dutch locations since 2016.
BEERS INCLUDE: light IPA **Sessie** (4.5%: ★★+); sharpish milk stout **Melk** (4.5%: ★★+); American-style wheat ale **Neck** (4.5%: ★★+); hoppy IPA **Straf** (5.5%: ★★+); red IPA **Raket** (6%: ★★+); and standout bean-forward coffee stout **Ontbijt** (6.5%: ★★★).

Roze Varken

Trommelhof 17, 6852 TG Huissen
T 06 2278 3150
hetrozevarken.nl

Founded in Gelderland in 2013, the Pink Pig produces a range of around 15 beers at Huttenkloas, far too many to provide a complete list here.
BEERS INCLUDE: black IPA **Stootijzer** (5.6%: ★★+); floral, hoppy IPA **El Dorado** (6.3%: ★★+);

improving amber **Knorretje** (7.2%: ★★); coffee-leaning porter **Kaat** (7.4%: ★★+); sweetish tripel **TierlanTijn** (8.4%: ★★); and bitter-finishing imperial stout **Pionier** (9.8%: ★★+).

Rufus

Iras 28, 5591 SG Heeze
T 06 5232 6460
brouwerijrufus.nl

North Brabant-based company founded in 2015, brewing at 3 Horne.
BEERS INCLUDE: bitter blond **Prufus** (6%: ★★+); bittersweet amber **Macker** (6.7%: ★★+); dryish brown **Knoet** (8%: ★★+); fruity golden tripel **'Tism** (10%: ★★); and **Kwart** (13%: ★★+), a dangerously drinkable heavyweight quadrupel.

Sapmeester

Wilhelminastraat 30, 9611 JW Sappemeer
T 06 1884 6947
sapmeesterbier.nl

This brewer based in Groningen province produced its first beer, amber **Rooie Rinus** (6.3%), at Noord-Hollandse in 2018, and eventually aims to have its own kit.

Scheveningen

Televisiestraat 2, 2525 KD Den Haag
T 070 778 5860
brouwerijscheveningen.nl

This began as a physical brewery in 2015 following the closure of the nearby Brouwcafé, but ceased brewing in 2019 and plans to shift future production elsewhere.
BEERS INCLUDE: lightweight pilsener **Zuidwester** (4.8%: ★★); bitter blond IPA **Bomschuit** (5.5%: ★★+); and aromatic **Scheveninger Tripel** (7.5%: ★★+).

Schoentjes

Da Costastraat 4, 5025 TE Tilburg
T 06 1266 3702
facebook.com/BrouwerijSchoentjes

Founded in 2018 by two brothers, Little Shoes works at Tilburg brewery.
BEERS INCLUDE: IPA **$neakers** (7%) and quadrupel **Vierkaantuh Têenschoenuh** (10%).

Schuit

Bierkade 18, 2512 AB Den Haag
brouwerijdeschuit.nl

Founded by two friends, the Barge brewed its first beer, blond pale ale **Bukkûh** (7%), at Noord-Hollandse in 2019.

Sisters

Stationsweg 57, 3621 LK Breukelen
T 06 8123 4221
thesistersbrewery.com

Beers from this producer in Utrecht province, founded in 2015, are brewed at Fontein by the father of the sisters in question. Their family name is Beijeman (Beekeeper), hence the beer names.
BEERS INCLUDE: amber session IPA **Waggle Dance** (4.4%: ★★+); weizen **Hive** (5.3%: ★★); amber rauchbier **Smoker** (5.4%: ★★+); bitter porter **Drone** (5.8%: ★★+); improving dry-hopped IPA **Queen Bee** (7.7%: ★★+); sweetish blond **Honey** (7.9%: ★★); rich imperial porter **Drone2** (8.5%: ★★+); fruity tripel **Apis** 8.5%: ★★); imperial saison **Worker** (9.4%: ★★+); and quaffable blond barley wine **Nectar** (10.7%: ★★★).

Sjaak

Stellingmolen 126, 3352 BL Papendrecht
brouwerijdesjaak.nl

This South Holland homebrewer went pro in 2018 after winning a competition with his IPA, and now upscales home-developed recipes at Weerter.

BEERS INCLUDE: **Eigen Weizen** (5.5%); the award-winning **IPA** (7.5%); and **Sweet Tripel** (9.5%).

Skavuiten

Penningkruid 7, 5721 RK Asten
skavuiten.nl

Formed by a group of North Brabant friends in 2016, Pirates works at various locations.
BEERS INCLUDE: improving gold-blond **Dukater** (6%: ★★) and unsubtle but decent dark barley wine **Dronker** (11%: ★★+).

Smaak

Tijsselinglaan 2, 3772 NM Barneveld
brouwerijsmaak.nl

A Gelderland company since 2015, Taste currently brews large-scale batches at Argentum.
BEERS INCLUDE: **Blonde Duif** (6.5%: ★★); fruity amber **Edele Hert** (6.5%: ★★); and imperial stout **Zwarte Schaap** (9%).

Smeijsters

Koestraat 40, 5688 AJ Oirschot
smeijstersbier.nl

A North Brabant company launched in 2018 with recreations of beers devised by the brewer's father for the ertswhile family brewery, in operation between 1890 and 1955. We are not certain where the first beer, dark lager **Munich** (7%), was made, but Vandeoirsprong in the same street is the prime suspect.

Smokkelaar

Vosbultkamp 72, 7586 GS Overdinkel
brouwerijdesmokkelaar.nl

Based in a former smuggling village in Overijssel, the Smuggler brewed its first commercial beer, strongly bitter **La IPA Bonita** (6.4%: ★★+), at Rigters in 2018.

SNAB

PO Box 204, 1440 AE Purmerend
T 0229 248751
snab.nl

Stichting Noordhollandse Alternatieve Bierbrouwers (North Holland Alternative Beer Brewers' Foundation) began in 1991 by reviving styles that were then rare but which have since become mainstream. The beers are still very good but have long been made at Proef in Belgium.
BEERS INCLUDE: tasty amber **1410** (5.5%: ★★+); malty English-style bitter **Otter S.B.** (5.6%: ★★); smoked porter **Roock** (6.5%: ★★+); floral hoppy **Pale Ale** (6.2%: ★★+); sweetish honeyed **Koning Honing** (7.5%: ★★+); amber barley wine **Speculator** (8%: ★★+); darker, richer barley wine **Maelstrøm** (9.2%: ★★★); and complex imperial stout **Czaar Peter** (9.5%: ★★★).
SEASONAL: autumn **IJsbok** (9%: ★★+); **IJsbok Hout** (★★★+), an oaked version of the same; and porter-like winter **Ezelenbok** (7.5%: ★★+).

Sneker Pypke

Zonnedauw 35, 8607 DX Sneek
bieruitsneek.nl

Established in Friesland in 2018, brewing at Vechtdal.
BEERS INCLUDE: sweetish **Blond** (6%: ★★); a **Dubbel** (6.5%); and a **Tripel** (8.5%).

Snor

Jacob Cremerstraat 20, 6821 DD Arnhem
T 06 5198 5743
brouwerijdesnor.com

Moustache, founded in Gelderland in 2018, brews at an unknown location.
BEERS INCLUDE: weizen **Wijze** (6.9%); crisp, ginger-spiced blond **Gele** (7.2%: ★★); and fruity IPA **Stoere** (7.2%).

Solobeer

Binderseind 31, 5421 CH Gemert
T 06 5705 0008
solobeer.nl

Active in North Brabant since 2016, brewing at De Leckere.
BEERS INCLUDE: fruity **Raspberry Session IPA** (3.5%: ★★+) and airhead **Blond** (6%: ★★).

Staalbaard

Molenkampsteeg 49, 9751 TS Haren
staalbaard.nl

Steel Beard, founded in 2016 in Groningen province, brews its only beer, lightly fruity **Blond** (6%: ★★), at Huttenkloas.

Stapzwan

Springweg 476, 3511 VZ Utrecht
stapzwan.nl

Begun by two friends in a former cloister in 2014 and brewing at Noord-Hollandse.
BEERS INCLUDE: weizen/IPA fusion **UPA** (4.9%: ★★+) and burnt sugar-edged **Porter** (6.9%: ★★+).

Stramme Kabouter

Lijsterstraat 15, 5451 XJ Mill
facebook.com/StrammeKabouter

Another amateur competition winner, North Brabant-based Stiff Gnome went pro in 2015 and we believe brews its **Kabouter** range at De Maar.
BEERS INCLUDE: thinnish witbier **Zwoele** (5.4%: ★★) and spiced tripel **Stramme** (8%: ★★).

Strieper

Nieuwe Waalreseweg 141, 5552 EH Valkenswaard
striepercraftbeer.nl

North Brabant company active since 2016,
brewing beers at Weerter that are perfectly
reasonable, but somewhat less special than
their daftly hyperbolic names imply.
BEERS INCLUDE: dry, nutty IPA **Amazing
Single Hop Galena Worship Gear** (6.2%: ★★);
average dubbel **Incredible Double Zen
Boosting Chill Machine** (6.8%: ★★); and
fruity tripel **Uplifting Triple Decker Flying
Apparatus** (8.5%: ★★).

Strong Ant

Laan van Broekpolder 423, 1967 KJ Heemskerk
strongant.nl

Six North Holland homebrewing friends who
went pro in 2018, currently working at De Werf.
Beers include bitter American pale ale **Ant
Sam** (4.7%: ★★) and bock **BB Ant** (6.5%).

Suzecinq

Melkweg 127, 1448 VX Purmerend
suzecinq.nl

North Holland company founded in 2017 by
five (*cinq*) francophile friends. They claim to
develop the recipes in Burgundy, but upscale
them locally at Berging.
BEERS INCLUDE: a gold-blond **Tripel** (9%).

Swarte Os

Kerkpad NZ 59, 3764 AJ Soest
T 06 5498 5287
swarteos.nl

Active in Utrecht province since 2016, Black Ox
works up its homebrewed pilot recipes at Loon.
BEERS INCLUDE: bitter amber **6** (6%: ★★+);
honeyed blond **8** (8%: ★★) and dark quadrupel
10 (10%: ★★+).

Tamesteut

Cézannehof 118, 1628 XE Hoorn
facebook.com/brouwerijtamesteut

A one-man North Holland operation founded
in 2018, working locally at De Werf.
BEERS INCLUDE: coffee-tinged imperial stout
Naughty Badass Modder Fokker (8.5%: ★★+).

Terschellinger

Baaiduinen 32, 8884 HJ Baaiduinen
T 0562 448797
terschellinger-bieren.com

Active on Terschelling since 2011, this brewer
makes beers at Wolf in Belgium using grain
from the island.
BEERS INCLUDE: hefeweizen **4** (4%: ★★);
blond **5** (5.6%: ★★); Belgian-stlye pale ale
Scelling Koan (6%: ★★); strong blond **7**
(7.4%: ★★); and sweetish stout **8** (8.5%: ★★).

Thorhem

Woudenbergseweg 19 D4, 3707 HW Doorn
T 0343 212002
brouwerijthorhem.nl

Founded in 2016 under the same umbrella
group (dbbt.nl) as A Brewery, brewing on the
latter's kit.
BEERS INCLUDE: blond **Thor!** (5.5%); malty
blond **Loki** (6.5%: ★★); and tripel **Odin** (8%).

Tiecelijn

Professor ten Doesschatestraat 125, 1963 AT
Heemskerk
facebook.com/tiecelijn

One-man North Holland operation founded
in 2016, brewing at Noord-Hollandse.
BEERS INCLUDE: thinnish, nutty English-style
brown ale **Locomotion** (4.8%: ★★); fruity,
bitter American pale ale **Kalypso** (5.3%: ★★+);
and cocoa-edged porter **Nyx** (6.5%: ★★+).

Strieper, Ir
Double Zer
Chill Mach

Tongval

Sluiskade 7, 1721 CB Broek op Langedijk
T 06 4397 6777
tongval.com

A North Holland-based brewer since 2014,
Dialect has its beers made at Hofbrouwerijke
in Belgium.
BEERS INCLUDE: hazy blond saison **Lichte
Tongval** (5.4%: ★★); standard brown **Dubbele
Tongval** (7%: ★★); and overbearingly sweet
Zware Tongval (9%: ★+).

Torenbier

Peperstraat 4, 1502 AH Zaandam
torenbier.nl

North Holland company brewing seasonals
only at Noord-Hollandse since 2014.

Trots

Sonmansstraat 7b, 3039 DG Rotterdam
T 06 5559 6344
trotsbier.nl

Founded in 2014, Proud brews beers at
Steffelaar for the local market.
BEERS INCLUDE: witbier **Wit** (5%); dry **Blond**
(5.9%: ★★+); and a decent **Tripel** (8%: ★★+).

Tureluur

Maasboulevard 100, 3063 NS Rotterdam
brouwerijtureluur.nl

One of the three friends who founded this
company in 2018 is a co-owner of Vet & Lazy,
where the business is based and the beers
are brewed.
BEERS INCLUDE: **Vol Blond** (6.2%) and herbal
Rozemarijn Tripel (7.8%) with rosemary.

Two Brew

Zandpad 44a, 3621 NE Breukelen
T 06 4781 5282
nijenrodebier.com

Small-scale outfit run by an Englishman in
Utrecht province since 2010, brewing his only
beer, dry blond **Nijenrode** (6.8%: ★★), at Proef
in Belgium.

Utberg

Sieverdingweg 8, 7134 NH Vragender
T 06 1058 9134
utbergbeer.com

Gelderland brewer active since 2019, big on
Viking-themed marketing but a little vague on
where its **Special Pale Ale** (6%) is made.

Vals Nat

valsnatbier.nl

Early beers from this business founded in 2016
– pale ale **Blonde Klasbak** (3.5%: ★★+) and
session **EPO IPA** (3.5%: ★★) – were made at
now-defunct InBier, and it may be dormant.

Van Slag

Weeshuishof 12, 2311 RM Leiden
vanslagbier.nl

South Holland homebrewer who went pro in
2017 after becoming a finalist in the Brand
Session IPA competition. The successful recipe
became the first commercial beer **De Tijd
Drinkt** (3.7%: ★★+), which was followed by
weizen **Wijzer** (4.7%). Heineken may have a
finger in the pie.

Van Weerdenburg

Concorde 19, 4116 HA Buren
brouwerij.vanweerdenburg.com

One-man operation founded in 2018, brewing
at an unknown location. The first beer was
Robuuste Weizen (5%), with **Burens Wit** and
Krachtig Blond expected to follow.

Vecht

Oud Over 8, 3632 VD Loenen
brouwerijdevecht.com

Utrecht-based duo working together since 2016 at Troost.
BEERS INCLUDE: session IPA **Abcoude** (4%: ★★+) and fruity IPA **Loender** (5.5%: ★★+).

Veenendaal

Wildeman 5, 3905 TK Veenendaal
facebook.com/stadsbrouwerijveenendaal

Utrecht province company currently making its flagship beer, **Gilbert Blond** (6%: ★★), at Heidebrouwerij, with vague plans to open a brewery in its home town.

Vergulde Lam

Waterhoen 33, 3752 ZH Bunschoten
T 06 4674 0756
hetverguldelam.nl

The former homebrewer who in 2017 founded the Gilt Lamb, named after one of the oldest buildings in her home town, brews her **Bunschoten** beers at Noord-Hollandse.
BEERS INCLUDE: fruity golden **Saison** (6%: ★★) and malty amber **'The King' A.P.A.** (6.5%: ★★).

Verlanghe

Vleutloop 12, 5384 WZ Heesch
derverlanghe.nl

Seven North Brabant friends who brewed their first commercial beer, **Blond Der Verlanghe** (6.2%), at Het Veem in 2018.

Vessel 11 (V11)

Wijnhaven 101 B, 3011 WN Rotterdam
T 010 840 4730
vessel11.nl

This business has been making beers in vaguely English styles since 2014, primarily for a like-named lightship which now houses a British restaurant. Its **V11** range, currently brewed at Steffelaar, is also sold elsewhere.
BEERS INCLUDE: **Classic Red Ale** (4.8%: ★★), with caramel notes; sweetish **Golden Blond** (5%: ★★); middling **Session Stout** (5.5%: ★★); and standout fruity-hoppy **IPA** (6.4%: ★★+).

Vijfhoeck

Kamstraat 26, 5701 PW Helmond
T 0492 834544
devijfhoeck.nl

Founded in 2013 and with its own taproom since 2018, Pentangle has its beers brewed at Anders in Belgium.
BEERS INCLUDE: crisp, superior **Pils** (5%: ★★+); its unfiltered version **Ongefilterd** (5%: ★★+); flagship blond **Vijfhoeck's 1515** (6%: ★★); and dry amber **Kasteel Bier** (6%: ★★).

Vissenberg

Markt 38, 4701 PG Roosendaal
bierbrouwerijdevissenberg.nl

North Brabant company brewing its single beer, blond **Lekker Weertje** (6.2%), at other locations since 2015, but planning its own place in the village of Oudenbosch "some day".

Voorschoten

Johan Willem Frisolaan 63, 2252 HD Voorschoten
T 06 4216 7172
facebook.com/brouwerijvoorschoten

South Holland company founded in 2018, making **Voorschotens** beers at Klein Duimpje.
BEERS INCLUDE: a **Pale Ale** (5.5%); **Blond** (6.5%); and **Tripel** (8.4%).

Voortsche

Zeumerseweg 5a, 3781 PB Voorthuizen
voortschebieren.nl

This Gelderland brewer has had a small kit for workshops since 2015 but its beers are brewed commercially at Grain d'Orge in Belgium.
BEERS INCLUDE: sweetish witbier **Vlier** (5%: ★★), with elderflower; coriander-spiced fruity amber **Dwaes** (7%: ★★); and amber winter ale **Vorst** (8.8%: ★★).

Vos

Oostendorperstraatweg 7, 8081 RH Elburg
facebook.com/stadsbrouwerijvos

A Gelderland brewer since 2016, Fox is based near and makes its beers at Eembier.
BEERS INCLUDE: US-hopped but sweet IPA **Vesting Session** (3.5%: ★★); dark, bitter, cocoa-laden **Vispoorter** (6.5%: ★★+); sweetish tripel **Ondeugende Gappie** (8%: ★+); rounded imperial **Stoute Vos** (9.3%: ★★+); and nutty barley wine **Don Aart** (9.5%: ★★★).

Wapen Van Well

Grotestraat 34, 5855 AN Well
facebook.com/wapenvanwell/

North Limburg company founded in 2015, dormant for a while but now brewing again at Herder.

Warnsfelder

Goldkampstraat 6, 7722 RN Dalfsen
warnsfelder.nl

Overijssel brewer active since 2017, making weizen **Oswald** (5%), **Mien Blonde** (6%), and tripel **Henrick 1661** (8.5%) at Huttenkloas.

Waterpoart

Houtdraaiersstraat 6p, 8601 VG Sneek
waterpoart.frl

Friesland brewer which made its first beer, blond **Waterpoartsje** (4.5%), at Troost in 2018.

Watertoren

Bachstraat 35, 4571 XS Axel
watertorenbier.nl

Zeeuws-Vlaanderen homebrewer who made his first commercial beer, **Goud Blond** (7%), in 2018 at De Cock in Belgium.

Wereld

Oudestraat 218–220, 8261 CA Kampen
T 038 337 1721
facebook.com/brouwerijdewereld

Overijssel company based since 2016 at the Stomme van Campen (see cafés), brewing **Kamper** beers at an unspecified location but with a long term plan to install its own kit locally.
BEERS INCLUDE: spiced blond **Princesse Bier** (4.5%: ★★); solid **Espresso Stout** (6%: ★★); banana-edged **Proef Blond** (7.5%: ★★); and bubblegum-flavoured red **M.IPA** (7%: ★★).

Westhoek

Burghseweg 53, 4328 LA Burgh-Haamstede
T 0111 652415
pannekoekenmolen.nl

Zeeland brewer making various limited-edition beers with local ingredients at Vermeersen for sale at a pancake restaurant since 2018.

Westlander

Poeldijkseweg 1c, 2681 LT Monster
T 06 1379 6753
westlanderbier.nl

South Holland company founded in 2016, working at Troost.
BEERS INCLUDE: **Weizen** (5%) and Belgian-style blond **Original** (7%).

Westlandse

Naaldwijkseweg 72, 2291 PA Wateringen
T 0174 506951
westlandsebieren.nl

Not to be confused with the above, this South Holland company gives its founding date as 2006, although its beer only appeared much later. There are rumours, which we are unable to confirm or deny, that the **Westlands** range is simply Budels beer with different labels.

White Dog

Bakema-erf 130, 3315 JC Dordrecht
T 06 5188 8101
facebook.com/WhiteDogBrewer

South Holland homebrewer who turned pro in 2018 and now makes beers at Weerter. *BEERS INCLUDE:* Citra dry-hopped double IPA **Cloud** (8.5%) and tripel **Pluvio** (9.3%).

Wijsbier

Weijpoort 12, 2415 BV Nieuwerbrug aan den Rijn
T 020 624 0436
cafewijs.nl

South Holland company active since 2013, making beer at De Molen exclusively for its Hofje van Wijs café (Zeedijk 43, Amsterdam), mostly flagship **De Blonde Poes** (4.7%: ★★).

Wild Mill

Raadhuisstraat 52, 4701 PV Roosendaal
T 016 553 3900
wildmill.nl

North Brabant-based company since 2018, owned by Dutch TV celebrity barbecue chef Jeremy Vermolen, who has his dry **Blond** (6.5%: ★★+), cherry juiced **Red** (8%:★★), and golden **Tripel** (8.5%: ★★) made at Vermeersen.

Witte Anker

Haven 19, 4811 WL Breda
T 06 3409 2312
witteanker.nl

Founded in 2017, White Anchor makes beer at the local Breda brewery, mostly for the Dok 19 café, its *de facto* taproom. *BEERS INCLUDE:* flagship hoppy witbier **Hopwit** (5.5%: ★★+); above-average **Blond** (6%: ★★+); a decent **Tripel** (8%: ★★+); and dark, liquoricey **Quadrupel** (9.5%: ★★+).

Witte Buizerd

De Zuylenkamp 21, 6999 CA Hummelo
facebook.com/Hummelobier

A Gelderland company since 2018, White Buzzard used Wittenburg to make its first commercial beer, American IPA **Hummelsche Hoppa** (5.5%).

Witte Konijn

Hof 8, 3811 CJ Amersfoort
T 033 737 0467
wittekonijn.nl

The White Rabbit (see cafés) has been tapping beers made under its own name at various locations since 2019. It also boasts a 1.5hl kit currently used for occasional test brews, and if any of these are ever sold, it will qualify as a brewpub. *BEERS INCLUDE:* dry-hopped 'New Zealand' lager **Rapeti** (3.9%: ★★★); dry and noble-hopped blond **Hop Hop Hop** (6%: ★★+); and **Pluis** (9%: ★★★), a moreish imperial stout.

Wild Mi

Witte Leeuw

Beelhof 29, 8091 WP Wezep
T 06 3629 2689
brouwerijdewitteleeuw.nl

The White Lion is a Gelderland husband and wife team active since 2011, content to brew commercially at Scheldebrouwerij in Belgium.
BEERS INCLUDE: hoppy blond **Amarillo Sun** (6%: ★★+); triple-hopped IPA **Stroatige Jannus** (7.5%: ★★+); and improving tripel **Hopus Dei** (8%: ★★+).

X-Brewing

Rijnstraat 104, 2223 EC Katwijk
x-brewing.com

Founded by a South Holland couple in 2019, brewing at Noord-Hollandse.
BEERS INCLUDE: cucumber weizen **Two Big Friends** (6.5%: ★★+); rounded IPA **Fruity Madness** (6.5%: ★★+); and bean-laden imperial stout **I Love the Smell of Coffee in the Morning** (10%: ★★+).

Zeeburg

1e van Swindenstraat 433, 1093 GB Amsterdam
T 06 1153 2914
brouwerijzeeburg.nl

Zeeburg has been promising a physical brewery since soon after it began 2009 but there's no sign of it so far. At first the beers were brewed at Proef in Belgium, but production has now switched to Naeckte Brouwers nearer to home.
BEERS INCLUDE: quaffable **Weizen** (5.7%: ★★); sweetish **Tripel** (8.2%: ★★); and roasted malty seasonal **Dubbelbock** (8.2%: ★★+).

Zeglis

Oudegracht 214,1811 CR Alkmaar
T 06 1240 0665
brouwerijzeglis.nl

North Holland-based Zeglis has been brewing with some finesse at four different Dutch locations since 2016.
BEERS INCLUDE: fruity Norwegian farmhouse ale **Kruisbeskveik** (6%: ★★) with gooseberries; bitter IPA **Eersteling** (6.2% ★★+); single-hopped blond **Andermaal** (6.2%: ★★+); fruity rauchbier **Zinder** (6.5%: ★★+); amber **Naalden Dennenbier** (7%: ★★+), perfumed with pine tops; dark vanilla stout **Temeer** (8.5%: ★★+); and barley wine **Krachtige Kveik** (9%: ★★+).
SEASONALS INCLUDE: autumnal **Herfsthout** (7.5%: ★★+), with smoked cherrywood malt.

Zevenstar

Winkelcentrum Nedereind 10,
3431 ER Nieuwegein
T 06 3009 5597
zevenstar.nl

Seven Star, active in Utrecht province since 2014 and named after a local brewery that burned down in 1765, brews at Huttenkloas.
BEERS INCLUDE: solid if unassuming **Blond** (5.9%: ★★) and quadrupel **Schavuit** (9.4%).

Zuidas

IJsbaanpad 9–11, 1076 CV Amsterdam
zuidasbier.nl

Named after its location when founded in 2017, Southern Axis brews at Naeckte Brouwers.
BEERS INCLUDE: quaffable **Amsterdam Pale Ale** (5.5%: ★★+); standard witbier **Wit** (6%: ★★); and wild-hopped **IPA** (6%: ★★).

Zwarte Pad

'Brouwerij' Het Zwarte Pad
Disneystrook 49, 2726 SP Zoetermeer
brouwerijhetzwartepad.nl

Black Path are two South Holland friends making beer at Loon since 2018.
BEERS INCLUDE: bittersweet **Pixie Blond** (5.5%: ★★) and double IPA **Hop Hydra** (7.5%: ★★+).

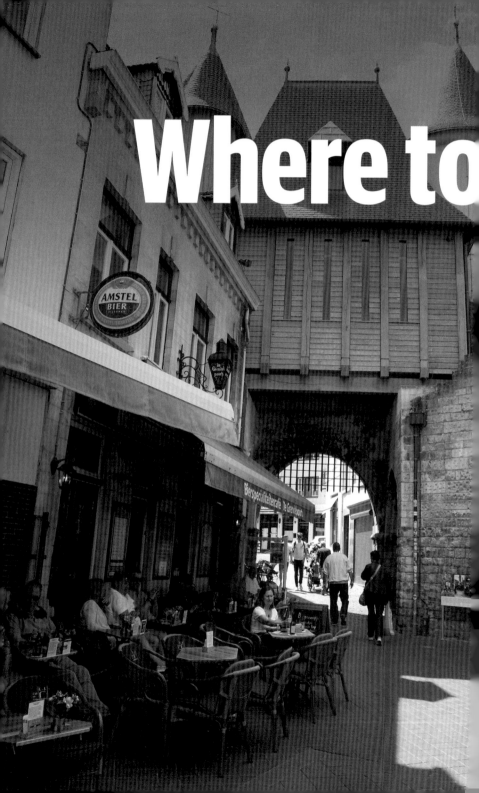

find beer

The Netherlands has a rapidly changing beer culture, we are a tiny operation, and it takes time to turn researched words into a book, so we are bound to be out of date, though not by much, we hope.

If you find somewhere as good or better for beer than the places we list, or that those we favour have been closed or ruined, please let us know via **timskelton@hotmail.com**.

WHAT WE LIST

We have included both drinking venues and places to buy beer to take home. Here are the standards we apply.

Beer cafés

A few exceptional cases notwithstanding, our loosely applied arbitrary cut-off to define a bar, tavern, *kroeg* or eating house as a specialist beer venue is that 60 or more beers appear on its menu. A healthy interest in local Dutch and/or international craft brews will get a place a full entry below this figure, as will somewhere with true architectural or historical signifcance. In such cases we try to justify why we are recommending the place. A menu stuffed full of the usual Belgian suspects found in every bar in the Netherlands will struggle to get our attention.

Taprooms

Brewpubs, taprooms and *proeflokalen* (literally 'tasting rooms') attached to breweries and certain other beer-makers are listed regardless of how many other beers are served, so long as they have regular and reliable opening times.

Bottle shops

For bottle shops and warehouses, the qualifying standard is generally 500 or more beers, although we make exceptions for smaller but noteworthy ranges.

HOW WE LIST IT

The selection is ordered alphabetically by province, then by town, and finally by venue name. For some towns we sweep up any oddities and near misses under 'Other venues' after the main listings, followed by any shops and warehouses under 'Beer to go'.

We have anglicised some province names by changing Noord- to North and Zuid- to South.

We have also imposed the English alphabet by placing 'ij' between 'ii' and 'ik', instead of the Dutch convention of placing it between 'x' and 'z', which we only do when the preferred local spelling is with an old-fashioned 'y'.

Pub names have usually been simplified, dropping pronouns and other qualifiers. Hence 't Kuipertje becomes Kuipertje, In de Wildeman becomes simply Wildeman, and so on. Addresses are given in Dutch order with the house number following the street name.

Opening times

Many bars list their hours simply as 'From 11.00' or similar, and stay open so long as someone is buying and not misbehaving. Alternatively, if it's quiet or the person in charge gets bored and wants to go home, they can shut early. We try to list all closing times earlier than midnight.

poort,
urg, Limburg

UNDERSTANDING DUTCH CAFÉS

The terms *bruin café*, translated here as 'brown café', and *kroeg* mean a traditional café with ceilings browned by tobacco smoke since long before the smoking ban. These will have most or all of the following: a wooden floor; dark wood tables, chairs and other fittings; smoke-stained walls and ceilings. The ambience grows from there.

Etiquette

Dutch cafés are generally convivial places but the staff have an annoying habit of assuming that everyone knows how to behave.

If you need to order at the bar it is usually obvious. The majority of cafés have table service so someone will take your order eventually, though attracting a waiter's attention is an art form, especially on a crowded terrace in summer. Staff often appear to have special training in how to look busy while scanning a room or terrace attentively without actually spotting anyone in the sea of thirsty punters frantically waving at them.

In many parts of the world, saying that you would like a beer will elicit a brief explanation of the options. In most Dutch cafés, this request will result in the appearance of a small (20cl) glass of industrial pilsener, poured fast until its foamy head spews over the top of the glass, only to be flattened with a deft flick from a white plastic spatula, the discarded froth going straight down the drain.

If you want a particular beer, find a menu and ask for it by name. Then, when the waiter fails to understand your effort to pronounce it in Anglo-Dutch, point and say, "That one." Most Dutch people speak English far better than the vast majority of English speakers who attempt Dutch.

Many bars will serve you a measure close to a pint (500ml) if you ask, though in doing so the word 'tourist' will appear on your forehead as a virtual tattoo. The arguments for drinking from these small glasses, which confusingly to English speakers are known as *pintjes* (little pints), are that you can finish them before they get warm, as industrial pils fares badly at any temperature where the flavour becomes apparent, and that people drink more of them.

Finally, many traditional pubs have a bell by the bar. Do not ring this. Unless you intend to buy everyone inside a drink, as that is the signal you will just have given.

Is there any interesting beer?

Even with the rise of craft beer, pilsener remains the overwhelmingly dominant species. The major brewers share the market between them. Market leader Heineken is particularly prevalent in its North and South Holland homeland; Grolsch rules the eastern Netherlands; Swinkels (Bavaria) is strongest in North Brabant; and AB InBev crops up everywhere, although it is annoyingly fond of promoting decidedly ordinary Jupiler ahead of home-grown names.

The bulk of cafés are controlled by these same big boys and while not excluding products from other brewers altogether, only a few competitors are allowed. In the majority of cases this means a handful of Belgian abbey beers, or real Trappist ales if you are lucky, plus a few familiar standard imports to bring the range up to around 25. This is typical of 90% of the country's bars.

ar Alt,
rdam
.246)

Smoking is still legally permitted, at least for now, on café terraces, but more and more places are introducing voluntary bans there as well. Check first before lighting up.

Food

Where we describe a place as selling 'snacks' we mean the likes of *bitterballen,* or a hefty plate filled with cubed cheese and/or salami, while the term 'nibbles' means nothing larger than a small side dish of nuts or crisps.

Tipping

Tipping in bars is optional. If only buying drinks, it is perfectly acceptable to pay the exact amount. In restaurants, or if ordering food in a café, round up the bill to any convenient amount, adding no more than five to 10%. These days, with many venues preferring electronic card payments, even restaurant tipping is far less common than it was.

SHOPS

We've listed all the specialist bottle shops with a range that really impresses us. In addition to these, three major retail chains sell beer. The best remains **Mitra** (mitra.nl), which was forced to slim down after experiencing financial problems but still has over 100 outlets nationwide, most of which stock several hundred beers. The largest chain, **Gall & Gall** (gall.nl) carries a far less inspiring list – we have not found a single store meriting special mention. Faring somewhat better is the chain of independently titled **Uw topSlijter** stores (uwtopslijter.nl), many of which are OK beer-wise.

One area in which the beer retail scene has developed massively since the previous edition of this guide was published has been the supermarkets. Even the major chains are now on-message, and most stock a decent range, usually with a few small local brewers making it onto the shelves.

Warning signs that you may be in for disappointment include plasticised generic beer menus, or beers on chalkboards being hailed simply as 'wit', 'tripel' or 'dubbel' etc, without reference to a specific brewer, a sure sign of disinterest. Any café with a good beer range will usually make a song and dance about it. Look for boards on the street advertising the numbers in stock or big chalkboards covering most interior walls.

Age limits

The minimum drinking age in bars is 18. There are no age restrictions on children entering bars, although common sense applies: taking a toddler into a local boozer at midnight is certain to raise eyebrows. On the other hand, many larger places provide play areas and games to distract youngsters while mum and dad sup.

Smoking

It is illegal to smoke anywhere inside any bar, café or restaurant. There are a dwindling number of die-hard places, usually run by nicotine-addicted landlords, that persist in flouting this law. To understand the Dutch history of introducing laws and then ignoring them, see prostitution, cannabis and others.

Drenthe

Groningen

Friesland Veenhuizen

Assen

E232

Emmen

Hoogeveen

Meppel

Coevorden

Overijssel

10 km

LARGEST CENTRES: **Assen, Emmen, Hoogeveen**
MORE INFORMATION: drenthe.nl
SELECTED BREWERIES: **Gulzige Gans**, *Coevorden;*
Jonge Beer, *Hoogeveen;* **Maallust**, *Veenhuizen;*
Veteraan, *Emmen*

EMMEN
Emmen

Drenthe's largest city (pop 107,000) is a classic
example of 20th-century Dutch town planning.
It only appeared in the 1950s, as modern suburbs
built around farming communities expanded
and merged. The souped-up 'adventure zoo'
Wildlands (**wildlands.nl**) attracts 1.3 million
visitors per year.

Brasserie

Hoofdstraat 53 · **T** 0591 616675
debrasserie.nl
Fr from 09.00; Su from 11.00; others from 10.00

Large café on the main square, with a terrace
and conservatory. Inside, a British telephone box
breaks up otherwise brown decor. Above that, a
Heath Robinson series of interconnected ceiling
fans are all driven by a single belt. Upstairs, an
old-fashioned all-wood bar is billed as a Belgian
beer café, but is often only open for events.
Food served all day. The beer list has expanded
to a healthy 125+ including 10 taps, but remains
dominated by safe Belgians, now with a few
Dutch choices and plenty of global Trappists.

HOOGEVEEN
44km NE from Zwolle off A28 exit 26
Hoogeveen

Quiet provincial town (pop 55,000) that
remained fenland until the railways arrived.
Its wide, grid-like street pattern preserves the
lines of canals formed by peat cutting but filled
in by cold-hearted town planners in the 1960s.

Now a flat, sparsely populated (492,000),
largely agricultural province, back in the
Bronze Age Drenthe was relatively crowded.
Visible evidence of this are the 53 megalithic
tombs, or *hunebedden* (dolmens), that have
dotted the countryside for around 5,500 years.

Before World War II, the Dutch government
built a camp near Hooghalen to house Jewish
refugees fleeing Hitler's Germany. With bitter
irony, during the occupation it became a transit
camp for Dutch Jews on their way to concentration and extermination camps further east.
Anne Frank went to Auschwitz on the last
train to leave from here in September 1944.

Drenthe is a deeply Protestant province
and for nine years from 1993 it had no breweries at all. This is changing slowly, but the
provincial capital Assen still has no real
beer destinations.

While beer-poor, the province boasts one
major sporting drawcard. The Assen motor
racing circuit hosts the annual Dutch TT
motorcycle event, attracting in excess of
100,000 fans every June. Unless you are
attending, or enjoy sitting in traffic, the area
is best avoided that weekend.

Dégust

Hoofdstraat 38 · **T** 0528 233475
degust.nl
Shut Mo&Tu; others from 17.00

This excellent beer café-restaurant on the
main square has been the provincial star for
a number of years. The tiled floor interior has
an 'ancient and modern' feel and includes a
champagne rack. The food (*until 22.00, snacks
until 23.30*) is great, and so is the beer menu,
mainly selected for pairing potential. The
100+ range is dominated by Dutch micros,
including locally-brewed Mommeriete and
Berghoeve, and the wine list is almost as long.

OTHER BEER VENUES
Hare Majesteit (Grote Kerkstraat 8 – **T** 0528
261899 – **cafedeharemajesteit.nl** – *shut Su-Mo
&We; Fr&Sa from 15.00; others from 16.00*) has
colourful murals, chandeliers, wooden-
beamed ceilings and 50+ beers.

BEER TO GO
Bij Marcel (Alteveerstraat 6 – **T** 0528 264583
– *Shut Su; Mo 13.00-18.00; Fr 09.00-21.00;
Sa 09.00-17.00; others 09.00-18.00*) stocks 500+
beers arranged by style, with a decent Dutch
and local craft selection.

MEPPEL

25km NNE from Zwolle off A32 exits 1-3
🚊 Meppel

The God-fearing townsfolk of Meppel (pop
33,000) were once known as Meppeler Muggen
(Meppel midges) due to an apocryphal tale
that they once mistook a swarm of midges
for the church tower being on fire.

If you get thirsty shopping (below),
Clouso (Zuideinde 25 – *Shut Mo; Su 15.00-22.00;
others from 15.00*) is a grungy brown café with
occasional live music, a beer garden at the back
and around 50 sometimes interesting beers.

BEER TO GO
Kisjes (De Putstoel 2 – **T** 0522 255923 –
kisjes-slijterijen.nl – *shut Su; Mo 12.00-18.00;
Fr 09.00-21.00; Sa 09.00-17.00; others 09.00-18.00*)
has 500+ Dutch and international beers.

VEENHUIZEN

15km W from Assen on N919
Bus 14

Spread-out village (pop 1,200) with a unique
history as Europe's only 'colony within a country'.
In the 1820s the Maatschappij van Weldadigheid
(Society for Benevolence) bought the land to
house and provide work for the poor, who
worked blocks of farmland, most of which
remain as they were. When the society went
bust the land passed to the Justice Department
and was turned into a penal colony, with
three prisons. Visit the National Prison
Museum (Nationaal Gevangenismuseum,
gevangenismuseum.nl) for a peek inside one
of them. The whole colony may become a
UNESCO World Heritage site in 2020.

Maallust

Hoofdweg 140 · **T** 0592 388971
maallust.nl
Shut Mo; others 11.00-18.00 (Nov-Mar also shut Tu-Th)

Brewery and tap in former grain mill with
scenic terrace out front. Watch your head
on the wooden beams inside. If you have a
meeting planned, there's a circular conference
room above. Simple lunches feature bread
baked with spent grain and cheese made next
door, alongside apple pie and snacks. All the
house beers are available on tap and in bottle,
with tasting flights and takeaway gift packs.

Maallust taproom, Veenhuizen

Flevoland

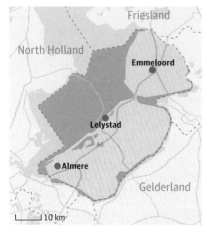

Created mostly on land reclaimed from the IJsselmeer and Markermeer lakes in the 1950s and 1960s, the Netherlands' newest province (pop 408,000) only became official in 1986. Its two cities are not much older, Lelystad being founded in 1967 and Almere in the 1970s. We would love to tell you they were created by forward-thinking town planners who found room for picturesque squares surrounded by cafés but it would not be true.

Fifteen years into the 'craft beer revolution', Flevoland still struggles to get the message, with more breweries than decent bars. Almere, the country's seventh-largest city, has a brewpub and a diner with a half-decent selection. Provincial capital Lelystad has nothing. We hope to be proved wrong one day, but at least the corpse is twitching.

Not everything is modern urban planning. The train between Almere and Lelystad passes through the Oostvaardersplassen nature reserve, an area used for 'rewilding' large herds of deer and Europe's largest population of wild horses.

LARGEST CENTRES: **Almere, Lelystad**

MORE INFORMATION: visitflevoland.nl

SELECTED BREWERIES: **Bierfabriek**, *Almere*; **Kemphaan**, *Almere*; **Stijl**, *Almere*; **Praght**, *Dronten*

ALMERE
🚉 Almere Centrum

New town (pop 197,000) that was fields barely half a century ago, built on land that was water 30 years before that. Despite its size it comes across as functional rather than fun. Most locals appear to use the centre for shopping, then travel into nearby Amsterdam for a night out. Still, there are now a couple of beer options, which is something.

Bierfabriek
Koetsierbaan 2 · **T** 036 782 0500
bierfabriek.com/almere
Sa from 15.00; Su 15.00–23.00; others from 16.00

The third outlet in the Beer Factory brewpub empire is in an oddly shaped brown building that looks small from the outside but like a TARDIS is cavernous within. There is a beer garden at the rear. The  modern interior follows the house style: brewkit in the middle, open kitchen, peanuts in shells and some tables with taps where you can pour your own beer. Food is fried chicken and similar. House beers are the same as in the two sister branches in Amsterdam and Delft (below).

Lou
Grote Markt 84 · **T** 036 525 3046
loustreetfoodbar.nl
Daily 11.00–23.00

This 'street food bar' with a terrace is more diner than pub, but as close to a beer café as Flevoland currently gets. The minimalist interior has brick and star-tiled walls. Food (until 22.00) is burgers, hot dogs and tacos. A list of around 60 beers with a decent range of Dutch micros would scrape into the book anywhere else, but here it is positively revolutionary.

Friesland (Fryslân)

The Netherlands' most independent province (pop 647,000), and the only one with a local language that enjoys equal official status. Historically, Frysk, or Frisian, is closer to English than Dutch, though it's understandably been much influenced by the latter. The province includes four of the populated Wadden Islands: Vlieland, Terschelling, Ameland and Schiermonnikoog.

Frisian history pre-dates the Romans. Before it was conquered by the Franks in the Middle Ages, its influence had at times stretched as far as modern Belgium and northwest Germany. Today what remains is sustained by agriculture and tourism.

The most-famous local event is the Elfstedentocht, a 200km ice skating marathon in which 16,000 racers speed through 11 towns along frozen canals. Because it requires a prolonged cold snap it does not happen that often: the last was in 1997.

A long history of conservative Calvinism once ensured any form of fun was frowned upon. This prompted an ancestor of this book to suggest fostering beer culture here was

like 'trying to whisk honey'. Since then the mixture has become decidedly frothier.

And yes, this is where the cows came from.

LARGEST CENTRE: **Leeuwarden**

MORE INFORMATION: friesland.nl

SELECTED BREWERIES: **Admiraals**, *Aldtsjerk*; **Amelander**, *Ameland*; **Bonifatius 754**, *Dokkum*; **Brouwdok**, *Harlingen*; **Dockum**, *Dokkum*; **Friese**, *Bolsward*; **Schoemrakker**, *West-Terschelling*.

AMELAND – NES
10km NW from Holwerd by ferry

In the 1870s, Ameland (Amelân), one of the Wadden Islands, was briefly connected to the mainland by a dyke, breached in a storm in 1882. The spit leading to Holwerd ferry port is all that remains. This was also one of the last places in Europe liberated by Allied forces at the end of World War II. Being of limited strategic value, the occupying forces did not surrender until June 2 1945, four weeks after hostilities had officially ended.

Today Ameland is mainly sand dunes and farmland, with birdwatching the main draw. Nes (pop 1,200) is its second-largest village, ferry port and tourist hub.

HOTEL TIP: **Hofker ★★★**, J. Hofkerweg 1 (hotelhofker.nl) is both central and near the ferry.

179

Nes Café

Van Heeckerenstraat 10 · **T** 0519 542760
nes-cafe-ameland.nl
Shut Mo–Th (Jan–Mar); others from 10.00

It's a café and in Nes, so what else could they call it? Beyond the front terrace is a bar area designed primarily for drinking and a semi-conservatory for dining. Centre stage among the beer pumps is a model of Ameland's distinctive lighthouse. A shelf behind the counter inevitably contains instant coffee jars. Foodwise, the house speciality is steaks cooked in a 'Green Egg' barbecue. The 60+ beers including 10 on tap often feature some from the local Amelander brewery.

BALK

40km SSW from Leeuwarden off N359
Bus 47 from Sneek

Small town (pop 4,000) with one long main street, spliced lengthwise by a canal.
HOTEL TIP: the **Teernstra★** (below) has basic rooms.

Teernstra

Van Swinderenstraat 69 · **T** 0514 601013
hotelteernstra.nl
Daily from 10.00

Hotel, restaurant and café halfway along the main street, with bench seating outside and a canalside terrace over the road. The largely wooden interior is divided in two: to the left is a locals' bar with billiards table, to the right a more formal restaurant (*from 17.00*). Empty beer bottles and enamels dominate. Lunch (*until 17.00*) and snacks are served in the bar. Maallust and De Molen feature prominently on the 90+ beer list.

BOLSWARD

27km SW from Leeuwarden off A7 exit 18
Bus 92, 350

Small town (pop 10,100) on the Elfstedentocht skating route, home to the province's oldest brewery. Check out the magnificent 17th-century town hall and the Boerekerk church, left as a striking glass-roofed ruin after it was gutted by fire in 1980.

Stadhuis, Bolsward

Us Heit

Snekerstraat 43 · **T** 0515 577449
usheit.com
Shut Su–We; Sa 10.00–18.00; others 15.00–18.00

Friese brewery taproom housed in a former food and drink technology college, with a first-floor tasting room in the old canteen serving draught and bottled house beers, and a downstairs shop selling takeaway bottles. A mural covers one wall and brewing equipment is scattered about elsewhere. There is also a small terrace. Nibbles only. The name, also used as the beer brand, translates as 'Our father', the first words of the Lord's Prayer in Frisian.

DOKKUM

28km NE from Leeuwarden off N361
Bus 51

Another picturesque old town (pop 12,500) on the Elfstedentocht route, with plenty of well-preserved medieval houses and cobbled streets. Devon-born Saint Boniface was murdered here in 754, lending his name for posterity to the venue below.

Bonifatius 754

Diepswal 5 · **T** 06 1368 7839
bonifatius754.nl
Shut Su-Tu; Fr 13.00-21.00; Sa 11.00-17.00; others 15.00-18.00

Small, cute taproom with small, cute canalside terrace in the centre of a small, cute town. The one-room brick-walled café has a smart Delftware tap on the counter. The brewery is on the floor above, although most of the range is actually made at its larger neighbour Dockum (below). Sausage and cheese snacks only. House beers are available on tap and in bottle.

tius 754, Dokkum

Dockum

Hogedijken 20 · **T** 0519 740004
brouwerijdokkum.nl
Shut Mo-We; Su from 14.00; others from 16.00

Shiny modern taproom and restaurant on the eastern edge of town, in a black wood and corrugated metal building with a terrace.

The high-ceilinged airy bar area has glass windows behind the counter looking onto the adjacent brewery, which produces beers under the name Kâld Kletske. Dinners and snacks are served, while house beers and some guests are poured from 18 taps.

HARLINGEN

27km W from Leeuwarden off N31
Harlingen Haven

Fish restaurants abound in this attractive harbour town (pop 15,800) and ferry port for Wadden islands Terschelling and Vlieland. Ancient quays stretch into the commercial heart, lining the streets with sailing boats.

Brouwdok

Nieuwe Willemskade 8 · **T** 06 4486 2255
hetbrouwdok.nl
Fr-Su 13.00-21.30; others 15.00-20.00

Dockside taproom in former warehouse a short walk south from the station. The terrace has one table raised to absurd heights for sunset views over the harbour wall. The interior has mismatched jumble sale furniture that includes a sofa corner. It was high-ceilinged on our last visit but plans are afoot to insert a mezzanine. Nuts, cheese and sausage as snacks. The full house range is served from 11 taps and some bottles, alongside collaboration brews and a few guests.

Brouwdok, Harlingen

LEEUWARDEN

🚉 Leeuwarden

The provincial capital (pop 107,000) is a pleasant place with canal-filled streets. This was the birthplace of Margaretha Zelle, the exotic dancer known as Mata Hari, who was shot as a spy in 1917. Another famous son was graphic artist M.C. Escher, he of those 'impossible' drawings with endless staircases. For a different kind of perspective, try the Fries Museum (**friesmuseum.nl**) of local history.

HOTEL TIP: **Alibi Hostel**, Blokhuisplein 40 (**alibihostel.nl**) is a restored ex-prison, its rooms former cells.

Freezone

Grote Hoogstraat 24
poolcafeleeuwarden.nl
Daily from 15.00

Friendly pool café with tiny terrace. The bar is at the front of the carpeted interior, with seven pool tables and four dartboards further back. Toasties and crisps only. Around 75 beers are mainly Dutch craft, Belgian and a few German and US interlopers. The list changes often so check the blackboards.

Markies

Groot Schavernek 19   ·   **T** 06 4125 9568
de-markies.nl
Shut Mo; Su 15.00–21.00; Fr&Sa from 15.00; others from 16.00

The province's best beer outlet is the Marquis, a friendly brown terrace café on a small square near the centre. Once a much smaller pils swillers' hangout, it first widened its beer offer in 2010, then expanded into a neighbouring building, its list growing accordingly. Brewery enamels occupy most of the walls. Snacks only, though most are substantial sharing platters. The 260-odd beers are well chosen, with short shrift given to crowd-pleasers, and plentiful local and Dutch craft on offer. Ten of the 12 taps dispense rotating guests.

Strohoed

Eewal 72
cafedestrohoed.nl
Daily from 15.00

Creaky-floored brown café the Straw Hat is one of those reassuring places seemingly unchanged since the Earth cooled, with a comforting musty smell when the place is quiet. The name derives from a former owner's fondness for Buster Keaton, and decor includes old British station signs, and wooden UK pub signs salvaged from an era before branding. Snacks only. The 70+ beers stick largely to safe Belgians, with a few Dutch offerings.

OTHER BEER VENUES

Spoek (Sint Jacobsstraat 29 – **T** 06 4547 0877 – **cafedespoek.nl** – *Su 15.00–23.00; others from 15.00*) has Warholesque screen prints of The Beatles at the bar, good music, 85 whiskies, and around 50 beers with a focus on Eem and Maallust.

OENTSJERK

12km NE from Leeuwarden on N361

Small village (pop. 1,750) known by its Fries name, more formally Oenkerk in Dutch.

It Wapen fan Fryslân

Rengersweg 51   ·   **T** 058 256 1747
kafee.nl
Shut Mo; Su 16.00–22.00; Tu 14.00–20.00; We 14.00–23.00; Th from 14.00; others from 11.00

Village local the Friesland Arms has a terrace and a carpeted interior with billiard table,

dartboards and a cast-iron stove backed with Delft tiles. It also has Hammerschlagen, a game that originated at the Munich Oktoberfest and involves banging nails into a tree stump, ideally without ending up in hospital. Rolls and snacks all day, dinners from 17.00. The beer range of around 150 may dwindle as the landlord puts more emphasis on the tap selection, which was 18 in 2019 but could grow.

SINT NICOLAASGA

38km S from Leeuwarden off A6 exit 19
Bus 41 from Heerenveen

Small provincial town (pop 3,300) with no pubs of note, but a shop that makes the journey worthwhile.

BEER TO GO
Box of delights **Lekkerbier** (Tsjûkemarwei 20 – **T** 0513 410190 – lekkerbierdebierwinkel.nl – *shut Su&Mo; Th 10.00–18.00; Fr 10.00–20.00; Sa 10.00–17.00; others 13.00–18.00*) stocks 1,200+ beers from all over and has an online store (bier-winkel.com).

SNEEK

27km SSW from Leeuwarden off N354
🚾 Sneek

Attractive old town (pop 34,000) best known for the highly photogenic Waterpoort, a canal-straddling city gate that dates from 1492. *HOTEL TIP:* Stay at the bar below, also a hotel.

3B
Wijde Noorderhorne 2 · **T** 0515 418707
biercafe3b.nl
Su 14.00–22.00; others from 14.00

The three Bs are Beer, Bed & Breakfast, as there are hotel rooms at the back. A white tile-fronted bar is straight ahead as you enter from the front terrace. To the left is a lounge with button-back sofas, to the right a modern café, with a bottle-lined staircase up to the mezzanine. Snacks and full meals (*until 21.00*) include pulled pork and stamppot. Besides 25 taps and 200+ bottles and cans with plenty from local craft micros, you can choose from an additional 50 cellar-aged 75cl bottles.

TERSCHELLING – MIDSLAND

25km NW from Harlingen by ferry
Bus 1 from West-Terschelling (below)

Historically, Terschelling (pop 5,000) was a popular spot for shipwrecks. With few trees on the windswept island, most farms and barns were built using salvaged timber. Things falling off container ships still wash up here, though the main income is tourism and much of the land is a nature reserve.

Book early if visiting during the the popular 10-day island-wide Oerol arts festival (oerol.nl) in mid-June.

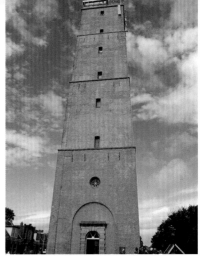

Midsland (pop 1,000), logically enough, is midway along the only main road, which connects the ferry port at West-Terschelling with Oosterend (Eastern End).

HOTEL TIP: **Wapen van Terschelling ★★** (below) has basic rooms.

Wapen van Terschelling

Oosterburen 25 · **T** 0562 448801
twapenvanterschelling.nl
Daily from 10.00 (may shut We in winter)

The Terschelling Arms is a two-room beer café with a terrace on the main street. The left side dining room is beer-themed, with enamels everywhere. Conversely, the walls in the main bar area carry enamel grocery adverts and the ceilings are hung with kitchen utensils and musical instruments. A ship's figurehead mermaid is thrown into the mix. An extensive food menu includes the house special schnitzels. Local Schoemrakker features among the 90+ beers, along with several mainland Frisian brewers.

TERSCHELLING – WEST-TERSCHELLING

25km NW from Harlingen by ferry

Dominated by a large square lighthouse several hundred metres inland, West-Terschelling is the ferry port for the mainland and the place where more than half the island's residents live (pop 2,600). The pedestrianised main street linking the lighthouse with the water is lined with bars and restaurants, including both entries below.

Mention this quietly, but in 1666 the English fleet sailed into the harbour and destroyed 150 ships, burning the town to the ground for an encore. Many locals considered the Great Fire of London later that year as divine retribution. It also provoked one of the most famous defeats inflicted by the Dutch on the English outside of a football stadium, when Admiral De Ruyter sailed up the Medway in 1667 to ransack Chatham.

HOTEL TIP: **Storm** (below) has hotel rooms.

Storm

Torenstraat 27 · **T** 0562 443232
storm-terschelling.nl
Daily from 11.30

Modern café and Schoemrakker taproom in a stepped-gabled building with front terrace. Bare brick walls inside are hung with arty photos on a vaguely nautical theme. The brewery is through the anonymous-looking door at the back. Lunches served until 17.00; heftier pub grub thereafter includes fish and chips. The house beers are served on tap alongside a dozen or so guests selected to appease the corporate landlord.

Zomer

Torenstraat 19 · **T** 0562 850714
cafedezomer.nl
Daily from 15.00

Summer is a cosy café with a terrace a few doors from Storm. It claims to be the country's northernmost beer café, although the entries above in Midsland and Nes might dispute that. The light wood interior has a sofa corner and a schematic mural of the brewing process. Tapas-style snacks served. Around 120 beers include plenty of local and Dutch craft choices.

Gelderland

The Netherlands' largest province (pop 2,000,000) and a beer hunter's paradise, Gelderland boasts some of the country's best breweries, beers and bars. It is divided into three vague regions, with its main cities running down the middle like a zipper.

To the north and west is the Veluwe, an undulating region of heathland and forest, much of it within the Hoge Veluwe national park, home to the Kröller-Müller Museum (kmm.nl) and its collection of Van Goghs. Several major rivers run through the southwest, with industrial cities lining their banks. The east, bordered on two sides by Germany and known as the Achterhoek (literally 'back corner'), feels pastoral and remote.

LARGEST CENTRES: **Apeldoorn, Arnhem, Nijmegen**

MORE INFORMATION: **gelderland.nl**

SELECTED BREWERIES: **Bronckhorster**, *Rha*; **Burg**, *Ermelo*; **Cambrinus**, *Zutphen*; **Drul & Stollenberg**, *Groesbeek*; **Eem**, *Elburg*; **Erve Kots**, *Lievelde*; **Hemel**, *Nijmegen*; **Kuipertje**, *Heukelum*; **Nederlands Openluchtmuseum**, *Arnhem*; **Nevel**, *Nijmegen*; **Oersoep**, *Nijmegen*; **Vlijt**, *Apeldoorn*; **Wageningen**, *Wageningen*; **Wentersch**, *Winterswijk*; **Wittenburg**, *Zevenaar*.

AALTEN

50km SW from Enschede off N318
⬛ Aalten

Quiet Achterhoek backwater (pop 27,000). Its biggest claim to fame is that AC/DC's geriatric schoolboy Angus Young has a house here, as his wife is from the town.

Oerkroeg Schiller

Prinsenstraat 4 · **T** 0543 472230
oerkroegschiller.nl
Shut Mo; Tu&We from 19.00; Th from 16.00; others from 14.00

Characterfully ancient brown café with blackened ceilings, wood everywhere, a collection of old radios on one shelf and a partly covered rear terrace with a mosaic-tiled outdoor bar in summer. The front room is 350 years old and the *trompe l'oeil* marble columns are original features. There is a separate dining room for food (*Th–Su 17.00–21.00*). The 50+ beers, including local Wentersch, wouldn't normally rate a full entry but the ambience gets it over the line.

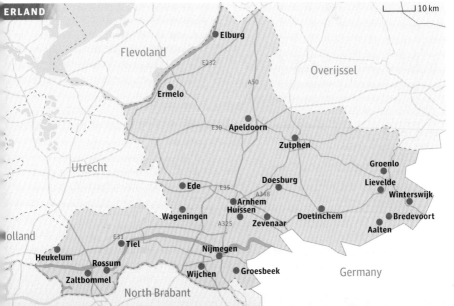

APELDOORN
🚆 Apeldoorn

Modern provincial town (pop 158,000).
The Dutch royal family liked the area enough
to build a country seat here: Paleis Het Loo
(**paleishetloo.nl**). Besides that, lovers of history
and twee architecture will be disappointed,
but railway nuts should note that in summer
a steam train (**stoomtrein.org**) runs between
here and Eerbeek/Dieren.
HOTEL TIP: **Paris ★★★**, Raadhuisplein 5-7
(**paris.nl**) has rooms above a central café.

Ale House

Hoofdstraat 202
facebook.com/alehouseapeldoorn
Shut Mo-We; Su 16.00-22.00; others from 16.00

Friendly brown café with terrace in a row of
lively bars. The dimly lit interior has colourful
lampshades, framed copies of oil paintings
on the ceiling, and an almost life-sized Virgin
Mary statue at the rear. Nibbles only. The 75+
beers include 16 taps, but the real stars lurk
among the bottles and cans, which on our
last visit featured around 50 US craft micros
rarely spotted this side of the Atlantic.

Graaf van Vlaanderen

Hoofdstraat 165A · **T** 055 576 7701
degraafvanvlaanderen.nl
Sa&Su from 14.00; others from 16.00

The Duke of Flanders is a large grand café
with a terrace and four 1890 tile murals
depicting the seasons in its single room
interior. Other features were rescued from
a 1920s Ghent bar. Full dinners served. The
200+ beer list was once exclusively Belgian
but a healthy number of Dutch craft names
are making inroads.

Vlijt

Vlijtseweg 114
veluwseschavuyt.nl
Sa&Su only 14.00-18.00

Brewery in an early 20th-century former
pharmaceutical factory, a 15-minute walk
north from the centre. The grand taproom was
once the laboratory and the impressive
mahogany and glass bar front was the
pharmacist's counter. Heavy wood furniture
and a red ceiling dominate, with a photo
mural of old Apeldoorn on one wall. Cheese
and sausage snacks are made with house
Veluwse Schavuyt beers. All regular beers
and one seasonal are on tap, with bottles to
take away.

OTHER BEER VENUES
In an elegant 1910 building with a peaceful
rear garden, **Achterom** (Mariastraat 2H –
proef-locaalhetachterom.nl – *Shut Mo-Th; others
15.00-20.00*) was the Veluwse Schavuyt tap
before production moved to De Vlijt (above).
Nieuws van Apeldoorn (Leienplein 12 – **T** 055
522 0566 – nieuwsvanapeldoorn.nl – *shut Mo;
Th&Fr from 14.00; Sa from 12.00; others from 15.00*)
is a lovely brown café with 40 beers.

ARNHEM
🚆 Arnhem Centraal

The site of the infamous battle in 1944 that
was 'a bridge too far', Arnhem (pop 153,000)
suffered heavy damage during World War II,
leaving fewer than 200 houses intact.
The Airborne at the Bridge Museum
(**airborneatthebridge.nl**) tells the story.
    It was a genteel resort in the 19th century
and is still noted for its parks, as well as for
having the country's only trolleybus network.

For a somewhat hair-raising pigeon's-eye view of the city, take the lift to the top of the Eusebius Church tower (**eusebius.nl**) and step out onto the glass-floored balconies. Just outside town is the Netherlands Open Air Museum, about which more below.

TRIVIA FOR FILM BUFFS: the 1977 movie *A Bridge Too Far* featured the bridge in Deventer, as budgetary constraints and permissions prevented Arnhem's bridge from being used. And Audrey Hepburn went to school here.

HOTEL TIP: **Vesting10** ★★★, Coehoornstraat 4 (**vesting10.nl**) has modern rooms in an old bulding, and is convenient for the station.

Beugel

Duizelsteeg 20 · **T** 026 351 9440
debeugel.com
Shu Mo; others from 17.00

Compact, cosy place down a narrow alley just south of busy Korenmarkt, with a mezzanine above a split-level bar, gothic arches and walls decorated with *trompe l'oeil* peeled paint. Good-value dinners cover all meat, fish and veggie bases. Around 60 beers include plenty of Dutch and local craft micros.

Budel

Nederlands Openluchtmuseum
(Dutch Open Air Museum)
Schelmseweg 89
openluchtmuseum.nl
Apr-Oct: daily 10.00-17.00. Shut Nov-Mar

The museum tram stops right outside the door of the Openluchtmuseum brewery tap, though you'll need an admission ticket to reach it. The Brabantian farmhouse is part of a fascinating collection of over 100 historic buildings transported here from across the country. It dates from 1700, its interior styled as it would have been in 1900: a tiled-floor parlour with rustic furnishings and a handsome ceramic and brass German beer tap. Food is snacks and sandwiches. House Goeye Goet beers are served.

Caspar

Elly Lamakerplantsoen 2 · **T** 026 840 3524
caspararnhem.nl
Daily from 09.00

Literally the wrong side of the tracks, but worth it. North of the railway, 200m west of Velperpoort station, or 10 minutes' walk east from the main station, this chic modern café has lampshades made from recycled glass, floor-to-ceiling windows (with unimpeded views of passing trains), and a leafy terrace. Food starts with breakfast. Few among the 100+ beers are run-of-the-mill, with plenty of Dutch and international craft options and the landlord's own CC brands, cuckoo-brewed elsewhere.

DAVO

Rijnkade 41
T 026 848 1881 · **davobieren.nl**
Shut Mo&Tu; Sa&Su from 12.00; others from 15.00

Modern bar run by the like-named Deventer brewery, with industrial lighting, posters of house beers and competition certificates on its blue-painted walls, and a partially riverside terrace. Food runs from snacks to burgers and pulled pork. House beers fill around 10 of the 15 taps, while 60+ bottles and cans are a global craft beer tour.

Leroy Brown

Stationsplein 3 · **T** 06 2474 7525
leroybrownbrewery.com
Th-Sa from 15.00

The brewery itself is across town, but this taproom is directly opposite the main station, with views of the bus station from its terrace. A plywood bar, hop plants and beer bottle lampshades decorate the modern interior, as do album covers by Bad Bad Leroy Brown songwriter Jim Croce. Snacks available alongside a handful of mains. At this writing the taps were exclusively guests with the house range sold in bottle, but this may change in future.

Leroy Brown

Meijers

Beekstraat 2
cafemeijers.nl
Mo-We 09.00-19.00; Su 13.00-19.00; others from 09.00

This city institution, a café for more than 80 years, has recently begun developing craft beer credentials. The stained wood interior of the 1895 building was last renovated in the 1970s though it looks much older, while a popular terrace catches the afternoon sun. Simple lunches; snacks only at other times. Aside from Trappists and a few crowdpleasers, the 65+ beers are mainly from craft micros. The WCs are 'through the menu' on the wall beside the bar.

Moortgat

Ruiterstraat 35 · **T** 026 445 0393
moortgat.nl
Sa from 12.00; others from 15.00

Longstanding beer pub in an old brick house that looks like a barn with a terrace. Amiably

rough-edged with battered furniture, it has smoke-darkened posters on the ceiling and billiards at the back. Toasties and snacks only. The 120+ beers are listed on a hotchpotch of randomly scattered chalkboards, with laminated menus for those who need order in their lives.

Nescio

De Wilstraat 51a · **T** 026 388 4669
cafenescio.nl
Shut Mo&Tu; Su from 15.00; others from 16.00

Suburban local NE from the station with a street corner terrace and modern brown interior: old wood chairs and tables, but a turquoise ceiling and white walls hung with photos of musicians in full flow. Snacks only. The 100 beers with 15 taps lean towards Belgium, but do feature Lowlander, Jopen and 't IJ.

Taphuys

Jansplein 56 · **T** 026 202 0258
taphuys.nl/arnhem
Daily from 11.00

Bar popular with a younger crowd in a former post office, a monumental red-brick building from 1889 with a large terrace and interior seating around a central tap station. Full food menu served. Plenty of craft options among the 100 self-service taps: buy a card, add credit, insert above the tap of your choice and the system debits as you pour, with no minimum spend.

Taphuys

Van Pernis (Prinsessestraat 34 – **T** 026 442 1918 – **slijterijvanpernis.nl** – *shut Su&Mo; Sa 09.30–17.00; others 09.30–12.30 & 13.30–18.00*) is a cellar-like backstreet shop stocking 1,000+ well-chosen beers.

BREDEVOORT
45km SW from Enschede off N318
Bus 191 from Aalten

This tiny town (pop 1,600) in the remote Achterhoek is known as 'Book Town' as, much like Hay-on-Wye in Wales, it's become a hub of the secondhand book trade.

Borghman
't Zand 25 · **T** 0543 450089
borghman.nl
Shut Mo; Tu&We 13.00–17.00; Th&Su 13.00–22.00; others from 13.00

A 1950s former school building, reinvented as a mock-medieval multi-roomed brewpub with walls full of armour, weapons and stuffed owls and squirrels. There is an admittedly weak excuse for the decor as between the 12th and 18th centuries a castle occupied the site: its footprint is marked on the terrace. Burgers, snacks and other meals available. The 75+ beers include the house range, also sold in gift packs.

DOESBURG
18km E from Arnhem off N317
Bus 26 from Dieren; 27, 29 from Arnhem

Well-preserved Hanseatic city (pop 11,300) with several museums and monuments including the Waag (below) and one that celebrates the city's former status as the Dutch mustard capital (**doesburgschemosterd.nl**).

Waag
Koepoortstraat 2–4 · **T** 0313 479617
waagdoesburg.nl
Daily from 10.00

This 1478 weigh house is the country's oldest café: an annexe has served beer for over five centuries. The grand red-brick stepped-gabled building has wooden window shutters and a terrace opposite the near-identical town hall. Giant scales hang from the ceiling in the barn-like interior. The food menu features an award-winning mustard soup. The 45+ beers, including several changing guests, would not warrant attention but for the historic location.

DOETINCHEM
30km E from Arnhem off A18 exit 3
Doetinchem

Tidy market town (pop 45,000) in the Gelderland Achterhoek.

HendriXen
Grutstraat 31 · **T** 0314 820993
grandcafehendrixen.nl
Shut Mo; Su from 15.00; others from 16.00

Grand café doubling as the Doetinchem tap: the brewhouse is in a separate building at the rear. There are terraces front and back; inside, dark wood and brass abound. Food stretches to full dinners. Besides the house Walters beers, most of the 80+ guest options are Belgian, although there are some Dutch craft choices.

ELBURG

20km SW from Zwolle off N309

Bus 514 from 't Harde, 100 from Zwolle
Well-preserved medieval town (pop 23,100)
founded in the ninth century. Its grid layout
dates from the end of the 13th century, when
is was rebuilt after a flood.

Aan de Gracht

Havenstraat 5 · **T** 0525 844676
aandegracht.nu
Shut Su; others 09.00–18.00

This former eel smokery is now Eembier's
taproom, although they run as separate
businesses, with the brewery next door.
The name means 'On the Canal' and the
scenic waterside terrace doesn't disappoint.
The bright interior has modern decor and
watery views through the windows.
Breakfast, lunch and high tea served. Eem
beers are sold on tap and in bottle, alongside
those from Vos, which also brews here.

OTHER BEER VENUES
Though the previous entry has stronger
credentials, sprawling **Haas** (Jufferenstraat 21
– **T** 0525 681737 – restaurantdehaas.nl – *Shut
Mo; Su from 13.00; others from 09.30*) has a loose
claim to being the Vos taproom, including
both Vos and Eem beers in its 30+ range.

Aan de Gracht, taproom and brewery (to the left), Elburg

ERMELO

22km NE from Amersfoort on N303
Ermelo

Provincial town (pop 26,700) with a beer café,
brewery and shop, all in a neat row.

Hazeburg

Putterweg 43 · **T** 0341 564934
hazeburg.nl
*Shut Mo; Sa from 11.00; Su 15.00–21.00;
others from 15.00*

This wood-dominated café with open hearth
and front terrace is both a specialist beer outlet
and the Burg taproom. Lunches until 17.00;
heartier dinners to 21.00. Snacks all day. Five of
the 23 taps dispense house beers, with a limited
number of crowd-pleasers in bottles and cans
in the fridge. If that's not enough, all the more
than 3,000 bottles and cans from the Burg
Bierwinkel (below) are also available to drink
in, ordered by number from the tablet menu.
They arrive on a cooling conveyor through a
'beer tunnel' running under the brewery to
reach the bar at serving temperature, their
progress monitored on CCTV.

Uddelaer

Staverdenseweg 283A · **T** 06 5377 8994
uddelaer.nl
Shut Mo–Tu; others 14.00–18.00

Despite its postal address, this brewpub is
9km east of Ermelo: bus 104 stops outside.

brewery, Ermelo

Brewery and bar are in the brick-floored stables and coach house of a grand white 17th-century chateau, moated on two sides and with a terrace on a third: you might find a table in a former horse stall. Nibbles only. All house beers are served on tap and in bottle, with tasting flights and takeaways.

BEER TO GO

Beside the brewery and café, **Burg Bierwinkel** (Putterweg 45 – T 0341 564934 – burgbieren.nl – *shut Su; Mo 13.00-18.30; Fr 09.30-21.00; Sa 09.00-17.00; others 09.30-18.30*) is the Netherlands' biggest beer shop, with more than 3,000 choices including swathes of hard-to-find Dutch options.

GROENLO

30km SW from Enschede off N18
Bus 73 from Winterswijk

Formerly known as Grol or Grolle, this small town (pop 10,000) in the Achterhoek near the German border was the original home of the Grolsch brewery and has regained some of its beer interest in recent years. In 1627, during the Eighty Years War, the Spanish-controlled town was besieged and ultimately conquered by the Protestant Dutch, a key moment in the development of the modern Netherlands which is reenacted in spectacular style during October in odd-numbered years (slagomgrolle.nl).

Brouwersnös

Eibergseweg 1 · T 0544 221009
brouwersnos.nl
We-Su 11.00-23.00

The directors of Grolsch once lived in the Villa Adriana. This stately home with a terrace overlooking a lake has since become a taproom, centred on a flame effect gas fire. A cannonball from the 1627 siege found in the nearby canal is kept by the door. The brewery is in the modern building with the wooden facade across the park. Lunches and dinners served (*until 20.30*). The 12 taps embedded in a blue-tiled wall dispense the house range, with tasting flights available and a shop for takeaways.

Brouwersnös, Groenlo

Streets

Kevelderstraat 26 · T 06 3741 7296
wijnbarstreets.nl
Shut Mo-We; others from 12.15

Friendly tiled-floor wine bar, brasserie and beer café on side street near de Lange Gang (below). Mock interior windows appear to look out onto arty photos of beaches, cobbled streets and Havana. Food has global influences, with sharing platters and more conventional burgers. The 65+ beers are Belgian-dominated but more Dutch are appearing.

OTHER BEER VENUES

Lange Gang (Kevelderstraat 15 – T 0544 464860 – langegang.nl – *shut Mo-We; others from 16.00, from 12.00 in Jul&Aug*) was Brouwerij de Klok, Grolsch's original 1615 incarnation. Brewing ceased in 1922 but the building remains a restaurant and has a museum in its cellar (see Beer tourism).

GROESBEEK

10km SE from Nijmegen
Bus 5

Smallish quiet town (pop 16,000) next to the key parachutist landing zone for Operation Market Garden in 1944. The National Liberaton Museum (**bevrijdingsmuseum.nl**) on the edge of town commemorates this.

D'n Drul

Dorpstraat 7 · **T** 024 207 0045
brouwerijdendrul.nl
Shut Mo–Th; Fr from 16.00; Sa from 14.00; Su 14.00–20.00

Modern taproom in former blacksmith's shop set back from the street. Its former use explains the hooks and chains that hang from the wood-beamed ceiling in the stone-floored interior with distressed furnishings. Snacks only. House beers on tap are joined by 100+ guest bottles. The venue's future is uncertain following the merger of Drul and Stollenberg breweries and the construction of a new brew-house elsewhere, so check before travelling.

HEUKELUM

10km NE from Gorinchem off N848
Bus 141 from Leerdam

Small village (pop 2,000) that transferred to Gelderland from South Holland in a 1986 boundary change.

Kuipertje

Appeldijk 18 · **T** 0345 611839
hetkuipertje.nl
Sa only 14.00–19.00

Semi-rural taproom of the Little Cooper brewery, 1km from the village centre. The dilapidated brick building could use some tender loving care: though it has a door, in summer the accepted way of getting from terrace to slightly musty bar area is to dodge through the window. Crisps only. A few changing draught house beers are served alongside a bought-in pilsener.

HUISSEN

7km S from Arnhem
Bus 33, 300

Attractive small town (pop 17,000), effectively a suburb of Arnhem but with its own charter since 1314.

Moment

Vierakkerstraat 28 · **T** 026 325 2586
cafehetmoment.nl
Shut Mo–We; Th from 19.00; Su 14.00–2300; others from 14.00

Friendly corner modern brown local with terrace around two sides. Wooden Westvleteren crates and photos and pencil drawings of notable regulars serve as decor. Occasional live events in a room at the back. Snacks only. The 150 beers are mainly Belgian include 12 on tap and a range of cellar-aged 75cl bottles, with a few Dutch entrants.

LIEVELDE

32km SW from Enschede off N18
⊠ Lichtenvoorde–Groenlo

Hamlet (pop 1,500) in the heart of nowhere.
HOTEL TIP: **Erve Kots** (below) has hotel rooms.

Erve Kots

Eimersweg 4 · **T** 0544 371691
ervekots.nl
Daily 10.00–20.00

Around 1km northwest of the station, beside the like-named open air museum, the Erve Kots taproom is accessible without paying an admission charge. In 1627, during the siege of nearby Groenlo, this was the headquarters of Frederik Hendrick, Prince of Orange. The interior has oak-beamed ceilings and brick floors, with period furnishings including a stuffed fox, cast-iron sewing machines and a massive fireplace. Food is pancakes and other light meals, with more expensive offerings in an attached restaurant, open evenings only. House beers are sold on tap and in bottle, also stocked in the museum shop. A second, modern bar inside the brewery is open to Bier Experience visitors (see Beer tourism).

NIJMEGEN

 Nijmegen

Three cheers for Nijmegen, pound-for-pound possibly the nation's beeriest place. Gelderland's largest city (pop 170,000) is also the Netherlands' oldest. Mentioned in the first century BC, when there was a Roman military camp nearby, it celebrated its 2,000th birthday in 2005. American bomber pilots caused major damage to the city centre in 1944 when they mistook it for Kleve in Germany. Few ancient remains are visible but there are fragments of city wall and the Valkhof Museum (**museumhetvalkhof.nl**) contains Roman artefacts.

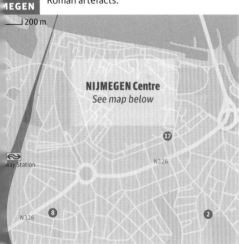

NIJMEGEN Centre
See map below

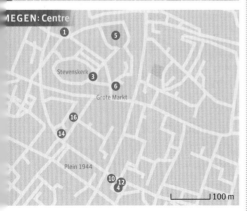

Forget about finding a room during the Nijmeegse Vierdaagse international four day 'Walk of the World' march in July: this tortuous event, which entails walking 30–50km each day, attracts 40,000 participants.

HOTEL TIP: **Credible ★★**, Hertogstraat 1 (**in-credible.nl**) is a quirky designer hotel in a central location.

Beer & Bites ❶

Priemstraat 9 · **T** 024 323 2075
beer-en-bites.nl
Daily 16.00–00.00

This cosy bar down the hill from Hemel (below) has a chic interior with beer bottle light fittings. Don't be fooled if you come in by accident from the Uilenspiegel restaurant around the corner as the two are conjoined under the same management. A full food menu is served. Around 75 beers are largely Belgian but the guests among the 14 taps are often worth a second look.

Beij Ons ❷

Daalsedwarsweg 21 · **T** 024 323 7020
beijons.nl
Daily 11.00–02.00

Modern corner café with split-level interior and small terrace 500m south of the centre, halfway to Jos (below). Lunches and dinners, with snacks all day. The 100-strong beer list is making healthy steps towards a more local focus, with at least 15 Dutch microbreweries represented last time we stopped by.

Blaauwe Hand ❸

Achter de Hoofdwacht 3 · **T** 024 323 2066
indeblaauwehand.nl
Sa from 13.00; Su from 14.00; others from 15.00

Near the Grote Markt, the Blue Hand is the city's oldest bar, dating from 1542. It was rebuilt after the war, not that you'd notice given the atmospheric dark wood interior. There's a small terrace and a lengthy snack menu which includes meal worms for those who really want to experience the pub grubs. One constant among the 60+ beers is the house Rooie Tiep Top tripel, commissioned from De Hemel.

Blaauwe Hand, Nijmegen

Deut ④

Koningstraat 36 · **T** 024 323 8110
cafededeut.nl
Su from 10.00; others from 10.00

One-room beer café, with a terrace on a small square. Smoke-darkened ceilings, ageing wallpaper, candlelit tables and assorted bric-a-brac create an atmosphere of *fin-de-siècle* kitsch. Rolls served until 16.00 with snacks at other times. The 100-strong beer list usually finds room for a few good lambics and some from locals Oersoep and Nevel.

Hemel ⑤

Franseplaats 1 · **T** 024 334 3094
restaurantdehemel.nl
Sa from 11.00; others from 12.00

Heaven is the Netherlands' longest-established microbrewery, located in the cellar of an ivy-clad 12th century cloister with bar and restaurant above. The cobbled terrace is a peaceful retreat, while the pictorial clock indoors is a work of art: the workings are on the far side of the room. Lunches, high tea and dinners served. House beers are sold on tap and bottle, also to take away: for a taster of all the draught options, order the Hemelse Proeverij. No credit cards.

Jan ⑥

Grote Markt 32 · **T** 024 323 3033
stadscafejan.nl
Daily from 09.30

Grand café on the main square with a large terrace in the shadow of the church. The corrugated zinc sheets lining the bar came from Rotterdam harbour in 1970, while 6,800 five cent coins decorate the toilet floors. Full food menu for lunch and dinner. The 100+ beers are mainly Belgian, with a small Nijmegen section.

Jos ⑦

Daalseweg 309 · **T** 024 323 2001
cafejos.nl
Sa&Su from 14.00; others from 15.00

Walk 15 minutes south on Daalseweg or take bus 8 to Badhuis to discover Jos, the kind of corner local that reaffirms your faith in corner locals. Its terrace occupies two sides of a leafy residential square, while the L-shaped interior has beer memorabilia and a bit of an equestrian theme. Snacks and toasties only. The 200+ beers include 33 on tap, with a growing Dutch craft presence. Ask for the cellar-aged menu, and if that doesn't finish you off, the 130 whiskies will.

Kluizenaar ⑧

Burghardt van de Berghstraat 96
T 024 322 1235
dekluizenaar.nl
Sa&Su from 14.00; Fr from 15.00; others from 16.00

Local with small terrace in Bottendaal, a residential neighbourhood just south of the centre. The name means 'hermit' and if you look through a small glass window on the right as you enter, you'll see one writing at the desk of his cell. Dinners from 17.30 feature spare ribs and burgers, with snacks all day. The 90+ beers include De Hemel's Botterik, originally brewed exclusively for outlets in this area.

Kroon 9

Daalseweg 361 · **T** 024 360 8860
cafe-dekroon.nl
Fr–Su from 14.00; others from 15.00.
Opens 1 hour later Nov-Mar.

The Crown is a corner one-room local with a streetside terrace in a southern suburb near Jos (above). The interior has a rug on the wooden floor and enamels on the walls. Snacks and toasties only. The 90+ beers include 50 guests, with plenty of Dutch craft. Use caution when ordering from the VSOB (Very Special Old Beer) list, which is largely an exercise in shifting out-of-date stock at discounted prices.

Mug 10

Pauwelstraat 9 · **T** 024 845 2673
cafedemug.nl
Shut Mo; Sa&Su from 12.00; others from 13.00

The Midge is a compact local with a small terrace on a central shopping street. The removal of the carpets from the interior tables has been its nod to modernisation. Food is light lunches and toasties; snacks at other times. There's a permanent tap for Schelde Mug Bitter among 80+ other choices, with enough highlights to warrant a visit, usually including a few from Oersoep.

Nevel 11

Waalbandijk 8D · **T** 06 2720 5494
nevel.org
Shut Su–Th; Fr 16.00–22.00; Sa 14.00–22.00

Simple taproom and basic terrace fronting the brewery proper, with a few leather sofas backed by rows of wooden barrels brightening up otherwise spartan furnishings. Basic sausage and cheese snacks. Six taps feature

house beers and a few craft guests. Most of the bottles are 75cl, also sold to take away. Tasting flights available.

Opera 12

Koningstraat 34 · **T** 024 323 2197
cafedeopera.nl
Su from 11.00; others from 10.00

Modern mock-Art Nouveau café and neighbour of the Deut (above), also with a terrace on a small square. The name has no bearing on the choice of background music. Light meals and snacks available. Five of the 20 taps are guests, and around a dozen of the 90 bottles and cans are from local micros.

Piet Huisman 13

St Jacobslaan 30 · **T** 024 355 2286
piethuisman.nl
Daily from 14.00

Suburban beer café a few km south of the centre: buses 1 or 14 to Akkerlaan drop you outside. Unassuming on the outside, the TARDIS-like interior finds space for several billiards and pool tables, with a brown pub at the front and empty bottles filling any wall space not occupied by fridges. Snacks only. The beer list has gone through the roof, with 500+ well-chosen options including a legion of Dutch and international craft micros. The same range is sold in the **Biermenneke** shop next door (St Jacobslaan 26 – **T** 024 204 9623 – **biermenneke.nl** – *Shut Su&Mo; Th 11.00–20.00; Sa 11.00–17.00; others 11.00–18.00*).

Samson

Houtstraat 4 · **T** 024 323 3023
cafesamson.nl
Su from 12.00; others from 10.00

Longstanding central beer joint with terrace fronting a semi-dark warren of rooms, named after the family who moved their café here in the 1950s. Light meals served all day. A few locals from Oersoep always lurk among the 100+ beers, alongside many from other Dutch micros.

Stoom ⑮

Waalbandijk 20 · **T** 024 202 0010
stoomnijmegen.com
Shut Mo; Th–Su from 16.00; others from 14.00

Steam is Oersoep's expansive taproom in an industrial complex 1.5km west of the centre, around the corner from Nevel (above) and a few metres from the river Waal, though an embankment blocks the view. Bus 5 stops nearby. Inside, a scantily decorated bar has an expansive seating area around the back, with a mezzanine above. Food is pulled pork and similar. All available house beers are served, mostly on tap, alongside an equally impressive range of craft guests.

Van Ouds ⑯

Augustijnenstraat 33 · **T** 024 323 3625
cafevanoudsnijmegen.nl
Fr from 14.00; Sa&Su from 13.00; Mo from 19.00; others from 16.00

Friendly local on a pedestrianised street south of Grote Markt, dominated by dark wood and white-painted walls. Snacks only, but these use products from local suppliers. The beer list has come on in strides and now tops 200, with plenty of room for Dutch craft and several imports not from Belgium.

OTHER BEER VENUES

Faber ⑰ (Van Broeckhuijsenstraat 12–14 – **T** 024-848 4411 – **cafefaber.nl** – *Su from 12.00; others from 11.00*) is a chic 'mock old' corner bar with leaded windows, glass chandeliers, evening pizzas and a list of 50 beers that just falls short of meriting a full entry.

BEER TO GO

Bierbrigadier (Nieuwe Markt 8 – **T** 06 2876 4727 – **debierbrigadier.nl** – *shut Su&Mo, Th 11.00–20.00; Sa 11.00–17.00; others 11.00–18.00*) has 400+ local, Dutch and international craft beers in premises shared with a hipster barbershop. **Bierhoeder** (Bloemerstraat 86 – **T** 024 360 1620 – **debierhoeder.nl** – *shut Su&Mo; Tu&We 12.00–19.00; Sa 11.00–18.00; others 12.00–21.00*) goes for a well-chosen selection of a few hundred international craft brews.
Biermenneke: see Piet Huisman above.

ROSSUM

15km N from 's-Hertogenbosch off N322
Bus 267 from Zaltbommel

Sleepy riverside village (pop 2,600).

De Pub

Waaldijk 1 · **T** 0418 664223
pubrossum.nl
Shut Mo; others 11.00–23.00

To find this compact wood-clad bar, a former Irish pub beside a dyke, look for the In Petto bistro sign: the pub is under the same management but around the back on the floor below. A small menu of hipster pub grub like pulled jackfruit is available. The beer range has crept upwards and passed 100, encompassing Dutch mini-majors such as Jopen and IJ: not everything is on the menu so you may need to ask.

TIEL

35km NE from 's-Hertogenbosch off A15 exit 33
 Tiel

Busy riverside town (pop 41,500) that bills itself as a fruit city. The town symbol is a frankly disturbing 'blackberry with a head' boy called Flipje with his own statue on the Markt. To boost your vitamin C levels, visit the annual Fruit Corso festival in September (**fruitcorso.nl**), which promises 'fruit like you've never seen'. Don't say we didn't warn you.

De Beurs

Korenbeursplein 2 · **T** 0344 627959
debeurstiel.nl
Shut Mo; Sa from 13.00; Su 15.00–22.00;
others from 15.00

One-room bar in a smart whitewashed
neoclassical building with a terrace on a quiet
square. The interior has grand old clocks and
guitars on the walls and a stage for live
events. Food is snacks only, but the same
owner runs the Olijf Italian restaurant and
Jus bistro next door and you can order the
same drinks in all three. Around 80 beers are
largely Belgian, but we found plenty from
Amsterdam's Oedipus on our last visit.

WAGENINGEN

18km W from Arnhem on N225
Ede-Wageningen, then bus 88

Provincial university town (pop 37,500), one
of the largest places in the country not on
the rail network, as Ede-Wageningen station
is 7km north, a 15-minute bus ride away.
The German surrender in the Netherlands
was negotiated and signed on May 5 1945
in the Hotel de Wereld (5 Mei Plein 1), now
a national monument.
HOTEL TIP: **De Wereld** (hoteldewereld.nl)
has modern bedrooms and public rooms
restored to how they looked in 1945.

Onder de Linden

Haagsteeg 16 · **T** 0317 843559
onderdelindenwageningen.nl
Mo&Tu from 15.00; others from 11.30

Edge-of-town taproom with tree-shaded
beer garden to one side, a 15-minute walk
northwest from the centre. The building dates
from 1717 and became a pub not long after.
It retains a period charm in the front bar where
only creaking floorboards and the ticking
of a clock break the silence at quiet times.
A second more modern rear room has a wall
of wine bottles, while the brewery is across
the courtyard. Lunches until 14.50; snacks
thereafter. Dinners from 17.00 are We–Fr only.
The house blond is on tap, with others in 75cl
bottles, alongside around 20 guests.

Onder de Linden

Rad van Wageningen

1e Kloostersteeg 3 · **T** 06 2425 8665
caferadvanwageningen.nl
Shut Mo–Tu; Sa from 14.00; Su 14.00–23.00;
others from 16.00

The Wheel of Wageningen, the town's other
house brewery, is a more modern affair
than Onder de Linden above, with a terrace,
simple furnishings and a central bar. Arty
beer-themed photos dominate. Food is
burgers (*Fr&Sa only 18.00–21.00*), with locally
sourced snacks at other times. Most of the
12 taps dispense house Wageningen beers,
supplemented by a few guests, with tasting
flights available. The 25 bottles include
several Belgian lambics.

Vlaamsche Reus

Hoogstraat 21 · **T** 0317 412834
vlaamschereus.nl
*Shut Mo; Sa from 14.00; Su 14.00–19.00;
others from 15.00.*

The dependable Flemish Giant has been
a specialist beer outlet since 1984, and is a
founding member of ABT. It has a terrace
on a small square, and beer memorabilia
everywhere inside, from enamels to cans
via Germanic glasses and steins. Snacks are
mainly Belgian cheeses and most of the 200+
beers are from south of the border too, but
the Dutch presence is growing and there's
also a selection of aged Fuller's Vintage Ales.

Zaaier

Herenstraat 33 · **T** 0317 410806
facebook.com/DeZaaier
Daily from 15.00

The Sower is a small café with a terrace
around several sides, the back one practically
contiguous with the Rad van Wageningen
(above). The interior mixes old and new,
agricultural equipment rubbing shoulders
with music posters. Snacks only. Among the
60+ mainly Belgian beers are a few UK
imports, alongside plenty of jenevers.

WIJCHEN

9km SW from Nijmegen off A326
Wijchen

Picturesque small town (pop 33,000) centred
on moated Wijchen Castle, founded in the
14th century and much rebuilt 200 years later.

Zus

Spoorstraat 4
cafezuswijchen.nl
*Shut Mo-Tu, Fr from 16.00; Sa&Su from 15.00;
others from 19.00*

The Sister is a friendly corner light-brown café
just west of the main square, in a white-painted
brick building with a small terrace. Inside is all
wood and beer enamels, with an accordion as
token ceiling tat. Nuts only. Around 85 beers

are mostly Belgian standards, with De Molen
and La Trappe keeping the Dutch flag flying,
plus occasional guests. Nothing from Wijchen
brewers though.

WINTERSWIJK

40km S from Enschede off N319
Winterswijk

Small town (pop 23,600) in the corner of the
Achterhoek, surrounded on three sides by
Germany. Dutch abstract artist Piet Mondriaan
spent much of his childhood here, and the house
where he lived for 12 years is now a museum
(**villamondriaan.nl**).

Lamme Hertog/ Hertog Karel van Gelre

Markt 25 · **T** 0543 518585
hertogkarelvangelre.nl
Karel: *Su from 12.00; others from 11.00.*
Lamme: *daily from 17.00.*

Ostensibly two separate operations but in
practice one as they are linked by open doors.
Hertog Karel (Duke Charles) at the front has
rococo mirrors and a posh tearoom interior,
with chandeliers and a terrace by the church.
The Lame Duke at the back has a second bar
and more of a pub feel, with table carpets and
a Bruegel-esque mural. Full food menu at the
front; snacks at the rear. Around 80 beers include
Texel, IJ and sometimes local Wentersch.

ZALTBOMMEL

16km N from 's-Hertogenbosch off A2 exit 17
🚄 Zaltbommel

Well-preserved riverside town (pop 12,500) with plenty of cobbled streets. The 100m tower of St Maarten's church dominates the area: it was even taller until a lightning strike removed the spire in 1538.

Orion

Nieuwstraat 6 · **T** 06 1649 9070
zaltbommelse-stadsbrouwerij.nl
Shut Mo-Tu, We&Th 15.00-23.00; Su 15.00-22.00; others from 15.00

Pass through an old gateway to reach the Zaltbommelse taproom in a garage-like building with a courtyard terrace. Quirky decor includes rugs on the wooden floor and a Black Forest theme with cuckoo clocks, stag heads and light fittings made from beer bottles. Snacks only. Beyond the house Kroniek beers, most of the 24 taps and 150 bottles are Belgo-centric.

ZEVENAAR

15km SE from Arnhem off A12 exit 29
🚄 Zevenaar

Quiet provincial town (pop 32,500) badly damaged in the war and rebuilt from scratch.

Wittenburg

Markt 25 · **T** 06 2050 8058
stadsbrouwerijwittenburg.nl
Shut Su&Mo; Fr 10.00-18.00; Sa 12.00-18.00; others 10.00-16.00

Brewpub which moved in 2014 to a larger location on the main square, with a big terrace. The wood-dominated interior has pop art portraits of luminaries like Hendrix and Marley on the walls and an old silver cash register on the counter. The copper brewery is through glass at the rear. There is a very good full food menu. Around 12 house beers on tap and in bottles, also sold to take away.

ZUTPHEN

22km SE from Apeldoorn off N345
🚄 Zutphen

Attractive town (pop 47,400) with Hanseatic connections. The chapter house of St Walburgis church boasts one of only five surviving medieval libraries in Europe. Books are chained to ancient desks, just as they were centuries ago to prevent them being nicked.

Cambrinus

Houtmarkt 56B · **T** 0575 546688
hanze-stadsbrouwerij.nl
Shut Tu; Th from 15.00; others from 10.00

Brewpub in a row of venues with lively terraces. Copper brewing vessels dominate a modern interior but the cellars are 800 years old. Food (*from 12.00*) is all-encompassing, from snacks to burgers. There are 16 taps and another 16 self-tapping points, with six house brews appearing on both. Guests don't double up: the bar choices tend to be more industrial, the self taps more crafty. Tasting flights available.

OTHER BEER VENUES

Camelot (Groenmarkt 34 – **T** 0575 511804 – *Fr&Sa from 12.00; others from 14.00*) has mock-medieval shields and banners and a mural depicting the Round Table but, while improving, its 55 beers are not yet the stuff of Arthurian legend.

Groningen

Outside the provincial capital of the same name, Groningen (pop 584,000) feels far from anywhere. To the east is German Lower Saxony; to the north the Wadden Sea. It is flat and agricultural, mainly comprised of reclaimed sea marsh. Its flatness reveals an awful lot of sky.

The east has a long history of political class struggle: from 1982 to 1990 the country's first and only communist mayor presided over the municipality of Beerta.

In the first edition of this guide the province had only one physical brewery. By late 2019 that number was well into double figures.

LARGEST CENTRE: **Groningen**
MORE INFORMATION: visitgroningen.nl
SELECTED BREWERIES: **Bax**, *Groningen*; **Corviri**, *Glimmen*; **Dokjard**, *Groningen*; **Martinus**, *Groningen*; **Parkzicht**, *Veendam*; **Rockin' Ludina**, *Groningen*; **Vandenbroek**, *Midwolde*; **Witte Klavervier**, *Bad Nieuweschans*.

GRONINGEN
Groningen

During the Middle Ages, Groningen was a regional power base, operating as a semi-independent state within the Hanseatic League. The central Martinikerk, which hosts a major beer festival each April, somehow escaped damage in the war.

Today this is the biggest city in the north (pop 200,000) and a university town with some 60,000 students, many from overseas, giving the place a cosmopolitan feel. This, and its relative remoteness, mean Groningen has a thriving nightlife. For something more cultured, the Groninger Museum (groningermuseum.nl) has some of the country's best contemporary art.

HOTEL TIP: **Martini** ★★★, Gedempte Zuiderdiep 8 (martinihotel.nl) has modern rooms in an old building in the city centre.

Bax

Friesestraatweg 201/2a · **T** 050 211 2041
baxbier.com
Shut Mo–We; Sa 14.00–22.30, Su 14.00–21.00; others 16.00–22.30

Brewery tap in a former sawmill with a canalside terrace northwest of the centre: take bus 7 or 17 to Siersteenlaan. The large bar has glass windows looking into the brewhouse, a pool table, sofa corner and wood-burning stove. Sausage, cheese and toasties. Half the 12 taps dispense house brews and another dozen guests appear in bottles, with a shop for takeaways.

Chaplin's Pub

Gedempte Zuiderdiep 73 · **T** 050 314 8864
chaplinspub.nl
Fr–Su from 16.00; others from 17.00

Cosy central English-style pub with a small
terrace on a busy street. The candle-lit interior
has old smoke-stained maps, a chess set on
the ceiling and some token Chaplin images.
If you're a ninja you can exit through the roof
(you need to be there...). Snacks only. The
beer range has yo-yoed, but was last seen
above 100, with Dutch micros and a healthy
showing of unusual European imports.

Concerthuis

Poelestraat 30 · **T** 050 230 4250
hetconcerthuis.nl
Daily from 10.00

Trendy café on a popular nightlife street,
with a terrace. The vaguely theatrical and
cinematic-themed interior includes a front
foyer bar and a rear seating area with 'living
room' corners. Lunches and dinners served,
the core theme being sharing plates. The
beer list hovers around 60 but has enough
local craft interest to stay in our good books.

Dog's Bollocks

Oude Boteringestraat 17 · **T** 050 230 8403
thedogsbollocks.nl
Fr from 16.00; Su from 14.00; others from 17.00

Unfortunately-named flashy British-style pub
under same ownership as Chaplin's (above),
with loud music attracting a younger crowd.
Dinners revolve around burgers and pub grub
classics like fish and chips. The, ahem,

Battered Bollocks snacks are, fortunately,
simply *bitterballen*. The beer list of 100+ has
some interest in local and imported craft,
including Thornbridge and BrewDog to
represent the home nations.

Dokjard

Noorderhaven 63 · **T** 050 364 2420
dokjard.nl
Shut Mo; Sa&Su from 14.00; others from 15.00

Modern canalside brewpub created by
someone who knows about interior design,
with rounded edges everywhere creating a
relaxed feel. The brewing kit is at the front,
with a circular sitting area around a central
hearth, a raised bar area at the back and
mezzanine above. Dinners include spare ribs.
The house beer, only one at the time of writing,
sits alongside a decent if short list of around
30 guests, several from the Groningen area.

Koffer

Nieuwe Blekerstraat 1 · **T** 050 313 6251
dekoffer.nl
Fr–Su from 14.00; others from 16.00

In a residential neighbourhood just west of
the centre, the unassuming simply furnished
Suitcase could easily slip under the radar of
the casual imbiber but is well worth seeking
out. Snacks only. The whole beer list was
once written up on the various blackboards
around the room but the staff now can't
write small enough to fit all 330 choices in.
Beside a core range of standards, around half
are changing Dutch and global craft guests.
An '050' menu named after the local area
code lists those from Groningen.

Martinus

Kostersgang 32–34 · **T** 050 318 3307
brouwerijmartinus.nl
Shut Mo–We; Sa from 14.00; Su 15.00–20.00;
others from 15.00

Enter through the ground-floor brewery to
find the taproom on the second floor of this
building just south of the centre, with battered
furniture, an industrial chic vibe and a balcony
terrace affording views of the Martini church.

A first-floor restaurant (*Th–Su only, 17.30–22.00*) serves daily specials incorporating house beers, with snacks at other times. All the brewery's beers are usually available on tap and in bottles.

Mout

Gedempte Zuiderdiep 43 · **T** 050 204 1350
proeflokaalmout.nl
Shut Mo; others from 15.00

Malt is a friendly corner café with picture windows, a small terrace and a stylish light-brown split-level interior. Snacks only, mostly cheese, sausage and olives. All 100+ beers, including 10 on tap, are quality choices from Dutch micros, with around 60 brewers represented at the last count and no fillers whatsoever. There's even a small beer shop on site (*open until 22.00*) to take home your favourites.

Pintelier

Kleine Kromme Elleboog 9 · **T** 050 318 5100
pintelier.nl
Daily from 15.00

Down a side street called Little Crooked Elbow, this café with a small terrace has been a beer lovers' favourite for two decades. The smoke-yellowed, dimly lit interior is decorated with brewery enamels and oversized bottles. Music is drowned by conversation. Snacks only. The 100+ beers include 27 taps, half of them rotating guests; the bottled range is largely Belgian, with some local options.

Pintelier

Prael

Boterdiep 75 · **T** 050 211 5313
deprael.nl
Shut Mo&Tu; Sa&Su from 12.00; others from 11.30

The fourth outlet in the growing Prael brewery empire is a large industrial-chic bar in a smart blue and white brick building north of the centre, with colourful art on the walls, umbrellas hanging from the ceiling and a chandelier formed from glass bottles. Snacks and full meals are prepared in an open kitchen. Around 15 house beers are sold, mainly on tap.

Singelier

Coendersweg 44 · **T** 050 526 0724
singelier.nl
Su from 14.00; others from 16.00

Corner local in a southern suburb: take bus 50 or 51 to Van Iddekingeweg. The cosy brown café has chalkboard menus, beer enamels and endearingly tatty furniture. Snacks only. There's a good Dutch representation among the beers from three guest taps and around 60 bottles, and each has a suggested spirit pairing from an extensive list including multiple jenevers.

Toeter

Turfsingel 6 · **T** 050 312 4499
cafedetoeter.nl
*Mo&Tu from 19.00; Fr&Sa from 15.00;
others from 16.00*

Large brown café with music theme in sound (mostly rock) and vision (instruments on the ceiling). Full dinners served. Part of the terrace is on a barge which once housed Rockin' Ludina brewery, and though this has moved, its beers still feature among 19 taps and 200 bottles and cans, alongside those of numerous other Dutch craft producers. The bar also invites customers to explore its range of 350 single malts with tasting plank samplers. The café helped to found the Groningen Bierfestival held each April, and its terrace now hosts a parallel side event.

Toeter, ningen

OTHER BEER VENUES

Elegant **Hooghoudt** (Grote Markt 42 – **T** 050 312 8258 – cafehooghoudt.com – *Su 11.00–22.00; Mo 11.00–23.00; others from 11.00*) has good food and around 55 beers with several local craft choices.

Opened in 1923, lovely **Wolthoorn & Co** (Turftorenstraat 6 – **T** 050 312 0282 – cafewolthoorn.nl – *Fr&Sa from 15.00; others from 16.00*) has 25 beers and preserves red flock wallpaper in a back room that seems barely changed for years.

BEER TO GO

Just In Bier (Folkingestraat 18 – **T** 06 4346 9823 – justinbeer.nl – *Shut Mo&Tu; We 13.00–18.00; Th 11.00–21.00; Fr 11.00–19.00; Sa 11.00–18.00; Su 13.00–17.00*) has 500+ top-end global craft beers with good Dutch coverage.

Slijterij Groningen (Vismarkt 36 – **T** 050 313 3654 – slijterijgroningen.nl – *shut Su; Mo 13.00–18.00; Tu&We 10.00–18.00; Th 09.00–21.00; Fr 10.00–19.00; Sa 09.00–18.00; Su 13.00–17.00*) has around 1,000 beers. A second outlet (Beren 56) has fewer.

Van Erp (Grote Kromme Elleboog 16 – **T** 050 312 6414 – vanerpwijn.nl – *shut Su Mo 13.00–18.30; Sa 10.00–17.00; others 10.00–18.30*) stocks 500+ beers and has second outlet in the town of Roden (Raadhuisstraat 11) if you're passing that way.

VEENDAM

30km SE from Groningen off N33
Bus 171

Provincial town (op. 20,000) noted for its Veenkoloniaal Museum (veenkoloniaalmuseum.nl) which tells the story of the region's peat-digging history and its strong links with Dutch maritime power.
HOTEL TIP: **Parkzicht** ★★★ (below) has quiet rooms.

Parkzicht

Museumplein 3 · **T** 0598 666 888
parkzicht.com
Fr&Sa from 11.00; others from 10.00

The Park View is a sprawling complex comprising hotel, Bogdike brewery, taproom restaurant and multiple function rooms, all fronted by a leafy terrace. Front left is a conservatory, to the right a seating area containing its noteworthy glass brewing kettles. A full restaurant menu is served. House beers number among the tap selection, with tasting flights available, while around 30 guests include M-Bier, made here by the same brewer.

WINSCHOTEN

36km E from Groningen off A7 exit 47
Winschoten

Sleepy town (pop 18,500) that is almost in Germany.

Carambole

Blijhamsterstraat 2 · **T** 0597 424190
carambole-winschoten.nl
Shut Mo-We; Th from 19.00; Su only for events; others from 15.00;

Old-established café south of the main square, named after a variety of billiards without pockets in which players cannon ('carom') balls off others. Once there were numerous tables for this purpose in a back room, but they've since been removed to make space for live music. The front bar, dimly lit by mosaic glass lamps, has gentlemen's club comfy armchairs and barrel tables. Snacks only. The beer list of 80 reflects the proximity to Germany.

Limburg

Long, thin Limburg (pop 1.1 million) is 110km from north to south but at is narrowest point separates Belgium from Germany by a mere 5km. Along its length is the widening river Maas (Meuse) and its valley. The northern portion is flat farmland, while the far south merits that most un-Dutch of topographical descriptions, hilly.

Being the most Catholic, least Calvinist part of the country, Limburg likes to enjoy itself.

Its rich beer culture is evidenced by the presence of many of the nation's oldest-surviving breweries and some excellent bars.

Limburg is also (in)famous for its pre-Lent *carnaval*, which every village celebrates with fervour from mid-November onwards. If you're not keen on fancy dress, excruciating oompah music and allegedly watered-down beer, avoid the area around the last week of festivities.

The local language Limburgs, or Limburgish, a divergent dialect of Dutch that overlaps with neighbouring German dialects, has semi-official status, but attempting to master it is pointless: every village has its own variant, each less intelligible than the last.

LARGEST CENTRES: **Heerlen, Maastricht, Venlo**

MORE INFORMATION: vvvlimburg.nl

SELECTED BREWERIES: **Alfa**, *Schinnen*; **Ambrass**, *Sittard*; **Brand** (Heineken), *Wijlre*; **Brouwschuur** (Weerter), *Weert*; **Fontein**, *Stein*; **Gulpener**, *Gulpen*; **Hertog Jan** (AB InBev), *Arcen*; **Lindeboom**, *Neer*; **Maar**, *Jabeek*.

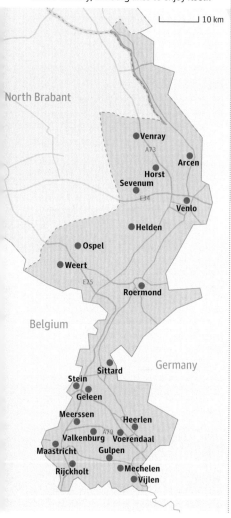

ARCEN

15km N from Venlo off N271
Bus 83 from Venlo

Small village (pop 2,200) with a castle. The latter's surrounding gardens, originally laid out in the 16th century, are now among the Netherlands' finest.

Hertog Jan Proeverij

Kruisweg 43 · **T** 077 473 9160
hertogjanproeverij.nl
Sa 11.00-00.00; Fr&Su 11.00-22.00; others 11.00-20.00

Brewery tap near the Maas, 1km north of the village, also reachable from Venlo by taking bus 29 to Broekhuizen Hoogstraat and catching the free ferry. Linked by an umbilical pipe to the brewery, though we doubt much beer passes along it. The café's Germanic feel is enhanced by 2,000 steins hanging from the ceiling. Simple lunches are served until 17.00; more elaborate fare thereafter. Besides the full house range there are around 50 guests.

GELEEN

20km NE from Mastricht off A76 exit 2
🚃 Geleen Oost or Geleen-Lutterade

Nondescript small town (pop 32,800), worthy of a stop-off to stock up.

BEER TO GO

Vos (Hegstraat 3 – **T** 046 474 9661 – **vosdranken.nl** – *shut Su&Mo; Sa 09.00–17.00; others 09.00–18.00*) is a Belgian-style drinks warehouse with 750+ Limburg, Dutch and international craft ales, and many whiskies.

GULPEN

16km WSW from Maastricht on N278
Bus 350

Attractive village (pop 3,700) with a large brewery at its heart.

Brouwlokaal

Rijksweg 19 · **T** 043 450 7558
gulpenerbrouwlokaal.nl
Su 11.00–20.00; others 11.00–22.00

Gulpener's taproom has a terrace out front, a beer garden at the rear and a 2.5hl experimental microbrewery within. Sparse furnishings include some wooden crate tables. Snacks and stews on the food menu use only locally sourced ingredients. There are 16 house beers on tap including one-offs, plus a shop for takeaways. Card payments only.

OTHER BEER VENUES

Zwarte Ruiter (Markt 4 – **T** 043 450 4635 – **herbergdezwarteruiter.nl** – *shut Tu; others from 10.00*) was Gulpener's brewery tap and is still the best place to drink their Mestreechs Aajt, matured here in huge vats visible through glass.

HEERLEN

25km ENE from Maastricht off A79
🚃 Heerlen

Provincial town in the nation's bottom right-hand corner (pop 86,800). Although the settlement has Roman origins, it only grew to a significant size during a 19th-century coal mining boom. The mines are long gone, their slag heaps now planted with greenery as newly honed hills, but you can learn about them from ex-miners in the Nederlands Mijnmuseum (**nederlandsmijnmuseum.nl**).

Beerkompanie

Pancratiusplein 46 · **T** 045 571 1877
beerkompanie.nl
Daily from 11.00

Modern brewpub and Alfa taproom. There are Bacchus gargoyles everywhere, while a yellow and white mosaic filling a back wall adorned with memorabilia depicts a giant glass of beer. Food all day. Beers from the Heëlesche Sjtadsbroewerie appear sporadically, made using the copper kit upstairs, otherwise expect to find the core Alfa range.

D'r Klinge

Pancratiusplein 47 · **T** 045 574 1441
drklinge.nl
Daily from 12.00

Friendly dark brown café with polished wood and beer enamels and a terrace staring out at Beerkompanie next door. The photos of children on the walls are regulars in their youth and their offspring. A slightly unnerving clown adorns the lamp at one end of the bar. Snacks only. Around 100 otherwise Belgo-centric beers include some Dutch craft choices.

HELDEN
17km SW from Venlo on N562
Bus 370 from Venlo or Weert

Small town (pop 6,200) with one excellent reason for showing up.

Zoes
Molenstraat 7 · **T** 077 307 1457
dezoes.nl
Shut Mo&Tu; Su from 11.00; others from 12.00

The bus stops a few paces from the small terrace of this chic café with a sprawling interior featuring bare brick, hipster lighting and modern wood furnishings. At the back, a glass floor panel peers into the cellar below. There is a full food menu. The 300+ beer list, including 16 taps with 10 changing guests, covers Trappists as well as Dutch and international craft. Bottles and cans pack glass chillers beside the bar, while 75cl sharing bottles are aged in the aforementioned cellar.

HORST
17km NW from Venlo via A73
 Horst-Sevenum (3km S) then bus 70, 79 or 87.

Small provincial town (pop 12,700).

Blok 10
Wilhelminaplein 10 · **T** 077 397 1224
blok10horst.nl
Shut We; others from 11.30

Modern café with a terrace on the main square. The austere, bright, almost diner-like interior has bench seating at the front, while a second room behind hosts occasional live bands. Lunches (*12.00–15.00*) and dinners (*17.00–21.30*) served, with snacks filling the gaps. Around 120 beers err on the safe side but with enough Dutch craft to keep us happy.

Proeflokaal van Horst
Wilhelminaplein 13 · **T** 077 398 6001
proeflokaalvanhorst.nl
Jun–Aug: *Shut Mo; Tu from 08.00; Sa&Su from 10.30; others from 14.00.*
Sep–May: *Shut Mo; Fr from 16.00; Sa&Su from 10.30; others from 19.00*

Friendly café with large terrace. Green and black floors and coloured chairs make a refreshing change from brown. Walls are hung with old photos of Horst, while Statler and Waldorf from the Muppets keep tabs on everyone from above the bar. Snacks only. The guests among the 140 beers are in a 'walk-to' fridge: go there, select a beer, hand it to the staff. There are 75 whiskies too.

Zoes, Helden

MAASTRICHT

Maastricht

One of the Netherlands' oldest and most attractive cities, Maastricht (pop 122,500) is a popular spot for signing treaties, as well as being a Premier League beer destination. It straddles the Maas, with the station on one bank and the old town on the other.

The Romans built the first river crossing here on the Via Belgica in the year AD 50. It lasted until 1275, when it collapsed killing 400 people. The current St Servatius pedestrian and cyclists' bridge is somewhat sturdier.

The 10th-century Romanesque St Servatius Basilica dominates the Vrijthof square. Onze Lieve Vrouwebasiliek (Basilica of Our Lady) was begun around the same time. Parts of the medieval wall still stand, including the 13th-century Helpoort, the country's oldest surviving city gate. Even the tourist office (VVV) is in the 15th-century former town hall and law courts.

City Hall, Maastricht

The town's beer culture is so embedded that the VVV carries a leaflet advising where to find local speciality Mestreechs Aajt. In early spring, Maastricht is the epicentre of the pre-Lent carnival: dress up, or leave town.

HOTEL TIP: **Poshoorn ★★** (below) has been refurbished and is within staggering distance of most places.

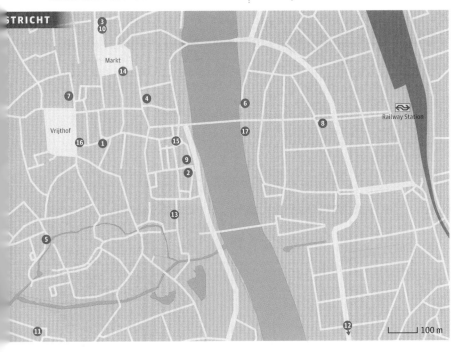

Falstaff

St. Amorsplein 6 · **T** 043 321 7238
cafe-falstaff.com
Daily from 10.00

Lively café with a terrace on a tiny square. It underwent a major refit in 2019 and is now a modern, bright place with lots of light wood. Lunches and dinners focus on burgers; finger food and sharing platters served all day. The beer list has improved immensely: around half the 120 options, with 22 taps, are global craft guests.

Frape

Het Bat 7 · **T** 06 4865 8918
Shut Tu; Mo&We 10.00–20.00; Th 15.00–22.00; Fr&Sa 09.00–00.00; Su 11.00–20.00

A must-visit slice of beer heaven by the Maas, with a river view terrace. This simple tiled-floor brown café has empty bottles lining shelves and windowsills. Snacks only. The beer selection is exceptional, running to 500+ Dutch and international brews. Only some more popular brands are listed, so convey your wishes to the knowledgeable landlord and he will find something to suit from his extensive cellar.

Gouverneur

Boschsstraat 105a · **T** 043 852 1125
degouverneurmaastricht.nl
Fr from 08.30; others from 10.00

Grand café in former brewery with large terrace just north of the Markt and next to Rozenhoedje (below). A sitting area at the front has beers on bookshelves, with a long bar behind and open kitchen at the rear. Full food menu served. The 250 beers are mainly Belgian including numerous lambics, with some Dutch and local micro choices.

Knijnspiep

Muntstraat 45 · **T** 043 321 4065
knijnspiep.nl
Fr&Sa from 10.00; Su 11.00–19.00; Mo 12.00–19.00; Th 10.00–23.00; others 10.00–19.00

The narrow-fronted Rabbit Hole, on a street too narrow for a terrace, is typical Burgundian Maastricht: a dimly lit brown café with bare walls and crystal chandeliers. Snacks only. It's technically the Klinker taproom as the owner is the brewer's father. The other 40 beers are less exciting.

The Lab

Ezelmarkt 15 · **T** 06 1516 2936
facebook.com/thelabmaastricht
Shut Su; We 18.00–22.00; Sa from 17.00; others from 18.00

Hipster bar and restaurant in a former barn south of Vrijthof square. There's a bar below and mezzanine above, with minimalist black decor and a wood-fronted counter. Dinners feature burgers, pizza and noodles. The 65+ beers go down the international craft route and one-third of the list is barrel-aged.

Maastrichter Maltezer

Oeverwal 12 · **T** 043 855 3258
stadsbrouwerijdemaastrichtermaltezer.nl
Shut Tu; Mo 16.00–23.00; others 11.00–23.00

Chic brasserie and taproom reviving beer production in the former Ridder brewery, closed by Heineken in 2002. Beyond the riverside terrace is a long, narrow interior with tiled floors and minimalist decor. Lunches, dinners and sharing tapas platters. The 16 draught and around 75 bottle and can options include house beers among a mix of Dutch and Belgian, industrial and craft.

Naovenant

Helmstraat 16b · **T** 06 2152 6789
naovenant.nl
Shut We; Fr-Su from 11.00; others from 18.00

Unassuming popular local with a cramped terrace and simple interior a few steps north from Vrijthof square. Snacks only. The 80+ beers tend towards local, but here that means more Belgian Limburg than Dutch, with several lambics.

Poshoorn

Stationstraat 47 · **T** 043 321 7334
poshoorn.nl
Daily from 09.00

The Post Horn is a lively pub with a large terrace near the station, its L-shaped interior dominated by hexagonal white tiling following a recent makeover. Breakfasts and lunches are padded out with all-day burgers, salads and sharing platters. The 90+ beers include several from Maastricht micros and plentiful Dutch IPAs.

Pothuiske

Het Bat 1 · **T** 043 321 6002
pothuiske.nl
Fr-Su from 10.00; others 11.00-00.00

The name of this riverside café with terrace recalls the boiling cauldron which was kept here for many years from the mid-15th century to provide safe drinking water to passing locals. The tiled-floor interior goes for wooden seats and beer ads, with a row of glass-fronted chillers behind the bar. Lunch and snacks available. The 80+ beers stay mainly Belgian, but there are a few Limburg locals.

Rozenhoedje

Boschstraat 109 · **T** 043 321 4575
Shut Mo; Fr from 08.00; others from 10.00

The Little Pink Hat is an old brown café with a terrace beside the Gouverneur (above). The cosy interior has a battered lived-in feel with tiled floors and walls decorated with old clocks and copies of oil paintings. Beware the live accordion music on some Friday afternoons. Snacks only. Around 100 mostly Belgian beers include a good choice of Trappists.

Tapijn

Tapijnkazerne 20 · **T** 043 311 7588
tapijn.nl
Daily 10.00-23.00

The Zuyd brewery is in the basement of this former barracks with a leafy terrace and a World War II-themed interior, with uniforms, helmets, radiograms and period music. Lunches and dinners served. Beers include Project-K, brewed exclusively for the café, other Zuyd lines and 30 guests chosen by the Hoppy Brothers (Beer to go below). Check before travelling as both brewery and café may have to move in 2021 if Maastricht University takes its building back.

Thembi

Dopplerdomein 20a · **T** 043 361 3621
thembi.eu
Daily from 15.00

Bustling suburban café on a housing estate, a 15-minute walk down the east bank of the Maas from the centre, or five minutes west from Maastricht Randwijk station. Décor is modern, with a view of houses from the terrace. Dinner served 16.00-22.00; snacks all day. The beer list of 250+ makes impressive reading: Limburg and the wider Dutch craft scene are well-represented, while the Belgian range includes harder-to-find options.

Witloof ⑬

Sint Bernardusstraat 12 · **T** 043 323 3538
Witloof.nl
Shut Mo&Tu; We&Th 17.30–21.30; Fr&Sa 17.00–22.00; Su 17.00–21.30

Flemish restautant with regularly changing décor that on our last visit included several Mannekens Pis, and a bicycle on the bar. Don't miss checking out the bottles in the self-proclaimed 'Beer Heaven' cellar. Food is as expected: mussels, *stoofvlees* stew, and of course *witloof* (chicory). Each dish has three suggested beer pairings. All 300+ brews are Belgian, with a huge range of lambics, the aforementioned cellared options and modern craft.

Zwaan ⑭

Markt 68 · **T** 043 321 5421
dezwaanmaastricht.nl
We&Fr from 07.30; others from 08.30

Corner modern brown café with a terrace beside the city hall. The walk-in fridge beside the bar dominates the wooden-floored room. Full food menu. Order from 200+ beers on the printed menu or simply take your choice from the fridge to the bar. The range leans towards Dutch craft.

OTHER BEER VENUES
The **Karkol** ⑮ (Stokstraat 5 – **T** 043 321 7035 – **indekarkol.nl** – *daily from 12.00*) is a gorgeous old brown café that oozes character from everywhere except the corporate beer list. All dark brown and creaky floors, **Ouden Vogelstruys** ⑯ (Vrijthof 15 – **T** 043 321 4888 – **vogelstruys.nl** – *daily from 09.30*) is the most characterful place on Vrijthof square.

Beside the like-named bridge, **Servaas** ⑰ (Cörversplein 10 – **T** 043 321 7669 – **servaascafe.nl** – *daily from 10.00*) reopened in 2019, having previously morphed into a tapas bar, and has resumed selling a small but interesting craft beer range.

BEER TO GO
Sandwiched between the Maastrichter Maltezer brewery and its taproom, **Hoppy Brothers** (Kotterweg 12 – **T** 06 5493 8559 – **thehoppybrothers.com** – *shut Mo&Tu; Su 13.00–17.00; others 11.00–18.00*) has 300 beers with a strong Dutch and local craft focus. **Keepin' it Hoppy** (Brusselsestraat 3B – **T** 06 5326 7715 – **keepinithoppy.nl** – *shut Su; others 13.00–22.00*) has 500+ international craft ales, half of them stored ready-chilled.

MECHELEN

20km E from Maastricht off N278
Bus 57 from Gulpen or Maastricht

Not to be confused with the Belgian city, this quiet village (pop 1,500) is blessed with two great pubs adjacent to each other. It also has several attractive half-timbered houses.

Kroeën

Hoofdstraat 23 · **T** 043 455 1262
cafeindekroeen.nl
Shut We&Th; others from 12.00

Just downhill from the church, the Crown opened in 1874 and has been in the same family for generations. The village water pump is on the terrace, while plastic ivy decorates the bar of the 'old and new' interior. Bottles line up in the windows. Lunches and dinners served. The growing list of 300+ beers is predominantly Belgian, but is strong on international Trappists and does feature some more local breweries.

Pintje

Hoofdstraat 25 · **T** 043 850 0270
tpintjemechelen.nl
Shut Mo&Tu; Su 10.30–21.00; others from 10.30

The Wee Pint also has a terrace on the main road beside its beerier neighbour. Inside is a charming warren of rooms, with a wood-burning stove in most. Food runs the full gamut from snacks to lunches and dinners. The 60 beers are mainly Belgian but include local guests and a few other Dutch micros.

MEERSSEN

6km NE from Maastricht off A79 exit 1
 Meerssen

Quiet village (pop 5,900) just outside of, and a dormitory for, Maastricht. An attractive Gothic church dominates the central square.

Keizer

Markt 14 · **T** 043 364 3919
cafedekeizermeerssen.nl
Th from 12.00; Fr from 16.00; Sa from 14.00; Su from 10.00; others from 18.00

This old-fashioned locals' brown café has a terrace opposite the main church, with tiled floors, bare brick walls and a few beer enamels as interior decor. Snacks only. Around half the 170+ beers are Belgian, the rest Dutch and global craft, with the landlord displaying a clear liking for hoppy IPAs.

RIJCKHOLT

6km S from Maastricht off A2 exit 57
Bus 57 to Gronsveld Vroendalsweg then 15 minutes walk S

Blink-and-you-miss-it village (pop 1,000) near the motorway heading south to Belgium.

Riékelt

Rijksweg 184 · **T** 043 408 1366 · riekelt.nl
Daily from 11.00

Large café and B&B with a roadside terrace opposite woods and fields. The multi-roomed interior has classic beer enamel decor and the bar at its core. Full lunch and dinner menu served, the latter including mussels. House beer Kuusjke amber is from Gulpener; otherwise the 110+ beers err on the safe Belgian side with a few Dutch surprises.

ROERMOND

 Roermond

Riverside town (pop 57,700), once strategically important but now mostly popular with regional shoppers thanks to its 200-store Designer Outlet complex.

Heilige Cornelius

Zwartbroekplein 6 · **T** 06 5200 4680
denheiligecornelius.nl
Shut Mo&Tu; We&Th from 19.00; others from 16.00

Tatty but friendly brown café with creaky floorboards and a 50-year history, wearing its wear and tear with pride. Live music several times a month. Cheese and sausage snacks, with peanuts in shells for floor preservation. A growing list of 200+ beers is split roughly equally between Belgian standards, Dutch micros and international craft.

Tramhalte

Stationsplein 17 · **T** 0475 854725
cafedetramhalteroermond.nl
Daily from 10.00

The Tram Stop is a longstanding brown café near the station with carpets on the tables and occasional live music. Snacks only.

Previously a beer champion, it went off the rails but is now back on track with a beer list of almost 100 and rising, albeit mostly Belgian with only a few Dutch making it on board.

OTHER BEER VENUES

Resistent (Looierstraat 2 – **T** 0475 334891 – **caferesistent.nl** – *shut Tu&We; Sa from 11.00; others from 14.00*) is an amiably rough and ready brown café with a short list that includes a house beer brewed by Fontein.

BEER TO GO

Bierbrigadier (Hamstraat 8 – **T** 06 2936 2143 – **debierbrigadier.nl** – *shut Mo&tu; Th 11.00–19.00; Sa 12.00–17.00; others 11.00–18.00*) has 400+ global craft options.

SEVENUM

12km NW from Venlo off N556
↝ Horst-Sevenum

Large village (pop 6,700) surrounded by farms.

Sevewaeg

Markt 3 · **T** 077 467 1345
desevewaeg.nl
Sa from 11.00; others from 10.30

Large modern brown café with a terrace by the church, 2km south from the station by bus 70 or 87. The wall behind the counter is lined with glass-fronted fridges. Old clocks and steins dominate and mock-art deco lighting abounds. Full food menu. The 85+ beers lean towards Belgium with a fair smattering of Dutch craft: check the board by the bar for the latest guests.

SITTARD

25km NE from Maastricht off A2 exit 48
↝ Sittard

Small provincial town (pop 38,000) with a picturesque market square. In theory, the Ambrass taproom (Gats 13) is open to visitors Fr 13.00–19.00 & Sa 13.00–20.00 but in practice they would prefer you to reserve in advance.

Gats

Markt 20 · **T** 046 850 8058
tapperiedegats.nl
Shut Mo; Tu from 17.00; Th from 10.00; others from 11.00

Olde worlde café in a yellow half-timbered building dating from 1535, with terrace out front. The cluttered interior is all wood-beamed ceilings and bric-a-brac like bugles and bird cages, with a raised seating area at the back. Lunches include *flammkuchen*; dinners are schnitzels and burgers. Around 90 beers include Ambrass, brewed just 100m away.

Gats, Sittard

Hophuys

Markt 15 · **T** 06 4693 4080
hophuys.nl
Shut Mo&Tu; We&Th 16.30–23.30; others from 12.30 (from 14.00 Nov–May)

Friendly beer bar with small terrace tucked into a corner of the main square. The interior is dominated by a mural of the brewing process. Snacks only. Around 120 beers including 20 taps featuring a bold and regularly changing range of global craft ales. There is a bottle-sharing session on the first Saturday of every month (*14.00–18.00*).

STEIN

16km NNE from Maastricht off A2
Beek—Elsloo (3km S)

Small town (pop 12,000) next to a colossal chemicals plant that is fortunately obscured from the local brewery.

Fontein

Ondergenhousweg 15 · **T** 046 426 2858
brouwerijdefontein.nl
Shut Mo&Tu; others 10.00–21.30

To reach this cosy, semi-rural taproom in a renovated farmhouse, take bus 33 from Beek–Elsloo station to Omphaliusstraat then head 800m WSW. Beside an inner bar with a wood-burning stove are a semi-glazed conservatory and a courtyard terrace. Simple meals served. The expansive house range is available on tap and in bottle, the latter also sold to take away.

VALKENBURG

12km ENE from Maastricht off A79
Valkenburg

Picturesque town (pop 6,200) in the Geul valley, a tourist hotspot since what is now the country's oldest railway station opened 160 years ago. Attractions include Valkenburg Castle and 'grottos' that are actually the remains of Roman stone quarries.

HOTEL TIP: **Sjoemkraag** (below) is a B&B.

Grendelpoort

Muntstraat 17 · **T** 043 601 2640
Shut Mo; others from 12.00

Lovely beer café with terrace beside the like-named 14th-century portcullis gate. Shelves inside are crammed with beer bottles. Snacks only. If the choice of 14 draught lines and 200+ bottles and cans crammed into chiller cabinets isn't enough, and shop temperature is acceptable, you can also order from a spectacular 2,000 options in the adjacent **Zythotheek** store, an Aladdin's Cave of beery wonders (Muntstraat 15 – **T** 043 311 0999 – **zythotheek.nl** – *shut Mo; Su 11.00–16.00; others 11.00–18.00*). House Gringel beers are brewed at Proef in Belgium.

Sjoemkraag

Wilhelminalaan 72–74 · **T** 043 204 1361
desjoemkraag.nl
Shut Tu; Mo from 14.00; We&Th from 13.00; Fr from 12.00; others from 10.00

Beer café with a terrace on a busy street, opened in 2019. The spacious modern interior has minimal decor in light shades. Snacks only, but the range is extensive. The 100+ well-chosen beers include several Dutch craft options, though the bottles and cans are more exciting overall than the draught choices.

OTHER BEER VENUES
In a 1668 stone farmhouse on the western edge of town, near Houthem-St. Gerlach station, **Burgemeester Quicx** (Sint Gerlach 17 – **T** 043 608 8888 – *daily 10.00–18.00*) is noteworthy as almost all its 25+ beers are from hard-to-find Limburg micros.

Burgemeester Quicx, Valkenburg

Pumpke (Daalhemerweg 2 – **T** 043 601 3721 – **pumpkevalkenburg.nl** – *shut Mo&Tu; Sa&Su from 12.00; others from 14.00*) is a friendly brown café stuffed with musical instruments and other bric-a-brac, but with a less-than-stuffed beer list.

BEERS TO GO
Zythotheek: see Grendelpoort above.

VENLO

60km E from Eindhoven off A67
⮄ Venlo

Provincial border town (pop 100,500) with a railhead linking to the German network.

Brouwersplaats

Parade 5e · **T** 077 772 5074
brouwersplaats.nl
Shut Mo, Fr from 15.00, Sa&Su from 12.00; others from 16.00

Modern pub with front terrace and rear beer garden. The interior is brushed wood, bare brick and metal pillars, with international hop-growing regions marked on a wall map. Lunches served Sa&Su only; snacks at other times. The beer menu of 120+ balances familiar stalwarts with a good smattering of more adventurous craft.

Klep

Keizerstraat 13 · **T** 077 463 3287
cafedeklep.nl
Shut Mo&Tu; others from 12.00

Friendly café hidden down an alley, with a terrace in the shadow of a church. The interior has an ecclesiastical theme, with iconography, pews and statues. A stove provides non-denominational heat. Light meals until 20.00; snacks all day. Numerous Dutch highlights on the 130+ beer list include the house Klep range brewed at Fontein by the landlord.

VENRAY

25km NW from Venlo off N270
⮄ Venray (3km E from centre)

Small provincial town (pop 28,000) which saw heavy fighting during the liberation of 1944. Learn more at the nearby Overloon War Museum (oorlogsmuseum.nl).

Goesting

Henseniusplein 13 · **T** 0478 855621
proeflokaalgoesting.nl
Fr–Su from 14.00; others from 16.00

Flashy modern beer bar with a terrace on a square just south of the centre. The mainly black interior has carpets on one wall and a glass-fronted cold room taking centre stage. Lunches and dinners served from an open kitchen. The 20 taps and 300 bottles and cans feature a cavalcade of Dutch and global craft stars.

Klokkenluider

Grote Markt 23 · **T** 0478 503470
cafedeklokkenluider.nl
Tu from 14.00; others from 12.00

Characterful old one-room café with sheltered terrace tucked in one corner of the main square. Bells hanging from the ceiling and an absurdly large example by the door reference the 'bell ringer' name, although it also means 'whistleblower' in Dutch. An upper seating area has a central hole in the floor, making it almost a mezzanine. Snacks only. The 100 mainly Belgian beers include a near-complete global Trappist selection.

BEER TO GO
Mr Hop (Raadhuisstraat 36A – **T** 085 065 6231 – **misterhop.com** – *shut Su&Mo; Fr 11.00–21.00; Sa 10.00–17.00; others 11.00–18.00*) has 1,400+ Dutch and international craft choices.

VIJLEN

15km S from Heerlen off N278
Bus 59 from Vaals, 350 from Gulpen

At a giddy 200m, this is the Netherlands' highest village (pop 1,500). The country's overall highest point, 321m above sea level, lies 5km to the southeast at Drielandenpunt, where the Netherands, Belgium and Germany meet.

Hijgend Hert

Harles 23 · **T** 043 306 2499
boscafe.nl
Sa&Su 09.00–21.00; others 11.00–21.00

It's worth the 2km climb along a lane from the village to reach this self-styled mountain hut, one of the country's cutest pubs. At 260m above sea level, its huge terrace roamed by chickens affords sweeping views. Behind the conservatory with its antler light fittings is a stone-walled bar with an open hearth that fills the air with wood smoke on most days. Food is served from an extensive menu. House Hert beers are brewed in Belgium, like most of the other 75 beer choices.

VOERENDAAL

4km W from Heerlen off A79
Voerendaal

Small dormitory village (pop 3,000).

Pintelier

Valkenburgerweg 33 · **T** 045 575 3214
facebook.com/pinteliervoerendaal
Shut Tu&We; Fr from 14.00; others from 16.00

Large brown corner local with rear terrace 1km south of the station. The interior has a floral ceiling hand-painted by a local artist, an old stove and an upright piano. There is a full food menu. The 100+ beer list is mostly Belgian, except for a few familiar Dutch faces.

WEERT

30km SE from Eindhoven off A2
Weert

Mid-sized industrial town (pop 51,000) that prospered thanks to its railways and canals.

Richard's Bar

Beekstraat 87 · **T** 06 2257 2060
richardsbar.nl
Shut Mo; Sa&Su from 14.00; others from 19.00

Irish pub with a warren interior, including a cosy bar area, snug, and pool and darts at the back. Leo, a South American parrot, often holds court by the bar and may join the conversation. Officially snacks only, but these run to fish and chips and sometimes Irish stew. Dutch craft options find space alongside more predictable Anglo-Irish fare on the 70+ list, along with a good range of whiskies.

Weerter Stadsbrouwerij, Weert

Weerter Stadsbrouwerij

Parallelweg 143/5
Shut Mo-We; Th 17.00-23.00; Fr 16.00-23.00; Sa 14.00-23.00; Su 14.00-21.00

The Brouwschuur taproom a few hundred metres north of the station has lime-washed brick walls, lampshades made from plastic kegs and a picture window looking onto the brewhouse. Food is scarce. Most of the 60 bottles and 10 taps come from the host Brouwschuur and the assembled masses who also brew here.

Wertha Brewpub

Bassin 6 · **T** 06 5241 5859
werthabrewpub.nl
Shut Mo; Tu&We 19.00-23.00; Su 13.00-23.00; others 13.00-01.00

Simple one-room café with a terrace opened in 2019. A large photo on the back wall dominating the interior depicts the view from outside around a century ago. Snacks only. The 'brew' part of the name was due to materialise in 2020, but the 100+ local and international craft beers on sale more than warrant inclusion without it.

OTHER BEER VENUES
On the outskirts of town, **Dennenoord** (Voorhoeveweg 2 – **T** 0495 532884 – **welkombijdennenoord.nl** – *shut Mo&Tu; Sa&Su from 10.00; others from 11.00*) has a fabulous lakeside terrace, a modern interior and some decent choices among its 50 beers.

North Brabant

North Brabant (Noord-Brabant), Brabant for short, is among the largest and most populous provinces (pop 2.5 million). It was once part of the much bigger medieval Duchy of Brabant, most of which is now in Belgium. South of the big rivers it is unrelentingly flat, and outside the major towns is largely farmland, fen and heathland broken up by canals.

Though still largely Catholic, the people of Brabant were never as zealous as those further south, so for much of its life the area was a buffer zone keeping the warring branches of Christianity apart. Its boundary with Belgium, especially around modern-day Baarle-Hertog/Nassau, is a lesson in how not to draw a border.

Brabant is among the beeriest regions of the country, with a high concentration of production breweries and in our view the best array of country pubs. If in doubt, aim for any village church: it's highly likely there's a decent watering hole close by, ready to replenish the sins of the repentent.

LARGEST CENTRES: **Breda, Eindhoven, Helmond, 's-Hertogenbosch, Roosendaal**

MORE INFORMATION: visitbrabant.com

SELECTED BREWERIES: **013**, Tilburg; **Budels**, Budel; **Croy**, Aarle-Rixtel; **Deftige Aap**, Helmond; **Dommelsch** (AB InBev), Dommelen; **Drie Horne**, Kaatsheuvel; **Eindhoven**, Eindhoven; **Frontaal**, Breda; **Kievit**, Zundert; **Koningshoeven**, Berkel-Enschot; **LOC**, Tilburg; **Muifel**, Oss; **Oijen**, Oijen; **Pimpelmeesch**, Chaam; **Ramses**, Wagenberg; **Sint Servattumus**, Schijndel; **Swinkels Family Brewers** (Bavaria), Lieshout; **Van Moll**, Eindhoven; **Vandeoirsprong**, Oirschot.

AARLE-RIXTEL
17km ENE from Eindhoven off A270
Residential village (pop 5,800).

Croyse Hoeve
Croylaan 9 · **T** 0492 381348
desmaakvancroy.nl
Su from 12.00; others from 17.00

Croy's taproom is a rural tavern with an open hearth 1.5km southwest from the village: take bus 25 from Helmond to Verliefd Laantje and walk 20 minutes west down Grote Overbrug. The terrace looks onto a hop field with Croy castle beyond. Food (*until 21.00*) includes dishes made with house beers. Four or five beers are usually on, with bottles to take away. The brewery next door has a separate bar for group tastings.

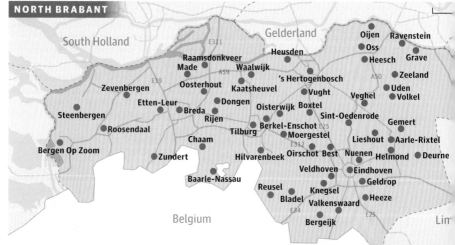

NORTH BRABANT

South Holland · Gelderland · Belgium · Lim

Oijen · Ravenstein · Oss · Heusden · Heesch · Grave · Raamsdonksveer · Made · Waalwijk · Zeeland · Zevenbergen · Oosterhout · Kaatsheuvel · 's Hertogenbosch · Uden · Vught · Veghel · Volkel · Etten-Leur · Dongen · Oisterwijk · Boxtel · Steenbergen · Breda · Rijen · Sint-Oedenrode · Gemert · Roosendaal · Berkel-Enschot · Tilburg · Moergestel · Lieshout · Aarle-Rixtel · Chaam · Bergen Op Zoom · Zundert · Hilvarenbeek · Oirschot · Best · Nuenen · Helmond · Deurne · Veldhoven · Eindhoven · Baarle-Nassau · Geldrop · Reusel · Knegsel · Heeze · Bladel · Valkenswaard · Bergeijk

BAARLE-NASSAU
27km SW from Tilburg off N260
Bus 132 from Tilburg or Breda

Two towns and countries in one: three-quarters is Dutch Baarle-Nassau, the rest Belgian Baarle-Hertog. In this medieval mess of ongoing boundary disputes, individual plots belong to different countries, creating Belgian enclaves in the Netherlands and enclaves within enclaves. National flags on the house numbers help, and street markings inform you when you cross borders, which is often. The whole set up is endearingly crap. Despite everything, national characters shine through: Belgian houses look scruffier, Dutch homes better-tended. The local brewery, **Dochter van de Korenaar**, is in Belgium but run by a Dutchman and would be in the Netherlands if it moved a few metres. Its taproom (Oordeelstraat 3B, Baarle-Hertog – **T** +32 14 699800 – dedochtervandekorenaar.be – *Fr 12.00-20.00; Sa&Su 11.00-19.00*) is worth a visit.

BEER TO GO

One of the world's oddest beer shops, **Biergrens** (Molenstraat 26 – **T** 013 507 7878 – debiergrens.be – *shut Mo; Sa 10.00-17.00; Su 10.00-16.00; others 10.00-18.00*) has a name meaning 'beer border' and indeed straddles a border, with two addresses (according to the Belgian mail system it's at Molenstraat 98) and phone numbers and a line on the floor to tell you which country you're standing in. Its 600+ beers are mainly Belgian.

BERGEIJK
21km SW from Eindhoven off N397
Bus 18, 318

Dormitory town (pop 8,800) for Eindhoven and Tilburg commuters.

Hofkaemer
Hof 18 · **T** 0497 571396 · hofkaemer.nl
Shut Mo&We; others from 10.00
(Jul&Aug: also open We)

Friendly village local with a terrace by the bandstand and secluded garden at the rear.

The cosy front bar has a wood-burning stove and one wall consisting entirely of wooden drawers. At the back is a larger dining area. The restaurant – light lunches and more substantial dinners – uses Brabantian ingredients and dishes come with beer recommendations. Around half the 100 beers are local.

BERGEN OP ZOOM
16km WSW from Roosendaal off A58 exit 27
Bergen op Zoom

The name of this attractive town (pop 66,000) implies hills, though the landscape remains resolutely flat: it actually refers to the way an ancient dyke built up naturally and kept out the surrounding marshes. Star attraction is the Markiezenhof (**markiezenhof.nl**), a beautiful brick palace built in 1485. This is also a city that celebrates the pre-lent carnival for longer, and takes it more seriously, than most others – you have been warned.

HOTEL TIP: **De Draak ★★★★**, Grote Markt 36 (**hoteldedraak.nl**) is the Netherlands' oldest hotel, dating back to 1397.

Loco
Markt 11 · **T** 0164 250321
biercafedeloco.nl
Shut Mo-Tu; We&Th 12.00-23.00; Su 12.00-21.30; others from 12.00

Formerly the Lokomotiefke, this brown café with a terrace on the main square has had a beery makeover, though it retains a great deal of its former cluttered charm. Food is predominantly *flammkuchen*. The 100+ beers balance safe Belgians with Dutch and international craft.

Provoosthuis
Potterstraat 36 · **T** 0164 257978
Mo-We from 19.00; others from 13.30

One block west of Grote Mark, this imposing 1783 brick and stone building was once the town garrison provost's house, a military court and prison. Nowadays it is a pool and snooker hall. Décor is limited to a few enamels and a pair of old skis above the bar. No food, except for occasional barbecues in the rear beer garden. Around 70 beers are mainly Belgian with local names like HillDevils now appearing.

BEER TO GO

In a suburban mall, **Zeeland** (Markiezaatsweg 11 – **T** 0164 712288 – **slijterijdezeeland.nl** – *Fr 09.00-20.00; Su 10.00-17.00; others 09.00-18.00*) stocks 700 international craft beers.

BERKEL-ENSCHOT
6km ENE from Tilburg off A65 exit 2

Dormitory town (pop 10,500) near Tilburg, best known in beer circles for its brewing monastery, though this is actually 6km from the town centre, between Tilburg and Moergestel and closer to both.

Koningshoeven

Eindhovenseweg 3 · **T** 013 572 2650
latrappeTrappist.com
Su 12.00-19.00; others 11.00-19.00; closes 18.00 in winter

This taproom is a purpose-built thatched barn with a huge terrace beside the celebrated Trappist monastery: to reach it by bus from Tilburg don't go to Berkel-Enschot but take the 141 bus which stops outside (Morgestel Kl. Koningshoeven). Inside is a high-ceilinged refectory with leather couches. Simple lunches (*12.00-17.00*) use organic local ingredients, including monk-made breads and cheeses. Snacks all day. The bar sells La Trappe draught and bottled beers, brewed on site, with bottles also on sale in the abbey shop.

BEST
10km NW from Eindhoven off A2 exit 28
Best

Not the Netherlands' worst small town (pop 29,800) but the name is a little hyperbolic. It's effectively a northern suburb of Eindhoven, but don't tell the residents we said that.

FF
Nieuwstraat 69 · **T** 0499 872089
eetcafeff.nl
Shut Mo; Su from 16.30; others from 17.00

This chic café-cum-restaurant has wooden floors, chandeliers, a conservatory at the front which opens up to become a terrace in fine weather and a spiral staircase in the middle. Steaks are the main focus of the dinner menu. Around 75 mainly Belgian beers including 16 taps with some Dutch options such as Muifel and Jopen.

BLADEL
27km WSW from Eindhoven off N284
Bus 19, 319

Modern village (pop 10,500) with a charmless main square.

D'n Bel
Markt 50 · **T** 0497 840687
facebook.com/cafednbel
Shut Mo; Fr&Sa from 15.00; Su from 14.00; others from 18.00

The dartboard and large TV screen give this loud, modern pub a sports bar feel. With the music turned up high, the only respite may be on the terrace outside on the square. Nibbles only. The 100+ beers compensate, with several local offerings and the odd surprise among the Belgian majority.

BOXTEL
25km NW from Eindhoven off A2 exit 25
Boxtel

Neat commuter town (pop 24,400). The Battle of Boxtel in 1794 was part of a failed Anglo-Austro-Dutch attempt to invade Napoleon's France via Flanders. One of the British brigade commanders present was a certain Lt-Col Arthur Wellesley, later the Duke of Wellington.

Becoloth

Rozemarijnstraat 2–2a · **T** 0411 673673
becoloth.nl
Fr from 10.00; Sa&Su from 15.00; Mo from 16.00;
others from 11.30

Multi-roomed place with a small terrace, one side of the interior decorated to look like a 1930s café, the other only open at weekends. A winter garden at the back has a Roman villa theme. Snacks only. The official beer range stretches only to 70 or so but ask about the 'secret' list of around 30 often more interesting additions brought in for tasting events.

Kerk

Oude Kerkstraat 10 · **T** 0411 674735
eetcafedekerk.com
Shut Mo–Tu; others from 14.00

The Church is a cosy corner café in the lee of – yes – a church. The large clock hanging from the ceiling beams in the red-walled bar with its brick arches looks lovely but doesn't work. Dinners revolve around burgers. The regular beer range is around 60, but the place qualifies for a full entry because on our last visit there was a small 'dark list' of unadvertised guests, so show interest and ask.

N9ne

Parallelweg zuid 35 · **T** 0411 687382 · n9ne.nl
Shut Mo–We; others 16.00–23.00

Semi-rural restaurant by the railway, 800m south of the station. It has an informal terrace and conservatory, and a smarter restaurant with carpet, red vinyl chairs and wine glasses on the tables. Sit at the bar if you just want to drink. Every dish on the extensive dinner menu comes with recommended beer pairings. Around 75 beers include several from Dutch micros and the house Nr. N9NE, a saison/tripel hybrid made by St Servattumus.

BREDA
Breda

Brabant's third city (pop 181,000) is ringed by canals, with parks roamed by feral chickens. The centre has a medieval elegance despite a 1534 fire that left just 150 buildings standing. The Grote Kerk, under construction at that time, is one of the country's finest Gothic cathedrals.

During Cromwell's Commonwealth in England, King Charles II spent much of his time in exile here. His Declaration of Breda in 1660 pardoned all enemies who recognised his restoration to the throne. Five years later he fought the Second Anglo-Dutch War – there's gratitude for you.

Aogse Markt

Haagse Markt 5 · **T** 076 205 0505
aogsemarkt.nl
Shut Mo; others from 11.00

Grand café in the Princenhage suburb near Don Qui-John and the Bierreclamemuseum (below). Take bus 4 to Dreef. The grey-painted townhouse has a burgundy door, an old postbox in the outer wall and a terrace on a market square. The eclectic interior has embossed metal ceilings, colourful murals and ketchup bottles on a metal beam. Light lunches and burger-style dinners. They admit to 180 beers, although only 100 of these appear on the menu. The house Daelder amber is made at Ramses.

Aogse Markt, Breda

Beer & Barrels

Ceresstraat 15a · **T** 076 303 6200
beersbarrels.nl/brouwhuis-breda
Daily from 15.00

Popular multi-level café in the former Drie Hoefijzers (Oranjeboom) brewhouse, part of a growing chain. The lower bar area sits beneath the giant disused copper kettles. There's a mezzanine above that and further up a second bar used for events. Food is on-trend pulled stuff and burgers. A list of 80 beers mixes safe Belgians with Dutch and local Breda choices.

Beyerd

Boschstraat 26 · **T** 076 521 4265
cafedebeyerd.nl
Shut We; Sa from 12.00; others from 10.00

The old-established and popular Carillion is a founding member of ABT and since 2004 a brewpub. The first café in the country to stock Belgian beers, it was opened in 1967 by beer hero Piet de Jongh, who died in 2019, and is still run by his sons. The front terrace seems perpetually full. Inside, traditions are upheld with carpeted tables and billiards, although it is normally too crowded to play. Brewery and restaurant (*evenings only*) occupy the back room, while lunches and snacks are served in the bar. The 120 beers include three or four house brews on tap, a reasonable Dutch selection and a strong range of Belgian lambics.

Bierreclamemuseum

Haagweg 375 · **T** 076 522 0975
bierreclamemuseum.nl
Su only 11.00–23.00

A standout oddity in a quiet suburb 3.5km southwest of the city centre, this is a warren of a pub that doubles as a free museum, packed to bursting with beer memorabilia. Take bus 4 (Princenhage) to Nieuwe Heilaarstraat and you can't miss it: look for the blue truck and British phone box on the terrace. There's a beer garden at the back and sometimes live music from 17.00. Snacks only. Only 45 or so mainly Belgian beers, but the uniqueness of this place gets it in.

Boterhal, Bre

Boterhal

Grote Markt 19 · **T** 076 889 8180
deboterhal.nl
Daily from 12.00

The former butter exchange spreads over two huge floors and a large terrace but often gets packed with a mainly youthful crowd. A characterful cellar bar housing the St Joris brewery is officially only open for groups, but if a visit is in progress you can sometimes sneak down for one. Lunches until 16.30; tapas thereafter. Besides the house brews, the bulk of the 125 beers are Belgian, but the list changes regularly and local craft is making inroads.

Brack

Speelhuislaan 175
brackbreda.nl
Shut Mo–We; Th&Fr 16.00–23.00; others 14.00–23.00.
NB Closed in winter: check before travel

Very much a work in progress, the joint taproom of Ramses and Bliksem opened in 2019 inside the shell of a huge former industrial building 1km northwest from the station. Its entire south wall was missing at the time of writing, leaving the bar area open to the elements, but warmed by wood-burning hearths. Over the lifetime of this guide the plans are to add a restaurant, a brewhouse for experiments by both brewers, and, yes, a fourth wall. The bar is already fully functional, serving house beers from 20 taps.

Catch-22

Vismarktstraat 14 · **T** 076 521 2936
facebook.com/Catch22Breda
Shut Tu; Sa&Su from 16.00; others from 18.00

Convivial pub with small terrace near a busy square. The focus is on drinking, with loudish music and minimal decor beyond beer enamels and chalkboard menus. Some well-worn tables have ludo and chess boards inlaid in them. Nibbles only. A constantly-refreshed range of 80 beers provides a good local and international mix.

DOK-19

Haven 19 · **T** 06 3409 2312
dok19.nl
Mo from 15.00; others from 11.00

Popular pub with canalside terrace. The spacious split-level, modern-brown interior has black and white tiles below, wood floors above at the back, and candles in beer bottles on the tables. Lunches and snacks only. Around 80 beers include the house Witte Anker range brewed at Stadsbrouwerij Breda.

Frontaal

Liniestraat 31
brouwerijfrontaal.nl
Shut Mo&Tu; others 12.00–23.00

Follow the signs to the back of an industrial complex just northeast of the station to find this taproom. The barely decorated bar has an arty mural on one wall, hanging plants, steel pillars, and a red container-like wall behind the counter housing the 31 taps. Snacks, rolls and soup served. Around half the beers are from the brewery through doors at the rear, the rest are global and Dutch craft guests.

Kleine Wereld

Grote Markt 59 · **T** 06 3819 0975
cafedekleinewereld.nl
Shut Mo-We; Su 15.00–22.00; others from 16.00

A cutesy café in a 1585 stepped-gabled building below the looming walls of the Grote Kerk, the Small World has a tiny conservatory and an equally tiny front terrace. The compact interior has bright white walls, with wood elsewhere. Snacks only. Around a quarter of its 60 beers are local and international craft guests.

Moeke

Ginnekenmarkt 17 · **T** 076 560 7020
moekeginneken.nl
Daily from 10.00

Beside the former town hall of the once-separate suburb of Ginneken, this grand brick building has both a front terrace and rear beer garden, and is reached by southbound buses 6 or 7. The high-ceilinged interior was once a hotel lobby. A full food menu is served. The 70 beers include a few Dutch classics such as Zundert and Jopen.

Samsam

Grote Markt 2 · **T** 076 522 7526
samsambreda.nl
Daily from 10.00

Longstanding café on the main square, diagonally opposite Zeezicht (below) and with a practically adjoining terrace. The interior mixes old and new, with Delftware plates adorning the walls and stylish modern furnishings. Simple lunches and snacks. The bulk of the 200 beers are Dutch and stocks are kept deliberately low to ensure a fast turnover.

Studio Dependence

Vismarktstraat 2 · **T** 076 521 0167
studiodependance.nl
Daily from 11.00

Long, narrow, student-friendly brown café with a front terrace. The wood-floored interior has half wood-panelled, half red-painted walls, ceiling fans and sport on TV. A second bar at the rear opens at peak times. Snacks only. Around 100 beers include a changing guest selection with plenty of Dutch micros and a featured brewery of the month.

Zeezicht

Ridderstraat 1 · **T** 076 514 8248
zeezichtbreda.com
Su from 11.00; others from 10.00

Corner bar with a terrace on Grote Markt and casual light-brown café interior. Simple lunches (*until 17.00*) and snacks served in the bar; dinners in an upstairs restaurant. Its collection of 80 beers is a treasure trove, with an ever-changing array of global craft gems on 22 of its 30 taps, usually with a fair showing from North America. There's a good range of whiskies and wines too. The one thing the Sea View does not have is a sea view, but then you are 80km from the coast.

OTHER BEER VENUES
A couple of doors down from Moeke (above), frozen-in-time brown café **Boerke Verschuren** (Ginnekenmarkt 13 – **T** 076 565 3220 – boerkeverschuren.nl – *daily from 10.00*) dates from around 1660, with carpets on some tables, inlaid games on others, gingham curtains and a few interesting beers.
Don Qui-John (Haagsemarkt 20 – **T** 076 514 7669 – donqui-john.nl – *shut Mo; others from 11.00*) is a suburban restaurant near the Aogse Markt (above), with good food and 40 well-chosen beers, strong on Dutch micros.

BEER TO GO
South of the centre, **Bierhuis** (Van Goorstraat 5 – **T** 076 522 8394 – hetbierhuis.nl – *shut Su&Mo; Sa 10.00-17.00; others 10.00-18.00*) stocks 700+ international beers.
Streken (Haagdijk 80 – **T** 06 8197 6418 – strekenbreda.nl – *shut Su-Tu; Th 13.00-21.00; Sa 09.30-19.00; others 13.00-19.00*) has 450+ global craft beers and growlers.
Bier Lokaal (Boschstraat 150 – **T** 06 4803 2137 – bier-lokaal.nl – *shut Su&Mo; Tu 12.00-18.00; Sa 09.00-17.00; others 11.00-19.00*) has 500+ beers and hosts tasting events.

CHAAM
13km S from Breda on N639
Bus 132

Sleepy village (pop 3,800) pronounced 'Kaam', which is logical in neither Dutch nor English. A former raspberry capital, it now makes its living from tourism.

Toontje Schoen

Ginderdoorstraat 4 · **T** 0161 496610
bijtoontjeschoen.nl
*Shut Mo all year & Tu-Fr (Oct-Apr);
others 10.00-20.00*

A 20-minute walk south from the village, the de facto Pimpelmeesch tap is not linked officially, but physically only a glass wall separates them inside a restored 18th-century thatched *langgevel* farmhouse: one end once housed the farmer, the other livestock. The terrace is opposite fields, with cows lowing in nearby sheds and pastures. Snacks include apple pie. The beer list is mainly Pimpelmeesch beers, among them a house Toontje Schoen blond.

DEURNE
24km E from Eindhoven off N270
🚆 Deurne

Quiet Brabant town (pop 24,500) surrounded by farmland.

De Brouwer

Markt 7 · **T** 0493 842215
debrouwer-deurne.nl
*Shut Mo; Fr&Sa from 14.00;
Su from 12.00; others from 19.00*

Large central café into which someone has ploughed large sums of cash. The modern interior, brightened by a skylight at the rear, has flagstone floors, dartboards and big-screen TVs. Snacks are international tapas, including sushi and bruschetta. The beer list of 300 is a good mix of familiar faces and unusual craft micros, both from home and abroad.

DONGEN

16km NW from Tilburg off N260
Bus 327 from Tilburg or Breda

Small commuter town (pop 23,500) that once had a leather industry.

Hamse Bok

Hoge Ham 45 · **T** 0162 313256
hamsebok.nl
Shut Su-Tu; others from 16.30

Multi-roomed brown café with a revolving door entrance, a traffic light at the back, lampshades made from red plastic keykegs and a rear garden terrace. At the centre is a tiny stage with a pole, if the mood takes you when things get lively. The dinner menu (*until 21.00*) is extensive. The 70+ beers are mainly Belgian but include locals Opener and Ramses.

Janssen & Janssen

Hoge Ham 59 · **T** 0162 319850
eetcafejanssenenjanssen.nl
Shut Mo; others from 11.30

English-speakers familiar with Tintin will know Janssen & Janssen as the Thompson Twins, as becomes evident when you enter this vast village local with three bars, a rear beer garden and a terrace opposite the domed St Laurentius church. There is a full food menu. The Belgian-led 150-strong beer menu also has a few Dutch and international choices.

EINDHOVEN

Eindhoven Centraal

Despite receiving city rights in 1232, the Netherlands' fifth city (pop 223,000) remained a backwater until a certain Gerard Philips began manufacturing light bulbs here in 1891. Its subsequent growth is almost entirely down to the global electronics giant his family business became, even if nowadays most manufacturing has relocated to the Far East and the former factories are now leisure facilities. To see what they used to make visit the Philips Museum (**philips-museum.com**).

Major war damage led to a radical redesign – for which read flattening – of the centre, and few old buildings remain. Modern Eindhoven views itself as a design capital, which manifests itself in some unusual buildings like the Evoluon and the Blob.

Recent years have seen a healthy flowering in this former beer desert and after a gap of 60 years there are now three breweries in town. Central Stratumseind – 'the Strat' – is a notorious street of bars, with around 50 lining up shoulder to shoulder. Most are aimed at students, with loud music and middling beer, but several exceptions appear below.

HOTEL TIP: **Glow ★★★**, Keizersgracht 13 a-b (**odysseyhotels.nl**) is a central boutique hotel.

100 Watt

Bleekweg 1 · **T** 040 842 8000
cafe100watt.nl
Mo&Tu 12.00–22.00; others from 12.00

Modern taproom of Stadsbrouwerij Eindhoven in a former carpet factory with an attractive riverside terrace and an inner courtyard. Large windows let the light flood into a spacious and stylishly minimalist interior. Lunches and dinners both feature salads and burgers. The full range of house beers and some guests are served from the 14 taps and in bottles.

Belgisch Biercafé

Stratumseind 95 · **T** 040 844 3312
belgischbiercafe-eindhoven.nl
Shut Mo&Tu; We&Th from 17.00; Su 14.30–23.00; others from 16.00

On the face of it, just another drinking den on the main nightlife street, until you see the drinks list. The brown café interior has Belgian provincial flags on the ceiling. Dinners include mussels, but no snacks. The 200+ exclusively Belgian beers including 25 on tap cover the usual bases but also cutting-edge names such as Struise and De la Senne.

Bierprofessor

Stratumseind 33 · **T** 06 5535 5572
bierprofessor.nl
Shut Mo; Fr from 16.00; others from 20.00

This very basic small café with a tiny terrace is another standout on the Strat. Snacks include 'Dutch Balls', by which they mean *bitterballen*. A beer list of 250 is rising slowly, with an improving range from smaller Dutch brewers: bottles on the wall are a better guide to availability than the printed menu.

Centraal

Markt 8 · **T** 040 245 2689
centraaleindhoven.nl
Su from 11.00; others from 10.00.

Long-established grand café with large terrace and spillover upstairs dining room for weekends. Full food menu. Its 70+ beers, with six guest taps, comprise the best range on the main square, which continues to improve with more Dutch craft getting a look in. History buffs should note that this is also where the author drank his very first Beer in the Netherlands, in 1989.

Drinker's Pub

Kerkstraat 11 · **T** 040 246 8121
drinkerspub.nl
Fr–Su from 13.00; others from 14.00

Deep narrow pub with a tiny terrace. The rough and ready interior has concrete floors and battered furniture. Finger food and main dishes served. The spectacular choice of around 1,000 beers from a seemingly endless parade of fridges behind the counter covers every base of the craft beer universe. Oldskool and Germany's Schneider Weisse get top billing among the 28 taps.

The Jack

Stratumseind 55
cafethejack.nl
Shut Mo&Tu; Fr from 15.00; Sa from 17.00; Su from 14.00; others from 19.30

Tatty, rough-edged rock café providing another oasis of beeriness on the Strat, with a small terrace, no-frills interior, pool table

and occasional live music. Look out for the guitar and medieval helmet behind the bar. No food. The 100+ beers are a pleasing mix of Dutch micros and imported craft.

Miss Paddle

Wal 7 · **T** 040 244 8756
misspaddle.nl
Shut Su–Tu; others from 12.00

Cosy café with modern wood furnishings, tiled floors and a curious inside-out bar where 10 taps dispense on the public side. Other diversions include a shuffleboard game and a skylight at the back looking up at nearby Catharinakerk. Despite what some minds may infer, the 'paddles' are wooden scoops used to serve the house speciality *flammkuchen*. Notably, all 60+ beers are from Dutch Brabant, mostly from local micros.

Van Moll

Keizersgracht 16A · T: 040 848 7255
vanmollcraftbeer.com
Shut Mo; Tu&We from 17.00; others from 15.00

Central brewpub with small terrace. A split-level industrial chic interior was formerly an office but now exhibits bespoke art illuminated by former runway lights from Eindhoven Airport. Snacks only. Half the 24 taps dispense beers from the brewery in the cellar, while the others, alongside 150+ bottles and cans, pluck the best from Dutch and international craft brewers. There are regular tap takeovers.

Eindhoven

Veem

Torenallee 86 · **T** 06 1381 2616
brouwerijhetveem.nl
Shut Mo–Tu; others 12.00–00.00

Modern brewpub in a former Philips factory
west of the centre, now the Vershal indoor
market. The taproom has picture windows
down one side, a bar down the other and the
brewery at the end. Snacks only, or bring in
anything from the adjacent food outlets. The
24 taps feature the house range and guests,
with 50-odd guest bottles and cans. A next-
door bottle shop under the same name
(Torenallee 86 – **T** 06 1381 2616 –
brouwerijhetveem.nl – *Su 12.00–19.00;
others 10.00–19.00*) has 600+ choices.

OTHER BEER VENUES
Central Irish pub **O'Sheas** (Jan van
Lieshoutstraat 9 – **T** 040 246 6213 –
osheaseindhoven.com – *daily from 13.00*)
has 50 beers, half of them from small
Dutch micros.
An oddity south of the centre, **Paviljoen
Genneper Parken** (Antoon Coolenlaan 2a – **T**
040 252 4632 – **paviljoengenneperparken.nl** –
shut Mo; Sa&Su 10.00–2.00; others 11.00–22.00) is
the café of a minigolf course with 55+ beers,
mostly from Eindhoven and Brabant micros.
Sala Thai (Staringstraat 31 – **T** 040 243 4101 –
restaurantsalathai.nl – *daily 17.30–22.30*) is a
restaurant combining excellent Thai food
with 20 or so mostly local craft beers.

BEER TO GO
Bierbrigadier (Bergstraat 41 – **T** 06 4352 3195
– **bierbrigadier.nl** – *shut Mo; Tu 12.00–18.00; Fr
11.00–20.00; Sa 11.00–18.00; Su 12.00–17.00; others
12.00–20.00*) has a growing range of 600+
global craft gems.

With a combined beer and wine range
arranged from light to dark and heavy, **Bottle
Shop** (Geldropseweg 86 – **T** 040 737 0504 – *Sa
10.00–18.00; Su&Mo 12.00–18.00; others 10.00–20.00*)
focuses on quality above its limited quantity.
West of the centre, **E Drinks** (Hurksestraat 44
– **T** 040 252 5856 – **edrinks.nl** – *shut Su;
Mo 13.00–18.00; Fr 10.00–20.00; Sa 09.00–17.00;
others 10.00–18.00*) stocks 600+ beers.
Veem: see above.
Suburban drinks warehouse **Wijnhuis Eindhoven**
(Vlokhovenseweg 46 – **T** 040 206 5560 –
wijnhuiseindhoven.nl – *shut Su; Mo 13.00–18.00;
Fr 09.00–20.00; Sa 09.00–17.00; others 09.00–18.00*)
has a growing range, 750 at the last count.

ETTEN-LEUR
10km W from Breda off A58 exit 18
🚄 Etten-Leur

Two neighbouring provincial towns that were
forged into one in 1968 (pop 43,000).

Pastoor

Lange Brugstraat 15 · **T** 076 503 5194
cafe-depastoor.nl
Daily from 11.00

Friendly suburban local northeast of the
centre: take bus 215 or 216 from the station.
The brown café interior has beer enamels for
decor and a billiards table. Full lunch menu;
snacks and tapas thereafter. The 100+ beers
are mainly Belgian but the menu highlights
local brewers with a handy red-white
chequered Brabant flag. There is also a guest
crate of some 20 changing beers in very
limited quantities.

GELDROP
6km ESE from Eindhoven off A67 exit 34
🚄 Geldrop

Quiet town (pop 28,800) near Eindhoven, home
to the nation's favourite brand of *ontbijtkoek*
('breakfast cake', a traditional spiced cake),
after which the entry below is named.

Peijnenburg

Heuvel 1 · **T** 040 286 7000
kaffeepeijnenburg.nl
Daily 10.00–00.00

This café with a spacious terrace functions as the Nijver taproom. The modern interior is themed with breakfast cake memorabilia and posters while the brewery is in the adjacent hotel. Lunches and dinners are from an open kitchen, with snacks served all day. House beers are poured from 75cl bottles alongside 50-odd guests including some from small Dutch micros.

GEMERT

24km NE from Eindhoven off N272
Bus 322

Large village (pop 15,900) in the Brabant hinterland. At the centre is the Heilige Losbol, a statue of a decapitated St Dionysius. He was beheaded by pagans around the year 250 for building a church where Notre Dame now stands in Paris, though quite what that has to do with Gemert is not clear.

Gij & Ik

Ridderplein 35 · **T** 06 1004 5316
gijenik.nl
Daily from 11.00

Thou & Me is a large local with a terrace beside the Losbol statue. One interior wall is covered in beer enamel-smothered carpet,

Gij & Ik

while lampshades are made from rings of upended bottles. A glass beer fridge dominates behind the bar. Full food menu served. The 150+ beers are largely Belgian but branch out with several local and other Dutch craft options.

GRAVE

15km SW from Nijmegen along N324
Bus 9, 99

Small settlement (pop 8,700) beside the Maas that got its town rights in 1233. It is much jollier than English speakers may assume from the name, especially during the pre-Lent carnival.

Maaspoort

Maasstraat 20 · **T** 0486 475618
maaspoort-grave.nl
Shut We; others from 11.00

Popular light-brown café with a terrace almost overlooking the river. Hanging plants, accordions, beer enamels and a wall of bottles dominate the decor. An open kitchen produces lunches and dinners. The 150 beers are mostly Belgian but find space for some Dutch: the list on the wall is a work of fiction so ask for the paper menu.

HEESCH

18km E from 's-Hertogenbosch off A59 exit 52
Bus 305 from Oss

Provincial town (pop 13,400).

Heesch Pannekoekenhuis

Osseweg 8 · **T** 0412 655545
pannenkoekenhuisheesch.nl
Shut Mo; Su 12.00–20.30; others 16.00–20.30

The bus passes the door of this large restaurant on the north side of village, with a vast terrace and a play area for kids. A brick-floored conservatory adjoins the main bar and restaurant area. The food menu is broad, but as the clue in the name hints, the stars are the 120+ pancake varieties. The beers only make half that number but include a full range from local Muifel.

HEEZE

13km SE from Eindhoven off A67 exit 34
🚉 Heeze

Quiet small town (pop 9,700) with a beautiful moated castle in the woods (**kasteelheeze.nl**).

Zwaan

Kapelstraat 23 · **T** 040 226 4357
tapperijdezwaan.nl
Daily from 10.00

The Swan is a white-painted village local with a terrace by the castle gates which has been serving booze in one form or other for 300 years. The brick and wood interior has partly stained-glass windows and wrought iron touches. A full food menu is available. The beer menu keeps creeping up and has passed 200, with plenty of Dutch micros in evidence.

HELMOND

14km E from Eindhoven on N270
🚉 Helmond

Medium-sized town (pop 90,000) with a well-preserved castle dating from 1350 and now housing the town museum (**museumhelmond.nl**). For a rundown of the local notables, see the row of mugshots opposite the Vijfhoeck (below).

Bascule

Havenweg 8–14 · **T** 0492 200020
facebook.com/cafebardebascule
*Fr&Sa from 15.00; Su 14.00–23.00;
others from 18.00*

Newish corner sports café with an almost-canalside terrace. The modern brown interior has art deco lighting and several TVs showing various sports simultaneously. Snacks only. Around 100 beers, including 20 taps, feature a decent selection of local and wider Dutch micros, among them the including the quite decent house Bascule Pale Ale, brewed by Hooglander.

Brouwer

Dorpsstraat 39 · **T** 0492 523998
cafednbrouwer.nl
*Shut We; Mo&Tu from 19.30; Su 12.00–22.00;
others from 12.00*

Suburban village local 3km northwest of town centre, on an inconvenient bus route that only operates when the pub is shut. The conservatory/terrace is the best part of this basic standing-only boozer. Simple lunches and snacks. The 100+ beers include local Kat and Strijder, but there's no printed menu and the landlord may try to steer you in the direction of his favoured Belgians.

Deftige Aap

Markt 14 · **T** 06 2152 7704
deftigeaap.nl
*Fr 11.00–23.00; Sa 09.00–22.00; Su 12.00–18.00;
others 10.00–22.00*

The Posh Ape brewpub is in a 1550 building given a modern makeover, its most striking feature being a high half-timbered ceiling. Down below is a nifty beer glass conveyor belt art installation, a bar counter lined with 'safe doors', and a brewhouse at the rear. Dinners and snacks served. Ten taps pour house beers and guests, with a similar range in bottles/cans.

Lokaal 42

Markt 42 · **T** 06 2354 2605
lokaal42.nl
Shut Mo&Tu; Su from 14.00; others from 12.00

Cosy music café with a terrace on the market square. The brown café interior is dominated by stage lighting used to for live bands. There is a full food menu. We were promised in the previous edition that the beer list would expand, and it's now nearing 100, with some local and wider Dutch craft options.

Muziekcafé

Zuid Koninginnewal 39
muziekcafehelmond.nl
Shut Tu; Fr–Su from 17.00; others from 20.00

One notch louder and three tattier than the previous entry, this grungy but friendly rock café features regular live bands, with a music-themed mural beside the stage and football shirts pinned to the ceiling. No food. The 65+ beers feature several Dutch craft options, but ordering one may cause heads to turn as most regulars swig the house pils from bottles.

Vijfhoeck

Kamstraat 26 · **T** 0492 834544
devijfhoeck.nl
Fr&Sa from 12.00; Su 12.00–23.00; others 16.00–23.00

Industrial-chic café in a former warehouse with view of Helmond Castle from the terrace. The bar has a glass-walled cold room at one end and mezzanine above. Full food menu served. Though its logo strapline proclaims it a *stadsbrouwerij*, the house beers are brewed in Belgium. The 130+ guest beers and 26 taps more than justify inclusion, however, with plenty of local colour.

's-HERTOGENBOSCH

🚆 's-Hertogenbosch

Brabant's attractive provincial capital (pop 151,000) is known universally by its colloquial name Den Bosch (pronounced 'denn boss'). The impressive 1530 St John's Cathedral was even grander before the western tower burned down in 1830.

The city's most famous son is Hieronymus Bosch, he of the nightmarish visions in paint, whose statue stands on the Markt square. Also notable is 13th-century De Moriaan, the nation's oldest brick house.

Basiliek

Hinthamerstraat 83 · **T** 073 737 0230
stadscafedebasiliek.nl
Shut Mo&Tu; Fr from 12.00; Sa from 10.00; Su 12.00–22.00; others from 15.00

This convivial ABT café near the cathedral has carnival-themed decor suggesting it is best avoided before Lent. A contraption above the billiard table can be lowered to create four extra tables. Snacks can include local speciality Bossche Bol, a giant chocolate éclair. A list of around 160 beers focuses on Belgium but includes local D'n Draok.

St John's (
's-Hertoge

Bossche Brouwers aan de Vaart

Tramkade 29 · **T** 06 2252 1380
bosschebrouwers.nl
Shut Mo–We; Th from 20.00; Su 14.00–21.30; others from 16.00

Canalside taproom in a former animal feed plant with numerous glass-bottomed hoppers still hanging above the industrial-chic bar. Live bands regularly perform on the podium. Snacks only. The availability of house beers is haphazard due to the relaxed attitude towards brewing here, but there are 100 guests including a strong Den Bosch and Brabant showing.

Jongens van de Wit

Hofvijver 4 · **T** 073 302 0014
jvandew.nl
Shut Mo; others 11.00–23.00

Bossche Stadsbrouwerij brewpub south of station, with glass frontage, large terrace and brewery on a mezzanine. A full food menu is served (*12.00–21.00*). The 100+ beers include 24 taps, with the house range sold on draught and in litre bottles to carry out. An eclectic guest range throws up occasional local and international surprises.

Jongens v
's-Hertoge

Keyzer

Korte Putstraat 24 · **T** 06 2239 3075
tapperijdekeyzer.nl
Shut Mo–We; Th&Fr from 16.00; others from 14.00

This charming one-room bar with a tiny terrace on a narrow street has an Edwardian parlour vibe: rugs on seats and tables as well as the floor, mirrors, chandeliers and a bookcase with leather-bound volumes. Free tapas are served with each round ordered before 20.00. Space limits draught options to three taps but the 90 bottles include some local brewers.

Le Duc

Korenbrugstraat 5 · **T** 073 613 6915
cafebarleduc.nl
Su from 12.00; Mo from 13.30; others from 11.00

This long-established and often crowded pub is now the Van Kollenburg taproom. Beyond the terrace, the interior bric-a-brac has a vaguely aquatic theme, a raised seating area at the rear and a stash of stuffed frogs above the front window. Full food menu served. Six draught house Kolleke brews figure among a range of 100+ including guest taps, once mainly Belgian but becoming more international.

M'n Tante

Korenbrugstraat 7 · **T** 073 613 4030
Fr&Su from 14.00; Sa from 11.00; others from 15.00.

My Auntie is a convivial light-brown café with a small, often-packed terrace. Black and white photos of worthy ladies (aunts, we assume) adorn the wall of the bricktile-floored interior. Snacks only. Cabinets opposite the bar display the range of 80-odd beers, once top-heavy with Belgians but now with an increasing Dutch presence.

Palm

Hinthamerstraat 82 · **T** 073 851 8663
cafedepalm.nl
Sa&Su from 12.00; others from 15.00

Compact and busy modern brown café with a front terrace. Beer menus occupy most wall space, interspersed with arty monochrome photos. A full dinner menu includes tapas, burgers and satay; snacks and toasties at other times. The 70+ beers are Belgian-oriented but include a few Dutch microbrews and several global craft options.

Paultje

Lepelstraat 31a · **T** 073 612 4441
tpaultje.nl
Daily from 13.00

Little Paul is a popular beerhunter's paradise in an unassuming modern brick building with a terrace and a light-brown interior. Snacks available. The beer list is a joy: only 11 taps but more than 400 bottles and cans, with an impressive core list and 80 or more sometimes spectacular guests. If that doesn't satisfy, they stock 60 whiskies.

Tap Punt

Minderbroedersstraat 28 · **T** 073 303 1600
tappuntzuid.nl
Shut Mo&Tu; Su from 13.00; others from 12.00

This modern, tile-floored café has a terrace out front and a mezzanine above. The front bar is dominated by a giant lighting display advertising the 10 taps. Food is mostly *flammkuchen*. Locals are well-represented besides international craft choices across both taps and around 100 bottles and cans. There is a tap takeover every last Wednesday of the month.

Thornbridge Pub

Koninginnenlaan 28–30 · **T** 073 888 9264
thornbridge.nl
Su from 11.00; Mo&Tu from 15.00; others from 13.00

The Derbyshire brewery's first pub outside the UK is a co-production with the owners of Paultje (above). This delightful boozer north of

Kareltje, Heu...

the station has tiled floors and a wood-beamed ceiling. Dinners (*from 17.00*) and a Sunday-only breakfast (*until 14.30*); snacks at other times. The 22 taps include three cask handpumps, keg options also from Thornbridge and eight lines reserved for interesting guests.

Veulen

Korenbrugstraat 9a · **T** 073 612 3038
hetveulen.nl
Fr from 14.00; Sa from 11.00; Su 14.00–23.00; others from 15.00

Like its immediate neighbours Le Duc and M'n Tante (above), this bustling café is often standing room only even on the terrace. The interior is largely wood and mirrors, with bar stools but few tables. Snacks only, but including snails. Among the 60+ beers are several from La Trappe and a house blond commissioned from Eem.

OTHER BEER VENUES
Bar35 (Lepelstraat 35 – **T** 073 720 0877 – bar35.nl – *Mo 16.00–23.00; others from 09.30*) is a modern burger bar with 40+ beers, mostly from Dutch micros.
Open since 1917, characterful tiny local **Bonte Palet** (Hinthamerstraat 99 – **T** 073 613 2532 – *shut Mo&Tu; others from 15.00*) nearly collapses under the weight of its collected bric-a-brac.

BEER TO GO
North of the centre, **Copernicus 2000** (Gruttostraat 21 – **T** 073 613 8824 – copernicus2000.nl – *shut Su; Mo 10.00–18.00; Tu&We 08.00–18.00; FSa 09.00–17.00; others 08.00–21.00*) has 600 beers.

HEUSDEN

15km WNW from 's-Hertogenbosch off N267
Bus 135

Attractive, fortified village (pop 5,500) with cobbled streets leading to a little riverside harbour with a wooden drawbridge and windmill – as Dutch as you can get without a woman in clogs selling tulips and a man dragging on a joint while lobbing an old bicycle into the water.

Kareltje

Burchtplein 5 · **T** 0416 660039
kareltje.info
May-mid-Sep: shut Mo&Tu; We from 19.00; others from 12.00. Mid-Sep–Apr: shut Mo–We; Sa from 14.00; Su from 12.00; others from 19.00

Possibly the only brewery to share its name with its resident spaniels: Kareltjes 1 and 2 patrol the pub and terrace. The cutely compact two-room pub has copper pipes going everywhere. Snacks only. There are usually two or three house brews among the 30+ beers, plus a range of house-made liqueurs.

OTHER BEER VENUES
The lovely harbourside **Havenzicht** (Vismarkt 2 – **T** 0416 662723 – **havenzicht.nl** – *daily from 10.00*) is the perfect spot for a brew with a view.

HILVARENBEEK

10km S from Tilburg off N269
Bus 142, 143

A town in name (pop 8,600) but with a village green, the Vrijthof, at its heart, albeit without the crack of leather on willow.
HOTEL TIP: **Sint Petrus** ★★, Gelderstraat 1 (**sintpetrus.nl**) is beside and run by the Taverne Paulus (below).

Gouden Carolus

Gelderstraat 20 · **T** 013 505 3178
goudencarolus.nl
Fr from 16.30; Sa from 20.00; Su 13.00–21.00; others from 19.00

Corner local with hearth, billiard table and ceiling hung with instruments and marionettes. Hanging on a back wall is a line of possibly 10 green bottles – insert your own gag. Two antique porcelain taps sit atop the bar. Snacks only. The 100+ beers include, unsurprisingly, the full Gouden Carolus range from Het Anker in Belgium as well as some local De Roos.

Roos

St. Sebastiaanstraat 4 · **T** 013 505 5045
museumbrouwerij.nl
Shut Mo&Tu (all year), We&Th (Sep–Jun);
others 13.00–17.00

Brewery tap and museum café north of Vrijthof.
There's no admission charge to reach the bar
in a wooden loft, which like museum and
brewery is staffed by volunteers, hence the
limited hours. Nuts only. There are usually
six house beers on tap plus whatever bottles
are in stock, also sold to take home.
See also Beer tourism.

Schouwke

Vrijthof 18 · **T** 013 505 3554 · **tschouwke.nl**
Shut Mo; Th&Su from 10.00; others from 11.30

Café with a terrace beside the village green.
The modern brown interior has wood-beamed
ceilings, a cast-iron stove and hipster lampshades. Lunches (*12.00–17.00*) and dinners
(*17.00–20.00*) served; snacks at other times.
Around 50 core beers are supplemented by
40 guests mostly from Dutch micros, bought
in small batches to ensure turnover.

OTHER BEER VENUES
Paulus (Gelderstraat 3 – **T** 013 505 5833 –
tavernepaulus.nl – *Su from 15.00; others from
16.00*) is a cosy tavern with leather armchairs,
fireplaces and around 40 beers.

KAATSHEUVEL

15km N from Tilburg via A261/N261

Small town (pop 16,600) known chiefly for
the Efteling amusement park (**efteling.com**).

Roestelberg

Roestelbergseweg 2 · **T** 0416 333079
de-roestelberg.nl
Mo from 10.30–20.30; others 09.15–20.30.

Country pub in an attractive location beside
the Loonse en Drunense Duinen, an area of
inland dunes: there's no convenient bus,
though it's a pleasant 3km walk mainly on
footpaths south and east from Vaartstraat
bus stop in Kaatsheuvel, on the 300 or 301

bus route from Tilburg. The expansive terrace
is almost on the sand, while the massive
interior seems set up for coach parties. The
food menu features 40 different pancakes.
The 60+ beers include local St Crispijn and the
house Roestelaere amber from nearby 3 Horne.

KNEGSEL

12km WSW from Eindhoven
Bus 294 from Vessem

You do pronounce the 'K' of this leafy village
(pop 1,300).

Kempen

Het Groen 14 · **T** 040 205 5032
dineecafedekempen.nl
Daily from 10.00

Large central modern café with black slate
floors, stylish furnishings and large terraces
front and back. Lunches and dinners served,
with snacks in between. Most of the interest
among the 100 beers is Belgian, but there are
Dutch interlopers on the IPA side. The house
H.E.N.K. is a blond ale made at Ramses.

LIESHOUT

15km NE from Eindhoven off N615
Bus 322

Brabant village (pop 4,300) dominated by the
country's largest independent brewery. Most
locals will know someone who works there.

Bavaria Brouwerijcafé

Heuvel 5 · **T** 0499 425585
bavariabrouwerijcafe.nl
Mo from 12.00; others from 10.00

Modern brasserie with two terraces 100m
from the brewery, and which functions as its
taproom. The decor misses no opportunity to
promote the brand. Lunch and dinner served.
Besides the house range, there are 50+ beers
from the many other beery pies in which
Bavaria has its fingers: La Trappe, De Molen,
Palm and Maallust, to name a few.

MADE

12km N from Breda off A59
Bus 123

Small commuter town (pop 12,000) near Oosterhout.

The Pub

Kloosterstraat 36 · **T** 0162 690590
thepubandchurchill.nl
Fr-Su from 12.00; others from 16.00

English-style pub and beer garden with Chesterfield sofas and fireplaces. Food is pub grub including fish and chips. The 10 taps include several cask handpumps, a rarity in the Netherlands, and the casks themselves are visible in the open cellar. The 90-odd bottled and canned selection presents some local Brabant offerings, with a few cellar-aged brews.

MOERGESTEL

7km ESE from Tilburg off A58
Bus 141

Small town (pop 6,000) that functions as a sleepover for Tilburg workers.

Reuselhoeve

Heizenschedijk 1 · **T** 013 503 6031
reuselhoeve.nl
Fr-Su 10.00-23.00; others 10.00-21.00
(winter hours may vary)

The barn-like Reuzen taproom, 3km from the village and with no handy bus, has a bucolic

terrace for birdwatching and a rope garden for kids. The brewery is on the first floor, the taproom below, with conditioning tanks visible through a glass floor panel in the latter. Simple lunches available; apple pie all day. The house beers are served on tap and in bottle.

Veerkes

Sint Jansplein 3 · **T** 013 513 2405
deveerkes.nl
Shut Mo&Tu; Th from 19.00; Su 13.00-23.00;
others from 14.00

Friendly local with worn floors and green walls. Its terrace is on the main square, which would be more attractive were it not otherwise a car park. Snacks and toasties only. The improving selection of 90 beers includes plenty of changing guest bottles and everything from its two near neighbours, La Trappe and Reuzen.

NUENEN

7km ENE from Eindhoven off A270
Bus 6, 321, 322

Attractive village (pop 19,900) with a central green. Van Gogh lived here when he was struck with the painting muse: visit the Vincentre (vangoghvillagenuenen.nl) to learn more.

Ons Dorp

Parkstraat 1 · **T** 040 842 8879
cafeonsdorp.nl
Shut Tu&We; Su&Mo from 13.00; others from 15.00

Friendly corner local with a sheltered terrace south of the green. Inside is a compact one-room café with barrels for some tables and a menu of bottles on the wall. Snacks only, but the list is long. The 100+ beers have a good local and regional bias. Also check out the 'beer safe' to the left of the bar filled with limited editions.

OIJEN

25km NE from 's-Hertogenbosch off N329

Small village (pop 1,100) on the south bank of the Maas.

Oijen

Oijense Bovendijk 61 · **T** 0412 492217
speciaalbierbrouwerij.nl

Apr–Oct: Sa&Su from 10.30; others from 11.00.
Nov–Mar: Shut Tu; Fr–Su from 11.00; others from 17.00

Take bus 296 from Oss to Macheren Dorpstraat and walk 15 minutes northwest to find this rural taproom with a large terrace. The extensive multi-room interior has higgledy-piggledy charm, with a long wooden conservatory down one side and a part-farmhouse, part-barn interior featuring low doors and gingham curtains. There is a full food menu; dinners sometimes include a *braai* barbecue. House beers are sold on tap, in bottle and to take away.

OIRSCHOT

17km NW from Eindhoven off A58
Bus 141, 142 from Best

Small town (pop 11,500) with cobbled streets and a disproportionately large church.

Vandeoirsprong

Koestraat 20 · **T** 0499 572002
vandeoirsprong.nl

Shut Tu; Fr 16.00–23.00; Sa 12.00–23.00;
Su 12.00–22.00; others 16.00–22.00

From the Source is a large taproom with a big terrace in the bottling plant of the former Kroon brewery. The interior goes for industrial chic, with bare brick walls and upcycled wooden tables. Snacks and burgers available. Up to a dozen house beers are on tap or sold in bottles to take home. To see the orignal 1665 Kroon brewery tap, book a brewery tour (see Beer tourism).

OTHER BEER VENUES

Contrasting with the above modernity, **Oud Brabant** (Markt 14 – **T** 0499 575509 – oudbrabant.nl – *shut Tu; Sa from 12.00; Su from 11.00; others from 14.00*) is a traditional village pub with carpeted tables and few local beers.

OISTERWIJK

11km E from Tilburg off N65
🚄 Oisterwijk

Small town (pop 19,800) with a tree-lined avenue, De Lind, running through its heart and a picturesque fenland nature reserve to the south.

Bierbaronnen

Lindeplein 11 · **T** 013 203 6026
bierbaronnen.nl

Shut Mo&Tu; others from 12.00

Modern terrace café with a terrace, and beer-themed murals on brick and plaster walls inside. Snacks and lunches served. Whilst there are a couple of international gatecrashers among the 16 taps, the remarkable 250+ bottled and canned range is exclusively from North Brabant, including many hard-to-find nanobrewers.

Boshuis Venkraai

Bosweg 162 · **T** 013 528 2396
boshuisvenkraai.nl

Su 09.00–19.00; others 10.00–19.00

To find this lovely café with a large terrace surrounded by woods, fens and ponds 2.5km south of the station, follow Stationsstraat to its end, through several name changes, turn right and left and continue on the path when the road runs out. The interior is typical brown café, with simple meals. The beer list hovers around 60 including local Reuzen.

Gelagh

Lindeplein 3 · **T** 013 522 0127
proeflokaaltgelagh.nl
Shut Tu; Fr–Su from 13.00; others from 15.00

Large two-roomed beer café with front terrace, equipped with wood-panelled walls that granted it instant authority when it opened in 2009. Snacks only. The 180 beers lean mainly to Belgium but include more local choices like Jopen and Vandeoirsprong plus a few UK and US imports. There's an impressive range of 230 malt whiskies.

OOSTERHOUT
10km NW from Breda off A27
Bus 325, 326, 327

Large town (pop 55,000) without a station.

Beurs

Klappeijstraat 4 · **T** 0162 453477
cafedebeurs.nl
Sa&Su from 11.00; others from 14.00

Expansive beer café near the main square, with a detached terrace on that square. The interior contains a British telephone box filled with the extensive whisky selection. Ceiling fans give the whole a whiff of colonial club. Snacks only. The 200+ beers are strong on local, Dutch and US craft, with house Goud Tripel and Zilver Blond brewed by Pimpelmeesch.

OSS
18km E from 's-Hertogenbosch off A59 exit 52
Oss

Tidy town (pop 57,800) with a modern centre. *Os* is Dutch for 'ox', hence the cattle heads that appear as pedestrian crossing lights. Trivia for football fans of a certain age: Ruud van Nistelrooy was born here.

H32

Heuvel 32 · **T** 0412 856128
h32.nl
Su&Mo from 10.30; others from 10.00

Modern multi-room grand café with an expansive terrace on the main square and a part-tiled, part-parquet interior. A full restaurant menu is prepared in an open kitchen. Around 75 beers include a 'self-service wall' with 12 taps which is often where the main interest lies: Uiltje, Kees! and Van Moll have all been spotted. There's a bottle shop at the rear.

Kaatje

Oostwal 196
cafekaatje.nl
Shut Mo–We; others from 20.00

A corner local since 1882 and currently a delightfully tatty rock music pub. Behind the pool table and stage is a mural that will be familiar to those who associate Rainbow with music, not kids' TV. The ceiling is plastered with album covers and vinyl from the classic rock era. Snacks only. The 150 beers justify a visit, with a good range of Dutch and international craft.

Nieuwe Wereld

Heuvel 29 · **T** 0412 658424
dnw-oss.nl
Tu from 10.00; Su from 12.00; others from 11.00

Stylish café with a terrace on a square and
a mezzanine at the back. A clock on one
wall masquerades as an altimeter, while
an anglepoise 'tarantula' chandelier takes
centre stage. Copper tanks behind the bar
are a nice touch. Food is posh pub grub.
The 55+ beers are borderline full entry,
but a strong showing of Dutch craft, with
Uiltje and local Muifel, gets it the nod.

OTHER BEER VENUES
Groene Engel (Kruisstraat 15 – **T** 0412 405504
– **groene-engel.nl** – *Mo-We from 14.00; Su from
13.00; others from 12.00*) is a theatre café with
a decent selection of 50 beers.

BEER TO GO
Wijnhuis (Zaltbommelseweg 22 – **T** 0412
632504 – **wijnhuisoss.nl** – *shut Su; Mo 13.00-18.00;
Th 09.00-21.00; Sa 09.00-17.00; others 09.00-18.00*)
is a large suburban off-licence with 600+
international beers.

RAAMSDONKVEER

20km NNW from Breda off A59 exit 34
Bus 326

Quiet provincial town (pop 12,300).

Twee Leeuwen

Keizersdijk 5c · **T** 06 5731 1866
detweeleeuwen.com
Fr 14.35-22.30 & Su 14.35-20.30 only

You'll find the Two Lions brewery and
taproom down a small alley off the main
street. Bare brick walls, wooden ceiling and
simple furnishings suggest the main funding
priority was the copper brewing kit in one
corner. Snacks only. Twelve house beers are
served on tap, with bottles to take away.

RAVENSTEIN

20km WSW from Nijmegen off A50 exit 17
Ravenstein

Cutesy old Brabant village (pop 3,500)
with narrow cobbled streets that used to
be a Vrijstad, a Catholic enclave amid
a sea of Protestantism.

Wilskracht

Molensingel 6 · **T** 06 5570 8153
stadsbrouwerijravenstein.nl
Shut Mo-Th; Fr-Sa 10.00-18.00; Su 13.00-18.00

Brewery tap in Brabant's tallest smock mill.
A cobbled terrace has fine views, courtesy of
the raised mound on which everything perches.
The brewery is glassed off at the back of an
adjoining building that also houses a café, part
of the old fortifications guarded by a cannon
outside the window. Nuts only. House beers
are sold in bottles to drink in or take away.

REUSEL

28km WSW from Eindhoven among N284
Bus 319

Quiet village near the Belgian border
(pop. 8,500)

Ouwe Brandtoren

Burgemeester Willekenslaan 2 · **T** 0497 620311
ouwe-brandtoren.nl
Fr-Su 09.30-22.00; others 09.30-18.00
(22.00 in high summer)

This lovely countryside tavern beside the
climbable forest fire lookout tower from
which it takes its name is a stiff half-hour

walk south from the nearest bus stop: bring stout shoes and GPS. There's a large green terrace and a tiled-floor interior with a wood-burning stove and heavy Germanic wooden furniture. Simple meals, snacks and ice cream available. Around 70 beers are mainly Belgian but more local offerings include Reusel's own Vergulde Pul range.

RIJEN

11km E from Breda off N282
🚃 Gilze-Rijen

Mainly residential provincial town (pop 16,800). If you hear choppers, it is because the nearby airfield is home to the Dutch Air Force's helicopter fleet.

Rijens Vat

Julianastraat 112 · **T** 0161 226850 · rijensvat.nl
Shut Su; Fr&Sa from 15.00; others from 19.00

The exterior of this whitewashed village local beside the station looks unassuming and its interior is hardly more exuberant: plain brown café with pool table and dartboard, and food that begins and ends with peanuts. But all will become clear once you see beer list: 250+ options with numerous craft contributions from around Europe and beyond.

ROOSENDAAL

🚃 Roosendaal

Provincial border town (pop 77,000), the last railway stop before Belgium. Fans of tacky ostentation should nip into the Passage shopping mall and check out the Milano Café. Hang around and you may see Marco Polo and Christopher Columbus perform a country and western duet. We'll say no more.

Brembos

Bergsebaan 164 · **T** 0165 379218
Shut Mo–Tu & Th; Tu 13.00–18.00; Fr from 16.00; Sa from 14.00; Su from 13.00 (14.00 in winter)

In the middle of nowhere, 3km south of Roosendaal and a 20-minute walk from the

closest bus stop (1 or 842 to Jasmijnberg), this place is worth the effort: a wonderfully woody old-fashioned local of the type they don't make 'em like any more, complete with a billiard table. Nibbles only. Around 90 beers, with plenty of Trappists and a good local showing from HillDevils. Check before travelling as it is often closed for private events.

Brembos Roosend...

Captain Cook's

Markt 17 · **T** 0165 599669
captaincooks.nl
Su from 11.30; others from 10.00

Popular grand café with rear beer garden, front terrace and an interior typically mock-aged with dark wood and polished brass. Apart from a few portraits of Hawaii's first celebrity murder victim, we are unsure of the link with the famous British explorer. Lunch and all-day tapas served downstairs; dinner upstairs from 17.00. Many global Trappists appear on its list of 65+ beers, alongside local Witte Anker.

Sjoes

Markt 16 · **T** 0165 564345
sjoes.nl
Shut Tu; Mo&Th from 19.00; Sa from 13.00; others from 14.00

This large boozer with a terrace is one of few on the main square to focus on beverages rather than food. Red walls and stucco ceilings make a change from standard-issue brown. Live blues music some nights. Snacks only. The growing beer list had reached 125 at the last count, with an increasing inclination towards Dutch and international craft.

SINT-OEDENRODE

17km N from Eindhoven off A50 exit 9
Bus 156, 157, 305
Neat, prosperous commuter town (pop 17,800).

Gasthuishoeve

Kremselen 2
gasthuishoeve.nl
Shut Mo-Tu; others 10.00-17.30

The RBM brewery and taproom operates
alongside a clog factory and bakery on this
farm amid countryside 3km west of the town
centre. A quaint old café is used for colder
weather, with a bar in a greenhouse that
features an indoor duck pond for when it's
warmer. Greenery abounds and the counter
is decorated with clogs. Lunches and snacks
served. Four or five house beers are served
in bottles and sold to take home.

STEENBERGEN

15km NW from Roosendaal off N259
Bus 111, 310 from Bergen op Zoom

Small town (pop 13,900) near the Zeeland
border, an important port in medieval times
with a harbour linked to the Rhine and Maas
delta. Wing Commander Guy Gibson of
Dambusters fame and his co-pilot Jim Warwick
lost their lives here in 1944 when their
Mosquito crashed on its way home from a raid:
they are buried in the Catholic cemetery.

Z'Onder Zeil

Kade 3 · **T** 0167 538399 · **zonderzeil.nl**
Shut Tu&We; Su from 14.00; others from 16.00

Friendly café with waterside terrace by a small
harbour. The nautical-themed interior has ships'
bells, sails and wheels. Karel the dead parrot
perches on a bell, even though he is no more
and has ceased to be. Dinners and snacks.
Around 80 beers include the house Z'Onder
Baard, a California common ('steam') ale made
by Ramses, and a vintage list of cellared
Belgian bottles.

TILBURG

Tilburg

Brabant's fast-growing second city (pop
217,000) and stepping off point for the Efteling
theme park. For quieter pastimes, the National
Textile Museum (**textielmuseum.nl**) reflects
its heritage as a centre of the wool trade.
HOTEL TIP: **City★★★**, Heuvelring 128
(**cityhoteltilburg.nl**) is a modern central hotel.

Anvers

Oude Markt 8 · **T** 013 583 3533 · **anvers.nl**
Su from 10.30; others from 10.00

A sprawling warren of a café with a large
terrace. The interior fills several rooms, all with
dark wood and white walls, the tallest of which
reaches all the way up to exposed rafters.
Food covers all bases from early to late. The
100-strong beer list is a mix of Dutch micros,
Belgian stalwarts and global craft.

Bakker

Heuvel 44-45 · **T** 013 889 7444
cafebakker.nl
*Shut Mo; Fr from 15.00; Sa&Su from 14.00;
others from 16.00*

Modern bar with brewing-themed murals,
homely lounge-styled area, front terrace and
rear beer garden. A full food menu is available.
The 70 beers are exclusively Dutch and mostly
from interesting craft micros, once you get
past the corporate owner's house brands.

Buitenbeentje

Heuvel 15a · **T** 013 536 0466
Daily from 15.00

Fabulously scruffy café and terrace on a
street of bars, with scuffed and barely
functional furniture. Works by Vermeer on
the walls are possibly not the originals.
The bar is sunken, requiring you to perch on
oddly low stools: if you order standing up,
the bar staff stare at your midriff. We
understand this is to reduce the steepness
of the descent to the cellar. Nibbles only.
You'll need to ask about the 120+ beers as
the list on the wall is largely historic.

Burgemeester Jansen

Piushaven 22 · **T** 013 545 1008
burgemeesterjansen.nl
Shut Mo; Su from 14.00; others from 15.00

Mayor Jansen is a cavernous one-room bar
with a terrace beside a gentrified industrial
harbour, with wall maps and what appears to
be an Aztec pyramid of Westvleteren crates
perched above the door. Snacks include
soups and toasties. A beer list of 200 with 22
taps divides itself between familiar Belgians,
and local, Dutch and international craft.
They also stock a big range of whiskies.

Jack's

Tuinstraat 81 · **T** 013 542 6322
cafejacks.nl
Shut Su&Mo; others from 20.00

Basic local two blocks south of the station.
A bar area at the front gives way to sporadic
seating at the back, while beer enamels
and three dartboards adorn otherwise plain
walls. Food is snacks, with occasional burger
nights. The 100-strong list fluctuates with
the moment as a large proportion comprises
guest beers, often from local micros.

Kandinsky

Telegraafstraat 58 · **T** 013 544 4924
biercafe-kandinsky.nl
Daily from 15.00

Long a beer oasis, this one-room corner bar
has plentiful breweriana and a narrow side

terrace. Snacks only. International craft brewers
have made significant inroads into a 250+ beer
list once slanted towards Belgian stalwarts.
And no, we don't know why it is named after
a Russian expressionist painter, though it does
provide an excuse to make a funky doodle out
of the café logo.

Little Devil

Stationsstraat 27 · **T** 013 545 2140
littledevil.nl
*Shut Mo; Sa from 15.00; Su from 13.00;
others from 17.00*

Rock music café near the station, feeling like
a regular brown café with a pool table when
there is no live music in the back room. No food
that we know of, beyond the food of love, in
which case play on. Guests from the global craft
scene account for a fair chunk of 70+ beers.

LOC

Burgemeester Brokxlaan 8–84
locbrewery.com
Fr&Sa only 16.00–22.00

Taproom in an ex-railway building NE of station.
A cluster of sofas adds a touch of comfort to
the basic interior, with brewery in one corner,
fermentation tanks behind glass and some
residual railway equipment. Snacks only. Beers
brewed on site are served from tap and bottle.
No cash payments.

Slagroom

Piusplein 6a · **T** 013 582 0070
slagroomtilburg.nl
Daily from 10.00

Whipped Cream is a grand café with a terrace on a popular square, its typical brown interior heavily featuring beer enamels. Rolls and toasties for lunch broaden into full dinners from 17.00. The 70+ beers are mainly corporate, but a healthy showing of Dutch craft guests such as Uiltje and Kompaan merits a full entry.

Spaarbank

Noordstraat 125 · **T** 013 543 8331
stadscafedespaarbank.nl
Su from 11.00; others from 10.00

Trendy corner café with rear beer garden and front terrace spilling over the road into a pocket park. The Savings Bank (its former life) has two semi-separate high-ceilinged bars, with a wood-burning stove at the back and seating rescued from rail carriages at the front. Lunches and dinners served; snacks all day. A third of the 75+ beers are Trappist ales.

Stadsbrouwerij 013

Piushaven 1 · **T** 013 207 0098
stadsbrouwerij013.nl
*Fr&Sa from 12.00; We&Th 12.00–23.00;
others 12.00–22.00*

Brewpub in an Amsterdam School-ish building with a terrace opposite the harbour. The brewery is on the left as you enter, while the café to the right has a black and white theme with booth seating down one side. Lunches, dinners and posh snacks served. House brews are joined by around 25 guests, mainly from the local area, with tasting flights available.

Taphuys

Piusplein 11–12 · **T** 013 203 3365 · taphuys.nl
Daily from 11.00

Modern polished wood and shiny metal place on a lively square. There is a full food menu including tapas-style dinners (*16.00-22.00*) designed for sharing in quantity. The 100+ beers include a decent range of 40 self-tapping options with no minimum volume: buy credit on a chip card, insert into the tap of your choice and pour.

Troubadour

Capucijnenstraat 54 · **T** 013 542 3438
troubadourtilburg.nl
*Shut We; Fr from 16.00; Sa&Su from 14.00;
others from 19.00*

Established and friendly billiards local on a quiet residential street south of the centre. Tables embedded with game boards such as Monopoly occupy the interior, alongside various bric-a-brac including an ornamental water pump behind the bar. Snacks only. Everything here is old-fashioned apart from the 150 beers, which include plentiful modern Dutch microbrews. Visiting brewers host regular tasting events.

Stadsbrouwerij 013, Tilburg

Zomerlust

Oisterwijksebaan 15 · **T** 013 542 5292
cafezomerlust.nl
*Shut Tu; Su 10.00–22.00; others from 11.00
(may open later in winter)*

One of the country's first specialist beer
cafés, Summer Madness has been family-run
since 1936 and remains a must-visit. Around
3km from the centre and 1km east of the
Sint-Josephstraat bus stop (141, 142, 143 from
Tilburg station), it's just beyond a canal
marking the city's eastern boundary, with a
terrace overlooking fields. The lovely interior
is lit by candles and art deco lamps. Simple
lunches until 18.00; snacks thereafter,
except for a book-ahead set meal on Fridays.
The 90 beers always include local 3 Horne's
Wiegeleier tripel on tap.

OTHER BEER VENUES
Ecclesiastically themed **Elfde Gebod**
(Paleisring 23 – **T** 013 536 6869 –
hetelfdegebod.eu – *Sa from 10.30; others
from 11.00*) is a charming brown café with
around 50 beers.
North of the station, **Lambiek**
(Wilhelminapark 66 – **T** 06 3603 7064 –
kaffeelambiek.nl – *Shut Tu; We 16.00–20.00;
Sa from 19.00; others from 16.00*) is a friendly
brown café with regular live rockabilly
music, but its once-proud beer list appears
to be on the slide.

BEER TO GO
Bierbrigadier (Telefoonstraat 39 – **T** 06 5232
1199 – **debierbrigadier.nl** – *shut Su&Mo;
Th 12.00–21.00; Sa 11.00–17.00; others 11.00–18.00*)
stocks 400+ global craft ales.
T-Drinks (Heuvelring 145 – **T** 013 580 1126 –
tdrinks.nl – *shut Su&Mo; Th 10.00–21.00; Sa 10.00–
17.00; others 10.00–18.00*) stocks 600+ beers,
with a good regional Dutch selection.

UDEN

28km ESE from 's-Hertogenbosch off A50
exit 13
Bus 305 from Eindhoven, 306 from
's-Hertogenbosch

Quiet provincial town (pop 36,300) that can trace
its origins to the 12th century. Little evidence of
its past remains, but there is one excellent
reason to visit.

Cravt

Markt 28 · **T** 06 1212 0043
cravtbrouwlokaal.nl
Fr-Su from 13.00; others from 16.00

Ultra-modern pub with a terrace on the main
square. The brick-walled interior has a world
map on one wall, plastic foliage on another
and a mock copper kettle at the rear. The space
between is dominated by a glass coldroom.
Snacks only, but the choice is substantial. The 16
taps could be more adventurous, but there's no
denying the calibre of the 300 bottles and cans,
with plenty of Dutch and international craft.

VALKENSWAARD

10km S from Eindhoven along N69
Bus 317, 318

Small town (pop 30,600) with a lively main square.
The name derives from its former position on a
falcon migration route, and many birds were
caught here for domestication in medieval days.

Bel

Markt 26 · **T** 040 204 7688
cafe-de-bel.nl
Daily from 10.00

Modern grand café with terrace and conservatory
in a row of modern grand cafés. Inside are brick
cobblestone floors and a large area at the back
that verges on a sports bar, with big screens and

pool tables. There is a full food menu. The 100+ beer list mainly consists of the usual Belgian suspects with an occasional Dutch craft surprise.

Fantast

Frans van Beststraat 9 · **T** 040 207 5822
fantast.nl
Shut Mo-We; Th from 20.00; Fr from 16.00; others from 15.00

Simply furnished light-brown café 400m east of the main square, with small terrace and live music on some weekends. Snacks only, but dinners are served at the adjoining Willem II, under the same management and with the same well-chosen beer list. Around 70 beers include plenty of local options such as Van Moll, with tasting flights available.

OTHER BEER VENUES
Tucked into one corner of the main square, **Swaen** (Markt 51 – **T** 040 201 2615 – **indeswaen.nl** – *shut; Th from 07.00; Su from 11.00; others from 15.00*) bills itself as a Trappist beer café, and heavenly ales account for virtually all the 45-odd choices.

VEGHEL

23km N from Eindhoven off A50 exit 11
Bus 305

Both our entries for this provincial town (pop. 31,500) are in a repurposed industrial area west of the centre, now a cultural complex with shops, bars and theatres.

Wittern

Verlengde Noordkade 4 · **T** 0413 782800
wittern.nl
Shut Mo-Tu; others from 12.00

Sprawling café and Vleeghel taproom with canalside terrace, vine-filled conservatory and brewhouse behind glass. Old hoppers and a 'stacked animal' sculpture in one corner allude to the building's former life as an animal feed plant. Full lunch and dinner menu. The house beers are served on tap alongside several corporate choices.

BEERS TO GO:
Uw Bierspecialist (Verlengde Noordkade 14; uwbierspecialist.nl; *Fr 10.00-21.00; Su 12.00-18.00; others 10.00-18.00*) is an Aladdin's cave with an impressive 1,700 global beers.

VELDHOVEN

6km SW from Eindhoven off A2 exit 30a
Buses: numerous from Eindhoven

Modern satellite town (pop 45,000), joined at the hip to Eindhoven.

Buurman

Heuvel 42 · **T** 06 2303 4132
biercafebuurman.nl
Shut Mo& Tu; Fr&Su from 16.00; others from 19.00

Bus 14 from Eindhoven to Heuvelstraat drops you 100m from this friendly modern local with a terrace beside a village green with bandstand. The sparsely furnished interior has recycled wood tile flooring, while glass fridges fill the wall behind the counter. Snacks only, with occasional soup and rolls. The 100+ beers include a good smattering of Brabant micros.

Wittern, Veghel

VOLKEL

30km ESE from 's -Hertogenbosch off N264
Bus 25, 26 from Uden

Small village (pop 3,400) near a military
airbase: you may get buzzed by fighter jets
if you sit outside.

Brabantse Hoeve

Zeelandsedijk 29 · brabantsehoeve.nl
Daily 10.00–22.00 (Nov–Mar: shuts 20.30 Mo–Th)

Country pub east of the village, with roadside
terrace, rear beer garden and B&B rooms.
The tiled-floor interior has a high ceiling with
wooden rafters, while beer enamels and a
chandelier constitute decor. Light lunches
served. There's local interest from Muifel
and Wijchense Schone among 160 otherwise
Belgian-leaning beers.

VUGHT

5km S from 's-Hertogenbosch off A2 exit 24
⊠ Vught

Tidy small town (pop 26,400) with a mix of
old and new architecture.

Oud Zuid

Marktveld 18 · T 06 2362 1501
cafe-oud-zuid.business.site
Shut Mo; Tu-Th from 16.00; others from 14.00

Friendly modern café with a terrace just east
of the centre. Mostly green lighting lends
a moody ambience to walls hung with beer-
themed pastiches of iconic paintings given a
witty makeover by an American artist. Snacks
only. Around 100 beers are mainly Belgian,
but locally brewed Uthoka has been spotted.

WAALWIJK

16km N from Tilburg off N261
Bus 300, 301

Largeish town (pop 47,500) lacking a rail
connection, but with several prominent 1920s
and 1930s buildings that give it a curious
modernist feel.

Proeflokaal

Grotestraat 222 · T 0416 534727
hetproeflokaalbrabant.nl
*Shut Mo-We; Th 14.00–23.00; Su 13.00–21.00;
others from 14.00*

Modern, airy bar decorated with oil drum lights
and ship's chains. It may one day become the
Nemeton taproom, once they sort out the
licences. Lunches and snacks served. The 32
taps and 100 bottles/cans cover a good range
of international craft. In theory you can also
order anything from among the 800+ choices
at the adjoining **Vinotake** shop (Grotestraat 222
– T 0416 534727 – hetproeflokaalbrabant.nl –
*shut Su-Tu; Fr 10.00–20.00; Sa 09.00–17.00; others
10.00–18.00*), which also boasts an extensive
range of whiskies and wines.

Proeflok...

Sint Crispijn

Winterdijk 10 · T 0416 745417
brouwerijsintcrispijn.nl
Shut Mo-We; Th&Fr from 16.00; others from 14.00

Taproom with informal terrace in a former
grain warehouse west of the centre.

Eclectically decorated, with rugs warming a concrete floor, a sofa corner and the brewery through glass at the rear. A photo on one wall shows the building in its former guise, while a painting of the brewing process adorns another. Snacks only. The house range is served on 10 taps, with bottles to take away.

BEER TO GO
Vinotake: see Proeflokaal above.

ZEELAND

25km SW from Nijmegen off N277
Bus 99 from Nijmegen or Uden

Neat Brabant village (pop 6,100), not to be confused with the province of the same name.

Brouwer

Kerkstraat 62 · **T** 0486 450886
herbergdenbrouwer.nl
Daily from 11.00

Sprawling complex comprising a bar, restaurant and B&B in a building that was once a brewery. The left half is chic brasserie, the right a brown café, with a large terrace that looks across at the village church. Choose your lunch or dinner from menus made from old vinyl album covers. At least 300 beers include local choices from Muifel, Wilskracht and others.

ZEVENBERGEN

18km NW from Breda off N285
Zevenbergen

Quiet provincial town (pop 14,300).

Bakkerij

Markt 7 · **T** 0168 327140
cafedebakkerij.nl
Shut Mo; Tu-Th from 14.00; others from 12.00

Brown café and Brood taproom, with a terrace on an attractive square: the brewery itself is in a nearby side street. The tiled-floor bar has musical instruments hanging from the ceiling, a pool table at the back and live

music some nights. Toasties and other snacks. Besides the house beers, 120 others include local Ramses and other Dutch craft.

ZUNDERT

16km SW from Breda on N263

Brabant village (pop 7,900), home to the eponymous brewery.

Den Hoek

Rucphenseweg 14 · **T** 076 597 2300
den-hoek.com
Shut Th; Su from 09.30; Mo&Tu from 13.00;
We from 18.00; others from 12.00

A café for over 90 years, the Corner is an unassuming rural local just beyond the village's western outskirts. It's a little tricky to reach: take bus 115 from Breda to Zundert Berkenlaan and walk 1.5km northwest, using a map to find the quickest route. Lunches and dinners (until 21.00) are often seasonal. Unsurprisingly, the 60+ beers include local Zundert alongside plentiful lambics and changing guests.

North Holland

North Holland (pop 2.8 million) is divided into two unequal halves by the IJsselmeer lake and the series of canals and locks linking it to the North Sea, allowing ludicrously oversized cruise ships to reach Amsterdam. The densely populated southern half runs from Haarlem to Hilversum, with industrial docklands occupying much of the waterside. Things get quieter and more agricultural as you travel north up the peninsula between lake and sea.

At the tip of the mainland you can continue by ferry to Texel, the largest of the Wadden Islands. Alternatively, veer northeast across the 32km Afsluitdijk, one of the 20th century's great engineering marvels. When completed in 1933, it converted the former Zuiderzee bay into the 1,700 sq km IJsselmeer, Western Europe's largest freshwater lake, itself later split in two by the dyke from Flevoland to Enkhuizen that created the Markermeer.

Considering Amsterdam's role in the international beer trade over centuries, it is no surprise to find the province has a high concentration of breweries.

LARGEST CENTRES: **Alkmaar, Amstelveen, Amsterdam, Haarlem, Hilversum, Purmerend**

MORE INFORMATION: iamsterdam.com; www.noord-holland-tourist.nl

SELECTED BREWERIES: **Butcher's Tears**, *Amsterdam*; **Dampegheest**, *Limmen*; **Egmond**, *Egmond aan den Hoef*; **Gooische**, *Hilversum*; **Hoop**, *Zaandijk*; **IJ**, *Amsterdam*; **Jopen**, *Haarlem*; **Naeckte**, *Amstelveen*; **Noord-Hollandse**, *Uitgeest*; **Oedipus**, *Amsterdam*; **Prael**, *Amsterdam*; **Schans**, *Uithoorn*; **Texelse**, *Oudeschild* (Texel); **Tommie Sjef**, *Den Helder*; **Troost**, *Amsterdam*; **Two Chefs**, *Amsterdam*; **Uiltje**, *Haarlem*; **Walhalla**, *Amsterdam*; **Waterland**, *Monnickendam*; **Zeven Deugden**, *Amsterdam*.

ALKMAAR
🚉 Alkmaar

This attractive ragbag of cobbled streets and canals (pop 107,000) attracts thousands to its Friday cheese market (*Apr–Sep: 10.00–12.30*). Expect vendors in traditional costume to mug about rolling industrial cheeses theatrically for camera-wielding hordes. More thematic is the National Beer Museum (see Beer tourism), while the Beatles Museum (**beatlesmuseum.nl**) is one fan's obsessively accumulated memorabilia collection.

Alkmaars Koffiehuis

Gedempte Nieuwesloot 42 · **T** 072 531 8712
alkmaarskoffiehuis.nl
Shut Mo&Tu; others from 12.00

The de facto Zeglis taproom is a trendy, eclectic café with a terrace on a busy shopping street, rug-covered floors and large windows. Snacks and light meals served, including pancakes. Coffee is the main focus here but Zeglis beers are sold on tap and in bottle alongside around 60 other choices.

Boom

Houttil 1 · **T** 072 511 5547
proeflokaaldeboom.nl
Sa from 11.00; Mo from 14.00; others from 13.00

The Tree, an attractive old-fashioned café with a canalside terrace, nestles in a semi-cellar below the abovementioned beer museum. Dimly lit at night, it has chalkboards, bottles and beer enamels covering most walls. Snacks only. Interesting Dutch micros and international guests often appear on a regularly changing list of 70+ beers.

Kleine Deugniet

Gedempte Nieuwesloot 117 · **T** 06 5278 5991
proeflokaal-de-kleine-deugniet.business.site
Sa from 13.00; Su 15.00-22.00; others from 16.00

The Little Rascal has moved location since the previous edition of this guide and is now a much larger brown café with a terrace on a shopping street. Snacks only. The beer list has also expanded to 150+, including four or five changing guests among its 17 taps and a good local focus, with Moersleutel and Uiltje featuring prominently.

Scrapyard

Pettemerstraat 23 · **T** 072 531 6793
facebook.com/Moersleuteltaproom
Shut Mo-We; Th&Fr 15.00-00.00; others 12.00-00.00

Moersleutel's taproom is a makeshift greenhouse-type affair in a commerical area north of the centre, opposite the Beatles Museum.

There are colourful wooden chairs on a terrace decorated with, yes, scrap. It's still a work-in-progress and may evolve. The 20 tap beers are dominated by house creations with some guests, and more of the same in can and bottle.

OTHER BEER VENUES
Kooltuintje (Kooltuin 11 – **T** 072 515 9555 – kooltuintje.nl – *Sa from 12.00; others from 14.00*) is an endearingly grungy canalside dive bar with around 30 beers.

BEER TO GO
Bierwinkel Alkmaar (Ridderstraat 14A – **T** 06 2428 9009 – bierwinkelalkmaar.nl – *shut Mo&Tu; Th 12.00-21.00; Sa 10.00-18.00; Su 12.00-17.00; others 12.00-19.00*) is a knowledgeable place with a strong Dutch focus among 500+ craft beers.

AMSTELVEEN
Metro 51, Tram 5 from Amsterdam

Technically a separate town (pop 90,000) but physically contiguous with Amsterdam. As the nearest city to Schiphol Airport, it provides an office base for KLM. Or it will do until 2024, when the airline has plans to move its HQ into the airport.

Anna

Amsterdamseweg 22 · **T** 020 889 0731
anna-amstelveen.nl
Shut Mo-We; Su 11.00-20.00; others 11.00-23.00

Naeckte's taproom is in a former church with vaulted ceilings and stained glass in abundance. The brewing kit is at one end, with the bar on one side flanked by pipes from the church organ. Several retro-style lounge areas have sofas, old TVs and radiograms. Lunches and dinners served. The 21 taps make room for the full house range plus some guests.

AMSTERDAM

Amsterdam Centraal (CS),
Amstel, Lelylaan, Sloterdijk

The nation's capital and its largest city (pop 863,000). For many it is a hub for loveless sex and the smoking of semi-illicit herbs. Others know it as a cutesy place criss-crossed by canals and cobbled streets that are painful to walk along. It is also home to the world's most intolerant cyclists: furious mutterings and impatient bell tingling greet the presence of half a toe on their bike path, and they will gleefully run down any pedestrian attempting to cross the road on a green signal.

We apologise for the area outside the magnificent Centraal Station, which is a grim mêlée of lost tourists, wheelie luggage, drug addicts, pickpockets, sex museums and pizza. Plough on through, head down, to reach the real Amsterdam.

With a barrow-load of great cafés, it should be first on the team sheet when compiling a Dutch, or indeed European, beer tour, part of its charm being the longevity of some of the best bars in this most cosmopolitan of cities.

HOTEL TIPS: stay in Haarlem, Zaandam or any of several other towns easily reachable by rail. Good places fill up quickly and are far from cheap; any remotely affordable rooms are usually rubbish.

Alt ❶

Stadionplein 103 · **T** 06 3094 1899
bar-alt.com
Shut Su&Mo; others 17.00–00.00 (also Th-Sa 12.00-14.00)

This large restaurant near the Olympic Stadium is the Two Chefs tap. The modern interior has hipster lighting, a bar to one side and open kitchen at the back. Food is upscale bistro. Sit at the bar or on the terrace for drinks. Of the 20 taps, half are Two Chefs, the rest often very special guests, with a good number of sours and saisons among 100 bottled options.

Arendsnest ❷

Herengracht 90 · **T** 020 421 2057
arendsnest.nl
Daily from 12.00

The elegant Eagle's Nest is a place of pilgrimage for beer lovers beside the stately Herengracht canal. The Eagle is beer icon Peter van der Arend, who runs four places in town (**morebeer.nl**). Snacks only. The original intention of the exclusively Dutch beer list to list at least one beer from every brewery has been abandoned for the happiest of reasons, but the 52 taps and 100+ bottles and cans still provide a perfect snapshot of the national craft scene, often showcasing obscure and hard-to-find micros.

Beer Loves Food ❸

Lange Leidsedwarsstraat 4-6 · **T** 020 223 7562
beerlovesfood.nl
Daily from 16.00

The fourth outlet in the Morebeer empire is a cosy one-room café with a small terrace, barrels on one wall and a beer-themed mural opposite. Burgers and pulled this 'n' that populate the hip food menu.

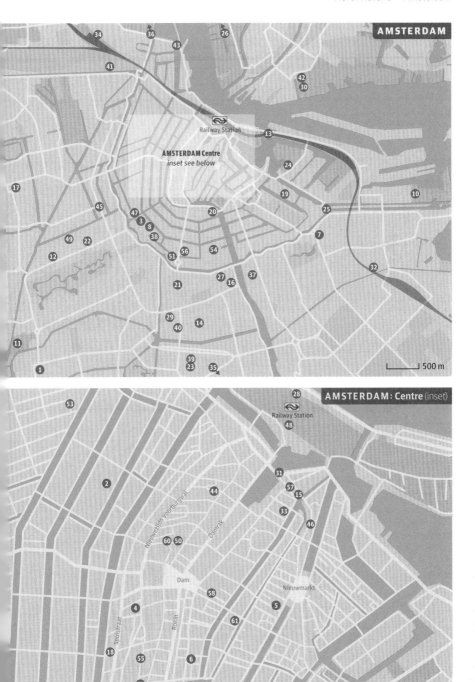

AMSTERDAM

34 36 26

41

43

42
30

Railway Station

13

AMSTERDAM Centre
inset see below

24

17

19

10

45

47
3 8
38

20

25

49 22

12

51 56 54

7

27 37

21 16

32

29
40 14

11

39
23 35

500 m

AMSTERDAM: Centre (inset)

28

53

Railway Station

48

31

2

44

57
15

Nieuwezijds Voorburgwal

Damrak

33

46

60 50

Dam

58

Nieuwmarkt

4

5

Rokin

61

Spuistraat

18

55

6

52

59
9

100 m

The 30 tap beers, mostly modern craft, always include the house Morebeers and several from BrewDog. Bottles and cans lift the full range above 60.

Beer Temple

Nieuwezijds Voorburgwal 250 · **T** 020 627 1427
beertemple.nl
Daily from 12.00

Contrasting with the Arendsnest (above), Peter van der Arend's second bar focuses on international craft. The interior goes for Americana, with a display of tap handles from former guests. Snacks include beef jerky. The commissioned house ale is Uiltje's sensational Big Fat Double 5 IPA, alongside 200+ other beers, 35 of them on draught, primarily from the US with a scattering from elsewhere. Tasting events every Sunday at 15.00 explore the range.

Bekeerde Suster

Klovenniersburgwal 6 · **T** 020 423 0112
debekeerdesuster.nl
Fr&Sa from 12.00; others from 15.00

The Reformed Sister brewpub has a small terrace just off Nieuwmarkt. The expansive low-ceilinged interior has a mezzanine above and copper kettles at the rear, with more seating beyond that. Lunches and full dinners are served (*until 22.30*). All the house brews are available on tap, supplemented by around 35 mainly Belgian guests, mostly in bottles.

Bierfabriek

Nes 67 · **T** 020 528 9910
bierfabriek.com
Sa&Su from 13.00; others from 15.00

The Beer Factory brewpub shed its skin in 2016 and moved lock, stock and many barrels to larger premises one block east. Brewing kit takes centre stage in the modern interior. Some tables have self-pour taps and most have free peanuts in their shells. Slow-roast chicken is the food star. Three of the four house beers are brewed on site.

Biertuin (Linnaeusstraat)

Linnaeusstraat 29 · **T** 020 665 0956
debiertuin.nl
Daily from 11.00

Near the Tropenmuseum, the Beer Garden's beer garden is actually a terrace. Bare brick walls down one side add rusticity to the minimalist interior. There is a full food menu. The beer list of 85 has a strong showing from local Amsterdam brewers such as Oedipus and Walhalla and half of the 17 taps dispense Dutch brews.

Biertuin (Prinsengracht)

Prinsengracht 494 · **T** 020 737 2941
debiertuin.nl
Sa&Su from 12.00; others from 15.00

Opened in 2018, the second in this empire of two has an almost-canalside terrace and a long narrow front bar area that opens up at the back. A side room on the right is a replica of Freddy Heineken's office. Meat dominates the food menu. The 140+ beers include 28 taps, many of them reserved for Amsterdam and Dutch craft offerings.

Brabantse Aap

Spui 30 · **T** 020 622 5110
debrabantseaap.nl
Daily from 11.00

The Brabant Ape enjoys a prime spot on a square where tourists and locals converge. Be skimmed by trams passing the terrace, or seek refuge in the conservatory or the ramshackle interior. There is a full lunch and dinner menu. The 60-ish beers include 16 taps, among which are three or four from the Bekeerde Suster brewery, under the same management.

Bruut

Cruquiusweg 83D · **T** 020 331 2727
bruutbier.nl
Sa&Su from 14.00; others from 15.00

This taproom with a terrace is out of the centre in the Eastern Docklands – bus 22 to Zeeburgerdijk gets you close. The modern bar is inside an old brick building, the former

Bruut

head office of a coconut oil manufacturer, with the brewery behind glass. Snacks only. Around 10 house beers plus a handful of guests on tap and in bottle.

Butcher's Tears

Karperweg 45 · **T** 06 5390 9777
butchers-tears.com
Shut Mo&Tu; We&Th 16.00–21.00; Su 14.00–19.00; others 16.00–23.00

Brewery tap in a former industrial area in southern Amsterdam: take tram 16 to Haarlemmermeerstation. The bright café has white-tiled walls and homemade art, with functional bench seating inside and out. Food is cheese with Swedish crispbread, reflecting the brewer's nationality. All the house beers are available in bottle and/or on tap.

Craft & Draft

Overtoom 416 · **T** 020 223 0725
craftanddraft.nl
Sa&Su from 14.00; others from 16.00
(shop closes 22.00)

Completing the Morebeer quartet, this is both shop and bar. The latter has a terrace at the front and a modern, minimalist interior, with a heavy bar counter of smoked oak and the house logo standing proud on a rear wall. Snacks only. The 40 taps and 200 bottles focus on global craft, with numerous hard-to-find items on a regularly changing list. The shop not only sells bottles but all the draught options from the bar in one litre growlers.

Delirium Café ⑬

Piet Heinkade 4–8 · **T** 020 811 0381
deliriumcafeamsterdam.nl
Th–Sa 16.00–00.00; others 16.00–22.00

Part of a Belgian chain, this waterside bar sits beneath a main road opposite the Muziekgebouw concert hall. Branding

dominates the decor, with pink elephants all over the terrace and on trays covering the ceiling. Burgers dominate the food menu. The 20 taps and 700 bottles/cans tilt towards Belgium but perhaps unexpectedly include plenty of Dutch and international craft.

Dopey's Elixer

Lutmastraat 49 · **T** 020 671 6946
dopeyselixer.nl
Sa from 16.00; Su 16.00–23.00; others from 13.00

Longstanding local with front terrace and daft name in a residential area of fashionable De Pijp. One end of the dark brown bar opens into a conservatory, above which is a collection of signs harvested from cycling events. Dinners available; snacks at other times. A growing list of 24 taps and 60 bottles includes several Amsterdam brewers.

Elfde Gebod

Zeedijk 5 · **T** 06 3062 6373
gollem.nl
Fr–Su from 14.00; others from 16.00

The old-established 11th Commandment ('thou shalt enjoy life') has been absorbed by the Gollem chain but retains its original branding. Religious artefacts dot the wood-panelled interior and church pews line one side. Nibbles only. The change of ownership has seen the beer list rise to 120, with more Dutch micros challenging the previous Belgian hegemony.

Foeders

Ceintuurbaan 257h · **T** 06 3659 3100
foeders.amsterdam
Daily from 14.00

This unassuming yet welcoming beer bar sits on a street busy with trams. The interior has a modern tasting room feel with bare brick and wood-panelled walls. Snacks only. Foremost among an impressive range of 42 draught lines and around 50 bottles is a mouthwatering selection of lambics and other wild and mixed fermentation brews, including rare vintages, many served by the glass or in tasting flights from 75cl bottles. Most are sourced from Belgium, reflecting the owner's origins, with some from Dutch micros and others.

Foeders

Frits

Jan Evertsenstraat 135 · **T** 020 233 9796
frits-amsterdam.nl
Daily from 16.00

Corner burger bar with a terrace on a busy square in Amsterdam-West: take tram 7 or 13 to Mercatorplein. Inside is a brick and wood-panelled one-room café. Snacks supplement the burger options. Around 65 beers lean towards local micros but also feature a fair number of UK and other international craft guests.

Gollem

Raamsteeg 4 · cafegollem.nl
Fr–Su from 12.00; others from 16.00

The capital's first specialist beer café opened in 1974 and is now part of a growing chain. The cramped wooden interior is often standing room only at the front, with tables on a raised area at the back. Most wall space is given over to old beer bottles and blackboard menus. No food. The 200+ list, once heavily biased towards Belgium, now admits a few representatives of the local craft scene.

Gollem aan het Water

Entrepotdok 64a
facebook.com/cafeGollementrepotdok
Sa from 12.00; others from 14.00

'Gollem 5' is one of a long line of former warehouses with a canalside terrace across the water from Artis Zoo. Inside, the bijou bar area is dominated by blackboards, with a more spacious sitting area above. Snacks include *flammkuchen*. A decent range of 85 beers is mainly Belgian but with some Dutch craft.

Gollem Amstelstraat

Amstelstraat 34
cafegollem.nl
Fr–Su from 12.00; others from 14.00

The fourth venue in the Gollem portfolio, on a busy street with trams rattling past the window, dares to differ beer-wise. Much of the interior wall space is covered by chalkboard menus while bottle labels are gluded to tabletops. Snacks only. The list of 30 draughts and 250 bottles and cans has more swagger than the food, and is a world tour of craft brewing.

Gollem (De Pijp)

Daniel Stalpertstraat 74
cafegollem.nl
Sa&Su from 14.00; others from 16.00

Gollem's first child, in trendy De Pijp, remains a must-visit, laid out like an enlarged and modern-ised version of its parent café, with front bar area leading to a raised mezzanine behind. Snacks only. As at other branches, the menu is scattered round the room on chalkboards, here boasting 180+ beers with plenty of Belgian and some Dutch craft options.

Gollem's Proeflokaal

Overtoom 160–162 · **T** 020 612 9444
cafegollem.nl
Fr–Su from 12.00; others from 13.00

Completing the Gollem quintet, the Tasting Room is a light-brown café with a terrace on a busy street near the Vondelpark. Food includes daily specials, some cooked with beer. Chalkboard menus list 175+ beers including 22 taps. A previously strong Belgian slant has softened, with more star billings for top Dutch brewers.

Goos

Maasstraat 74 · **T** 020 679 3443
cafegoos.nl
Daily 10.00–00.00

It's worth a trip on tram 12 to Maasstraat to visit this bright, modern terrace café and its neighbour Tap Zuid (below). The airy interior has overhead ceiling fans and wall posters advertising arty events, with a full food menu on offer. Around 50 of the 80+ beers are sourced from around 20 North Holland micros.

Homeland **24**

Kattenburgerstraat 5 · **T** 020 723 2550
pensionhomeland.com
Hours flexible

Hotel, brewery and tap with harbourside
terrace in a former naval officers' mess
overlooking the Dutch East India Company
ship *Amsterdam*, part of the Scheepvaart
Museum (**hetscheepvaartmuseum.nl**).
Merchant vessels once loaded beer for
export here. The bar area has a 1960s feel
with vinyl chairs and music including live
bands on some nights. Snacks only, but there
is a separate restaurant with the brewery
behind it. House beers are dispensed on tap
and in cans alongside a handful of guests.

IJ **25**

Funenkade 7 · **T** 020 261 9801
brouwerijhetij.nl
Daily 14.00–20.00

Popular tap of Amsterdam's oldest
operational brewery near Artis Zoo.
The windmill overlooking the terrace
belongs to the neighbours. The café,
a former bathhouse with tiled
walls, has a central serving area
surrounded by oak tables. Snacks
only. All the house brews are sold
on tap, with tasting flights available.
The brewery has a second outlet in
the Blauwe Theehuis (Vondelpark 5 –
daily 09.00–00.00), an iconic pavilion in
the Vondelpark.

IJver **26**

Scheepsbouwkade 72
T 020 247 1001
ijveramsterdam.nl
Daily from 09.00

Near the NDSM ferry terminal, this Russian
doll-like affair is a new 'warehouse' built
inside an old warehouse, the latter also home
to many art studios, with an indoor/outdoor
terrace. The slick, modern high-ceilinged
interior has beer fridges lining one wall.
Lunches and dinners served. Twenty taps and
100 bottles include plenty of local interest.

Lion's Head **27**

Van Woustraat 34 · **T** 06 4845 0378
lionsheadbrewing.com
Shut Mo&Tu; Sa from 13.00; others 17.00

The German and South African origins of
the couple behind this gastro brewpub are
betrayed by both food and beer. There is an
upscale restaurant on one side and a more
basic bar to the left. The brewery is in the
cellar, visible through a glass panel. Food is
modern, with Bavarian pork knuckle thrown
in. Half the 15 beers are brewed in house.

Little Delirium **28**

De Ruyterkade 42A · **T** 020 337 7971
littledelirium.nl
Daily 11.00–23.00

Slick, glass-sided café overlooking the IJ at the
back of Amsterdam Centraal station concourse.
Pink elephant decor reflects the branding of
its Belgian parent chain. Lunches and dinners
served; snacks all day. Twenty taps and 100+
bottles lean towards the owner's Huyghe
brands but Dutch craft also gets a fair crack.

Lokaal de Pijp **29**

Dusartstraat 51 · **T** 020 673 2487
lokaaldepijp.nl
Sa&Su from 11.00; others from 15.00

Compact corner café with a terrace on two
sides and a bar with wooden tables and large
picture windows. Arty posters advertising
forthcoming events take up most wall space.

Dinners include burgers. We applaud the fact that though the 60+ beer list isn't vast, it is overwhelmingly local. Pub quiz in English every other Thursday.

Oedipus

Gedempt Hamerkanaal 85 · **T** 020 244 1673
oedipus.com
Shut Mo-We, Th 17.00-22.00, Su 14.00-22.00; others 14.00-23.00

Taproom in an industrial building in Amsterdam-Noord, close to Walhalla (below): take the metro to Noorderpark or the free ferry. Brewing kit fills part of a colourfully painted interior otherwise occupied by tables that spill out onto a terrace. Food (*Su 16.00-20.00; others 17.00-21.00*) is predominantly burgers. Most of the 12 taps dispense house brews, with occasional guests.

Old Nickel

Nieuwebrugsteeg 11 · **T** 020 846 5575
oldnickel.com
Daily from 09.00

The endearingly crusty Old Nickel is a place of many characters. Some afternoons the carpeted interior may be semi-deserted, with only the odd barfly for company, but in the evenings it transforms into a convivial wood-panelled tavern. You can stay in the hotel above. No food. The 70+ beers are a mix of Belgian, German and Dutch.

Poesiat & Kater

Polderweg 648 · **T** 020 333 1050
poesiatenkater.nl
Sa&Su from 10.00; others from 11.00

Taproom in the ammonia plant of a former gasworks near Muiderpoort station. The bar has a mezzanine above, while the brewery is in the next room. Poesiat and Kater were employees of the long-gone Gekroonde Valk brewery, the original home of the Van Vollenhoven beers now made here: their portraits are displayed on one wall, the old brewery's crowned falcon logo on another. Lunches and dinners served. All beers on sale are brewed on site.

Poeslat & Ka

Prael Oudezijds

Oudezijds Armsteeg 26 · **T** 020 408 4469
deprael.nl
Su 12.00-23.00; others from 12.00

Down an alley beside the brewery shop, this split-level taproom's concrete and industrial edge is softened by eclectic furnishings. A lower bar area has brick flooring, while the upper level seems half café, half living room with sofas and armchairs. Main dishes are available until 22.00; snacks to 23.00. Around 10 house beers are served on tap.

Prael Houthavens

Nieuwe Hemweg 2 · **T** 020 215 3400
deprael.nl
Shut Mo; Tu&We 11.00-22.00, Fr 11.00-00.00; Su 12.00-22.00; others 11.00-23.00

Prael's second outlet is in a former postal building northwest of the centre: take bus 22 to Spaarndammerdijk. Like its sister the interior contains battered furniture, with a wooden bellows serving as one table. There is live jazz every Sunday (*15.00-18.00*). Lunches and dinners served. The 16 taps dispense house beers. Card payments only.

Proefzaak

Hullenbergweg 6 · **T** 020 210 1703
deproefzaak.nl
Shut Su-Mo; Tu 11.30-17.00; We 11.30-22.00; others 11.30-00.00

Near Bullewijk metro, Kleiburg's taproom is in a green Nissen hut that stands out from the surrounding offices and a giant Ikea.

Proefzaak, Kleiburg's taproom

Large windows light up the simple interior, with the brewery at one end. Full meals available. Six house beers are served on tap. Cards only. Check before travelling as there are plans to build a hotel on the site.

Proost & Stroop

Meteorenweg 272 · **T** 020 331 2351
proostenstroop.nl
Stroop: Shut Tu; Sa&Su 10.00–21.00; Mo 11.00–19.00 others 11.00–21.00
Proost: summer only Shut Mo–Th; Fr 16.00–23.00, Sa&Su 15.00–23.00

The Friekens taproom is sandwiched between allotments and a community vineyard in a small park in northwest Amsterdam: bus 35 to Meteorenweg gets you close. Proost is an outdoor taproom with a grassy beer garden, while the Stroop pancake house above is a less official tap but with longer hours. Both serve house beers, along with a few local guests.

Ruyschkamer

Ruyschstraat 34 · **T** 20 670 3622
deruyschkamer.nl
Shut Mo&Tu; Su 15.00–23.00; others from 17.00

This low-ceilinged bar resembles a bomb shelter at the front, with a mezzanine too low for chairs where customers slouch on cushions. It opens up at the back into cosy sofa areas where mirrors and skylights create a sense of space. Dinners include pizza and pasta. All 70+ beers are in self-service glass fridges, with plenty of local options: grab a bottle and someone will bring an opener and glass.

Spuyt

Korte Leidsedwarsstraat 86 · **T** 020 624 8901
cafedespuyt.nl
Sa&Su from 15.00; others from 16.00

A longstanding favourite east of cheesy Leidseplein, this unassuming one-room café with bijou terrace and simple interior is happy to stay off the high-volume lager-swillers' radar. Food is snacks, paninis and toasties. The 150+ list posted on the wall opposite the bar gives ample space to Dutch micros and global craft.

Tap Zuid

Maasstraat 70 · **T** 020 205 2002
tapzuid.amsterdam
Daily from 12.00

Two doors from Goos (above), this bright, trendy bar has a terrace out front. If you were doubting where you were, the large red and white illuminated sign behind the counter will set you straight. *Flammkuchen* and burgers dominate the food menu. Around half the 125 beers, including 25 on tap, are local, with some 30 different Amsterdam brewers represented.

Troost

Cornelis Troostplein 23 · **T** 020 737 1028
brouwerijtroost.nl
Sa&Su from 14.00; others from 16.00

Troost's original brewpub in De Pijp has a front terrace and a rear conservatory, though the brewery visible through glass inside is nowadays only used for small runs and experiments. Food is *flammkuchen*, and pub grub including fish and chips. All house beers are served on tap with tasting flights available. Card payments only.

Troost Westergasfabriek

Pazzanistraat 25–27 · **T** 020 737 1028
brouwerijtroostwestergas.nl
Sa&Su from 12.00; others from 16.00

Troost's second brewery in an old gasworks in the Westerpark is now its main power base and the source of most of its beers. The high-ceilinged industrial taproom beyond the front terrace has a mezzanine at the back. It serves the same food as the original site (above).

Troost Westergasfabriek

Around 12 house beers are on tap, with tasting flights available. Card payments only.

Walhalla

Spijkerkade 10 · **T** 06 1139 1675
walhallacraftbeer.nl
Shut Mo-Th; Fr 16.00-23.00; Sa 14.00-23.00; Su 14.00-20:00

This taproom with a small terrace in Amsterdam-Noord is handily just 100m from Oedipus (above). The interior is a spartan but cosy brick-lined space with a single long table down the middle and a few others around the sides. The brewing kit is in the next room. Snacks and toasties only. All the house beers are served on tap, in tasting flights if required.

Westerdok

Westerdoksdijk 715/A · **T** 020 428 9670
cafewesterdok.nl
Shut Mo; others from 16.00

A 15-minute walk (or bus 48) west from Centraal station, this welcoming corner pub has wallpaper and wood-panelled walls and an upright piano that gets an occasional workout. Hot and cold snacks available. 100+ beers are selected according to the tastes of the British landlord, but Dutch offerings usually include Bronckhorster. Four of the 13 taps are dispensed through a ship's throttle.

Wildeman

Kolksteeg 3 · **T** 020 638 2348
indewildeman.nl
Shut Su; others from 12.00

Founded in 1986, In de Wildeman remains an essential destination for beer lovers the world over. A former jenever distillery, the two-room interior has tiled floors, olive-green walls and a rack of old spirit casks. An absence of music helps foster a communal hum of conversation and appreciative sampling. Bar snacks only. The 270+ list is half Belgian and one-third Dutch, with the remainder imported from all over. The 18 taps are as cleverly chosen as you will find, often including one-off, barrel-aged or tweaked versions of familiar names.

Zest

Bilderdijkstraat 188 · **T** 020 412 9631
zestamsterdam.nl
Fr&Sa from 17.00; others 17.00-23.00

This dim, candlelit, split-level restaurant on a busy shopping street is also the Asperius taproom, the kit visible through glass at the rear of a sunken brick-walled bar area. Food is burgers, plus dishes that reflect the Bulgarian owner's heritage. The beer list limits itself to three or four house brews plus a handful of guests.

Zilt

Zeedijk 49 · **T** 06 2527 7244
cafezilt.nl
Daily from 17.00

This chic one-room café eschews tradition by preferring green and turquoise shades to brown. Live music some Sundays is classical and jazz. Nibbles only. The beer list has risen to 120 and the bottled range now leans towards 75cl sharing bottles, many containing Belgian lambics and oak-aged ales. They also stock 130+ whiskies.

In de Wildeman

Zotte (47)

Raamstraat 29 · **T** 020 626 8694
facebook.com/sosdezotte
Daily from 16.00

The Fool, a block west of Leidseplein, has a small terrace and a dimly-lit interior with candles to help you glimpse what you are drinking. Food (*until 21.30*) includes a selection of dinner mains. A list of 100+ beers remains resolutely Belgian but includes upstarts such as Brussels Beer Project.

OTHER BEER VENUES
For the best and widest-ranging guide to Amsterdam's other beer bars we recommend *Around Amsterdam in 80 Beers* by one Tim Skelton (Cogan & Mater, available from booksaboutbeer.com).
The sumptuous art nouveau **1e Klas** (48) (Stationsplein 15 – Platform 2b, Amsterdam CS – **T** 020 625 0131 – restaurant1eklas.nl – *daily 09.30–23.00*) is to 19th-century station cafés what the Taj Mahal is to mausoleums.
Friendly **De Bar** (49) (Jan Pieter Heijestraat 119D-h – **T** 020 854 52 77 – gebrouwendoorvrouwen.nl – *daily from 12.00*) serves Gebrouwen Door Vrouwen beers and would be their taproom if they ever get their own brewery.
Once a fixture on the Amsterdam beer scene, **Belgique** (50) (Gravenstraat 2 – **T** 020 625 1974 – cafe-belgique.nl – *Mo-We from 15.00; others from 13.00*) has lost its former star appeal but still serves 50+ Belgian beers in cosy if cramped surrounds.
Styled as a Berlin living room café, **Brecht** (51) (Weteringschans 157 – **T** 020 627 2211 – cafebrecht.nl – *daily from 11.00*) has mismatched furniture and 30 German beers.
Family-run since 1798, tiny **Doktertje** (52) (Rozenboomsteeg 4 – **T** 020 626 4427 – *shut Su-Tu; others from 16.00*) is the city's smallest bar, with a candlelit interior held together by cobwebs and dust.
Timeless **Hegeraad** (53) (Noordermarkt 84 – **T** 020 624 5565 – *Su from 11.00; others from 08.00*) has carpeted tables and a pissoir almost in the bar.
In the same family since 1877, **Oosterling** (54) (Utrechtsestraat 140 – **T** 020 623 4140 – cafeoosterling.nl – *Su 08.30–20.00; Mo&Tu 08.30–21.00; others from 08.30*) has wooden casks, a low-slung bar and a sloping floor.
Pilsener Club (55) (Begijnensteeg 4 – **T** 020 623 1777 – *shut Su; others from 12.00*) is a characterful drinking hole with sandy floors, smoke-darkened everything else, and no bar counter, just a serving door. It is also charmingly known as de Engelse Reet (the English Arse).
Tiny **Taproom** (56) (Nieuwe Vijzelstraat 1 – **T** 020 221 2343 – taproom.nl – *Fr-Su from 12.00; others from 13.00*) has no space for bottles but most of its 24 taps pour local craft.

THE JENEVER CONVENTION

An older Amsterdam tradition than the beer bars is that of spirits houses, some of which are among the city's most atmospheric drinking places. A word to the unwary though: if tempted to add these onto a pub crawl, do so at the beginning, not the end. Wisdom is easier to bring to bear on larger drinks.
Bijou **Ooievaar** (57) (Sint Olofspoort 1 – **T** 06 3158 6941 – proeflokaaldeooievaar.nl – *daily from 12.00*) has been a jenever tasting room since 1782.

The unmissable and, to English speakers, amusingly named tasting room **Wijnand Fockink** (58) (Pijlsteeg 31 – **T** 020 639 2695 – wynand-fockink.nl – *daily 14.00–21.00*) has sandy wooden floors, no seats and a hatful of spirits. Equally central is the **Hoppe** (59) (Spui 18–20 – **T** 020 420 4420 – cafehoppe.com – *daily from 08.00*): head to the right to find its sandy-floored 1670 tasting room, a favourite haunt of Freddy Heineken.
Bols-owned jenever tasting

room **Drie Fleschjes** (60) (Gravenstraat 18 – **T** 020 624 8443 – dedriefleschjes.nl – *Su 15.00–19.00; others 14.00–20.30*) has been serving since 1650, though nowadays its locked private casks are mostly for show.
Bucking the old trend, **Kelkje** (61) (Oudezijds Achterburgwal 164A – **T** 06 2537 8104 – kelkje.nl – *shut Mo; Tu-Th 16.00–21.00; others 15.00–21.00*) is a newish 'mock-old' tasting room serving Nieuwe Diep spirits as well as Czech and German beers.

BEER TO GO

Among the country's finest specialist shops, **Bierkoning** (Paleisstraat 125 – **T** 020 625 2336 – bierkoning.nl – *Su 12.00–19.00; Mo 12.00–18.00; others 11.00–19.00*) finds space for 1,400 global craft beers. If you become Stendhalised, the enthusiastic staff can make suggestions. A smaller spin-off, **Bierkoning Oost** (Czar Peterstraat 233 – **T** 020 737 1950 – *shut Su-Tu; Fr 12.00–19.00; Sa 10.00–18.00; others 14.00–19.00*), has the best of its parent range.

Bier Baum (Sarphatipark 1 – **T** 020 779 2040 – bier-baum.nl – *Sa 12.00–22.00; others 14.00–22.00*) focuses on global craft with 300 beers. Open extraordinary hours and with an extraordinary range, **Sterk** (De Clerqstraat 1 – **T** 020 618 1727 – sterkamsterdam.nl – *Fr&Sa 09.00–03.00; others 09.00–01.00*) is a late-night deli claiming 3,000+ beers. We haven't counted to verify, but they do have a lot.

BEVERWIJK

13km N from Haarlem off A22
↩ Beverwijk

The proximity of this small provincial town (pop 38,500) to Amsterdam has ensured its popularity as an out-of-town retreat for wealthy traders since the 17th century.

Broer & Zus

Schans 10 · **T** 0251 228229
stadsbrouwhuisbroerenzus.nl
Shut Mo-Tu, Fr 15.30–00.00; Sa 14.00–00.00; Su 15–21.00; others 15.30–23.00

Brother and Sister is a modern taproom in a former church. A front room behind a small terrace has leather armchairs, with more seating in the larger bar area beyond, which also houses the brewing kit. Snacks only. House beers appear on 10 taps and in bottle alongside around 60 bottled and canned guests.

CASTRICUM

35km NW from Amsterdam off N203
↩ Castricum

Quiet provincial town (pop 35,400) with one good reason to swing by. Behind the station, Huis van Hilde (huisvanhilde.nl) tells the archaeological pre-history of the local area.

BEER TO GO

Bierhut (Burgemeester Mooijstraat – **T** 0297 769018 – bierhut.business.site – *shut Su; Th-Fr 10.00–19.00; Sa 10.00–17.00; others 12.00–19.00*) has 1,200 Dutch and international craft beers and another 800 assorted beverages.

DEN HELDER

41km N from Alkmaar along N250
↩ Den Helder

Naval and commercial port town (pop 55,000), the gateway to the Dutch North Sea gas platforms and the island of Texel.

Fort Westoever

Westoever 1 · **T** 0223 697842
fortwestoever.nl
Shut Mo&Tu; Sa&Su 10.00–23.00; others 11.00–22.00

Helderse Jongens brewery established itself in 2017 in the West Bank Fort, built to defend the port approaches in Napoleonic times. The taproom inside the low-slung building has brick vaulted walls and white ceilings, with side rooms that can be opened as required. Lunches and dinners served. House beers share space with 25 regional guests.

EGMOND AAN DEN HOEF

8km W from Alkmaar off N512
Bus 165

Sleepy village (pop 4,000) close to the
Egmond aan Zee beach resort. The remains
of 11th-century Egmond Castle amount to
little more than an outline and a moat.

Egmond

Weg over de Bisschop 1C · **T** 072 303 0404
brouwerijegmond.nl
May–Sep only: Shut Mo–Th; others 16.00–19.00

This large airy taproom is on a mezzanine
overlooking the Egmond brewhouse below.
A mural by a sofa corner depicts the like-named
abbey, 3km to the south in Egmond-Binnen.
Nuts only. The 10 taps dispense whichever of
the house Sancti Adalberti beers are available.

ENKHUIZEN

18km ENE from Hoorn off N302
🚉 Enkhuizen

Picturesque West Frisian harbour town (pop
18,400) with oodles of history, an important
port until the Afsluitdijk cut it off from the sea.
HOTEL TIP: **Compagnie** (below) has rooms.

Compagnie

Spoorstraat 10–14 · **T** 0228 323334
herbergdecompagnie.nl
Fr&Sa from 11.0; others 11.00–23.00

This large grand café was due to become a
brewpub until the idea morphed into De Werf
around the corner (below). The terrace has a
harbour view, if you stand on tiptoe. A full food
menu is served. The 80+ beers with 26 taps
are mainly Belgian but include options from
De Werf and other North Holland micros.

Werf

Paktuinen 6 · **T** 0228 222160
brouwerijdewerf.nl
Shut Mo–We; Th&Su 14.00–22.00; others 14.00–00.00

The Wharf taproom is refurbished warehouse
with a brewhouse at one end, storage at the

Werf

other, a bar in between and a harbourside
terrace. The modern interior has high stools
and tables and a sofa corner. Snacks and
dinners served. House beers are poured from
12 taps, with a few bottles. Tasting flights can
be ordered, and bottles are sold to take away.

OTHER BEER VENUES
Picturesquely located by a white drawbridge
and medieval city gate, **Ankertje** (Dijk 6 – **T**
0228-315767 – **cafe-ankertje.nl** – *Fr&Sa from 10.00;
others 10.00–23.00*) is a cosy nautical -themed
brown café and the BrouwVrouw taproom,
although the beers are made elsewhere.

Ankertje

HAARLEM
~~ Haarlem

The provincial capital (pop 161,000) is one of North Holland's prettiest cities, dominated by St Bavo church, or Grote Kerk, which looms over the Grote Markt. Go inside to marvel at its impressive organ, proof that size is important.

The museum named after the city's most famous son, the painter Frans Hals (franshalsmuseum.nl) exhibits its collection of old masters in a former cloister. Founded in 1784, the Teyler's Museum (teylersmuseum.eu) is the country's oldest, reflecting the eclectic tastes of an eccentric collector.

HOTEL TIP: Malts ★★★, Zijlstraat 56–58 (maltshotel.nl) is a central B&B.

Bierlokaal d

Bierlokaal De Uiver

Lange Begijnestraat 10 · **T** 023 576 9372
bierlokaaldeuiver.nl
Shut Mo; Fr–Su from 16.00; others from 17.00

Around the corner from, and not to be confused with, the timeless Uiver (below), this speciality beer bar has mock-old wooden floors and green wooden walls. Snacks only. The 40 taps are mostly Dutch and international craft rotating guests, grouped into fives by style, colour and so on. At least 40 bottles and cans bring the total choice above 80.

Bruxelles

Lange Wijngaardstraat 16 · **T** 023 531 4509
cafebruxelles.nl
Daily from 17.00

This popular, brightly coloured café down a narrow alleyway just north of Grote Markt has an elevated terrace at the rear of its first-floor dining room. Belgian-leaning food includes mussels and a cheap daily special. Despite the house name and Manneken Pis logo, around half the 80+ beers are now Dutch.

Jopen Waardepolder

Emrikweg 21 · **T** 023 533 4114
jopenproeflokaal.nl
Shut Su, Th&Fr 10.00–20.00, Sa 12.00–18.00; others 10.00–19.00

Taproom on industrial estate 2.5km northeast from the station: bus 15 gets you close. A shop and a bar above have views into the brewery, with a moveable bar counter in the centre. Meals and snacks served. The 20 taps and equal numbers of bottles are mostly occupied with house brews, plus a few guests. Combine a visit with the Uiltje tap around the corner (below).

Jopenkerk

Gedempte Voldersgracht 2 · **T** 023 533 4114
jopenkerk.nl
Daily 10.00–01.00

The original Jopen brewpub is impressively housed in the restored Jacobskerk, with a large terrace on a square. The modern interior acknowledges its former existence, not least in the floor-to-ceiling stained-glass windows.

Jopenkerk

Some ceilings are carpeted. Lunches and snacks are served in the bar downstairs, dinners in the mezzanine restaurant (*Tu-Sa 17.30-22.00*). All 24 tap beers are from the house, with some guests among the bottles.

Linde

Botermarkt 21 · cafedelinde.nl
Daily from 09.30

Old-established grand café with black and white photos on the mock-marble walls, a large terrace out front and a glassed-in conservatory. Lunches and dinners served; snacks all day. Jopen gets a look in on an otherwise Belgian-dominated list which now tops 100.

Lokaal

Koningsstraat 46zw · **T** 023 551 2129
lokaalhaarlem.nl
Shut Mo; Fr-Su from 16.00; others from 18.00

Run by the former landlord of the now-closed Briljant, this friendly one-room café has wallpaper, copies of Old Masters and maps on the walls and a small front terrace. A stage with a piano at the back hosts regular acoustic music events. Snacks and toasties served. Around 120 beers are almost exclusively small Dutch micros with a few Belgian stalwarts for the non-believers.

Roemer

Botermarkt 17 · **T** 023 532 5267
cafederoemer.nl
Su from 12.00; others from 10.00

On Haarlem's bustling Botermarkt, the Rummer, named after a bowl once used for drinking toasts, is one of five cafés in a row, each with large terraces. An inner terrace becomes a conservatory in winter. The spacious art deco interior includes a striking glass frieze behind the bar. There is a full food menu. The 80+ beers feature Jopen and a fine selection of craft IPAs.

Uiltje Bar

Zijlstraat 18 · **T** 023 844 6227
uiltjecraftbeer.com
Th 17.00-00.00; Fr from 15.00; Sa from 12.00; Su 12.00-22.00; others 17.00-23.00

This modern streetside café has a bare brick wall on one side and the brewery's distinctive owl logo dominating the other. A picnic table terrace appears in summer. Snacks run to cheese, pizza and toasties. Beside around 10 taps dedicated to house specials are another 20 guest lines plus 120 or so bottles and cans, together representing a melting pot of global craft brewing. A must visit.

Uiltje Bar

Uiltje Taproom

Bingerweg 25 · **T** 023 844 6395
uiltjecraftbeer.com
Shut Mo-We; Fr 12.00-22.00; Su 12.00-18.00; others 12.00-20.00

Brewery shop, taproom and terrace on industrial estate close to and easy to visit alongside Jopen Waardepolder (above). There's not much beyond a basic wood-covered bar with booths down one side. Snacks are pizzas. Ten taps dispense the brewery's latest creations and sometimes guests. Two cask handpumps are used only rarely.

OTHER BEER VENUES

Serving around 25 beers, **Koops** (Damstraat 4 – **T** 023 532 2760 – cafekoops.nl – *daily from 16.00*), with its gnarled tables, worn floors and mustard walls, is honed from another era.

Uiver

Hugely characterful **Uiver** (Riviervischmarkt 13 – **T** 023 532 5399 – **indenuiver.nl** – *daily from 16.00*) has a Delft tile and marble bar, an aeronautically themed central room, a snug with 17th-century leather wallpaper, and around 30 beers on its menu.

BEER TO GO

Melgers (Barrevoetestraat 13-15 – **T** 023 531 3149 – **melgers.nl** – *Th 09.30–20.00; Fr 09.30–19.00; Sa 09.30–18.30; Su 13.00–17.00; Mo 12.00–18.00; others 09.30–18.00*), just west of Botermarkt, stocks 1,000+ beers.

HEEMSKERK

20km N from Haarlem off A9 exit 9
🚃 Heemskerk, Uitgeest

Modern commuter town (pop 39,000).

Jack's

Kerkweg 9 · **T** 0251 252790
jackscafe.nl · *Shut Mo; others from 10.30*
This friendly, cosy beer and burger joint has a terrace near the central church and a wood-floored, brick-walled, modern brown interior. Burgers are the house specials until 21.00, with lighter lunches until 16.00 and snacks all day. The 50+ beer list sneaks in as it's increasing in extent and interest, with a fair smattering of Dutch micros.

OTHER BEER VENUES

Café and live music venue **Lokaal** (Anthonie Verherenstraat 5a – **T** 0251 249170 – **cafe-lokaal. nl** – *shut Mo&Tu; Fr&Su from 17.00; Sa from 19.00; others from 20.00*) strongly features Dutch craft choices among its 40 beers.

HENSBROEK

13km E from Alkmaar off N194
Bus 409 from Obdam

Tiny rural hamlet (pop 750).

Het Wapen van Wogmeer

Wogmeer 59 · **T** 0229 561325
wapenvanwogmeer.nl
Daily 11.00–23.00

Semi-rural local on the other side of a footbridge, a further 30 minutes on foot from the village bus stop. The café dates from 1918 but the original building burnt down and was replaced in 1926. Outside is a front terrace, with minigolf at the back, while the timeless interior has carpeted tables, billiards and a jukebox stocked with 1950s and 1960s vinyl. The food menu runs from snacks to steaks. The 80 beers are dominated by Belgian classics but local micros like Egmond and Dampegheest also appear.

HILVERSUM

🚃 Hilversum

This bustling city (pop 90,000) near Amsterdam is a good place for celebrity-spotting as it's long been the nation's media capital. It still provides a base for 10 or so TV and radio stations.

BarBier

Groest 92
biercafedebarbier.business.site
Daily from 15.00

In a former carpet shop, the Barber has a narrow frontage and small terrace, but opens up into a rear sitting area with leather sofas and a corrugated iron ceiling. A rusty moped acts as a conversation piece. Snacks only. The 100+ beers, including many Dutch and international craft options, are displayed on a wall of bottles, with a paper menu for traditionalists.

Mout

Marktplein 1
mouthilversum.nl
Daily from 09.00

The Gooische taproom is part of an expansive food hall with an open hearth firepit and large terrace.

The brewery is in one corner, with food outlets around the sides of an island bar. Food (*12.00–22.00 except bar snacks*) includes pizza, dim sum and fish. Around eight house beers are served, in tasting flights if required, alongside a handful of guests.

HOORN

Hoorn

Attractive city (pop 72,700) that was an important Zuiderzee port until a series of dykes blocked its access to the sea. Learn about the history of its heyday in the West Frisian Museum (**westfriesmuseum.com**), a lovely stone gabled building dating from 1632. Central Roode Steen square is one of the prettiest in the Netherlands.

Charlies

Dubbele Buurt 4 · **T** 0229 217798
charlies.nl
Shut Mo&Tu; We&Th from 16.00; Fr&Sa from 15.00; Su 14.00–22.00

Corner café northwest of the centre. A front bar has bits of Charlie Chaplin memorabilia and art deco light fittings. The back room picks up the cinematic theme and runs with it, with movie posters, projectors, canisters and strips of celluloid. Snacks only. About one-third of the 100 beers change seasonally, with plenty of Dutch craft micros on show.

Klinker

Roode Steen 13 · **T** 0229 213281
eetcafedeklinker.nl
Sat from 11.00; others from 12.00

Lively brown café with a large terrace on the main square. Sand-covered wooden floors and black and white portrait photos dominate the candle-lit interior. Food is 'large snacks': think mega-portions of nachos, and 'KFC' (Klinker Fried Chicken wings). A list of 65+ is strong on Dutch micro IPAs and six of the nine taps dispense changing guests.

Wout's Beer House

Kerkplein 33 · **T** 06 1164 6587
woutsbeerhouse.nl
Shut Mo&Tu; Fr from 16.00; Sa&Su from 15.30; others from 19.00

Simple wooden-floored corner local in the shadow of the main church. Seats are sparse so most people prop up the bar. Snacks only. With no printed menu, you'll need to inspect the glass-fronted fridge to choose from 75 beers, mainly Belgian but including local Egmond among the many abbey and Trappist options.

OTHER BEER VENUES
Beiaard (Kerkplein 3 – **T** 0229 270675 – **debeiaard-hoorn.nl** – *Shut Mo; Sa&Su from 15.00; others from 16.00*) remains a good place to eat but its list of 40 beers has lost its lustre.

BEER TO GO
Fust (Kerkstraat 11 – **T** 0229 214974 – **t-fust.nl** – *Shut Su-Mo; Sa 09.30–17.00; others 09.30–18.00*)

stocks 500+ beers in addition to 500 whiskies and 800 wines.

Lokaal Oostwest – (Grote Oost 23 – **T** 06 2035 3602 – **lokaaloostwest.nl** – *shut Mo&Tu; We&Fr 12.00–20.00; Th 12.00–21.00; Sa 10.00–18.00; Su 12.00–17.00*) is a local produce store stocking 500 beers with a strong North Holland focus.

KROMMENIE

19km NNW from Amsterdam off N246
Krommenie-Assendelft

Small sleeper town (pop 17,400).

BEER TO GO

Drinks & Gifts (Heiligeweg 15a – **T** 075 640 5179 – **drinks-gifts.nl** – *shut Su; Mo 13.00–18.00; Th 09.00–20.00; Sa 09.00–17.00; others 09.00–18.00*) stocks an impressive 1,500+ beers including many from Dutch micros.

MEDEMBLIK

18km N from Hoorn off N240
Tram: Museum Stoomtram (**stoomtram.nl**, seasonal service), or bus 139

Cutesy town (pop 8,600) on the IJsselmeer, reachable in season by preserved steam tram. The 13th-century moated Radboud Castle was built by Floris V, Count of Holland. Jacobite Lord George Murray, who ended up in exile here after the Battle of Culloden, is buried in the churchyard.

HOTEL TIP: **Medemblik ★★★**, Oosterhaven 1 (**hetwapenvanmedemblik.nl**) has good rooms a few steps from the entry below.

Radboud

Gedempt Achterom 4 · **T** 0227 823393
stadsbrouwerijradboud.nl
Shut Mo&Tu; Fr&Sa 13.00–00.00; others 13.00–20.00

Taproom in an industrial building that was a brewery in the 16th century but more recently a car mechanic's workshop. The bar is between the brewhouse on one side and a kitchen used for cookery demonstrations on the other. Pizzas and snacks. House beers are

served on tap and in bottle, in tasting flights if preferred, with gift packs to take away.

MIDDENMEER

22km N from Hoorn off A7 exit 12
Bus 135

Quiet residential village (pop 3,600).

BEER TO GO

De Bierboetiek (Professor ter Veenweg 11b – **T** 06 5424 7349 – **bierboetiek.nl** – *shut Su-We, Th 13.30–18.00, Fr 13.30–20.00, Sa 11.00–17.00*) is a small but lovely emporium with 500 exclusively Dutch craft beers.

MONNICKENDAM

13km NE from Amsterdam off N247
Bus 314, 316

Touristy town (pop 9,900) beside the IJsselmeer.

Waterland

Galgeriet 4 · **T** 0299 407647
bierderijwaterland.com
Shut Mo&Tu; Fr 15.00–00.00; Sa 12.00–00.00; Su 12.00–22.00; others 15.00–22.00

The city's hop-on-hop-off sightseeing bus stops close to this taproom in a barn-like warehouse, with a terrace beside a yachting marina. The brewery is at one end, with a mezzanine designed as a viewing platform. At the other end is a taproom with lampshades recycled from wooden crates, an ice cream parlour, a beer shop, and a fish and

terland

sausage smokery. Food includes flatbread pizzas and burgers. All 13 taps dispense house beers, with tasting flights offered.

NAARDEN-VESTING

22km ESE from Amsterdam off A1 exit 6
Naarden-Bussum

Attractive, moated and fortified medieval town with cobbled streets. Modern Naarden (pop 17,000), 2km south, is less appealing but has the station.

Demmers

Marktstraat 52 · **T** 06 2551 6408
vestinggilde.nl
Su&Mo 16.00-21.00; others from 16.00

Atmospheric pub in old walled area: bus 110 stops a few minutes away in Westwalstraat. The 17th-century corner house has been a café since at least 1885, its wooden floors and beamed ceilings contributing to a general creakiness. Food is snacks and simple meals. The range of 50 beers isn't huge but charm and history get it in.

OUDENDIJK

9km WSW from Hoorn off N243
Rural farming hamlet (pop 450).

Les Deux Ponts

Slimdijk 2 · **T** 0229 541275
lesdeuxponts.nl
Shut Tu; others from 10.30

Several cafés could claim to have the nicest setting of any in this guide but this beats most. Bus 128 from Hoorn to Avenhorn Het Hoog

gets you within 1.5km. This whitewashed local has a superb canalside terrace overlooking reeds, grebes and the two bridges which give the place its name. The barn-like but charming interior is the hub of village life, something we hope will continue despite a change of ownership in 2019. Lunches and dinners served. The 50+ beers are largely predictable Belgian choices, but the location more than compensates.

PURMEREND

16km ENE from Amsterdam off N235
Purmerend

Market town (pop 80,000) that was originally a fishing port. Koemarkt (Cow Market) is one of the country's largest squares, though now with only a bovine statue as a reminder of the days before the cattle auctions moved to more practical premises in 2008.

Bonte Koe

Koemarkt 24 · **T** 0299 421124
biercafedebontekoe.nl
Summer: Shut Mo; Tu 09.00-18.00; Su 12.00-20.00; others from 11.00.
Winter: Shut Mo; Tu 09.00-13.00; We&Th from 16.00; Fr from 15.00; Sa from 12.00; Su 14.00-20.00.

Longstanding brown café the Spotted Cow has a terrace on the square and paintings that have adorned its walls since 1897. Glass cabinets at the rear house steins and other memorabilia. Lunches and dinners served. A list of 250+ beers including 21 taps has always championed small, local brewers alongside plentiful interesting imports, and there are 200 whiskies too.

OTHER BEER VENUES

Characterful brown café **Aad de Wolf** (Koemarkt 15 – **T** 0299 423974 – aaddewolf.nl – *Shut We; Tu from 09.00; others from 12.00*) has 40 beers with local SNAB to the fore. Bijou **Bakker** (Koemarkt 44 – **T** 0299 421262 – proeflokaalbakker.nl – *Shut Mo; Sa from 15.00; Su 15.00-22.00; others from 16.00*) has 40+ beers to enjoy under an old wooden ceiling that requires support from two slender columns.

TEXEL – DE KOOG
12.5km N of ferry port on N501

Ferry from Den Helder then bus 28 or Texelhopper

Outside the tourist season, sheep outnumber people on Texel (pronounced 'Tessel'), with just 13,600 permanent residents. Most of the island manages to retain a sleepy charm even in summer. Note the Texelhopper bus, which will also get you to the other recommended beer venues on the island, is partly an on-demand service requiring you to reserve your journey using an app or website: see **texelhopper.nl**. Bus 28 runs a scheduled service.

   De Koog (pop 1,300) is the island's kiss-me-quick holidaymaker's hub, with a main street lined with souvenir shops and bars. It is overrun in summer, dead in winter.

Paal 17
Ruyslaan 96 · **T** 0222 317614
paal17.com
Daily from 10.00

Until TX brewery began bottling in 2019, this beach bar in a splendid location southwest of De Koog was its only outlet, though the brewery itself is 8km away in another village The modern pavilion has a largely sand-covered wooden terrace with sea views. Lunches and dinners served, with three house beers usually on tap.

TEXEL – DEN BURG
7km NNE of ferry port on N501
Bus 28 or Texelhopper

The island's capital and home to half its residents (pop 7,000), with a charming town centre. *HOTEL TIP:* **Lindeboom ★★★**, Groeneplaats 14 (**lindeboomtexel.nl**) is on the main square.

Slock
Parkstraat 36 · **T** 0222 313161
deslock.nl
Sa from 15.00; Su from 12.00; others from 16.00

Around for over 50 years, the Slurp has evolved into Texel's best beer pub. Umbilically linked via shared toilets to its neighbour the Hollebol, now a separate business, this friendly local boozer welcomes all to a dark wood interior with a billiards table at the back. Nibbles only. Around half the 100 beers are from Dutch micros.

Tesselaar
Spinbaan 11 · **T** 06 3023 0277
biervantexel.nl
Shut Mo; others 15.00–18.00

This brewery on a business park north of the centre has a shop at the front and a cosy wooden taproom behind with a window looking onto the copper self-built brewhouse. Cheese, nuts and sausage snacks. House beers are served on tap and sold in bottles for take away. If booked on a tour you are welcome from 13.30.

Twaalf Balcken

Weverstraat 20 · **T** 0222 312681
12balcken.nl
Su from 17.00; others from 10.00

The front half of this large café near the main square is classic brown, while the rear is a lighter atrium with a gas-effect stove. Lunches and dinners served, with some dishes featuring local Texel lamb. Popular at weekends, so book ahead if you want to eat, otherwise stand at the bar. The 100+ beer list has some Dutch craft representation.

TEXEL – DEN HOORN

4km NW of ferry port

Small village (pop 450) in the southwest of the island.

Bonte Belevenis

Rommelpot 11 · **T** 0222 314180
landgoeddebontebelevenis.nl
Mid-Feb to Oct: Shut Mo, Fr&Su; others 10.00-17.00

The Boei taproom is the café of a farm museum, 1.5km north of Den Hoorn right by a Texelhopper bus stop. You will need a ticket to get in, which includes a brewery and distillery tour. The self-service café is rustic rather than bar-like: British readers should think National Trust tearoom. Simple meals served. Five or six house beers are poured from bottles, also sold in the museum shop.

TEXEL – OUDESCHILD

8km northeast of ferry port off N501

The island's commercial fishing port (pop 1,100) and home to one of the country's largest little breweries.

Texels Proeflokaal

Schilderweg 214 · **T** 0222 313229
texels.nl
Shut Su&Mo (all year), Fr (Nov-Mar) & Tu&Th (Jan-Feb); others 10.30-18.00

Taproom in the countryside west of Oudeschild, where sheep serenade you on the rear terrace: the Texelhopper bus stop nearby is reassuringly named Bierbrouwerij. Some interior walls are painted with pastoral and beach scenes, while others are brewery-themed. Snacks only. Around 12 house beers are served on tap and there's a brewery shop for takeaways.

UITHOORN

18km SSW of Amsterdam on N201

Small dormitory town (pop 29,000).

HOTEL TIP: **Schans** (below) has one B&B room.

Schans

Schans 17-21 · **T** 0297 522106
schansbier.nl
Taproom: Shut Mo-Th; Su 12.00-20.00; others 15.00-22.00. Shop: Shut Su-Tu; Sa 09.00-17.00; others 11.00-18.00

Brewery, distillery, taproom and bottle shop in a row of three houses dating from the 1700s. You'll find the shop with 400 beers and spirits at the front and a leafy back garden and bar at the back, where a handsome fox bust doubles as a model for the house spirits logo. Snacks sometimes include apple pie. Four house beers are usually on tap with others in bottle.

BEER TO GO
Drinkhut (Joost van den Vondellaan 33B – **T** 0297 769018 – drinkhut.nl – *Shut Su&Mo; Tu 12.00-18.00; We&Th 10.00-18.00; Fr 10.00-19.00; Sa 10.00-17.00*) has 1,500 global and Dutch craft offerings.

ZAANDAM

15km NNW from Amsterdam off A8 exit 1
Zaandam

As you leave the station and pass the extraordinary stack of buildings that forms the Inntel Hotel, this commuter town (pop 76,000) seems like Disney Holland, with everything orderly and nice, but it has history. Russian tsar Peter the Great worked incognito in the Dutch East India Company shipyards here in 1697 before moving on to Deptford in London as part of the same factfinding mission.

The house where he stayed is now a museum (zaansmuseum.nl/en/tsar-peter-house). *HOTEL TIP:* **Zaan Inn**★★★, Grenehout 22 (zaaninn.nl) beside the station can be a better-value alternative to Amsterdam.

The Black Smith

Hogendijk 46 · **T** 06 4860 9872
Shut Mo-We; others from 16.00

This lovely old bar is, as the name hints, in an 18th-century former smithy, now with wood everywhere and a tiny terrace. Red walls are smothered with old photos, while bottles line up on creaking wooden shelves behind the counter. Nibbles only. Around one third of the 60 beers are craft Dutch, the rest mainly Belgian, with some unusual finds on the guest taps.

Lab-44

Hembrugterrein, Middenweg 44 · **T** 020 237 4111
lab-44.nl
Shut Mo; others from 11.00

During World War I, the neutral Dutch profited from selling both sides the mustard gas invented in this former munitions factory laboratory, 2km south of central Zaandam and beside the ferry terminal for Amsterdam (**zaanferry.com**). Happily its products are no longer so sinister: it's Hoop's experimental brewery, with a high-ceilinged industrial-chic taproom serving a full food menu. Beers include one-offs brewed on site alongside the core range from the main brewery in Zaandijk (below), and there's a shop for takeaways.

BEER TO GO
Vonk (Tuiniersstraat 8 – **T** 075 616 9355 – slijterijvonk.nl – *shut Su; Mo 13.00-18.00; Th 09.00-21.00; others 09.00-18.00*) stocks 500 beers and 600 whiskies.

ZAANDIJK

20km NNW from Amsterdam off A8 exit 2
🚃 Zaandijk Zaanse Schans

Small town (pop 8,700) within the Zaanstad municipality, full of food factories such as a cocoa processing plant with its unmissable aroma. Across the river is Zaanse Schans, an open air museum, replete with more windmills than Don Quixote could tilt at.

Hoop

Hoop

Lagedijk 69-73 · **T** 075 204 7000
brouwerijhoop.nl
Fr&Sa from 11.00; others 11.00-23.00

Taproom and restaurant with a terrace and shop in a new building off an old-world street. The spacious modern interior has an open kitchen at the back, with the brewery next door behind glass. Lunches and dinners served (until 22.00). The house Hoop and sister Breugem beers are both sold on tap and in bottle, alongside several guests. There is also a shop for take aways.

OTHER BEER VENUES
Lovely old **Kruis** (Lagedijk 13 – **T** 075 621 5367 – **proeflokaal-dekruis.nl** – *Su&Mo 11.00-19.00; Tu 11.00-20.00; others from 11.00*) has wood from top to toe and 30 reasonable beers.

Overijssel

The name of this largely agricultural province means 'beyond the IJssel', referring to the river that forms much of its southwestern border with Gelderland. In essence this is two provinces, divided by Christianity. Its western half is historically Protestant, dotted with small, neat towns where people would never dream of washing their cars on Sunday, let alone drink beer. Decent drinking options were once correspondingly thin on the ground here but today cities like Zwolle and Kampen more than hold their own. The eastern part, bordering on Germany, is known as Twente and is more Catholic and relaxed, with most of the province's 1.1 million population living in the urban cluster between Almelo and Enschede.

LARGEST CENTRES: **Almelo**, **Deventer**, **Enschede**, **Hengelo**, **Zwolle**.

MORE INFORMATION: overijssel.nl; beleefoverijssel.nl

SELECTED BREWERIES: **Berghoeve**, *Den Ham*; **Eanske**, *Enschede*; **Grolsch** (Asahi), *Enschede*; **Hettinga**, *Zwolle*; **Huttenkloas**, *Albergen*; **Koperen Ster**, *Enschede*; **Mommeriete**, *Gramsbergen*; **Ootmarsummer**, *Ootmarsum*; **Pauw**, *Ommen*; **Stanislaus Brewskovitch**, *Enschede*

ALBERGEN

8km E from Almelo on N349
Bus 66

Semi-rural Twente village (pop 3,500). Theoretically you can also visit the Huttenkloas tasting room here (*We&Sa 14.00–17.00*) but this is usually best done on a tour (see Breweries).

Morshuis

Ootmarsumseweg 159 · **T** 0546 441238
morshuis.nl
Shut We; Mo&Th from 16.00; others from 09.00

This veteran beer-friendly café boasts a British telephone kiosk on its roadside terrace. The indoor space is filled with collectables, including a cast-iron stove and two disused cask handpumps, with an open fire and sunflowers painted on the ceiling. Food is simple lunches and snacks. The 100+ beers include plenty of local choices.

BEER TO GO

Beside the Morshuis, **Pakhuis Twente** (Ootmarsumseweg 159 – **T** 0546 442251 – **pakhuistwente.nl** – *Shut Su&Mo; Th 10.00–20.00; Sa 09.00–16.30; others 10.00–17.30*) is a drinks emporium stocked with 1,800 local, national and international craft brews.

ALMELO

17km NW of Hengelo off A35 exit 30
🚆 Almelo

Provincial town (pop 72,600) where one of the major employers is a uranium enrichment plant – if you see the locals glow in the dark, that is why.

België

Schuttenstraat 2 · **T** 0546 453365
proeflokaalbelgie.nl
Sa from 12.00; Th, Fr&Su from 14.00; others from 15.00

Corner local with an expansive split-level canalside terrace and typical cosy brown

interior. There is live music some nights and a monthly pop quiz. Snacks only. Unsurprisingly the 90+ beers are mainly Belgian, but with La Trappe and Zundert among the Trappists and a few German imports.

OTHER BEER VENUES
The atmospheric old **Hookhoes** (9 Grotestraat 126 – **T** 0546 814898 – hookhoes.nl – *Sa&Su from 14.00; others from 16.00*) remains a lovely café but its beer list has dwindled to 25.

DEURNINGEN

5km NE from Hengelo off N738
Bus 59

Sleepy village (pop 1,800) just outside the city.

Pelle's

Hoofdstraat 9 · **T** 074 851 1662
pelles.nl
Mo 16.00–00.00; Tu&We 16.00–23.00; others from 10.00

This friendly local in the style of an urban English tavern has a terrace looking out onto a village green and church. The interior has red-wallpapered walls covered with beer enamels, a motorcycle tyre on the ceiling and a covered winter garden at the rear. Full food menu available. One third of the 80 beers are Dutch, the rest Belgian.

DEVENTER

13km W from Apeldoorn off A1 exits 23&24
Deventer

Modern town (pop 100,000) with a historic heart: parts of the Proosdij, the nation's oldest stone house, date from 1130. This was once a centre of carpet making, though only one of the five factories survives, today making artificial turf. Visit during the December Dickens festival (**dickensfestijn.nl**) and you may encounter people dressed as Mr Macawber or Little Dorrit.

DAVO

Sluisstraat 6
davobieren.nl
Shut Mo–Tu; Sa&Su from 12.00; others from 15.00

Taproom with beer garden in an industrial space southeast of the centre where wooden windmills were once made. Behind the shop at the front is a bar area with a brewing kit at one end and a stove and sofa corner at the other. Burgers and snacks served. The 12 taps mostly dispense beers from the house, alongside an eclectic selection of guest bottles.

Heks

Brink 63 · **T** 0570 613412
deheks.nl
Daily from 14.00

The fact that the Witch is the only pub honoured in miniature in the Madurodam theme park in Den Haag is an acknowledgement of its longevity: hospitality has been offered on this site, on and off, for seven centuries. You'll find its terrace on the main square behind the Waag (weigh house): inside is a single room with witches flying from light fittings. Snacks only. The 120-strong Dutch and international beer list incudes 25 taps, one of them dedicated to house blond Pyromaan, brewed by Praght.

Persee

Brink 32
persee.nl
Summer: Th–Su from 13.00; others from 15.00.
Winter: Fr–Su from 13.00; others from 17.00

This bright café with a terrace on the main square has a dancefloor at the back where DJs entertain on Saturday nights. There are instruments on the ceiling, while the red-painted walls are the beer menu: bottles sit on individual shelves, each with its appropriate glass. Snacks only. The 12 taps and 120 bottles feature many Dutch micros including nearby DAVO.

ENSCHEDE
⟷ Enschede

Close to the German border, Overijssel's largest city (pop 158,500) is known in local dialect as Eanske. Over the years it has been periodically rebuilt and redesigned, following a series of fires that earned the townsfolk the nickname *brandstichters* (arsonists). A monument on the Grote Markt commemorates the biggest conflagration that razed the town in 1862. Ironically, Enschede last hit the international headlines in 2000 when a fireworks warehouse exploded, destroying an entire neighbourhood.

Today it is known for being the home of both the Grolsch brewery and FC Twente, the football club where Steve McLaren acquired a Dutch accent. Willem Wilmink, 20th-century writer of much-loved poetry for children, was born here, and murals celebrating both him and poetry in general are dotted around the centre.

HOTEL TIP: **InterCity** ★★★, Willem Wilminkplein 5 (**intercityhotel.com**) is modern and central.

Beiaard

Oude Markt 24 · **T** 053 430 6267
beiaardenschede.nl
Sa from 12.00; Su from 13.00; others from 14.00

Terrace café on the main square, formerly part of the like-named group but now independent. The bar is dominated by its remarkable light fitting, a tangle of twisted metal and glass hanging from a four-panel painted ceiling representing the seasons. Dinners and snacks include dishes cooked with beer. The 150 beers, with 24 on tap, include house Zwarte Ros (Black Rose) brews made at Rigters. Bottles are discounted 40% after 21.00 on Sunday.

België

Oude Markt 20 · **T** 053 574 5616
proeflokaalbelgie.nl
Sa from 10.00; Mo from 14.00; others from 12.00

Sister of the like-named café in Almelo, with a terrace on the main square. The large one-room interior has chandeliers dangling from a high ceiling. Food is snacks, toasties and apple pie. The 90+ beers, including eight draught guests, are nearly all Belgian with a handful of Dutch, including local Eanske, and a couple from Germany.

Stanislaus Brewskovitch

Stadsgravenstraat 59 · **T** 053 203 2470
stanislausbrewskovitch.nl
Shut Mo; Fr-Su from 13.00; others from 16.00

Central brewpub with a small rear beer garden in a white-fronted former church building. The interior is industrial chic, with spotlit pink saint statuettes a token nod to its former role and a brewhouse behind glass. A mezzanine above has album covers on the walls. Lunches, dinners and snacks served. Half the 30 taps are house brews, while the others, and 100+ bottles and cans, present the best of Dutch and international craft. A shop sells bottles to take away.

Vestingbar

De Hems 10 · **T** 053 489 4530
vestingbar.nl
Shut Su; Tu from 20.30; others from 21.00

On the UTwente campus, this student pub welcomes everyone: take bus 1 to UT/Bastille or 9 to Kennispark/UT and look for the cartoon cow. The dive bar interior has a vinyl floor for spillages, no decoration or windows, and 60+ beers including some Dutch craft. Food is from a snack bar dispensing the kind of unhealthy deep-fried fare the regulars prefer.

Vluchte

Oldenzaalsestraat 153a · **T** 06 4661 3680
devluchte.nl
Shut Su&Mo; Sa from 20.00; others from 19.00

Another oddity, this suburban youth centre hidden from the road has billiards, darts, card tables and bowling lanes. No food and no service, unless you want a tap beer. Its treasures are to be found in the chilled Aladdin's Cave beside the bar, stocked with 100+ bottles: help yourself to one of these and a glass and use the button on the floor to get out. Your personal opener harvests the bottle tops used to calculate the bill. Simple. There are also six self-service taps with changing guests.

BEER TO GO
Hennie Berendsen (Deurningerstraat 27 – **T** 053 431 5264 – **slijterijberendsen.nl** – *shut Su; Mo 13.00–18.00; Th 09.00–21.00; Sa 09.00–17.00; others 09.00–18.00*), **north of the station, stocks 1,000 global beers and 1,200 whiskies.**

GRAMSBERGEN

45km WNW from Zwolle off N34
Gramsbergen

Village (pop 3,100) in the northeast of the province. The nearest town, Coevorden, is in Drenthe.

Mommeriete

De Oostermaat 66 · **T** 0524 562511
mommeriete.nl
Daily from 10.00

Brewpub in a former lock-keeper's cottage, a lovely building with shuttered windows and flower boxes. The picturesque canalside terrace is beside a wooden drawbridge. One interior room looks unchanged for 100 years, with a hearth backed with Delftware tiles and a built-in box-bed. Brewing kit occupies another room, and there is a conservatory with an open

hearth. Light lunches; snacks thereafter. Five or six house brews are available.

HENGELO

8km NW of Enschede off A35 exit 28
Hengelo

Provincial city (pop 81,000) that developed with the arrival of the railways. Accidentally flattened by Allied bombing raids, its quick-fix rebuild lacks historical appeal.

HOTEL TIP: **City** ★★★★, B.P. Hofstedestraat 50 (**cityhotelhengelo.com**) is a modern central place.

Pleintje

Burgermeester Jansenplein 25 · **T** 074 291 2425
biercafehetpleintje.nl
Sa from 12.00; Su from 14.00; others from 11.00

Central café with large terrace, the Siamese twin of the adjacent Twee Wezen, which shares a rear kitchen and also offers Pleintje's beers. Indoors is packed to the gills with neon signs, beer ads and enamels. Lunches and dinners served. The 90+ beer list has grown more adventurous, with as many Dutch craft options as safe Belgians.

Twentse

Haaksbergerstraat 51 · **T** 074 250 0681
twentsebierbrouwerijproeflokaal.nl
Shut Mo; Fr 13.00–23.00; Sa 14.00–23.00; Su 14.00–22.00; others 13.00–22.00 (opens later Jul-Aug)

Bus 53 to Vockersweg stops outside the semi-rural terrace of this chic modern bar, which relocated from the city centre to an out-of-

entse, Hengelo

town business park in 2018. Although it has the appropriate kit, no beer had been brewed here as of 2019, so its status as a brewery and taproom is arguable. There is a full food menu. Seven or eight of the 15 taps are house beers brewed in Belgium; others local guests.

Uurwerk

Langestraat 25 · **T** 06 4542 0161
cafehetuurwerk.nl
Shut Su; Fr from 15.00; Sa from 14.00; others from 16.00

The Clockwork is a friendly local with a terrace just north of the centre. Inside, wooden walls, floors and low ceilings give the impression of a ship's cabin or a giant coffin, but with a bar. Snacks only. The 120 beers, some of them displayed in a glass wall cabinet, include local choices to balance the familiar Belgians.

KAMPEN

15km WNW from Zwolle off N50
Kampen

This charming medieval town (pop 36,600) in Overijssel's top-left corner is the last stop before the Flevoland no-fly zone for beer lovers. Three of its seven medieval city gates remain intact and its long main streets are linked by impossibly narrow alleys.

HOTEL TIP: **Stadsboerderij**, Groenestraat 148 (stadsboerderij.nl) is a friendly central B&B.

Stomme van Kampen

Oudestraat 218-220 · **T** 038 337 1721
destommevankampen.nl
Shut Su&Mo; Fr&Sa from 15.00; Tu from 19.00; others from 17.00

The lovely Mute of Kampen is two premises in one. The main bar has panelled walls and a Delftware tile fireplace featuring a depiction of the *Kogge* galleon. A more recent side area has a copy of the 17th-century painting by Hendrick Avercamp which lends the pub its name. Dinners include burgers and spare ribs. Among 16 taps embedded in a copper back bar are some for house De Wereld beers, based here but brewed elsewhere, with tasting flights available. The 70-odd bottles include a good Dutch showing.

OLDENZAAL

10km N from Enschede off A1 exit 32&33
Oldenzaal

Market town (pop 32,000) with possibly the only church in the world dedicated to St Plechelm, an eighth-century Irish monk who moved here from Lindisfarne. Among the exhibits at the Palthehuis Museum (palthehuis.nl) is the custom-made chair in which local 18th-century serial killer Klaas Annink (1710-1775), better known as Huttenkloas, was restrained for 114 days before his trial and subsequent execution by being broken on the wheel.

Engel

Markt 14 · **T** 0541 521903
bierlokaaldeengel.nl
Sa&Su from 12.00; others from 14.00

The Angel is a friendly local with a large terrace, one of those comfortable places where it is too easy to become ensconced for an evening. Every inch of interior wall and most of the wood-beamed ceiling is covered with bric-a-brac, including several cherubs but surprisingly few angels. Snacks and toasties only, with peanuts and occasionally other nibbles handed out for free. The 100+ beers are balanced between modern Dutch and established Belgian choices, though only 60 are listed on the printed menu, with a more current and comprehensive list on the website.

OOTMARSUM

17km E from Almelo on N349
Bus 64

Attractive small town (pop 4,400) close to the German border, tracing its origins back to around AD770. The Open Air Museum (**openluchtmuseumootmarsum.nl**) has regional farm buildings and equipment including some handsome traction engines built in Leeds, with Ootmarsummer beers on sale in its shop.

Oatmössche, Ootmarsum

Oatmössche

Commanderieplein 3/4 · **T** 0541 291330
oatmossche.nl
Shut Mo; others from 11.00

Ootmarsummer's brewery was once hidden on an industrial estate but has relocated in style. Copper kettles dominate the bar area of a chic taproom, with a conservatory on one side overlooking a hop garden. The courtyard terrace has views of another building with conditioning tanks connected to the bar by underground piping. Lunches, dinners and snacks served. Up to 10 house beers are available on tap or in bottle.

RAALTE

25km SE fromZwolle off N35
Raalte

Small modern market town (pop 17,000) that was once home to a brewery used by half the nation's homeless brewers, since relocated east to Albergen.

Zuiderbuur

Grotestraat 28 · **T** 0572 351301
zuiderbuur.nl
Shut Mo&Tu; Su from 14.00; others from 11.00

The Southern Neighbour is a corner café with large artificial grass terrace. The modern and airy interior has light shades with beer enamels on the walls and and a tile theme on the ceiling and bar counter. Tapas, snacks and full meals. Around 120 mostly Belgian

beers include cellar-aged Straffe Hendrik of various vintages and a changing list of limited-quantity guests that sell out quickly.

ZWARTSLUIS

20km N from Zwolle on N331
Bus 71

Quiet harbour village (pop 4,800) linked to Zwolle by the Zwarte Water canal, once an important commercial waterway but now used mainly by recreational boats.

Sluus

Schoolstraat 2 · **T** 06 5364 5714
cafedesluus.nl
Sa&Su from 12.00; others from 15.00

Friendly one-room corner local with a bijou terrace, a medieval-style village map painted on the ceiling, and eclectic paraphernalia that runs from a motorbike engine casing to tea caddies, via rope rigging and a Michelin man. Snacks run to soup, toasties and uitsmijters. Around 100 beers include plenty of Dutch micros.

ZWOLLE

Zwolle

Attractive provincial capital (pop 124,000) and former Hanseatic city. Its ancient fortifications have almost all vanished except for city gate the Sassenpoort, built in 1409, and a moat that still surrounds the centre.

HOTEL TIP: **Hanze ★★★**, Rodetorenplein 10-11 (**hanzehotel.com**) is small and central.

Belgische Keizer

Melkmarkt 58 · **T** 038 421 1011
belgischekeizer.nl
Su from 12.00; others from 10.00

The Belgian Emperor is a lovely pub with not-quite-vertical interior walls and a terrace on a square. Amazingly, the ancient wooden-faced clock incorporated into the back bar is still working. Lunches and dinners served; snacks all day. Most of the 70+ beers reflect the pub's name, including welcome choices like Dupont.

Gezelligheid

Gasthuisplein 11 · **T** 038 331 9140
cafedegezelligheid.nl
Daily from 14.00 (16.00 in winter)

As a friendly one-room brown café, the Cosiness lives up to its name. Beer enamels tick the decor box, alongside some brewing-themed photos. Snacks only. The beer range of 80, including 16 taps, is Belgian-dominated but finds room for local offerings like Witte Leeuw and Axes Castellum.

Hete Brij

Nieuwe Markt 9 · **T** 038 421 7526
cafedehetebrij.nl
Fr-Su from 14.00; others from 16.00

The expresssion *om de hete brij heen draaien* means to delay tackling something difficult, literally to circle round the hot porridge, so the suggested translation is Hot Potato. This friendly café has a small terrace and an 'old and new' interior with carpeted tables. Illustrations on the toilet doors leave little to the imagination: we'll just say 'Adam and Eve' and drop the potato. Snacks only. Dutch beers on the 80+ list include several Bronckhorster, among which Blonde Brij and Bokkige Brij are brewed for the house.

Refter

Bethlehemkerkplein 35a · **T** 038 303 1841
hetrefter.com
Daily from 12.00

Large café with terraces front and back in the Bethlehem cloister: the name means a monastic refectory. The vast main hall has beamed

ceilings and tiled floors, stained-glass highlights in the windows and shelves of custom-ised bottles. Other halls can be rented for events. A full food menu is available. The 250 beers, 20 of them on draught, include a fine selection of local, Dutch and international craft ales.

Woodies

Melkmarkt 34 · **T** 038 458 2213
woodies-zwolle.nl
Shut Mo; Fr&Sa from 10.00; Su 13.00–22.00; Th from 11.00; others 11.00–23.00

Bright and lively grand café with terrace. The vast interior is an eclectic joy for jaded beer writers struggling to find new ways to describe 50 shades of brown: a Mona Lisa copy, a Liberty statue draped in the Stars and Stripes, musical instruments, chandeliers and more. Lunch and dinner are served from an open kitchen. The 160 beers include Dutch craft options from Bird to Van Moll.

OTHER BEER VENUES

Tapas restaurant **Bapas** (Grote Kerkplein 9 – **T** 038 422 1844 – bapaszwolle.nl – *Shut Mo; Th 12.00–23.00; Fr&Sa from 12.00; others 12.00–22.00)* pairs its dishes with 35 beers.
Ramshackle, grungy **In De Buurt** (Luttekestraat 6 – **T** 038 423 5010 – jebentindebuurt.nl – *shut Mo; others from 14.00)* has crafted peeling plaster, bare brick walls and 50 beers.

South Holland

A densely-populated region (pop 3.65 million) that, together with the southern part of North Holland and Utrecht, forms the Randstad, a conurbation of 8.2 million people. But it's not all tower blocks: the north of the province, home to most of the country's famous bulb fields, explodes into glorious technicolour in spring.

The central strip is dominated by the megalopolis encompassing Rotterdam, Den Haag and the industrial docklands of the Europoort. Outside the built-up areas, most of what's left is covered by more than 100 sq km of greenhouses which every year produce hundreds of thosands of tonnes of pretty but largely flavourless tomatoes and other fruit.

Things get quieter further south where the rivers Nederrijn (Lower Rhine) and Maas (Meuse) break up into intertwining channels, creating a network of fertile islands. Near Rotterdam is the attraction responsible for more chocolate box lids and jigsaws than anywhere else: the 19 windmills of the Kinderdijk.

The province's beer credentials are secure, with numerous breweries and the three cities of Delft, Den Haag and Rotterdam worth the journey in themselves. At the other end of the scale is fast-growing Zoetermeer. Fifty years ago just 7,000 people lived there; today 125,000 do, but none of them has yet opened a decent beer bar. If you find yourself stuck there, the best place we've found so far is the Old Blind Mole Irish pub (Dorpsstraat 100a; theoldblindmole.nl) with 40 beers.

LARGEST CENTRES: **Alphen aan den Rijn, Delft, Dordrecht, Gouda, Den Haag, Leiden, Rotterdam, Schiedam, Spijkenisse, Vlaardingen, Zoetermeer.**

MORE INFORMATION: vvvzhz.nl

SELECTED BREWERIES: **Animal Army**, *Den Haag*; **Delftse**, *Delft*; **Dukes**, *Gorinchem*; **Heineken**, *Zoeterwoude*; **Kaapse**, *Rotterdam*; **Klein Duimpje**, *Hillegom*; **Kompaan**, *Den Haag*; **Koperen Kat**, *Delft*; **Leidsch**, *Leiden*; **De Molen**, *Bodegraven*; **Noordt**, *Rotterdam*; **Pelgrim**, *Rotterdam*; **Pronck**, *Leiden*.

ALPHEN AAN DEN RIJN

15km E from Leiden off N11

🚆 Alphen aan den Rijn

Largely modern town (pop 73,000) on the Oude Rijn (Old Rhine), home of the impressive Avifauna bird park (**avifauna.nl**) which claims to have 1,800 species.

HOTEL TIP: Van Der Valk Avifauna ★★★★, Hoorn 65 (**vandervalkavifauna.nl**) is beside the bird park.

Hendrick's Pub

Prins Henrikstraat 119 · **T** 0172 493323
hendrickspub.nl
Shut Mo&Tu; Fr from 15.00; Sa&Su from 14.00; others from 16.00

White-painted corner local with side terrace just south of the centre. Inside is half brown café, half British-style pub with carpeted floors and a dartboard. Food is snacks and toasties, except Thursday when a 'pub grub' main is served. The 100+ beer list is Belgian-oriented but with enough Dutch micros and global imports to maintain interest.

Natte

Julianastraat 19 · **T** 0172 426193
biercafedenatte.nl
Shut Su; others from 16.00

Well-established narrow bar on a shopping street, with a small terrace and an unusually high, beamed ceiling accommodating a mezzanine with extra seating. A glance at the cupboard-sized kitchen beside the bar will explain why the food is limited to snacks and toasties. The 170 beers include some good local choices and a 'specials' list of mostly Dutch barrel-aged stouts and barley wines.

BODEGRAVEN

27km NE from Rotterdam off A12 exit 12/12a

🚆 Bodegraven

Once a sleepy manicured backwater, this small town (pop 20,000) is now firmly on the world beer map thanks to a globally famous craft brewery and two excellent shops. Despite this, many residents still look on in bewilderment when their home is occupied by international beer geeks during the Borefts festival in September.

HOTEL TIP: Stay in **Alphen aan den Rijn** or **Woerden**, each one train stop away.

De Molen

Overtocht 43 · **T** 0172 610848
brouwerijdemolen.nl
Shut Mo&Tu; others from 12.00

The Mill taproom, terrace and restaurant is in the Arkduif (Ark Dove) windmill, built in 1697 but renamed in 1956 following a competition. The bar has wooden ceilings and whitewashed walls, with a canal view at the back. Lunches and dinners use local ingredients and the menu changes seasonally. Around half the 20 taps dispense house brews, also served in tasting glasses. There's also a shop (**demolenbeershop.com** – *shut Mo&Tu; others 12.00-17.00*) selling bottles and cans from dozens of the world's best brewers besides the brewery's own products.

BEER TO GO
De Molen has a first-class shop: see above.
Speciaalbierwinkel (Overtocht 6 – **T** 0172 615558 - **speciaalbierwinkel.be** – *shut Su-We; Th 09.00-18.00; Fr 09.00-20.30; Sa 09.00-17.00*) stocks 500+ beers, around 90% from small Dutch breweries, including the owner's own Kraan (Tap) range brewed at the back.

BRIELLE

26km SW from Rotterdam off N218
Metro Line D to Spijkenisse Centrum, then bus 106

This picturesque fortified town (pop 16,900) has a charming centre laced with cobbled streets. The capture of Brielle in 1572 by Dutch Protestants was a key moment in the Eighty Years' War, as at the time the Spanish occupying forces were on the brink of quashing the uprising.

Kont van 't Paard

Kaatsbaan 1 · **T** 0181 416161
kontvanhetpaard.nl
Daily from 17.00 (phone ahead as it is often booked for private events)

To find the characterful Horse's Arse brewpub, head west from the central square and turn right at the cast-iron cannon and stocks. The old inn has undergone several changes in use, including a stint as a slaughterhouse. The higgledy-piggledy interior has low oak-beam ceilings, with the brewery in a room at the back. Dinners served (*until 21.30*). A couple of house brews are usually available, but if not there are 80+ alternatives.

OTHER BEER VENUES
In the 1788 guardhouse on the picturesque main square, **Hoofdwacht** (Markt 7 – **T** 0181 418393 – **dehoofdwacht-brielle.nl** – *daily from 09.00*) stocks 50 beers.

DELFT
8km SSE from Den Haag off A13 exit 9
⟷ Delft, Delft Zuid

If all towns were as beery as Delft (pop 101,000), this book would double in size. This miniature, more sedate version of Amsterdam has canal-filled streets lined with gabled houses. The precarious 14th-century tower of the Oude Kerk (Heilige Geestkerkhof 25) is notable for its top being two metres out of whack with its base. Those with an interest in history should visit the Prinsenhof museum (**prinsenhof-delft.nl**) where Dutch founding father Willem van Oranje (William the Silent) was shot dead in 1584: the bullet holes are still visible in the wall.

HOTEL TIP: **Leeuwenbrug ★★★**, Koornmarkt 16 (**leeuwenbrug.nl**) is canalside and friendly.

Bebop
Kromstraat 33 · **T** 015 213 5210
jazzcafebebop.nl
Sa&Su from 15.00; Mo from 20.00; others from 16.00

Down a narrow alley, this dimly lit, laid-back jazz café has a small beer garden at the back. Photos of musicians adorn the walls, and brass instruments dangle from the ceiling, as does a pair of skis. Did these belong to Dizz-ski Gillespie, we wonder? There are jam sessions from 20.30 on Thursdays. Snacks only. The improving 90-odd beer list now balances Belgian standards with craft IPAs.

Oude Kerk, D

Bierfabriek
Burgwal 45-49 · **T** 015 364 6154
bierfabriek.com
Fr&Sa from 12.30; Su 12.00–23.00; others 16.00–00.00

Aiming at the young and loud crowd, this central brewpub with a front terrace follows the same formula as its Amsterdam sibling. A spacious interior with brewing kit taking centre stage, surrounded by some self-tapping tables and peanuts in their shells. The food star is charcoal-grilled chicken. Three house beers are served alongside Alfa's unfiltered pils.

Delfts Brouwhuis
Hippolytusbuurt 43
delftsbrouwhuis.nl
Shut Mo; others from 11.00

Central brewpub with a beer garden beside the Oude Kerk. A front bar area splits into a sunken semi-cellar with remnants of 700-year-old stone vaulting, and a double mezzanine above with brewhouse on one side, seating opposite. Lunches and dinners served. Half the 20 taps pour house beers; the remainder being reserved for (mainly Dutch) craft guests. Tasting flights available.

Doerak

Vrouwjuttenland 17 · **T** 06 4569 4928
cafedoerak.nl
Sa from 12.00; Su from 13.00; others from 15.00

The Rascal is an airy and bright corner café with a canalside terrace. Empty Westvleteren crates are a common decorative item in Benelux pubs but here they are a statement of intent, used to decorate the counter. Food stops at snacks, but 180 beers will feed your soul, with an ever-changing cavalcade of Dutch and international craft choices amid more-familiar Belgian names.

Kat in de Stad

Markt 33 · **T** 015 737 0291
dekatindestad.nl
Shut Mo; Tu&We 16.00–23.00; others from 13.00

The Cat in the City is a small café with a terrace beside the town hall on the main square. The interior has tiled floors and 'Delftware' wallpaper featuring the house cat logo. Quiet music and convivial discussions permeate the air. Snacks only. The list of 100+ beers is exclusively Dutch and mainly from craft micros including co-owner Koperen Kat.

-Kat in de Stad

Klomp

Binnenwatersloot 5 · **T** 015 212 3810
bierhuisdeklomp.nl
Daily from 16.00

The Clog was founded in 1652 in a 1538 building, making it Delft's oldest pub. The wooden front bar creaks every time anyone gets up. Behind it is a lighter snug and a tiled

17th-century scullery with a brick floor that conjures up images of Vermeer. Snacks only. It would be worth a visit even if the beer list were rubbish, which it happily is not, with 90 choices including Kees! and local Koperen Kat, alongside 60 jenevers.

Klooster

Vlamingstraat 2 · **T** 06 4569 4928
cafehetklooster.nl
Sa&Su from 14.00; others from 16.00

Corner bar the Cloister has a micro terrace and a macro beer list. A change of ownership has seen its old-school brown decor morph into hipster minimalism with bare-brick chic. Snacks only. The beer menu of 170+, including 20 draught choices, is now mainly modern craft, with on-trend IPAs, stouts and sours both locally sourced and imported from Europe and elsewhere.

Koperen Kat

Schieweg 15M · **T** 06 4212 3398
koperenkat.nl
Shut Mo–We; Th from 21.00; Fr 16.00–21.00; others 14.00–20.00

Taproom in old cable factory five minutes walk from Delft Zuid station. The bar is directly beside the brewing kit, and a terrace opens in summer. Be warned that Thursday is karaoke night, with live music on most Sunday afternoons. Snacks only. House beers are served from 12 taps.

Locus Publicus

Brabantse Turfmarkt 67 · **T** 015 213 4632
locuspublicus.nl
Su from 12.00; others from 11.00

First opened in 1978, this cramped and popular brown café gets narrow at the back, where customers sit elbow-to-elbow at busy times as if on a rush-hour train. If you can find space, the front terrace offers respite. Inside, beer memorabilia adorns every inch of wall and ceiling. Simple lunches and snacks available. The 200+ beers lean heavily towards Belgium, with a growing number of Dutch microbrewed gatecrashers.

Proeflokaal

Gasthuislaan 36 · **T** 015 212 4922
facebook.com/ProeflokaalDelft
Sa&Su from 12.00; others from 16.00

Large canalside pub with polystyrene ceilings that suggest a 1970s origin. Round the central bar are two seating areas, one decked out with football scarves and TVs showing live games, the other half a standard brown café. Snacks only. The 100 beers include several from Dutch micros and a few UK and German imports.

OTHER BEER VENUES
In an industrial building south of the centre, **Huszar** (Hooikade 13 – **T** 015 262 6562 – huszar.nl – *daily 11.00-00.00*) stocks 40+ beers with a strong Dutch bias while sharing in 'Vermeer's View', the outlook over the river Schie made famous by the baroque painter. **Waag** (Markt 11 – **T** 015 213 0393 – de-waag.nl – *Su from 11.00; others from 10.00*) is a 17th-century weigh house with a stone facade, a grand interior and a less grand 40 beers.

BEER TO GO
Flink Gegist (Oosteinde 227 – **T** 015 785 1308 – flinkgegist.nl – *shut Mo&Tu; Fr 12.00-21.00; Sa 10.00-18.00; others 12.00-18.00*) stocks 700+ beers from around the world.

DEN HAAG

🚉 Den Haag CS & Den Haag HS

Officially known as 's-Gravenhage, and to English speakers as The Hague, Den Haag (pop 528,000) is the nation's centre of government but not its capital city – Amsterdam does that. The royal family maintains a residence here, alongside many multinational companies and foreign embassies.

Despite its size, it can seem oddly quiet at times. It's not overwhelmed with tourists and bicycles like Amsterdam and lacks the metropolitan atmosphere of Rotterdam. Indeed it is quite a pleasant place, even if most visitors are here on business and fail to notice.

Two wildly different art galleries are worth your time. For Old Masters by Vermeer and Rembrandt, visit the Mauritshuis (**mauritshuis.nl**). Down the road is Escher in

het Paleis (**escherinhetpaleis.nl**), filled with the works of MC Escher, whose mind-bending graphics are best seen before rather than after a session in the pub. If on a short visit to the Netherlands just head to Madurodam (**madurodam.nl**), a unique permanent exhibition of virtually every important Dutch building or monument shrunk to 1:25 scale.
HOTEL TIP: Patten ★★★, Wagenstraat 127–129 (**pattenhotel.nl**) has rooms close to the centre.

Beer Garden

Kerkplein 1–3 · **T** 070 326 0937
beergarden.nu
Daily from 15.00

Despite the name, this place is below ground in a 14th-century vaulted cellar, with a terrace beside the Grote Kerk. The interior goes minimalist with few frills. Eating options are, in their words, "organic sophisticated junk food", meaning posh hot dogs and burgers. The 120+ beers, 12 on tap, include plenty of Dutch craft choices, albeit with few surprises.

Brody's

Korte Molenstraat 2 · **T** 070 215 5827
brodys.nl
Shut Mo; Fr–Su from 14.00; others from 16.00

This self-styled American taphouse is a large, slick, modern place with loud music and plenty of reflective bling on the ceiling and bar counter. Snacks only. The 25 taps showcase an ever-changing parade of US craft imports rarely seen on this side of the Atlantic, although prices often reflect that exclusivity.

De La Gare

Nieuwe Schoolstraat 13A · **T** 070 744 6255
delagare.nl
Shut Mo; Fr–Su from 16.00; others from 16.30

The Station Café is in a former coaching inn, with a terrace on a quiet square two blocks behind the opulent Hotel des Indes. The tiled-floor light-brown interior gains further atmosphere after dark when staff light candles on tables. Snacks only. The 150 bottles lined up on the back wall illustrate the beer choice, among them numerous Dutch craft options.

Fiddler

Riviervismarkt 1 · **T** 070 365 1955
fiddler.nl
Mo from 16.00; others from 12.00

Large brewpub with wood everywhere, including casks used as tables. It ups its British pub credentials with a red phone box and a history as one of the overseas outposts of the now-defunct UK-based Firkin brewpub chain. Food is burgers and pub grub, with fish and chips and all-day English breakfasts. The Animal Army brewery, in a side room, produces cask ales that feature on the handpumps. Beyond that, a list of 200+ guests renders this place unmissable.

Franklin

Valkenbosplein 24 · **T** 070 785 1412
cafefranklin.nl
Sa&Su from 15.00; others from 16.00

Popular suburban local with terrace beside busy junction: tram 3 stops outside. The stylishly modern interior has parquet floors and a sofa corner with wood-burning stove for winter evenings. Dinners (*from 17.00*) include steak and mussels. Several guests, often from local brewers, rotate among its 60+ beers. Card payments only.

Hoppzak

Papestraat 26A · **T** 070 744 9673
facebook.com/bierspeciaalcafehoppzak
Shut Mo; others from 16.00

This central cellar bar is a place to unwind quietly at the end of a long day, with low lighting and non-intrusive music creating a laid-back vibe. The bijou one-room bar has ample seating at the back and a bottle cellar on display around the corner. Snacks and toasties only. The 180 beers include 15 draughts, with a fine Dutch and international range. There are also 80+ whiskies.

Huppel the Pub

Oude Molstraat 21 · **T** 070 360 9113
dehuppel.nl
Sa&Su from 15.00; others from 16.00

Located on a narrow shopping street, this friendly bar is a popular city centre gathering point. The split-level brown café interior has wood and beer enamels aplenty. Food is toasties and snacks. The beer list of 60 is dominated by local and Dutch micros, but even this is eclipsed by the whiskies, with 150+ single malts on offer, also served in tasting flights.

Kompaan's taproom

Kompaan

Saturnusstraat 55 · **T** 070 762 2494
kompaanbier.nl
Shut Mo-We; Sa 11.00–01.00; Su 11.00–22.00; others 16.00–01.00

Kompaan's taproom is a warehouse with canalside terrace on an industrial estate southeast of the centre: take bus 26 or 46. The interior is a collage of cutaway shipping containers, with the brewery in the next room and a mezzanine above the main bar. Lunches and dinners served. The 20 taps pour house beers, also available as tasting flights, with a handful of guests. Card payments only.

Lokaal Duinoord

Obrechtstraat 198 · **T** 070 743 0000
lokaalduinoord.nl
Daily from 16.00

In an up-and-coming area west of the centre
– take tram 3 or 11 – this corner local has a
streetside terrace and a brown café interior
with on-trend light fittings adding a
contemporary touch among the beer
enamels. Mirrors on one wall give a distorted
sense of space. Dinners served (*17.30–22.00*).
Around 70 well-chosen beers focus on local-
ish micros from the Randstad.

Murphy's Law

Dr. Kuyperstraat 7 · **T** 070 427 2507
murphysjazz.nl
Shut Su; others from 16.00

The name and cosy red-ceilinged interior of
this friendly local near the city centre suggest
an Irish theme, but beyond a couple of
corporate taps this doesn't influence the 90+
beer selection. There were more Estonian
choices than Irish on our last visit, the rest
leaning towards Dutch and global craft.
Snacks only, and live music occasionally.

Paas

Dunne Bierkade 16a · **T** 070 360 0019
depaas.nl
Sa&Su from 15.00; others from 16.00

Just north of HS station, with a terrace partly
on a canal barge, light-brown café Easter is a
well-established drinking institution. White-
tiled walls and marble-topped tables make a
change from wood. Snacks only, but the range
is extensive. The beer list hovers around 180,
with Dutch micros and other international
stars gradually displacing the Belgian majority.

Prael

Esperantoplein 20 · **T** 070 568 0834
depraeldenhaag.nl
*Shut Mo; Sa 12.00–23.00; Su 12.00–22.00;
others 09.00–23.00*

Prael's third venue is a vast pub with a canalside terrace below a modern office block northwest of the centre: take tram 11. A display of
global craft bottles on one wall is arranged
to resemble a world map. Food from an open
kitchen includes daily special offers. Draught
and bottled house beers are served.

Rootz

Grote Marktstraat 14 · **T** 070 363 9988
rootz.nl
Daily from 10.00

Popular grand café with terrace near Grote
Markt. Once a coach house, the building
displays something of its heritage, with
old brick walls and ceiling beams inside.
Candlelit tables expand into a dining room
above. Lunch and dinner served. The double-
sided beer menu has 150 Dutch craft options
on one side and 150 Belgians on the other.

Van Kinsbergen

Prins Hendrikplein 15 · **T** 070 310 7892
gastropubvankinsbergen.nl
Sa&Su from 10.00; others from 11.00

Swish gastro brewpub in a grand brick building
on a circular 'square' north of the centre: take
tram 16. The interior has black and white tiled
floors, pot plants and big windows. Lunches
and dinners served. The house Pale Ale is
brewed elsewhere, but others are from the
brewing kit in the glassed-off room to one
side. Around 80 guests are mostly Dutch
and international craft.

OTHER BEER VENUES

In the former butter market, atmospheric **Boterwaag** (Grote Markt 10 – **T** 070 365 9686 – boterwaag.nl – *daily from 10.00*) has high ceilings, brick floors and around 50 beers.

Gekke Geit (Lutherse Burgwal 5 – **T** 070 220 4026 – *Su 09.00-22.00; others from 16.00*) is an informal hostel café with occasional live music and 40 often-interesting beers.

In the suburb of Zuiderpark, concert venue **Musicon** (Soestdijksekade 345 – **T** 070 368 6800 – musicon.nl – *Sa&Su from 15.00; others from 17.00*) has regular gigs and a list of 50+ beers.

BEER TO GO

Free Beer Co (Prinsestraat 59 – **T** 070 331 1392 – freebeerco.com – *shut Mo; Su 12.00-17.00; Tu&We 12.00-18.00; others 12.00-21.00*) is a bijou place with a small but excellent range of global craft ales and a growler station. Despite the name, they expect payment.

In an 1826 building near Voorburg station, **Voorburgs Bierwinkel** (Wielemakerssloop 8, Voorburg – **T** 070 444 8632 – voorburgsebierwinkel.nl – *shut Su&Mo; Sa 09.00-17.00; others 10.00-18.00*) has wood-beamed ceilings, a fireplace and 400+ mostly local and Dutch beers.

DEN HAAG – Scheveningen

5km N from Den Haag
Tram 1 from Den Haag city centre,
11 from HS station

This coastal suburb of Den Haag functions almost as a separate town, and is a major beach resort. Its name is legendarily unpronounceable to non-Dutch speakers and was allegedly used as a means of detecting undercover German agents during World War II.

Brouwcafé de Hofnar

Dr. Lelykade 28 · **T** 070 354 0970
hetbrouwcafe.nl
Mo from 11.00; others from 10.00

Despite its name, the harbourside Court Jester is no longer a brewpub as its kit was removed to make extra space for drinking, but it still stocks a worthwhile beer range.

The modern interior has a photo mural on one wall of an overcrowded beach scene. Lunches and dinners served. Its 80 beers include the Scheveningen range, now brewed elsewhere.

DORDRECHT

22km SE from Rotterdam off A16 exit 21
Dordrecht

Provincial city (pop 119,000) with an old-world core evoking memories of its centuries as a global trade hub beside a great river. Things nearly came splashing to a halt in 1421 when a flood inundated much of the city: a stained-glass window in the wonky-towered Grote Kerk commemorates this.

De Tijd

Voorstraat 170 · **T** 078 613 3997
detijddordrecht.nl
Fr from 15.00; Sa&Su from 14.00; others from 16.00

For three decades this one-room terrace café has ploughed a lonely furrow as the beer world's sole local torchbearer. Behind a stepped-gabled facade from 1603 is a pleasingly scruffy interior with marble-topped tables. Food runs to snacks and toasties. The 160+ beers, with 14 on draught, remain Belgian-oriented, but nearby producers and pan-European craft influences are increasingly creeping in.

GORINCHEM

37km ESE from Rotterdam off A15 exit 27

🚆 Gorinchem

Known locally as Gorcum, this attractive old town (pop 35,000) is filled with narrow cobbled streets, although its sole entry here is neither old nor cobbled.

Dukes

Dr. H. B. Wiardi Beckmanplein 60
T 0183 750297
stadsbrouwerijdukes.nu
Th&Fr only from 17.00; & 1st Su of month 14.00–19.00

Modern brewpub in an eastern suburb, in effect the bar of an adjoining sports centre: take bus 1 from the station. The mock-old brown café has brewing kit behind glass, a mezzanine and a terrace. Snacks and schnitzels for food. House beers are served on tap and sold in bottles to take home.

GOUDA

24km NE from Rotterdam off A12 exit 11

🚆 Gouda

This vehicle-unfriendly small city (pop 72,300) is indelibly associated with the nation's best-known dairy product, though it's made on farms in the surrounding countryside rather than in the city itself. At the cheese market

on the main square every Thursday morning, men in fancy dress rearrange piles of orange wax-coated wheels for tourists to photograph. The giant wedding cake that is the 15th-century town hall makes a great backdrop. Products actually made in town are mostly not as photogenic: they include clay pipes, candles and *stroopwafels* (syrup waffles).

HOTEL TIP: **Utrechtsche Dom★★**, Geuzenstraat 6 (**hotelgouda.nl**) is central, small, and friendly.

Goudse Eend

Wilhelminastraat 66 · **T** 06 5120 7944
cafedegoudseeend.nl
Shut Mo; Fr&Sa from 14.00; others 14.00–22.00

The city was crying out for a serious beer contender when the Gouda Duck appeared like a knight in hop-clad armour. This convivial one-room corner local near the centre has a classic interior with tiled floors and partly wood-panelled walls. Snacks only. The landlord's beer credentials include a stint as chair of the PINT beer consumer group. His 160+ well-chosen offerings including nine taps feature many local and regional brewers.

OTHER BEER VENUES
Opened in 1916, **Central** (Markt 23 – **T** 0182 512576 – **grandcafecentral.nl** – *shut Mo; Th&Fr from 09.00; Sa from 08.30; Su 10.00–23.00; others 09.00–23.00*) has 30 beers and murals from 1924 that claim to be the missing link between art nouveau, art deco and De Stijl.

BEER TO GO
A treasure trove in a lovely old building, **Der Gouwen Aar** (Oosthaven 6 – **T** 0182 581958 – **slijterijdengouwenaar.nl** – *Mo 12.00–17.00; Th 10.00–21.00; others 10.00–18.00*) **stocks 1,000 beers and hosts regular tastings.**

HILLEGOM

12km SSW from Haarlem on N208

🚆 Hillegom (2km NW of town)

Small town (pop 21,000) among the bulbfields. From mid-March to mid-May the nearby Keukenhof gardens (**keukenhof.nl**) are home to seven million tulips and almost as many tourists.

Klein Duimpje

Hyacintenlaan 2A · **T** 0252 531186
kleinduimpje.nl
Shut Mo–Th; Fr&Sa 13.00–20.00; Su 13.00–18.00

The best way to this taproom is on bus 50 from Haarlem or Leiden or 361 from Schiphol or Noordwijk: get off at Hillegom Steenfabriek to find it in a semi-rural industrial building behind the petrol station. A canalside terrace fronts the modern, functional interior. Bar snacks only. Six house beers are on tap, with tasting flights, and many others in bottle, also on sale to take home.

OTHER BEER VENUES

Zomerzorg (Meerlaan 70 – **T** 0252 515228 – zomerzorg.nl – *shut We; Sa&Su from 11.30; Mo 15.00–23.00; Tu 15.00–21.00; others from 15.00*) is a friendly corner local with good food and 50+ beers, including Klein Duimpje, that just misses a full entry.

LEIDEN

16km NE from Den Haag off A44 exit 8
Leiden

Picturesque old streets and canals abound in this university city (pop 121,500), along with a few intact city gates. In 1620, it was home to a group of English Puritans who, on deciding that the Netherlands was no more godly a place than their immoral homeland, set out for a new life in the New World. First returning to England on the *Speedwell*, they joined up in Plymouth with a likeminded group on another ship, the *Mayflower*, before crossing the Atlantic to reach what is now New England and become collectively known as the Pilgrim Fathers.

It is said that a mere decade later, local physician Franciscus Sylvius became the first person to flavour grain alcohol with juniper, creating the world's oldest jenever, or gin, a story only spoiled by the fact he was not born for another century and jenever is known to have existed in Flanders two centuries earlier. But that is strong drink for you.

HOTEL TIP: **Mayflower ★★★**, Beestenmarkt 2 (hotelmayflower.nl) enjoys a prime central spot.

Lemmy's

Morsstraat 24 · **T** 071 512 6402
biercafe.nl
Sa&Su from 15.00; others from 17.00

One-room wooden-floored rough and ready rock and blues bar with photos of music stars on the walls, the titular Lemmy included. There are a few tables, but it is mostly standing room only, with occasional live music. Snacks only. Some 100+ beers on a well-chosen list hail from as close by as local Leidsch and as far afield as New Zealand.

Meneer Jansen

Nieuwe Rijn 21 · **T** 071 513 3197
cafemeneerjansen.nl
Daily from 10.00

One of several bars in town with a terrace on a canal barge, this one's selling points are a decent beer list and a fine view across to the historic Vismarkt. The compact light-brown interior has a raised stage area at the back where musicians sometimes play. Snacks only. The 70 beers include a dozen options from local micros Pronck, Leidsch and Neptunus.

Olivier

Hooigracht 23 · **T** 071 512 2444
leiden.cafe-olivier.be
Fr&Su from 12.00; Sa from 11.00; others from 16.00

Built in 1892 by Franciscan sisters, this was a hospital before it became part of a Belgian-themed chain, with a grand wood-panelled main bar and rear dining room. Food is mostly Belgian, including mussels, but burgers also appear. Maximus, Jopen and other Dutch entrants may lurk among an otherwise all-Belgian beer cast of 80.

Stadsbrouwhuis Leiden

Aalmarkt 1–3f · **T** 071 532 7646
stadsbrouwhuis.nl
Shut Mo&Tu; Sa&Su from 11.00; others from 15.00

Canalside brewpub with terrace by a cobbled bridge. The wonky building looks old outside but is modern within, with beer enamels, glasses and bottles on shelves and brewing kit visible through glass at the back. Food is Dutch pub grub (satay and burgers). Around five house beers number among the 20 draught options, with tasting flights available.

OTHER BEER VENUES

Lovely **Bonte Koe** (Hooglandsekerkkoorsteeg 13 – **T** 071 514 1094 – **cafedebontekoe.net** – *Sa from 12.30; Su from 13.30; others from 16.00*) has tiled murals with an art nouveau bovine theme: it was originally intended as a butcher's shop but became a pub with 30 beers instead.

De Twee Spiegels (Nieuwstraat 11 – **T** 071 887 3943 – detweespieghels.nl – *Sa from 14.00; Su from 15.00; others from 16.00*) is a cosy jazz café with live music most nights and the full range of local Pronck beers.

Ancient **Vergulde Kruik** (Haarlemmerstraat 22 – **T** 071 512 0509 – verguldekruik.nl – *Sa from 11.00; Su 12.00–22.00; others from 15.00*) boasts porcelain urinals dating from 1881 and the only two surviving silver beer taps in the country, as well as 45 beers.

BEER TO GO

Bierwinkel (Hartesteeg 9 – **T** 071 566 5770 – bierwinkel-leiden.nl – *shut Su; Mo 12.00–17.00; Th 12.00–21.00; Sa 10.00–18.00; others 10.00–18.30*) is a cramped central shop with 500 beers and 200 whiskies.

Drankenhandel Leiden (Zeemanlaan 22B – **T** 071 240 0285 – **speciaalbierpakket.nl** – *shut Su; Sa 08.30–18.00; others 09.00–18.00*) stocks 500+ beers with a good Dutch selection and has an online store.

NIEUWKOOP

10km ENE from Alphen aan den Rijn off N231
Bus 147

Semi-rural town (pop 9,400) once declared the nation's safest. If driving, do not approach from Bodegraven: as we learned from experience, Ziendeweg looks like a short cut but must be the Netherlands' busiest single-track road.

Hollandsche Leeuw

Dorpsstraat 75 · **T** 0172 755009
hollandscheleeuw.nl
Shut Mo–Tu; Su 15.00–21.00; We-Th 15.00–22.00; others from 15.00

The oldest building in town, the Holland Lion is a lovely thatched pub with a side terrace. The ancient interior has precariously leaning walls covered in oil paintings and ageing wallpaper. Live music some weekends. Dinners and snacks available. Around 100 beers include local De Molen and changing guests on an otherwise Belgian-heavy menu.

sche Leeuw, Nieuwkoop

NOORDWIJK

12km NNW from Leiden on N444
Bus 20

Former fishing port, now a seaside resort (pop 25,900). The biggest employer outside tourism is ESTEC, the European Space Agency's research and technology centre. If it is European and connected with space travel, it was probably designed here.

Harbourlights

Koningin Wilhelmina Boulevard 9
T 071 361 7705
harbourlights.nl
Su from 12.00; others from 16.00

Coastal brown café, although dunes block the sea view. The dominant theme of the interior is nautical, with lanterns, buoys and bells on the ceiling and a ship's wheel on the wall. Food is burgers and satay, with fish and chips the only reminder of the bar's origins as a British-style pub. Around 20 of the 100 beers are from Dutch micros, the rest Belgian.

NOORDWIJKERHOUT

12.5km N from Leiden on N206

Bus 57 from Hillegom, Leiden or Voorhout Small town (pop 16,400) among the bulb fields, with a cutesy white church at its heart, imaginatively named de Witte Kerk (the White Church).

Van Der Geest

Zeestraat 7a · **T** 0252 372306
cafevandergeest.nl
Mo 14.00–22.00; others from 14.00

Central local with a terrace on a pedestrianised street: alight at Victoriberg if using bus 57. The bright interior has blue walls hung with enamels and copies of oil paintings. Food is toasties and snacks, with a few dinner mains that will send vegetarians sprinting for cover. Half the 100 beers are Dutch, with 20+ small brewers represented and a guest tap reserved for local brewers such as Leidsch and Klein Duimpje, which also feature among the bottles.

ROTTERDAM

Rotterdam CS, Rotterdam Blaak

The Netherlands' second city (pop 624,000) is an industrial, commercial and maritime hub. The Port of Rotterdam, including the city docks and Europoort, is the largest and busiest in Europe, covering a 100 sq km swathe westwards to the North Sea.

The city was badly damaged in World War II, particularly in one bombing raid on May 14 1940 during the Nazi invasion which made 85,000 people homeless. For a poignant reminder, follow the Fire Line, a string of lights in the pavement that marks the boundary of the area destroyed.

A few districts, notably Delfshaven, escaped unscathed and retain their historic character. Elsewhere, post-war policy has encouraged top architects to build high and build flashy, creating a metropolitan cityscape unlike anywhere else in the Netherlands and sometimes dubbed Manhattan-on-the-Maas. For a bird's eye view, ascend the 185m Euromast (**euromast.nl**), and don't miss the spectacular Markthal (**markthal.nl**) indoor market, displaying an 11,000 sq m mural that is the world's largest painting. More traditional fine art can be found in the Museum Boijmans Van Beuningen (**boijmans.nl**), with a collection that's among the best in the country.

HOTEL TIP: **Breitner ★★★**, Breitnerstraat 23 (**hotelbreitner.nl**) is central, but on a quiet street.

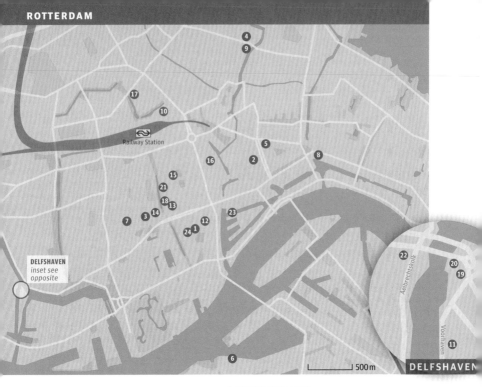

Bierboutique ❶

Witte de Withstraat 40B · **T** 010 223 5442
bierboutique-rotterdam.nl
Shut Mo; Fr-Su from 12.00;
others from 16.00

Chic modern bar with a small terrace.
The interior pulls out all the fashion stops:
black and white 'zebra' floor tiles, dark wood,
mirrors, a faux stag's head and designer
lighting. Lunches and dinners are served
from a kitchen resembling a deli, its windows
hung with food. Corporate offerings dominate
the 10 taps but 80 bottles and cans include
beers from several Rotterdam brewers.

Bokaal ❷

Nieuwemarkt 11 · **T** 010 720 0898
bokaalrotterdam.nl
Daily from 11.00

This modern café near Blaak station has mostly
glass walls, industrial chic architecture,
salvaged wood features and a large terrace.
The full food menu goes pan-European,
with steak tartare, risotto and fish and chips.
The 80-ish beers are half Dutch, half Belgian,
with a good portion from local brewers.

Boudewijn ❸

Nieuwe Binnenweg 53A-B · **T** 010 436 3562
bbcboudewijn.nl
Daily from 12.00

Large café with front terrace, rear garden and
split-level interior which is partly subterranean.
A mostly Belgian food menu includes mussels
but also burgers. Despite this officially being a
Belgian beer bar and naming itself after several
of that nation's kings, it stocks considerable
numbers of local and other Dutch gatecrashers
among a list of 220+, including 28 taps.

Brewpub Reijngoud

Vijverhofstraat 8-10 · **T** 010 503 6327
brewpubreijngoud.nl
Shut Mo&Tu; others from 15.00

Brewpub with terrace, built in the arches
beneath a disused railway northeast of
Centraal station, under the same ownership
as Boudewijn (above) and Reijngoud (below).
The long narrow interior is filled with
hanging plants, with the brewery behind
glass at one end. Food includes hot dogs,
flammkuchen and burgers. House beers and
guests are dispensed through 40 taps.

Faas

Zwaanshals 248 · **T** 010 341 5097
facebook.com/proeflokaalfaas
Sa&Su from 14.00; We&Th from 16.00;
others from 17.00

Friendly corner local with a terrace, north of
the centre. The brown café interior has a sofa
corner, wood-panelled walls with red above,
large windows, a bit of Delftware tiling
behind the bar and occasional live music.
Nibbles only. Around 100 beers, including
15 draught, encompass a decent selection
from local brewers and other Dutch micros.

Gele Kanarie

Goudsesingel 284 · **T** 010 333 5444
degelekanarie.com
Daily from 11.00

Yellow Canary is a modern brewpub with a
streetside terrace on a busy junction. The
spacious interior has a central serving area,
floor-to-ceiling windows and a gas-effect
hearth, with the brewery in the cellar.
Lunches and dinners served. Forty or so
beers include house brand Hoppie Blond
among a strong Dutch showing.

Kaapse Proeflokaal

Veerdijk 19d · **T** 010 218 0853
kaapsebrouwers.nl
Shut Mo; others 12.00-23.00

Kaapse's taproom is part of the Fenix Food
Factory, a collective of outlets in a docklands
warehouse. The waterside terrace has views
of the Kop van Zuid skyscrapers and the Hotel
New York. The brewing kit is at one end of
the spacious bar area. An outdoor oven bakes
flammkuchen when weather allows; otherwise bring in food from one of the neighbours.
The 20 taps dispense house beers and craft
guests, with a bottle shop around the side.

Kraft Bar R'dam

Nieuwe Binnenweg 99b · **T** 010 843 3842
kraftbarrdam.nl
Shut Mo&Tu; Sa&Su from 12.00; others from 16.00

Part of a growing empire that includes
Boudewijn (above) and the Reijngoud (below),
this modern corner bar has stools and high
tables, a raised platform at the back and a
huge mural of the view from the Euromast.
Food is *flammkuchen* and snacks. Around 80
beers, with 22 taps, include a good Rotterdam
selection and several global craft imports.

Locus Publicus & Locus International

Oostzeedijk 364 & 358B
T 010 433 1761 & 010 412 6606
locus-publicus.com
Daily from 16.00 (International: Shut Su&Mo)

Two pubs in one. Open since 1988, Locus
Publicus remains one of the country's most
respected beer cafés. The one-room pub in
a 1904 building that survived the war has an
open wood fire and tiled wall friezes depicting
farming scenes and spice growing, recalling its
former use as a grocer's shop. Locus International, three doors down, arrived in 2014 with
more modern decor. Snacks only at both.
Draught beers tend towards traditional in the
former, contemporary global craft in the latter,
but the 200+ bottle list is the same in both.

Noordt

Zaagmolenkade 46 · **T** 010 223 0566
brouwerijnoordt.nl/taproom
Shut Mo-We; Th 15.00-19.00; Fr 15.00-21.00;
others 14.00-19.00

Taproom in a warehouse north of the centre:
take tram 7 or bus 38. The basic interior has
concrete floors and chipboard walls, with tanks
lined up along one of them. Snacks only.
Most of the 20 taps serve the house range,
and there's a shop for takeaways (*also open
Mo-We 09.00-18.00*). Card payments only.

Noordt

Le Nord

Proveniersstraat 33A · **T** 010 265 4438
lenord.nl
Su 11.30–23.00; others from 11.00

Corner pub with a terrace in a residential area near Centraal station. A ground-level front bar splits into a sunken brown café and an upstairs space with button-back sofas and 'old stuff': a telephone, radio and typewriter. Further back is a more formal restaurant. Full meals and snacks. Around 65 beers err on the safe side but include IJ and Texels.

Oude Sluis

Havenstraat 7 · **T** 010 477 3068
cafedeoudesluis.nl
Sa&Su from 14.00; others from 12.00

A café since 1912, the characterful Old Lock sits at the north end of the historic Delfshaven harbour – a terrace and rear conservatory both look out over the water. Interior walls are dominated by wooden bas reliefs featuring scenes of revelry inspired by the paintings of Jan Steen. Snacks only. The 80+ beers are Belgium-focussed but very strong on global Trappists.

Pelgrim

Aelbrechtskolk 12 · **T** 010 477 1189
pelgrimbier.nl
Shut Mo&Tu; Su 12.00–22.00; others 12.00–00.00

Delfshaven brewpub beside the Pilgrim Father's church, in the building where the travellers assembled for departure in 1620: a passenger list from the *Mayflower* is on display. The brewery is to the left, the café with its low beamed ceilings and chiming clocks to the right, with a courtyard garden and front terrace. Lunches and dinners served. Around six house draught beers are available: go for the tasting flight if unsure.

Reijngoud

Schiedamse Vest 148 · **T** 010 414 6050
proeflokaalreijngoud.nl
Daily from 12.00

Modern street corner bar with a large terrace west of the Maritime Museum. The light,

airy interior has high ceilings and minimalist furnishings, with exposed concrete and a mezzanine above. Food (*11.30–22.00*) covers many bases including rolls, burgers and *flammkuchen*. You'll find plenty of local, Dutch, German and UK craft options on the 200-strong beer list, with de la Senne and De Ranke among the Belgians. Half the 24 taps are allocated to changing guests.

Sijf

Oude Binnenweg 115 · **T** 010 433 2610
sijf.nl
Daily from 09.30

Classic art nouveau corner café with a terrace on a busy shopping street. The high-ceilinged front section splits into an upstairs-downstairs sitting area at the rear. Food starts with breakfast and goes all the way through. The 100+ beers veer a little towards Belgium but include local Noordt and Amsterdam's Oedipus.

Stalles

Nieuwe Binnenweg 11a · **T** 010 436 1655
cafestalles.nl
Daily from 12.00

Central multi-roomed brown café with front terrace and pool tables upstairs. All-day pizzas form the core of the menu, alongside toasties which stop early. The 100 beers, 22 on tap, include plenty from small Dutch brewers. The whisky list is even longer, and some of the empty bottles have ended up as light fittings.

Steak & Bier

Karel Doormanstraat 290 · **T** 010 433 2582
steakenbierrestaurant.nl
Daily 11.00–22.00

Pelgrim, R…

This modern joint with a terrace on the theatre square is more all-day restaurant than pub, with framed photos on the walls and plushly upholstered seating. There's a clue in the name about the dining options, but other foodstuffs are available. The list of 70 beers is mostly predictable but with enough Rotterdam brewers to hold our interest.

– **proeflokaal-de-ooievaar.business.site** – *shut Mo; Su from 12.00; others from 11.30*) is a lovely old-fashioned brown café by Delfshaven with 30 beers.

Traditional brown local the **Riddert** ㉑ (Mauritsweg 28 – **T** 010 226 1068 – riddert.nl – *daily from 17.00*) has 25 beers and claims to be Rotterdam's smallest café, and having squeezed our way in, we cannot argue.

Another grand old Delfshaven corner local, **Vanouds 't Kraantje** ㉒ (Schiedamseweg 2A – **T** 010 477 0153 – biertapperij.nl – *daily from 12.00*) has 50 beers and stained glass windows with art deco details.

A 1951 lightship that once protected the Welsh coastline, **V11** ㉓ (Wijnhaven 101 – vessel11.nl – *Fr from 12.00; Sa from 11.00; Su 11.00-23.00; others 12.00-23.00*) is now an English-style pub brewing its own beers at Steffelaar, not technically real ales though dispensed for show through traditional handpumps. With a half-decent selection of 50+ beers, central brown café **Witte Aap** ㉔ (Witte de Withstraat 78 – **T** 010 414 9565 – dewitteaap. nl – *Sa&Su from 12.00; others from 15.00*) gets packed late at night as it stays open long after all the rest have closed.

BEER TO GO

Bier en Zo (Hoogstraat 54a – **T** 010 411 2496 – bierenzo.nl – *shut Su&Mo; Sa 10.00-17.00; others 11.00-17.30*) stocks 600+ brews, with quality in all areas, also available to order online.
De Biergids (Vlietlaan 18 – **T** 010 242 0336 – *shut Mo 13.00-19.00; others 10.00-19.00*) has a modest selection of a few hundred beers hand-picked by the knowledgeable owner.
Hop In (Zwaanshals 484 – hop-in.nl – *shut Mo&Tu; We 12.00-18.00; Th&Fr 12.00-19.00; Sa 11.00-18.00; Su 11.00-17.00*) has a carefully chosen range of 400 local and global craft, with a focus on vintage and barrel-aged ales.

Thoms Stadsbrouwerij ⑯

Halvemaanpassage 1 · **T** 010 333 5322
thoms.nu/stadsbrouwerij
Shut Mo; Su 12.00-23.00; others from 12.00

Not to be confused with other cafés in the Thoms chain, this brewpub is in a large building behind the city hall shared with the City Museum (museumrotterdam.nl). The high-ceilinged interior has a long bar, brewhouse near the door and indoor trees shading floor-to-ceiling windows. Food includes sharing plates and burgers. Draught house beers are served, with self-tapping points on some tables.

Walenburg ⑰

Walenburgerweg 62b · **T** 010 466 9577
cafewalenburgrotterdam.nl
Daily from 14.00

Friendly corner local 400m north of Centraal station and opposite a park. The one-room brown café has a colourful barrel and hop-themed mural on one wall. Snacks and light meals served. Around 80+ beer options include 26 draught lines, with some local interest such as Noordt and Hoevebrugsch, the latter once brewed in a room above the bar. The emphasis may shift more from bottle to tap in future.

OTHER BEER VENUES

Kaapse Maria ⑱ (Mauritsweg 52 – **T** 010 842 3978 – kaapsemaria.nl – *shut Mo-Tu; others 15.00-00.00*) is the brewery's central restaurant with 24 taps and food pairings: see also taproom above.
Ooievaar ⑲ (Havenstraat 11 – **T** 010 476 9190

SCHIPLUIDEN

5km SW from Delft off N468
Bus 33

Small village (pop 4,500) with an attractive canal running through the centre.

Raadhuis

Dorpstraat 12 · **T** 015 785 0049
raadhuisschipluiden.nl
Shut Mo&Tu; Sa&Su 10.00–17.30; others 09.00–17.30

A lovely canalside café with rear beer garden, the tHuis taproom is in a building which has been a town hall, a garage and a bike shop, the last of which explains the stag heads sculpted from saddles and handlebars decorating the interior. Breakfasts and lunches feature local ingredients. Up to six house beers are poured from bottles. The brewery is in the process of moving a few kilometres to Harnaschdreef 7, Den Hoorn, with a new taproom serving draught beer due to open in 2020.

SOMMELSDIJK

45km SW from Rotterdam off N215
Bus 436, 437

Village (pop 7,400) on Goeree-Overflakkee, an island surrounded by the river delta.

Solaes

Oostdijk 36
solaes.nl
*Shut Su-Tu & Th-Fr; We 10.00–17.00; Sa 13.00–19.00
(& 1st Fr of the month 16.00–20.00)*

Tiny taproom with bijou green and gold bar equipped with an old Germanic ceramic tap. The character holding sway in the mural photo opposite the bar is a former landlady who lived in the back room, now a second seating area. Brewing kit is downstairs. Nibbles only. Beers are served on tap, with bottles also sold in takeaway gift packs.

VLAARDINGEN

9km W from Rotterdam off A20 exit 8&9
≈ Vlaardingen Centrum

A picturesque boat-lined harbour stretches north from the Maas into the heart of this Rotterdam commuter suburb (pop 71,000), a reminder of its past as a thriving fishing port.

Antonius

Hoogstraat 21 · **T** 010 434 8811
bierlokaalantonius.nl
Shut Mo&Tu; Su 16.00–23.00; others from 16.00

Friendly local with a terrace on the high street. White walls dotted with beer enamels, and a central brass light fitting add an understated elegance, as does the ancient cash register on the bar counter. A full dinner menu is offered. Local and other Dutch micros are slowly gaining a foothold on a Belgian-dominated list of 70+ beers.

OTHER BEER VENUES
Friendly brown café **Oude Stoep** (Smalle Havenstraat 5 – **T** 010 434 7502 – oudestoep.nl – *shut Tu; Fr–Su from 14.00; others from 16.00*) has 50 beers, and many jenevers and liqueurs.

VOORHOUT

9km N from Leiden off N444
≈ Voorhout

Quiet small town (pop 16,200), the birthplace in 1668 of scientist and humanist Herman Boerhaave. An all-round renaissance man who worked at Leiden University, he invented the concept of university teaching hospitals. The gardens of the house where he was born, behind the main church, are a fine place for a stroll if you arrive before opening time. *HOTEL TIP*: the entry below has rooms.

Boerhaave

Herenstraat 57 · **T** 0252 211483
boerhaave-voorhout.nl
Shut Mo; others from 16.00

This sprawling modern local with a terrace on a busy street is the hub of town nightlife. Displays of beer bottles take up much of the wall space in the extensive tiled-floor interior. Dinners served; snacks at other times. A list of 120 beers includes 20 draught options, with a small but adventurous selection of rotating guests among the Belgian stalwarts.

Solaes, Som

Utrecht

Utrecht is the Netherlands' smallest province by area, though densely populated, with most of its 1,290,000 residents living in and around its eponymous main city. The bishopric of Utrecht was founded in the year 722 by Northumbrian monk and missionary Willibrord, patron saint of the Netherlands and Luxembourg, and in its day was among the most powerful city states in Europe.

The eastern part of the province, its soil too poor for agriculture, has remained largely forested. Elsewhere, water dominates. The south is criss-crossed by canals and rivers, while the boggy countryside of the north was exploited for peat, leaving a patchwork of artificial lakes.

No historical breweries survive – the current longest-running, Drie Ringen, was founded in 1989 – but the growth of beer culture here has been more dramatic over the past decade than in any other province. *LARGEST CENTRES:* **Amersfoort, Utrecht, Veenendaal**
MORE INFORMATION: **visit-utrecht.com** (city); **utrechtyourway.nl** (province)
SELECTED BREWERIES: **Drie Ringen,** *Amersfoort;* **Duits & Lauret,** *Everdingen;* **Kromme Haring,** *Utrecht;* **De Leckere,** *Utrecht;* **Maximus,** *Utrecht ;* **Oproer,** *Utrecht;* **Rock City,** *Amersfoort;* **Oudaen,** *Utrecht;* **vandeStreek,** *Utrecht;* **Volle Maat,** *Leusden.*

AMERSFOORT
22km ENE from Utrecht off A28 exits 5–8
🚆 Amersfoort

Besides Utrecht, the province's only other major city (pop 152,000). One of the most impressive sights in its attractive medieval core is the 15th-century Koppelpoort, a combined land and water gate. The station, 1km to the west, is an important rail hub.

Amersfoort's nickname is Keistad (Boulder City), derived from a nine tonne lump of rock found out on the moors. In 1661, a local land-owner bet a friend he could persuade the townsfolk to drag it into town. He won by bribing 400 people with beer and pretzels, and the stone now sits on a pedestal on Arnhemsestraat as a monument to human folly.
HOTEL TIP: Tabaksplant ★★★, Coninckstraat 15 (tabaksplant.nl) is friendly and central.

Boothill Saloon
Krankeledenstraat 16 · **T** 033 461 8007
boothillsaloon.nl
Fr–Sa from 12.00; others from 14.00

Central rock music café with a tiny terrace and canalside beer garden. The mainly-brown interior wraps around three sides of a serving counter, with a pool table at the back. No kitchen, but burgers, hot dogs and burritos can be ordered in. The 60 beers continue the American theme, with one chiller cabinet dedicated to US craft imports.

Dikke Koning
Appelmarkt 18 · **T** 033 202 5991
facebook.com/dedikkekoning
Shut Mo&Tu; FR&Sa from 13.00; Su 13.00–19.00; others from 15.00

On a small square with a smaller terrace, the friendly Fat King, formerly the Zomaar, has a wood-beamed ceiling, board games for the bored and a gas-effect fire. Snacks only. The 100+ beers are a little Belgo-centric but more local brews are appearing among them.

Drie Ringen

Kleine Spui 18 · **T** 033 465 6575
dedrieringen.nl
Shut Mo (all year) & Tu (Nov-Mar); Fr-Su 13.00-19.30;
others 14.00-19.30

Taproom enjoying a scenic canalside location
by the Koppelpoort. The bright interior is
dominated by the copper brewing kettles.
Snacks include help-yourself free boiled
eggs. Eight taps dispense at least three
house beers and several from Gulpener.

Lobbes

Hof 10a · **T** 033 461 0637
mamaroux.nl/bruin-cafe-lobbes
Fr&Sa from 11.00; Su 12.00-21.00; others from 12.00

One-room brown café with a terrace on
a lively square, beer enamels and smoke-
stained ceilings. Snacks only. The 90+ beers
are mostly Belgian, though with occasional
surprises, found mainly in the 'outside the
card' section at the end of the menu.

Marktzicht

Lieve Vrouwekerkhof 2 · **T** 033 448 0767
facebook.com/marktzichtamersfoort
Daily from 11.00

The Market View is one of several bars with
terraces on Lieve Vrouwekerkhof square.
The woody interior is broken up by mirrors,
beer enamels and bookshelves with games.
Snacks for food, plus the same order-in menu
as nearby Boothill Saloon (above). The 70+
beer list includes several local choices.

Rock City Brewpub

Mijnbouwweg 15 · **T** 033 202 2230
rockcitybrewpub.nl
Shut Mo&Tu; Sa 14.00-23.00; Su 14.00-21.00;
others 15.00-23.00

Brewpub in an industrial park: take bus 1 to
Mijnbouwweg. The warehouse-like interior,
kept cosy by underfloor heating in winter,
has a kitchen and bar at the front, with the
brewery behind. Food (*until 21.00, 20.00 on Sun*)
is mainly US-style fare like hot dogs and Philly
cheese steaks. House beers and occasional
guests pour from 20 taps and a few bottles,
with takeaway beer in bottles and growlers.

Witte Konijn

Hof 8 · **T** 033 737 0467
wittekonijn.nl
Shut Mo; Fr&Sa from 11.00; Su 12.00-00.00;
others from 14.00

This showcase for the Witte Konijn brewery
opened in 2019 on the same square as Lobbes
(above). Beyond the terrace, the modern
interior has minimalist furnishings and a 150l
pilot brewing kit. Lunches and dinners served.
Some 20 taps dispense a mix of occasional
one-off and experimental beers brewed in-
house, core house beers made elsewhere
and craft guests, alongside a mouthwatering
local and global list of 270+ bottles and cans.

OTHER BEER VENUES

Long John's Pub (Krankeledenstraat 20-22 –
T 033 461 8897 – longjohnspub.nl – *daily from
09.00*) is a basic local but with plenty of UK
craft choices among its 40 beers.

BEER TO GO

Bierwinkel Hop (Achter Het Oude Stadhuis 2
– **T** 06 2207 2678 – bierwinkelhop.nl – *shut
Mo&Tu; We 12.00-18.00; Th 12.00-21.00; Fr 10.00-
18.00; Sa 10.00-17.00; Su 10.00-17.00*) stocks 500+
global craft beers.
In a modern suburb near Vathorst station,
Hoptimaal (Leeghwater 14 – **T** 085 130 1591 –
hoptimaal.nl – *shut Mo; Fr 10.00-21.00; Sa 10.00-
17.00; Su 12.00-17.00; others 12.00-18.00*) offers
800 beers split evenly between Dutch
microbrews and international craft.

Rock City Brewpub, Amersfoort

Fortbrouwerij Duits & Lauret, Everdingen

EVERDINGEN

24km S from Utrecht off A2 exit 12

Tiny village (pop 1,300).

Fortbrouwerij Duits & Lauret

Noodweg 2 · **T** 06 1425 1923
forteverdingen.com
*Shut Mo–Th; Fr 12.00–18.00; Sa 11.00–18.00;
Su 10.00–18.00*

From Vianen take bus 146, alight at Diefdijk then walk 1km north to find this intriguingly sited taproom. The brewery and adjacent campsite are within the grounds of Fort Everdingen, part of the New Holland Waterline, a string of defences built to protect Amsterdam and Utrecht following the defeat of Napoleon but only completed in the 1870s. Behind a terrace is a green wooden shed containing a swish bar and a brewhouse behind glass. Snacks and toasties. House beers are served from tap and bottle, the latter also available from a shop across the courtyard.

HOUTEN

12km SSW from Utrecht off A27 exit 29
Houten

Dormitory town (pop 49,000), faceless and modern around the station but far more charming around the historic central square where both our recommendations are found.

Roskam

Plein 25 · **T** 030 208 0944
deroskamhouten.nl
Su 11.00–00.00; others from 09.00

The 16:30 brewery tap is in a building dating from 1630, with a terrace by a white church. The split-level interior has a chic restaurant at the front and more informal pub area behind. Lunches and dinners served. The brewing kit, at the back of the building behind several function rooms, is only used occasionally so house beers aren't always available, but 100+ guests, half of them Dutch craft, will stave off any disappointment.

Zwijger

Plein 21 · **T** 030 636 9719
tapperijdezwijger.nl
Sun 11.00–22.00; others from 11.00

Steps from the Roskam, the Taciturn is a fine old brown café with a terrace on the square. Dark wood abounds in the split-level bar, with beer chalkboards on several walls and a doctored painting of William the Silent in shades on another. Lunches and dinners served. Around 70 beers with 10 on tap include the entire range from local Hommeles.

UTRECHT
Utrecht CS

Before the ascendancy of Amsterdam, Utrecht was the most important settlement in the region and the centre of a powerful theocracy. It's still the Netherlands' fourth largest city (pop 353,000) and the hub of the rail network. Half of all Dutch train lines pass through and transport buffs should not miss the National Railway Museum (**spoorwegmuseum.nl**). The city's icon and its most prominent building is the Domtoren, the country's highest church tower, and any proposal for a new building which surpasses its 112m height is met with controversy.

Arguably the two most famous Utrecht natives in history had radically different career paths. In 1522, Adriaan Boeyens was elected Pope Adrian VI, the last non-Italian pontiff before John Paul II in 1978. More recently, actor Sylvia Kristel made her name starring as Emmanuelle.

Today the unusual split-level banks of the Oudegracht canal snaking through the centre are filled with bustling café terraces, but for many centuries they were lined with brewhouses. The city boasted 22 breweries in 1610

and remained an important brewing centre until the early 20th century. A few remnants can still be seen if you know what you're looking for: including the main building of the most famous historic brewery, De Boog (The Bow), now converted to flats. Apart from Oudaen (below), the modern micros currently restoring Utrecht's beer mojo are outside the centre.

HOTEL TIP: Despite its upmarket chain image, **Park Plaza ★★★★**, Westplein 50 (radissonhotels.com) often has some of the best-value rooms near the centre.

Beers & Barrels Downtown ❶

Oudegracht a/d Werf 125 · **T** 030 636 8744
beersbarrels.nl
Daily from 16.00

Trendy, subterranean brick cellar bar and restaurant with a small canalside terrace on the lower level of Oudegracht. Sit by the open kitchen at the back to watch your steaks and burgers be flame-grilled before your singed eyes. The 70+ beers, with a lot of Dutch craft on show, include 20 or so from the Utrecht area.

Beers & Barrels at the Harbour ❷

Veilinghavenkade 177 · **T** 030 293 7563
beersbarrels.nl
Daily from 10.00

The above entry's sister is a slick restaurant 1km southwest of Centraal station. Sadly, a wall beside the terrace largely blocks the view of the adjoining harbour. The modern interior has a lower seating area around a central serving island and a mezzanine above which provides the best view of the water. Food is steaks and burgers. A range of 80 beers shows a strong Dutch craft interest.

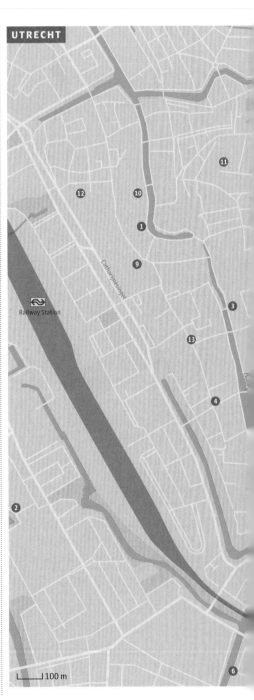

UTRECHT

Railway Station

100 m

België

Oudegracht 196 · **T** 030 231 2666
kafebelgie.nl
Su&Mo from 13.00; others from 11.00

Longstanding Utrecht institution just south of the Domtoren. The lack of table service and barren decor give it a student vibe, the café logo on the back wall and a casually reclined full-sized plastic cow above the bar adding style of sorts. No food, but you can bring your own. Despite the name, a growing number of the 200+ beers are Dutch, including house Kamikaze UPA brewed by Maximus, and non-Belgian imports.

dBs

CAB – rondom 100 · **T** 030 293 8209
dbstudio.nl
*Sa&Su from 12.00; others from 09.30
(opens later mid-Jul to mid-Aug)*

Beside Utrecht Zuilen station, this music venue and rehearsal space with a small terrace occupies the same building as Oproer (below). Previously a bus drivers' canteen, the bar is now decorated with album covers and other music-related items. Snacks only. Some 70 beers include 20+ changing guests, mostly sourced locally.

Derat

Lange Smeestraat 37 · **T** 030 231 9513
cafederat.nl
Daily from 14.00

This convivial and very popular corner café has well-worn tables and an upright piano, while rat memorabilia are kept to a tasteful minimum. Snacks only for food, but toast and cheese are free on Saturday afternoons. Around a third of the 120+ beers are lambics, with rarities from De Cam, Hanssens and 3 Fonteinen. The remaining selection is a well-chosen balance of locals and imports from the global craft scene.

Drie Dorstige Herten

Lange Nieuwstraat 47 · **T** 030 888 4430
dedriedorstigeherten.nl
Shut Mo&Tu; We&Su 15.00–19.00; Th 15.00–22.00; others 15.00–23.00

One block east of Oudegracht, the welcoming Three Thirsty Harts is another shining jewel in the Dutch beer treasure box. This small, tile-floored bar is filled with basic wooden furniture. Snacks only. Of 150+ beers, around 100 are from small Dutch breweries, the rest top names from Europe and the US, including a fine selection of lambics and a long list of barrel-aged stouts.

Gist

Helling 9 · **T** 06 1844 5344
taplokaalgist.nl
Fr–Su from 14.00; others from 15.00

Under the same ownership as Derat (above), Yeast is a canalside place beside the Helling concert venue, with a chic dining and bar area, a mezzanine above and a roomy terrace by the water. Hefty snacks and daily changing dinner mains are served. Thirty taps almost all dispense Dutch and international craft, while most of the 30 or so bottles are 75cl specials, leaning towards sours and lambics.

Gist

Jan Primus

Jan van Scorelstraat 27–31 · **T** 030 251 4572
facebook.com/Cafejanprimus
Daily from 15.00

This craft beer veteran is a suburban corner pub on a busy junction: take bus 4 to Prins Hendriklaan. The interior is comfortably battered, with big windows for watching traffic. Besides beer enamels, a lone oar acts as token bric-a-brac. Snacks only. The 60+ beers encompass a few Dutch options, including occasional commissioned brews from local Brouwerij 74. They are not connected, but 1974 was the birth year of both brewers and café.

Kromme Haring

Europalaan 2C
dekrommeharing.nl
Shut Mo&Tu, Sa&Su from 14.00; others from 16.00

The Crooked Herrring brewpub is on a small industrial site southwest of the centre, a 10-minute walk west from Vaartsche Rijn station. The simple bar area with a terrace out front is on the south side of the building, away from the road. The brewing kit is at the back. Snacks only. The 12 taps dispense house beers, collababorations, experiments and a few guests, with more of the same in bottles.

Ledig Erf

Tolsteegbrug 3 · **T** 030 231 7577
ledigerf.nl
Daily from 10.00

Cosy corner café at southern end of Oudegracht, with a relaxing terrace on a small square. Colourful stained glass above the windows lights up an otherwise simple interior. Snacks only. The 60+ beer list had long been solid if unspectacular, but appears to be gaining an interest in local micros and global craft.

Lijn 4

Twijnstraat 3 · **T** 030 231 5481
cafelijn4.nl
Sa&Su from 14.00; others from 16.00

Trendy brown café on a narrow street south of the centre, with leather-quilted booths and views of the Oudegracht through the back window. Mirrors and a collection of black and white photos fill the walls. Snacks only. The 60-strong beer selection is Belgian-led with just enough local and wider Dutch representation to provide variety.

Lombok

Vleutenseweg 228 · **T** 030 294 5952
cafelombok.nl
Mo&Tu from 17.00; others from 12.00

Lively corner local with a terrace on a busy street just northwest of Centraal station. The simply furnished interior has a bar down one side and brightly painted walls elsewhere, some hung with vinyl album covers. Lunches

and dinners served (*until 22.00*). The 50+ beer list is modest in number but almost entirely comprised of Dutch microbrews, most from the local region.

Maximus

Pratumplaats 2A · **T** 06 8345 0013
brouwerijmaximus.nl
Shut Mo&Tu; Su 12.00-20.00; others 14.00-22.00

Out-of-town taproom: take bus 4 to De Woerd. Behind the large terrace beside a tiny hop garden, the interior has concrete floors, plywood walls, a bar made from pallets and a brewing kit behind picture windows. Lunches and dinners served. House beers, specials and guests appear on the 22 taps, with tasting flights on offer and more beer in bottles, also sold to take away.

Maxim...

Olivier

Achter Clarenburg 6 · **T** 030 236 7876
utrecht.cafe-olivier.be
Su&Mo from 11.00; others from 10.00

If you want to admire an impressive organ whilst supping, look no further. This former church retains much of its original 1860 interior, including the high ceilings, with a small terrace expanding the drinking space outside. Lunches and dinners display Belgian tendencies, as do the 90 beers, but with a few local influences to keep things in check.

Oproer

CAB-Rondom 90A
oproerbrouwerij.nl
Shut Mo&Tu; We 17.00-22.00; Th 17.00-23.00;
Fr 17.00-00.00; Sa 15.00-00.00; Su 15.00-22.00

Taproom with terrace in an industrial building beside Utrecht Zuilen station. The brewing kit moved down the road in 2018 to create more space, since filled with sofas and plants. Vegan street food is served. Thirteen taps dispense house beers alongside a handful of guests, with a similar number of guest bottles and cans.

Oudaen

Oudegracht 99 · **T** 030 231 1864
oudaen.nl
Daily from 09.00

If you want to get married somewhere that is both a castle and a brewery, this is the place, a towering building partly dating from 1267. The brewing kit is in the basement, and a canalside terrace spreads over two levels. The imposing main bar was a medieval banqueting hall but has had a modern makeover. Full meals served. House beers are available on tap.

VandeStreek

Ontariodreef 43 · **T** 030 737 1255
vandestreekbier.nl
Shut Su-Th; Fr 16.00–23.00; Sa 13.00–21.00

Taproom in an industrial area north of the centre – take bus 3 from Centraal station. The large bar area backed by containers has a mirror ball chandelier and sofa corner, with the brewery behind. Snacks and filled pitta breads are available. The 16 taps pour house beers with a similar number in bottles and cans, also sold for takeaway.

Werkspoorcafé

Tractieweg 43 · **T** 085 273 3455
werkspoorcafe.nl
Sa&Su from 13.00; Mo&Tu from 11.30; others from 10.30

De Leckere's taproom was the paintshop of a plant that made steel products for the Dutch railways. The brewery itself is around the corner. The interior space, dominated by a central tree, has a glass wall looking out onto a dockside terrace. Food runs from snacks and sharing plates to barbecue meals. Twelve taps and some bottles cover the full house range.

OTHER BEER VENUES

Guusjes (Van 's-Gravesandestraat 27 – **T** 030 272 3450 – etenbijguusjes.com – *Su-Tu 08.30-23.00; others 08.30-00.00*) is a fashionable neighbourhood corner café with good local representation among its 50 beers.
Central music café **Hofman** ⑪ (Janskerhof 17a – **T** 030 230 2470 – hofman-cafe.nl – *Su&Mo 12.30-23.30, Tu&We 11.00-23.30; Sa from 10.00 others from 11.00*) also has 50 beers with Dutch and imported craft options.
Chicken restaurant **Kloek** ⑫ (Vredenburg 31 – **T** 030 879 2999 – kloekutrecht.nl – *Fr-Su from 12.00; others 12.00-23.00*) has 40 beers, half of them from small Utrecht brewers.
Arthouse cinema **Springhaver** ⑬ (Springweg 50 – **T** 030 231 3789 – springhaver.nl – *Sa&Su from 10.00; others from 11.00*) has a café serving 40 decent beers.

BEER TO GO

Bierman & Bierman (Biltstraat 46 – **T** 030 662 4544 – biermanenbierman.nl – *Mo 13.00-19.00; Th 11.00-21.00; Sa 10.00-18.00; Su 13.00-18.00; others 11.00-19.00*) keeps 500+ beers in store and sells 1,800 through its website.
Central **Bierverteller** (Twijnstraat 47 – **T** 030 737 1306 – debierverteller.nl – *shut Mo; Sa 10.00-18.00; Su 12.00-18.00; others 11.00-19.00*) has 700 beers and a programme of workshops and tasting events.
Little Beershop (Hardebollenstraat 7 – **T** 06 4826 9387 – littlebeershop.nl – *shut Su-Tu; We 12.00-18.00; Sa 11.00-18.00; others 12.00-21.00*) stocks 250+ beers that change regularly, and has a second outlet, **Drie Meter Bier** (Amsterdamsestraatweg 379 – *shut Mo; Su 11.00-17.00; others 10.00-18.00*), at the back of a deli.
Van Bieren (Nachtegaalstraat 65 – **T** 030 633 2929 – vanbierencadeau.nl – *shut Mo; Fr 10.00-19.00; Su 12.00-17.00; others 10.00-18.00*) has a small but well-chosen selection of 200, with a strong Dutch focus.
Off licence **Zuilen** (Amsterdamsestraatweg 595 – **T** 030 244 1850 – slijterijzuilen.nl – *shut Su; Mo 13.00-18.00; Th 11.00-19.00; Fr&Sa 10.00-18.00; others 11.00-18.00*) has 600 beers equally split between Dutch, Belgian and international craft.

VEENENDAAL

35km E from Utrecht off A12 exit 23

〰️ Veenendaal Centrum

Conservative modern city (64,600).

Plantage

Markt 8 · **T** 0318 526225

brasseriedeplantageveenendaal.nl

Shut Mo&Tu; Sa from 11.00; others from 16.00.

Large modern café with a terrace beside a white-painted church. Button-back sofas, armchairs, church panelling and pews break up the brown wood interior. Lunches and dinners served, the latter revolving around steak and burgers. Around 70 beers are Belgian-dominated with some interesting Dutch guests.

Robert's Pub

J.G. Sandbrinkstraat 1a · **T** 0318 508866

robertspub.nl

Sa from 13.00; others from 14.00

Popular brown-café-cum-English pub with terrace at foot of modern brick apartment building. British and Belgian beer ads and enamels decorate the walls and there's occasional live music. Snacks only. The 120 beers err towards caution but small Dutch micros are making inroads: check the fridge for items not listed on the menu.

BEER TO GO

Pollekebier (Zandstraat 25 – **T** 0318 553180 – **pollekebier.nl** – *shut Su&Mo; Fr 11.00–21.00; Sa 09.00–17.00; others 11.00–18.00*) has 600 mostly Belgian and Dutch beers and goes nuts on the other side of the room – the foodstuff, that is.

VIANEN

13km S from Utrecht off A2 exit 11 or A27 exit 27 Bus 74

Small town (pop 20,400) with an ancient moated centre. The broad main street is like an oddly elongated square, with a 15th-century city gate at one end and the imposing stone facade of the 1425 town hall its other prominent feature.

Rooie Reiger

Voorstraat 68 · **T** 0347 320295

cafederooiereiger.nl

We 11.00–23.00; Fr&Sa from 12.00; Su 12.00–21.00; others 12.00–23.00

The Red Heron is a friendly modern café with a terrace on the main street, with photos of local views displayed on its brown wood walls. Lunch (*daily*) and dinner (*Mo–Sa*); snacks at other times. The 65+ beers are mainly Belgian, including the house beers brewed at Van Steenberge, but with just enough Dutch surprises to grab our attention.

WOERDEN

22km W from Utrecht off A12 exit 14

〰️ Woerden

Provincial town (pop 36,800) with an early 15th-century moated castle.

Bierhuys

Van Oudheusdenstraat 3a · **T** 0348 418766

bierhuys.nl

Shut Mo&Tu; others from 14.00

Friendly one-room corner café with terrace on residential street west of centre. The wood-laden interior has a gas hearth for winter nights. Live music includes an open podium acoustic night twice a month. Main meals until 21.00; snacks all day. Around 200 beers astutely balance Belgian standards with local and regional Dutch brews. The sign on the wall reads *gevaarlijk gezellig* (dangerously convivial) and it's not wrong. Round the corner is the associated **Bierhuys** bottle shop (Meulmansweg 6 – **T** 0348 508705 – **bierhuyswinkel.nl** – *shut Su-Tu; We 10.00-19.00; Th 12.00-19.00; Fr 12.00-21.00; Sa 10.00-18.00*) with 500 Dutch and international brews.

BEER TO GO

See **Bierhuys** above.

Zeeland

Nowhere else is the Netherlands' sometimes fraught relationship with the sea more obvious than in this relatively deserted province (pop 400,000). Once a series of isolated islands in the tangled streams of the Schelde (Scheldt) and Maas (Meuse) deltas, its dots have been joined together by bridges, dykes and polders, though 30% of its potential area remains underwater.

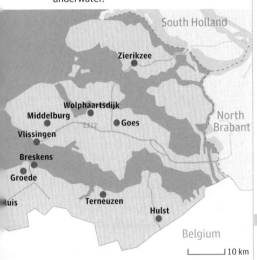

The region's vulnerability to the forces of nature was brought into focus in January 1953 when dykes burst during a storm, inundating everywhere and killing 1,800 people. In response, the government constructed one of the world's great engineering marvels, a massive line of sea defences known as the Delta Works. For the full story, visit Deltapark Neeltje Jans (**neeltjejans.nl**), part theme park, part engineering expo, where you can go inside a dam to get a close-up of the tidal flows gushing through the sluices.

The area south of the Westerschelde, Zeeuws-Vlaanderen, shares its land border with Belgium. Until the opening of the 6.6km Westerschelde Tunnel in 2003, it was connected to the rest of the Netherlands only by ferry.

LARGEST CENTRES: **Middelburg**, **Vlissingen**

MORE INFORMATION: **vvvzeeland.nl**

SELECTED BREWERIES: **Brouwerslokaal**, *Groede*; **Gansje**, *Goes*; **Kees!**, *Middelburg*; **Middelburg**, *Middelburg*; **Slot Oostende**, *Goes*; **Vermeersen**, *Hulst*.

BRESKENS

61km (by road) S from Vlissingen off N675

Ferry from Vlissingen (**westerscheldeferry.nl**) Harbour town (pop 4,800), on the south bank of the Westerschelde estuary. It is a long slog from anywhere by car but a regular ferry carries people, mopeds and bikes on a 5km trip to and from Vlissingen in 25 minutes.

Ons Dagelijks Kost

Spuiplein 39 · **T** 0117 381866
onsdagelijkskost.com
Shut Mo; others 10.00–21.00

Our Daily Fare is a modern local with a terrace on a square close to the harbour and ferry. Inside is a cosy stove-and-armchair corner with a few token beer enamels on the wall. A full food menu features burgers. The 90 beers are mainly Belgian, including several 75cl bottles; a quaffable house blond is brewed at Slot Oostende.

Slot Oostende

GOES
28km E from Middelburg off N289
≋ Goes

Small town (pop 27,000) with a long history. In 1572, during the Eighty Years' War, the city was besieged by Dutch and English Protestants. The siege failed when Spanish troops waded across the Schelde estuary to surprise the multinational task force from behind. The Goes-Borsele steam train runs from here in summer (destoomtrein.nl).

HOTEL TIP: **Slot Oostende** (below) also has rooms.

Eric's (La Strada)
St.Jacobstraat 48 · **T** 0113 212669
Shut Mo-We; Sa from 14.00; Su from 15.00; others from 17.00

Although technically Eric's, many people still use this central local's former name La Strada. There's just enough space on the narrow street for a tiny terrace, while the interior has mats covering wooden floors, house plants and a British red phone box. There is regular live music. Snacks only. The 80-100 beers are mainly Belgian with a few Dutch guests.

Gansje
Magdalenastraat 9 · **T** 0113 269416
hetgansje.nl
Shut Mo&Tu (& 1st Su of the month); We&Su 14.00-18.00; others 14.00-22.00

In a former jenever tasting room dating from 1903, the Little Goose brewpub is a simply furnished place with vinyl records for music. The bijou copper brewing kit on one shelf was retired when it started leaking, replaced by a barely bigger kit in the kitchen at the back of the room. Snacks include *bitterballen*. Six beers are served on tap and another dozen or so in bottles, also sold to take away.

Slot Oostende
Singelstraat 5 · **T** 06 1456 2981
slotoostende.nl
Daily from 10.00

This brewpub in a tastefully rebuilt ruined castle has a central restaurant and bar with the brewery on the mezzanine above. You may also find a conservatory, shop, upstairs dining areas and a motorbike in a cupboard. The 13th-century vaulted cellars are open for special occasions and visited on pre-booked heritage tours. A full food menu is served. The 85+ beers include 20 from both Slot Oostende and Emelisse, alongside a mix of Dutch and international craft. The castle has no connection to the Flemish port but instead to a now-submerged Zeeland village of the same name.

GROEDE
15km SSW from Middelburg by crow, 60km by road on N675
Bus 42 from Breskens (for ferry to Vlissingen) or Brugge (Bruges, Belgium)

Tiny village (pop 1,100) closer to Bruges than to anywhere in the Netherlands. It lay underwater and abandoned for 30 years after surrounding dykes were deliberately broken during the Eighty Years War. In 1944 it housed a Red Cross base accepting wounded from both sides during the battle to control the Schelde delta, so was spared the shelling that destroyed many other Benelux towns and villages.

HOTEL TIP: **Natte Pij ★★★**, Slijkstraat 1 (**denattepij.nl**) is an atmospheric inn on a historic museum street themed to recreate life in 1900.

Drie Koningen

Markt 30 · **T** 0117 371511
dedriekoningen.com
Daily 11.00–21.00

At the time of writing, the Three Kings is the Brouwerslokaal tap, although that honour may shift to a new location around the corner (Blekestraat 16) in 2020. Resembling a traditional inn from the outside, the interior is modern, with the brewery behind glass at the rear. Lunches and dinners served. House Marckensteijn and Dutch Bargain regular and experimental brews are served on tap and in bottle, with occasional surprise guests appearing on a 'black list'.

HULST

57km SE from Middelburg off N290
Bus 22, 43 from Sint-Niklaas (Belgium),
20 from Terneuzen

Small town (pop 11,000) in Zeeuws-Vlaanderen. The nearest big city is Antwerp in Belgium, and the moated old town has a more Flemish than Dutch feel. Outside the main church is a statue of Reynard the Fox, eponymous hero of a classic medieval European folk tale, as several places in town are name-checked in the Dutch version.

Biecht

Steenstraat 1 · **T** 06 5742 6403
Shut Mo&Tu; We&Th from 16.00; others from 14.00

In a lovely old stepped-gabled building, this sparsely furnished pub has a wood-beamed ceiling, a chalkboard beer menu on one wall and large black and white photos on another. Snacks only. The 100+ beers including 12 taps lean towards the southern neighbour but include the full range from local Vermeersen and several from other Zeeland brewers.

OTHER BEER VENUES
In the town's former station, **Oud Hulst** (Stationsplein 7 – **T** 0114 728027 – oudhulst.nl – *shut Mo&Tu; others from 11.00*) has 45 beers, a grand interior and a terrace looking across at the adjacent but unconnected Vermeersen brewery.

MIDDELBURG

Middelburg

Pretty provincial capital (pop 41,600) dating back to the ninth century and retaining its medieval character. It was originally an island fortified to protect the mainland against Viking raiders. Both the flamboyant Gothic town hall and the abbey are worth a look: the latter is home to the Zeeuws Museum (zeeuwsmuseum.nl). For panoramic views, climb Lange Jan (Long John), a 91m church tower.

HOTEL TIP: **Nieuwe Doelen** ★★★, Loskade 3 (hoteldenieuwedoelen.nl) is handy for both centre and station.

Desafinado

Koorkerkstraat 1 – **T** 0118 640767
desafinado.nl
Shut Su&Mo; others 11.00–00.00

This jazz café and restaurant with occasional live music has a front terrace in the lee of the Lange Jan tower. The low-ceilinged interior has blue walls and a piano key motif decorating the bar counter. A full food menu is served. Local beers from Kees! are permanent fixtures on a growing beer list of 120+ which otherwise balances familiar Belgian faces with Dutch and international stars.

Stadsbrouwerij Middelburg

Korte Geere 17 · **T** 06 8107 9149
stadsbrouwerijmiddelburg.nl
Shut Su-We; Sa 14.00–23.00; others 15.00–23.00

This bijou central brewpub has a tiny terrace, a small taproom at the front and a brewery

behind glass at the rear. Candles on tables provide a restful ambience. Nibbles only. A dozen or so house beers are available, with eight on tap and others in 33cl and 75cl bottles, also sold to take out, plus a handful of guests.

Vliegende Hollander

Damplein 48 · **T** 06 3163 3237
biercafemiddelburg.nl
Shut Mo (all year), Tu-We (winter), Th & Su from 20.00, Fr from 16.00, Sa from 15.00

Despite the old-fashioned name, the Flying Dutchman is Middelburg's most switched-on beer bar. The single-room café with a terrace on a picturesque square has a vaguely nautical theme amid the usual breweriana, with well-stocked fridges lined up behind the bar. Snacks only, but the choice is extensive. Eighteen taps and 300+ bottles and cans fly the flag for both Dutch and international cutting-edge brewers.

OTHER BEER VENUES
Brooklyn (Markt 81 – **T** 0118 650949 – grandcafebrooklyn.nl – *Su from 11.30; others from 10.30*) is a hip modern grand café with Triumph motorbike decor and 40 decent beers.

BEER TO GO
Pocket-sized **Hoplala** (Gravenstraat 14 – **T** 06 5188 7000 – hoplala.nl – *shut Su-Th; Fr 14.00-18.00; Sa 13.00-17.00*) only has space enough for a few hundred carefully chosen brews.

SLUIS

23km SW from Middelburg by carrier pigeon (70km by road), off N253
Bus 42 from Breskens (for ferry to Vlissingen) or Brugge (Bruges, Belgium)

Tiny town (pop 2,300) on the Belgian border in Zeeuws-Vlaanderen, the westernmost in the Netherlands, a cutesy place with a much-visited 1739 windmill and a reputation as a culinary hub. The nearest city is Bruges, and most visitors are Belgian.

Garage 3

Plompe Toren 3 · **T** 0117 462253
garage3.nl
Shut Mo-We; others 10.30-18.00

Belying the quaint feel of the rest of town, this modern café with a small terrace is indeed in a former garage workshop. The interior is part motorbike-themed, part 1950s American diner, with spare parts, whole bikes, tyres and lampshades made from cogs. Burgers form the centrepiece of the food menu. The 80 beers are mostly Belgian but include a smattering of Dutch micros and several international Trappists.

TERNEUZEN

34km SE from Middelburg via N62 (Westerschelde Tunnel)
Bus 50 from Middelburg

The position of this Zeeuws-Vlaanderen town (pop 25,500) at the point where the Ghent-Terneuzen canal meets the Westerschelde estuary has turned it into the country's third-largest port. The rest of the Netherlands is across 5km of water, plied by giant ships heading for Antwerp. Its most famous resident was fictional: Captain Van der Decken cursed God and was condemned to sail the oceans aboard the doomed ship The Flying Dutchman in Frederick Marryat's novel *The Phantom Ship* (1839), based on the same legends as Richard Wagner's well-known opera.

Vriendschap

Noordstraat 1 · **T** 0115 612593
Daily 11.00–19.00

The Friendship is a brown café the like of which they make no more: a dilapidated building now isolated in a sea of characterless modern constructions. Classic old school, it has creaking floorboards, solid unyielding chairs, and table-top carpets, as well as a vague nautical theme to the decor, with model ships and ship's wheels. A squirrel holding sway over the bar is just one of several stuffed animals. Simple lunches and snacks. The 80+ beers are mainly Belgian. A collection of old bottles on the first floor bills itself with some hubris as a museum.

OTHER BEER VENUES
Bée (Noordstraat 85 – **T** 0115 696414 – *daily from 15.00*) is a quirky joint with such a dense mass of brass and copper pots hanging from the ceiling that it could be an antiques shop, but only around 25 beers.

VLISSINGEN

 Vlissingen

As both a major port (pop 33,000) and beach resort, Vlissingen is the kind of place that ought to be endowed with great beer pubs, but we haven't found one yet. Please enlighten us if we are wrong. The city's English name, Flushing, is rarely used today but has stuck to its namesake in New York City. It was the home port of Vice Admiral Joost de Moor (1548–1618), an ancestor of this guide's esteemed editor and a modestly important participant in several naval battles during the Eighty Years War who also helped frustrate the Spanish Armada when it threatened England.

BEER TO GO
Inside an Emté supermarket, **Paauwenburg (Acedrinks)** (Van Hogendorpweg 93 – **T** 0118-465781 – acedrinks.nl – *shut Su; others 08.30–18.00*) has 500+ beers, with a strong focus on international craft, and an online store.

WOLPHAARTSDIJK

9km NW from Goes off N668
Bus 582

Tiny village (pop 2,100) in an area badly affected by the 1953 flood.

Den Baas en Zijn Madam

Watersportweg 4
T 0113 769088
denbaasenzijnmadam.nl
Daily from 12.00

The Boss and his Madam and its terrace are on a short jetty, surrounded by a yachting harbour 2km north of the village. Pennants and a ship's wheel lend a nautical touch to the modern interior. You will meet Madam if you visit the loos. Food is Belgian, with mussels featuring prominently. House Baasje beers are brewed on site but informally and not as a fully fledged brewery; 170 other beers are mostly Belgian but include some from Slot Oostende.

ZIERIKZEE

42km NE from Middelburg off N59

Characterful port town (pop 10,500) with medieval charm.

Gekroonde Suikerbiet

Nieuwe Haven 141 · **T** 0111 413825
cafedebiet.nl
Daily from 11.30

A pub since the 19th century, the Crowned Sugar Beet, de Biet to its friends, is in a 1645 building with a harbourside terrace. A single bar loops around both halves of a two-room interior. Fragments of a mural depicting cherubs, believed to date from 1920, are protected by glass on a rear wall, while porcelain beer pumps are of similar vintage. Food is full gastropub, with posh burgers to the fore. Ninety beers feature an increasing number of Zeeland micros and other Dutch options.

OTHER BEER VENUES
Modern **Werf** (Vissersdijk 2a – **T** 0111 414244 – **grandcafedewerf.nl** – *shut Mo; others 11.00–21.00*) has a scenic terrace, good food but a short beer list.

Late arrivals

Listed below are a few more worthwhile cafés, which opened while this guide was already in production – plus two that almost snuck under the radar.

EDE (Gelderland)

Substitute

Nieuwe Stationsstraat 27 · **T** 0318 617730
substitute.nl
Sa from 13.00; others from 15.00

This friendly beer pub with a terrace and dark wood-dominated interior sits in a row of lively bars opposite Ede Centrum station. Snacks only, but portions of chips can be ordered in by the bag. Around 120 beers are a good mix of Belgian classics and Dutch and international craft.

's-HERTOGENBOSCH (North Brabant)

Jeronimus/Warenhuis

Markt 8/Markt 2 · **T** 073 612 8765/073 689 7190
jeronimus-cafe.nl & hetwarenhuisdenbosch.nl
Jeronimus: Mo&Tu from 17.00; Fr&Sa from 10.00; others from 11.00. Warenhuis: daily 08.00–23.00

Two adjoining cafés on the main square that share a terrace, beer and food menus. Jeronimus is a cosy brown pub with art deco stained glass; the Warenhuis is more austere hip with white tiles and dining on two floors. Full food menu served. The 250 beers have a strong Belgian bias, but with some local representations.

AMSTERDAM (North Holland)

Eeuwige Jeugd

Linnaeusstraat 37A · **T** 020 235 7171
deeeuwigejeugd.nl
Sa&Su from 11.00; others from 15.00

Home of the like-named brewing company with a sheltered terrace opposite Oosterpark. The stylish interior has fringed tables, shuffle-board, and a rear living room and mezzanine. Glass wall cabinets contain toys. Snacks include *poutines* – chips with pimped toppings. The 16 taps mainly dispense house beers, while most of the 35+ bottled guests are Amsterdam micros.

Lagerhuys

Rokin 84 · **T** 06 3659 3100
lagerhuys.amsterdam
Daily from 09.00

Opening its doors just as we went to press, this chic semi-subterranean cellar bar just south of Dam Square is run by the same management as Foeders (page 249). The all-day food menu has global influences, as do the 50 craft taps, most of which switch to a different brewery when each keg empties.

Tears Bar

Jan van Galenstraat 10 · **T** 020 354 2176
tears-bar.co
Shut Su&Mo; Fr–Sa from 15.00; others 15.00–23.00

Butcher's Tears second taproom is a sparse affair in Amsterdam West that takes the minimalist theme of its parent (page 248) and runs with it. The only colour palette comes from the street scenes beyond the large windows. Food is French fries and nuts. House beers are served from 10 taps and a few bottles.

UTRECHT (Utrecht)

Taphuys

Mariaplaats 3 · **T** 030 633 9706
taphuys.nl/utrecht
Daily from 11.00

This bright central bar is the third in a growing chain with siblings in Tilburg and Arnhem. Much of the interior is taken up by 68 beer and 64 wine taps. In between, neon lighting and hanging plants dominate. The extensive food menu covers bases from toasties to curry. The taps are self-pour, with a 1cl minimum: to operate, buy a card and top with credit.

Beer tourism

BEER PLACES TO VISIT

Brewery tours

Of the bigger names, Brand, Budels, Grolsch, Gulpener and Hertog Jan all run regular tours that individuals can join, but you must book ahead by phone or online. Budels tours are very irregular (around six per year). Bavaria (Swinkels) only runs group tours, but will try to find space for individuals to join if you ask. Heineken offers no tours of its breweries, but expects you instead to visit the Heineken Experience (below).

Of the smaller breweries, Brouwdok, Burg, Dordrecht, Hemel, Huttenkloas, 't IJ, Sint Crispijn, Tesselaar and Texelse are among those that run fixed-time tours open to individuals without pre-booking. Others require reservation in advance, sometimes for individuals but usually only for groups, while a few will simply show you around if not busy. In the latter case, call ahead to make sure someone is there. See the breweries section for details.

Organised tours

We know of no tour companies currently offering dedicated beer tours to the Netherlands from the UK. From the US, Chris Bettini of **Pub Culture Beercations** (pubculturebeercations.com) leads extended tours of the country's beeriest venues and other European destinations several times per year. Mike Arra and Ruth Berman of **Bon Beer Voyage** (bonbeer.com) organise an annual beer-themed canal cruise from Amsterdam to Bruges, including visits to De Molen and La Trappe among others.

Both **Podge's Belgian Beer Tours** (podgebeer.co.uk) from the UK and **beertrips.com** from the US have been known to slip across the border on their visits to neighbouring beer lands, although neither do so on a regular basis. **AleHunters** (alehunters.co.uk) currently only runs trips to Belgium from the UK, but maybe one day we can tempt them to the dark side.

Once in the country, **Brews & Tales** (brewsandtales.com) are two young women who run personalised craft beer tours of Amsterdam for small groups (eight people or fewer).

Another local enthusiast offers a way to keep fit and drink in the same breath. Maarten Exel of **Bierwandeltochten** (bierwandeltochten.nl) arranges guided walks that begin with some fresh air and finish with a brewery visit and tasting. Most are 12-15km.

MUSEUMS

Bier Experience

Eimersweg 4, 7137 HG Lievelde (Gelderland)
T 0544 371691
brouwhoesachterhoek.nl
We-Su 11.00-18.00

Audiovisual experience in the Erve Kots brewery. Interactive displays activated by a personalised card take you on a journey through the brewing process, with themed tasks to perform and a tasting at the end, in English on request.

Bierreclamemuseum

Haagweg 375, Breda (North Brabant)
T 076 522 0975
bierreclamemuseum.nl
Su only 11.00-23.00

An out-of-hand collector's hobby, this suburban house is stuffed with beer enamels, brewing equipment, neon signs, glasses, labels, ashtrays and beer mats. There are 1,000+ items, most dating from 1900-1960. The upper floor is a recreation of a 1930s café. Downstairs is the real bar. When there's live music it gets packed – come early. Entrance is free.

Bonte Belevenis

Rommelpot 11, Den Hoorn, Texel (North Holland)
T 0222 314180
landgoeddebontebelevenis.nl
Mid-Feb to Oct: Tu-Th&Sa 10.00-17.00

Small countryside farm museum that is home to both the De Boei brewery and a distillery. Tours of both are included in the ticket price.

Brouwerij Bosch

Wycker Grachtstraat 26, Maastricht (Limburg)
T 043 325 2121
brouwerijbosch.nl
Sa only at 14.00 (for groups at other times on request)

Historic brewery founded in 1758 and closed in 1970, with its equipment intact, some of it from the late 19th and early 20th centuries. Tours, which last around two hours including time for a tasting, start at the Tourist Office (VVV), Kleine Staat 1. Buy tickets there in advance, or reserve online. House beers are currently commissioned from Belgium, although an on-site microbrewery is planned.

Heineken Experience

Stadhouderskade 78, Amsterdam
T 020 261 1323
heinekenexperience.com
Sep–Jun: Fr–Su 10.30–21.00; others 10.30–19.30. Jul&Aug: daily 10.30–21.00

Effectively a corporate visitor centre and history museum in a building that hasn't brewed since 1988. You may learn little about how the company makes its products now but you will discover how brilliant they are at selling them. The entry fee entitles you to two beers – you'll never guess what those will be. Note: last entry is two hours before closing.

De Lange Gang (Grolsch Brouwhuys)

Kevelderstraat 15, Groenlo (Overijssel)
T 0544 464860
langegang.nl
Fr–Su 11.00–18.00 (pre-booking required)

The former Klok brewery was the original home of Grolsch from 1615 to 1876, even though it would not assume its current name until a merger in 1922. In the cellar museum, virtual characters from the past pop up to recount key moments from the company's 400-year history. Tours end with a tasting in the ground-floor café.

Museumbrouwerij de Roos

St. Sebastiaanstraat 4, Hilvarenbeek (North Brabant)
T 013 505 5045
museumbrouwerij.nl
Sep–Jun: Sa&Su 13.00–17.00. Jul&Aug: We–Su 13.00–17.00

Former village brewery restored and opened as a museum, containing a wealth of information about

brewing – we did not know stingray pelts were once used to clarify beer – and records of closed breweries. Audio guides in English are included with the ticket, as is a beer in the bar at the end. Visits with a human guide are possible for groups of 10 or more.

Nationaal Biermuseum De Boom

Houttil 1, Alkmaar (North Holland)
T 072 511 3801
biermuseum.nl
Mo–Sa 13.00–16.00 (Fr 11.00–16.00 in 'cheese market season' – roughly Apr–Sep)

Housed in a former brewery, the National Beer Museum is one of the country's best exhibitions dedicated to all things hops and barley. It has displays of tools and brewing equipment, some 200 years old, including oddities like an ice sled used for transporting barrels. Bottles, glasses, posters and other memorabilia complete the show. Finish up in the Boom pub below (see cafés).

Nederlands Openluchtmuseum

Hoeferlaan 4, Arnhem (Gelderland)
T 026 357 6111
openluchtmuseum.nl
Daily 10.00–17.00

The Netherlands Open Air Museum is home to a full-scale brewery in a modern glass structure that sits rather incongruously amid a sea of medieval farmhouses. You are free to wander in and watch the brewers at work and there's a historical display to the side.

Vandeoirsprong

Koestraat 20, Oirschot (North Brabant)
T 0499 572002
vandeoirsprong.nl
Pre-arranged visits for groups of 10 or more

Visiting this one requires you to get a group tour together, but we have included it here for its historical significance. Vandeoirprong has only been brewing since 2014 but is on the site of the former Kroon brewery, which goes back 350 years. Several original buildings have been preserved as museum containing old equipment, some of which still works. The oldest-surviving copper brewing kettles in the Netherlands, dating from 1912, are here. The original Kroon taphouse dates from 165

Beer festivals and events

The number of beer festivals in the Netherlands has spiralled upwards. There are now half a dozen per year in every major city, and practically every weekend sees at least three or four happening somewhere. Some events become established and take place year after year while others come and go like mayflies. Even familiar faces are not immune to change: two long-standing stalwarts, Gouda's winter beer and Amsterdam's autumn bock festival, are no more.

Not only are festivals becoming more common, they are also increasing in popularity. In a bid to limit crowds and cut down queues, many have online pre-sales for entry tickets and some sell out before the day itself, meaning you won't be able to turn up on a whim. If you are thirsty, is keep an eye out on Facebook and other social media platforms where festival announcements are generally made.

Since this is one area that changes daily, we have not even attempted the impossible task of detailing every Dutch beer festival here but merely listed some of our favourites, as well as arguably the most important. Of the websites that attempt to keep tabs on everyone, **pint.nl/events** (in Dutch) probably gets closest.

Finally, a word of warning. There are a disturbing number of 'Oktoberfest-style' events, typically promoted with posters featuring young ladies in dirndls thrusting out oversized jugs. As these are merely excuses for drinking large quantities of bland pils, we ignore them.

MARCH

2ND WEEKEND: *Sa 14.00–22.00*
Noorderlijk Lentebierenfestival
Stadsschouwburg De Harmonie,
Ruiterskwartier 4, Leeuwarden (Friesland)
Indoor festival with around 15 local and regional breweries from the north.

3RD WEEKEND: *Su 11.45–15.45 & 16.30–20.30*
Barrel Aged Beer Festival
Brouwerij De Pilgrim, Aelbrechtskolk 12,
Rotterdam Delfshaven (South Holland)
Two sessions serving exactly what the name suggests, in the brewery taphouse. Advance registration essential as space is limited.

3RD WEEKEND: *Su 13.30–20.00*
Delta Bier Festival (deltabrouwers.nl)
De Goederen Loods, Albert Plesmanweg 23,
Goes (Zeeland)
Small but popular well-established indoor/outdoor festival with half a dozen brewers.

APRIL

2ND WEEKEND:
Th&Fr 19.00–23.00;
Sa 13.00–17.00 & 19.00–23.00
Groningen Bierfestival
(bierfestivalgroningen.nl)
Martinikerk,
Martinikerkhof 3,
Groningen (Groningen)
Around 40 Dutch and
international brewers
and masterclasses in
a medieval church,
with a beer dinner on
the evening before.
Advance booking advised.

Groningen Bierfestival

MAY

1ST WEEKEND: *Su 12.00–19.00*
Nederlands Speciaalbier Festival
(speciaalbierfestival.nl)
Parade, 's-Hertogenbosch (North Brabant)
Outdoor event beside the cathedral with 50 Dutch brewers, usually including a few making their festival debut.

2ND WEEKEND: *Sa 13.00–21.00*
Dutch Craft Beer Festival
Metropool, Willem Wilminkplein 2,
Enschede (Overijssel)
Indoor event with around 15 Dutch craft brewers and live music.

2ND WEEKEND: *Sa 12.00–19.00*
Utrechtse Bierbrouwers Festival
De Fabrique, Westkanaaldijk 7, Utrecht (Utrecht)
Indoor/outdoor festival with exclusively Utrecht provincial breweries. Check before travelling as there was no event in 2019 and, whilst we are assured it will return from 2020, it may be at a new location.

ASCENSION DAY (*Hemelvaartsdag*): *Th 13.00-20.00*
Brabants Bierfestival
Vandeoirsprong brewery, Koestraat 20,
Oirschot (North Brabant)
Outdoor festival with around 10 Brabant brewers.

Week van Het Nederlandse Bier (Dutch
Beer Week - weekvanhetnederlandsebier.nl)
11-day celebration of Dutch beer, usually held
in late May. Hundreds of nationwide events
in cafés and breweries, beginning with the
festival below. The second weekend is Open
Brewery Days.

3RD or 4TH WEEKEND: *Th 18.00-22.00;*
Fr 16.00-22.00; Sa 13.00-17.00 & 18.00-22.00
Nederlands Bierproeffestival
Grote Kerk, Rond de Grote Kerk 12,
Den Haag (South Holland)
Launch event for Dutch Beer Week with
50+ exclusively Dutch breweries plus
masterclasses and other fringe activities.

Nederlands Bierproeffestival

4TH WEEKEND: *Fr&Sa 14.00-22.00*
Middelburgs Abdij Bierfestival
(abdijbierfestival.nl)
Abdij van Middelburg, Onder den Toren,
Middelburg (Zeeland)
A dozen local brewers and half a dozen
others with an abbey link, held in a cloister.

LAST WEEKEND (or early June): *Fr 14.00-00.00;*
Sa 12.00-00.00
24uurs van Maastricht
Bernardustraat 24A, Maastricht (Limburg)
In and beside the city walls, with 20+
breweries and live music.

VARIOUS WEEKENDS
TAPT (taptfestival.nl)
Summer-long craft beer festival series at various
locations in different cities. Events were held in Alkmaar,
Amsterdam, Arnhem, Nijmegen and Utrecht in 2019.
It may spread elsewhere in future years.

VARIOUS WEEKENDS
MOUT (moutbierfestival.nl)
Similar to the above, with events in Arnhem,
Nijmegen, Enschede and Tilburg in 2019.

MAY/JUNE

WHITSUN WEEKEND (*Pinskterweekend*):
Sa&Su 13.00-00.00; Mo 13.00-21.00
Nijmeegse Bierfeesten
Valkhofpark, Nijmegen (Gelderland)
Outdoor festival with a daily changing cast of 25 brewers.

JUNE

1ST OR 2ND WEEKEND: *Su 14.00-20.00*
Twents Speciaalbier Festival
Twentse brewery, Haaksbergerstraat 51,
Hengelo (Overijssel)
Outdoor festival with 20+ regional brewers.

2ND OR 3RD WEEKEND: *Sa 13.00-20.00*
Noord-Holland Bierfestival
Grote Kerk, Koorstraat 2, Alkmaar (North Holland)
Twenty local brewers plus workshops.

2RD WEEKEND: *Th-Su times vary*
Carnivale Brettanomyces (wildegist.nl)
Amsterdam (North Holland)
A citywide weekend celebration of wild and
mixed fermentation beers, with dinners, tastings,
talks by brewers and other events.

3RD OR 4TH WEEKEND: *Sa 12.00-19.00*
PINT Ledenfestival
Location varies
Festival with around 10 breweries and other events, exclusively for members of the PINT consumer organisation (**pint.nl**).

LAST WEEKEND: *Su 12.30-18.30*
Tilburgs Bierfestival (tilburgsbierfestival.nl)
Heuvel, Tilburg (North Brabant)
Outdoor festival with 25+ brewers.

JULY

1ST WEEKEND: *Su 15.00-23.00*
Flink Gegist Festival
Vrouwjuttenland, Delft (South Holland)
Outdoor festival with 12+ Dutch brewers.

1ST WEEKEND: *Su 12.00-19.00*
Biermatinee (biermatinee.nl)
Lind Noord, Oisterwijk (North Brabant)
Outdoor festival with 20+ breweries.

LAST WEEKEND: *Su 12.00-19.00*
Gerstenat! (bierfestivalgerstenat.nl)
Markt, Valkenswaard (North Brabant)
Outdoor event with 15 Brabant breweries.

AUGUST

1ST WEEKEND: *Fr 15.00-22.00; Sa 12.00-20.00*
Burg Bierfestival (burgbieren.nl/bierfeest)
Putterweg 45, Ermelo (Gelderland)
Outdoor festival with 20 Dutch brewers on day one, doubling on day two.

4TH WEEKEND: *Sa&Su 13.00-21.00*
Van Moll Fest
Evoluon, Noord Brabantlaan 1A, Eindhoven, (North Brabant)
Beside an iconic UFO-shaped conference

centre, an outdoor festival with around 25 of the best Dutch and international craft breweries... and pedalos.

LAST WEEKEND: *Sa 17.00-22.00*
Speciaal Bierfestival
Café de Heks, Waag, Deventer (Overijssel)
Outdoor festival with 15 breweries.

LAST WEEKEND: *Su 11.00-19.00*
Bierfestival Delft
Brabantse Turfmarkt, Delft (South Holland)
Outdoor festival with 30 Dutch and other brewers.

SEPTEMBER

1ST WEEKEND: *Su 13.30-19.00*
Speciaal Bierfestival Grave (speciaalbierfestival-grave.nl)
Loswal, Grave (North Brabant)
Around 20 breweries and live music beside the River Maas.

1ST WEEKEND: *Sa&Su 13.00-19.00*
International Bier & Crafts Festival
Marktplein, Apeldoorn (Gelderland)
Outdoor beer, wine and food festival with workshops and other events.

1ST OR 2ND WEEKEND: *Sa 13.00-22.00*
Brewda
Brouwerij Frontaal
Liniestraat 31, Breda (North Brabant)
Outdoor festival with around 15 Dutch and international craft breweries.

2ND WEEKEND: *Su 12.00-19.00*
Gulpener Hopfest
Reijmerstokkerdorpstraat, Reijmerstok (near Gulpen, Limburg)
Food, beer and other events, held during the annual Gulpener hop harvest.

2ND WEEKEND: *Su 14.00-19.00*
Bierfestival pROOSt
Vrijthof, Hilvarenbeek (North Brabant)
Village green local crafts festival with a dozen brewers.

2ND WEEKEND: *Su 13.00-19.00*
Bierfestival Biereloth
Café Becoloth, Rozemarijnstraat, Boxtel (North Brabant)
Outdoor festival with 15+ brewers.

BAF (Borefts After Festival), Kaapse Brouwers, Rotterdam (South Holland)

LAST WEEKEND: *Fr&Sa 12.00–22.00*

Borefts Beer Festival

Brouwerij de Molen, Doortocht 4,
Bodegraven (South Holland)

Around 25 leading craft breweries from around
the world serving regular brews and experimental one-offs and attracting an equally international audience. Advance booking essential.

BAF (Borefts After Festival)

LAST WEEKEND: *Su 12.00–22.00*

Kaapse Brouwers, Fenix Loods, Veerlaan 19-D,
Rotterdam (South Holland)

Follow-up festival the day after Borefts,
favouring Dutch brewers with some
international guests

OCTOBER

1ST WEEKEND: *Fr 16.00–00.00; Sa 12.00–00.00;
Su 14.00–20.00*

Amersfoorts Bockbier Festival
(amersfoortsbockbierfestival.nl)

Krankeledenstraat 16-22, Amersfoort (Utrecht)

Around 20 Dutch brewers focusing on the
seasonal style.

2ND WEEKEND: *Su 13.00–18.30*

Bokbiermarkt (bokbierdag.nl/bokbiermarkt)

Zutphen (Gelderland)

Very popular citywide festival with 20 cafés
serving bocks.

LAST WEEKEND: *Fr–Su times vary*

Amsterdamse Bokbier Weekend

Designed to replace the now-defunct PINT
Bockbierfestival, with the partiticaption
of a dozen beer cafés across the city.

NOVEMBER

2ND WEEKEND: *Su 13.30–18.00*

Flevo Bierfestival

Poppodium de Meester, Rentmeesterstraat 2,
Almere (Flevoland)

Around 10 local brewers and
live music.

4TH WEEKEND:
Sa 13.30–17.30 & 18.30–22.30

Wild Festival Groningen
(wildfestivalgroningen.nl)

A celebration of wild beers, wines and ciders,
with a food court.

DECEMBER

1ST WEEKEND: *Sa 13.00–22.00*

Bier & Big Winterfestival

Ketelhuisplein, Eindhoven (North Brabant)

Outdoor beer and hog roast festival with braziers
and around 20 breweries. A similar End of Winter
event follows at the same location in March.

2ND WEEKEND: *Sa 15.00–21.00*

Winterbierfestival Wormer
(winterbierfestival-wormer.nl)

Sporthal Wormer, Spatterstraat 21,
Wormer (North Holland)

Around 20 Dutch brewers pouring both winter
and non-seasonal beers.

3RD OR 4TH WEEKEND: *Su 14.00–19.00*

Noorderlijk Kerst- en Winterbieren Festival

Plein, Hoofdstraat Noord, Hoogeveen (Drenthe)

Outdoor festival focusing on Christmas and winter
beers, with 10+ northern brewers and other stalls.

Further research

BOOKS

Benelux

Around Amsterdam in 80 Beers by Tim Skelton (Cogan & Mater, 2015; ISBN: 978-0-9547789-3-4). Features 80 venues with 80 different beers, an essential guide for those staying longer in the capital, in its 2nd edition.

Good Beer Guide Belgium by Tim Webb and Joe Stange (CAMRA Books, 2018: ISBN: 978-1-85249-341-7). The unique and original in-depth guide to all things beery in Belgium, now in its 8th edition.

The Beer Map of Netherlands/Dé Bierkaart van Nederland (De Bierverbinding, 4th edition expected 2020). At-a-glance map of beer pubs, shops, festivals and museums.

Wish You Were Beer by Jan Willem Kaldenbach & Edo Dijksterhuis (De Kring, 2018: ISBN 978-9-46297-113-4). The authors' personal selection of the top bars and breweries in Amsterdam.

International

Pocket Beer Book by Stephen Beaumont and Tim Webb (UK: Mitchell Beazley, 2017; ISBN 978-1-78472-336-1 and US: Hamlyn, 2017; ISBN 978-1-78472-336-1).

The World Atlas of Beer by Tim Webb and Stephen Beaumont (UK: Mitchell Beazley, 2016; ISBN 978-1-78472-144-2 and US: Sterling Epicure, 2016; ISBN 978-1-45492-217-9). New edition due in 2020.

Dutch language

Bier by Rick Kempen (self published, 2017: ISBN 978-9-02633-941-7). A guide to beer history, brewing and beer styles.

Bier aan Tafel by Arvid Bergström (Koken Met Krullen, 2018; ISBN 978-9-08238-446-8). Food pairing and recipes using beer.

Bier in Nederland: een biografie by Marco Daane (Atlas Contact, 2016; ISBN 978-9-04502-868-2). A history of beer and brewing in the Netherlands from ancient times to the craft beer era, challenging much received wisdom.

De Bierrevolutie by Jan Willem Kaldenbach and Edo Dijksterhuis (Terra, 2017: ISBN 978-9-08989-697-1). The in-depth story of the Dutch beer revolution.

Cafés by Fiona de Lange (Lannoo, 2019: ISBN 978-9-40145-768-2). Glossy coffee table guide to 250 selected Dutch cafés.

Dit is een boek over bier by Raymond van der Laan (Fontaine, 2017; ISBN 978-9-05956-734-4). General guide to brewing and beer styles, with recommended examples from each of the latter.

Rivier van Bier by Henri Reuchlin (Birdy, 2018: ISBN 978-9-49105-205-7). A personal beer-themed journey up the river Maas.

Utrecht Hop! by Kees Volkers (Gegarandeerd Onregelmatig, 2016; ISBN 978-9-07864-154-4). A trip around Utrecht province's beer history, breweries and bars.

MAGAZINES

Bier! (biermagazine.nl). Quarterly beer magazine.

Schuim (schuimmagazine.nl). Quarterly beer magazine.

Hopster (hopstermagazine.com), Free craft beer magazine, given away in bars and shops.

CONSUMER GROUPS, WEBSITES & OTHER INFO

PINT

Vereniging **P**romotie **IN**formatie **T**raditioneel Bier – pint.nl
The Dutch national beer consumer group, founded in 1980 by beer lovers appalled at the state of the national industry. PINT played a key role in turning things around, not so much by direct action as by nurturing the folks who made it happen. Its aims are "to promote beer culture in the Netherlands and to inform and promote the interests of Dutch beer consumers". With around 4,500 members, it is the nation's largest independent consumer association. Regional branches

organise tastings, brewery visits and festivals in their areas. The organisation publishes the bi-monthly *PINT Magazine* and the website has an events diary. PINT also organises campaigns, for example pushing for more informative beer labelling and protesting against disproportionate tax hikes on beer.

ABT

Alliantie van Bier Tapperijen – alliantie-van-biertapperijen.com
ABT was founded in 1986 as a community of specialist cafés, with the common aim of serving decent, properly kept beer. There is a truism that all ABT members are good beer cafés, but not all good beer cafés are ABT members. There are 31 outlets currently enrolled, all in this guide, but around 80 others have been members at one time or other. They join and leave for a variety reasons. A new operation might use it to gain exposure, while some leave because they dislike being tied to its Beer of the Month (*Bier van de maand*) scheme. A few have been loyal since the start. ABT represents members' interests in dealings with the press, breweries, wholesalers, consumer groups and public authorities. From a consumer viewpoint, an ABT café guarantees a wide range of well-kept beers, though not necessarily a high proportion of Dutch ones. It also means the menu will be clearly presented, the staff will know about what they sell and there should be no sloppy service.

EBCU

The European Beer Consumers Union – ebcu.org
EBCU was formed in 1990 as an umbrella organisation, currently representing 19 national beer consumer groups and coordinating their lobbying and campaigning activities at a European level. Its aims and objectives are the preservation of European beer culture; the promotion of traditional beers; supporting traditional breweries in fending off consolidation; and representing beer drinkers in their campaign for choice, quality and value for money.

CRAFT

craftbrouwers.nl
Founded in 2003 as the Dutch Small Brewer's Collective (KBC), Craft represents the interests of around 160 small brewers, both with and without their own brewing equipment. Craft is run by and for the brewers, and gives them a platform for discussion and exchange of knowledge and experience. It aims to provide balance in the press to counteract the dominance of the major breweries. Craft also organises the annual Dutch Craft Beer Conference, held in January in Den Haag, and sometimes works alongside Nederlandse Brouwers (below) on matters of common interest.

Nederlandse Brouwers

nederlandsebrouwers.nl
A trade organisation with similar aims to Craft, but which represents the interests of the bigger players, with 10 members including multinationals like Heineken and AB InBev, but also larger microbrewers like Texels and De Leckere. Founded in 1939, it works to "allow Dutch brewers to produce and sell beer efficiently and responsibly in three key policy areas: responsible drinking; economic, taxation and legal affairs; and sustainability and delivery chain management".

Dutch Beer Challenge

dutchbeerchallenge.nl
The nation's primary beer competition, held in mid-March in Rotterdam. Only Dutch brewers are allowed to enter beers, which are assessed by a panel of Dutch and international beer judges. The winners in 24 style categories are announced in April, with the overall title of Best Beer in the Netherlands bestowed at the Bierproeffestival in Den Haag in May (above).

BAV

Bier & Verzamelaarsvereniging – bav.nl
The Beer and Collectors' Association was set up in 1983 as the Association of Brewery Items Collectors. It is now a body bringing together collectors, breweries, beer stores and publicans. Without these people we might have remained unaware of the art of tegestology.

StiBON

Stichting Bieropleidingen Nederland
(Dutch Beer Education Foundation) – **stibon.nl**
Offers Dutch-language beer sommelier courses
for brewers, café staff and others wishing to
expand and deepen their tasting and
appreciation skills.

WEBSITES

Blogs in English

010beerblog.com – beer sommelier and
Rotterdam resident Tina Rogers's blog
about the local and wider craft scene

barclayperkins.blogspot.com – beer historian
and Amsterdam resident Ron Pattinson's
blog makes occasional forays into Dutch beer

hopculturereference.com – Dutch beer travels
and opinion in a blog formerly known as
Dutch Beer Pages

mylifewithbeer.nl – the opinions of Dutch beer
connoisseur Rick Kempen

Blogs in Dutch

aroundthebar.nl – news and opinion
bier.blog.nl – beer news
bierathlon.nl – opinion and tasting notes
bierburo.nl – news and comment
biercolumns.nl – comment and opinion
bierista.nl– news and comment
bierliefde.nl – comment and opinion, with a
slight leaning towards food and beer pairing
biermetboot.nl – comment and opinion
blog.beerinabox.nl – comment and opinion
letsbier.nl – trip reports and opinion
speciaalbiertjesblog.nl – comment and opinion

Online beer stores

beerdome.nl
beerwulf.com (Heineken-sponsored)
bierenzo.nl
bierfamilie.nl
hetbiermoment.nl
brewpack.nl – online subscription club with
monthly beer packs
brouwmaatje.nl – homebrewing equipment
and supplies, no beer
buurtbier.nl – targets the Utrecht region

drankgigant.nl – also has a physical store with a
smaller range (Paspoortstraat 17, Oost Souburg)
hollandcraftbeer.nl – aimed at the brewing and
café trade
hopt.nl
speciaalbierpakket.nl

Other websites and apps

beeradvocate.com – international crowd-sourced
beer resource with some Dutch coverage,
listing and rating beers, brewers and beer
venues
bierboombierevents.nl – organises tastings,
festivals and meet the brewer events
bierbrouwerijen.nl – Dutch breweries, festivals
and other tasting events
biercuisine.nl – beer and food site, with recipes
for cooking with beer
biergenoten.nl – beer enthusiasts' Facebook group
bierisbest.nl – a listing of many breweries and
cafés
bierlokaal.nl – bilingual site with Dutch beer bars,
beer shops, news and events
biernet.nl – industry-sponsored news and
information
brewver.com – newly established social
networking app listing and rating beers,
brewers and beer venues along similar lines
to Untappd and Ratebeer
debierverbinding.nl – aims to bring breweries,
cafés and consumers together through
tastings and advice
europeanbeerguide.net – Ron Pattinson's
European beer guide
nederlandsebiercultuur.nl – a database of all
Dutch breweries and brewers and other
aspects of beer culture
pinkgron.nl – collector's site with beer labels,
and a Dutch brewery map.
ratebeer.com – international crowd-sourced
beer resource now owned by AB InBev, listing
and rating beers, brewers and beer venues.
untappd.com – beer-based international social
networking app with strong Dutch coverage,
listing and rating beers, brewers and beer
venues, some of which use it to list their menu.

And…

stiva.nl – STIVA: the Dutch Foundation for
Responsible Drinking

General index

Breweries and beers brands index

Below are listed the keywords within brand names that should enable you to find any beer we list. There are far too many beers to be able to index every one by name.

Thank you and acknowledgements

This book would not have been possible without the help of a great many people.

Firstly, a shout out to those who were involved in the production of this second edition. Big thanks to Des de Moor (desdemoor.co.uk), author of The CAMRA Guide to London's Best Beer, Pubs and Bars, for applying his inestimable beer knowledge and editing skills to help sharpen the text. To Dale Tomlinson for creating the fabulous layout and making the book look as excellent as it does. And thank you to John Macklin for providing the maps.

Thanks also to Tim Webb for his mentorship over the years and for his Foreword to this second edition. And to both him and Jo Copestick for their support in getting the original edition of Beer in the Netherlands made.

A great many of the breweries and cafés in this book came onto my radar as a result of having lived in the Netherlands for 30 years, but there were always going to be some I missed. I am thus grateful to Jan Ausems and Harry Pinkster and the rest of the nederlandsebiercultuur.nl team for their tireless attempts at keeping up with new breweries as they arrive. Likewise, thanks to the Ratebeer community, from whom I plundered many café tips.

In the same vein, thank you to all the following for their support and insider's tip-offs about bars, shops and festivals: Rob Alphenaar, Peter van der Arend, Xander van Balen, Stephen Beaumont, Chris Bettini, Rob Bours, Dirk Breedveld, Hans & Ria Buijtels, Martijn Buisman, John Carlton, John Clarke, Erwin de Cock, Marco Coenen, Marco Daane, Martijn van Damme, Brett Domue, Simon Duerden, Maarten Exel, Andreas Fält, Theo Flissebalje, Simon Fokkema, Yuri Hegge,

Jaap Hermans, Erik Hendriks, Han Hidalgo, Rianne Joosse, Rick Kempen, Dennis Kort, Wout Koster, Raymond van der Laan, Fiona de Lange, Jan Beekaa Lemmens, Bryan Longbottom, Bob Molenbroek & Nicole Warners, Erwin van Moll, Rick Nelson, Henk van Oijen, Menno Olivier, Ton van Opstal, Michel Orderman & Lydian Zoetman, Ron Pattinson, Casper Pennings, Marco Philipsen, Graham & Sarah Povey, Roger Protz, Henri Reuchlin, Andy Robb, Tina Rogers, Frans Ruiter, Alain Schepers, Frans van der Schot, Joe Stange Eugene Straver, Mike Thompson & Marlous Huesken, Dave Thornhill, Guy Thornton, Paul Travis, Laurens van Ulden, Willem & An Verboom, Fedor Vogel, Derek Walsh & Astrid Walsh-Adan, Jos Walstra, Tony Webb & Jean Longma Winfried Weel, Ferry Wijnhoven, Freek Willems, and Willem van Zanten.

And to the many brewers, café owners, PINT members and readers of both Beer in the Netherlands and Around Amsterdam in 80 Beers who have showed support and enthusiasm for this project – far too many to name check everyone.

A particularly big thank you to Amanda, for her suppor company and proofreading skills, and for agreeing to beco "Bob" the designated driver when our research trips to remoter locations demanded it.

Farewell and RIP to the sadly missed beer pioneers Piet de Jongh and Chris "Podge" Pollard, and to my dear old dae

And finally, a slightly more leftfield doff of the cap to the Grand Duchy of Luxembourg, without which the book wouldn't exist in this form. It's still a long story. Let's talk about it over a beer.